T0291377

# KEY PERFORMANCE INDICATORS

Key performance indicators (KPIs) are widely used across organisations. But are they fully understood in how they can properly shape, improve, or even undermine organisational systems and outcomes? This book presents a framework and tools for measuring and managing performance at various levels within an organisation, and helps managers re-think the ways KPIs can be implemented to meet organisational goals.

Innovative performance measurement and management is a vital function within any organisation irrespective of its size and industry. Measuring and managing performance (whether on an individual, team, or departmental basis) assists management in calibrating their established strategic goals by providing an insight into how well their employees and the organisation are doing and identifying areas of concern for rectification and improvement. This book focuses on the practicality of performance management tools (for example, Performance Analytics; Performance Reporting; Critical Success Factors; Balanced Scorecard; Benchmarking; Six Sigma; Business Excellence Models; Enterprise Risk Management) and illustrates their use, and the changing nature of how organisational performance will be evaluated in the future. This includes the application of Artificial Intelligence as an important trend in performance measurement and management.

This book provides a universal framework for implementing a performance measurement and management system that is applicable to both the private and public sectors. It is particularly relevant to HR and operational managers, and organisational leaders and public administrators at all levels.

**Emanuel Camilleri** is a visiting senior lecturer at Malta University and has authored several books. He has occupied senior management posts in industrial engineering, finance, and ICT sectors in Australia and Malta. Recently, he was appointed Chairman of the Planning Authority, Planning Board, Malta.

# KEY PERFORMANCE INDICATORS

## The Complete Guide to KPIs for Business Success

*Emanuel Camilleri*

Routledge
Taylor & Francis Group

LONDON AND NEW YORK

Designed cover image: © Getty Images / Jian Fan

First published 2024
by Routledge
4 Park Square, Milton Park, Abingdon, Oxon OX14 4RN

and by Routledge
605 Third Avenue, New York, NY 10158

*Routledge is an imprint of the Taylor & Francis Group, an Informa business*

*British Library Cataloguing-in-Publication Data*
A catalogue record for this book is available from the British Library

*Library of Congress Cataloging-in-Publication Data*
Names: Camilleri, Emanuel, author.
Title: Key performance indicators: the complete guide to KPIs for business success / Emanuel Camilleri.
Description: Abingdon, Oxon; New York, NY: Routledge, 2024. | Includes bibliographical references and index.
Identifiers: LCCN 2023047583 (print) | LCCN 2023047584 (ebook) | ISBN 9781032685458 (hardback) | ISBN 9781032648897 (paperback) | ISBN 9781032685465 (ebook)
Subjects: LCSH: Performance standards. | Performance—Management. | Organizational effectiveness.
Classification: LCC HF5549.5.P35 C36 2024 (print) | LCC HF5549.5.P35 (ebook) | DDC 658.3/12—dc23/eng/20231019
LC record available at https://lccn.loc.gov/2023047583
LC ebook record available at https://lccn.loc.gov/2023047584

ISBN: 978-1-032-68545-8 (hbk)
ISBN: 978-1-032-64889-7 (pbk)
ISBN: 978-1-032-68546-5 (ebk)

DOI: 10.4324/9781032685465

Typeset in Joanna
by codeMantra

Life and death flow from each other. I would like to dedicate this book to Candy, my English Cocker Spaniel, whom I loved as a puppy and still loved dearly as his life ebbed away in my arms as he took his last breath at the age of almost fifteen years. I knew that I would miss him, but I never imagined that it would be such a painful and heart-breaking experience. When my time is up and if I am worthy to enter the Kingdom of God, I will come looking for you at Rainbow Bridge where we can be together with all our loved ones for eternity. Life and death flow from each other, and during this period of grief came Ellie, our first granddaughter, who is giving Maryanne, my wife and I, so much joy and contentment.

# CONTENTS

# FIGURES

# TABLES

# FOREWORD

Peter Drucker is famous for saying 'if you can't measure it, you can't manage it.'

Excellence is not achieved by merely setting out clear targets or goals, but by also ensuring that they are measurable, and are continuously assessed. This book, authored by Dr Emanuel Camilleri, offers an extensive framework that does just that. It features a plethora of performance management tools that can be immensely useful for organisations seeking to improve their operations and achieve their goals. Moreover, the approach is one which is forward-looking, and the  book itself covers new developments, such as the use of artificial intelligence in performance measurement and management.

The book demonstrates, in a clear fashion, just how much management science has evolved over the years, and how operators in the private and public sectors can benefit from the adoption of new techniques. Many seem to associate increased productivity and efficiency solely with the adoption of technological developments, yet the reality is, that having access to the best technology is no guarantee of success if the organisations remain rooted in dated approaches to performance management. The adoption of innovative management systems is a key step forward for countries committed to successfully achieving the twin transformations of digitalisation and climate neutrality.

These challenges require a holistic reform of the way organisations set their goals and measure their performance. In this light, the tenets espoused in this book can be of great help to organisation leaders in the coming decades, where change will be a key part of organisational operations, and where the measurement of success will become ever more critical and challenging.

In contrast to many management science books, which tend to focus simply on theoretical constructs, this book is indeed practical, as the performance management tools described herein are applied on two authentic organisations: One from the private sector and the other from the public sector. This not only confirms the general applicability of the recommended performance management tools, but also shows how these can be tweaked to reflect very different goals that organisations set for themselves. Performance management is not only essential to enhancing profits or the balance sheet of an entity; it is equally important for public sector entities with wider goals, which may not be measured as easily.

The challenges of digitalisation and climate neutrality are complex, as over the coming decades many nations are expected to have an ageing workforce. The availability of human resources will become scarcer and there will be increased competition for talent. In such an environment, performance management will become even more important. Organisations will need to achieve more with fewer resources, and in order to do this they will need to plan better and pay more attention to how they deploy their limited resources.

I believe that the approaches outlined in this book present an important steppingstone for organisation leaders determined to transform their organisation. Dr Camilleri has done a great service to managers by putting this comprehensive guidebook together. I am confident that it will stand them in good stead in the years to come.

His Excellency Dr Robert Abela KUOM, BA, LLD, Adv Trib Melit, MP
Prime Minister, Malta

# PREFACE AND ACKNOWLEDGEMENTS

This book, entitled *Key Performance Indicators: The Complete Guide to KPIs for Business Success*, is not about performance but about performance measurement and management. This is an important distinction, because the word performance in its simplest form means the action of carrying out a task or function. Moreover, good performance is defined as conducting a task in a precise and consistent fashion that adheres to a well-defined process. However, none of these definitions refer to how performance is measured and managed. There is also a difference between measuring and managing the performance of an individual and an organisation. In fact, there is a range of performance measurement and management practices, with the individual at the lower end of the spectrum and the organisation at the top end, amongst teams, departments, divisions, products, and many others in between. Additionally, performance is dependent on many variables, some of which may be known and others unknown. Therefore, the performance of an individual or entity (and constituents in between this spectrum) is not measured by just one variable but through several variables. Moreover, these variables are indicative of the performance that is expected from the individual or entity. In other words, they are suggestive or emblematic.

On an individual level, research has shown that traditional performance management systems and their associated annual employee appraisal methods are time-consuming. Often a supervisor goes through the mechanics of the appraisal process without realistically assessing the extent to which an employee was contributing towards to the achievement of the organisation's strategic objectives. Experience has shown that these appraisal systems, particularly in the public sector, are a way of giving an employee a pay rise without upsetting the organisational salary scales that may have been negotiated with the trade unions. Performance at an organisational level is even more difficult to assess, particularly during a recession. Achieving results during a recession is much harder than during an economic boom. Yet, during a recession, managers are penalised when targets are not fully achieved. It has become apparent that better performance measurement and management systems are required.

This book is aimed at overcoming the anomalies described above. The book offers a common performance management framework that is supported by an extensive set of tools, which may be applied in various circumstances to satisfy the wide spectrum of roles, from the individual to the organisation level (and in between) in both the public and private sectors. The content of this toolbox is not prescriptive but provides suggestions. Most of all, the tools provided are meant to stimulate the manager's thinking to adopt and adapt these tools to their own organisational circumstances. Performance is like holding a bird. Squeeze it too hard and you are likely to stifle it; loosen your grip and you run the risk of losing control of it. Performance needs to be fairly measured and managed and be within reach. Performance is not only the outcome of hard work, but also the outcome of applying suitable tools that focus on the things that matter to make the organisation successful.

Finally, I would like to acknowledge the effort of all the staff at Routledge publishing, namely Rebecca Marsh, Lauren Whelan, Sarah Hudson and Jade Ridgill, who provided their invaluable and professional advice during the whole publication process, and the marketing team for the professional way they promoted this book. I would also like to thank my wife, Maryanne, who painstakingly checked all the chapters, and Aidan Cross, who meticulously carried out the copy-editing, ensuring that the book was to the highest standard possible.

Dr Emanuel Camilleri

# ABBREVIATIONS

| | |
|---|---|
| ABC | Activity Based Costing |
| AHT | Average Handling Time |
| ANOVA | Analysis of Variance |
| ASRS | Aviation Safety Reporting System |
| BQF | British Quality Foundation |
| BE | Business Excellence |
| BPE | Business Process Engineering |
| BPM | Business Performance Management |
| BSC | Balanced Scorecard |
| CAC | Customer Acquisition Cost |
| CBS | Cost Breakdown Structure |
| CMIS | Customer Management Information System |
| CPM | Corporate performance management |
| CRT | Current Reality Tree |
| CSCW | Computer-supported cooperative work |
| CSF | Critical Success Factors |
| CTQ | Critical to Quality |
| DFSS | Design for Six Sigma |
| DMADV | Define, Measure, Analyse, Design, Verify |
| DMAIC | Define, Measure, Analyse, Improve, Control |
| DPMS | Dynamic performance measurement system |

| | |
|---|---|
| DSO | Days Sales Outstanding |
| DSS | Decision Support Systems |
| EFQM | European Foundation for Quality Management |
| EIS | Executive Information Systems |
| ERM | Enterprise Risk Management |
| ERP | Enterprise Resource Planning |
| FAA | Federal Aviation Administration |
| FMEA | Failure Mode and Effects Analysis |
| FMIS | Financial Management Information System |
| GDPR | General Data Privacy Regulation |
| GPRA | Government Performance and Results Act |
| HRMIS | Human Resource Management Information System |
| ICT | Information and Communication Technology |
| IDP | Individual Development Plan |
| IoT | Internet-of-things |
| IRD | Inland Revenue Department |
| KPA | Key Performance Area |
| KPI | Key Performance Indicator |
| KPM | Key Performance Measure |
| KRA | Key Result Area |
| KRI | Key result indicator |
| LTV | Lifetime Value |
| MIS | Management Information Systems |
| MSSP | Measurement Systems Strategic Performance |
| NESC | NASA Engineering and Safety Center |
| NPS | Net Promoter Score |
| OCF | Operating Cash Flow |
| ODS | Operating Data Store |
| OKR | Objectives and Key Results |
| OLAP | On-Line Analytical Processing |
| OPM | Organisational Performance Management |
| PAF | Performance and assessment framework |
| PI | Performance indicator |
| PMI | Project Management Institute |
| PMM | Performance Measurement and Management |
| PMP | Performance management and planning |
| PMS | Performance measurement systems |

| | |
|---|---|
| PPM | People performance management |
| RACI | Responsibility assignment matrix |
| RADAR | Results, Approach, Deployment, Assessment, and Review |
| RDBMS | Relational Database Management Systems |
| RI | Result indicator |
| ROE | Return on Equity |
| ROI | Return-on-investment |
| RPR | Rapid Problem Resolution |
| SCR | Salary Competitiveness Ratio |
| SMART | Specific, Measurable, Achievable, Realistic, Timely |
| SQA | Singapore Quality Award |
| TJC | The Joint Commission |
| TOC | Theory of Constraints |
| TPS | Toyota Production Model |
| TQM | Total Quality Management |
| WAN | Wide Area Network |
| WBS | Work Breakdown Structure |

# PART I

## PERFORMANCE MEASUREMENT

### THE ESSENTIALS OF KEY PERFORMANCE INDICATORS

According to the Collins Dictionary, the word 'performance' means how successful someone or something is, or how well they do something. It is contended that the term 'performance' is illusive because it does not provide a specific meaning, or more precisely it is difficult to pin down its exact significance. For example, a student may obtain a mark of 90% in an exam, and one may describe his/her performance as being excellent. However, what if the exam was considered simple when compared to previous examinations on the same topic? How would you classify a student who obtained a mark of 75% in an exam that was considered difficult with a student who obtained 90% in an exam that was considered simple? Consider a student who obtains 70% for the simple examination. How would one describe his/her performance? Would it make a difference to our judgement of the performance of the student who obtained 70% if this student was dyslexic? The message being conveyed is that someone's or something's performance is dependent on certain variables, some of which may be known and others unknown. It is realised that the examples

DOI: 10.4324/9781032685465-1

provided are about individuals. However, similar types of examples may be applied to organisations as well.

Furthermore, performance of an individual or entity is not measured by just one variable but through several variables. Moreover, these several variables are indicative of the performance that is expected from the individual or entity. In other words, they are suggestive or emblematic. Therefore, in measuring the performance of an individual or entity, one must be aware that the measure is indicative depending on the circumstances and thus the variables selected to measure performance must be chosen carefully. The selected variables to measure the concept of performance must be considered as key performing elements. If these simple principles are understood, then the fundamental concept of Key Performance Indicators (KPIs) becomes clearer.

In simple terms, KPIs are a category of performance measurements that gauge the success of an organisation or of an activity in which the organisation participates. Hence, it is a measurable value that illustrates the degree of effectiveness an organisation achieves in implementing its fundamental business objectives. Additionally, organisations utilise KPIs at various levels to assess their achievement at attaining their targets. Therefore, high-level KPIs tend to focus on the holistic or general performance of the organisation. On the other hand, low-level KPIs are inclined to focus on activities or processes in departments, such as operations, marketing, quality control, personnel (HR), and administrative support, amongst others, depending on the industry the organisation operates in.

KPIs are important because they keep business objectives at the head of the decision-making process. This is the reason why an organisation needs to have an effective communications strategy to ensure that its business objectives are disseminated accurately across the organisation, so that employees grasp and become accountable for their own KPIs. This ensures that the organisation's key targets are embedded or entrenched in the employees' mindset as a way of routine thinking.

# 1

# PERFORMANCE MEASUREMENT

## KEY PERFORMANCE INDICATORS CONCEPTS

'Selecting the right measure and measuring things right are both art and science. And KPIs influence management behaviour as well as business culture.'
Pearl Zhu
Author

KPIs help an organisation to obtain consistent and acceptable results that will eventually enable the organisation to grow and succeed in a competitive and turbulent environment. However, these organisational results can only be realised when employees work as a well synchronised team that constantly achieves the organisational objectives and goals through the established KPIs. As defined previously, a KPI is a computed measure to assess how well individual goals and/or the organisational targets are being achieved. Normally, managers do not rely on just one KPI but tend to define several KPIs to determine how well departments, work teams, or individual employees are faring at performing the tasks allocated to them. This implies that there is a distinction between high-level KPIs (at departmental level) and low-level KPIs (at individual level).

DOI: 10.4324/9781032685465-2

For example, if a consultancy firm is evaluating how well an eGovernment application is working at the Inland Revenue Department (IRD) regarding the taxpayers' tax returns submissions and associated tax payments, it may establish a group of specific KPIs to determine the success of this specific eGovernment application. These KPIs may appraise different aspects, including:

(a) *Information Technology Reliability.* File Server and WAN are to have an uptime of 99.9%; less than three seconds response time; and no reported or observed security violations.
(b) *Information System Reliability.* The application system is to have an uptime of 99.9%; less than five seconds response time; and no reported or observed security violations.
(c) *Legal Framework.* Appropriate laws are in place to support the electronic transactions policy with no legal challenges in court regarding transaction authentication and verification policies.
(d) *Organisational Framework.* Appropriate human resource policies are in place that result in less than 10% staff turnover rate; an average of less than two days' sick leave per worker; an average of less than 50 client complaints per month; and an average decrease in operational cost per year of 7.5%.
(e) *System Utilisation by Taxpayers:* System penetration growth rate per month of 1.5%.

As one may observe, the above KPIs would be integrated in the IRD's strategy for implementing a particular eGovernment Taxpayer IRD service. There is no golden rule as to how KPIs are constructed and defined, but they should be quantitative, measurable, practical, and directional to assess whether the organisation is advancing in the defined strategic path. This example also illustrates the significance of KPIs as a facilitator of organisational growth, in this case the application system penetration rate in the taxpayer market space.

## Introduction

It has been established that KPIs are measurable factors that exemplify the effectiveness of an organisation to achieve its main business goals. However,

KPIs may be applied at two specific levels, namely high-level KPIs that high-light the generic performance of the organisation, and low-level KPIs that have at the centre of interest a particular organisational activity and/or individual. Therefore, KPIs are values, which are expressed in numerical terms that are intended to communicate as much information as possible in concise terms. Acceptable KPIs are those that are properly defined, are suitably presented, and generate opportunities and motivate action. KPIs are rarely presented as raw data; they are typically considered to be information, which is the outcome of processing raw data into a meaningful value, such as averages, percentages, and ratios. For example, the Current Ratio for a firm is calculated by dividing its Current Assets by its Current Liabilities. This ratio measures if the organisation under examination can currently pay off short-term debts by liquidating its assets. Hence, raw accounting data is transformed into meaningful information that summarises the organisation's liquidity position in concise and explicit terms.

A fundamental principle related to performance indicators is deciding which indicators are 'Key' to shedding light on the performance of the organisation under examination. This decision is normally assigned to the company executives who manage the organisation, namely the Board of Directors and Senior Management. According to PriceWaterhouseCoopers (2007), many Boards tend to be given financial performance indicators, even if these KPIs are communicating strategies, such as maximising customer experience, or attracting and retaining the best and brightest people. In their view, the main concern is whether the KPIs presented to the Board of Directors are those KPIs that provide the Board with the proper information to permit them (and those using the information) to appraise progress against the stated strategic objectives. A difficulty that may arise is whether the Board of Directors takes the initiative to define its KPI requirements. In many cases, this initiative is taken by the Chief Executive Officer and Financial Controller, which may not be desirable, particularly if the KPIs are used as the basis for computing their performance bonus payments. KPIs are also dependent on the industry and on the degree of operating leverage.

PriceWaterhouseCoopers (2007) cite an example where a firm in the retail industry might use sales per square foot and customer satisfaction as KPIs, whereas a company in the oil and gas industry may possibly choose measures related to the success in exploration, such as the value of new reserves. Furthermore, companies trade in different products with the result of having different operating leverage depending on the product being traded. For instance, if the operating leverage of a company is high, a small percentage increase in sales can produce a much larger percentage increase in net operating income. Hence, operating leverage measures the degree of sensitivity on the part of net operating income to percentage changes in sales. Thus, a company that makes few sales, with each sale providing a very high gross margin, such as selling luxury cars or up-market real estate, is said to be highly leveraged. However, a business that makes many sales, with each sale contributing a very slight margin, such as goods in a supermarket, is said to be less leveraged. Therefore, the KPIs for high operating leverage companies will need to be different for those companies with low operating leverage. Thus, a business that has a higher proportion of fixed costs and a lower proportion of variable costs is said to have used more operating leverage, and a business with lower fixed costs and higher variable costs is said to employ less operating leverage. Therefore, the KPIs for such companies need to reflect the nature of the business and their cost structure.

The above illustrates that it is essential for the KPIs to be relevant and applicable to that individual organisation. The ultimate objective of management is to implement the strategies defined and approved by the Board of Directors. Thus, the choice of KPIs for a particular organisation should support the strategic objectives. These KPIs must make available adequate details on how they are measured and the critical data set that needs to be collected to allow one to determine whether the KPIs are being achieved.

## Key Performance Measures

We have established that a KPI consists of two basic characteristics, namely: (a) it is a measurable value, and (b) this measurable value demonstrates to some extent the effectiveness with which an organisation is achieving its key strategic objectives. However, it may take several KPIs to demonstrate this level of effectiveness. Therefore, a combination of these two characteristics for several KPIs permits the organisation's management to assess the level of achievement an organisation has attained in conducting its activities. Hence, it is extremely important to identify the key performance measures that will be used to assess organisational or activity or individual performance.

In many cases, such as in manufacturing, success is merely the constant and continual periodic attainment of an established level of an operational goal. For instance, a manufacturing firm may have a quality control goal of zero component defects and/or keeping to (0% deviation from) the promised delivery schedule. An organisation offering computing services as a provider may aim for a 99.9% uptime in its computing facility and networking capability. Thus, key performance measures need to be selected carefully depending on the nature of the organisation and its business activities. Therefore, KPIs are established to reflect the desired organisational performance outcome, which is linked to the organisation's strategic objectives. In selecting the key performance measures, management requires a good understanding of what is essential and of significance to the organisation. This is precisely the reason why KPIs have been successfully exploited in manufacturing industries, particularly by those organisations that had initially implemented Activity Based Costing (ABC) systems, where the impact of the cost and profit drivers were fully understood. Hence, it is important that the operational intricacies of the organisation are fully understood before defining the organisational objectives and the associated key performance measures.

It is therefore essential that the organisational objectives are suitably defined. It is suggested that in defining the organisational objectives, the 'SMART' concept is applied. Organisational objectives define the general direction or path the organisation needs to take by providing management with the appropriate motivation and unambiguous focus. Hence, organisational objectives establish the targets that management should aim for. The SMART concept is an abbreviation or acronym that stands for Specific, Measurable, Achievable, Realistic, and Timely. It encompasses these five fundamental norms to assist one to focus its efforts and increase the possibility of achieving the established objectives. The SMART objectives are as follows:

(a) *Specific:* The objectives are to be precisely and unambiguously defined. Objectives that are precise and clear have a considerably greater probability of being achieved. To make a goal precise and clear, the five 'W' questions are to be reflected on:
   - Who: Who is involved in this objective?
   - What: What is to be accomplished by this objective?
   - Where: Where is this objective to be achieved?

- When: When is this objective to be achieved?
- Why: Why is this objective to be achieved?

For example, a general objective would be 'I want to increase productivity.' A more specific objective might be 'I want to increase capital investment by 10% to upgrade machinery at the foundry division by the end of the financial year to increase production by 25%.'

(b) *Measurable*: Objectives are to have explicit criteria for measuring the progress being made to achieve them. The aim is to have objectives that have a set of criteria for measuring progress. Unless this is done there is no way of determining whether progress is being made towards the set objective. Objectives may be made measurable by reflecting on the following:

- Quantity: How many or how much?
- Target: How does one know whether the objective has been achieved?
- Gauge: What is the indicator that determines the progress being made to achieve the objective?

For example, by end of this financial year I want to increase production at the foundry division by 25%.

(c) *Achievable*: Objectives need to be doable and reasonable to achieve. An objective must be within reach, manageable, and attainable so that one is motivated to work towards its achievement. The attainability of the objectives may be ascertained by addressing the following:

- Competency: Are the resources and capabilities available to achieve the objective?
- Assessment: What is required, if the resources and capabilities are not available?
- Look to the past: Has the objective been achieved successfully in the past?

(d) *Realistic*: Objectives must be manageable, practical, and pertinent. The objective must be realistic given that the objective needs to be practically accomplished within the available resource and time constraint. The objective's fulfilment may be assessed by asking the following:

- Practical: Is the objective reasonable, manageable, and within reach?
- Achievable: Is the objective doable, given the available time and resources?

- Commitment: Is the necessary commitment present for the attainment of the objective?

(e) *Timely*: Create a sense of urgency by having an unambiguous timeline, with a definite start and completion date. The objective must be time-bound with an explicit start and completion date, else there will not be the appropriate motivation to achieve the objective. The timeliness of the objectives may be assessed by asking the following:

- Does the objective have a deadline for its completion?
- What is the target date for achieving the objective?

For example, an objective would be 'I want to increase capital investment by 10% to upgrade the machinery at the foundry division by the end of the financial year to increase production by 25%, not later than the first quarter of the following year.'

The SMART concept mitigates failure. Often management will position itself for failure by establishing wide-ranging and impractical objectives, which are defined in vague terms with imprecise challenges that, instead of motivating employees, will demoralise them. SMART objectives lead to success by ensuring that objectives are specific, measurable, achievable, realistic, and timely. This helps to establish realisable challenges for employees that motivate them to put in extra effort for achieving the set objectives. Once the objectives have been defined, these need to be transformed into suitable KPIs. To avoid confusion, it must be stressed that KPIs are not the company objectives, goals, or targets themselves. They are a measurement of the objectives, goals, or targets (i.e., the key performance measures). For example, if your organisation's objective is to produce a certain volume of components each month, the KPIs will illustrate and gauge the extent to which the objective is being achieved.

A KPI in this situation may be reported weekly and thus indicate that the production team for a particular component is producing only 90% of the budgeted volume during that month. The KPI will alert the manager to this status and the reason for not achieving the required production volume, and allow him/her to take appropriate corrective action. Hence, when a manager can measure the objectives in this way, it gives him/her the opportunity to comprehend what is going on in the process and make decisions that help to achieve the objectives more rapidly and take whatever action is deemed necessary. This is the significance of KPIs.

KPIs also help to create a learning organisation through the ability to measure goals and discuss the cause of the variances that occur. Hence, the key performance measures lead to the establishment of KPIs, which are continuously monitored and discussed with the individual or team responsible for that specific activity and associated KPI. This provides management with the opportunity to coach employees to be innovative and show them how to do things differently to improve their performance, and thus achieve the established objectives. Moreover, the continuous monitoring of KPIs and the resultant analysis for the causes of any variances that may result provides an opportunity to review and, if necessary, amend KPIs to reflect current circumstances and thus ensure that the goals are practical and realistic to realise.

The key performance measures and resultant KPIs in combination provide an instantaneous holistic snapshot of the organisation's performance and allow management to drill down to reveal the causes of success and failure at an activity (or lower) level. The immediate information provided by KPIs permit management to make systematic modifications and fine-tuning to processes so that organisational objectives are attained, thus avoiding panicked actions to maintain the desired performance level as the end of a reporting period approaches. This is particularly important in a highly competitive market where the aim is not only to have a cost-effective organisation but also to keep ahead of competitors.

Various organisations exploit KPIs to determine whether they are succeeding in their social responsibilities, which are not directly related to financial performance. For instance, organisations are currently more conscious of issues related to 'climate change' and how they may contribute through green technology to mitigate the adverse effects their industry is causing. For example, the Department for Environment, Food and Rural Affairs of the United Kingdom issued a document entitled 'Environmental Key Performance Indicators: Reporting Guidelines for UK Business' (Defra, 2006). This document claims that reporting on environmental performance will benefit the organisation in two ways: (a) It will provide management information to help management to exploit the cost savings that good environmental performance usually brings; and (b) It gives management the opportunity to set out what it believes is significant in its firm's environmental performance. Hence, in this case the KPIs will assist companies in managing and communicating the links between environmental and financial performance.

The Defra (2006) guidelines establish 22 environmental KPIs, together with information on how environmental impacts arising from the supply chain and from the use of products can be considered. However, no one company is expected to report on all the defined KPIs. According to Defra, an analysis of business sectors suggests that around 80% of companies are likely to have five or fewer KPIs. It also claims that whilst some companies already have sophisticated reporting systems in place, the Guidelines aim to help many more companies reach a level where they understand their environmental performance and can improve it.

Information is the basis for all decisions. Hence, without KPIs depicting fundamental statistics about performance, management is at risk of reaching incorrect decisions about a host of situations. KPIs should be aligned with a responsibility centre. This responsibility centre could be an individual or work team. This way KPIs may be used as a tool to foster accountability for employees as individuals or as a team. Additionally, the analysis of the combined KPIs on a holistic organisational basis also encourages accountability for management in relation to organisational performance.

If KPIs are defined according to the SMART principles, they can motivate employees and increase job satisfaction, which will in turn facilitate organisational performance and organisational commitment, and build a culture of achievement. Therefore, it is important that KPIs are realistic and practical; otherwise instead of being a motivator, unachievable KPIs can demoralise both employees and management. Suitable KPIs create a sense of purpose that helps to maintain both the management team and employees alike, focused on achieving the established objectives. Key performance measures that are transformed into suitable and achievable KPIs help to achieve the defined organisational objectives and have the potential to stimulate both the management team and employees towards a higher level of performance on an individual level. However, identifying key performance measures is just one step in the desirable direction. What is also important is identifying the key result areas.

## Key Result Areas (KRAs)

According to The Economic Times (2021), key result areas (KRAs) refer to the general metrics or parameters which the organisation has fixed for a specific role; where the term outlines the scope of the job profile and captures almost 80% to 88% of a work role. KRAs refer to a short list of overall goals that guide an employee on how to conduct their function. KRAs may also be defined at a higher level so that they describe the general achievement and progress goals for an organisation or its individual divisions. Therefore, KRAs facilitate the scope definition for specific functions, departmental or divisional goals, and organisational objectives. Moreover, they help to define the optimum outcomes and results of daily work at the various organisational levels; thus they are essential for an employee, division, or organisation to be successful in achieving their daily tasks.

KRAs are those areas in which a manager has complete ownership and accountability. It is important for the manager of a KRA to itemise the daily tasks that are within the mandate of the KRA. The focus is on day-to-day activities. Therefore, KRAs will likely be different from one organisation to another and from one work area to another. There are no golden rules for defining KRAs; however, they generally summarise the job profile, including the key impact areas for which the employees are expected to deliver. Hence, KRAs largely describe the job profile of the various categories of employees so that they have a clear understanding of their practical role. Therefore, KRAs must be unambiguously defined, quantifiable, and easy to measure. The objective is to facilitate the alignment of the employees' role with that of the organisation.

KRAs are general issues or themes on which the employee must focus during the year. In practice, this means that a manager working at a manufacturing environment would have a different KRA than a manager working for a service-related organisation. For example, a manager working in a manufacturing organisation would need to focus on maintaining the production budget of the division, the safety level of the employees, coordination with different organisational divisions, staff development, and reporting, including launching new technologies to enhance productivity. Furthermore, management must identify and define the objectives and standards for each KRA that are clearly and easily quantifiable. This ensures that the employees have a clear comprehension of their specific KRA to conduct their various tasks efficiently.

As stated previously, KRAs vary a great deal, depending on the organisation, or the stipulated goals of a division within an organisation, or the specific role of an employee. Although KRAs vary, there are several major characteristics that are critical for developing a KRA; namely they must be specific, clear, and measurable. These criteria need to be addressed while the KRA is being defined and not after. In defining KRAs, it is critical that they are task-specific under the direct responsibility of an individual or a division and that they embrace a fundamental activity of the organisation.

## *Preparing Key Result Areas for Individuals*

The identification of KRAs is very important because if one applies the Pareto principle, 80% of the outcomes or after-effects of an activity or task is the result of 20% of the causes. Thus, if this principle is applied to how departments, divisions, organisations, or individuals perform their work, then 80% of the value of the work being done will result from 20% of the tasks or activities conducted. Consequently, it is vital that one recognises and comprehends the most significant 20% of the work being conducted, which will reveal the somewhat small portion of the work that produces the most value to the organisation. Developing KRAs requires a systematic process that is straightforward and includes the following:

- *Communicate*: Communication is seen as a two-way process. In other words, it is important that everyone is permitted to participate in the KRA definition process. When defining KRAs for a department or organisation, provide team members with the opportunity to discuss and decide the KRAs. If a KRA is being defined for an individual employee's post within the organisation, the employee should be consulted when defining the KRAs for the position. This consultation process allows employees and managers to share information related to what is under their direct control and what is important to achieving the organisation's goals. Using this approach everyone will understand the indicators that are appropriate to the KRAs. This approach will ensure that the KRAs are viewed as being reasonable and achievable, and have value for the individual and organisation.
- *Define the Job Profile*: The KRAs will likely itemise a list of functions and activities that are considered important to the success of performing the function. If the KRAs are being defined for a specific position, ensure that they broadly define that job function and provide the employee with clear and unambiguous understanding of their role within the organisation.

- *Confirm that the KRAs are suitable for the position*: KRAs should only require specific objectives from an employee if that employee has the capacity within the organisation's structure to achieve the defined objective.
- *Apply the SMART principle*: All KRAs should be specific, measurable, achievable, relevant, and time-bound.
- *Limit the number of objectives*: KRAs, whether for individuals, departments, or organizations, should reflect the most crucial objectives. Hence, limit the number of objectives to between three and a maximum of seven objectives. It should be noted that resources are required to monitor KRAs; therefore make sure that the process is manageable by having only significant objectives.
- *Categorise tasks*: To ensure the process is manageable by grouping related tasks together.
- *Document the KRAs*: The KRAs must be documented, evaluated, revised, approved, and signed by pertinent stakeholders. KRAs for individual employees should be discussed with the individual concerned with the aim of having a document that is signed by the individual.

In determining the appropriate KRAs for an individual it is necessary to firstly evaluate how the employee currently spends his/her time on the assigned job. Secondly, itemise the tasks the employee should be doing but is not currently doing, and thirdly ask and obtain responses to the following questions with the help of the employee:

(a) Why was the employee employed by the organisation?
(b) What is the employee expected to achieve?
(c) What are the employee's daily and weekly duties (as separate lists)?
(d) Which of the employee's daily and weekly duties are most important to the success of the organisation?
(e) Why is the employee's position important to the organisation's success?
(f) What makes the employee's position vital to the success of the organisation?
(g) What are the tasks that only the employee can do to attain definite results for the organisation?
(h) Are there tasks that are being done by the employee that can be delegated?
(i) What tasks are not essential for the employee to perform well, or are getting in the way of doing his/her job well?

The KRAs should be reviewed frequently with the employee and amended when necessary. As a manager or supervisor, itemise what the unit or department should be doing to demonstrate its importance.

### *Preparing Key Result Areas for an Organisation*

When defining the KRAs for an organisation, these must focus on the critical areas that best support the organisation's strategic objectives, which directly provide the thrust for its success. Thus, it is important that an analysis is conducted with the participation of employees and managers to define the success factors. Furthermore, the organisation's strategic objectives and the KRAs for the various divisions and functional areas are congruent across the organisation. Hence, it is essential that employees in an organisation work as a well synchronised group pulling in the same direction with the same priorities. This is achieved by having a realistic number of significant KRAs that support the strategic objectives. Moreover, it will ensure that the organisation will grow and succeed.

It should be noted that that each general KRA will have a detailed metrics, referred to as key performance indicators, which may be monitored to assess the progress that is being made in each area. Although the KRAs will vary from one organisation to another, there are several general areas that are part of the KRAs, which are common to various organisations, such as: Profitability; employee contentment; product quality; customer satisfaction; effective organisational management; and innovation.

In developing KRAs several barriers need to be overcome, such as: (i) ensuring that KRAs are unambiguous in relation to the main tasks and outcomes employees should focus on; (ii) ensuring that employees focus on daily tasks that are truly of value to the success of the organisation; (iii) ensuring that employees are involved in defining their KRAs, because the imposition of KRAs in an organisation will result in conflicts that generate a performance system that habitually fails.

The identification and monitoring of KRAs is fundamental for ensuring that the appropriate performance level is achieved by the employees and the organisation as a whole. The outcome without suitable KRAs that act as a tool for focusing efforts of employees is loss of effectiveness. Employees will be distracted by tasks that may appear important to them but may not add sufficient value to the organisation. Hence, the accumulation of these insignificant tasks may be substantial and hinder the organisation's performance. Defining KRAs, especially when employees are involved in their definition, will likely result in a significant growth in motivation and job satisfaction. Giving employees specific and realistic targets that they and their supervisors can monitor to assess progress is likely to motivate them to work harder.

The KRAs also help the holistic organisation to remain on track because KRAs compel the organisation to make a distinction between those activities that are important to focus on and those that are considered critical (firefighting). Apart from KRAs there are also Key Performance Areas (KPAs) that describe the general areas for which an individual or organisation may be responsible. However, unlike KRAs, the KPAs are not monitored because they merely describe the general areas of responsibility. For example, the general area of responsibility related to a specific organisational division may involve financials that include financial trends, expenditure, revenue, and net profits; customer satisfaction in terms of frequency of complaints and faulty product returns; and productivity related to achieving overall objectives, meeting growth estimates, and the customers' perception of the organisation and its services.

## Key Performance Indicators (KPIs)

In the previous section the concept of Key Resultant Areas (KRAs) was discussed, which basically explained that KRAs refer to a short list of overall goals that guide employees as to how to conduct their function. However, KRAs also consist of several Key Performance Indicators (KPIs) that segment the KRAs into lower-level goals. Typically, a KPI is any metric that measures whether an organisation is achieving certain defined objectives, whose outcome assists the organisation to be successful in its undertakings. Hence, KPIs may be expressed by ratios that reflect sales, productivity, rate of return on capital investment, and many other potential indicative figures that reflect performance.

Figure 1.1 depicts the concepts described in the previous sections. Figure 1.1 and Table 1.1 illustrate that a KRA is related to the KPAs but the KPAs are not monitored. In fact, a KPA assists with identifying the KPIs for a KRA. One needs to keep in mind that a KRA consists of several KPIs. Finally, the KPIs are directly related to the outcomes; that is, the achievement of the objectives. It should be noted that the Key Performance Measures as shown

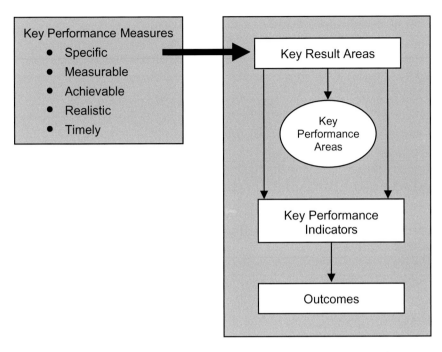

*Figure 1.1*  The Relationship between Key Performance Measures, Key Performance
Areas, and Key Performance Indicators

in the diagram are illustrating that the KRAs and KPIs must follow the
SMART concept of having a metric that is specific, measurable, achievable,
realistic, and timely. Therefore, the KPIs are viewed as being the measurements associated with the general objectives delineated in a KRA.

KPIs must be effective and specific to an organisation's operating environment. Often organisations adopt KPIs that may be industry-recognised
and find that they fail to affect any positive change. However, the common
reason for this is that the adopted KPIs do not reflect accurately their own
business activities. KPIs are an important communications tool and as such
must abide by a suitable set of guidelines that represent the most efficient
or sensible course of action in each business situation.

It should be noted that a KPI that is concise, clear, and consists of relevant information is much more likely to be understood and acted upon.
Therefore, when formulating KPIs it is best to first itemise and understand
the organisational objectives; secondly plan how these objectives are to be
achieved; and finally identify the person who would be responsible for

*Table 1.1*  Differences between KRAs, KPAs, and KPIs

|  | *Key Resultant Area (KRA)* | *Key Performance Area (KPA)* | *Key Performance Indicator (KPI)* |
|---|---|---|---|
| Definition | Areas of work that are critical to the performance of an employee, unit, division, or entity. | Overall segments of outcomes or accountabilities for an entity, division or individual. | A measure that assists in assessing performance in KRAs. |
| Scope | Measurability of key areas within an entity. | General description of work areas, particularly non-essential aspects of work that are not results-oriented. | A system of measurement e.g., explicit number or rate. |
| Objective | Target for unit or entity to be successful, including how employees are to conduct their work, providing overall attainment of goals. | Responsibility areas of entity, division, or individual. | Evaluated progress toward defined targets identified in KRAs. |
| Example | Growth of online sales. | Online sales expansion. | Growth in sales of a particular service from 8% to 15%. |

monitoring them and taking action. The full KPIs formulation process is iterative and encompasses feedback from the technical and managerial staff. Thus, with the passage of time and experience, employees in the organisation will better appreciate and comprehend the business processes that need to be measured and included in a KPI dashboard, and who should have access to this information. Defining KPIs is not as straightforward as it seems.

The essential overtone for KPIs is the word 'key' because each KPI should be related to a specific business consequence with a specific performance measure. Hence, KPIs are to be defined in a way that corresponds to the critical or core objectives of the organisation. In defining a KPI, the follow-ing should be taken into consideration:

- What is the required outcome?
- What is the significance of this outcome?
- How is progress to be measured?
- How will you know that the required outcome is being achieved?
- How frequently will progress be reviewed to ensure that you are mov-ing towards the required outcome?

For example, let us assume that the objective is to increase productivity this year and management has decided to call this the 'Productivity Growth' KPI. The 'Productivity Growth' KPI might be defined as follows:

a) *Required outcome*: Increase productivity by 20% this year.
b) *Significance of outcome*: By achieving this target the business will be able to deliver its product on time.
c) *Measuring progress*: Calculate the difference between promised delivery date and actual delivery date.
d) *Knowing that outcome is being achieved*: The production manager is responsible for this metric, with product delivery time variance to be close to zero. This will lead to a 20% increase in productivity by this year.
e) *Frequency of review*: The review of productivity variance will be daily.

KPIs differ from industry to industry, as illustrated by Table 1.2. However, as stated previously, KPIs should not be blindly accepted just because they are industry-recognised, but should be defined specifically for the organi-sation. Hence, Table 1.2 is being provided as an indication of what KPIs may look like for some specific industries.

It is important that only the performance measures that are essen-tial (key) to managing an organisation are included and these should be explained in sufficient detail to ensure everyone understands what is required. This facilitates KPI transparency. As noted above, KPIs should be specific to an organisation depending on its strategic objectives; therefore there is no golden rule that specifies how many KPIs an organisation should have. However, the literature related to KPIs suggests around a handful, but there is no precise amount. It must be remembered that the more KPIs an

Table 1.2  Significant Measures across Particular Industries

| Insurance | General Retail | Mining |
|---|---|---|
| Customer loyalty | Capital investment | Capital invested |
| Customer growth rate | Store product range changes | Exploration success rate |
| Credit rating | Projected return on latest stores | Equipment utilisation rate |
| Claims rate | Customer satisfaction rate | Extraction capacity |
| Insurance type | Same store comparable growth | Degree of anticipated reserves |
| Claim frequency | Sales per square metre floor space | Degree of confirmed reserves |

organisation has, the more management effort is required to collect the relevant data to monitor them.

An important consideration is for management to establish the process for collating the KPIs and reporting them internally. For instance, management should establish whether the KPIs convey the right message or seem correct when accumulated and reported at a group level. It may be more beneficial and practical to report the KPIs on a unit, department, or divisional level. KPIs should not be considered as being eternal. Hence, management needs to review the selected KPIs and determine whether they are relevant at any point in time. Moreover, organisational strategies and objectives are not static; they change over time. Therefore, the KPIs that were applicable to them will also change.

The choice of KPIs often depends on the information that is available at a specific point in time. Hence, new KPIs may be included, and others changed due to the ability of management to collect new information that permits them to compute new KPIs that provide a greater comprehension of business activity. An important issue related to KPIs is their reliability. There are no reliability standards that are applicable to specific KPIs. However, the definition of KPIs should be supported by underlying assumptions and any data restrictions or weaknesses. This will permit those exploiting the KPIs to evaluate the usefulness of the KPIs for themselves.

## Relationship between KRAs and KPIs

The relationship between KRAs and KPIs is better explained through sample reports, namely those on an individual basis and those on an organisational basis. Figure 1.2 provides a sample report that shows the KRAs definition design for an individual within an organisation and the associated KPI measures. Figure 1.2 is divided into three main reporting segments that illustrate the relationship between the KRAs and KPIs. The first report segment consists of the employee work position details, including the applicable supervisor and reviewer details. The second report segment describes the employee position mission (how it serves the organisation's strategic objectives) and the related growth plan. The third report segment consists of a detailed description of each KRA (job profile) in order of significance and associated KPI details, outcomes for each quarterly period, and overall goal. The information from the third segment signifies the relationship between the KRAs and the KPIs, and demonstrates how they are applied to assess the employee's performance in those specific areas. Figure 1.3 provides a sample report for an organisation (in this case a department within an organisation) and the associated KPI measures. Figure 1.3 is very similar to Figure 1.2, the only difference being the titles of the first and second report segments.

## Conclusion

This chapter has covered the fundamental principles regarding the definition and usage of key performance indicators (KPIs). It has shown that KPIs may be defined at different levels within the organisation. For example, KPIs may be established at organisational, divisional, departmental, activity, and individual levels. Hence, KPIs are about accountability of those who are responsible for a specific segment of the organisation.

The opening point of the KPI process is commitment of all the parties concerned, beginning with the Board of Directors, and cascading to the individual employees towards having a KPI methodology as the performance management appraisal system. Therefore, it is extremely important for all concerned to be closely involved in the KPI process. Furthermore, it is essential that all employees at the various organisational levels are aware of the strategic objectives of the organisation and how their specific

**Employee Details**

Name          Position          Commencement Date          I.D Number          Signature

**Workplace Details**

Department          Supervisor          Date          Supervisor Signature

**Reviewer Details**

Name          Designation          Date Last Reviewed          Reviewer Signature

**Position Mission**

Provide main purpose of your role and describe how it aligns with the overall mission of the department and organisation. List the key tasks that are carried out often by you to perform your role well.

**Growth Plan**

After the KRAs and KPIs are reviewed, describe what you intend on doing to focus on improving in the next period.

**Key Result Areas (KRA) in order of priority**

| KRA Description | KPI | Description of KPI | Results (per month) | | | | | | | | | | | | Moving Ave. | Goal |
|---|---|---|---|---|---|---|---|---|---|---|---|---|---|---|---|---|
| | | | M1 | M2 | M3 | M4 | M5 | M6 | M7 | M8 | M9 | M10 | M11 | M12 | | |
| KRA 1: | 1.1 | | | | | | | | | | | | | | | |
| | 1.2 | | | | | | | | | | | | | | | |
| | 1.3 | | | | | | | | | | | | | | | |
| | 1.4 | | | | | | | | | | | | | | | |
| KRA 2: | 2.1 | | | | | | | | | | | | | | | |
| | 2.2 | | | | | | | | | | | | | | | |
| | 2.3 | | | | | | | | | | | | | | | |
| | 2.4 | | | | | | | | | | | | | | | |
| KRA 3: | 3.1 | | | | | | | | | | | | | | | |
| | 3.2 | | | | | | | | | | | | | | | |
| | 3.3 | | | | | | | | | | | | | | | |

Figure 1.2  Key Result Areas for an Individual Within an Organisation

## Department Details

| Department | Supervisor | Date | Supervisor Signature |
|---|---|---|---|

## Reviewer Details

| Name | Designation | Date Last Reviewed | Reviewer Signature |
|---|---|---|---|

**Position Mission**
Describe main objective of the department. Describe how it aligns with the overall mission of the organisation.

**Growth Plan**
After the KRAs and KPIs are reviewed, describe what you intend on doing to focus on improving in the next period.

### Key Result Areas (KRA) in order of priority

| KRA Description | KPI | Description of KPI | Results (per month) | | | | | | | | | | | | Moving Ave. | Goal |
|---|---|---|---|---|---|---|---|---|---|---|---|---|---|---|---|---|
| | | | M1 | M2 | M3 | M4 | M5 | M6 | M7 | M8 | M9 | M10 | M11 | M12 | | |
| KRA 1: | 1.1 | | | | | | | | | | | | | | | |
| | 1.2 | | | | | | | | | | | | | | | |
| | 1.3 | | | | | | | | | | | | | | | |
| | 1.4 | | | | | | | | | | | | | | | |
| | 1.5 | | | | | | | | | | | | | | | |
| KRA 2: | 2.1 | | | | | | | | | | | | | | | |
| | 2.2 | | | | | | | | | | | | | | | |
| | 2.3 | | | | | | | | | | | | | | | |
| | 2.4 | | | | | | | | | | | | | | | |
| | 2.5 | | | | | | | | | | | | | | | |
| KRA 3: | 3.1 | | | | | | | | | | | | | | | |
| | 3.2 | | | | | | | | | | | | | | | |
| | 3.3 | | | | | | | | | | | | | | | |
| | 3.4 | | | | | | | | | | | | | | | |
| | 3.5 | | | | | | | | | | | | | | | |

Figure 1.3 Key Result Areas for an Organisation (Department)

function contributes towards the achievement of these strategic objectives. Once these basic principles are recognised, the actual KPI definition development may commence.

The KPI definition development process starts off by defining an implementation plan. This plan will set out when the various KPI implementation levels are scheduled to come on board, starting from the organisational holistic level and ending with the individual employees. The KPIs implementation plan must be realistic, with each phase defining in detail the tasks to be conducted at each specific level. These specific levels are referred to as Key Result Areas (KRAs).

The KRAs refer to a short list of overall goals and describe the general achievement and progress goals for an organisation, department, activity, or individual employees. Therefore, KRAs facilitate the scope definition for specific functions, departmental or divisional goals, and organisational objectives. Moreover, they help to define the optimum outcomes and results of daily work at the various organisational levels, thus they are essential for an employee, division, or organisation to be successful in achieving their daily tasks. KRAs are those areas in which a manager has complete ownership and accountability.

It is important for the manager of a KRA to itemise the daily tasks that are within the mandate of the KRA. The focus is on day-to-day activities. Therefore, KRAs will likely be different from one organisation to another and from one work area to another. The KRAs may (if deemed necessary) be segmented further into Key Performance Areas (KPAs) that describe the general areas for which an organisation, department, or individual may be responsible. However, unlike KRAs, the KPAs are not monitored, because they merely describe the general areas of responsibility.

Therefore, taking each specific level (KRA), identify the Key Performance Measures (KPMs) for that level. The KPMs will be used to assess the performance of the specific level, be it the organisation, department, activity, or individual. The KPMs are to follow the SMART concept, namely, being specific, measurable, achievable, realistic, and timely. The combination of the KRAs and KPMs will provide the KPIs for that specific organisational level. As one may appreciate, the KPI definition process is iterative. Hence, each KPI must be closely monitored and fine-tuned until management (and employees) are satisfied that the resultant KPIs are equitable and represent the realistic circumstances of the functional level being measured. Once the KPIs are recognised as being accurate and realistic, the KPIs are accepted as part of the performance dashboard for that specific organisational level.

Finally, there is a need to regularly review the KPIs, since these may not be appropriate if the strategic objectives of the organisation change at any point in time. Having said this, generally, if the KPIs are being achieved then the strategic objectives of the organisation are being accomplished, with the consequent desirable organisational outcome.

## References

Defra (2006). *Environmental Key Performance Indicators: Reporting Guidelines for UK Business.* Available at: www.defra.gov.uk (Accessed 20 November 2023).

Eby, K. (2019). *The Most Comprehensive List of Key Results Areas for Departments & Positions.* Available at: https://www.smartsheet.com/content/key-result-areas (Accessed 20 November 2023).

PricewaterhouseCoopers (2007). *Guide to Key Performance Indicators: Communicating the Measures That Matter.* Available at: https://www.pwc.com/gx/en/audit-services/corporate-reporting/assets/pdfs/uk_kpi_guide.pdf (Accessed 20 November 2023).

The Economic Times (2021). *Human-Resource: Definition of 'Key Result Areas'.* Available at: https://economictimes.indiatimes.com/definition/key-result-areas (Accessed 20 November 2023).

# 2

## PERFORMANCE MANAGEMENT CONCEPTS AND RELATED TOOLS

'If you don't collect any metrics, you're flying blind. If you collect and focus on too many, they may be obstructing your field of view.'

Scott M. Graffius
Author

There are several approaches to managing performance that complement the use of KPIs. Therefore, it is appropriate to provide an overview of the performance management concept and several associated tools. Traditional performance management approaches are based on appraising employees from time to time by assessing their effort and resultant productivity regarding their overall contribution to the defined organisational goals. Hence, the objective of this approach is highly regarded and there are still many organisations that apply this traditional approach. However, the traditional approach is commonly criticised as being burdensome and time-consuming, and found not to work in a practical sense. All too often those assessing employees go through the mechanics of the system without truly evaluating whether the organisational goals are being achieved.

DOI: 10.4324/9781032685465-3

This has made many organisations realise that a better system is needed for appraising employees and responsibility areas, such as departments. This realisation has resulted in several performance management systems being developed that are still evolving with the objective of significantly increasing organisational effectiveness and employee productivity. According to HR Tech (2021), the statistics show that:

- 80% of the younger generation desires direct gratification rather than a formal review, since an annual review results in a 12-month gap during which period special achievements would likely be forgotten.
- 90% of performance reviews are viewed as being emotionally and mentally distressing processes that may harm an employee's self-esteem.
- Only 5% of HR management view performance reviews as satisfactory.
- 95% of managers are disappointed with conventional performance management traditions.
- 51% of employees view annual reviews as grossly inaccurate and unfair.

The above information illustrates that a better performance management methodology is necessary. Azadinamin (2011) argues that older and traditional methods seem to fail in measuring performance under the current market structure and respective market rules. He argues that these methods are being modified and their focus is shifting from accounting-based methods towards an economic-oriented framework.

## Introduction

Performance management systems and their associated annual employee appraisal methods are not new and have been in use for at least a century. Initially these types of approaches were used to specifically identify poor performers with the objective of terminating their engagement or to reassign them to other duties. These systems grew in popularity over the years, especially during periods of high inflation, such as the 1970s energy crisis, where salary increases had to be tightly controlled. Thus, annual appraisals were viewed as a simple and practical way of achieving this. Employee appraisals became the basis for the adopted performance management systems and continued to be unchallenged in their use up to the early 2000s, at a time when flat organisation structures were the accepted norm. However, it soon became evident that conducting regular employee appraisals was a time-consuming activity and was not considered to be a practical solution for the supervisor. The common outcome was that the supervisor went through the mechanics of the appraisal process without realistically appraising whether and to what extent the employee was achieving the strategic objectives of the organisation. Hearn (2021, p. 3) cited research from a study conducted by Corporate Executive Board (CEB), which identified several concerns with the annual appraisals that are currently the basis of many performance management systems in organisations. These concerns include:

- 95% of managers are not satisfied with performance appraisals and dislike undertaking them. Hence, they frequently evade doing them, or at best they regard them as a tick-box exercise with little meaningful discussion taking place, particularly in relation to the achievement of the strategic objectives of the organisation.
- 75% of employees view performance appraisals as unfair and 66% see them as interfering with their productivity.
- Only 8% of organisations view performance appraisals as adding value and the majority of the organisations do not view them as an effective use of time.
- 30% of the performance reviews resulted in decreasing employee performance and a meta-analysis of 607 studies of performance evaluations found that appraisals were not improving employee performance and engagement.

Hearn argues that despite the above concerns with performance appraisals, organisations continue applying them. Citing CEB research findings, he maintains that there are two key explanations for this, namely: (a) to evaluate performance as a basis for pay and promotions decisions even though more than 75% of HR managers state that their performance review process does not accurately reflect employee contributions; and (b) to identify poor performers and hold them accountable. However, Hearn argues that managers are notable to effectively differentiate employee performance because of the halo effect, where managers consistently give selected employees high ratings and fail to recognise areas for improvement, and/or to reverse engineer performance ratings to provide the reward outcome they want.

Furthermore, he argues that less than 5% of employees in an organisation are typically poor performers, therefore it does not justify having extensive documentation for every employee, particularly if one accepts the fact that performance appraisals are not a reliable way of identifying poor performers. Hearn contends that performance appraisal methods are not effective drivers of performance and engagement for the following reasons:

(a) Performance appraisal methods strive to attain too many outcomes from one meeting, such as, reviewing performance compared with past objectives, assessing demonstration of competencies, giving feedback, recognising achievements, identifying performance problems, discussing career goals, setting a personal development plan, setting objectives for the forthcoming year and rating performance for pay purposes. He argues that dealing with all these component outcomes in a single meeting is not practical. Hence, he claims that typically none of the components end up being discussed in sufficient detail to be significant and thus the process becomes a tick-the-box exercise that disengages both the employee and the manager.

(b) Discussing performance once or twice a year is not adequate. Hearn argues that to improve the performance and productivity of employees requires more than one or two performance discussions a year; rather it necessitates frequent feedback, recognition, and coaching from managers for employees to perform to the best of their abilities. Moreover, he claims that getting feedback at an appraisal meeting about something that did or did not go well several months in the past will have little positive impact and typically leads to resentment.

(c) Appraisals are inclined to be focused on the past rather than being future-oriented. Hearn argues that appraisals typically focus on whether employees have achieved their objectives over the last year and whether they have demonstrated the appropriate behaviours or competencies. He further argues that to drive performance, dialogue is required with employees about past performance in combination with regular future-focused discussions.

The above demonstrate that performance management systems and their associated annual employee appraisal methods may not be the best approach to ensuring that employees work together for achieving the strategic objectives of the organisation.

## Overview of Performance Management and Tools

The above illustrate that the way performance management systems are being applied, using annual employee appraisals, may not be achieving the outcome for which these systems have been designed. Hence, it is appropriate to examine the basics of performance management. One may view a performance management system as being a continuous systematic process under the guidance of the HR Department that permits employees to participate in improving the success of the organisation, by achieving its defined vision, mission, and objectives. Therefore, performance management includes many of the human resource functions, such as: regular communication with employees, employee development programmes aimed at improving performance, introducing good work practices, establishing realistic goals, regular progress review, and immediate feedback from employees. A close examination of this performance management system description reveals that the annual employee appraisal aspect is not a key feature. An effective performance management system is one in which:

- The performance management cycle is not an annual affair but is essentially continuous.
- Senior management is strongly committed to performance management.
- Management is in the habit of making significant verbal statements of encouragement to employees related to their performance.
- Managers are eager and able to provide daily results-oriented performance management.
- The system is easy to use and is not burdensome.

Hearn (2021) argues that most organisations have some form of employee performance management or performance appraisal process, but he questions whether managers in many organisations genuinely know the motive behind why performance management is undertaken in their organisation. He contends that this question needs to be addressed if performance management is to be successfully implemented. There is consensus that the primary purpose of performance management should be aimed at making sure the strategic objectives of the organisation are being achieved and individual employees are contributing to this aim. However, many organisations use their performance management system to identify poor performers and to facilitate pay and promotions decisions that have been shown to result in diminishing employee performance rather than enhancing it. Hearn asserts that an effective performance management approach should be based upon five key principles, which collectively aim to improve employee performance and engagement:

- *Aligned, Near-Term Objectives*: Employees cannot perform adequately unless they understand in unambiguous terms what is expected of them. On the other hand, organisations cannot succeed unless their employees participate fully and contribute to the strategic objectives of the organisation. Hence, it is essential that employees, together with their manager, agree to specific objectives that are congruent with the goals of the organisation or work team. In other words, there must be an alignment of the work objectives of the employee with those of the organisation. Furthermore, the established employee objectives should not be established or reviewed on an annual basis, since they can easily become irrelevant, especially if business activities change during the 12-month period. Such circumstances may in fact demoralise employees because they will find it difficult to maintain the alignment of their established goals with those of the organisation. Hence, it is preferable to shorten the performance review time frame to monthly or quarterly periods. This provides employees with short-term milestones that make it easier for them to achieve and adjust to changing operating circumstances. In addition, employees need to be directly involved (together and in agreement with their manager) in establishing their objectives, providing that the defined objectives are aligned with the organisational goals. The alternative is for the employee objectives to be dictated from above, which will likely result in resentment and resistance.
- *Frequent Feedback*: The advantage of short-term milestones is that they provide an opportunity for regular and continuous feedback that has been found to significantly improve employee performance. Furthermore, feedback is most advantageous when provided frequently and immediately, rather than at the formal performance review meeting intervals.
- *Regular Support from Manager*: Employees cannot thrive in their respective roles and make significant progress unless they are frequently and consistently supported by their manager. Hence, performance reviews that take place annually or bi-annually are not enough. The support

from the manager is essential and does not need to be a formal affair. Moreover, managers need to be aware of how to conduct one-to-one engagements that help employees to remove the obstacles to success, put more effort on future activities, and learn from past experiences. The outcome of this will be positive and explicit action points for the manager and employees.

- *Employee Recognition*: Employee recognition is the sincere acceptance and expressed appreciation for employees' contributions to their organisation. Employee recognition contributes to increasing employee performance and engagement and is viewed as the timely, informal, or formal acknowledgement of an employee's behaviour and effort that supports the organisation's goals and values and exceeds the manager's normal expectations. Research has shown that organisations which adopt a 'high recognition' ethos have 30% lower voluntary turnover than average and are inclined to do better than their peers in a variety of other metrics.

- *Personal and Career Development*: Because performance reviews focus on assessing and rating performance of employees, they tend to pay lip service to discussing and agreeing development and career plans with employees. Research has found that organisations that do not allocate adequate and consistent time to discuss employee development tend to have lower employee organisational commitment, consequently having a higher turnover rate with the associated risk of losing their key talent.

## Aligning Organisational and Employee Needs

The starting point to establishing a performance management system is to examine the needs of the organisation and the needs of the employee, and align these needs. The needs of the organisation are basically defined in the agreed Organisation's strategy and associated strategic objectives. Hence, executive management are responsible for providing improvements in specific KPIs, such as generating revenue at a certain level, which should be specified as one of the strategic objectives. Therefore, organisational objective achievement is measured by metrics, such as KPIs, which determine whether the agreed goals have been achieved. Ideally, these goals should be defined as the 'Objectives and Key Results' (OKRs) for the organisation that are viewed as annual and possibly quarterly milestones. Typically, departments, units, work teams, or individuals depending on the system adopted by an organisation will align their goals using a suitable frame-work, such as OKRs. However, it should be recognised that not all the work effort in an organisation Is directly contributing to the strategic objectives of the organisation.

The work effort can be classified into two categories: Work effort that is directly linked to strategic objectives (OKRs), such as the core activi-ties (primary activities); and work effort that contributes to supporting the organisation, such as business-as-usual processes and jobs-to-be-done that maintain and improve specific areas of responsibility (secondary activities). In some cases, employees may have a mixture of the two categories of work effort. Therefore, it is important that every employee knows where they fit in the scheme of things and how their work effort contributes to the organisation's success. For this to happen, all employees must know in clear terms their specific role and associated goals, and how their work effort contributes to the organisation's business plan. This provides the employees' raison d'etre, their purpose in the organisation, which in turn is found to be rewarding and positively affects their job satisfaction, result-ing in productivity gains. Having a clear role and explicit goals ensures that the employees' work effort is relevant and is fully directed towards achieving the organisational plans and strategic objectives. Moreover, the general impact is the development of affective organisational commitment, namely the emotional attachment of an employee to organisational values. This contributes towards the capability of the organisation to appeal to and retain the ablest employees.

Furthermore, all levels of employees would rather know what is expected of them and how their role contributes to the organisation's success. Hence, it is important that the strategic objectives are conveyed to employees through a comprehensive communication strategy. This communication strategy should link the strategic objectives with the goals and role of the individual employees. Table 2.1 illustrates the relationship between the needs of the organisation and those of the employees, and the prerequisites that are required by the employees to achieve outstanding performance. Table 2.1 indicates that apart from appropriate skills and resources, employ-ees require continuous support from the systems they use; their manager and team members; and the overall organisational culture, and values, including learning and development opportunities, general wellbeing, and recognition of their efforts towards organisational success.

Table 2.1 Organisational and Employee Needs

| Organisation Needs | Employee Needs | What Employees Need to Achieve Outstanding Performance |
|---|---|---|
| Achievement of Strategy | Knowledge of strategy & its direction | Accessibility to resources & expertise |
| Upgrading the Metric (KPI) | Transparent and clear method of measuring achievement | Efficient systems & processes, supported by innovative technology |
| Alignment of objectives with strategy and its implementation | Involvement in defining goals | Extensive peer support |
| Determination | Sensitive and safe work environment | Consistent support from management |
| Attainment of objectives | Leadership support to attain goals | Worthy ethics and conduct |
| Capable & inspired employees | Having a learning organisation | Opportunities to learn and develop |
| Control and reporting | Considerate managers that develop and coach employees | Sensitivity to employee welfare needs |
| Responsiveness | Contributing to organisational success | Recognition and appreciation |
| Outstanding culture | A pleasing and supporting culture | Collaborative environment |
| Acquiring capable employees | Commend and acclaim the employer | Beneficial and responsible employer |
| Employee retention | Development of affective commitment | Organisational commitment |

The above requirements are highly dependent on the level of organisational leadership and management qualities. It is the function of management to bring the various behavioural and operational components together as a synchronised force to generate synergy by linking and reinforcing organisational, team and individual objectives. Moreover, management needs to provide continuous support and frequent feedback to employees that will assist them to enhance their performance. Collectively, these factors strengthen employee and management transparency and accountability, resulting in better organisational governance.

## *Achieving Sustainable and Enhanced Performance Management*

To achieve sustainable and enhanced performance management, an organisation requires a robust framework consisting of a suitable structure and responsive system that is supported by processes comprising of a series of actions or steps. This framework will need to provide a simple and precise indication of the objectives, information as to whether it is achieving its goals, and a data gathering process to gauge whether employees on an individual basis or work team are achieving the agreed performance level.

Once the assessment criteria are defined and there is agreement regarding these criteria between the manager and employees or work team, an evaluation process is undertaken. Using such a process means that the manager is unlikely to stereotype employees that may result in biased assessments. It is suggested that the following simple procedure and actions will assist in the creation of an effective performance management system. Many of these might even become OKRs. Additionally, the actions will likely lead to defining the objectives and key results (OKRs) for the employees or work team.

### *Frequent Review of Roles and Responsibilities*

The concept of having clear roles and responsibilities has already been discussed. However, it is worth mentioning that generally employees are taken on with a defined job description, which becomes integrated as an important component of their human resource dossier. Nevertheless, in a practical working environment, organisations, work teams, and individuals develop and change, thus job descriptions become quickly outdated and do not reflect reality. Another important aspect is to enhance the 'role fit' by ensuring that employees are assigned tasks that are most suited for them and for which they are enthusiastic about. Therefore, it is essential to have a process of reviewing job descriptions that reflect the current employee work status and ability, thus ensuring it provides an accurate basis for evaluating how individual employees contribute towards the work team effort and/or the organisation's overall performance.

| R = Responsible | A = Accountable | C = Consulted | I = Informed |
| --- | --- | --- | --- |

| Task / Deliverable | Accountant | Accounts Clerk | Procurement Clerk |
| --- | --- | --- | --- |
| Purchase approval. | R | I | A |
| Procurement of goods. | C | I | R/A |
| Delivery of goods. | A | I | R |
| Sign delivery-note for goods. | I | A | R |
| Invoice for goods received. | R | I/C | A |
| Invoice for goods verified. | I/C | R | A |
| Approval for payment of goods. | R | A | C |
| Prepare payment for goods. | R | A | C |
| Make payment for item. | R | A | C |

Figure 2.1  Example of Using RACI Matrix

This is accomplished by reviewing the tasks to be conducted and their respective deliverables assigned to employees or the work team, and matching these with the defined roles and goals to determine whether there are any gaps. A responsibility assignment matrix (RACI) may be used to identify these gaps. RACI maps the contribution by various roles in completing tasks or deliverables for a business process. Figure 2.1 provides an example of how to use a RACI matrix to map the roles and goals of employees in a clear manner. This example illustrates a simple procurement business process performed by three employees, namely the Accountant, Accountants Clerk, and Procurement Clerk. Note that work teams or sections of a department could have been used instead of the individual employees. The RACI matrix provides a two-dimension tablet, with the vertical section indicating the task and/or deliverable and the horizontal section showing the employees involved in the process. The corresponding cells in the table relate to the tasks/deliverables and the employees may take on four specific roles, namely who is responsible, accountable, consulted, and kept informed.

## Culture, Values, and Behaviours

There is wide consensus that organisation culture directly impacts the defined strategy, its delivery, and consequently the overall performance of the organisation. The key reason for this is that the organisational culture reflects the mindset and attitude of its leaders, who ultimately are responsible for defining and implementing the strategy. Furthermore, a common management quote in organisations is that the 'culture eats strategy for breakfast.' This quote means that no matter how strong the strategic plan may be, its effectiveness will be hindered by the organisation's members if they do not share the proper culture. The bottom line is that those implementing the plan are the ones that make all the difference between success and failure. Merchant (2011) contends that culture is all that invisible stuff that glues organisations together and includes things like norms of purpose, values, approach – the stuff that is hard to codify, hard to evaluate, and certainly hard to measure, and therefore hard to manage. She further argues that this 'invisibility' causes many managers to treat culture as a soft topic, but it is the stuff that determines how to get things done. Therefore, it is essential for management to know what kind of culture they desire, and how they may go about building and maintaining this desired culture. But as stated previously, culture is a tricky issue since it normally reflects the attitude of the organisation's leadership.

## Share your Mission, Vision, and Objectives

It is important that executive management has a communications strategy in place to make sure that their mission, vision, and objectives are made known to all employees. This will ensure that management shares the long-term strategy of the organisation and that everyone in the organisation pulls in the same direction.

## Define Yearly and Quarterly Business Objectives and Key Results (OKRs)

Examine closely the organisation's long-term vision/mission and the upcoming annual segment of the organisation's strategy so that the organisation's OKRs may be identified for the upcoming year. Coordinate discussions with work teams (and individuals if deemed necessary) to enable them to define their own OKRs, which are aligned with and support the overall organisation's OKRs. The work team and individual OKRs will be their goals and obligations for assisting the organisation to achieve its strategic objectives for the upcoming year. This way everyone knows what is required from them to achieve their own and the organisation's OKRs, either as an initiator/owner or as a contributor to the identified OKRs. Obviously, whether the individual is the initiator/owner or contributor to the identified OKRs depends on their assigned role and responsibilities. This approach and the generated OKRs facilitate clarity of roles and generate the appropriate culture that highlights the notable role each employee contributes to the organisation's achievement.

## Generation of Innovative Proposals

The OKRs will establish what needs to be measured to determine organisational success. Therefore, discuss the various identified and defined OKRs with the work teams (and individuals) to determine an innovative means of undertaking them. It must be recognised that conventional work methods may not provide the optimum outcome. It must be understood that the employees know all the fine points of their work and they can often suggest a better and more effective way of doing an activity. Hence, organisational success will be directly enhanced by these innovative proposals.

## Employee Development

Clear roles and identified OKRs that reflect an employee's responsibilities provide a solid foundation for defining an employee's development programme on an individual basis. An employee development programme does not just consist of training but provides a means of sharing experiences, discussing lessons learnt, and reviewing their ambitions in terms of what they would like to be doing to contribute to the organisation's success. These employees develop programmes that are executed on a regular basis and reviewed quarterly or biannually. The basic objective of this review process should be to align the employee's development with the defined OKRs.

## Maintain an Agreed Momentum

To ensure that the defined OKRs are sustained and adhered to, it is important for the supervisor to encourage a two-way communication process and maintain continuous impetus towards achieving the OKRs. This is an important key feature for a successful performance management system, which does not need to consume a lot of time in meetings. The supervisor must assume a coaching role through encouragement and maintaining momentum in the execution of productive activities.

## Knowledge Management

It is important that experiences learnt throughout the whole OKR process, and their implementation, are not lost. It is essential to encourage, accumulate, and document continuous feedback from different sources. The main source of feedback will likely come from employees, but it may come from other work teams, customers, and suppliers. No matter what source, the feedback needs to be documented in a knowledge repository.

## Performance Management Information Application Module

The various procedures and actions described above require a user-friendly system that make the whole process manageable and do not result in a burden to management. Ideally, a performance management information application module should be part of an Enterprise Resource Planning System (ERP). The ERP provides an integrated approach to conducting core business processes, and simplifies sub-module processes, such as Performance Management.

### Performance Management Tools

Performance management tools help an organisation to manage and monitor the delivery of the planned results and ultimately the implementation of the organisation's strategy. Therefore, these tools not only assist managers to develop their leadership skills but are also essential for the organisation's operational success. There are many tools for managing performance that one may apply to improve the organisation's operational functioning and resultant productivity. Some of these tools are described below. However, an important fundamental element for implementing these performance management tools is to develop a high-performance culture within the organisation at every hierarchical level. This will enable each employee to be aware of how they may contribute towards the organisation's defined overall corporate strategy. This makes it easier for management to track, monitor, and manage performance in an effective manner and ensure that the forecasted results are attained.

According to Marr (2021), performance management systems may be categorised under two general types, namely, corporate performance management (CPM) and people performance management (PPM). Corporate performance management is also referred to as enterprise performance management. As the name suggests, this type of performance management focuses on the entire organisation, with specific emphasis on strategic performance improvement. Hence, this type of performance management system assists management to monitor and measure performance for strategic decision-making purposes. Marr argues that the focus of CPM is on strategic performance improvement, which includes various types of processes that help to identify and define strategic objectives and monitor and measure performance.

According to Marr, the monitoring and measurement performance function includes tasks like analysing, reporting, and reviewing performance, and aligning the organisation's people and its culture with its strategic objectives. Marr (2021) identifies several CPM tools and techniques that include management dashboards, Balanced Scorecards, KPIs, analytics, strategic planning, budgeting, and forecasting, Benchmarking, business excellence models, Six Sigma, Enterprise Risk Management, project or programme management, and performance reporting.

The other category of performance management systems is people performance management (PPM). Marr (2021) contends that this focuses on the management of individuals, which aims at ensuring that their performance contributes to the holistic strategic goals of the organisation by aligning the performance of employees with the improvement of corporate performance. Marr views PPM as consisting of processes for communicating corporate goals and priorities, aligning individual goals with corporate goals, agreeing performance measures and targets, helping individuals understand how well they are performing, as well as developing the skills and competencies required to improve results. Thus, the focus of PPM is the individual and how the individual can contribute to corporate performance.

Marr argues that PPM consists of tools and processes that are typically applied for managing people performance that include appraisals, reward and recognition systems, personal development plans, performance targets, and performance review meetings. Some of these tools have already been described in the previous sections. However, it is pertinent to add that most of the CPM tools can also be applied at various hierarchical levels within the organisation, even at an individual employee level. Hence, the general centre of attention here is the treatment of CPM tools. Although the focus is KPIs, it is worthwhile to provide a general description of the CPM tools to provide the reader with a wider understanding of performance management systems and how these relate to KPIs in general. It is important to keep in mind that KPIs and the associated metrics provide a method of measuring how well an organisation, division, projects, or individual employees are performing when compared to the established strategic goals and objectives of their particular entity.

KPIs provide a specific measurement of what should be achieved to enable management to assess performance and make better decisions. However, KPI measures must be meaningful and selective. KPIs need to address the question: What specific goal will this KPI assist my entity to achieve, or what concern will it resolve? Hence, well defined and selected KPIs provide a clear depiction of the performance levels being achieved by the organisation and whether the organisation is strategically where it desires to be. Therefore, PPM and CPM methods that are based on measurements and metrics may be considered as belonging to the KPIs family. The methods may differ in the way they are defined and how the relevant information may be collected, but the fundamental principles of measuring performance are practically the same.

### Management Dashboards

A management dashboard is a performance management tool that provides a visual, meaningful, and self-explanatory presentation of key facts and figures showing key performance indicators (KPIs) that an organisation, division, or unit needs to attain to gauge whether its operations are on track to achieve the defined business goals. However, the fundamental basis of management dashboards is to know what indicators to display and their interpretation to enable managers to run their business in the most self-assured manner. Therefore, a management dashboard summarises the most essential information that a manager requires to make the appropriate decisions. An appropriate decision may include direct action to resolve a concern, and/or examining the underlying data to seek a deeper understanding of what is taking place.

The crux of the matter is to select the most essential or key information to be included in the management dashboard. Hence, to select the key information for inclusion in the management dashboard one needs to analyse the organisation's value chain by examining the processes that identify the areas which add value to the entity (or division or unit within the entity) under examination. Hence, the focus is on the processes that are viewed as delivering more value to the end customer. An important principle to remember is not to clutter the dashboard with irrelevant information, since this distorts judgement and does not add anything that assists in making proper decisions.

Another critical factor is that the KPIs selected for inclusion in the management dashboard must be manageable. They need to present numbers that are easy and unambiguous to interpret by those using them. In other words, they need to be easy to measure and have no likelihood for calibration errors. One needs to remember that the outcome of calibration errors is unreliable information leading to unreliable and defective judgement and decisions, even if the information is relevant.

The KPIs presented on the management dashboard are of two types: Some will represent results attained (e.g., revenue collected), and others will display trends, thus indicating whether the entity is heading in the right direction to attain its targets. Management dashboards should be generated frequently because they provide a pictorial representation of what is taking place at a particular point in time (i.e., a snapshot). Hence, the management team needs to be trained in interpreting the figures (KPIs), to be able to use them to ascertain the current position of the entity, and to be able to make an accurate prediction of future outcomes.

Furthermore, management dashboards need to be examined for content so that a decision is made regarding who is to access this critical and sensitive information. In many cases the management dashboards may be shared generally with employees. However, those management dashboards that contain strategic and sensitive information may need to be restricted to the senior management team only. Figure 2.2 provides a simple example of a management dashboard. This example provides two types of information. The upper text boxes show facts that are related to the results attained, whereas the graphs display trends so that management may predict future outcomes. This type of management dashboard could represent a holistic organisation or division or unit within a division. It could also represent a service or product line.

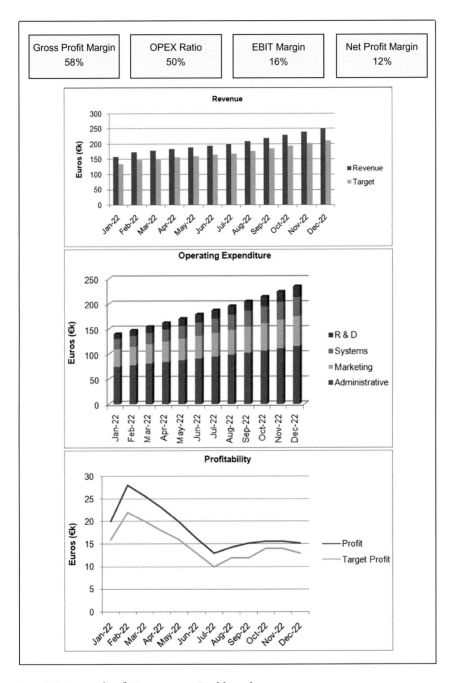

Figure 2.2  Example of Management Dashboard

### *Balanced Scorecards*

Balanced Scorecards (BSC) is an important performance management tool. The BSC is a corporate framework that is utilised for monitoring and implementing an organisation's strategy. The BSC framework is based upon key indicators, like KPIs. The BSC framework can be viewed as an approach for identifying and defining KPIs. As the name suggests, the BSC framework is based on the principle of balancing important (or key) indicators, specifically focusing on those indicators that are lagging (based upon past performance). These indicators are viewed as the drivers and outcomes of the organisation's goals. Hence, when applied in the BSC framework, these key indicators signify whether the established goals are being achieved and whether one is on the way to achieving future goals. Therefore, similar to the management dashboard, these indicators provide a snapshot of the current position and also give an indication of the future trend.

Generally, the BSC will allow management to describe the corporate, divisional or unit strategy; measure the strategy in meaningful terms; and enable one to monitor the actions being taken to improve performance (future outcomes). When building a BSC, one needs to define several parameters. The first parameter is to define the objectives. An objective is a high-level target. For example, a manager may have an objective of reducing operating costs by 25% by the end of the financial year. The second parameter is to define several measures to provide the manager with information as to whether the objective is being achieved. In other words, these measures allow the manager to determine whether the objective is being achieved. For instance, in the example of reducing operating costs, these measures may involve identifying various cost elements that comprise of the administration and operational costs.

The third parameter involves the identification of the initiatives or action that will be implemented to achieve the defined objective. For instance, taking the example a step further, this may include investing in the implementation of eCommerce software for online procurement, sales, payments, and generating sales revenue. In a practical sense, the third parameter is the identification of initiatives that will improve performance. The fourth parameter is to monitor the relevant measures to see whether the objective is being currently achieved (operational costs growth/decline rate over the previous period) and likely to be achieved (operational cost trend). It should be noted that the overall strategy may need to be reviewed if the outcomes are not achieving the desired results. For instance, in the example related to reducing operating costs by 25%, the strategy may be modified through giving a special discount for those customers ordering and paying online and intensifying the internal and external communications strategy to encourage the use of online services.

The three main advantages of using the BSC are to initiate and activate an organisation's corporate strategy for making holistic decisions; effectively communicating the corporate strategy across the organisation; and to monitor strategic performance by tracking performance through monthly, quarterly, and annual reports. The BSC approach is seen as an important tool and therefore a whole chapter will be dedicated to it (See Chapter 7).

## *Performance Analytics*

Performance analytics is an important component of performance management, particularly for the public sector. Performance analytics specifically refers to high quality analytics. Hence, it goes beyond just having a list of KPIs and well-designed management dashboards. Having a list of KPIs and well-designed management dashboards is still important, but these should be viewed as the basic data. In other words, they are merely indicators that may need further investigation. Performance analytics calls for a deeper examination of the figures because this provides an additional insight into the composition of the presented information, which assist managers define and design their products and services to attain much better outcomes. Hence, performance analytics is a results-based performance management framework complemented by high quality analytics, which continuously examines and reviews the strategic and non-strategic processes to improve operational decision-making.

All too often managers use KPIs and other performance management data to decide if they are on target or whether they are going to meet their targets. They may even take certain measures that in their judgement will correct or improve the performance status of the organisation. However, very often they take certain decisions purely on the face value of the presented data without delving deeper into the information to determine the rationale behind the performance indicators. Whilst performance management reveals the status of the organisation by getting managers and employees to debate the meaning of the data presented and probing the results, performance analytics provides the answers to these discussions and outcomes. Having said the above, the key components of performance management are still required. Therefore, under the Performance Analytics concept, the KPI method may be viewed as the beginning, not the end. The KPIs may allude to concerns that need to be examined in more depth by assessing the organisational data by analytical means.

On the management side, organisations still need the key ingredients for having a successful performance management culture, such as top management support to champion the performance management concepts; clear vision and mission; accountability and transparency; culture of learning by questioning past and current events; and engaging employees in the performance management process. However, performance analytics goes further by developing and implementing analytical skills across organisational boundaries.

This requires recruiting highly qualified employees that are familiar in the application of innovative tools and techniques. It is an undisputable fact that in the current digital era the availability of data is virtually unlimited and cheaper to attain and store by having a data repository or data warehouse. However, analysing the data requires highly skilled staff using data mining tools and a well-developed intelligence engine. This new breed of analysts requires the ability to convert current information into the prediction of future events. This requires creativity; technological expertise; intellectual inquisitiveness and a problem-solving mindset; analytical ability; effective communications; and adhering to the concept of information resource management, particularly related to sharing data across the organisation.

### Strategic Planning

Typically, the focus of performance management tools is the attainment of the organisation's strategic objectives. According to Taiwo and Idunnu (2010) and others, Strategic Planning can be defined as the process of using systematic criteria and rigorous investigation to formulate, implement, and control strategy, and formally document organisational expectations (Higgins and Vincze, 1993; Mintzberg, 1994; Pearce and Robinson, 1994). They argue that Strategic Planning is a process by which senior management can envision the future and develop the necessary procedures and operations to influence and achieve that future. Hence, these definitions imply that Strategic Planning is directly linked to performance, since it establishes targets to be attained by management. Strategic Planning may be viewed as establishing the strategic objectives of the organisation that management needs to strive to achieve.

Furthermore, the success for achieving the strategic plan depends on the tactics that are applied by management when implementing the strategic plan. These tactics may involve establishing divisional, unit, and individual targets that are required to be achieved within a specified timeframe. These targets need to be easily understood, measurable, and provide the drive to be monitored and be realisable in a short time interval. These characteristics tend to suggest that Strategic Planning may be used as a basis for identifying and defining KPIs on a corporate level, whereas the KPIs emerging from tactics are on a lower level (Divisional, Unit, and individual). This link between Strategic Planning and KPIs will be discussed in greater detail in an upcoming chapter.

Dusenbury (2000) generally supports this reasoning and contends that the strategic plan defines the performance to be measured, while performance measurement provides the feedback that keeps the strategic plan on target. He also argues that Governments have adopted the private sector's strategic planning approach to help set priorities and allocate scarce resources in a changing environment. However, he warns that often public-sector strategic planning is treated as a mere document and presented with much fanfare, which tends to evaporate over time, and is not in reality taken seriously. Dusenbury suggests that often public sector agencies expend a substantial effort to prepare a strategic plan to meet executive or legislative mandates but do not execute the plan to direct agency activities. Strategic planning should be seen as a continuous process that requires regular monitoring and feedback about how the current strategies are functioning in terms of performance.

According to Dusenbury, strategic planning takes a different perspective when discussing the private and public sectors. With the private sector, the reaction of the market expresses how it is performing in terms of profit levels, return on investments, and sales trends. These KPIs tend to keep the businesses informed of their achievement and may also suggest what action may be required to adjust their strategies and get back on track. Furthermore, further insights may be required by applying performance analytics to obtain a more detailed picture of what is affecting the organisation's performance. With the public sector, performance measurement (possibly through KPIs) provides similar and equivalent information because strategic planning looks ahead towards desired goals and performance measurement looks back at achievements (Dusenbury, 2000). Thus, strategic planning and performance measurement form a continuous loop of managing (private sector) or governing (public sector) for results. Thus, the strategic plan defines the performance to be measured, while the performance measurement aspect provides the feedback that keeps the strategic plan on target (Ibid.).

Moreover, Pirtea, Nicolescu, and Botoc (2009) argue that it is important to understand not only the potential of strategic planning but also its limitations. Hence, they maintain that a strategic plan is not just a wish list, a report card, or a marketing tool. They view the strategic plan as a tool that may provide an insight into an organisation's unique strengths and relevant weaknesses, enabling it to pinpoint new opportunities or the causes of current or projected problems. Pirtea, Nicolescu, and Botoc link strategic planning with performance management by highlighting the fact that a strategic plan can provide an invaluable blueprint for growth and revitalisation, enabling an organisation to take stock of where it is at, determine where it wants to go, and chart a course to get there. However, Dusenbury goes further by arguing that performance measurement relies on specified end outcomes and not just activities. He contends that the essential element is the result of those activities, and that the goals and objectives defined by the strategic plan focus the performance measurement on outcomes which assist to identify and define appropriate performance indicators (i.e., in other words, KPIs).

### Budgeting and Forecasting

The topic regarding budgeting and forecasting is a continuation of the previous section related to Strategic Planning and is a significant component of performance management. A strategic plan may be viewed as a long-term road map that describes where the organisation wants to be positioned in the future on a holistic level. However, budgeting and forecasting is an important part of the business plan, which is viewed as a short-term segment (usually one financial year) of the Strategic Plan. Additionally, budgeting and forecasting provide financial information at a lower organisational level. In other words, it describes financial information at a Divisional, Product, and Service level. Hence, whereas the KPIs associated with a Strategic Plan are at a corporate level, the KPIs associated with budgeting and forecasting are at a much lower level.

A budget defines what needs to be achieved in financial terms and assists management to anticipate issues and be prepared to respond to them if they occur. Budgeting and forecasting allow an organisation's management:

1.  *To determine and comprehend the organisation's current cash flow position.* A budget identifies and defines the cash flow requirements for the various divisions and units within the organisation. This assists management to know whether they can meet the current cash commitments and decide whether there are sufficient cash reserves to withstand possible disruptions to the organisation, such as an economic downturn. Knowing the organisation's cash flow permits management to take advantage of investment opportunities and be able to enter long-term commitments with suppliers, customers, and employees.

2.  *To monitor and remain on target in relation to the short and long-term business goals.* The budget being a financial plan assists management to implement activities that need to be achieved in the upcoming financial year. It also permits management to update its matrices to enable it to measure the level of success being achieved. These matrices are likely to be defined in terms of KPIs that provide an insight into the organisation's performance achievement level.

3.  *To measure and manage financial related risks.* This ensures the protection of the shareholder's investment in the organisation. It allows management to plan expenditure proposals and debt obligations.

4.  *To plan for the future.* The primary objective of budgeting is to enable management to plan its future activities in terms of the expected revenue and expenditure. This includes identifying various trends related to the services and products being provided to its customers, and the revenue and expenditure targets that it intends to achieve during the financial year. This process also includes prioritising capital and recurrent expenditure, and making sure that the liquidity of the organisation is adequate to see it through difficult periods, should a downturn in the economy takes place.

5.  *To monitor and appraise progress.* The budget combined with a variance analytical process provides management with a robust monitoring tool for tracking and evaluating progress. Furthermore, it permits management to identify where the organisation is achieving or failing to achieve its targets and the reason for the success or failure in doing this. Thus, giving management the opportunity to take timely corrective action

when things are not going to plan or to take advantage of the situation when things are going well. The budget also presents quantifiable data that measures performance against predefined targets, thus providing realistic KPIs that can be used as a basis for indicating the operational success of the organisation.

The above suggests that budgeting and the resultant business plan are critical for driving an organisation forward and can be applied in association with KPIs to assess the success of the various business divisions, units, products, and services.

## *Benchmarking*

The success of a performance management tool and the related performance measures depend on how well the performance measures are applied. Hence, to evaluate whether performance measures have meaning and provide useful information, it is critically important to make comparisons. According to Poister (2003), such comparisons may evaluate progress in achieving the given defined goals, appraise the trends in performance, or to match and assess the performance of one organisation against another. Benchmarking, as the term suggests, is a systematic process of measuring one's performance against recognised leaders as a basis of comparison to determine the perceived best practices that achieve superior performance if correctly applied.

Benchmarking is not useful when adopted in an ad hoc manner or as an informal approach. Hence, Benchmarking must be implemented as a structured and systematic process that has the full commitment of management. Thus, benchmarking is oriented towards best practice that is part of a continuous improvement and development plan, incorporating a feedback process. Like most other performance management tools, the fundamental principle of Benchmarking is to recognise and comprehend those things that are important to the organisation, which are the critical success factors, and to measure performance for these factors. These then become the key performance indicators. The gap or variance between actual performance and desired achievement is analysed to identify where improvements may be made and to detect the cause of the inadequate performance. This is followed by exploring best practices that may be utilised to facilitate in addressing the performance concerns.

Zairi and Leonard (1996) argue that Benchmarking is not a measurement itself but a process of establishing gaps in performance, and as such ensuring that an action plan is put in place to close the identified gaps and measuring it to verify the closure. Thus, confirming that there is a direct linkage between Benchmarking and performance measurement. The concept is based upon continuous improvement, through TQM, then determining gaps by Benchmarking, leading to a new standard. Although this is not a new notion, they contend that the positive process may have limitations since the improvements attained may not be enough for establishing highly competitive standards. However, they maintain that the Benchmarking process ensures continuous improvement, where continuous improvement is viewed as being external in terms of the competitive standards it realises. Furthermore, they argue that if performance measurement is only internally focused, it may have greater limitations, since it could be considered as focusing on effectiveness rather than competitiveness. Thus, the objective of Benchmarking is to ensure that performance establishes competitiveness (as a priority) and best practice (effectiveness) through doing the right things the first time around (TQM) from the perspective of the customer.

The link between Benchmarking and performance measurement is achieved since Benchmarking leads to an action-orientated mindset that mitigates (and often eliminates entirely) complacency. Benchmark findings and the operational principles based upon them are transformed into specific realisable tasks with an associated mechanism being implemented for periodic measurement and evaluation of achievement. Furthermore, metrics (like KPIs) provide a direct link between Benchmarking and performance measurement by presenting a relationship between the desired standards and the standards achieved to attain superior performance in comparison with competitors. Like other performance management tools, such as performance analytics, Benchmarking goes beyond the definition of matrices. However, the matrices (that form the basis for KPIs) are still the source for the Benchmarking-performance linkage process.

Benchmarking should be viewed as a performance management tool that is applied at various hierarchical levels across the organisation. Benchmarking can also be used in a project implementation environment with data being gathered and entered on a project milestone level, which may be accumulated on the project level. At a milestone level, Benchmarking can be exploited to detect certain features that are indicative of potential difficulties. This would allow the manager to pinpoint certain aspects of project management, such as risk management, that require special focus to ensure project success. Furthermore, Benchmarking may assist in the conduct of project decisions. This is particularly important at the post-project phase, where Benchmarking is used to evaluate the overall performance of project delivery, thus enabling management to document lessons learned and feedback, which may be used to establish benchmarks for future assessment. To be successful, Benchmarking requires full management and employee commitment at the various hierarchical organisational levels.

## Business Excellence Models

Another useful performance management tool is Business Excellence Models (also known as Quality Models). These have the key objective of improving organisational performance through the recognition of best practice in the different operational areas. Generally, Business Excellence Models have the same objective as benchmarking. These models are used as a quality improvement tool for evaluating an organisation in comparison with the competitors. When reference is made to Business Excellence it is important that one understands the meaning of this term. Business Excellence means superiority and high-quality standards (excellence) in strategies, business practices, and stakeholder-related performance results, which have been confirmed by evaluation through robust measurement and the application of verifiable business excellence models that attain tenable outstanding performance. It should be noted that the terms Business Excellence and Performance Excellence are synonymous.

Business Excellence (BE) models have the objective of guiding organisations towards sustainable top-notch business results that are founded on proven business principles. The business principles or core values are similar for most BE models and are designed to assist and show management the way to improve organisational performance. There are around eighty BE models worldwide that are sponsored by National Institutions to enhance national economic performance and as a basis for award programmes. Promoters of the BE models claim the following benefits on a corporate or organisational level: (a) Provide the basis for enhancing organisation performance; (b) Present a robust structure for developing and improving various performance segments; (c) Facilitate the achievement of organisational goals; (d) Reveal interdependencies and relationships between the operational divisions within the organisation; and (e)

Impart a performance benchmarking plan, which ensures that the business is frequently evaluated against the primary components of the BE model.

Most BE models are based on a self-assessment mechanism that identify the organisation's strengths and opportunities with the objective to improve performance. Thus, once the self-assessment exercise is completed, the organisation's management develops and executes the improvement action plans. The BE model concept may also be applied by management to improve the organisation's culture by fostering the use of best practice in those business segments where the impact will be most advantageous to enhance performance. The following are the most common BE models adopted on a national basis:

- United States of America: Baldrige Criteria for Performance Excellence (BCPE).
- European Union: European Foundation of Quality Management's EFQM Excellence Model.
- Japan: Deming Prize and the Japan Quality Award.
- South America: Ibero American Excellence Model for Management (I.E.M.).
- India: Confederation of Indian Industry award, CII/EXIM Bank Award for Business Excellence.
- New Zealand: Baldrige Criteria for Performance Excellence (BCPE)
- Australia: Australian Business Excellence Framework (ABEF)
- Singapore: Singapore Quality Award Criteria (SQAC)

Figure 2.3, which is adapted from the Business Excellence Model developed by the European Foundation for Quality Management, illustrates the EFQM BE model. This European Union (EU) model (like other BE models) is very comprehensive and appears to be quite complex. According to EFQM (2021), the focus of the EFQM BE Model is the primacy of the customer; the need to take a long-term stakeholder-centric view; and understanding the cause-and-effect linkages between why an organisation does something, how it does it, and what it achieves because of its actions. The EFQM BE model is an EU development that is based upon European Values. The model is based on three concepts, namely 'Direction', 'Execution', and 'Results'. The 'Direction' concept is viewed in terms of organisational objectives, vision and strategy, and organisation culture and leadership. The 'Execution' concept has three components, consisting of stakeholder

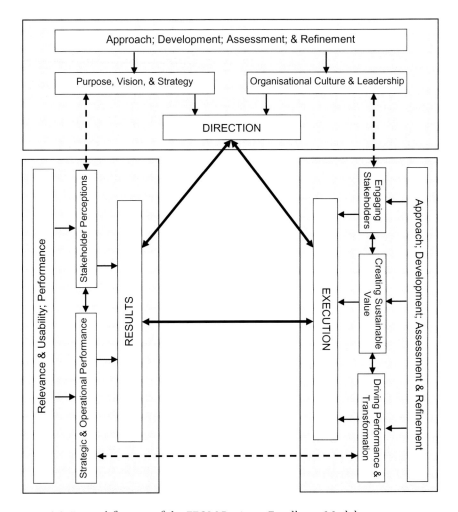

*Figure* 2.3  Exemplification of the EFQM Business Excellence Model

engagement, creating sustainable value, and driving performance and transformation. The 'Results' concept, meanwhile, is attained through strategic and operational performance, and stakeholder perceptions. The three concepts (Direction, Execution, and Results) are closely integrated in a continuous self-monitoring loop to ensure that the model achieves excellence in organisational performance.

According to Seddon (2021), the EFQM BE model (like most other BE models) is based on a self-assessment exercise that compares the organisation under examination with the model. Seddon argues that the model presents plausible logic through the key concepts of 'Results' and 'Enablers.' The results component is related to financial performance, customer satisfaction, people satisfaction, and the impact on society. The results component is achieved through the other key component, being the Enablers that consist of leadership, policy and strategy, people management, resources, and process management. Seddon explains that the rationale underlying this BE model is that by improving the 'how,' this will lead to improving the results (i.e., the 'what'). However, Seddon places doubt on how well Self-Assessment describes the relationships between results and enablers, and whether managers can act with confidence in their actions leading to improvement.

Seddon contends that numerous early users of the Model are disappointed since they have not experienced the promised rise in quality, excellence, or the bottom line. From qualitative research, he found that it is not advisable to start with comparing the organisation with the model, but to first concentrate on the work processes of the target organisation by defining them and focusing on value work in terms of how services are delivered and what is important to customers. Hence, Seddon contends that change should not start with comparison to a model but should commence with a meticulous understanding of the 'what and why' of current performance.

Seddon argues that the EFQM BE model has two weaknesses, namely the method and content. He contends that self-assessment by the comparison of the organisation to the Model is an unreliable approach for starting change, since in many cases it does not lead to a good understanding of what is going on in an organisation, therefore defining a solution becomes haphazard with fruitless actions for improvement. Furthermore, Seddon views quality as a better way to carry out work. He argues that most organisations are planned and managed on mass-production principles, with top-down hierarchy, functional specialisation of work, measurement of budgets, targets, standards, and so on. However, he maintains that quality guides managers to work in a different and better way; thus, rather than thinking top-down, they need to think outside-in. He argues that the work design and content is less concerned with functional issues and more concerned with the nature of demand and flow. He contends that this way of thinking is very different from mass-production orientation. He asserts that the current BE model guidance is interspersed with 'mass production' ideas and thinking, which is not consistent with what is required.

Generally, BE models appear to be complex in the way they should be implemented and monitored. Furthermore, there appears to be some disagreement in the way these models should be adopted by organisations regarding whether a comprehensive study of processes should be undertaken and documented before any other activities. Most of the BE models are defined by National Governments (or Government Agencies) to be used by private sector enterprises. This may explain why most BE models are considered bureaucratic in nature. Moreover, the research suggests that these types of models are more suitable at a corporate level. Hence, unlike many performance measurement tools that can be used at different hierarchical organisational levels, even down to individuals, the BE models are more restrictive and focus on the uppermost strategic level. However, BE models may be used in conjunction with other models, such as KPIs, where the applied BE model is used for strategic purposes and KPIs are used for the various organisational levels (i.e., divisions, units, products and services, and individuals). A more detailed examination of BE models will be dealt with in a later chapter.

### Six Sigma

The Six Sigma approach is considered as an important performance management tool. The Six Sigma concept is all about the streamlining of quality management, where the level of the quality control level is viewed as a key performance measure. Six Sigma is defined as a methodology that streamlines quality control with the objective of improving the processes, products, or services being conducted by an organisation through the discovery and elimination of defects. This means that the improvement being made in the processes, products, or services results in the mitigation (as much as possible) of variances so that the statistical dispersion (standard deviation) in the normal distribution is decreased to an absolute minimum. The symbol sigma ($\sigma$) in statistical theory signifies the standard deviation.

In 1993, Motorola registered 'Six Sigma' as a trademark to denote that the Six Sigma method was expected to be defect-free 99.99966 percent of the time, which translates to 3.4 defective features for every million occurrences. Initially, Motorola established this target for its manufacturing operations. However, this became a widely used standard by many large organisations as a key quality management approach. It is commonly accepted that Six Sigma gained prominence when the methodology was adopted successfully by General Electric in 1998.

Six Sigma defines a series of steps around a specific target by identifying and eliminating the defects that cause variations in quality. Target values are normally the qualitative or quantitative parameters that are required to achieve quality for the customers and may adopt different modes based on what and how the target is being measured. Hence, this methodology has the intention of facilitating the identification of errors and defects that will affect quality in an objective manner by applying a statistical approach. There are basically two Six Sigma methods, namely DMAIC, which is applied to improve existing business processes, and DMADV, which is used to generate new processes, and new products or services. The acronyms DMAIC and DMADV each consist of five steps, with each step represented by its first letter. Hence, DMAIC represents:

- **D**efine the concern (which could be a specific problem, customer, ot project needs) and the eventual goals and expectations of the customer.
- **M**easure the performance of the current process by instituting a data gathering plan to ascertain defects and assemble the appropriate metrics.
- **A**nalyse the process to determine the root cause of the variations and defects, thus identifying the concerns with the current strategy that are acting as barriers to the achievement of the end target.
- **I**mprove the process by removing the root causes of the defects through the implementation of innovative solutions.
- **C**ontrol the new process to elude past ways of doing things and to ensure that the new process keeps on track.

Similarly, DMADV is represented by:

- **D**efine realistic goals that align with the customer's needs and/or the business strategy.
- **M**easure and determine the customer's critical to quality (CTQ) needs and transform them into unambiguous and transparent project goals.
- **A**nalyse the various alternatives available to the customer in conjunction with the approximate holistic life cycle of the project.
- **D**esign the process, starting at a high level and moving down by adding more detail that will eventually become the model to detect errors and make the necessary change.

- **V**erify that the final product or process model is accepted by all internal and external customers/clients.

The projects that are appropriate for the Six Sigma approach must have a process with clear inputs and outputs. Before undertaking a Six Sigma project ensure that data is available regarding the variations in the process inputs. It is important to have an open mind without any bias for a pre-determined solution. The focus should be on mitigating variations in the operation of the process that minimise disruption to employees, and how to control and eliminate defects. There are several criticisms of the Six Sigma method. Studies have shown that the Six Sigma approach is only suitable for large organisations that have a workforce of 500 employees or over. Moreover, Six Sigma certification is not a simple process and requires a high level of support and qualified staff.

The Six Sigma method focuses on enhancing current processes, but many solutions tend to revolve around new technology. This may limit improvements and innovation since Six Sigma tends to support legacy systems and existing products and services. Thus, the method does not easily permit disruption or developing innovative products and services. Hence, business process reengineering may still be required to increase process effectiveness to mitigating waste and cost.

### Enterprise Risk Management

Enterprise Risk Management (ERM) is a valuable performance management tool because its focus is the identification and evaluation of the risk associated with the attainment of the organisation's strategic objectives. Typically, ERM is a process whereby an entity's management undertakes to identify and evaluate the collective risks that impact the entity's value, and thus helps to define a holistic entity strategy to address these identified risks. The outcome of the process is an effective risk management strategy that maximises the entity's holistic value.

The basis of ERM is to understand the various risks that impact the organisation and the ability of management to successfully address them through a comprehensive risk management strategy that is aimed at achieving the defined business strategic objectives. Hence, it is essential that the risk management strategy adopted by management supports the organisation's performance objectives by being congruent with these objectives.

Risk can never be eliminated but it can be mitigated to allow management to accomplish the defined goals and performance objectives. By defining and implementing an enterprise risk management strategy, management will be able to mitigate risk and become accustomed to transformational change, thus achieving an increase in growth. This will boost performance across the organisation.

ERM goes beyond traditional risk management. Traditional risk management addresses a particular cost centre within an organisation, such as a Section or Department that mainly focus on exposure type risks. Therefore, traditional risk management is not an appropriate method for addressing risk at a holistic enterprise level. ERM complements the traditional risk management approach by assisting management to focus on three general aspects, namely, strategic issues; applicable risks; and performance indicators.

ERM has a strategic orientation since it does not limit risk to a specific cost centre but rather addresses risk on an enterprise-wide basis that fosters perpetual reviews and facilitates the achievement of value-based objectives. The applicable risks consist of all types of risk that impact the organisation. These are addressed so that the defined objectives are not hindered but are fully achieved. Performance indicators or metrics are integral to an organisation's success and are defined as the facts and statistics representative of an organisation's actions, abilities, and overall quality. Since ERM's focus is on results-based performance measurement by applying risk management tools during the execution of a business goal, it assists in the mitigation of residual risk at all organisational levels and reduces the undesirable outcome related to neglected opportunities.

The ERM framework provides several advantages for the organisation since it endeavours to optimise performance through strategic means. The ERM framework improves enterprise robustness by strengthening the organisation's capacity to predict and act in response to change. By being risk-based, ERM enhances the spectrum of opportunities that are available to an enterprise by examining each possibility, irrespective of whether these are positive or negative, and evaluating alternative responses. Since ERM takes an enterprise-wide view of risk, it identifies and manages risk on a holistic basis, but it still makes an allowance for the effect of risk on every aspect of an organisation, irrespective of the circumstances.

The continuous risk identification and control features of ERM mitigate adverse disruptions and enhance positive outcomes. This helps to provide stable organisational performance rather than having performance fluctuating, since ERM predicts the likely risks that impact performance and allows management to take appropriate action, thus mitigating disruptions. A risk-based approach, such as ERM, focuses on anticipating disruptions, thus allocating appropriate resources to those organisational sectors that require immediate support to overcome the predicted concerns.

An ERM framework is not very beneficial unless it is integrated as part of an enterprise-wide strategy and performance system. Hence, the starting point in implementing an ERM approach is having a proper strategic definition mechanism and a workable performance management system. Therefore, it is essential that the ERM framework is congruent with the organisation's strategy, which reflects the organisation's mission, vision, objectives, and performance targets. Hence, the ERM approach needs to consider the possibility (i.e., probability or risk) of not achieving the strategy and its respective objectives. Hence, ERM helps the organisation's management to identify, evaluate, and monitor the various risks that are applicable to the strategy, and to take the proper response. The ERM framework is based upon several principles to ensure its alignment with the defined strategy and performance system, namely:

- The organisation must be maintained by suitable Governance and Culture that fosters proper values and supporting operational management structures, which exhibit commitment to the core values and apply significant risk management control.
- The organisation requires a mechanism for defining its organisational strategy and associated objectives. This mechanism is to consider and assess alternative strategies.
- Management needs to ensure a specified performance level by implementing a risk management system that identifies and prioritises risks by assessing their gravity, defining the risk responses for each type of risk, and continuously monitoring each risk and applying the appropriate risk response if the risk occurs.
- Management requires a process that continuously reviews the identified risks and performance goals and takes corrective or adjusting action for improvement.
- Management must define and implement a communications strategy that conveys meaningful information to relevant stakeholders related to risk occurrence, risk response, and performance outcomes through a suitable information system.

The above principles will ensure that the organisation has an appropriate enterprise risk management framework that provides management with the information for managing and mitigating the risks related to the defined strategy and associated strategic objectives.

## Project/Programme Management

Performance management tools are not restricted to organisations that are dominated by operational functions; some tools are also applicable to project-oriented organisations. While the terms project and programme management are very similar in meaning, they have several distinctive features that contribute to the organisation's effectiveness in different ways. The Project Management Institute (PMI) defines programme management as a group of related projects managed in a coordinated manner to obtain benefits not available from managing them individually.

PMI maintains that program management is achieved by effectively monitoring and controlling the strategic, financial, and operational risks of major undertakings. Hence, project programs are viewed as a related group of projects that endeavour to attain similar organisational objectives. However, the projects within a program may be managed by different project managers and thus assigned to separate project teams. The important feature is that the projects within a programme aim for the same strategic objective. Thus, program management is a means of implementing the organisation's project strategy by having different project teams working across the organisational boundaries with a mutual and untied objective. Moreover, a key objective of programme management is the optimum use of human and other resources.

Unlike project management, which is mainly aimed at achieving the project activities on schedule, program management is focused on strategic planning, continuous improvement, and the attainment of project value. Therefore, program management ensures that the organisation makes the best use of its resources with minimal conflicts that may result in time delays and adverse financial issues. This ensures that these resources are better aligned to the organisational functional strategies. Program management is viewed as the transformation of strategic objectives into quantifiable business goals.

Project management tends to focus on the implementation of a specific project. However, a specific project could be part of a programme or portfolio of projects. Hence, project management complements programme management. PMI defines a project as a temporary undertaking that has a specific beginning and end to create a unique product, service, or result, and typically involves a team effort designed to achieve a specific objective. Individual projects may vary in magnitude and scope, thus requiring different amounts and types of resources. Project management is a tool for implementing undertakings and assumes that the project being implemented is aligned to the organisation's strategy.

Traditional project management consists of several steps that include five key activities, namely: define project scope; define project organisation; define project team; define the project plan; and project monitoring and control. The project plan also consists of several steps that include: Identifying the project components; preparing a work breakdown structure (WBS); breaking down each project component into activities; determining the physical, technological, resource, and management constraints; determining the relationships between the activities; preparing the project network diagram; preparing the utility data for the activities; preparing the cost breakdown structure (CBS); and scheduling activities based on time, cost, and resources. It should be noted that planning a project requires a considerable amount of manual and mental effort, and rigorous human interaction. Furthermore, numerous computer software packages are available to aid the project team with project scheduling, but the preceding steps require information and manual decision-making at a micro human level.

Whilst programme and project management disciplines are well-developed and greatly assist in the organisation and the implementation of the activities involved in a project that result in executing projects successfully, these disciplines require processes related to project performance management to ensure strategic success as well. All too often organisations undertake projects without having a project performance management mechanism in place, leading to wasted resources. Instead of focusing purely on the implementation of activities, project performance management is about the overall holistic management of the organisation's strategy.

Typically, project performance management is the process of generating, executing, and administrating (monitoring and control) projects that significantly contribute to the positive performance of an organisation and its strategy. Project performance management links the projects undertaken by the organisation to its strategy, by tracking project performance over time and reviewing the completed projects with the objective of making future improvements to the project implementation process. It is important that before a project is undertaken, a study is conducted to ensure that the project is aligned with the organisation's strategy. Any activity that does not support or benefit the organisation's strategy is applying resources in a wasteful manner. Only projects that move the organisation forward should be undertaken. Furthermore, tracking the performance of the undertaken projects on a frequent and regular basis is essential not only to ensure that project activities are delivered on time, to specifications and budget, but also to ensure that the executed project activities are truly generating the intended outcomes.

It is also important that management conducts a post-project review to determine what went right and wrong in the project execution phase to improve the project implementation process and to assess whether the project goals were achieved. Therefore, project performance management should be viewed as a vital part of the holistic performance management process that is applied for leveraging the undertaken projects to implement the organisation's strategy. Hence, project performance management is all about the successful implementation of the organisation's strategy and remaining competitive (for the private sector) or sustainable (for the public sector).

An issue that at times arises is related to the relationship between project performance management and organisational performance management (OPM). OPM is all about defining the organisational goals, how these goals are measured, and what action is taken to achieve the desired outcomes. Therefore, organisational performance management addresses issues regarding how one communicates the goals and their respective measurements and actions across the organisation, whilst ensuring that the undertaken organisational activities are aligned and support the organisational strategy. As has already been demonstrated in previous sections, the Balanced Scorecard, Business Excellence Models, and Six Sigma, amongst others, are all frameworks that assist in managing corporate performance. Hence, project performance management is viewed as a subcategory of organisational performance management.

One should also not confuse project performance management with employee performance management. Employee performance management is a subcategory of human resources that focuses on enhancing employee productivity, job satisfaction, and operational competency. Thus, the focus of employee performance management is on developing competencies, bridging skill gaps, and developing employees' career paths through regular reviews. Therefore, the relationship between employee performance management on one hand, and project performance management and organisational performance management on the other hand, is the fact that organisations require trained and professional employees to execute projects and require suitable employees with the appropriate skills for their specific role to implement the defined organisational strategy.

The actual measure of a successful project is not just whether the project was implemented on time and to budget, but whether the project truly contributes to the organisation's strategic objectives. The Project Performance Management framework consists of six key phases. This framework ensures that project implementers are able to go beyond merely successful project management, making sure that projects optimally contribute to the strategic goals of the organisation. Firstly, it is important that a business case is prepared for the project, which justifies its undertaking due to its direct or indirect contribution to the organisation's strategy.

In preparing the business case, management must consider alternative project options to the one being proposed to ensure that the option which generates the most value is selected for implementation. The next phase is to define the project goals because these stipulate a clear direction for the project and explicitly identify what the project is to achieve. It may be appropriate at this stage to link the expected project achievement to the organisation's KPIs to demonstrate how investing in a specific project will drive long-term results. This will ensure that project funding is visibly and transparently linked to the organisation's strategy. Another important phase is to establish suitable project data points (usually milestone based) to measure project outcomes. These project data points are integrated with the organisation's performance management process to enable management to monitor and keep track of progress.

This phase supports the next stage in the Project Performance Management framework, which is to identify specific milestones that provide possible action response and time limits. Project networks have many dependencies, therefore a delay of a specific milestone may disrupt others. Hence, this stage will help management to decide whether to expedite certain activities to mitigate disruptions. It is also important that regular and frequent progress meetings are organised to ensure that the project is kept on track. These progress meetings should not merely discuss what has been executed but should look ahead for future activities to establish whether there are any anticipated difficulties in commencing them according to the agreed schedule, and whether there will be any repercussions to other projects within the project portfolio.

The final phase of the Project Performance Management framework is conducting a post-implementation project review to formally close the project and moving the project outcome to the operational phase. This final phase will need to document a project summary and describe what went right and wrong during project execution, and how things may be improved in conducting similar projects.

## *Performance Reporting*

Performance management is highly dependent on the quality of the performance reports generated by the system. However, performance reporting is oriented towards achieving outcomes by having an integrated system of planning and reporting. The two key components of performance reporting are planning that includes establishing priorities and the overall strategy, and reporting that includes the monitoring of the plans and generating the reporting requirements. The performance reporting process has several key objectives, namely, to facilitate the clarification of organisational goals and instructions; unambiguously communicate the priorities of the organisation to all employees; monitor progress and implement continuous improvements; maintain budgeting and resource distribution decisions; and provide accurate and timely information to relevant stakeholders.

Reporting on performance is not a goal that is pursued to the exclusion of others; rather it is viewed as an essential feature of effective management, transparency, and accountability. It is vital to recognise that planning and reporting are both regarded as an integral part of an organisation's ongoing operations and decision-making process. Management should promote performance reporting because it helps to encourage a 'continuous improvement' response cycle where reports on activities and performance provide significant information to permit the best possible decision-making for the next planning cycle.

Planning is the foundation of the performance reporting process because a sound plan will define the objectives, priorities, and activities the organisation is to achieve subject to the limitations of the available resources. However, as the plan is being implemented, the organisation's management will need to monitor progress and make the necessary modification to the plan. Hence, planning is not static but an iterative process. At suitable time intervals (weekly, monthly etc.) the organisation's management will report on the performance achieved by the organisation and the attainment of the established priorities, goals, and actions. In other words, this process is specifically reporting on the defined and agreed plan. This reporting process is cyclical because the reporting aspects will likely impact future planning and resource allocation. Hence, in this performance reporting approach, the planning and reporting aspects are two ends of the same process. It should be recognised that the planning and performance reporting process take place across organisations in numerous configurations and for different varied reasons. However, normally the primary reason for having a planning and performance reporting process is transparency and accountability.

Performance reporting is essential for organisations. It should be noted that a performance report is a document that the management of an organisation prepares to define and measure its overall success. Thus, it is intended to provide a summary of how the organisation is performing. Hence, performance reports consist of information that is gathered regarding specific work performance, and this information is analysed and interpreted to provide recommendations that assist management in making decisions. A performance report can drill down and focus on the performance of a specific activity, product, service, and/or client. It can also focus on the entire enterprise depending on the needs of management.

While performance reports can have different configurations, they typically comprise of similar data and data processing fundamentals that examine the objectives of an organisation; the strategic long-term vision; established KPIs; the regularity of the KPI measurement; and data sources being applied for monitoring and control functions. Performance reports can take several formats, such as progress reports, project status reports, marketing trend reports, operational standard cost variance reports, and forecasting reports, amongst many others. Performance reports can be text, tabular, graphical, or specifically designed dashboards that all aim to give an unambiguous and accurate depiction of the performance of the organisation.

Although the intention of a performance report may differ, they are typically generated to provide an overview by recording and describing the activities being undertaken; identifying whether the activities being conducted are assisting the organisation to expand and achieve its goals; and identifying the strengths and weaknesses of the business segment under examination. However, there are several specific reasons for generating performance reports, these include establishing benchmarks that determine and measure targets as a comparison with competitors or best practise organisations to identify sectors that are underperforming and outperforming. This assists management to identify solutions and resolve specific concerns, through the provision of relevant data for analytical purposes that reveal opportunities.

Another significant reason for performance reports is related to monitoring employee performance to encourage continuous improvement within the organisation and ensuring a customer-oriented approach to increase customer satisfaction. Performance reports may also be required to satisfy regulatory obligations, such as annual reports and financial statements, and providing a narrative for explanatory notes. Timely, meaningful, and accurate performance reports provide vital immediate information about the organisation that accumulates and feeds into knowledge-based systems for the identification of the strengths and weaknesses of the organisation and the development of realistic and achievable strategies. Finally, a well-designed performance report with suitable dashboards is an excellent communication tool that helps to determine the strengths and weaknesses of the organisation; understand employees and their performance levels; and provide added knowledge about the organisation's customers' needs and preferences.

## Conclusion

This chapter has examined performance management concepts and several associated performance management tools. This chapter has illustrated that performance management systems have traditionally been based upon annual employee appraisal methods. These methods had been in use for at least a century. However, their utility in the modern era has been questioned. Initially employee appraisal methods had been designed to specifically identify poor performers with the objective of terminating their engagement or to reassign them to other duties. Hence, these systems grew in popularity, especially during periods of high inflation, such as in the 1970s energy crisis, where salary increases had to be tightly controlled. Under a high inflation scenario, annual employee appraisal methods were viewed as a simple and effective way of controlling salary increases.

Thus, employee appraisal methods were adopted as the preferred performance management system and continued to be unchallenged in their use up to the early 2000s, at a time when flat organisation structures were the accepted norm. However, with the passage of time, it became apparent that carrying out regular employee appraisals was a very time-consuming activity and was not taken seriously by supervisors. In fact, it was not considered to be a practical solution for the supervisor, since often supervisors went through the mechanics of the appraisal process without realistically appraising whether and to what extent the employee was achieving the strategic objectives of the organisation. Therefore, it became evident that a performance management system was required to be linked to the organisation's strategic objectives so that some measure of corporate success could be established and determined. Hence, the contribution to the achievement of the organisation's strategic objective was soon adopted as the basis for measuring performance, whether at an individual level or at the various hierarchical organisational levels.

Key Performance Indicators have become the accepted norm in many industries and their utilisation has been adopted in most performance management systems. Hence, there are several performance management approaches that complement the use of KPIs. This chapter has provided an overview of performance management concepts and several associated performance management tools, all of which utilise matrices and KPIs as the basis for measuring performance at various levels. Performance management tools may differ in the way information about an organisation's performance may be gathered and analysed, but the common theme is the defined KPIs. Hence, KPIs provide a common thread between the various performance management systems and associated tools. Performance management systems are still evolving with the objective of significantly increasing organisational effectiveness and employee productivity.

# References

Azadinamin, A. (2011). *Modern Tools for Performance Measurements*. SMC University. Available at: https://www.researchgate.net/publication/230687444_Modern_Tools_for_Performance_Measurements (Accessed 20 November 2023).

Dusenbury, P. (2000). *Governing for Results and Accountability: Strategic Planning and Performance Measurement*. Washington, DC: The Urban Institute.

EFQM (2021). *The EFQM Model Revised 2nd edition*. Brussels: EFQM.

Hearn, S. (2021). *Continuous Performance Management: Your Definitive Guide to Success*. Clear Review. Available at: https://resources.clearreview.com/continuous-performance-management-ebook (Accessed 20 November 2023).

Higgins, J.M. and Vincze, J.W. (1993). *Strategic Management: Concepts and Cases*. Chicago, IL: Dryden Press.

HR Tech (2021). *Performance Management System – A Complete Guide*. Available at: https://www.techfunnel.com/hr-tech/performance-management-system/ (Accessed 20 November 2023).

Marr, B. (2021). *What is Performance Management? A Super Simple Explanation for Everyone*. Available at: https://bernardmarr.com/what-is-performance-management-a-super-simple-explanation-for-everyone/ (Accessed 20 November 2023).

Merchant, N. (2011). Culture Trumps Strategy, Every Time. *Harvard Business Review*. Available at: https://hbr.org/2011/03/culture-trumps-strategy-every (Accessed 20 November 2023).

Mintzberg, H. (1994). 'The Fall and Rise of Strategic Planning.' *Harvard Business Review*, 72, pp. 107–114.

Pearce, J.A. and Robinson, R.B. (1994). *Strategic Management: Formulation, Implementation and Control*. Homewood, IL: Irwin.

Pirtea, M., Nicolescu, C., and Botoc, C. (2009). 'The Role of Strategic Planning in Modern Organisations.' *Annales Universitatis Apulensis Series Oeconomica*, 11(2).

Poister, T.H. (2003). *Measuring Performance in Public and Non-profit Organizations*. San Francisco, CA.: Jossey-Bass.

Seddon, J. (2021). *The Business Excellence Model – Will it Deliver?* Available at: https://beyondcommandandcontrol.com/wp-content/uploads/2015/07/the-business-excellence-model.pdf (Accessed 20 November 2023).

Taiwo, A.S. and Idunnu, F.O. (2010). 'Impact of Strategic Planning on Organizational Performance and Survival.' *Research Journal of Business Management*, 4(1), pp. 73–82.

Zairi, M. (2005). *Benchmarking for Best Practice: The Power of Its Adoption and the Perils of Ignoring Its Use in a Modern Business Environment*. Pakistan's 9th International Convention on Quality Improvement November 14–15, 2005 – Karachi, Pakistan.

Zairi, M. and Leonard. P. (1996). *Practical Benchmarking: The Complete Guide: A Complete Guide*. Dordrecht: Springer (Science and Business Media).

ZOKRI (2021). *The Complete Guide to Performance Management in 2021*. Available at: https://zokri.com/performance-management-guide/ (Accessed November 20 2023).

# 3

# ROOT CAUSE ANALYSIS AND ITS IMPACT ON PERFORMANCE MANAGEMENT

'Data Driven Decision making is a cultural intervention which requires habit change from the leaders to the frontline employees.'

Harjeet Khanduja
Author

Problems plague all businesses regardless of their size or industry, and these will impact the general level of performance throughout the organisation. Treating just the symptoms will not make the problems disappear. A band-age may cover an injury, but it will not heal it. Hence, addressing only the symptoms of the organisation's performance issues will not eliminate the problems; they will merely return, probably more aggressively.

Serious shortcomings that require regular firefighting by providing swift repairs and that keep management speculating as to what may go amiss next are indicative that a radical change is required. Hence, to improve performance, one cannot just address the symptoms but must reveal the underlying causes of the problems and apply the appropriate treatment that will eradicate the problem permanently. Unless the root of the concerns

DOI: 10.4324/9781032685465-4

become known and treated, they will continue to reappear. It is important that a problem-solving process is put in place to address and eliminate the difficulties at their root by taking a proactive approach instead of being reactive. A reactive standpoint usually results in having short-term firefighting types of solutions because of the ensuing emergency and consequential panic. A proactive outlook promotes a careful long-term resolution of the problems, because management may meticulously examine the situation and provide the required action without being under excessive tension that will lead to panicked thinking and flawed decisions, with dismal consequences.

## Introduction

Root Cause Analysis is linked to service and product quality. It is an approach that reveals in a very explicit way the source of a problem, in terms of when, where, and why the problem has occurred. What is special about Root Cause Analysis is that it does this proactively, before the problem can flow out and impact the customer (internal or external) a second time. It must be recognised that problems in organisations can be mitigated but can never be eliminated. Hence, the essence of the approach is to ensure that while a difficulty or glitch can occur, it does not reoccur a second time or ever.

Often employees, either as individuals or as teams, spend a significant amount of their time addressing symptoms without delving deeper to discover the roots of the concerns being encountered; unfortunately, these same concerns are very likely to reoccur. However, by making an extra effort and digging deeper to reveal the source of the concern, they can resolve the issues being encountered permanently, thus saving time and money. There is the need to determine precisely why certain difficulties occur to identify the cause of the problem. Understanding how to track and locate the adverse effects back to their primary cause or revealing the interrelated causes is critical in achieving a higher level of performance by attaining a greater level of quality and having satisfied customers. This is what Root Cause Analysis is all about.

There is a need to have a systematic mechanism in place to not only identify the problems, but to discover what is causing the problems. Resolve the cause and the related problems will disappear. Root Cause Analysis is a deductive problem-solving methodology that is widely applied throughout every industry and organisational function, from software development to engineering, operations and administration, and marketing, amongst many others. Using Root Cause Analysis means mitigating the use of firefighting and crisis management to an absolute minimum as a primary mode of resolving difficulties across the organisation.

## Development of Root Cause Analysis

The basis of Root Cause Analysis is an ancient practice. However, Root Cause Analysis as a systematic problem-solving mechanism is a relatively modern phenomenon that has developed due to various industrial and engineering incidents and accident investigations. As illustrated above, Root Cause Analysis is an approach for evaluating problems based on their root causes, thus analysing the causal elements in any given adverse circumstances by identifying the source of the problem and taking corrective measures to rectify the situation.

The uniqueness of Root Cause Analysis is its distinctive feature of probing deeper to reveal solutions based on unknown or obscure causes and their effects, instead of just examining the surface and examining what is most apparent. Root Cause Analysis has been labelled as a reactive process because it is enacted following an adverse event taking place. However, as soon as Root Cause Analysis is implemented systematically, it rapidly becomes an extremely valuable tool by anticipating problems before they occur, thus taking a proactive role. Root Cause Analysis takes on a circular aspect because identifying the root causes in a given circumstance appears to be the most significant feature of resolving the problem. However, these root causes are of secondary importance when compared to the solutions being pursued to avoid a repetition of the occurrence in the future.

Root Cause Analysis as a modern methodology is credited to Sakichi Toyoda, who was the founder of Toyota Industries. Sakichi Toyoda (1867–1930) is known as the 'King of Japanese Inventors' or the 'Japanese Thomas Edison' who referred to the approach as the 'The Five Whys.' The basis of the method was to ask WHY five times or until the root cause of a problem is revealed. However, there are examples of similar methods being used in the Tay Bridge collapse of 1879 and the New London school explosion of 1937. These incidents required more meticulous investigative methodologies to be sought to determine the exact cause of problems that categorically could not be allowed to reoccur. Other incidents that contributed to refine the method were the West Gate Bridge disaster of 1970 and the Challenger space shuttle disaster of 1986.

## Tay Bridge Disaster

The Tay Bridge disaster occurred on a stormy night at around 7.15pm on 28 December 1879, when the central navigation spans of the bridge that carried a single rail track collapsed into the Firth of Tay at Dundee, Scotland, destroying a train with six carriages and killing 75 persons. The bridge, which was nearly two miles long, was considered at that time to be the longest bridge in the world. It had only been opened 19 months previously and had been declared as safe by the Board of Trade. The incident is one of the most notorious bridge failures and to date it is still viewed as the worst structural engineering catastrophe in the British Isles. The bridge consisted of 85 spans, 72 of which were shored up on spanning girders below the level of the track, and the rest (13 navigation spans) were spanning girders above the level of the track, thus the train travelled through a tunnel of girders.

It was these navigation spans that collapsed, leaving most of the girders below track level standing. In fact, the girders below track level that remained standing were transferred to the present-day Tay rail bridge. The Court of Inquiry established to determine the reason for the collapse concluded that the root cause of the accident was the insufficiency of the cross bracing and its fastenings to sustain the force of the gale. The Court of Inquiry revealed that if the piers, specifically the wind bracing, had been suitably constructed and maintained, the bridge could have withstood the storm that night, albeit with a low factor of safety. The bridge designer was primarily blamed for the collapse due to not making adequate allowance for wind loading (the designer used a wind pressure of 10 pounds force per square foot for the design of the Tay Bridge).

## New London School Catastrophe

An explosion occurred at the New London School, located in Texas, United States, at 3.17pm on 18 March, 1937, when 18 students at the school gymnasium were about to prepare for the next day's Inter-scholastic meeting in Henderson. On entering the gymnasium, which was filled with a mixture of gas and air, the instructor turned on a sanding machine. The switch ignited this mixture and carried the flame into a nearly closed space beneath the building, 253 feet long and 56 feet wide. Witnesses claimed that the explosion seemed to lift the building into the air, shattering it to the ground. The explosion was heard four miles away.

The incident caused 295 fatalities out of 500 students and 40 teachers, with only about 130 students escaping serious injury. An investigation was immediately initiated. Experts from the United States Bureau of Mines concluded that a faulty connection to the residue gas line allowed gas to leak into the school. However, the root cause of the accident was the fact that natural gas is invisible and is odourless, and therefore the leak went unnoticed. To mitigate the damage of future leaks, the Texas Legislature within weeks of the explosion made it mandatory for thiols (mercaptans), which have a strong odour, to be added to natural gas. This measure made leaks quickly noticeable, and the practice was swiftly adopted worldwide.

### West Gate Bridge Tragedy

On 15 October 1970, the West Gate Bridge collapsed into the Yarra River in Melbourne, killing 35 and injuring 18 construction workers. This was Australia's worst ever industrial accident. The West Gate Bridge was nearing completion when an 11 cm gap was observed between two spans. The engineers applied kentledge weights, which are often used as counterweights in cranes, to force down the structure and realign the girders. However, it appeared that too much weight had been applied, causing the bridge to buckle. Consequently, the engineers attempted to straighten out the buckle, but at around noon, a 112-metre span between two piers, weighing 2000 tonnes, plunged 50 metres into the mud of the Yarra River.

Many of those who died were on their lunch break in the workers' huts underneath the bridge, which were crushed by the falling span; the others were working on the span when it fell. The noise from the collapse was heard 20 kilometres away and buildings that were hundreds of metres from the disaster were shaken and sprayed with mud. A royal commission into the disaster was appointed by the Premier of Victoria, Australia. The royal commission, which concluded its findings in 1971, recommended the strengthening of occupational health and safety laws in Australian workplaces. Thus, the root cause was the lack of occupational health and safety laws. Work on the bridge project resumed in 1972, and West Gate Bridge opened in 1978. Currently some fragments of the collapsed bridge are on permanent display at Monash University's Clayton campus gardens to remind students of the potentially tragic consequences that can result from errors in engineering.

## Challenger Space Shuttle Misfortune

During its 10th scheduled flight, on 28 January 1986, the space shuttle Challenger exploded 73 seconds after lift-off, killing the seven crewmembers. An inspection of the launch pad before launching showed a large amount of ice accumulating due to unusually cold overnight temperatures. The temperature of a previous launch was 20 degrees warmer. NASA had no experience launching the shuttle in such cold temperatures. As the temperatures dipped below freezing, some of the shuttle's engineers were anxious about the reliability of the seals on the solid rocket boosters in such low temperatures. The company commissioned to the build the solid rocket boosters informed NASA that in their opinion, the O-ring seals in the solid rocket boosters would perform adequately in the cold. Each solid rocket booster had four hull segments filled with powdered aluminium (fuel) and ammonium perchlorate (oxidiser).

These fuel segments were assembled vertically, with field joints containing rubber O-ring seals being installed between each fuel segment. Unfortunately, it transpired that the O-rings were never tested in extreme cold, thus on the morning of the launch, the cold rubber became stiff, failing to fully seal the joint. As the shuttle ascended, one of the seals on a booster rocket opened enough to allow a plume of exhaust to leak out. Consequently, hot gases soaked the hull of the cold external tank full of liquid oxygen and hydrogen until the tank ruptured. Hence, at an altitude of 9 miles (14.5 km) the shuttle was torn apart by aerodynamic forces. The crew compartment rose to an altitude of 12.3 miles (19.8 km) before dropping into the Atlantic Ocean.

A presidential commission was appointed to investigate the incident. The Commission concluded that the entire failure could be traced to an O-ring, a rubber seal on the solid rocket boosters that degraded in the cold weather of the launch. However, the O-ring was not considered the root cause of the problem. The root cause was the fact that NASA chose to launch on a day with very low temperatures. A US House of Representatives report from the Committee on Science and Technology concluded that it was a long-standing failure in safety protocols, combined with an unsustainable launch rate, that led to the disaster. After making extensive technical changes to the shuttle and promoting a safety and accountability culture of its workforce, the shuttle program resumed flights in 1988.

### Sakichi Toyoda and Others

As stated previously, it was Sakichi Toyoda who formally developed a method for identifying root causes to problems to solve or prevent damaging situations. The method he developed was referred to as the '5 Whys.' Previously, Sakichi Toyoda devised the Jidoka principle, which immediately stopped a machine when a problem occurred. Afterwards he offered Jidoka's patent to a British firm for $150,000. This was his seed money to fund the setting-up of Toyota, which became the world's second largest car manufacturer. Hence, it was Toyota Motor Corporation that used the Root Cause Analysis approach as a systematic method for resolving manufacturing process problems called the '5 Whys' in 1958.

It was mandatory at Toyota that new employees had to learn the '5 Whys' process as part of their induction training into the Toyota Production System. Basically, the '5 Whys' method asks 'why' five times until the main cause of the problem is revealed. This approach analytically excludes other causes every time a 'why' is asked. After a while the system was viewed as being too basic, since it did not probe deep enough to reveal the understanding needed to discover the right causes. Another difficulty with using the method was a lack of standardisation for formulating the 'why' questions. Hence, employees tended to formulate the 'why' questions based upon their own individual experiences and depth of knowledge, without truly knowing whether the questions being asked were the right questions for the current circumstance.

Root Cause Analysis has evolved over time to address various circumstances. Hence, several approaches based upon the root cause principle have emerged to cater for specific situations, such as safety, focusing on occupational safety and health, in addition to incidental analysis; production, focusing on manufacturing, specifically quality control; processes, focusing on business and manufacturing methods; failure incidents, focusing on engineering and maintenance environments; and systems that focus on a mixture of approaches, and incorporating certain aspects related to systems analysis and design, change management, and risk management.

Several derivatives of Root Cause Analysis have been developed by major organisations. For example, in 1975, the Federal Aviation Administration (FAA) defined the Aviation Safety Reporting System (ASRS) to execute its safety management policies. These standards were applicable to the aviation industry to reduce accidents to an absolute minimum by improving quality control, mitigation of errors, and risk management. These standards have lowered the death rates from airline accidents by 80%. The ASRS, whilst funded by FAA, is administered by NASA, with its risk management system success being attributed to the separation of authority.

Another significant development occurred in 1986, when Motorola introduced a new approach for risk management called Six Sigma. Six Sigma applies Root Cause Analysis by using specific methods, including statistical information. The Six Sigma quality standards have achieved a high criterion of risk management measured at 3.4 errors or defective products per million (or 99.99966% acceptance rate). Although Six Sigma has been implemented by many large manufacturing companies, such as General Electric, it has also been adapted for the service industries. However, studies have shown that the Six Sigma approach is only suitable for large organisations that have a workforce of 500 employees or over (see Chapter 2, Section 2.2.3.8).

In 1999, the US health care system viewed Root Cause Analysis as a potential method for addressing the high quantity of adverse cases related to patient safety and hospitalisation standards. Medical errors were the eighth primary cause of death in America. The Institute of Medicine (now known as the National Academy of Medicine) argued that errors can be prevented by implementing processes that make it difficult for individuals to make a mistake and easy for individuals to do things correctly. They contended that other industries had found ways to prevent adverse incidents. Hence, there was no logical reason why similar principles could not be applied to health care.

It was maintained that a safer system in health care entailed having procedures which certify that patients are safe from accidental injury. It was posited that when agreement to follow a course of medical treatment has been attained, patients must have the assurance that this agreed medical treatment will proceed correctly and safely so that they will have the best chance possible of achieving the desired outcome. Therefore, it was decided that root cause analysis was to become the preferred method in health care risk management. Root Cause Analysis was adopted by The Joint Commission (TJC), which is a major accreditation body of health care systems in the US as part of its assessment standards. The Joint Commission's Framework for Root Cause Analysis and Action Plan provides an example of a comprehensive systematic analysis, consisting of 24 analysis questions that are intended to provide a template for analysing an event and an aid in organising the steps and information in a Root Cause Analysis.

The above examples illustrate the importance of Root Cause Analysis as a problem-solving tool. From a management perspective, pointing the finger at individual employees for inattention or negligence hardly ever accomplishes anything productive, whereas using occurrences of human negligence to develop more robust processes and practices that prevent such personal errors from reoccurring or happening in the first place can achieve outstanding results. These examples also illustrate that most problems can seldom be ascribed to a single specific cause. In fact, problems are often the outcome of a succession of interlinked 'causal factors.' These causal factors may range from poorly trained employees, design issues, and flawed engineering methods, amongst many others. The causal factors underlying any difficult event can be categorised in terms of causal culpability, while concurrently recognising that all the factors were contributing as conditions that, collectively, escalated into an accident.

## Root Cause Analysis

Root Cause Analysis is based upon the premise that the organisation's processes are usually viewed as the root causal components. However, the response of the employees in relation to how they conduct themselves in performing the processes are the impact or outcomes, which are viewed as the symptoms. Therefore, Root Cause Analysis focuses on the identification of defective or imperfect processes as a way of preventing undesirable symptoms before they reoccur. Hence, pointing the finger at an individual may not be very helpful, but having a system that regularly reviews the way that individual's work is being conducted may be effective to prevent undesirable outcomes.

## 5-Whys Approach

It is important to understand what Root Cause Analysis is about. The simplest application of Root Cause Analysis is using the Sakichi Toyoda approach, namely the 5-Whys approach. The 5-Whys approach is fundamental for devising more complex methods of inquiry. The 5-Whys approach involves having an employee behaving like an inquisitive child by simply asking the question 'Why?' five times in progression, or as often as may be needed to obtain a suitable deduction (refer to Figure 3.1).

The easiest way to explain the 5-Whys Root Cause Analysis approach is by considering the following example: *I often developed headaches because I was dehydrated. Usually, my headache would cease when I took Panadol. However, the next time it happened I neglected to drink sufficient water and I suffered another aching headache.* Hence, in this situation the Panadol was treating the symptom, not the root cause of the headache. The example in Figure 3.2 applies the 5-Whys to determine the root cause of why sufficient water was not consumed.

The above example provides a general overview of the 5-Whys approach. However, if the root cause is not revealed on the fifth question, further questions would be needed to drill deeper into the actual specifics of the issues. Considering the spectrum of causal factors, from processes to people to materials and equipment, they commence with a concern and work back to its causes (or vice versa) depending on the circumstance being

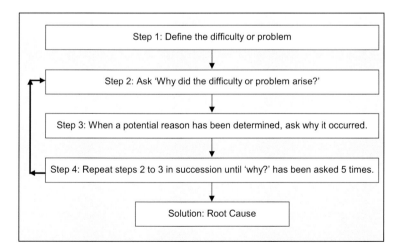

Figure 3.1  The 5-Whys Approach

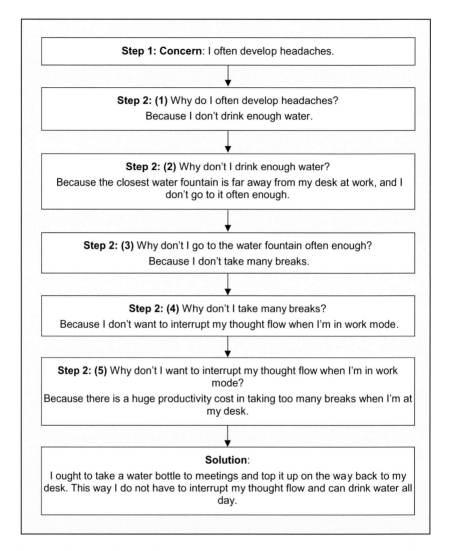

*Figure* 3.2  Example: The 5-Whys Approach

examined. Hence, the 5-Whys and other Root Cause Analysis methods of causal mapping typically depict in a visual method the process of revealing the solution or root cause. Other methods include: The challenger interview, role playing, flowcharts, fishbone diagram (cause-effect graphs), and Ishikawa diagrams.

## *Challenger Interview Method*

The Challenger Interview is similar to the 5-Whys; however, its focus is not on asking why something has occurred, but why the event even matters. The Challenger Interview explains the employee's underlying goals and motivations to reveal the real problem, concern, difficulty, or opportunity that should be resolved. The Challenger Interview process is as follows:

- Step 1: Make clear the problem with the individual (or team) that is experiencing it.
- Step 2: Probe by asking: 'Why does this problem matter to you?' Express this question in a compassionate way by not sounding judgemental. You need to project a sympathetic attitude.
- Step 3: When the reason has been revealed, enquire why that matters to them.
- Step 4: Keep doing this (successively) until the individual's (or team's) underlying goals or motivations are understood.

Let's take an example. When high-rise buildings were being constructed, builders had to find a way of conveying people to their respective apartments or offices in an efficient manner. Thus, the elevators were developed and installed. However, people grumbled that the elevators were too slow. At rush hour, a person may be waiting many minutes with other people who needed to get off at many different floors. There was a general attitude developing that unless something was done to speed up elevators, people and companies would resist moving into high-rise premises and seek alternative floor space. Elevator manufacturers responded by developing faster elevators to significantly increase performance. However, there was a limit to this improvement and people still complained. One of the engineers thought more profoundly into the problem and decided to investigate the situation of why people complained and were upset so much about several minutes' waiting time, particularly during rush-hour.

The engineer decided to ask workers using the elevators: *Why does waiting several minutes in an elevator matter to you?* The general response from the workers was that they were just standing and waiting, with nothing to do. Hence, the engineer was able to clarify the problem as being a matter of dullness and boredom. After considering the matter and discussing the issue with colleagues to come up with some options on how to resolve the problem, it was decided to install mirrors on the inner walls of the elevator. This solution drastically reduced the complaints and constant grumbling.

People just wanted something to do while in the elevator and the mirrors provided them with the opportunity to observe and watch others. This example illustrates that the assumed problem was to reduce elevator carriage times; however the real problem was that people were bored doing nothing in the elevator. Hence, reducing the elevator carriage time would not have resolved the problem fully, because no matter how fast an elevator is, a certain amount of waiting time at rush-hour would still result. Challenging the situation (i.e., the difficulty) in a pleasant and sympathetic way permitted the actual problem to be revealed and resolved.

### Role Playing Method

The role playing method is based upon putting yourself (as the investigator) in someone else's shoes (role). Therefore, viewing the situation or circumstance from someone else's standpoint can divulge profound understandings into the root cause of the problem or difficulty being encountered. This approach is particularly prevalent in the innovative industries related to technology and consumer packed products. Hence, an individual working in the organisation or someone who could be a potential customer may be enduring a problem that you want to solve. In these innovative industries, product and/or service managers and customer perception investigators typically apply role playing as a means of resolving concerns. Like other Root Cause Analysis methods, the role playing approach involves four steps as follows:

- Step 1: Define the role character to be playacted by describing the character's attitudes, motivations, and goals. The role character can be a real person, or a typical person within a group.
- Step 2: Describe the problem, setting, other people involved, and scenario your character is playacting.
- Step 3: Visualise yourself as the play character by dressing and behaving like the play character.
- Step 4: Playact your visualised character by trying to resolve their problem or circumstance. Note down new discernments into the problem being resolved.

Take the previous example regarding the long waiting time in an elevator to reach a building floor destination.

- Step 1: Define the character: A specific office worker arriving at the office building wanting to take an elevator to its place of work.
- Step 2: Define the scenario: The specific office worker enters the elevator with 20 other persons all wanting to reach different floors in the building. The specific office worker has their office on the 30th floor and is likely to be the last person out.
- Step 3: Get into character: Talk to people who use the elevator and enquire how they felt about the waiting time in the elevator. They all felt bored with nothing to do in the company of people they do not know or work with.
- Step 4: Playact the role. I enter the elevator with many others. We do not make conversation because we do not know each other. I try to pass the time by discretely trying to watch the others but it's very difficult when you are standing, and your surrounding vision is limited. However, I think that if the elevator walls had a reflecting surface, one may pass the time observing the others, what they are wearing, who they are, and trying to guess what they do. In no time the elevator reaches where I want to step off and I do not notice the several minutes that I have spent in the elevator because my mind was occupied with watching others.

The concern is resolved by simply removing the boredom from the daily routine of using the elevator to reach the place of work.

### *Process Maps (Flowcharts)*

Process maps (or flowcharts) are an excellent visual tool because they describe the logical flow of all the steps that comprise a process in a comprehensible rational diagram. Process maps enable one to examine the activity in detail and permit any inconsistencies in the procedure that are at the root of a process dissection to be easily detected. Process maps are a common tool used in business process reengineering to map the flow of the various steps in a transactional procedure. They are normally used to streamline processes by removing non-added value activities that consume resources but do not contribute to the efficient performance of activities and related tasks. Process maps are a fundamental basis for the Total Quality Management (TQM) concept. Hence, process maps are an essential tool for quality management at many companies around the world. The creation of a process map basically consists of five steps as follows:

- Step 1: Identify and define the target process that is of interest.
- Step 2: Conduct a brainstorming session to ascertain all the various steps and decision points for the selected process.
- Step 3: Identify the starting and finishing points of the selected process. Place these on the initial process map as a foundation.
- Step 4: Using the information from Step 2, enter the middle steps of the process in the initial process map that was defined at Step 3, including the routes for any decision points.
- Step 5: Verify the process by checking that all steps and decision points identified at Step 2 have been included. Request a colleague to assist in the verification process and note any new breaking points in the process.

Let us take an example. Assume that a university is having some difficulties with the admission registration process of new students, in that some applicants are complaining that they have not received any feedback from the university about their admission registration. This is causing a great deal of discomfiture to the manager and employees at the university admissions office. To resolve the issue, the manager and employees at the university admissions office meet to conduct a brainstorming session with the objective of mapping out the admissions process to ensure the process is reliable. The outcome of the meeting results in the process map shown in Figure 3.3. The brainstorming team finds that the problem arose because the Administration Office was updating the students' personal files with the rejection notifications but was not sending the rejection notification letters to the students (see shaded tasks with dotted lines on Figure 3.3). Hence, the process map revealed two vital missing action points.

Process mapping as a procedure is an iterative process, which means that there may be several process map versions before one is satisfied that the process map accurately represents the process activities. Furthermore, the above example is relatively simple. However, some problematic situations may require very complex causal-factor process maps to arrive at the root cause(s).

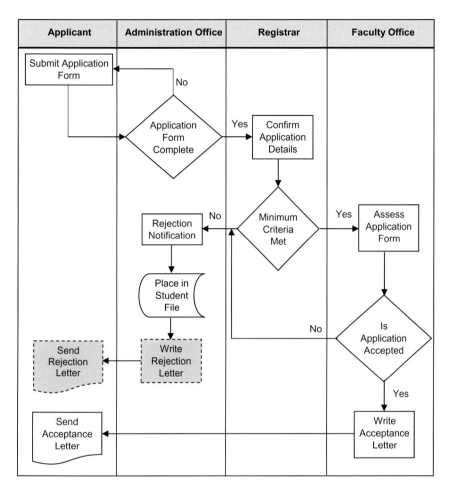

Figure 3.3  Example: Process Map – University Admissions Process for New Students

As has been illustrated, Root Cause Analysis basically defines or resolves in a very explicit way the nature of the problem, in terms of when the problem occurred, where the problem occurred, and the reason why the problem occurred. The objective is to ensure that the problem does not reoccur.

## Ishikawa Diagram or Fishbone Diagram

The Ishikawa Diagram is named after Kaoru Ishikawa, who was a Japanese organisational theorist and an engineering professor at the University of Tokyo. He was noted for his quality management innovations. The Ishikawa

Diagram or the Fishbone Diagram (or cause-and-effect diagram) is often used in the analysis of industrial processes as a causal analysis tool and is viewed as one of the seven basic quality tools. Its primary purpose is to identify the many possible causes for an effect or problem. Because the Ishikawa Diagram instantly sorts ideas into useful categories, it can be applied to structure brainstorming sessions. It is very useful when identifying possible causes for a problem and when a team's thinking may be likely to fall into a pattern of behaviour that is dull and unproductive and hard to change.

The procedure to prepare an Ishikawa Diagram is relatively simple and only requires a marking pen and a whiteboard or flipchart. Like similar tools, the procedure to complete an Ishikawa Diagram is an iterative process. Hence, it may take several revisions before a satisfactory diagram is created. The process to complete an Ishikawa Diagram is as follows (also refer to Figure 3.4, which illustrates these steps):

- Step 1: The team is to agree on a problem statement, which is viewed as the effect. This is written in a rectangular box at the centre (vertically) and to the right (horizontally) of the whiteboard.
- Step 2: Draw a horizontal arrow running to the problem definition box.
- Step 3: Conduct a brainstorming session to categorise the causes of the problem. If categorising the causes of the problem becomes difficult, use the broad headings of Methods; Machines (equipment); People (manpower); Materials; Measurement; and Environment.
- Step 4: Write each identified category of the causes as branches from the main arrow.
- Step 5: Conduct a brainstorming session regarding all the possible causes of the problem.
- Step 6: Ask the question: Why does this happen? As each response (idea) is provided, the appointed scribe writes it down as a branch from the suitable category. If the causes relate to several categories, they can be written for each category.
- Step 7: Repeat the question: 'Why does this happen?' about each cause, writing the sub-causes branching off the causes. Carry on asking 'Why?' and produce deeper levels of causes. Note that layers of branches indicate causal relationships.
- Step 8: When the brainstorming team has exhausted all ideas, it should focus attention on the areas on the diagram that have generated few ideas.

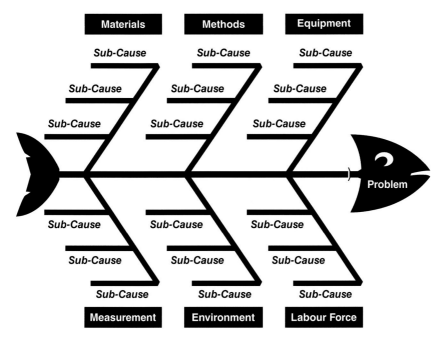

*Figure* 3.4  Example: Constructing an Ishikawa Diagram

The Ishikawa Diagram has several advantages. It is a highly visual brainstorming instrument that can generate added examples of root causes and can swiftly detect if the root cause is found multiple times in the same or different causal tree. It also permits one to view all causes concurrently and provides helpful visualisation for displaying concerns to stakeholders. Its main disadvantages are that complex deficiencies may generate numerous causes, which may clutter the diagram, with interrelationships between the causes not easily revealed. An Ishikawa Diagram is a highly structured method and an excellent aid for conducting brainstorming sessions to detect possible causes of a problem and sorting thoughts into suitable categories; thus making it very suitable for brainstorming causes of a problem, particularly when using the Five-Whys tool.

As Figure 3.4 illustrates, the problem (or effect) is shown at the head or mouth of the fish. Possible causes are recorded on the smaller 'bones' under various cause categories. The diagram is very helpful in detecting likely causes for a problem that may not otherwise be considered by the brainstorming team, enabling them to explore the categories and reflect on alternative causes. The brainstorming team should consist of members who have personal knowledge and experience of the procedures and systems involved in the problem or event to be examined. The root causes of the event (or occurrence) are the underlying process and system problems that permitted the contributing factors to culminate in a detrimental event. Remember that there can be multiple root causes. Moreover, when the root causes and contributing factors are identified, each root cause and contributing factor will need to be addressed in an appropriate manner.

## Other Root Cause Analysis Methods

Apart from the methods described in the previous section, there are also several other methods for detecting the root cause of a specific problem. However, the applicability of these other approaches is contingent on the industry and problem types, and include the following:

- Rapid Problem Resolution (RPR) Problem Diagnosis.
- Failure Mode and Effects Analysis.
- Current Reality Tree.

### *Rapid Problem Resolution (RPR) Problem Diagnosis*

The Rapid Problem Resolution (RPR) Problem Diagnosis method ascertains the root cause of recurring grey problems in the ICT field. Grey problems are problems where the causing technological factor is unknown or unconfirmed, such as intermittent errors in IT equipment; intermittent incorrect output in sensing apparatus; or transitory performance problems in newly installed information systems. These types of problems make it very difficult for IT personnel to allocate the problem to a technical support team.

Figure 3.5 provides a model that combines the frequency of problem occurrence with the causing technology to illustrate the level of complexity of the problem being encountered and thus determine the level of difficulty to investigate the problem. The problem types that are shown in each quadrant have specific attributes. For instance, the problem types that are shown in Quadrant-One have firm faults that are straightforwardly diagnosed and traced to a causing technology where the technical support team can deal with them without difficulty. These problem types are the typical

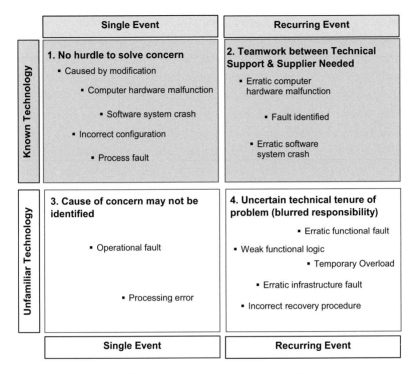

*Figure* 3.5  Identification of Recurring Grey Problems Model

day-to-day occurrences and there is no difficulty in resolving the concern. The problem types indicated in Quadrant-Two are recurring and at times occur due to a known error or are clearly being caused by a specific hardware or software component. Hence, these problem types are reasonably easy to resolve but require a high degree of collaboration between the technical support team and the suppliers.

Difficulties in resolving problems are usually encountered for problem types that occur in Quadrant-Three and Quadrant-Four. Problem types occurring in Quadrant-Three are usually a single incident (one-off) and do not normally reoccur, hence the cause may never be revealed. However, problem types itemised in Quadrant-Four are usually of a reoccurring nature, but their technical ownership is unclear and therefore they are labelled 'Grey Problems.' These are the problem types that require special attention.

It must be recognised that RPR does not cater for all types of problems but addresses specific IT problem areas, such as application software failures, incorrect output, and performance issues. Furthermore, its key use is in the diagnosis of ongoing and recurring problems that have an unclear technical ownership. The method consists of the core process and supporting techniques. The core process defines a step-by-step approach to problem diagnosis and has three phases. The first phase is the discovery stage, which focuses on collecting and reviewing relevant existing information, and defining an agreed understanding of the issue being investigated.

The second phase is the investigation stage, which focuses on creating and implementing a diagnostic data capture plan; analysing the results and if necessary, repeat the analysis task until the analysis process is exhausted; and identify root cause. The third and final phase is the problem resolution stage, which focuses on translating the diagnostic data and interpreting the analysed results; deciding on a solution and implementing it; and verifying that the root cause (problem) has been addressed. The supporting procedures specify how the objectives of the core-process steps are achieved, referring to examples that use tools and techniques, which are at the disposal of the organisation under examination.

It must be noted that the RPR approach is an evidence-based method that is focused on three key principles, namely that an investigation is focused on a single symptom; having conclusive diagnostic data that is gathered when the specific symptom occurs; and that the diagnostic data is always collected for a real problem in a live environment. It is important that the diagnostic data is definitive (i.e., conclusive, and complete) and that it is recorded for diagnostic events, which are directly correlated to the user's experience of the symptom.

### *Failure Mode and Effects Analysis*

Failure Mode and Effects Analysis (FMEA) is a highly structured and systematic tool for failure analysis that was conceived in the 1940s to analyse problems that might arise from malfunctions of military systems. It is based on inductive reasoning (forward logic) and a proactive approach for evaluating a process to identify where and how it might fail and to assess the relative impact of different failures, with the aim of identifying the segments of the process that are most in need of change. FMEA is based on recording the failure types and their outcome effects on the rest of the system in a specific FMEA template (worksheet). The FMEA template varies according to the type of process being examined but its core application is related to reliability engineering, safety engineering and quality engineering. FMEA's primary objective is to facilitate the identification of potential failure modes based on experience with similar products and processes.

The aim is to identify the true failure modes at all system levels, commencing with the functional analyses to estimate the failure probability or its mitigation by understanding the failure mechanism. This will enable management to structure the mitigation for risk reduction based on the failure effect severity reduction or based on reducing the probability of failure or both. Therefore, FMEA may include information on causes of failure to mitigate the probability of occurrence by eliminating the identified (root) causes. The FMEA process addresses three key questions:

- What may go wrong? This identifies the failure modes. The failure modes are the various ways in which something might fail in practice.
- Why would the failure happen? This identifies the failure causes. Failures are any potential or actual errors or defects that affect the end-user or customer.
- What would be the consequences of each failure? This identifies the failure effects, which refer to studying the consequences of those failures.

Addressing these three questions enables FMEA teams to assess the processes for likely failures and proactively correct any detected defective processes. Thus, the approach is a failure preventive measure, since the defective process is corrected before it occurs rather than correcting it as a reaction to adverse events after a failure has occurred. Hence, the focus on prevention mitigates the operational risk that may adversely affect the organisation. The FMEA approach is extremely effective when assessing a new or modified process before its implementation to detect any likely failure points. Likely failures are ranked on three key factors, namely by how serious their consequences are; how frequently they are likely to occur; and how easily they can be detected.

The primary objective of FMEA is to take the appropriate measures to eliminate or mitigate failures, commencing with the highest-priority ones. FMEA is an essential component of continuous improvement programmes since the analysis documents current knowledge and actions about the risks of failures in a proactive manner. The approach is firstly applied during the process design to prevent failures and once the process is implemented it is used as a control measure, before and during the ongoing operation of the process. Hence, FMEA should be applied at the conceptual stages of the process design and continued throughout the product/service life cycle.

The FMEA approach may be applied in several instances, specifically after quality function deployment at the design or redesign stage in the development of a process, product, or service; after using an existing process, product, or service in a new or modified application; prior to the defining control plans for a new or revised process; once enhancement targets are planned for an existing process, product, or service, such as KPIs; after analysing failures of an existing process, product, or service; and at regular intervals during the process, product, or service life cycle.

### Failure Mode and Effects Analysis (FMEA) Procedure

Typically, Failure Mode and Effects Analysis follows a structured approach consisting of various steps. It should be noted that before undertaking an FMEA exercise, the assigned team should consult the standards (if any are available) within the organisation and/or industry. Figure 3.6 provides the typical procedure to be followed in conducting an FMEA assignment.

Figure 3.6 illustrates the deductive and structure approach of FMEA. It consists of a series of steps that must be undertaken in a meticulous manner. A description of the various steps are as follows:

1.  It is important that a cross-functional team with a diverse knowledge of the process, product or service, and customer requirements must be established. This cross-functional team is to consist of members who are knowledgeable about the process, product, or service in terms of its design, production, quality, assessment, reliability, maintenance, procurement, sales, marketing, and customer service.
2.  Define the FMEA scope. Treat the FMEA exercise like any other project, therefore determine the type of task that will be addressed. For instance, is the FMEA exercise to address a process or a product, or a service, or a specific production unit. Establish the scope parameters or boundaries. Decide on the level of detail that should be undertaken. Apply a diagramming tool, such as a project network or flowchart,

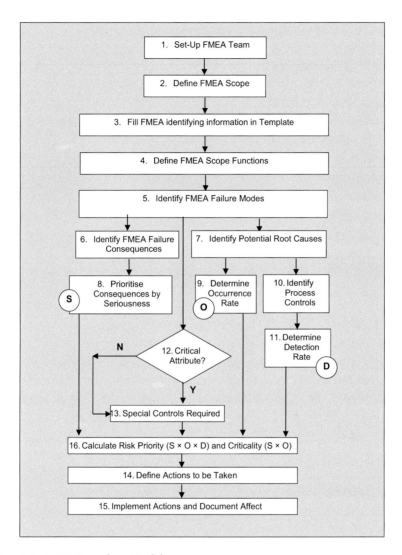

*Figure* 3.6  FMEA Procedure Model

to define the scope, ensuring all team members fully understand the defined scope.

3.  Adapt and use an FMEA tabular template for entering information related to the specific issue being investigated (refer to Table 3.1). Note that Table 3.1 may need additional columns to cater for the specific need of the organisation.

Table 3.1  FMEA Tabular Template

| 1 | 2 | 3 | 4 | 5 | 6 | 7 | 8 | 9 | 10 | 11 | 12 | 13 |
|---|---|---|---|---|---|---|---|---|----|----|----|----|
| FMEA Ref. No | Item | Potential Failure Mode | Potential Failure Outcomes | Gravity (S) | Root Cause | Occur Rate (O) | Present Controls | Detect Rate (D) | Special Controls (Y/N) | Risk Priority (SxOxD) | Actions | Effect |
| | | | | | | | | | | | | |

4. Identify the functions that comprise the FMEA scope. The functions may be identified by examining the aim the FMEA scope is tackling, such as a system, design, process, product, or service, and define the associated customer expectations. The functions may be identified by breaking down the scope into components, such as system modules, assemblies, items and parts of assemblies, or process steps.

5. Identify the failure modes for each function. These are the potential ways a failure may occur. The FMEA procedure model is an iterative process, so it may be necessary to revert and rewrite the function in more precise detail so that the failure modes are revealed in full.

6. Once the failure modes are identified for each function the procedure branches in three directions, namely identifying the consequences of the failure, identifying the root causes of the failure, and whether a specific failure mode has critical characteristics that require special attention.

7. First Branch: Identify all the consequences for each failure mode related to the nature of the subject under examination, such as a system, system module, process, associated processes, product, service, customer, or regulatory requirements. Establish and define what the customer is likely to experience if this failure occurs. In other words, what happens if this failure occurs?

8. Prioritise the consequences by determining the level of seriousness of each identified consequence. This establishes the severity rating (referred to as 'S'), which has a scale from 1 to 10, where 1 is insignificant and 10 is catastrophic. Note the severity rate on FMEA template (if a failure mode has more than one effect, write only the highest severity rating for that failure mode).

9. Second Branch: Determine all the potential root causes for each failure mode by using the cause analysis techniques described in previous sections. Also apply the knowhow and experience of the FMEA team. Note all the possible causes for each failure mode on the FMEA template.

10. Determine the occurrence rating for each cause (referred to as 'O'). The occurrence rating is the probability of a failure occurring for each specific cause during the life cycle of the FMEA scope. Occurrence is rated on a scale from 1 to 10, where 1 is extremely unlikely and 10 is inevitable. Note the occurrence rating for each cause on the FMEA template.

11. Identify existing process controls for each cause. The process controls are checks, procedures, or other devices that are currently in place to

prevent failures from impacting the customer. These controls attempt to remove or mitigate the cause from happening or detect failure after the cause has occurred but before it has impacted the customer.

12. Determine the detection rating for each control (referred to as 'D'). This rating appraises the effectiveness of the controls to detect the cause or its failure mode after they have occurred but before they impact the customer. Detection is rated on a scale from 1 to 10, where 1 means the control is certain to detect the problem and 10 means the control is certain not to detect the problem (or no control exists). Note the detection rating for each cause on the FMEA template.

13. *Third Branch*: This procedure step is only necessary if there are government regulatory safety or compliance requirements that need specific controls, referred to as critical attributes. Determine whether the failure mode is associated with any critical attribute. Simply note on the FMEA template 'Y' or 'N' to indicate whether special controls are needed. Typically, if 'Y' is noted the severity rate would normally be 9 or 10, and occurrence and detection ratings above 3.

14. *Applicable to all branches*: Compute the risk priority number, or RPN, which equals (S × O × D) and criticality, which equals (S × O). Enter the results of these computations on the FMEA template. The results of these calculations provide a general ranking for potential failures so that they may be addressed.

15. Define recommended actions. The recommended actions aim to lower severity (S) or occurrence (O). These actions may be viewed as additional controls to enhance detection. It is also important to enter the target completion dates and the person responsible for the actions on the FMEA template.

16. Update FMEA template with the completed actions. Enter the completed actions and their affects (new S, O, or D ratings and new RPNs) on the FMEA template.

The above procedure provides a systematic process for conducting an FMEA analysis.

### Current Reality Tree

Current Reality Tree is based on Theory of Constraints (ToC). ToC is a highly logical and analytical approach of reasoning about how systems work, and how to facilitate their improvement. According to ToC, every system has a single constriction referred to as a bottleneck, which restricts how the whole system performs. Hence, when a bottleneck is removed, the constraint moves somewhere else in the system. Hence, if each respective constraint is not addressed, the investment associated with that system will be wasted because the overall system performance will not be enhanced. The ToC process consists of several collaborative 'thinking tools', which despite being very similar in the manner they operate, are augmented to be used in different circumstances.

Basically, the objective of these tools is to assist management to address three fundamental issues, namely: what needs to be changed; what is the change that is required; and how will the required change come about. Once these issues are addressed, management can implement the required changes that will bring about organisational improvements. One common and useful ToC tool is the Current Reality Tree (CRT). The CRT tool is a process that is used to examine simultaneously many organisational problems. CRT is intended to assist the analyst to reveal and recognise the linkage between the various issues, and to specifically identify the most important issue that should be prioritised and resolved. The CRT process consists of four fundamental steps:

- Identify and attain agreement of the system or process scope that needs to be understood. It is important that the team undertaking the CRT exercise has the knowhow, expertise, and the authority to initiate and implement improvements. Identifying and agreeing on the scope of the analysis will facilitate the process of selecting the appropriate team that can contribute to the understanding of the overall system that is under study.
- List all the existing undesirable effects in the current circumstances. An ideal list consists of between five to ten undesirable effects for analysis. A list with too many undesirable effects is likely to indicate that the team is looking at too much detail at this preliminary stage. Furthermore, determine whether each undesirable effect listed is valid by evaluating whether they really exist in the present environment and have an impact. Ensure that each effect is suitably described by an appropriate statement. Describe the undesirable effects in positive and present terms, including the preferred solution. For example, the undesirable effects of a customer care service point may include the

following: Frequently incidents are poorly managed; Often there are repeat incidents; Customer Care Officials have insufficient experience to handle incidents; Customers are unhappy with the service they receive; There is a very high turnover of Customer Care Officials; and Reported incidents are not resolved in a timely manner.

- Analyse the cause/effect relationships between the listed undesirable effects and identified inherent causes that contribute to them. In the example described in the previous step, it may seem evident why customers are not satisfied with the service, namely that the service does not resolve the incident in a timely manner and often the incidents are of a repetitive nature. This relationship is shown in Figure 3.7. Note that this is not a logical flowchart but a method of making cause/effect links apparent.

- Draw a consolidated cause/effect tree by linking the cause/effect relationships. The analysis is completed by searching and placing each of the undesirable effects to the Current Reality Tree (CRT). At this stage it is likely that additional causes for some of the undesirable effects on the list will be identified, which will be included on the CRT. Figure 3.8 illustrates this point, for instance 'Not many new problems are identified' is an added cause for 'Often there are repeat incidents.' The construction of the CRT is an iterative process, with new versions being created until all the undesirable effects have been entered and joined appropriately, and with the CRT team being satisfied with the resultant outcome. A CRT is likely to be completed when it can be reasonably and fluently read from top to bottom (and vice-versa) using the statements in each box.

The CRT will enable the team to identify all the issues that need to be tackled first. Note that the CRT tells the team what needs to be changed and not

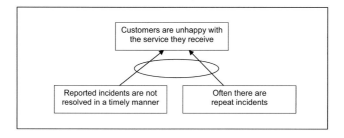

*Figure 3.7*  Example: Cause/Effect Relationships – Customer Care Service

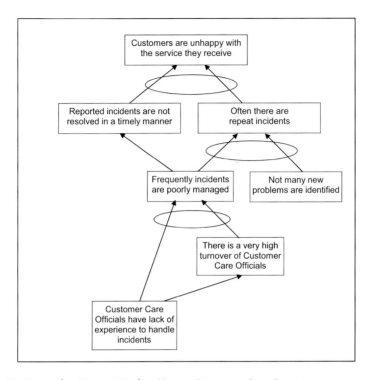

*Figure* 3.8  Example: Current Reality Tree – Customer Care Service

what action is required. The action that is required and how the action is to be implemented comes at a later stage. However, the CRT assists the team to identify what needs to be corrected (the problem area).

## Root Cause Analysis: Finding the Cause of Performance Issues

A fundamental principle regarding Root Cause Analysis is to think outside the box. Problems, especially repetitive ones, all impact the organisation's performance. A problem consumes time and energy for it to be resolved, thus affecting the performance of employees. However, if the problem impacts the product or service in terms of functionality and quality, then the impact becomes more serious because it not only consumes time and energy of employees to resolve, but also directly impactsthe customer in a negative way.

It is also important to apply Root Cause Analysis proactively by identifying the most critical reoccurring problem being encountered by the organisation. This may be done by examining the organisation's performance data and obtaining customer feedback. Common reoccurring problems are often related to missed targets, with the consequence of late shipments to customers. Hence, repetitive problems need to be addressed without delay. It is also important to review the current process by assembling an appropriate team to discuss their hindrances, customer interfaces, and which processes are inhibiting performance. Such a team will be able to explore and see issues that management are not aware of by holding brainstorming sessions to identify problems and reveal the root cause.

This will provide sufficient information for the team to ascertain where and when performance issues are arising so that they may evaluate the cause of the problems. Having a cross-functional team with each member having distinct experience and knowledge establishes the right synergy for revealing and agreeing on the root causes and enabling the team members to realise that there may be several interrelated factors causing the issue. Once the root causes have been identified, an action plan is required to address each root cause with the view of eliminating them and enhancing performance at various levels, namely at employee, divisional, and organisational levels. This plan should be detailed and specific, utilising the information and suggestions put forward by the team. The plan may consist of implementing several control points in the delivery process, such as reporting on activities that are to occur soon (say a week beforehand) to ensure that the inputs for a specific activity are guaranteed and are therefore the envisaged performance level achieved.

However, an action plan is itself theoretical; it must be implemented, and the outcome evaluated for it to become reality. Implementing the action plan is not a difficult matter but it requires a monitoring mechanism to ensure that the activities are being conducted according to the timeline and that the implemented measure can be evaluated to assess its effectiveness and impact on the performance. It is essential that team members are continuously involved in the implementation process to ensure there is consensus among the team members that the measures are succeeding in resolving the identified root cause of the problem and that performance is on track. Hence, it is important to maintain momentum in implementing the action plan and ensuring that the modified process or system remains under scrutiny. This can be achieved by maintaining a log of performance measurements, and persistently training team members (new and regular) to ensure that the progress registered is not lost over time, and the root causes are permanently eliminated, hence making certain that the performance goals are achieved.

## Conclusion

As stated in the introduction of this chapter, Root Cause Analysis is related to service and product quality that impacts the eventual performance of the organisation. Root Cause Analysis explores and exposes in a very definite way the source of a problem, in terms of when, where, and why the problem has occurred. Although problem solving appears to be a reactive activity, Root Cause Analysis acts as a proactive tool because it ensures that the problem can be prevented from flowing out and impacting the customer (internal or external) a second time. The fundamental principle is to dig deeper into the problem area to discover the root cause of the problem rather than wasting time addressing the symptoms.

Addressing the symptoms merely masks the problem; it will not prevent it from reoccurring. Hence, there is the definite need to determine completely why certain difficulties have occurred and to identify the cause of the problem. Root Cause Analysis is all about understanding how to track and locate the adverse effects back to their primary cause or revealing the interrelated causes. This is critical in achieving a higher level of quality and having satisfied customers. There is an essential need to have a systematic process in place that not only identifies the problems or what went wrong but uncovers the causes of the problems, since resolving the cause will automatically eliminate the problem.

Applying the Root Cause Analysis approach effectively will be governed by established principles, such as reliable and detailed documentation; attaining the optimum and often the lowest cost solutions; identifying all the root causes; defining incidents and failures fully and correctly; and determining a timeline, such as a Gantt Chart. Once these principles are accepted as the fundamental basis of the methodology, a step-by-step approach can be adopted to successfully conduct a Root Cause Analysis. The following suggested steps may be used to implement the Root Cause Analysis process. These suggested steps should be viewed as a typical process and may need to be revised to suit a particular industry or specialisation:

1.  Describe and document the full occurrence or incident. This documentation is to be a realistic and truthful explanation of the event (incident).
2.  Collect as many facts (evidence) as possible to confirm the description of the incident.
3.  Chronologically categorise (rank) all the events that happened leading to the final failure incident.
4.  Adopt the 'Five-Whys' approach for each event leading to the failure incident to help identify the causes.
5.  Segregate (set apart) all the root causes for each event leading to the failure incident that affected the incident from the casual causes that did not have a direct impact. In other words, for each event leading to the failure incident, separate the root causes that did not have a direct impact from those that did.
6.  Determine all the preventive activities, with the easiest and most cost-effective activities at the top.
7.  Further categorise the preventive activities by identifying those activities that have team agreement and that are expected to have the top-most possible rate of preventing the problem in the future without generating other disruptions.
8.  Explore other tools that may be applied to determine the root cause of the problem being examined.
9.  Implement the agreed corrective activities to confirm the future prevention of the failure incident and its adverse consequences.

Remember that Root Cause Analysis is a deductive problem-solving methodology that is widely applied throughout every industry and organisational function, from software development to engineering, operations and administration, and marketing, amongst many others. Using Root Cause Analysis means mitigating the use of firefighting and crisis management to an absolute minimum as a primary mode of resolving difficulties across the organisation.

# References

Aboagye, R., Cherala, S., Senesac, P., and Johnston, J. (2016). *Quality Improvement (QI) in Evaluation: Ask Why Again and Again and Again.* Centre for Health Policy and Research (CHPR) Publications. Available at: https://escholarship.umassmed.edu/healthpolicy_pp/197 (Accessed 21 November 2023).

Institute of Medicine. (2009). *To Err is Human: Building a Safer Health System.* Washington, DC: National Academy Press.

Shirouzu, N. and Murphy, J. (2008). 'Toyota to Change Leader Amid Global Sales Slump.' *Wall Street Journal*, 24 December 2008.

# 4

# PERFORMANCE MANAGEMENT FRAMEWORK

'A performance management system is the foundation of performance excellence in an organization and therefore it should be simple, straight-forward, and intuitive, aligned with organizational goals and have flavours of organization values.'

Kaustubh Sonalkar
CEO, Essar Corporate Services LLP

The performance management framework adopted is a fundamental and strategic pillar of any organisation. But often organisations turn this signifi-cant pillar into a bureaucratic nightmare. It is important for the management team, as guardians of the process, to ensure that the performance manage-ment framework implemented in their organisation does not lose its signifi-cance. As has been illustrated in Chapter 2, the traditional year-end employee appraisal systems, which were designed in the 1940s to specifically identify poor performers with the objective of terminating their engagement or reassigning them to other duties, and their successor systems of the 1970s, are now questioned and are viewed by most as being ineffective.

DOI: 10.4324/9781032685465-5

The performance management framework needs to shift its focus from the achievements of the individual employees to assessing the contributions of employees as a team, and thus on the team's impact on the strategic objectives of the organisation. There is no magic wand solution. An organisation must determine its position within its life cycle and adopt a performance management framework that suits its current circumstances and specific needs. In other words, the performance management framework that is adopted must be meaningful and specifically aimed at gaining corporate success. Hence, the model to be adopted must have a combination and complementary number of ingredients related to mutual trust, clarity of roles, diversity of talents, and a practice of providing equal access to opportunities and resources for people who might otherwise be excluded. Designing metrics that cater for these aspects will require a major rethink about the tools and approaches that are to be adopted as part of the performance management framework.

## Introduction

Previously, it was established that the performance management framework of an organisation is a fundamental and strategic pillar of that organisation. It was also argued that often organisations turn this significant pillar into a bureaucratic nightmare. Hence, a fundamental issue that needs to be addressed is to allocate this fundamental task and responsibility to the appropriate management level. Defining the performance management framework that is to be implemented cannot be delegated. Those heading the organisation have the specific and key responsibility for defining and leading the process of performance management.

The performance management framework of an organisation needs to reflect the culture and core values of the organisation, which normally reflects the leadership style and values of those who run it. Furthermore, these qualities are reflected and form an integral basis for the organisation's strategy and its respective strategic objectives. Unless those who head the organisation drive the performance management process, the integration of their vision, values, and strategic direction will not be incorporated completely within the performance management framework and the established business goals will not be achieved. The driving of the performance management process by those who run the organisation does not mean having an autocratic process. It means taking the lead with the collaboration of many others in the organisational hierarchical structure, typically from senior management and executives to general employees.

A performance management system needs to promote performance excellence in an organisation and therefore must be easily understood and manageable. In other words, the performance management process must support the organisational values, be easy to apply, form an integral part of the organisation, and be congruent with the organisational goals. These attributes are essential because the process must support and be aligned with the organisation's strategic direction, its tactical policies and practices, and determine the performance outlook for its employees. Hence, the process needs to be simple and satisfying, and should be viewed as an effortless process that adds value to the organisation's operations.

The performance management framework to be adopted will depend on the organisation's industry sector and its culture and inherent complexity in terms of its size and activity domain, since this will determine the appropriate performance management tools and respective accuracy level that may be applied. The performance management framework adopted in an organisation must generate the proper type of organisational commitment. Organisational commitment facilitates better organisational performance through the achievement of the strategic goals, because employees experience a strong bond to the organisation, and are thus more productive and dedicated to their work.

Organisational commitment has a positive relationship with employee engagement, job satisfaction, performance, and distribution of leadership. However, a proper type of commitment needs to be fostered that promotes a strong bond between the employees and the organisation they work for, which will likely increase an employee's chances of staying with the organisation for a longer period. Often the term 'employee engagement' is confused with employee commitment. However, there is an important difference – engagement refers to how happy an employee is in their job, while commitment refers to how much effort an employee puts into their job. Hence, an engaged employee will not automatically be a committed employee, and vice-versa.

The type of organisational commitment and level of employee engagement are influenced by the organisational culture. Creating a culture where management is responsive to new ideas and permits these ideas to be executed at any level of the organisation will genuinely make the most of the diversity that the workplace has to offer. This type of organisational environment encourages employees to be passionate about the work they perform. Avoid the creation of organisation commitment based on financial rewards; this type of commitment is short-term.

As was stated earlier, there is no magic wand solution. There is no such thing as the best performance management framework. An organisation must modify its performance management framework to reflect the changes taking place within the organisation and the industry it operates in, and modify its performance management framework to reflect the changes taking place within the organisation and the industry it operates in. Hence, the performance management framework must be flexible and adaptable to changing circumstances. All performance management frameworks are acceptable providing they support the achievement of the organisational goals. The performance management framework must be designed to be congruent and specifically aligned with overall business goals.

## Creating the Right Organisational Environment

The above illustrates that a mandatory factor in defining and implementing an appropriate performance management framework is the creation of a proper organisational environment in terms of leadership, commitment and employee engagement, communication, and training. This will ensure that employees develop a higher level of job satisfaction and motivation that become a primary thrust in attaining higher performance through the achievement of the established organisational goals.

### *Developing a Proper Management and Leadership Approach*

The philosopher Lau Tzu (600BC) is reputed as stating that:

> To lead people, walk beside them... As for the best leaders, the people do not notice their existence. The next best, the people honour and praise. The next, the people fear; and the next, the people hate... When the best leader's work is done the people say, 'We did it ourselves!'

This quotation implies that good leaders need to inspire confidence in themselves and take the initiative. However, truly great leaders inspire confidence within the people they lead to exceed their normal performance level. Hence, those that head an organisation must directly lead the performance management process, but it is the employees that should be the driving force in its implementation. Leaders are made not born; they need to develop the proper skills and interact with others. Leadership is a process by which an individual can influence others to achieve an objective and directs the organisation in a way that makes it more cohesive, coherent, and productive. Having authority to manage the organisation does not make an individual a leader. Authority or power within an organisation provides the individual with the mandate to direct the organisation, but leadership makes employees want to follow the leader to achieve high performance goals.

The contingency leadership theory of the 1960s and 1970s conceptualised leadership as accommodating the complexities of leadership due to the impact of different situations. Although this contingency theory had five streams, the Path-Goal Theory developed by House (1971) is the most prevalent of the contingency theories and contributed to recognising the fact that no single pattern of behaviour will be effective in all situations. The Path-Goal theory places importance on how leaders affect their subordinates' perceptions of their work and personal goals, and the direction they take to achieve their goals. Furthermore, this theory posits that a leader becomes effective because of the impact they make on their subordinates' level of motivation, resulting in the subordinates' ability to perform effectively. The theory attempts to describe the consequences of four specific styles of leadership behaviour on three subordinate attitudes, namely: Satisfaction of subordinates; subordinates' acceptance of the leader; and the subordinates' expectations that their effort will result in effective performance, and that this effective performance is the route to rewards. House and Mitchell (1974) conceptualised the Path-Goal theory by integrating previous leadership research into a multi-dimensional model that depicted four leadership styles:

(a) Instrumental or directive leadership. With this style the leader informs subordinates what is expected of them; provides subordinates with specific support as to what tasks are to be carried out and how they are to be executed; indicates and explains the role of each subordinate in the group; upholds specific standards of performance; and requests that group members adhere to standard rules and regulations.

(b) Supportive leadership. The leader under this style is viewed as being friendly, showing particular interest in the status, well-being, and needs of subordinates. A supportive leader is amenable, doing little things to make the tasks more satisfying, and considers members as equals.

(c) Participative leadership. A participative leader seeks opinions from subordinates and genuinely takes these suggestions into account before deciding.

(d) Achievement-oriented leadership. This type of leader sets demanding and stimulating goals, where subordinates are expected to perform at their highest level. Besides, the leader constantly looks for ways to improve performance, and displays a high level of trust that will stimulate subordinates to take on the prerequisite level of responsibility, by exerting the necessary effort to achieve the established goals.

According to House and Mitchell (1974), these leadership styles must correspond to both environmental and subordinate contingency factors. The environmental attributes that moderate the impact of a leader's behaviours are task structure, including the level of repetitiveness; formal authority system; and the work group. Whilst the subordinate attributes that moderate the impact of a leader's behaviours are locus of control; experience; and ability. An improvement to the contingency leadership theory was the visionary or charismatic leadership theory that is based on a study conducted by Bass (1990) related to successful business leaders managing their organisations through change. Generally, Bass posited that there are three basic ways to explain how people become leaders: (i) some personality traits may lead people naturally into leadership roles; (ii) a crisis or important event may cause a person to rise to the occasion, which brings out extraordinary leadership qualities in an ordinary person; and (iii) people can choose to become leaders by learning leadership skills. Bass identified three types of leadership:

(a) Laissez-faire leadership. This type of leader avoids making decisions, attempts to relinquish responsibility whenever possible, and does not exercise authority.

(b) Transactional leadership. This style places importance on contingent rewards, rewarding team members for meeting performance targets, and fosters management by exception by acting when tasks are not according to schedule.

(c) Transformational leadership. This style focuses on the attributes of the leader, such as charisma, developing a vision, and rousing self-esteem, respect, and trust. Furthermore, the leader is seen as providing inspiration, motivating subordinates by initiating high expectations and being a role model for proper behaviour. The leader will also be sensitive to the individuals' needs, paying personal attention to the individuals in the group and showing them respect and dignity. Moreover, the leader will provide intellectual stimulus, and provoking group members with fresh ideas and approaches.

In practice, the combination of the latter two leadership types will be suitable in diverse operational conditions. However, transactional leadership assumes that the manager has the authority to reward the team members. This is not always the case, such as in the public sector. In this situation transformational leadership becomes more important. A further development was the emotional intelligence school that emerged in the late 1990s and is based on the premise that emotional intelligence will have a greater impact on being a successful leader in terms of achieving higher team performance than intellectual ability (Goleman et al., 2002).

Turner and Müller (2005) argue that the current trend is the competence school of leadership. The competence school of leadership embraces all the earlier leadership theories by giving the term competence a wide meaning. Crawford (2003) defines competence as knowledge, skills, and personal characteristics that deliver superior results. The fact that this theory promotes the concept that different competence profiles are suitable under diverse conditions aligns it to the contingency leadership school, whilst the elements that make up the attributes of knowledge, skills, and personal characteristics embrace all the other various leadership schools.

The above leadership concepts have evolved over time, with the general conclusion that what constitutes an effective leader will depend on the circumstances. The major turning point in the leadership theories without doubt is the contingency school of leadership. The leadership theories that have followed have tended to fine tune the contingency leadership school concept. Moreover, it may also be concluded that leadership can be learnt, although some are more predisposed to leadership roles than others.

Hence, personal characteristics appear to be important, but their level of importance varies according to the circumstances. The analysis of the various leadership theories and research findings suggest the following major leadership attributes:

- Be friendly and sociable;
- Have a vision that stimulates employees;
- Have energy, aspiration, and an optimistic outlook;
- Be honest, reliable, and trustworthy;
- Have communications skills and negotiating ability;
- Be sensitive to the needs of employees;
- Foster teamwork and collaboration;
- Be flexible in the application of rules and regulations;
- Allow employee participation in formulating decisions and in decision-taking;
- Inform subordinates what is expected of them, explaining their role in the process;
- Be concerned for productivity by upholding a specific standard of performance;
- Provide support as to what and how tasks are to be conducted.

In general, the leadership style, apart from reflecting the physical and technical nature of the task itself, must give great importance to the different needs and concerns of the individuals that make up the team. Hence, managers need to adopt their leadership behaviour to match different individuals' needs and circumstances. Managers must know and understand the people that they are leading. The previous sections have mainly focused on leadership styles. However, organisational leaders need to focus on several aspects to ensure that they contribute to building a high performing and competitive organisation:

(a) *Organisational Business Strategy.* It is important that management define the strategic direction of the organisation and ensure that all employees comprehend the strategic goals. Everyone needs to be knowledgeable about the outputs of the organisation in terms of the services and products that are being offered now and in the future. From this knowledge, these leaders must be able to know what core competencies are required to attain client orders; what existing capabilities must be enhanced; what competencies should be developed to satisfy future outputs; how priorities in terms of utilising resources are to be decided; and what key performance indicators are to be adopted to measure success in attaining objectives.

(b) *Resource Optimisation.* Management must allocate resources in a way that maximises the organisation's performance outcome. This is never an easy task and typically is a source of conflict. Management is to have a system in place that informs them of the resource availability at any one time, in terms of human resource skills, equipment, and finance. It is important that any undertaking is supported by the appropriate resources and that disputes between teams vying for resources are avoided.

(c) *Outcome Quality.* It is critical for activities to be closely monitored for quality. Too often managers tend to focus on time and cost with not enough attention being devoted to quality. Managers must define suitable quality indicators and monitor them at frequent intervals.

(d) *Conflict Resolution.* Conflict will always arise. However, it is vital that conflicts are not allowed to linger on. Conflicts must be resolved absolutely and quickly. Management must establish procedures for escalating any issue so that it is resolved in a timely fashion.

(e) *Leadership Style.* Managers must be aware of the prevailing circumstances and be able to read the signs, switching styles as necessary. Managers must keep their ears to the ground and have sufficient knowledge of the individual team members and address their individual concerns when necessary.

(f) *Communication Strategy.* Managers must ensure that channels of communication (and authority) are explicitly defined to create clear communication that works without causing confusion.

(g) *Performance Appraisal.* It is essential that key performance indicators are defined. These help to create a performance environment to reward team members for their effort, not only in financial terms but also in terms of satisfaction, personal development, and advancement. Therefore, it is imperative that the performance environment establishes clear responsibilities and objectives; allocates adequate resources with the appropriate skills to achieve specific functions; provides sufficient support; and imparts ample feedback in relation to their performance and management expectations.

The above provide a general description of certain areas that management leaders should generally focus upon in running their organisation.

## Developing the Right Type of Organisational Commitment

Reichheld (1996) stated: '*Loyalty is by no means dead. It remains one of the great engines of business success.*' A committed employee is an individual who supports the organisation through good and bad times; attends work on a regular basis; defends the organisation; contributes a full day's effort and more; and is supportive of the organisations' goals and objectives. In other words, committed employees are loyal and devoted to the organisation they are working for. Commitment is generally viewed as the employees' emotional attachment and identification with the organisation, and their strong desire to maintain membership with the organisation. Research suggests that employee commitment has a favourable impact on job performance by lowering absenteeism, lateness, and turnover. Hence, having committed employees has positive outcomes for organisational performance.

However, there may be a negative aspect to commitment as well. For example, having employees committed to the organisation solely due to financial reasons. Such commitment normally grows fainter and diminishes completely during adverse or declining economic conditions. Equally risky is to have passive or blind commitment, where employees remain silent and do not provide their feedback. In other words, their level of participation is low or non-existent. Such an environment could stifle creativity and result in an organisation lagging in the innovative process. It is therefore essential for management to identify and develop the proper type of employee commitment. Furthermore, employees must be encouraged to participate in the formulation of decisions and in decision-taking. An appropriate level of employee participation fosters their understanding of the activities being undertaken and will influence them to increase their commitment to the organisation in general.

Commitment is viewed as an attitude towards the organisation that links the identity of the individual to the entity. According to Meyer and Allen (1991), commitment is a psychological state that characterises the employee's relationship with the organisation and has implications for the decision to continue membership of the organisation. Meyer and Allen (1997) extended the meaning of commitment as referring to the employee's emotional attachment to, identification with, and involvement in the organisation, and the employee's feeling of obligation to remain with the organisation taking into consideration the costs that the employee associates with leaving the organisation. Although there may be differences amongst researchers as to the precise meaning of commitment, Meyer and Allen (1997) argue that the various definitions suggest three broad propositions, namely that commitment may be viewed as indicating an affective orientation towards the organisation; recognition of the costs associated with leaving the organisation; and exhibiting a moral obligation to remain with the organisation.

The various definitions of commitment share a common proposition, in that commitment is a bond or linking of the individual to the organisation. The definitions differ in terms of how this bond is considered to have developed. For example, some researchers refer to attitudinal commitment. This is defined as the relative strength of a person's identification with and involvement in a particular organisation. Conceptually, these researchers characterised commitment by at least three factors: (i) strong belief in and acceptance of the organisation's goals and values; (ii) willingness to exert considerable effort on behalf of the organisation; and (iii) strong desire to maintain membership of the organisation.

A second form of commitment is referred to as calculative commitment, which is defined as a structural event that occurs because of individual-organisational transactions and alternatives in side-bets over time. Through calculative commitment, individuals become bound to an organisation because they have invested in the organisation (e.g., a pension plan) and cannot afford to separate themselves from it. Other types of commitment have emerged, including normative commitment that describes a process whereby organisational actions, such as selection, socialisation, and procedures, as well as individual pre-dispositions, such as loyalty attitudes, lead to the development of commitment. Meyer and Allen (1991) developed an integrated approach, utilising the concepts put forward by various researchers, and have defined commitment as consisting of three components:

(a) *An affective component.* This refers to the employee's emotional attachment to, identification with, and involvement in the organisation. Those with strong affective commitment continue employment with the organisation because they genuinely want to do so. They see the organisation or project team as being part of themselves.

(b) *A continuance component.* This refers to commitment based on the costs that the employee associates with leaving the organisation. Employees whose primary link to the entity is based on continuance commitment remain with an organisation because they need to do so and have no other viable alternative.
(c) *A normative component.* This refers to the employee's feeling of obligation to remain with the organisation. Employees with a high level of normative commitment feel that they ought to remain with the organisation because they are grateful to it.

Management behaviour can influence an employee's commitment type, in terms of whether an employee is more affectively committed. Some of the contributing factors that make employee work commitment imperative include: The trend to organisational downsizing; employment mobility; job satisfaction; and the economic environment. Even though organisations are becoming leaner, they must maintain a core of committed individuals who are the source of organisational activity. Those who remain represent the 'heart, brain, and muscle' of the organisation (Meyer and Allen, 1997). It is therefore important to retain employees who will provide the greatest benefit to the organisation in general.

Workers who become less committed to an organisation will route their commitment in other directions (Ibid.). These employees may start to evaluate their skills and experience in terms of their marketability outside the organisation, rather than by their implications for their current or future jobs in the organisation. Management must invest in employees that want to remain members of the organisation.

Research suggests that employees who develop a high level of work commitment are more inclined to be highly satisfied and fulfilled by their jobs. Therefore, employee work commitment is essential in the development of proactive and innovative organisations. In the current turbulent global economic scenario, organisational change is a continuous process that requires support of all employees in the hierarchical structure. Having employees with the appropriate levels of commitment facilitates the change management process and ensures its successful implementation. Furthermore, human resources strategies related to employee recruitment, retention, and reward and incentive policies need to be defined in a holistic manner with the primary aim of encouraging employees to possess the appropriate type and level of commitment. It is therefore essential for management to comprehend the dynamics that influence the development of commitment and take proactive initiatives to ensure that employees want to remain members of the organisation not because they have no other alternative, but because they genuinely want to be part of the organisation.

Research illustrates that affective, continuance, and normative commitment are all related to employee retention, but in different ways. Given that an employee with strong affective and normative commitment feels an emotional attachment to, identification with, and involvement in the organisation, and has a feeling of obligation to remain with the organisation, then this individual is likely to have a higher motivation level to contribute meaningfully to the organisation than would an employee with weak affective and normative commitment. Therefore, it is reasonable to suggest that those employees with strong affective and normative commitment are more likely to be absent less often and motivated to give a higher performance.

This contrasts with individuals who have strong continuance commitment. These individuals appear to become bound to an organisation because they have invested in the organisation and cannot afford to separate themselves from it. Thus, employees with strong continuance commitment are likely to decide to remain with the organisation based on the costs that they associate with leaving the organisation. Hence, these individuals are likely to abandon the organisation if they find an opportunity elsewhere that pays them more.

In practice, management wants more from committed employees than simply membership of the organisation. Various research findings suggest that employees with strong affective and normative commitment are more valuable. When commitment reflects an emotional link, the organisation may benefit through reduced turnover, increased productivity, and higher job satisfaction among employees. However, when the commitment by the employee is based primarily upon financial aspects (costs associated with leaving) then the organisation may experience higher employee retention at the expense of reduced job satisfaction and self-esteem and higher employee stress. It is therefore suggested that organisations should implement HR policies to develop the right type of commitment. For example, strategies such as rapid promotions and the development of departmental specific skills all tend to increase continuance commitment that may eventually work against the organisation.

Although continuance commitment measures may contribute to assure that an employee stays with the organisation, they may not encourage them to contribute to the organisation's benefit. Instead, some employees may want to quit, but may not be able to afford to do so. Some employees may be motivated to do just enough to maintain their jobs. On the other hand, affective commitment is harder to achieve. However, research has shown that it is strongly related to the results that organisations value, such as high job satisfaction and a strong motive to contribute to the organisation's effectiveness.

It is therefore important that organisations develop the right type of organisational commitment. The literature indicates that employees who perceive their organisations as being supportive tend to become affectively committed. Those who perceive that they have made a substantial investment, which would be lost if they left, develop continuance commitment. Those employees who think that loyalty is expected of them become normatively committed. It is therefore essential for management to influence the employees' perceptions so that the right type and level of commitment is developed. Meyer and Allen (1997) and others contend that management must aim to directly develop affective commitment; develop human resources management policies that encourage affective commitment; and manage the change management process. According to Meyer and Allen, affective commitment develops in the following settings:

- Making every effort to treat employees with respect and consideration. Employees must feel that they are valued and appreciated by their supervisors and the division that employs them.
- Managers should provide a clear signal to all employees that the organisation is highly concerned with quality and customer service.
- Managers should clearly define the employees' job and responsibilities. Job clarity refers to how precisely supervisors communicate to their employees, what must be done, and what their expectations are, rather than a detailed job description.
- Managers should design and assign tasks that allow the employees to use their aptitudes, professional knowledge, and judgement, offering them job enrichment.

- Managers should communicate quality information on divisional plans and activities to employees. This is particularly vital during periods of extreme organisational change, when employees feel insecure and uncertain about their future.
- Empirical research suggests an organisation that is concerned about controlling its costs and increasing productivity is more likely to have employees who identify with it than organisations that are loosely managed.

Human resource management policies may greatly influence employee work commitment. Therefore, suitable practices are needed for the following:

- *Recruitment and selection.* When recruiting, management should avoid using the conventional approach, but provide practical job previews that describe both the positive and negative aspects of the job. This allows applicants to determine whether the tasks will meet their specific needs; therefore if successful, they are likely to find these tasks satisfying. Being fully informed about the job allows applicants to become fully aware of the choice they must make and are likely to be more committed once the choice is made.
- *Socialization and training.* Reinforcing the employees' sense of self-worth and providing a supportive environment appears to entrench a strong sense of employee work commitment. Training can lead to different forms of commitment. Employees who receive training, particularly training intended to provide them with the opportunity for advancement, might perceive that the organisation values them as individuals and therefore they tend to develop stronger affective commitment. However, the same training could lead to the development of continuance commitment if it is perceived as providing organisational specific skills that contribute to status or economic advantage within the project or division that will not transfer to jobs outside the organisation.
- *Promotion.* A policy of promoting from within may be perceived by employees as an indication that the organisation is committed to them. This may lead the employees to reciprocate. A policy of promoting from within conveys the message that the organisation is committed to the development of the employees' careers.
- *Assessment.* The perception of fairness in the evaluation and promotion process is very important. Affective commitment is likely to decrease

when an employee fails to be promoted. If the decline in affective commitment is accompanied by an increase in continuance commitment, the organisation might find that it is retaining employees who are not highly motivated to do more than what is required in order to keep their jobs. Therefore, it is important to ensure that affective commitment is maintained by providing these employees with assistance in gaining opportunities elsewhere within the organisation.

- *Compensation and benefits.* If an employee views a compensation and benefit contract from a purely financial angle, then continuance commitment is likely to increase. However, if the employee perceives the organisation as one that is concerned and as being fair in its dealings with employees, then affective commitment is likely to develop. Therefore, management must ensure that compensation and benefits packages place emphasis on the nonfinancial features, even though the result may be an increase in the employees' financial position.

Many organisations undergoing extensive change end up undertaking organisational downsizing. An outcome of downsizing is uncertainty and the potential for increasing responsibility among the non-managerial grades due to the cutback of management layers. Research indicates that employee turnover is a concern following layoffs and that often, the increasing turnover is among the organisation's most valued employees. Researchers also suggests that those who are most confident in their abilities are most likely to consider leaving the organisation at these times. Hence, it is essential to find ways of maintaining the commitment of employees when important organisational change is taking place. The following are suggested:

- Redundant employees are to be given adequate compensation and support. This may involve generous termination pay or aiding them with relocating inside or outside the organisation. It is essential that the redundancy policy is communicated to employees.
- The selection of those employees to be made redundant or relocated must be perceived by all the employees to be fair, and the action taken must be seen as a measure to increase the job security of those remaining.
- Management must convince the employees that the implemented changes will lead to job enrichment and greater job satisfaction.

- Management must put in place a comprehensive communication strategy prior, during, and after the changes are to take place to mitigate uncertainty among the employees.

All the above measures are intended to increase the level of affective commitment of employees. Finally, it should be emphasised that having a committed workforce will result in operational effectiveness and will facilitate high levels of cooperation during difficult times when that extra effort is required to tilt the balance towards having a successful organisation through the attainment of higher performance levels.

### Enhancing Employee Participation

Employee participation reflects a participative style of leadership and encompasses a wide variety of activities that are aimed at increasing the employees' understanding of the organisation's strategic objectives; using the employees' abilities and talents; giving employees the opportunity to influence decisions; and nurturing the employees' commitment to the established organisational goals. Employee participation is closely linked to the organisation's communication process. It is important to recognise that communication is a two-way process.

Employees want guiding principles from their manager and management desire feedback from the team members. This two-way interactive process is likely to encourage employee participation. Most organisations have little difficulty passing information downward. However, their difficulty stems from obtaining an upward information flow since it is viewed as being more demanding. A lack of employee participation (input) may lead to negative outcomes for the organisation, such as missed opportunities, failed initiatives, neglected performance improvement and project delays. Research suggests that benefits generated by employee participation include improved efficiency; enhanced quality and competitiveness; increased job satisfaction and work motivation; closer collaboration; and better employee-leadership relationship.

Management must strive to develop a quality interactive process between the management team and employees through employee participation. There are basically two major methods of encouraging employee participation: (i) Indirect involvement, where employees are represented by a delegate or an association, as in collective bargaining or joint consultation; and (ii) Direct involvement, where employees actively participate in making decisions about work practices. The focus of this section is related to direct employee involvement. There are four basic elements that promote direct employee involvement, namely communicating the needs; skill and knowledge sharing; creating a communication culture; and creating an empowering environment.

Employees must be told that communication is a two-way process and therefore they have a responsibility to provide their input. Employees should be encouraged to inform management of their concerns and how these concerns may, in their view, be mitigated by management. Management, on the other hand, must repeatedly reinforce the organisational vision and show how the current objectives contribute to this vision. Furthermore, management must explain the necessity for the employees' participation by providing input towards achieving the defined vision.

When employees impart their advice regarding a specific situation, these employees are utilising their experience to reach a particular conclusion. This is what employee participation is all about. However, some employees may need to be prompted to provide their input. Hence, having a dialogue session with employees regarding their task process and concerns, reviewing factual data, or discussing a client's survey results can stimulate and encourage employees to offer their suggestions. Discussing 'what if' situations based on proposals made by employees may enable employees to comprehend their role on the organisational outcomes and will prompt the employees to contribute to the process.

The extent of management input in keeping employees informed is a major contributing factor in motivating employees to provide feedback and making suggestions for improvements. This process achieves an appropriate level of employee participation. However, appropriate techniques must be utilised to make the communication process easier and more effective, such as organising team meetings specifically designed to allow employees to share their ideas; setting aside a half-day session to conduct open discussions that specifically address their concerns; and providing short one-to-one sessions between managers and employees to discuss employee issues.

To attain employee participation through empowerment, employee input needs to be documented and acted upon once agreement has been reached. Before assigning tasks, managers are required to discuss specific goals and parameters with the team, so that the team members accept their responsibilities and make any necessary adjustments to ensure success. Effective employee participation leads to feelings of empowerment for employees. This helps to reduce their feelings of anxiety and uncertainty during periods of organisational change or when an organisation is encountering difficulties. However, employee empowerment does not occur automatically. Empowerment results when management consciously and actively provides its employees with the knowledge, skills, information, and resources, together with the authority to use these elements without always having to seek approval.

These work practices can generate the type of discretionary behaviours that lead to enhanced performance in a wide range of aspects, including increased client satisfaction, profitability and productivity, and reduced employee turnover. One should note that a high employee turnover rate is a frequent factor that contributes to delaying projects. Employee participation motivates employees to identify themselves with the organisation and seek to remain members of that organisation. In other words, employee participation helps to motivate employees to directly contribute to the success of the organisation's performance.

### *Developing and Sustaining Employee Engagement*

Employee engagement is all about creating the right conditions for employees in the workplace so that they give their best effort each day, are committed to the organisation's goals and values, are motivated to contribute to the success of their organisation and have an enhanced sense of their own well-being. The underlying foundation for employee engagement is two-way commitment and communication between the organisation and its employees, leading to a higher level of trust and integrity. Employee engagement positively impacts both organisational and individual performance, thus it is likely to increase the probability of business success.

When employees engage with the organisation, they fully understand their individual role in the organisation and have a clear insight of where they fit in with achieving the organisation's purpose and objectives. An important outcome of employee engagement is a heightened sense of inclusion of employees as members of the organisation, who are fully focused on clear goals, are trusted, and empowered. Moreover, these employees receive frequent and constructive feedback in recognition for their work and are supported in developing new skills. In other words, employee engagement is based on robust and authentic organisational values, with clear indication of trust and fairness based on mutual respect, where two-way assurances and commitments between employers and employees are understood and fulfilled. Employee engagement generates positive attitudes and behaviours from employees that result in enhanced business outcomes, which cause and strengthen one another. Employee engagement means that employees work harder, stay longer with the organisation, and motivate other employees to do the same.

There is some consensus regarding the definition of employee engagement, with many definitions emphasising some aspect of an employee's commitment to the organisation or the positive behaviours an engaged employee may exhibit. For example, Quantum Workplace (2021) views employee engagement as the strength of the mental and emotional connection employees feel towards their places of work, while Gallup (2017) describes engaged employees as employees who are involved in, enthusiastic about, and committed to their work and workplace. Additionally, Willis Towers Watson (2021) considers employee engagement as the willingness and ability of employees to contribute to company success. Whilst the precise definition of employee engagement is still fluid, there is agreement between researchers that disengaged workers feel no real connection with the roles they perform and tend to perform at the bare minimum.

Disengagement may be revealed in worker behaviour, such as a 9-to-5-time clock mentality, a reluctance to take part in social events, or an inclination to isolate oneself from peers. Disengaged employees may show antipathy towards their jobs, with constant griping to colleagues that tends to promote low morale at the workplace. SHIRM (2021) defines the difference between engaged and disengaged employees in terms of several characteristics. They view engaged employees as being optimistic, team-oriented, going above and beyond what is expected of them, solution-oriented, selfless, passionate about learning, and content to pass along credit where it is due and accept blame. However, they see disengaged employees as being pessimistic, self-centred, high in absenteeism, negative in attitude, egocentric, focused on monetary aspects, and having a tendency to accept credit but pass along blame. Quantum Workplace (2021) generally views employee engagement as measuring how employees feel about their organisation, arguing that based on the perceptions of their workplace, employees are classified into four main groups, namely:

- Highly engaged employees. These employees feel connected to their teams, love their jobs, and have positive feelings about their organisation. These employees are likely to want to stay with the organisation and make an extra effort to make sure that the organisation succeeds; they promote their organisation to family and friends and encourage other employees to do their best.
- Moderately engaged employees. These employees like their organisation but see opportunities for improvement. Hence, these employees are less likely to request more responsibilities and may underperform; thus there is something that holds them back from full engagement.
- Barely engaged employees. These employees are unresponsive about their workplace and usually lack motivation, doing only as much as they can to get by and sometimes even less. These employees are likely to be searching for other jobs and are a high turnover risk.
- Disengaged employees. These employees are completely disconnected from the mission, goals, and future of the organisation. They lack commitment and unless handled correctly, they may even have a negative impact on the performance of the employees around them.

There appears to be some convergence between employee engagement and organisational commitment. However, there is a difference between these two concepts. Employee commitment tends to refer to the level of employee dedication towards completing a particular task or activity, whereas employee engagement involves the employees' contribution towards the attainment of organisational goals. Furthermore, employee commitment is built with the satisfaction level of the employees to work in the organisation, whereas engaged employees are those who are emotionally attached to the organisation and are always trying to give their maximum contribution towards its betterment.

Unfortunately, it is doubtful whether Meyer and Allen (1997) would agree with these differences, since they view organisational commitment as also being an emotional attachment to the organisation. It is appropriate to state that engagement tends to refer to how happy an employee is in their job, while commitment refers to how much effort an employee puts into their job. Hence, an engaged employee will not automatically be a committed employee and vice-versa. There is no doubt that the type of organisational commitment and level of employee engagement are influenced by the organisational culture that the employees work for. There is also considerable disagreement about the differences between employee engagement and job satisfaction. These terms at times are used synonymously. Like organisational commitment, there is some overlap between employee engagement and job satisfaction, but there are also some differences.

Employee engagement tends to describe the employees' frame of mind (like organisational commitment) in terms of how they feel focused, enthusiastic with a sense of urgency, and intensely involved in the work they do. Employee engagement views employees as being determined, proactive and going beyond their formal job descriptions by being adaptive in ways that expand the job roles as necessary. Satisfied employees feel pleasant, content, and gratified about the work they perform and often associate with aspects over which the organisation has control, such as pay, benefits, and job security, whereas engagement levels are impacted by the employees' supervisor through the assigned tasks, personal trust and recognition, and day-to-day communications, amongst others.

Quantum Workplace (2021) has found that employee engagement has several key benefits, such as increased employee productivity, where research suggests that engaged employees are 17% more productive. Furthermore, employee engagement results in higher employee retention because employees feel recognised for their contributions; see opportunities for professional growth and career development; and better understand why and when organisational change occurs. Quantum Workplace contends that employee engagement increases customer satisfaction because these employees intensely care about their jobs, and hence their customers. It also found that engaged employees have lower absenteeism and record lower workplace injury, since they are more aware of their environments and can focus on the task at hand.

According to SHIRM (2021), research suggests that there are both organisational and managerial drivers that influence employee engagement levels. They cite several employee engagement drivers at an organisational level that have the greatest impact; namely having leaders that are committed to making the organisation a great place to work in; trusting the leaders of an organisation to define the correct road map for organisational growth;

having faith that the organisation will be successful in the future; having employees that understand how they fit into the organisation's future plans; having organisational leaders that value employees as their most valuable asset; and having an organisation that invests in making its employees more successful.

From a managerial perspective they cite the following key drivers, namely, employees experiencing a good relationship with their supervisor; employees having the essential tools and authority to perform their job well; and employees having the freedom to make work decisions. Quantum Workplace argues that the prerequisites for employee engagement include having: (a) motivating work, since employees desire challenging jobs; (b) inspiring teams and leaders, since employees would like to work in environments that put people first, value employee contributions, and show integrity; and (c) organisational commitment because employees would like to work for organisations that have a strategy built for success where they can contribute to that success. Moreover, employee engagement may be improved by several methods, which include:

- Giving precedence to organisational culture
- Motivating employees through the organisation's mission, vision, and values
- Upgrading and preparing managers as coaches
- Creating excellent communication practices
- Generating a forceful feedback ethos
- Communicating employee feedback and exploit this feedback where possible
- Depicting a well-defined image of success at every hierarchical level
- Acknowledging employees' contributions
- Ensuring that employees have access to development opportunities
- Focusing on employee welfare and being flexible in the application of rules
- Leveraging technology to apply the above methods.

The above has provided the basic principles regarding the importance of employee engagement in an organisation and how it may be developed. The concept of employee engagement overlaps with other important practices, such as leadership and organisational commitment, which have been described in previous sections. Additionally, it also overlaps with communications and employee development, which will be discussed in the next sections.

### Enhancing Communication within the Organisation

Effective communication and employee involvement were key factors identified as contributing to high performance teams. However, research suggests that in many organisations both employees and their managers are not satisfied with these key aspects. The employees were often confused by conflicting messages; were overloaded with information; had difficulty prioritising their activities; and felt there was insufficient leadership. On the other hand, managers have had to contend with rapid changing business conditions that result in a radical change to their business strategy.

This scenario suggests that there is a need for management to introduce a communication configuration that enables the management team to formulate and impart clear and consistent messages to all the employees. Furthermore, there is a need for management to display leadership by having face-to-face meetings with employees and holding regular briefing sessions. Moreover, a communication strategy becomes effective when it is a meaningful two-way process. Employees, either as individuals or as a team, must be given the opportunity to provide their feedback. However, the provided feedback must be perceived as being seriously taken into consideration by management and be visibly seen to be applied in the organisation's decision-making process.

Effective communication facilitates and enhances organisational performance. But for this to happen, management must treat its employees as if they were part owners of the organisation. Thus, as perceived shareholders, employees through employee-management meetings will be informed about the organisation's corporate and functional strategies, and about the organisation's results. With suitable impetus, the communications process can develop into a programme for different types of organisational improvements, particularly if the process is linked to the organisation's incentive scheme. Employee-management meetings should be characterised by a non-threatening environment, complete openness, and honest spontaneous responses to all types of questions, acceptance of constructive criticism, and a request for feedback.

The setting for these meetings must be based on mutual trust where all cards are placed on the table. It is through such a process that everyone in the organisation is focused on the vision, mission, strategies, and objectives of the organisation. Thus, the communication process provides direction in terms of where the organisation is heading, defines clear objectives in terms of expected productivity and quality levels, provides momentum by focusing everyone on a common goal, and offers an opportunity to senior management to demonstrate leadership qualities and develop further their leadership competencies.

A study of UK organisations (Blue Rubicon and Henley Management College, 2002) shows that the methods business leaders use to communicate with their employees considerably influences their profitability. Furthermore, the authors of this study argue that a performance culture stresses goal attainment and the value of effort and quality, while a people culture emphasises employee involvement, trust, and commitment. Both cultures are important and largely stem from the top management layers. However, the study results show that a staggering 93% of managers think that the purpose of employee communications is to keep staff well informed, with only 57% thinking that the purpose is to give staff the opportunity to provide input into company strategy.

These results suggest that organisations lack sincerity to the principle of employee communication and are not utilising it as a means of advancing their business. In a similar study, regarding human capital and financial management related to US and Canadian employers, Marshall and Heffes (2006) found that companies with the most effective communication programs returned 57% more to their shareholders; achieved a 91% total return to shareholders; are associated with a nearly 20% increase in market value; and were 20% more likely to report lower turnover rates. An effective communication strategy provides the common relationship between the different groups to promote within the organisation a universal set of attitudes, beliefs, values, and a common appreciation of the organisation's objectives. An effective communication strategy promotes the formulation and implementation of a shared organisational vision that is supported by the defined corporate strategy. The literature suggests that an effective communication strategy will help to:

- Motivate the organisation's entire workforce;
- Acquire acceptance of the organisation's corporate and functional strategies;

- Encourage employees to put more effort into the tasks that are assigned to them;
- Clarify policies and how these are linked to the overall organisational vision;
- Ensure employees understand their individual roles and expectations;
- Monitor and evaluate performance through employee input;
- Demonstrate in real terms management commitment;
- Identify potential organisational areas for improvement.

Although the benefits of effective communication are well known, there may be barriers to proper communication. For example, an organisation culture where management talks down to employees allows only one-way communication. An effective communication process allows two-way communication to take place. This communication process is built on a partnership between management and employees working together for the mutual good of the organisation and ultimately for their own individual mutual benefit. The most difficult barrier in the communication process is deciding how much to say, when, and to whom. On the other hand, in a proper communication environment, openness, honesty, sincerity, and trust are essential. If the employees perceive that the purpose of the communication strategy is to manipulate them, then only failure will result, with very serious negative performance consequences.

Blue Rubicon and Henley Management College (2002) found that the most effective channels of two-way communications were appraisals; regular team meetings with quality and assurance sessions; talk back sessions with senior management; feedback forums; one to one staff dialogue; interactive conferencing; and intranet site with bulletin board. This study suggests that face-to-face meetings are seen as being much more effective than e-communication methods. For instance, less than 3% of respondents considered interactive conferencing to be effective.

Research is consistently indicating that an organisation's communication strategy coupled with employee involvement has an important influence on organisational effectiveness by supporting business and individual results and performance, building corporate culture and values, and developing individuals. Furthermore, a communication strategy should not be viewed as being a purely HR function, to be defined and managed by the HR Department. A communication strategy is a collective effort, embracing all different types of employees to perform a variety of job functions and occupy diverse hierarchical levels within the organisation.

Employee involvement reflects a participative style of leadership and encompasses a wide variety of activities that are aimed at: increasing the employees' understanding of the organisation; using the employees' abilities; giving employees the opportunity to influence decisions; and nurturing the employees' commitment to the established project and organisational goals. Employee communication is a two-way process. Employees want guiding principles from their manager, and management desire feedback from the team members. Most organisations have little difficulty communicating downward, however obtaining an upward information flow is more demanding. A lack of employee input may lead to negative outcomes, such as missed opportunities, failed initiatives, neglected performance improvement, and project delays. Research suggests that benefits generated by employee involvement include improved efficiency; enhanced quality and competitiveness; increased job satisfaction and work motivation; closer collaboration; and better employee-leadership relationship.

Management must strive to develop a quality interactive process between the management team and employees through employee involvement. There are basically two major methods of encouraging employee involvement: (a) indirect involvement where employees are represented by a delegate or an association, as in collective bargaining or joint consultation; and (b) direct involvement where employees participate actively in making decisions about work practices. There are four basic elements that promote direct employee involvement:

(a) **Communicating the needs**. Employees must be told that communication is a two-way process and therefore they have a responsibility to provide their input. Management, on the other hand, must repeatedly reinforce the organisational vision and show how the current objectives contribute to this vision.
(b) **Skill and knowledge sharing**. Employees may need to be prompted to provide their input. Hence, having a dialogue session with employees regarding their task process and concerns, reviewing factual data, or discussing a client's survey result can stimulate and encourage employees to offer their suggestions.

(c) **Creating a communication culture**. The extent of management input in keeping employees informed is a major contributing factor in motivating employees to provide feedback and making suggestions for improvements.

(d) **Create an empowering environment**. Employee input needs to be documented and acted upon once agreement has been reached. Managers, before assigning tasks, are required to discuss specific goals and parameters with the project team, so that the team members accept their responsibilities and make any necessary adjustments to ensure success.

Effective employee involvement leads to feelings of empowerment for employees that help to reduce their feelings of anxiety and uncertainty during periods of organisational change or when the organisation is encountering difficulties. However, employee empowerment does not occur automatically. Empowerment results when management consciously and actively provides employees with the knowledge, skills, information, and resources, together with the authority to use these elements without always having to seek approval. These work practices can generate the type of discretionary behaviours that lead to enhanced performance in a wide range of aspects, including increased client satisfaction, profitability and productivity, and reduced employee turnover. Employee involvement motivates employees to identify themselves with the organisation and seek to remain members of that organisation. In other words, employee involvement helps to motivate employees to directly contribute to the project's success.

Often transforming an organisation's vision to reality requires a total change in the established attitudes and culture within an organisation. Unfortunately, the bias towards the continuation of past modes of behaviour is powerful in many organisations. Furthermore, employee communication is generally acknowledged as the key to effective management; however it must be enduring, coherent, and discernible. Establishing a shared vision requires a well-defined employee communication strategy that disseminates high quality information horizontally and vertically throughout the organisation, with the capability of being receptive to the views of the recipients. Establishing a shared vision is an iterative process commencing with top management; is disseminated to all the organisational levels; provides a mechanism for employee feedback; allows for vision fine tuning; and is effectively communicated to all the organisational levels as the final vision. Some key principals to keep in mind to meet the communication challenge include:

- Communication takes effort. Devote adequate time to it.
- Communication is not habitual; it must be planned and scheduled.
- Communication requires honesty.
- Consider various communication approaches.
- Link the communication strategy to business goals and management concerns.
- Communicate the future not the past.
- Ensure the communication strategy is economically feasible.
- Develop a regular communication program for a specific period.
- Communication strategy requires perseverance and commitment.
- Communication strategy is to convey a consistent message.
- Develop communication skill competencies.
- Monitor the communication strategy.

It is important for management to monitor the communication strategy and be particularly aware of any employee grievances about communication. Grievances about communication may suggest a concern that needs to be addressed. The above principles will help managers to send sufficient and unambiguous information to their employees and provide them with an opportunity to give their views, hence achieving two-way communication. It is important that the provided feedback is visibly seen to be applied in the organisation's decision-making process. Such a process will build the required leadership-employee trust for implementing a thriving communication strategy.

### *Employee Development and Training*

Training helps employees to become more efficient and flexible in carrying out their functions. In the context of performance management, organisations must develop creative ways to help employees make the most of their training by focusing on the performance management process and the competencies required to effectively execute this process. An important objective of training is to help employees develop their potential fully in their chosen profession. However, one should note that this objective is not something that can be achieved completely because the development of employees is a continuous process and the competencies required by an organisation are also in an ever-changing mode. Therefore, both employees and organisations are confronted with a situation where the organisational needs and the employee development goalposts are always in motion. Organisations must recognise this condition and continually seek feasible opportunities to be effective and efficient in the training activities undertaken.

All too often training programmes in organisations fail to achieve their objectives. It is not uncommon for many to proclaim that training does not work, and to some extent this may be true. If training is seen to be disjointed because it does not form part of an overall strategy, then it will not provide the optimum return and at times may turn out to be a waste of effort. From an organisational perspective a training programme must support the organisation's strategic direction and address the following questions: What competencies does the organisation currently possess? What competencies does the organisation need now and, in the future, to sustain and enhance its competitive position? How can the organisation develop the full potential of its employees to motivate and attain their commitment and trust? From the employees' perspective a training programme must cater for the individuals' development needs. To define these training requirements, management needs to answer the following: What are the current competences of the employees? What competencies need to be strengthened and developed? What is the mismatch between the current employee and organisational competencies requirements? What is the best way for an organisation and its employees to bridge the competency gap?

To establish a successful training program, an organisation must focus on creating the proper environment by developing a sense of commitment, motivation, and trust in the workplace. However, this is only achieved by having strong leadership. Leaders produce the environment that directly affects the employees' capacity and desires to perform at their highest potential. Research shows that the employees' perception of the organisation in terms of how well the organisation is being managed has a strong association with individual and organisational performance. A major objective of training is to develop employees as being the best in their industry and for the employees to act as being the best. However, for this to happen employees need to be in no doubt that the organisation knows where it is headed. It is important for the management to define a training model that describes the process for defining the training requirements of an organisation. Such a model is likely to be based on five major activities: (a) defining the competencies that are required by the organisation to carry out its strategy; (b) identifying the competencies that the organisation already has; (c) assessing the organisational competencies gap; (d) defining a training programme; and (e) implementing the defined training programme.

Competencies are identified behaviours, skills, and knowledge that have a direct and positive influence on the success of employees and the organisation. Furthermore, these competencies must be compatible with and aligned to the organisation's mission and business strategies. Therefore, it is important for an organisation to identify and define its business product and service lines by having a comprehensive business strategy. The defined business strategy will outline the current and future direction of the organisation. At this stage an organisation would need to address an essential question: What competencies does the organisation need now and, in the future, to achieve its defined strategy and enhance its competitive position?

Once the competencies required by the organisation have been identified, it is essential to determine the competencies that are currently available to the organisation. Comparing the competencies required with those that are available to the organisation will provide the competency gap that needs to be filled. Details of the existing organisational competencies may be gathered by the Human Resource Department for each employee, or alternatively the information may be extracted from the HR Management system. The comparison and combination of the competencies required by the organisation and those available to the organisation enable management to determine the magnitude of the competency gap within the organisation for each functional area.

The completed training programme will consist of three major elements, namely, the competencies to be developed; the employees who are to be the recipients of the competency development; and the time schedule for the competency development to take place. The training programme is defined by using two inputs:

(a) Organisational competencies gap analysis. This identifies the competencies that the organisation needs, while currently experiencing a shortfall in the number of employees who possess the identified competencies. Hence, it measures the magnitude and identifies the competency gap in terms of number of employees. The organisational competency gap analysis answers the questions: What competencies does the organisation need to develop? How many employees need to be trained for the identified competencies?

(b) Employee competency details. This identifies the competencies possessed by individual employees for their respective role within an organisational functional area. Moreover, by inference, it identifies those employees who do not have competencies and need training in specific sectors. Therefore, the employee competency details answer the question: Who are the employees who are to be trained in the identified organisational competencies gap?

Hence, the training programme provides information about three major elements, namely, the competencies to be developed; the participants that will take part in the training; and the training schedule when the competency development will take place.

## Performance Measurement Framework: Is There a Difference between Public Sector (and Non-Profit Entities) and Private Sector?

The implementation of different performance measurement systems (PMS) in public and non-profit sectors over the last three decades has generated a lot of interest. According to De Waele and Polzer (2021), performance measurement is viewed as a sub-process of performance management that generally deals with identifying, monitoring, and communicating performance targets, throughputs, and results using indicators. However, there is no doubt that the distinguishing factor between Public (and non-profit) organisations and private sector organisations is the focus on profit maximisation. Hence, private Sector organisations tend to focus on the bottom line against which performance can eventually be measured.

According to Boland and Fowler (2000), most public and non-profit sector organisations depend on the State for their revenue generation and are accountable to several stakeholders. However, Pollitt and Bouckaert (2017) recognised that the boundaries of administrative models are not always clear-cut, especially with respect to the core ideas conveyed. As an example, the measurement of outcomes related to government action cannot be consigned to a single model, since public management spans across all administrative modules.

De Waele and Polzer argue that over time, there has been a shift towards a multi-dimensional view on organisational performance in the public sector in line with an expansion of the number of 'pillars of administration' (Amirkhanyan et al., 2014). They cite Boyne (2002) and Carter (1989), who both state that performance has been constructed around pillars such as 'efficiency,' 'effectiveness,' and 'economy,' often referred to as the 'three pillars of public administration' or '3E model.' They also cite Fredrickson (1990, 2010), who suggested the inclusion of a fourth pillar, namely '(social) equity,' expanding the '3E' to a '4E model.'

De Waele and Polzer also contend that organisational performance is conditional on factors such as the organisation's purpose. For instance, Behn (2003) found that different managerial objectives require diverse performance measures, such as public services related to social welfare, education, and health care. Harris (1998) argues that motivations for adopting coherent performance models originate from at best four factors: A contemporary view of the state, limited resources, the quest of efficiency, and demands for accountability. Evans and Bellamy (1995) contend that because of severe budget cuts, more government organisations in Australia exploited performance measures as a means of allocating scarce resources. Thus, a drive was initiated to improve performance measures and to identify value added both in dollars and in physical terms.

Additionally, an attempt has been made to adapt private sector performance measurement frameworks and their respective tools for the public and non-profit organisations without considering their distinctiveness. Moreover, although literature exists that addresses specific performance indicators, no integrated framework has been devised that embraces the various organisational features that require evaluation. Van Peursem et al. (1995) highlight two main weaknesses when using performance indicators in the assessment of management, namely that performance indicators are deceptive because they falsely convey an impression of objective truth and that by making certain aspects of performance visible, they marginalise other management activities. However, one must also make a distinction as to whether the performance management system adopted is measuring management performance or organisational performance. For the two performance measurements aspects to be comparable, the foundation of the performance management framework would need to be based upon the strategic objectives of the organisation, irrespective of whether the organisation is belongs to the private or public sector.

Micheli and Kennerley (2005) argue that despite the appeal for improving government, many state and local governments have not developed performance-measurement systems, and even fewer use these systems to improve decision-making. When examining some of the earlier literature, the discussion of performance tends to focus on two aspects, namely policy adoption and actual implementation. The former relies more on factors from rational and technocratic theory, whereas the latter is influenced by factors addressed by political and cultural considerations (de Lancer Julnes and Holzer, 2001). A difficulty with this view is that there seems to be no reference to the strategic objectives of the organisation. Hence, there appears to be a shift of emphasis from having a performance measurement system that evaluates the achievement of the strategic objectives of the organisation to a system that assesses the readiness of the organisation to develop and implement performance measures; the identification and involvement of the organisation's internal and external interest groups; the involvement of employee unions; awareness and culture that the adoption of performance measures can create; and the existence of a performance measurement culture (Ibid.).

Micheli and Kennerley point out that literature regarding performance management focuses on the lack of capabilities, infrastructures, and flow of information. This view confirms the shift of emphasis from having a performance measurement system that evaluates the achievement of the strategic objectives of the organisation to a system that considers the ability to develop performance goals and measures and to overcome such conceptual barriers as distinguishing outcomes from outputs, and the nature of support, especially from top management, for performance measurement (Berman and Wang, 2000). Once again, this literature appears to ignore the central purpose of a performance measurement system, namely, to measure the achievement of the strategic objectives of the target organisation in objective terms.

A vast majority of the literature of the 1990s and early 2000s appears to focus on the barriers or challenges to defining and implementing performance management systems in the Public Sector. For instance, Halachmi and Bouckaert (1994) highlight the importance of technology and organisational features; and Tourish and Hargie (1998) mention the relevance of internal communication. However, once again, no mention is made regarding the fundamental requirement of the performance management system, namely introducing a system that measures the achievement of the organisation's strategic objectives.

On the other hand, Atkinson and McCrindell (1997) are closer to the focal topic by describing a strategic performance measurement model and the four main implications for governments regarding: Developing and publicly disclosing their objectives and principles; defining in clear terms their objectives and commitments; developing of performance measures relating to objectives and secondary measures that reflect the broad stakeholder principles of the government; and identifying how each of the organisation's responsibility units contribute to its objectives and evaluating each unit's contribution to achieving the organisation's objectives. These principles are very similar to the aims of private sector performance measurement systems.

Other researchers applied private sector principles to the public/non-profit sector of frameworks. For example, Boland and Fowler (2000) recommend the construction of a location/action matrix model and the application of system theory to public sector performance management, while Wilson and Durant (1994) place emphasis on the potential uses of total quality management. Osborne et al. (1995) and others talk about the attributes of a rationalist model of performance assessment by exploring the assessment of performance in complex public environments. These researchers argue that the suggested framework can be adapted to the needs of a wide range of public and voluntary organisations delivering public programmes.

Henry and Dickey (1993) posit that the research and development (R&D) approach, which includes activities that companies undertake to innovate and introduce new products and services, may offer benefits when implementing performance measurement systems both in the private and public sectors. They contend that the R&D approach requires commitment, patience, and openness to ideas and changes, with these attributes requiring significant organisational change and additional resources that are applicable to the public sector.

McLaughlin and Jordan (1999) argue that the logic model, which describes the chain of causes and effects leading to an outcome of interest, may be adopted in the public sector since managers would be able to meet accountability requirements and present a logical argument for their programme; therefore, they are able to measure outcomes and use measurement to stimulate improvement. This approach consists of five key steps to develop performance indicators, namely, collecting the relevant information; clearly defining the problem and its context; identifying the elements of the logic model; showing a diagram of the logic model; and verifying the logic model with interested parties.

Other researchers suggested the modification of existing private sector models to be applied for specific public sector areas. For example, Gooijer (2000) adapted the balanced scorecard (BSC) and the concerns-based-adoption-model (used to understand, lead, and monitor the change process) to develop two methods for evaluating knowledge management in the public sector (specifically the Victoria Department of Infrastructure, Australia). The first method known as the knowledge management performance scorecard maps the objectives for knowledge management across the balanced scorecard's key outcome areas.

The second method, known as the knowledge management behaviour framework, identifies levels of practice demonstrated by individuals and defines seven levels of knowledge management skills for exhibiting collaborative behaviour (i.e., typical behaviours of managers and the roles they would assume in relation to individuals at each level). Another example is the holistic approach adopted by Chow-Chua and Goh (2002), which merges the Singapore quality award (SQA) model of business excellence with the BSC approach in a health care scenario. These authors contend that, despite the prevailing confines and implementation challenges, their initial findings indicate that this approach may be applicable in hospitals to generate sustainable improvement in patient satisfaction and better inter-departmental communication. According to Sanderson (2001), other business-like management approaches have been applied that include strategic management, cost-centre management, business planning, and marketing and quality management.

There have been several attempts to develop a generic performance measurement framework for public and non-profit sectors. For example, the English performance and assessment framework (PAF), which the British government intends to apply, uses as a strategic measurement tool for benchmarking and for improving the National Health Service (NHS) performance due to its similarities with the BSC. Chang et al. (2002) argue that PAF is similar, but not identical to BSC. They contend that the BSC method has been modified to match the distinctive context of the NHS. Another example is the Scottish performance management and planning (PMP) framework that was specifically defined to support Scottish councils.

This framework had the objective to achieve and demonstrate continuous performance improvement. Wisniewski and Stewart (2001), in their evaluation of this approach, suggest that the audit framework assisted councils in identifying areas where improvement is needed. However, they argue that the effectiveness of the PMP audit can only be realistically assessed when councils' effort at achieving the improvements identified through the audit process is evaluated. Curtright et al. (2000) studied a PMS that was specifically designed for the Mayo Clinic (Minnesota). They found that the PMS process aligned the concept of measuring organisational performance with meeting Mayo's vision, primary value, core principles, and operational strategies. Thus returning to the original purpose of a PMS, which is the achievement of the strategic objectives of the organisation.

One should note that there is an intensive trend in the American public sector to measure performance. This is confirmed by legislative initiatives such as the Government Performance and Results Act (GPRA). The GPRA of 1993 requires federal agencies to prepare a strategic plan covering a multiyear period and requires each agency to submit an annual performance plan and an annual performance report. Rosenblatt et al. (1998), in studying the California System of Care Model for youths with severe emotional disturbances, demonstrated how ongoing assessment of the costs and outcomes of service delivery can be an integral part of a service delivery model.

In their study they defined a planning process to assist in the care system development and implementation that identified a five-step approach, namely, define the target population; establish the goals; develop the necessary inter-agency partnerships; develop the services that will result in the achievement of goals for the clients and the system; and develop methods for monitoring client and system outcomes and providing feedback on these outcomes for client and programme decision-making. Thompson (2001) suggested a framework for evaluating the performance in New Zealand's museums. He concludes that the New Zealand accounting profession's specification of service performance reporting is flawed. The author suggested guidelines with a focus on the nonfinancial reporting aspects, specifically related to problems in applying definitions of things that are difficult to measure that may lead to likely defects in the frameworks because of the exclusion of applicable parameters.

The Balanced scorecard (BSC) has emerged as the most popular PMS in the private and public sectors, because it allows organisations to evaluate both their financial and non-financial performances. Oliveira (2001) conducted a study regarding the application of the balanced scorecard in the health care sector and recommended a framework in relation to how the BSC is to be implemented, namely, building the business case; identifying strategies; identifying tactical objectives; identifying performance measurements; identifying data sources; creating the data warehouse; selecting information technology; creating the balanced scorecard; managing the strategy; and refining and reusing the process. There are many similar studies that are too numerous to document in this text. The above research findings suggest the following:

- The PMS methodology applicable in the Public Sector is a political decision and is likely to be based upon the need for accountability.
- The public sector has a huge spectrum of activities and related services, therefore there is not a single PMS framework that is applicable to all situations. Hence, it is likely that the PMS adopted will need to be modified to cater for a specific organisation.
- There is a need to understand what should be included in the PSM model. Hence, management needs to be selective in relation to what data is be collected and reported. The PSM model must support the strategic objectives of the organisation in a similar way as in the private sector.

A difficulty in applying performance measurement systems in the public sector is the conflicting objectives. For instance, like the education and public health sectors, transport generates positive and negative externalities (Moriarty and Kennedy, 2015). An externality is a cost or benefit caused by a producer that is not financially incurred or received by that producer. For example, Moriarty and Kennedy (2015) conducted a case study related to the state highway authorities of Victoria, Australia, where the producer is the state highway authorities. They argue that positive externalities do not pose a difficulty because the general benefits are likely to be advertised by the relevant authorities. However, negative externalities become a problem because they make it difficult for the relevant authorities to define a coherent set of objectives that will generate a meaningful set of performance measures.

The reason for this is that road traffic, apart from being a major contributor to greenhouse gas emissions and oil depletion, can also create other problems such as noise and air pollution, difficulty for non-motorised modes, and separation of communities, and can require much land, leading to loss of homes or parkland. These side effects provide environmentally focused groups with the impetus to contest the objectives that the highway authorities would set themselves in the absence of this pressure. For example, the extension of the Eastern Freeway in Melbourne, Victoria, illustrates how objectives can be in conflict. According to Gibson (1990), a government-appointed panel to assess the options for this extension found that upgrading and extending the public transport system would be the most cost-effective option as well as the best environmentally nonthreatening option. However, an internal study by VicRoads (the state highway authority), which completely contradicted the first report, was accepted by the state government even though it was viewed as the worst option from the environmental viewpoint.

Therefore, subject to those environmental effects being ignored, the state highway authorities can themselves ignore conflicting objectives. On the other hand, if environmental objectives become important constraints because of concerns related to climate change and oil depletion, the authorities themselves could experience real organisational difficulties (Moriarty and Kennedy, 2015). Benchmarking (a private sector performance measurement tool) may be applicable in this case. For instance, different transport types have different fatality rates per 100 million passenger-kilometres and highway authorities dedicate much of their efforts to reducing their number and severity. However, the authorities tend to make traffic fatality comparisons between the various states of Australia, and with countries overseas, but they rarely make comparisons with public transport fatality rates. Hence, performance targets may be established with the much lower rates for rail travel as the relevant benchmark (Ibid.).

Some may see this comparison as unfair because the rail mode of travel utilises well-trained drivers, has its own right-of-way, and runs on fixed rails that makes it naturally safer. However, if safety is important, then there is ample justification for adopting it as the benchmark. Intrinsically, the decision as to which benchmark is deemed appropriate is a political one. Thus, defining objectives for government client sector agencies is likely to become a major concern in the future because the concept of the post-war era welfare state is no longer applicable or acceptable. There is a change in culture, where issues such as the alternative lifestyles, equal opportunities, and rights of minority groups are seen as important, and are influencing government policy. Furthermore, environmental and resource availability problems, including air quality, water, agriculture, forests, and energy supply, as well as transport and urban planning, are also likely to change the way that these are conceptualised and thus influence government policy.

Another example where a performance measurement system has been applied successfully and resembles private sector principles is at Centrelink Australia, which is the agency that processes social security payments and services to Australians. In 1999, Centrelink adopted a version of the Balanced Scorecard to improve its performance (Moriarty and Kennedy, 2015). This organisation has over 24,000 employees, and 6.3 million customers throughout Australia, with payments exceeding $A 51.7 billion. Centrelink's management established a set of Key Performance Indicators (KPIs) for each identified organisational goal and issues monthly performance reports against the selected KPIs to its Board of Management. Centrelink administers policy on behalf of its diverse client agencies. However, due to the increasing heterogeneity of the Australian population, Centrelink encounters difficulties due to the increased complexity of customer inquiries and needs. These are catered for in the applicable KPIs for customer satisfaction. Hence, Centrelink's KPIs for customer satisfaction with the service, such as 'appointment wait time' and 'call wait time,' are like the indicators used in a private sector (Centrelink, 2001).

Unlike the previous example regarding the state highway authorities, Centrelink was successful in implementing the Balanced Scorecard approach since its objectives were clearly defined and narrowed down to essential elements, such as the effective delivery of government services to eligible customers. However, one needs to be aware that Centrelink's dominant activity is to cater for the customers of the various client agencies, with policy making and their respective objectives being the responsibility of the various client agencies. Therefore, Centrelink is viewed as purely a customer service organisation with its sole responsibility being service delivery.

As the examples above demonstrate, the core difficulty confronted by public sector organisations is the existence of externalities that create problems in defining customers and in formulating coherent objectives. Furthermore, policy decision-making becomes complex as the numbers of objectives and stakeholders increase. This is particularly difficult in the health care sector, where there is a wide spectrum in the types of services, types of delivery methods, and types of customers that are catered for. According to Carlin (1999), performance measurement matrices require understanding of the relative weight to be placed on each performance target.

Private sector organisations do not have a problem in doing this, since they have a rather limited number of strategic objectives. However, this is often a difficulty in the public sector because it is questionable whether the different stakeholders can reach consensus on the relative importance of the different objectives since the trade-offs can only be achieved by the political process. Hence, it is important that public sector organisations do not seek a holistic solution, but to separate the various functions within the organisation and implement a performance management system for each function with their own limited number of objectives. For instance, in the example of the highway authorities, it would have been better to have three separate functions, namely state and urban transport planning; road design and construction; and traffic management. This would enable each functional area to design a specific performance measurement system and associated KPIs to cater for a more simplified cluster of related strategic objectives (i.e., limited to engineering functions), irrespective of whether there are major shifts in government transport policy.

Moriarty and Kennedy (2015) argue that the public sector can only successfully adopt performance measurement to the extent that they resemble private businesses. They contend the performance measurement in the private sector is possible because these organisations have relatively limited objectives, such as to make a profit for their shareholders, subject only to constraints imposed on their operation by government legislation and by ethical considerations. The major issue is whether there is a difference between private sector and public sector performance management frameworks. As highlighted above, the difficulty with the public sector performance management framework is the tendency of viewing Government or a Ministry or a Department holistically.

Viewing these organisations holistically makes it extremely difficult to identify the appropriate KPIs and to reconcile them with the strategic objectives of the organisation. Hence, it is important that public sector organisations do not seek a holistic solution, but to separate the various functions within the organisation and implement a performance management system for each function (and in many cases sub-functions) with their own limited number of objectives and resultant KPIs. For example, trying to establish a performance management system for a public hospital as a holistic entity becomes extremely complex and is likely to fail. However, if management identifies the different functions within a hospital, the task of establishing a performance management system for each singular function (or sub-function) becomes possible and much easier.

For instance, the hospital function related to the operating theatres can apply a standard costing system and associated Variance Analysis tools (as in the private sector) to adequately measure performance for a specific type of intervention. Hence, in this case the function would be the operating theatres and the sub-function would be the type of intervention. Many types of interventions follow a standard procedure in terms of time, operating team (by profession and grade), consumables, and fixed and variable overheads. Variance Analysis tools may be applied to establish the performance for the specific intervention and establish the reason why the intervention had a positive or negative deviation from the established standard. Furthermore, there is no lack of computer application software that supports standard cost systems, and many types of interventions have been performed often enough for the relevant data to be available and standards established.

## Performance Management Framework

The performance management framework described in this section is applicable to both the private and public sectors. This is possible because the research in the previous section revealed that the segmentation of the organisation into functional (and sub-functional) areas permits the identification of a small number of pertinent objectives and associated key performance indicators. Furthermore, the suggested performance management framework can also be adapted to several settings, such as individual employees, organisational units, products, services, and individual clients.

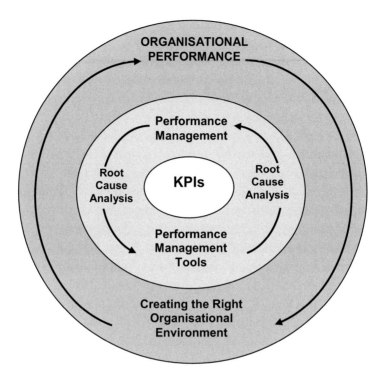

*Figure 4.1* Top Level Performance Management Framework

The proposed Performance Management Framework may be described at the various levels, with each level being more specific and detailed. The first level of detail is illustrated by Figure 4.1. Figure 4.1 indicates that organisational performance is contingent on creating the right organisational environment in terms of leadership approach, suitable type of organisational commitment and employee participation, development of employee engagement and enhanced internal communication, and developing an employee development and training programme. Moreover, Key Performance Indicators (KPIs) are established after conducting a Root Cause Analysis of the identified problematic area, and selecting the appropriate performance management tool, leading to the definition of the relevant KPIs.

The second level of detail is illustrated by Figure 4.2, which provides a systematic process for the proposed Performance Management Framework. Figure 4.2 demonstrates that the proposed Performance Management Framework consists of several stages that describe general procedures. The first stage reveals the process for preparing the organisation to create the

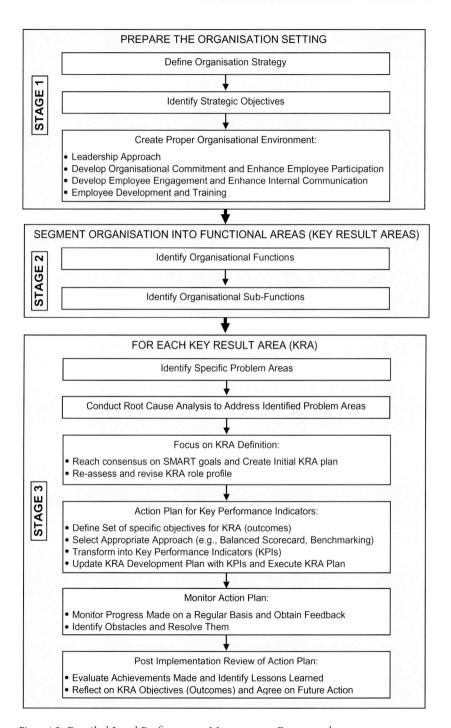

**STAGE 1**

**PREPARE THE ORGANISATION SETTING**

Define Organisation Strategy

Identify Strategic Objectives

Create Proper Organisational Environment:
- Leadership Approach
- Develop Organisational Commitment and Enhance Employee Participation
- Develop Employee Engagement and Enhance Internal Communication
- Employee Development and Training

**STAGE 2**

**SEGMENT ORGANISATION INTO FUNCTIONAL AREAS (KEY RESULT AREAS)**

Identify Organisational Functions

Identify Organisational Sub-Functions

**STAGE 3**

**FOR EACH KEY RESULT AREA (KRA)**

Identify Specific Problem Areas

Conduct Root Cause Analysis to Address Identified Problem Areas

Focus on KRA Definition:
- Reach consensus on SMART goals and Create Initial KRA plan
- Re-assess and revise KRA role profile

Action Plan for Key Performance Indicators:
- Define Set of specific objectives for KRA (outcomes)
- Select Appropriate Approach (e.g., Balanced Scorecard, Benchmarking)
- Transform into Key Performance Indicators (KPIs)
- Update KRA Development Plan with KPIs and Execute KRA Plan

Monitor Action Plan:
- Monitor Progress Made on a Regular Basis and Obtain Feedback
- Identify Obstacles and Resolve Them

Post Implementation Review of Action Plan:
- Evaluate Achievements Made and Identify Lessons Learned
- Reflect on KRA Objectives (Outcomes) and Agree on Future Action

*Figure 4.2  Detailed Level Performance Management Framework*

proper organisational environment, cited in Figure 4.1. This basically consists of defining the organisational strategy and identifying the strategic
objectives, leading to the prerequisites for creating the proper organisational environment as described previously. The second stage proposes the
segmentation of the organisation into functional areas, referred to as the
Key Result Areas.

The Key Result Areas are described in detail in Chapter 1 and can target different organisational aspects, such as functions, sub-functions, individual employees, organisational units, products, services, and individual
clients, amongst others. This segmentation permits the Performance Management Framework to be applicable to both the private and public sector
organisations. The third stage, shown at Figure 4.2, provides the necessary
steps for the implementation of the Performance Management Framework.
These steps are applicable to each targeted Key Result Area (KRA). The
implementation phase consists of six processes:

(a) Identifying specific problematic areas (if any).
(b) Conducting Root Cause Analysis to address the identified problematic
    areas.
(c) Focusing of the KRA by generating SMART goals (see Chapter 1), creat-
    ing an initial KRA development plan, and reassessing and reviewing
    the KRA role profile (goals).
(d) Preparing an action plan for defining KPIs for the KRA by identifying
    specific objectives (outcomes), selecting the appropriate performance
    management tool (see Table 4.1), transforming the objectives into KPIs,
    revising the KRA development plan with the KPIs, and implementing
    the KRA development plan.
(e) Monitoring the implementation of the KRA development plan on a
    regular basis and recording feedback, and identifying and resolving
    any encountered obstacles.
(f) Conducting a post-implementation review of the KRA development
    plan by evaluating the achievement made, identifying, and recording
    lessons learnt, reflecting on the KRA objectives (outcomes), and agree-
    ing on any future actions that may be taken, such as reviewing KRA
    objectives and related KPIs.

Note that KRAs refer to a short list of overall goals that guide employees as to how to conduct their specific function. KRAs also consist of

Table 4.1  Applicable Tools for the Proposed Performance Management Framework

| Performance Management Tools | Applicability |
|---|---|
| Strategic Planning | High applicability in Private and Public Sector |
| Budgeting and Forecasting | High applicability in Private and Public Sector |
| Variance Analysis (production and service industries) | High applicability in Private and Public Sector |
| Performance Analytics | High applicability in Private and Public Sector |
| Performance Reporting | High applicability in Private and Public Sector |
| Critical Success Factors | High applicability in Private and Public Sector |
| Balanced Scorecard | High applicability in Private and Public Sector |
| Benchmarking | High applicability in Private and Public Sector |
| Business Excellence Models | High applicability in Private and Public Sector |
| Enterprise Risk Management | High applicability in Private and Public Sector |
| Project/Programme Management | High applicability in Private and Public Sector |

several related Key Performance Indicators (KPIs) that segment the KRA into lower-level goals. Remember that a KPI is any metric that measures whether an organisation is achieving its defined objectives, whose outcome assists the organisation to be successful in its undertakings. Hence, KPIs may be conveyed as ratios that reflect productivity, service time rates, rate of return on capital investment, and many other potential indicative amounts that reflect performance. KPIs are directly related to the outcomes, that is, the achievement of the objectives, and must follow the SMART concept of being specific, measurable, achievable, realistic, and timely. Therefore, the KPIs are viewed as being the measurements associated with the general objectives delineated in a KRA. It is important that KPIs accurately reflect the business activities of the organisation, specifically the KRA. In defining a KPI, the following should be taken into consideration:

- What is the required outcome?
- What is the significance of this outcome?
- How is progress to be measured?
- How will you know that the required outcome is being achieved?
- How frequently will progress be reviewed to ensure that you are moving towards the required outcome?

The proposed Performance Management Framework is a practical and easy approach for measuring performance in both the private and public sectors and provides the advantage of allowing management to implement the process in a phased manner and at a pace that is manageable to a specific organisation.

## Conclusion

The performance management framework adopted is a fundamental and strategic instrument of any private or public sector organisation. However, performance management framework must be easy to apply and can be implemented gradually throughout the organisation. It is also important that senior management are directly involved in establishing and implementing the adopted performance management framework. Furthermore, the performance management framework must shift its focus from the achievements of the individual employees to assessing the contributions of employees as a team, and thus on the team's impact on the strategic objectives of the organisation.

Every organisation is unique is some ways or other, therefore each organisation must examine its particular circumstances and adopt a performance management framework that matches its specific needs. There is no doubt that the model to be adopted must be based upon mutual trust, clarity of roles, diversity of talents, and a practice of providing equal access to opportunities and resources for people who might otherwise be excluded. Therefore, designing metrics that cater for these aspects will require a major re-evaluation about the tools that are to be adopted as part of the performance management framework.

Moreover, a performance management system needs to promote performance excellence in an organisation and therefore must be easily understood and manageable. The performance management framework to be adopted will also depend on the organisation's industry sector and its culture and inherent complexity in terms of its size and activity domain. This will determine the appropriate performance management tools and respective accuracy level that may be applied.

Before a performance management framework may be implemented successfully, management must create the right organisational environment, in terms of the leadership approach, generating the proper type of organisational commitment, having a high level of employee engagement, enhancing internal communication, and encouraging employee participation at all levels. There is no such thing as the best performance management framework. Each organisation must examine its circumstances and adopt a performance management framework that suits its specific needs and that reflects the changes taking place within the organisation and the industry it operates in. Hence, the performance management framework must be flexible and adaptable to changing circumstances. All performance management frameworks are acceptable providing they support the achievement of the organisational goals. The performance management framework must be designed to be congruent and specifically aligned with overall business goals.

# References

Amirkhanyan, A.A., Kim, H.J., and Lambright, K.T. (2014). 'The Performance Puzzle: Understanding the Factors Influencing Alternative Dimensions and Views of Performance.' *Journal of Public Administration Research and Theory*, 24(1), pp. 1–34.

Atkinson, A.A. and McCrindell, J.Q. (1997). 'Strategic Performance Measurement in Government.' *CMA*, 71(3), pp. 20–23.

Bass, B.M. (1990). 'From Transactional to Transformational Leadership: Learning to Share the Vision.' *Organizational Dynamics*, 18(3), pp. 19–31.

Behn, R.D. (2003). 'Why Measure Performance? Different Purposes Require Different Measures.' *Public Administration Review*, 63(5), pp. 586–606.

Berman, E. and Wang, X. (2000). 'Performance Measurement in US Counties: Capacity for Reform.' *Public Administration Review*, 60(5), pp. 409–420.

Blue Rubicon and Henley Management College (2002). *Employee Communications and Relationships Report 2002*.

Boland, T. and Fowler, A. (2000). 'A Systems Perspective of Performance Management in Public Sector Organizations.' *International Journal of Public Sector Management*, 13(5), pp. 417–446.

Boyne, G.A. (2002). 'Public and Private Management: What's the Difference?' *Journal of Management Studies*, 39(1), pp. 97–122.

Camilleri, E. (2002). 'Some Antecedents of Organizational Commitment: Results from an Information Systems Public Service Organization.' *Bank of Valletta Review*, 25, pp. 1–29.

Camilleri, E. (2006). 'Towards Developing an Organizational Commitment-Public Service Motivational Model for the Maltese Public Service Employees.' *Public Policy and Administration*, 21(1), pp. 63–83.

Camilleri, E. and van der Heijden, B. (2007). 'Organizational Commitment, Public Service Motivation, and Performance within the Public Sector.' *Public Performance and Management Review*, 31(2), pp. 241–274.

Carlin, T. (1999). 'Simplifying Corporate Performance Measurement.' *Australian CPA December*, pp. 48–50.

Carter, N. (1989). 'Performance Indicators: "Back Seat Driving" or "Hands Off" Control?' *Policy and Politics*, 17(2), pp. 131–138.

Centrelink (2001). *Annual Report 2000–01*. Centrelink, Sydney.

Chang, L., Lin, S.W., and Northcott, D.N. (2002). 'The NHS Performance Assessment Framework: A Balanced Scorecard Approach?' *Journal of Management in Medicine*, 16(5), pp. 345–358.

Chow-Chua, C. and Goh, M. (2002). 'Framework for Evaluating Performance and Quality Improvement in Hospitals.' *Managing Service Quality*, 12(1), pp. 54–66.

Crawford, L.H. (2003). 'Assessing and Developing the Project Management Competence of Individuals,' in J.R. Turner (ed.), *People in Project Management*. Aldershot, UK: Gower Publishing Company Limited, pp. 13–29.

Curtright, J.W., Stolp-Smith, S.C., and Edell, E.S. (2000). 'Strategic Performance Management: Development of a Performance Measurement System at the Mayo Clinic.' *Journal of Healthcare Management*, 45(1), pp. 58–68.

De Lancer Julnes, J.P. and Holzer, M. (2001). 'Promoting the Utilization of Performance Measures in Public Organizations: An Empirical Study of Factors Affecting Adoption and Implementation.' *Public Administration Review*, 61(6), pp. 693–708.

De Waele, L. and Polzer, T. (2021). 'A Little Bit of Everything? Conceptualising Performance Measurement in Hybrid Public Sector Organisations through a Literature Review.' *Journal of Public Budgeting, Accounting & Financial Management*, 33(3), pp. 343–363.

Evans, P. and Bellamy, S. (1995). 'Performance Evaluation in the Australian Public Sector: The Role of Management and Cost Accounting Control Systems.' *International Journal of Public Sector Management*, 8(6), pp. 30–38.

Frederickson, H.G. (1990). 'Public Administration and Social Equity.' *Public Administration Review*, 50(2), pp. 228–237.

Frederickson, H.G. (2010). *Social Equity and Public Administration: Origins, Developments and Applications*. Armonk, NY: M.E. Sharpe.

Gallup, Inc. (2017). *State of the American Workplace*. Available at: https://www.gallup.com/workplace/238085/state-american-workplace-report-2017.aspx (Accessed 23 November 2023).

Gibson, H. (1990). *Eastern Arterial Road and Ringwood Bypass Panel of Review*. Report to the Victorian Government, Australia.

Goleman, D., Boyatzis, R. and McKee, A. (2002). *The New Leaders*. Boston: Harvard Business School Press.

Gooijer, J.D. (2000). 'Designing a Knowledge Management Performance Framework.' *Journal of Knowledge Management*, 4(4), pp. 303–310.

Halachmi, A. and Bouckaert, G. (1994). 'Performance Measurement, Organizational Technology and Organizational Design.' *Work Study*, 43(3), pp. 19–25.

Harris, J. (1998). 'Performance Models: Enhancing Accountability in Academe.' *Public Productivity and Management Review*, 22(2), pp. 135–139.

Henry, G.T. and Dickey, K.C. (1993). 'Implementing Performance Monitoring: A Research and Development Approach.' *Public Administration Review*, 53(3), pp. 203–212.

House, R.J. (1971). 'A Path-goal Theory of Leader Effectiveness.' *Administrative Science Quarterly*, 16 (September), pp. 321–338.

House, R.J. and Mitchell, T.R. (1974). 'Path-goal Theory of Leader.' *Contemporary Business*, 3 (Fall), pp. 81–98.

Marshall, J. and Heffes, E.M. (2006). 'Communication: Employee Communication Linked to Performance.' *Financial Executive*, 22(1), pp. 11–12.

McLaughlin, J.A. and Jordan, G.B. (1999). 'Logic Models: A Tool for Telling Your Programs Performance Story.' *Evaluation and Program Planning*, 22(1), pp. 65–72.

Meyer, J.P. and Allen, N.J. (1991). 'A Three-component Conceptualization of Organizational Commitment.' *Human Resource Management Review*, 1, pp. 61–89.

Meyer, J.P. and Allen, N.J. (1997). *Commitment in the Workplace: Theory, Research, and Application*. Thousand Oaks, CA: Sage Publications, Inc.

Micheli, Pietro and Kennerley, Mike (2005). 'Performance Measurement Frameworks in Public and Non-profit Sectors.' *Production Planning & Control*, 16(2), pp. 125–134.

Moriarty, P. and Kennedy, D. (2015). *Performance Measurement in Public Sector Services: Problems and Potential*. Department of Mechanical Engineering, Monash University-Caulfield Campus, Caulfield East, Victoria, Australia.

Oliveira, J. (2001). The Balanced Scorecard: An Integrative Approach to Performance Evaluation. *Healthcare Financial Management*, 55(5), pp. 42–46.

Osborne, S.P., Bovaird, T., Martin, S., Tricker, M., and Waterston, P. (1995). 'Performance Management and Accountability in Complex Public Programmes.' *Financial Accountability and Management*, 11(1), pp. 19–37.

Pollitt, C. and Bouckaert, G. (2017). *Public Management Reform. A Comparative Analysis – into the Age of Austerity*. Oxford: Oxford University Press.

Quantum Workplace (2021). *What is Employee Engagement? What, Why and How to Improve It.* Available at: https://www.quantumworkplace.com/ future-of-work/what-is-employee-engagement-definition (Accessed 21 November 2023).

Reichheld, F.F. (1996). *The Loyalty Effect.* Boston: Harvard Business School Press.

Rosenblatt, A., Wyman, N., Kingdon, D., and Ichinose, C. (1998). 'Managing what You Measure: Creating Outcome-driven Systems of Care for Youth with Serious Emotional Disturbances.' *Journal of Behavioural Health Services and Research*, 25(2), pp. 177–193.

SHRM (2021). Developing and Sustaining Employee Engagement. Available at: https://www.shrm.org/resourcesandtools/tools-and-samples/toolkits/ pages/sustainingemployeeengagement.aspx (Accessed 21 November 2023).

Thompson, G.D. (2001). 'The Impact of New Zealand's Public Sector Accounting Reforms on Performance Control in Museums.' *Financial Accountability and Management*, 17(1), pp. 5–19.

Tourish, D. and Hargie, O. (1998). 'Auditing Staff–management Communication in Schools: A Framework for Evaluating Performance.' *International Journal of Educational Management*, 12(4), pp. 176–182.

Turner, J. R. and Müller, R. (2005). 'The Project Manager's Leadership Style as a Success Factor on Projects: A Literature Review.' *Project Management Journal*, 36(2), pp. 49–61.

Van Peursem, K.A., Prat, M.J., and Lawrence, S.R. (1995). 'Health Management Performance: A Review of Measures and Indicators.' *Accounting, Auditing and Accountability Journal*, 8(5), pp. 34–70.

Willis Towers Watson (2021). *Employee Insights for a Better Employee Experience.* Available at: https://www.willistowerswatson.com/en-BE/Solutions/ employee-engagement (Accessed 21 November 2023).

Wilson, L.A. and Durant, R.F. (1994). 'Evaluating TQM: The Case for a Theory Driven Approach.' *Public Administration Review*, 54(2), pp. 137–146.

Wisniewski, M. and Stewart, D. (2001). 'Using the Statutory Audit to Support Continuous Improvement in Scottish Local Authorities.' *International Journal of Public Sector Management*, 14(7), pp. 540–555.

# PART II

## PERFORMANCE MANAGEMENT TOOLBOX

### METHODS FOR DETERMINING KEY PERFORMANCE INDICATORS

Part I of this book included the four previous chapters, which laid the foundation regarding performance management and measurement principles. It was shown that key performance indicators (KPIs) may be defined at different levels within the organisation, such as corporate, divisional, departmental, activity, and individual levels. KPIs may also be defined on a product or service level or for specific customers. Hence, KPI methodologies are extremely versatile and may be adapted for the private and public sectors. It must be recognised that KPIs are about accountability of those who are responsible for a specific duty, role, or segment of the organisation. The success of the KPI process depends on the commitment level of all the parties concerned towards having a KPI methodology as the performance management appraisal system, beginning with the executive team, and cascading down to the individual employees. It is also critical that all employees are aware of the strategic objectives of the organisation and how their specific function contributes towards the achievement of these strategic objectives.

DOI: 10.4324/9781032685465-6

The KPI process requires an implementation plan that defines when the various KPI implementation levels are scheduled, starting from the organisational holistic level, and ending with the individual employees. The KPIs implementation plan must be realistic, with each phase defining the tasks and overall goals to be achieved at each specific level known as Key Result Areas (KRAs). KRAs are those areas in which a manager has complete ownership and accountability, and which permit the identification of the Key Performance Measures (KPMs) for that level. Thus, the combination of the KRAs and KPMs will provide the KPIs for that specific organisational level or function. As one may appreciate, the KPI definition process is iterative. Therefore, each KPI must be closely monitored and fine-tuned until management (and employees) are satisfied that the resultant KPIs are equitable and represent the realistic circumstances of the functional level being measured. Once the KPIs are confirmed as being accurate and realistic, the KPIs are accepted as part of the performance dashboard for that specific organisational level or function. Moreover, KPIs need to be regularly reviewed, specifically when there is a change to the organisation's strategic objectives.

The literature research revealed that initially employee appraisal methods had been designed to specifically identify poor performers with the objective of terminating their engagement or to reassign them to other duties. These systems were popular during periods of high inflation, such as the 1970s energy crisis, where salary increases had to be tightly controlled and annual employee appraisal methods were viewed as a simple and effective way of controlling salary increases. However, with the passage of time, employee appraisals were seen as a very time-consuming activity and were not taken seriously by supervisors. Often supervisors just went through the mechanics of the appraisal process without realistically assessing whether and to what extent the employee was achieving the strategic objectives of the organisation. Hence, the contribution to the achievement of the organisation's strategic objective was soon adopted as the basis for measuring performance either at an individual level or at various organisational functional levels. Thus, KPIs emerged as the accepted performance management norm in many industries.

Due to the wide spectrum of industries, there are many performance management and measurement approaches, and associated tools, all of which utilise matrices and KPIs as the basis for measuring performance. Performance management tools may differ in the way information about an organisation's performance may be gathered and analysed, but the common theme is based upon the defined KPIs. Hence, KPIs provide a common thread between the various performance management systems and associated tools. Performance management systems are still evolving with the objective of significantly increasing organisational effectiveness and employee productivity. However, poor organisational performance may be due to various causes that may not be related to the individuals carrying out the innumerable tasks in an organisation. Therefore, before KPIs may be established at the various organisational functional levels, it may be wise to examine the general cause of the performance problem.

Chapter 3 has shown that Root Cause Analysis is a valuable tool to investigate problematic situations because it explores and exposes in a very definite way the source of a problem, in terms of when, where, and why the problem has occurred. The literature research has shown that while problem solving appears to be a reactive activity, root cause analysis acts as a proactive tool because it ensures that the problem can be prevented from flowing out and impacting the customer a second time. Root Cause Analysis determines completely why certain difficulties have occurred and to identify the cause of the problem. Root Cause Analysis is all about understanding how to track and locate the adverse effects back to their primary cause or revealing the interrelated causes. This is critical in achieving a higher level of quality and having satisfied customers. Root Cause Analysis is a deductive problem-solving methodology that is widely applied in every industry and organisational function. Using Root Cause Analysis means mitigating the use of firefighting and crisis management to an absolute minimum as a primary mode of resolving difficulties across the organisation.

The research literature has also indicated that a performance management framework is essential since it is viewed as a fundamental and strategic instrument of any Private or Public sector organisation. Chapter 4 illustrated that a performance management framework must be easy to apply and that it can be implemented gradually throughout the organisation. It was also shown that senior management should be directly involved in establishing and implementing the adopted performance management framework. Likewise, it is important that the performance management framework must shift its focus from the achievements of the individual employees to assessing the contributions of employees as a team, and thus on the team's impact on the strategic objectives of the organisation.

Additionally, the research revealed that every organisation has some level of uniqueness, therefore each organisation must adopt a performance management framework that suits its particular circumstances and specific needs. However, no matter what the organisation's circumstances are, the model to be adopted must be based upon mutual trust, clarity of roles, diversity of talents, and a practice of providing equal access to opportunities and resources for people who might otherwise be excluded. Therefore, designing metrics, such as KPIs that cater for these aspects, will require a major re-evaluation of the tools that are to be adopted as part of the performance management framework. Moreover, a performance management system needs to promote performance excellence in an organisation and therefore must be easily understood and managed.

The performance management framework to be adopted will also depend on the organisation's industry sector and its culture and inherent complexity in terms of its size and activity domain. This will determine the appropriate performance management tools and respective accuracy level that may be applied. The research revealed that before a performance management framework may be implemented successfully, management must create the right organisational environment, in terms of the leadership approach, generating the proper type of organisational commitment, having a high level of employee engagement, enhancing internal communication, and encouraging employee participation at all levels. It is important to note that there is no such thing as the best performance management framework. Hence, the performance management framework must be flexible and adaptable to changing circumstances. All performance management frameworks are acceptable providing they support the achievement of the organisational goals. A performance management framework must be designed to be congruent and specifically aligned with overall business goals. Chapter 4 proposed a performance management framework that is robust and flexible, and yet easy to apply and applicable to both the private and public sectors.

Part II of this book will examine in much more detail several of the performance management tools that were considered in Chapter 2. These performance management tools are critical for the successful implementation of the proposed performance management framework described by Chapter 4. From a performance management perspective, viewing an organisation holistically makes it extremely difficult to identify the appropriate KPIs and to reconcile them with the strategic objectives of the organisation. An important principle of the proposed performance management framework is to separate the various functions within the organisation and implement a performance management system for each function (and in many cases sub-functions) with its own limited number of objectives and resultant KPIs.

It should be emphasised that each organisational function or sub-function may utilise different tools and methods for establishing and monitoring performance through KPIs. For instance, some functions may use balanced scorecards, others may utilise a standard costing system and associated variance analysis, yet still other functions may use benchmarking, and so on. This basic principle of segmenting an organisation into functional units (and even sub-units) for the purpose of performance management will permit the same performance management framework to be used by both the private and public sectors. This is possible because the research in the previous chapters revealed that the segmentation of the organisation into functional (and sub-functional) areas permits the identification of a small number of pertinent objectives and associated KPIs.

Furthermore, the suggested performance management framework can also be adapted to several settings, such as individual employees, organisational units, products, services, and individual clients. Part II of this book will specifically describe the various performance management and measurement tools as depicted by Figure 4.2 and Table 4.1 found in Chapter 4. As the reader may recall, Figure 4.2 illustrated a practical performance management framework. Part II will focus on Stage Three of the proposed performance management framework, specifically the action plan for KPIs, monitoring the action plan, and the post-implementation review of the action plan. Each chapter in Part II will focus on certain aspects of the tools shown in Table 4.1 of Chapter 4.

# 5

## STRATEGIC MANAGEMENT AND BUSINESS PLANNING AS A BASIS FOR ESTABLISHING KPIS

'Overcoming complacency is crucial at the start of any change process, and it often requires a little bit of surprise, something that grabs attention at more than an intellectual level. You need to surprise people with something that disturbs their view that everything is perfect.'

Dr John Kotter
Konosuke Matsushita Professor of Leadership,
Emeritus, Harvard Business School; Co-Founder and
Executive Chairman, Kotter International

Operating without a strategic plan is like sitting in a canoe that drifts along with the current. You see it gather speed and go faster, passing one milestone after another. Eventually, however, you helplessly watch as it moves without purpose over the rapids until it breaks apart and disintegrates. Strategic planning places you in the piloting position, where you paddle along with an objective in mind. It acts as a navigational map that identifies and defines the course that should be taken, highlighting potential danger zones so that they may be adequately managed

DOI: 10.4324/9781032685465-7

and possibly avoided. Organisations without a strategy will certainly under-utilise their resources and are likely to be misdirected until they fail completely.

Strategic planning is a systematic process that defines a roadmap regarding the direction to be taken by the organisation. Hence, it describes the organisation's objectives and actions that are required to achieve the management's vision and outlines the performance metrics for measuring success. Strategic planning provides 'the big picture' so that management may focus on the fundamental purpose of the organisation and the stipulated goals by developing and taking advantage of the opportunities presented. It should be noted that a strategic plan considers the long-term future of the organisation, which may be from three to five years. Hence, the strategic plan takes a high-level view of the organisation and where it wants to be positioned in the long-term.

On the other hand, a business plan is a short-term segment of the strategic plan that normally has a duration of one year. Hence, a business plan is more detailed, and the performance metrics are established at a lower organisational level. In a practical sense, a strategic plan is implemented through a series of annual business plans. For a strategic plan to be successful it must be implemented in a meticulous manner. Remember that typically a plan focuses on what, and why. However, implementing the plan focuses on who, where, when, and how.

Strategic plans fail for several reasons. It is important that there is the appropriate commitment to the strategic plan across the organisation. In other words, there needs to be a sense of ownership for the plan among the various stakeholders. This means having employees accountable for their actions and empowering them to take the appropriate action. It also means linking the strategy to employee incentives and linking the strategy to the budgeting process, including performance management and measurement. A suitable communications strategy must also be adopted to ensure that all relevant stakeholders understand and participate in the strategic planning implementation process. Management must assign responsibility for tasks amongst employees and adopt a suitable tracking and monitoring process that supports the performance management and incentive system. It is important for management to involve employees in structured performance conversations to review and monitor performance, particularly the assessment of the defined KPIs.

# Introduction

Pirtea, Nicolescu, and Botoc (2009) argue that strategic planning has long been used as a tool for transforming and revitalising corporations, government agencies, and non-profit organisations. However, they contend that scepticism about planning has been steadily increasing due to the political and economic uncertainty, and the rapidity of technological and social change. Hence, they maintain that this uncertain environment is making it difficult for the planning efforts to keep stride with developments, thus leading to some disillusionment. However, the issue is not whether strategic planning has lost its fundamental meaning and purpose, but whether the strategic planning process is being implemented in the proper way for it to succeed. For strategic planning to succeed it must follow a meticulous process in which the views of the relevant stakeholders are solicited, goals are realistic and clearly defined, and where an action plan is specifically identified, defined, and implemented. Pirtea, Nicolescu, and Botoc (2009) argue that a successful strategic planning process will examine and make informed projections about environmental realities to help an organisation anticipate and respond to change by clarifying its mission and goals; targeting spending; and reshaping its programs, securing funding and other aspects of operations.

It must be recognised that even though there is a very close relationship between operational planning and strategic planning, the latter must be the driver. As stated previously, the operational plan (i.e., business plan) should be viewed as a short-term segment of the longer-term strategic plan. Hence, the focus should be on the organisational strategy with everything else flowing from there. Pirtea, Nicolescu, and Botoc (2009) found that this focus is not always achieved, and very few organisations are succeeding in driving the organisation through the strategy, and integrating that strategy into the annual budget, and the objectives and actions of managers throughout the organisation.

Pirtea, Nicolescu, and Botoc (2009) argue that there is a very important relationship between strategic planning and performance management. However, the term performance management has a broad meaning. One may view performance management as establishing and achieving goals at the employee level and identifying and resolving the difficulties that act as obstacles to achieving these goals. On the other hand, one may question where the goals come from, and the response to this should be related to the strategic plan. After all, the key objective of strategic planning is identifying the goals that should be achieved by management and the respective employees under their specific responsibility. Hence, strategic planning permits an organisation and its individual work-units to define their goals and objectives. Moreover, these goals and objectives are applied to determine and analyse the goals and objectives of the work-units and their employees.

Additionally, goals and objectives can be transformed into key performance indicators at various levels, from individual employees to a corporate level (and in between). Therefore, for a strategic planning process to succeed, an organisation must have a robust integrated strategic plan driven by a clear vision and supported by a strong performance management system at every level of the organisation. Figure 5.1 provides a model for integrating the strategic and business planning processes with their respective performance management systems, utilising various tools that range from KPIs at various levels to performance analytics and performance reporting.

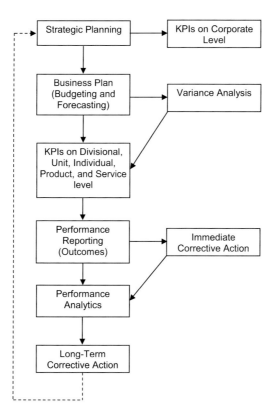

Figure 5.1 Integrated Strategic and Business Planning Performance Management Model

This chapter will discuss in some detail several performance management tools that were briefly mentioned in Chapter 2, including:

- Strategic Planning
- Business Planning (including Variance Analysis)
- Performance Analytics
- Performance Reporting

## Strategic Planning as a Performance Management Tool

It is not the intention of this chapter to describe the strategic planning process. The objective is to adapt strategic planning as a performance management tool for defining KPIs. Dye and Sibony (2007) argue that many companies fail to execute the chosen strategy and found that more than 25% of their survey respondents said their companies had plans but no execution path. Furthermore, they found that 45% reported that their planning processes failed to track the execution of strategic initiatives. Hence, they contend that putting in place a system that measures and monitors progress can greatly enhance the impact of the planning process.

Dye and Sibony also found that many organisations adapted budgets and operating reviews as the sole approach for monitoring progress of the strategy. Hence, they argue that managers tend to transform the decisions made during the planning process into budget targets or other financial goals. These researchers claim that while budget targets or other financial goals are necessary, practical, and reasonable, financial targets should not be the only approach for assessing the success of the strategic plan. For example, they argue that an entity undertaking a major strategic initiative to enhance its innovation and product-development capabilities must measure an assortment of input metrics, such as the quality of available talent, the number of ideas being generated, the number of projects at each stage in development, as well as output metrics related to the revenue generation from new-product sales.

Strategic-performance-management systems will differ from entity to entity depending on the type of product or service they provide, and the industry they belong to. It is argued that financial targets are classified as lagging indicators since they report past events. However, in addition to these lagging indicators, what is required is a strategic performance-management system that gives early warning signals related to the difficulties a specific strategic initiative may be encountering. This will enable management to take timely corrective action, including aborting the initiative.

Dusenbury (2000) argues that a strategic plan defines the performance to be measured, while performance measurement provides the feedback that keeps the strategic plan on target. Dusenbury views strategic planning as a continuous process that requires constant feedback about how the current strategies are working. For example, he argues that feedback from the market informs the private sector how it is performing through profit levels, return on investments, and sales trends. Thus, this feedback may also indicate that strategies need to be reviewed and modified. Feedback from the market may take a different form when dealing with the public sector; the performance indicators here are more related to customer satisfaction regarding the various services being provided.

Dusenbury views strategic planning as forward-looking to achieve desired goals, whereas performance measurement is historical, reviewing what has been achieved. He argues that a combination of strategic planning and performance measurement provides a continuous process of management-for-results in the private sector and governing-for-results in the public sector. Thus, he suggests that the strategic plan defines the performance to be measured, while performance measurement provides the feedback that keeps the strategic plan on track. He argues that the link between strategic planning and performance measurement strengthens both processes, since performance measurement depends on specified end outcomes, not just the undertaken activities.

In other words, it depends on the results of these activities. Hence, the strategic plan's goals and objectives focus on outcomes as the performance measurement elements that facilitate matters for management to define the appropriate performance indicators (Dusenbury, 2000). Furthermore, he argues that strategic plans must regularly reassess the goals, objectives, and outcome measures since circumstances change. Hence, regular reporting of key performance indicators (KPIs) makes available the required information to direct changes in the strategic plans, thus ensuring that the strategic plans remain on target and can adjust to environmental changes.

## Prerequisites for Selecting Strategic KPIs

However, before discussing the specific KPIs at a strategic level it is important to avoid several common mistakes that are typically made by organisations.

Firstly, make sure that the defined KPIs are aligned with the strategic objectives. Strategic objectives are defined at a corporate level and therefore the selected KPIs must also reflect this. There are numerous performance indicators that may be measured and collected. However, it is important for management to decide which performance indicators are 'key' for making the right strategic decisions. Therefore, determining that a performance indicator is 'key' is dependent on how much that specific performance indicator is congruent (aligned) with a specific strategic objective. For example, let us assume that a magazine publishing company has a strategic objective of increasing the number of magazine subscribers within the next financial year by 5,000, then a KPI labelled as 'Number of new subscribers' would correspond with this strategic objective. However, a KPI designated as 'Degree of Working Capital' is not consistent with this specific strategic objective.

Secondly, ensure that you do not limit the selected KPIs to those that are easily measured. All too often organisations select financial KPIs because they are easily available and measured. However, non-financial KPIs may not be easily attained, but are valuable performance measures. For example, if your organisation is a service provider, 'Customer satisfaction' would probably be an essential KPI. However, it would likely require a customer satisfaction survey to be undertaken at regular intervals, which is time consuming and costly, unlike accounting ratios that are readily available.

Thirdly, make sure that the selected KPIs do not give excessive significance to past events. Both backward and forward-oriented KPIs are important, but there must be a balance in their use. It is important that the selected KPIs do not solely focus on past outcomes. KPIs that only look to the past are called key results indicators (KRIs), which have been described in an earlier chapter. Looking only to past events may cause a serious strategic problem. For example, turnover (the amount of money taken by a business in a particular period) is required to determine how the business has ventured during a particular period. However, it is reporting a past event that cannot be altered. Hence, in addition to past events, forward-looking KPIs are required to provide stimulus to the future. For example, a strategic objective of 'Customer orientation', where an organisation puts the needs of the customer over the needs of the organisation, may assist to increase the growth of sales and therefore turnover.

Fourthly, do not use KPIs as a mechanism for controlling employees. Apply KPIs as a strategic tool to improve the performance of the organisation and not for manipulating and/or penalising employees. For example, a KPI such as 'Number of transactions per counter assistant' that appears to collect data on an individual basis may trigger deeds that hinder productivity. Hence, if employees sense that the data is being applied to penalise them, for instance by reducing performance allowances, this is likely to arouse resentment that hinders the attainment of a desired goal. For example, the counter assistant may speed up the transaction by having an unfriendly attitude, thus processing the customer's transaction at a faster rate. Finally, there is need to make a distinction between strategic and operational KPIs. Strategic KPIs are applicable and focus on the long-term performance. Hence, the frequency for collecting data related to strategic KPIs does not need to be as often in comparison to operational KPIs. For example, in many instances operational KPIs must be collected and monitored practically on a real-time basis. However, often strategic KPIs may be collected and monitored less frequently, say on a monthly or quarterly basis.

The above illustrate that strategic KPIs must align with the strategic objectives as much as possible. These KPIs must be significant to the strategy implementation process by ensuring that each KPI is directly linked to a specific strategic objective. For this to occur, the KPIs must be integrated in the strategic management framework adopted by the organisation. Moreover, make sure that there is a rigorous process in place for selecting the appropriate KPIs. Remember that too many KPIs will make the performance management system unmanageable; on the other hand, too few KPIs will make it meaningless. Therefore, have a robust KPI selection process, so that the KPIs which are eventually chosen to address specific strategic objectives are clearly defined, there is a blend of financial and non-financial KPIs, and there is a balanced combination of forward-looking and backward-looking KPIs. The focus in this section is related to strategy implementation. Obviously, strategic KPIs must be supported by operational KPIs, which will be discussed later in this chapter.

### *Financial and Non-Financial Strategic KPIs*

Before discussing specific strategic KPIs, it is important that a distinction is made between financial and non-financial KPIs. They are both important and non-financial KPIs are even more essential for the public sector due to its non-profit making characteristics. Financial KPIs are typically

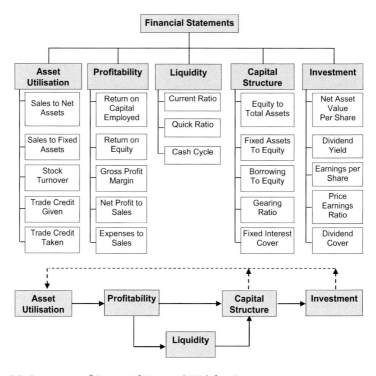

*Figure 5.2* Summary of Financial Ratios (KPIs) by Category

based on the financial statements of the organisation and refer mainly to the statement of financial performance (income statement) and statement of financial position (balance sheet). These financial statements provide an assortment of financial ratios that may be adopted as KPIs. Figure 5.2 provides a summary of the different categories of financial ratios, whilst Table 5.1 illustrates the numerous varieties of financial ratios that may be applied for strategic performance management. However, as stated previously, management must be selective in the KPIs that are chosen for performance measurement, otherwise the performance management system at a strategic level becomes unmanageable. It is suggested that a brainstorming session should be conducted by senior executive management with the objective of selecting around five KPIs to assess strategic performance.

On the other hand, non-financial KPIs are other measures applied to evaluate the activities that an organisation views as important to the achievement of its strategic objectives. Examples of non-financial KPIs include measures regarding customers, employees, operations, quality, and the components

Table 5.1a  Financial Ratios (KPIs) by Application Category

| Financial Ratio | Formulae | Remarks |
|---|---|---|
| **Liquidity:** | | |
| Current Ratio | Current Assets ÷ Current Liabilities | A current ratio of between 1.5:1 and 2:1 is generally considered practical although this depends on the nature of the business. Current assets should always be greater than current liabilities. |
| Liquid Ratio (Quick ratio or Acid Test) | (Current Assets − Stock) ÷ Current Liabilities | A liquid ratio of 1:1 is normally considered satisfactory but may be allowed to fall to 0.9:1 if the debtors pay promptly and there is a regular inflow of cash from them. |
| **Profitability:** | | |
| Return on Capital Employed (R.O.C.E) | $\dfrac{\text{Profit Before Interest and Tax}}{\text{Capital Employed}} \times 100$ | This ratio indicates management efficiency because it contrasts the earnings with the funds utilized to generate that profit. As a minimum management will aim to maintain the ROCE level.<br><br>Capital Employed = Total Assets − Current Liabilities. |
| Return on Equity (R.O.E) | Profit Before Tax (after preference dividends) ÷ (Ordinary Share Capital + Reserves) | The ratio measures profitability by revealing how much profit a company generates with the money shareholders have invested. Net income is for the full fiscal year (before dividends paid to common stockholders but after dividends to preferred stock.) Shareholder's equity does not include preferred shares. |

(Continued)

Table 5.1a  (Continued)

| Financial Ratio | Formulae | Remarks |
|---|---|---|
| Gross Profit Margin | Gross Profit ÷ Sales | The ratio shows the margin that is being earned on sales. It measures a company's manufacturing and distribution efficiency during the production process. Note that gross margin tends to remain stable over time. |
| Net Profit to Sales | Profit Before Interest and Tax ÷ Sales | The ratio indicates the overall performance of the company. |
| Expenses to Sales:<br>Operating Expenses<br><br>Selling/Distribution Cost<br><br>Administrative Expenses<br><br>Finance Charges | Total Operating Expenses ÷ Sales<br>Selling & Distribution Expenses ÷ Sales<br>Administrative Expenses ÷ Sales<br>Finance Charges ÷ Sales | Only four ratios are shown and focus on the performance of the company in terms of the proportion of each particular expense to sales. Other ratios may include any other expense item. These ratios provide a view of the company's cost structure. |

Table 5.1b Financial Ratios (KPIs) by Application Category (Continued)

| Financial Ratio | Formulae | Remarks |
|---|---|---|
| **Asset Utilisation:** | | |
| Sales to Net Assets | Sales ÷ Net Assets<br>Where: Net assets = Total Assets − Total Liabilities. | Unless the firm is over trading, a high ratio is a healthy indication.<br>A low ratio may indicate unused capacity, especially if accompanied with a high ratio of fixed overheads to sales. |
| Sales to Fixed Assets | Sales ÷ Net Fixed Assets<br>Where: Net Fixed Assets = Purchase price − Depreciation + Leasehold Improvements − Total Liabilities. | Measures the utilisation of fixed assets. A low ratio may suggest ineffective use of fixed assets. However, this may also be due to recent fixed capital investment. One may consider using the book value of the fixed assets for net fixed assets. |
| Stock Turnover (days) | (Average Stock ÷ Cost of Sales) X 365 days | Shows the number of days stock held before it is sold.<br>Average Stock = (Opening Stock + Closing Stock) ÷ 2 |
| Trade Credit Given (days) | (Average Debtors ÷ Sales) X 365 days | Measures the collection period in days of debtors.<br>Average Debtors = (Opening Debtors + Closing Debtors) ÷ 2 |
| Trade Credit Taken (days) | (Average Creditors ÷ Purchase) X 365 days | Measures the payment period in days of creditors.<br>Average Creditors = (Opening Creditors + Closing Creditors) ÷ 2 |
| Cash Cycle Duration (days) | Stock Turnover + Credit Period Given − Credit Period Taken | Measures the period of time between the purchase of stocks and receipt of cash from debtors for goods sold. |

(Continued)

Table 5.1b  (Continued)

| Financial Ratio | Formulae | Remarks |
|---|---|---|
| **Capital Structure:** | | |
| Equity to Total assets | (Capital + Reserves) ÷ Total Assets | Shows the percentage of total assets financed by the shareholders. |
| Fixed Assets to Equity | Net Fixed Assets ÷ (Capital + Reserves) | Shows the percentage of fixed assets financed by the shareholders. |
| Borrowing to Equity | (Long Term Liabilities + Current Liabilities) ÷ (Capital + Reserves) | Shows the proportion of external financing versus internal financing. |
| Gearing Ratio | Long Term Liabilities ÷ (Capital + Reserves) | Measures financial leverage, demonstrating the degree to which a firm's activities are funded by owner's funds versus creditor's funds. |
| Fixed Interest Cover | Net Profit Before Interest ÷ Fixed Interest Expense | Indicates how easily a firm can pay interest on outstanding debt. |

Table 5.1c  Financial Ratios (KPIs) by Application Category (Continued)

| Financial Ratio | Formulae | Remarks |
|---|---|---|
| **Investment:** | | |
| Net Asset Value per Share | Net Assets ÷ No. of Ordinary Shares<br>Where: Net assets = Total Assets − Total Liabilities. | Represents the value of a share and may be viewed as the price at which shares are bought and sold. |
| Dividend Yield | Dividend per Share ÷ Market Price per Share. | Measures the real rate of return on an investment since it is based on the market price and not the nominal value. |
| Earnings per Share | Net Profit After Tax ÷ No. of Ordinary Shares | Indicates level of profitability, but it is limited when compared to dividend yield since number of shares remain constant. |
| Price Earnings Ratio | Market Price per Share ÷ Earnings per Share | The lower the price earnings ratio, the quicker the capital outlay is recovered. |
| Dividend Cover | Net Profit After Tax ÷ Net Dividend | It shows the amount available for distribution and demonstrates the plough back and dividend distribution policies of the company. |

of the organisation's supply chain. Non-financial KPIs are not expressed as monetary values but focus on various other aspects of the organisation. However, this does not mean that these KPIs cannot be expressed in numeric terms. In fact, they may measure either quantitative or qualitative properties of the organisation. For instance, many organisations view their employees' 'soft skills' as significant contributors to non-financial performance that may be measured in several ways. These 'soft skills' refer to the personal attributes that enable someone to interact effectively and harmoniously with other people, such as leadership, teamwork, communications, problem solving, flexibility, and interpersonal skills. Additionally, non-financial KPIs are often forward-looking (leading) measures, whereas financial KPIs tend to be backward-looking (lagging) measures.

There are two main reasons why non-financial performance measures are important. Firstly, these measures help to explain and provide background support for financial KPIs. Financial KPIs are historical and therefore backward-looking (i.e., lagging measures); this facilitates their collectability and subsequent analysis. Hence, they report what has already happened, such as turnover for a specified period. However, financial data does not present the full picture. For example, financial data does not explain why certain events occur, such as the reason for a drop in profit in a particular month. But non-financial performance measures can provide additional information about the reason for the fall or increase in sales turnover. For example, if the advertising time was reduced or increased in a specific period, one would expect this to affect the sales turnover for that or the subsequent period.

Secondly, there may be several strategic objectives that are expressed in non-financial terms, making it simpler for non-financial KPIs to be directly associated with these types of strategic objectives. For example, if the organisation's mission emphasises the provision of the best customer service in the industry, profit or cost figures will not address this. However, a customer satisfaction survey will provide the appropriate scores for an assessment to be made in this regard. Tracking non-financial performance measures is important because they often denote the strengths and weaknesses of the organisation. For example, if one of the organisation's strategic objectives is service excellence to customers, the non-financial KPI through a customer survey will highlight the degree to which the customer service times are acceptable. Hence, such surveys provide measures that can help bring to light the organisation's core competencies and draw attention to failing areas that management was not aware of.

Non-financial KPIs can highlight the impact of certain events on business performance. The performance level of an organisation will eventually reveal itself in its level of profitability. Non-financial KPIs can provide sufficient information to reveal the root cause for this level of profitability (i.e., over or underperformance level). For example, a high employee turnover rate is likely to have a negative impact on recruiting costs and other related HR costs. Furthermore, customer service costs are likely to increase due to the learning curve of the new recruits. Non-financial KPIs can provide a better means for employees to give their feedback on how to achieve the strategic objectives. Information regarding KPIs related to employee turnover, late attendance, sick leave, and absenteeism allow employees to clearly know what is required from them to achieve their goals and learn to appreciate the impact these KPIs have on productivity. Hence, there is a clear link between the day-to-day events and the defined strategic direction. The above illustrates that it is important for an organisation to have a balanced mixture of financial and non-financial KPIs that support each other and specifically address certain aspects of the organisation's strategy.

### Suggested Financial and Non-Financial Strategic KPIs

As explained previously, KPIs are meant to measure organisational performance and help management to identify certain aspects that require improvement in the organisation's operations. As Table 5.1 illustrates, there are many KPIs that may be used to ensure that the defined strategy is implemented as planned. KPIs provide the direct evidence about the financial health of the organisation, the intensity of its status to undertake growth initiatives, and its ability to execute its strategic plans to achieve the defined goals and objectives. Figure 5.2 shows that there are various categories of KPIs that may be applied, including asset utilisation, profitability, liquidity, capital structure, and investment.

Recall that our current focus is the strategic level (i.e., the big picture). Hence, it is necessary to decide and select those key indicators that address the big-picture strategic planning for the future direction of the organisation. Subsequent sections of this chapter will deal with KPIs at the various hierarchical levels of the organisation to provide a complete picture of the performance management and measurement framework. Therefore, the issue at this stage is to address how to evaluate the success or otherwise of the organisational strategic planning implementation process. Remember that success and failure are always dependent on hard metrics, but it is important to realise that focusing on the essential indicators will determine whether a strategy is successful. However, each organisation has its unique features and therefore different KPIs may be important for a specific organisation. As a rule, it is suggested that the following financial KPIs are given special consideration:

(a) Working Capital: This measure represents the cash that is readily accessible to the organisation. It is computed by subtracting the organisation's financial liabilities from its current assets. Working capital includes short-term investments, cash, account receivables (debtors), accounts payable (creditors), loans, and expenses accrued. The working capital value indicates the financial position of the organisation, as exhibited by its current ability to meet short-term financial commitments with available operating funds. A low Working Capital amount suggests that the organisation has difficulties meeting its cash outlays, such as loan payments. A range of 1.2 to 2.0 is viewed as a healthy working capital ratio. However, if it decreases below 1.0 the organisation is in a risky zone, known as negative working capital. With more liabilities than assets, the organisation would have to sell its current assets to pay off the liabilities.

(b) Current Ratio: The current ratio is computed by dividing the organisation's total assets by its total liabilities to provide the proportion of the organisation's financial assets to its liabilities. This KPI discloses the extent to which the organisation is consistently able to cover its financial commitments when due and maintain the level of credit status necessary to acquire funding to achieve its strategic growth initiatives. Hence, the organisation would need to limit its financial liability to bring it to a level that is satisfactory to creditors and attractive to potential investors. Whether the organisation has a 'good' current ratio is dependent on the industry type. Often a current ratio between 1.5 and 3 is considered satisfactory. However, various investors or creditors may look for a slightly higher figure.

(c) Debt to Equity Ratio: This measures the organisation's profitability through the successful management of funds for the organisation's growth through the application of the shareholder's investments. This ratio is computed by dividing the organisation's total liabilities by the total of its shareholder equity (net worth) to reveal the amount of debt that has accumulated in developing a profitable organisation. A high debt-to-equity ratio suggests that an organisation has higher debt, while a lower debt-to-equity ratio signifies fewer debts. Generally, a good debt-to-equity ratio is less than 1.0, while a risky debt-to-equity ratio is greater than 2.0. An excessive debt ratio indicates a dependence on accumulating debt to fund growth. This may require the organisation to fund its growth through equity rather than borrowing.

(d) Operating Cash Flow: This measure reflects the organisation's capacity to pay its day-to-day operational expenses, such as utilities, materials, and supplies. This measure is computed by calculating the total operating income, adding back depreciation, and subtracting taxes, and adjusted for any changes to the amount of working capital. Operating cash flow (OCF) measures the amount of cash generated by an organisation's normal business operations. Operating cash flow indicates whether an organisation can generate sufficient positive cash flow to sustain and grow its operations; otherwise, it may require external financing for capital expansion. A ratio greater than 1.0 is preferred by investors, creditors, and analysts, since it means that an organisation can cover its current short-term liabilities and still have earnings left over. Organisations with a high or up-trending operating cash flow are generally considered to be in good financial health. Therefore, this KPI indicates the organisation's performance in generating enough cash to cover capital investments to grow the business. The KPI helps management to decide on new capital investment, as part of its growth strategy by assessing the percentage of the organisation's total employed capital (i.e., operating cash). This KPI reveals the financial strength of the organisation. This indicator may be strengthened to support management's growth plans by adjusting the budget and tightening operating expenditure controls.

(e) Customer Acquisition Cost to Lifetime Value: This measures the total of marketing and sales costs required in gaining a customer. This measure is computed by dividing the total cost of sales and marketing for an accounting period, by the total number of customers gained by the organisation during that period. This KPI evaluates the efficiency of the organisation's sales and marketing procedures and measures the organisation's commercial investment value. The Lifetime Value is the value that the organisation's customers are individually generating to the business, on average, over the total period that they continue doing business with the organisation. Additionally, the Customer Lifetime Value to Customer Acquisition (LTV:CAC) ratio measures the relationship between the lifetime value of a customer, and the cost of acquiring that customer. Where: LTV:CAC Ratio equals:

[(Revenue per Customer − Direct Expenses per Customer) ÷ (1 − Customer Retention Rate)] ÷ (No. of Customers Acquired ÷ Direct Marketing Spending).

If the LTV:CAC ratio is less than 1.0, the organisation is destroying value, and if the ratio is greater than 1.0, it may be creating value, but more analysis is required. LTV:CAC ratio of 2 suggests that the organisation is profiting 100% on its total sales and marketing investment. Generally, a ratio greater than 3.0 is considered a good indicator of likely long-term profitability, but this may not necessarily be the case. This KPI may be improved through the enhancement of the sales process and operations management by adjusting prices, customer services, quality processes, and other areas of the sales process and operations management.

(f) Inventory Turnover: This KPI provides the average inventory amount sold by the organisation in an accounting period. This KPI quantifies the organisation's success in selling its products, which results in the movement of inventory and the efficiency rates of the organisation's production system. This measure is calculated by dividing the total sales for an accounting period by the average amount of inventory in that period. It therefore measures the amount of inventory turnover that is occurring as the inventory is continuously moving in and out from the production areas and warehouses. A good inventory turnover ratio is between 5 and 10 for most industries, which indicates that the organisation is selling and restocking its inventory every 1 to 2 months. This strikes a good balance between having enough inventory on hand and not having to reorder too frequently. To improve this KPI one needs to examine the root causes for the sales order cancellation rates, order processing concerns, production workflows bottlenecks, and potential difficulties in warehouse systems, materials ordering processes, backlog management, and other critical processes.

(g) Return on Equity (ROE): This reveals the amount of the organisation's wealth, when compared with the net income the organisation is generating for its shareholders. This KPI is calculated by dividing the organisation's net income by the organisation's total of shareholders' equity. The ROE shows whether the net income for the organisation is sufficient for the magnitude of the total investment shareholders have poured into the organisation. The ROE ratio indicates the organisation's profitability and general management efficiency. As with return on capital, an ROE is a measure of management's ability to generate income from the equity available to it. An ROE ration of 15% to 20% is generally considered good in most industries. An improvement in the ratio suggests that management is effective towards maximising the shareholders' returns. The ROE may be improved by adjustments to pricing policies, enhancing the revenue networks, eliminating those channels that generate low margins, reducing spending and any other changes across the entire range of KPIs.

The above are Financial KPIs that are highly applicable to the private sector. However, one must be aware that most public sector organisations adhere to accrual accounting principles through the International Public Sector Accounting Standards (IPSAS) and therefore these financial KPIs may also be adapted to the public sector. Figure 5.3 provides an example dashboard that illustrates how the various financial rations may be depicted to management. Figure 5.3 may be enhanced by using a colour scheme to show the safe, warning, and danger zones, thus making it more meaningful for management. The presented dashboard illustrates the adage that a picture is worth a thousand words.

As was stated previously, there are also important non-financial KPIs that need to be evaluated since they are useful in strategic planning and may be more department-specific. For example, a Customer Satisfaction indicator provides an indication of the organisation's long-term sustainability by measuring the customer retention rate. This type of KPI is applicable to both the private and public sectors. For example, in the education sector for high schools or colleges, typical KRAs (Key Resultant Areas), which are a short list of overall goals that guide an employee on how to conduct their function, include the following: Improve quality of instruction; improve efficiency for quality instruction; engage students with quality instruction; and do a better job of preparing students for college or a career. The

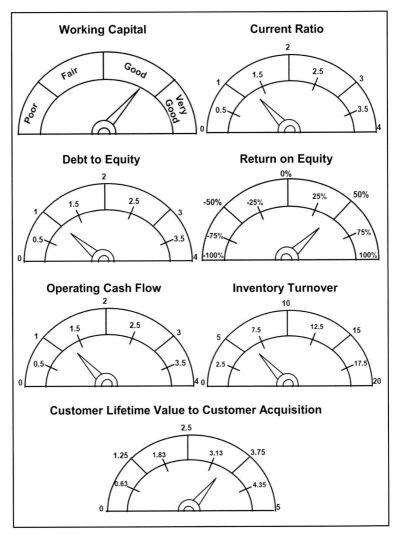

Figure 5.3  Example Dashboard for Financial KPIs Used in Private and Public Sector Organisations

associated KPIs for high schools or colleges would therefore include graduation rate; student daily attendance rate; student to faculty ratio; and cost per student.

In another example, typical KRAs for Customer Service Agents would include: Increase satisfaction levels with dissatisfied customers; and efficiently and appropriately handle customers' complaints. The resultant KPIs from these KRAs related to the Customer Service Agents would be: Customer satisfaction rates after engaging with Customers Service Agents; percentage of complaints resolved within an established time limit; percentage of completed call centre calls; average service response time for call centre calls; and average time to respond to email or other correspondence. Non-financial performance measures may generally be categorised under three key viewpoints in relation to strategic management as follows:

(a) Customer: Suggested KPIs under this category include:
   - *Conversion Rate*: The percentage number of customer contacts that result in a sale or service provision. The Conversion Rate KPI is calculated by dividing the Number of Customer Contacts with Completed Transactions by the Total Number of Sales or Service Provision Customer Contacts. For example, a conversion rate is the percentage of users who have completed a desired action and is calculated by taking the total number of users who 'convert' (e.g., by clicking on an advertisement), dividing it by the overall size of the audience and converting this figure into a percentage. The rating of the conversion rate depends on the application. However, generally a conversion rate of between 2% and 5% is considered average; 6% to 9% is considered above average; and anything over 10% is good.
   - *Retention Rate*: This is the percentage of existing customers who remain customers after a given period. The customer retention rate helps organisations to better understand what keeps customers with the organisation and may indicate opportunities to improve customer service. Generally, the better the customer retention rate, the more loyal the customers are. The Retention Rate KPI is calculated by dividing the Number of Customers Relinquish during a Given Period by the Total Number of Customers at the Start of a Given Period. Research shows that the current customer retention rates in the US average around 90% but vary by industry. Generally, an employee retention rate of 90% or higher is deemed good.
   - *Contact Volume by Channel*: The number of support requests by phone and email. This permits an organisation to compare which method customers prefer and to track the number of support requests month-to-month.

- *Customer Satisfaction Index*: This is an analytical tool for measuring customer satisfaction for a product, service, or an organisation. The data can be applied to help retain customers, transact more products and services, improve the quality and value of offers, and ensure a more efficient and economical operating environment. A six-point system is used to discover the customer satisfaction, meaning, contribution, and consent for a specific attribute. For example, the respondents may be asked to rate: 'How are you satisfied with the price/performance ratio of a [*product*]?' A score of 1 is definitely 'yes' and a score of 6 is definitely 'no.' Hence, a score of 1 is given 100 points, a score of 2 is given 80 points, and so on, with a score of 6 being given 0 points. The interpretation is as follows: A score of 0 to <70 is 'Below average satisfaction;' a score of 70 to 80 is 'Average satisfaction;' and a score of >80 is 'Above average satisfaction.'
- *Net Promoter Score*: The Net Promoter Score (NPS) measures customer experience and predicts business growth. It provides an indication of the likelihood that customers will recommend a brand or service to others. The NPS calculation is based on asking respondents one simple key question, namely: 'How likely is it that you would recommend [*brand or service*] to a friend or colleague?' The respondents, in answering this question, use a scale from 0 to 10. The respondents are then classified as follows: Promoters (score 9–10) are loyal enthusiasts who will keep buying (or use the service) and refer others, thus fuelling growth; Passives (score 7–8) are satisfied but unenthusiastic customers who are vulnerable to competitive or alternative offerings; Detractors (score 0–6) are unhappy customers who can damage your brand (or service provided) and impede growth through negative word-of-mouth. The NPS is calculated by subtracting the percentage of Detractors from the percentage of Promoters, which can range from a low of -100 (if every customer is a Detractor) to a high of 100 (if every customer is a Promoter). Hence, NPS = (Number of Promoters) - (Number of Detractors).

Figure 5.4 provides an example dashboard that illustrates how the various non-financial KPIs related to the customer may be depicted to management. The presented dashboard provides a simple but clear indication of the relationship between the customer and the organisation.

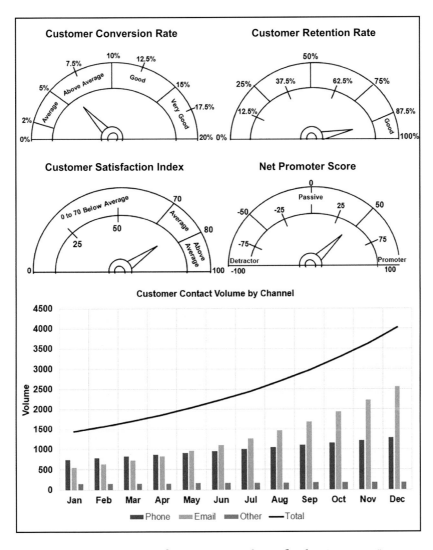

Figure 5.4  Example Dashboard for Non-Financial KPIs for the Customer Category

(b) Operations (i.e., internal processes): Suggested KPIs under this category include:

- *Customer Support Tickets*: A customer support ticket approach maintains a formal and certified record of a customer's request, including its current stage of progress, internal notes, and other context information regarding the issue. Hence, every ticket that is inputted into the system has a unique tracking number, enabling support agents to quickly locate, add information, or communicate a customer's request status. Moreover, in an omnichannel ticketing system, which is a multichannel approach to sales that focus on providing seamless customer experience whether the client is shopping online from a mobile device, a laptop or in a brick-and-mortar store, a ticket contains a complete flow of emails, chat messages, calls, or messages from other communication channels about the same issue reported by a customer. The Customer Support Tickets measure maintains a record of the number of new tickets, the number of resolved tickets, and resolution time. This enables the KPI 'Product Defect Percentage' to be calculated, which gives management the percentage of defective products in a specified timeframe. This KPI may be calculated by dividing the Number of Defective Units in a Specific Period by the Total Number of Units Produced in a Specific Period to give Product Defect Percentage. A Product Defect Percentage rate of 1% is considered as good. But this depends on the type of industry the organisation belongs to.

- *On-Time Rate*: This KPI measures the percentage of time products were delivered promptly as scheduled. This KPI is calculated by dividing the Number of On-Time Units in a Specific Period by the Total Number of Units Shipped in a Specific Period. A higher percentage the better.

- *Efficiency Rate*: The efficiency KPI is measured differently in every industry and is highly dependent on the nature of the work being performed. If a manufacturing environment is assumed, the efficiency rate may be computed by recording the number of units produced every hour and the machinery uptime percentage. The higher the calculated values the better.

- *Overdue Project Percentage*: This measures the number of projects that are late or behind schedule. This KPI may be calculated by dividing the Number of Overdue Projects in a Specific Period by the Total Number of Projects in a Specific Period. The lower the percentage the better.

Figure 5.5 provides an example dashboard that illustrates how the various non-financial KPIs related to the operations category may be depicted. The

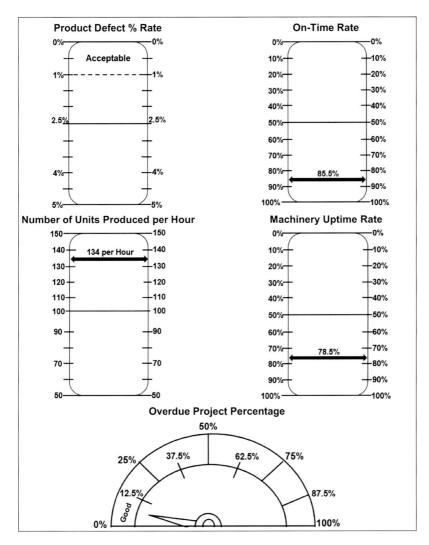

Figure 5.5  Example Dashboard for Non-Financial KPIs for the Operations Category

presented dashboard provides a simple but clear indication of the effectiveness of the organisation's operations environment.

(c)  Human Resources (i.e., learning and growth): Suggested KPIs under this category include:
  •  *Salary Competitiveness Ratio (SCR)*: SCR measures the extent that the current salary being offered by the organisation for specific job

roles is competitive when compared with the salary offered by competitors or the industry average. Hence, salary competitiveness can be measured against specific competitors or against the general market. SCR can be calculated by the following formulae: SCR = (Average Company Salary) ÷ (Average Salary Offered from Competitors [or Average Salary Offered by Industry]). The organisation should aim to offer employees a competitive salary of between 5% to 10% above the industry averages.

- *Employee Productivity Rate*: This KPI measures workforce efficiency over time and provides the organisation with a clear view of who is doing their job and who is not. The Employee Productivity Rate (EPR) may be computed by dividing the Total Organisation Revenue by the Total Number of Employees. A common cause of a decreasing EPR is overworking the employees to the point that they simply cannot come to work well-rested. Another cause for a decrease is neglecting to praise employees and tell them that they are doing a good job. Generally, the average worker productivity rating is 60% or less each day. However, the productivity rating for office workers drops significantly.

- *Turnover Rate for Highest Performers*: This KPI measures the success of the retention efforts to hold on to top performers and the plans for talent replacement. This measure is normally computed annually or at any given time when the HR team fails to retain its valuable human assets. Generally, research studies have shown that the loss to an entity when an employee leaves the organisation is about five times the employee's salary. The High Performer Turnover Rate is calculated by dividing the Number of High Performers Who Departed in Past Year by the Total High Performers Identified in the organisation. Research studies reveal that the turnover rate should be 0%, but at times even a 3% rate is acceptable. However, it depends on the industry type. For example, in the USA, the highest turnover rate for the highest performers is in the health and care sector, which is 18% for all institutions. It is suggested that an organisation calculates its Turnover Rate for Highest Performers and compares the result to other organisations in the same sector of expertise. This will help to possibly identify what is causing the situation.

- *Average Time to Hire*: This KPI measures the efficiency of the hiring process of an organisation in relation to the time to recruit, interview, and hire. The Average Time to Hire depends on the industry type. For instance, research shows that Construction, = 12.7 days; Leisure and Hospitality = 20.7 days; Wholesale and Retail = 24.6 days; Manufacturing = 30.7 days; and Government = 40.9 days. The organisation should calculate its Average Time to Hire and compare this with other organisations in the same sector of expertise. If the hiring process is too short (i.e., fast hiring), the organisation might not screen candidates thoroughly enough and risk making bad hires. On the other hand, slow hiring could result in competitors securing the best candidates. The objective is to speed up administrative tasks and streamline communication to candidates.
- *Internal Promotion Rate*: This measures the opened positions in an organisation that are filled internally by selecting the best talent to fill vacant positions. This process aids organisations to assess the internal talent's capability to satisfy different roles. The Internal Promotion Rate is viewed as measuring the successful retention and growth of top performers and is calculated by dividing the Number of Promoted Individuals by the Total Number of Employees. Generally, research suggests that organisations promote 8.9% of employees internally, while new recruits are typically at 30.2%. At the supervisory levels, organisations promoted more internally than they hired externally (17.2% of managers are promoted, while 15.6% are new hires).

Figure 5.6 provides an example of the HR dashboard. The presented dashboard provides a simple but clear indication of the effectiveness of the organisation's employee retention and recruitment process.

There are many more KPIs that may be shown. However, it is important to be selective and only the key ones should be displayed, otherwise the system will become unwieldy. One should note that management must track those non-financial performance measures that best fit the organisation's needs. There are literally hundreds of KPIs to choose from, so focus on the ones that make the most substance for your organisation's strategy.

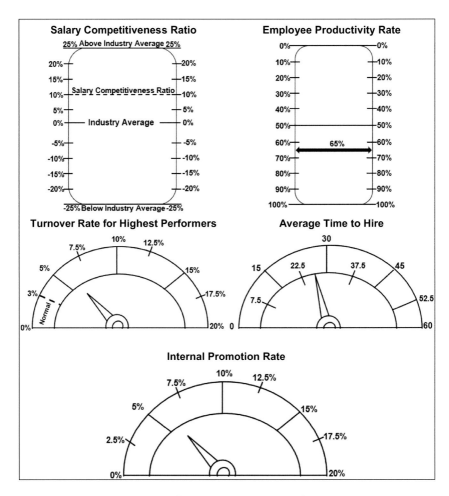

Figure 5.6 Example Dashboard for Non-Financial KPIs for the Human Resources Category

## Business Planning as a Performance Management Tool

In the previous section it was stressed that having a strategic plan is fundamental for ensuring an acceptable organisational performance level. It was also illustrated that a business plan and the associated budget was a short-term segment of the strategic plan. Therefore, having a budgetary process in place is viewed as the most effective way of keeping the organisation's business operations and its related finances on target. The focus of this section is to discuss the KPIs that are necessary at the business planning level. However, before discussing this it is important to provide an outline of the significance of budgets and business planning, and briefly explain how to go about defining them. It is contended that having various action points help management to administer the organisation's financial position more effectively and ensure that the generated business plans are practical and measure the organisation's business performance.

The business plan and the related budget act as a short-term roadmap for the future development of the organisation. It defines the organisation's business domain, its objectives, its financial forecasts, and its market. Hence, the strategic plan takes a holistic approach and views things from a higher level, whilst a business plan and its associate budget focus on the lower levels of the organisation to help management secure external finance, measure its success, and ensure sufficient business growth. Moreover, budgeting can be the most useful approach for controlling expenditure and cash flow, and permit management to invest in new opportunities at the appropriate time. Fundamentally, a budget is a financial plan to enable management to control finances, ensure the organisation can continue to fund its current commitments, enable management to make financial decisions and meet its objectives with a high degree of confidence, and ensure the organisation has sufficient cash to fund future projects. So basically, the budget provides a framework that shows how and on what the organisation will consume its available funds.

In a practical sense, a budget is not a forecast, because a forecast is a projection of the future, whereas a budget is a planned outcome that the organisation desires to achieve. The organisation's business budget generates several benefits, such as enabling management to oversee the organisation's money effectively; allocating appropriate resources to projects; monitoring financial performance and meeting the defined objectives; enhancing the decision-making process; anticipating and resolving difficulties before they occur; planning future activities; and improving the motivation of employees. Budgeting improves business growth because it enables management to:

1. *Understand the organisation's present cash flow*: Budgeting helps management to know in real terms its cash flow position, whether it can meet current obligations, determine the impact of engaging new employees, and ascertain whether it has sufficient cash reserves to withstand a

decline or disruption in the organisation's operations. Understanding the organisation's cash flow position enables management to consider investment opportunities and/or make long-term commitments to undertake its business transactions.

2. *Manage risk and establish how to strategically handle financial issues*: Budgeting helps management to protect the organisation's investment by identifying debt commitments and expenditures. It also assists management to plan for financial disruptions, such as a decrease in revenue, increasing costs, or logistics concerns affecting the delivery of materials.

3. *Remain on track in relation to short-term and long-term business goals*: A financial plan helps management to organise future operational activities for the year ahead. Having such a plan enables management to review progress and adjust on a periodic basis to ensure that targets are achieved. The resultant plan also provides management with an understanding of the underlying issues as an added input to decision-making and to identify the metrics that measure organisational success.

4. *Be future oriented*: Budgeting helps management to be forward-looking, mapping out the revenue and expenditures that are likely to be achieved in the short-term future. This may include ascertaining sales trends and targets, prioritising disbursements, defining a tax plan, and increasing the organisation's cash reserves to help it during difficult times.

5. *Evaluate the attained achievement*: A well-defined budget permits an organisation to monitor its progress and help management identify those actions that are giving the desired (or undesirable) results. A budget consists of quantifiable data that helps management to measure performance against expectations.

### *Defining the Budget for the Organisation*

As explained previously, generating, monitoring, and managing a budget is essential for organisational success. However, it is important to view the budget (and its associated process) as a key supporting pillar for the overall organisational strategy. Hence, the annual budget must be seen as a short-term segment of the organisational strategy. This point cannot be stressed enough. Budgeting is a fairly simple process that facilitates the allocation of resources where they are required most in the organisation as defined by the overall strategy with the aim of achieving the strategic objectives. An individual annual budget cannot be viewed in isolation; thus, a series of annual budgets contributes to the achievement of the overall organisational strategy, which is the long-term plan that defines the long-term strategic direction of the organisation. Moreover, the budgeting process may be viewed as an adjusting mechanism for the overall organisational strategy, since strategies are not cast in stone and must be modified according to circumstances and the outcomes being achieved.

The budget must reflect the strategic objectives by allocating what the organisation is likely to earn and spend to ensure that they contribute towards the achievement of the defined strategic objectives. Therefore, it should be recognised that budgeting is not merely an accounting exercise but has a much wider purpose and impact. Often organisations commence the budget process about two to three months before the start of a new financial year by firstly reviewing the overall organisational strategy and updating the business plan. Once the strategic review and business planning is completed, the budget team will determine the projected sales (or services) for the budget period based upon each individual product and/or service. The projected sales (and services) must be realistic and evidence-based, otherwise problems will arise at the implementation stage.

Next, the direct costs of the sales and/or services must be determined in terms of materials, components, subcontractors, and any other cost elements that are required to make the product or supply the service based upon each individual product and/or service. The next and final stage is to determine the fixed costs (or overheads). These fixed costs (or overheads) must be determined by type, such as:

(a) Cost of premises, including rent or loan payment, maintenance, insurance, and service charges.
(b) Employee costs, including salary, benefits, bonuses, National Insurance, other insurances.
(c) Utilities, including water and electricity, telephone, and internet connection.
(d) Software licences.
(e) Postage and stationery.

(f) Vehicle expenses, including fuel, service and maintenance, road licence, and insurance.
(g) Equipment costs, including service and maintenance.
(h) Advertising and promotion costs.
(i) Travel and subsistence costs.
(j) Legal and professional costs, including indemnity and other insurance.

The budget is segmented by the hierarchical organisation structure so that every division and department (and possibly unit) may be monitored. The budget will need to include every type of cost, including taxation and customs duties if any. A capital investment plan is also specified within the budget to allow for operational growth. The budgeting exercise must be completed by the start of the financial year so that its implementation may commence. Remember that the updated business plan reflecting the organisational strategy will facilitate the budgetary process when determining the projected sales, cost of sales, fixed costs, and overheads. Therefore, the budgetary process should be viewed as part of the business planning cycle. Also keep in mind that financial planning and the resultant budget is theory (i.e., what is expected to happen).

However, implementing the budget is reality (i.e., what is happening). The implementation of the budget is supported by the accounting system and needs to be constantly monitored and information collected to measure the established KPIs. This will enable management to know whether the organisation is operating according to the business plan and whether it is achieving its performance targets, and thus the strategic objectives. The full process allows management to examine the various costs and take action to reduce them, and it reveals whether the organisation is likely to have cash flow concerns. The budget process is an important tool for measuring organisational performance. It can provide information that support management decisions throughout the year and highlight how various costs and revenues are linked to each of the organisational activities. An important aspect of budgeting is that it may be used as a means of monitoring and controlling organisational activities using variance analysis, particularly if a standard cost approach is being utilised. This aspect will be addressed in more detail later in this chapter.

The budget can be used as a base line for measuring financial performance. By comparing the budget year on year, it can be used as an effective approach of benchmarking the organisation's performance. Furthermore, it is possible to compare projected margins and growth with those of other similar organisations in the same industry, or across different segments of the operational activities. KPIs may be applied to measure performance in different areas and to monitor the critical components that drive the organisation's activities. Since there are many factors that affect organisational performance, it is critical to focus on a handful of such factors and to monitor them very carefully. The three key performance drivers for most organisations are related to revenue generation, expenditure, and working capital.

These key performance drivers will in some way or other reflect the cash flow and profitability condition of the organisation. Therefore, deciding which KPIs to measure is important for having a successful performance management system. To be used as an effective performance tool, the budget must be continuously monitored and frequently evaluated and adjusted to ensure that in a practical sense the organisation is moving in the defined strategic direction. There is a need to analyse the reasons for any under or overperformance, to reveal what corrective action should be taken if underperforming or take advantage of opportunities being presented if overperforming. Analysing the variations will reveal the true reasons for current performance level and will assist management to navigate the organisation through the agreed roadmap (strategy) by refining the accuracy level of future budgets and permitting it to act when and where needed.

### Measuring Business Performance: KPIs for Budgeting and Forecasting at Departmental (or Responsibility Unit) Level

KPIs can provide organisations, irrespective of their size, with the ability to gain quick insights into their internal operations. KPIs for budgeting and business planning are very useful for monitoring and regulating the organisation's financial health and operational efficiency. As a rule, organisations with healthy KPIs are likely to meet all requisite liabilities and generate an acceptable level of revenue. Furthermore, it is important for management to understand and interpret the various financial KPIs that are available to be able to determine the performance rating of the organisation. KPIs for budgeting and forecasting are important because

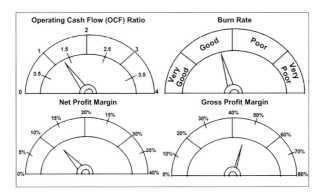

Figure 5.7 Example Dashboard for Financial KPIs for Cash Availability and Profitability Category

they indicate whether organisational departments or specific units are achieving the prerequisite targets for maintaining profitable operations. Some useful KPIs at a departmental level include the following (also refer to Figure 5.7 to Figure 5.13):

(a) *Operating Cash Flow (OCF)*: The OCF displays the total amount of earnings generated by a department or specific responsibility unit from its daily business operations. This KPI implies whether a segment (department or responsibility unit) of an organisation can sustain a healthy cash flow position required to take advantage of growth opportunities or needs external financing to deal with the outstanding expenses. In other words, OCF is a popular metric for assessing the department's (or responsibility unit's) ability to generate sufficient cash inflow through its business activities. OCF is calculated by two methods, namely the direct or indirect approach. For the direct method: OCF = Total Revenue − Operating Expenses and the indirect method, OCF = Net Income ± Changes in Assets and Liabilities + Non-Cash Expenses. The OCF ratio is calculated by dividing operating cash flow by current liabilities. Preferably, the OCF ratio should be close to 1:1, since a much smaller ratio suggests that the department or responsibility unit is obtaining a great deal of its cash flow from sources other than its core operating capabilities. It is suggested that OFC is contrasted to total capital employed (funds employed) to evaluate whether the department or responsibility unit generates sufficient capital to maintain positive

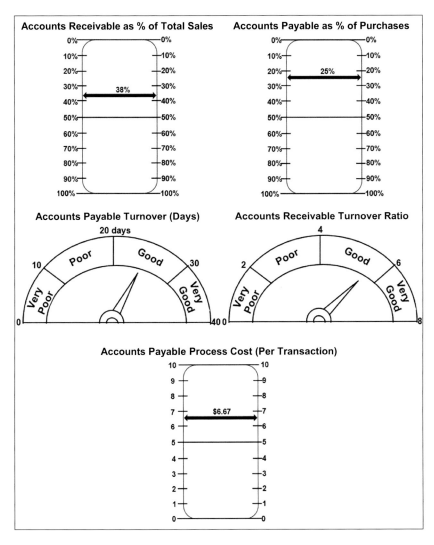

Figure 5.8  Example Dashboard for Financial KPIs for Cash Generation and Liquidity Category

accounts. Capital employed is the total amount of capital applied for the attainment of profits and is calculated by subtracting current liabilities from the summation of fixed assets and current assets.

(b) Burn Rate: This measure refers to the rate at which a department or responsibility unit consumes its cash cache in a loss-making scenario. This

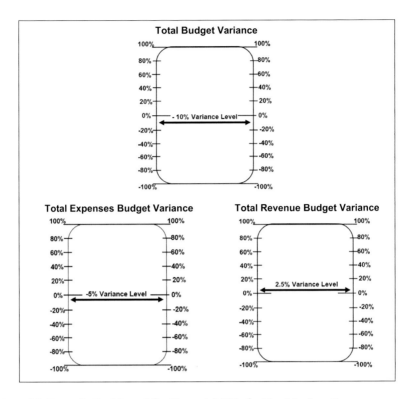

*Figure* 5.9  Example Dashboard for Financial KPIs for Total Budget Category

metric is used to assess the performance and valuation of organisations (departments or responsibility units), including start-ups. A start-up is often unable to generate net income in the early stages of its life cycle since it is normally focused on the growth of its customer base and enhancing its product or service line. Hence, a start-up is usually provided with seed money by investors or venture capitalists, but their funding needs to support the organisation's burn rate. When compared with Net Profit Margin and Revenue, the Burn Rate will reveal whether the organisation's operating costs are maintainable in the long-term. The Burn Rate may be expressed as Gross Burn Rate and/or Net Burn Rate. Gross Burn Rate is often calculated monthly by accumulating all the operating expenses, such as rent, salaries, and other overhead and is computed by dividing Cash (seed money) by the Monthly Operating Expenses. Basically, it highlights the cost drivers and efficiency, regardless of the revenue generated by the organisation under examination.

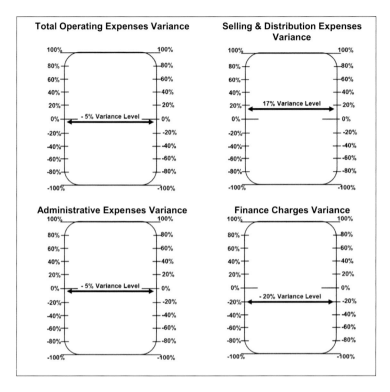

Figure 5.10 Example Dashboard for Financial KPIs for Budget Expenses Line Items Category

The Net Burn Rate is also calculated monthly and measures the rate at which an organisation is losing money. It is computed by dividing Cash (seed money) by Revenue less Operating Expenses (i.e., Net Burn Rate = Cash ÷ [Revenue - Operating Expenses]). The Net Burn Rate indicates how much cash an organisation requires to continue its operations for a specific period. A high burn rate indicates that the organisation under examination is consuming its cash supply at a fast rate, suggesting there is a high probability that it will be shortly in a state of financial distress. This implies that investors will likely be required to provide more cash and to grant more time for the organisation to increase its revenue and achieve profitability. Moreover, investors will also need to insistently establish definite goals for the organisation to achieve its revenue targets within agreed funding constraints. The Burn Rate may be mitigated by downsizing and pay cuts; achieving

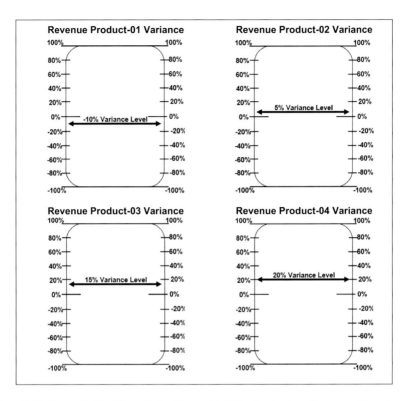

*Figure* 5.11  Example Dashboard for Financial KPIs for Budget Revenue Line Items Category

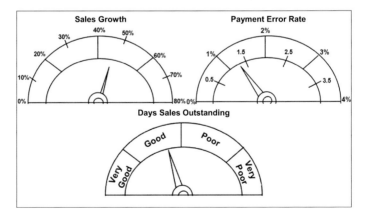

*Figure* 5.12  Example Dashboard for Financial KPIs for Sales of Products and Services Category

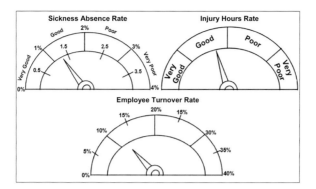

*Figure 5.13*  Example Dashboard for Non-Financial KPIs for Employee Characteristics
Category

growth and improving the economies of scale; and enhanced marketing to achieve growth and enhance the customer and/or product/
service base.

(c) *Net Profit Margin*: This metric measures how much net income or profit is
generated as a percentage of revenue and reveals the efficiency of the
organisation at generating profit compared to its revenue. Hence, this
is the ratio of net profits to revenues for an organisation or a segment
of the organisation. This KPI highlights how much of each currency
unit earned (e.g., dollar) by the organisation translates into profits and
is calculated by dividing the net profit by revenue. Thus, it reflects the
organisation's profitability and suggests the rate that the organisation
may grow in the long-term outlook. Generally, a net profit margin
greater than 10% is viewed as excellent; however, it depends on the
industry and the structure of the organisation being examined.

(d) *Gross Profit Margin*: This KPI measures the profitability of an organisation (or organisation segment) by revealing the amount of revenue
remaining in an accounting period after the organisation pays for the
cost of goods sold (i.e., labour and materials costs). The ratio indicates
the percentage of each currency unit (e.g., dollar) of revenue that the
organisation retains as gross profit. For example, if the ratio is calculated to be 25%, this means for every currency unit, such as a dollar of
revenue generated, $0.20 is retained, while $0.80 is attributed to the
cost of goods sold. This metric is a better indicator of an organisation's

financial health because it shows whether an organisation has the capacity of paying its operating expenses while having funds left for growth. This metric is calculated by dividing Cost of Goods Sold by Revenue. Hence, the higher the percentage, the more the organisation retains on each currency unit of sales to service its other costs and obligations. Typically, organisations have a somewhat stable Gross Profit Margin statistic unless the organisation has made several radical changes that affect production costs or pricing policies.

(e) *Current Accounts Receivable*: This KPI measures the amount of money owed to an organisation (or organisation segment) by its debtors. The Current Accounts Receivable metric facilitates the estimation of upcoming revenue and helps to plan cashflow in a timely and accurate manner. The Accounts Receivable are classified as an asset because they provide value to the organisation and refer to the money owed by the organisation's customers for goods or services they have received but not yet paid for. For example, purchases on credit by customers of goods and/or services is an amount that is added to accounts receivable. This metric helps management to calculate the average debtor days that indicates the average time for a debt to be paid. A high Current Accounts Receivable metric might suggest that the organisation is not efficient or competent in dealing with long-term debtors and is thus losing money. It should be noted that those individuals or entities that do not pay their invoices for goods and/or services received are in default.

(f) *Current Accounts Payable*: This is the reverse to the receivables. In other words, the Current Accounts Payable is an accounting entry that represents an organisation's obligation to pay off a short-term debt to its creditors. For example, electricity, telephone, and internet invoices, advertising, travel, entertainment, and office supplies or any other object that is purchased on credit are part of the Current Accounts Payable. Other examples include accrued expenses, such as logistics, licensing, leasing, raw material procurement, and job work. The Current Accounts Payable metric shows the amount of money that an organisation owes to suppliers, banks, and creditors and can be categorised by departments, divisions, responsibility units, and projects, thus providing a more detailed overview of the current payables. Current Accounts Payable is calculated by summating all liabilities that must be paid in a particular time frame.

(g) *Accounts Payable Turnover*: This metric shows how many times an organisation pays off its accounts payable during a period. Hence, this KPI suggests the rate that an organisation pays its average payable amount to suppliers, banks, and other creditors. The accounts payable turnover ratio reflects the efficiency of an organisation at paying its suppliers and short-term debts. The higher the accounts payable turnover ratio is, the quicker the organisation is paying its debts. Days payable outstanding (DPO) of 15 means that on average, it takes the organisation 15 days to pay its suppliers. Typically, a high DPO is viewed as being favourable since it indicates that the organisation can apply cash (that would have gone to immediately paying suppliers) to other uses for an extended period. If the turnover ratio is decreasing when compared to previous periods, it might indicate that the organisation is having difficulty paying back its debt. On the other hand, if the turnover rate increases, it may indicate that the organisation is paying back its suppliers at a faster rate than beforehand. To calculate the Total Accounts Payable Turnover, firstly compute the average Accounts Payable (AP) by summating the value AP at the beginning of the period and the AP at the end of the period and dividing this total by 2. Secondly, divide the total purchases for the period by average AP (i.e., Total Accounts Payable Turnover = Total Purchases ÷ ((Beginning AP + Ending AP) ÷ 2)). For example, assume an organisation makes $8 million value of purchases for the month of January. Further assume that on 31 December the Accounts Payable were $650,000 and on 31 January the Accounts Payable were $680,000. This means that the Total Accounts Payable Turnover is equal to $8 million ÷ (($650,000 + $680,000) ÷ 2) = $8 million ÷ $665,000 = 12.03. Therefore, Average Accounts Payable Days = 365 ÷ Total Accounts Payable Turnover. Hence, 365 ÷ 12.03 = 30.34 days.

(h) *Accounts Payable Process Cost*: This KPI indicates the total cost of processing all payments and invoices in a specific accounting period. The total cost to process accounts payable includes labour, systems, outsourcing, overhead, and other miscellaneous process costs. This metric is calculated by dividing the total cost to process the accounts payable by the total number of invoices processed by the organisation in a specific accounting period (i.e., Total cost to process an account payable = total cost to process accounts payable ÷ total number of invoices). For example, if the total cost to process 1500 invoices is $100,000, then the total cost to process an account payable = $10,000 ÷ 1500 = $6.67 per account payable. This KPI provides an indicative measure of the organisation's ability to process the accounts payable efficiently. The accounts payable process cycle includes many activities that contribute to the processing cost, such as coding invoices with correct account and cost centre, invoicing data entry, authorising invoices, matching invoices to purchase orders, and posting for payments. Thus, the cost of processing an invoice may increase due to several critical factors, namely slow processing, matching errors, exception invoices that may require manual follow-ups, unauthorised purchases, dispatching payment before delivery, missing invoices, and double payments. Generally, the number of invoices that may be addressed by an employee will depend on the sophistication of the accounts payable application system module. However, the average employee working in the accounting department is likely to process about 4 to 6 invoices per hour, or about 30 to 40 per day.

(i) *Accounts Receivable Turnover:* This KPI reveals the organisation's effectiveness in collecting debts and extending credits. Having high accounts receivables means that the organisation is providing interest free credit instead of collecting what is owned to it quickly to fund its growth strategy. Accounts Receivable Turnover ratio suggests how many times the accounts receivables have been collected during an accounting period. Accounts Receivable Turnover is calculated by dividing the net value of credit sales during a given period by the average accounts receivable during the same period (i.e., Accounts Receivable Turnover = net value of credit sales ÷ average accounts receivable). For example, assume that an organisation had $80,000 in net credit sales for the year, with average accounts receivable of $20,000 for the same period. Hence, the accounts receivable turnover ratio would be equal to four ($80,000 ÷ $20,000 = 4). Thus, the higher the turnover, the faster the business is collecting its receivables and the less likely that the organisation is striving to collect debts and payments and is more likely to have liquidity for investing in growth and innovation. There is no general rule to assess a good accounts receivable turnover ratio for an organisation. One would need to compare it with the average turnover ratios for the organisation's industry. Hence, using the previous example, if the industry average was three, then the organisation with a value of four would be ahead of its peers. Generally, a higher accounts receivable turnover rate is better because it means that the organisation is receiving payment for debts quickly, which increases the organisation's cash flow and allows it to pay its debts. It also means that the organisation's debt collection methods are effective, and that the organisation has a high proportion of quality customers that pay their debts quickly. Moreover, a high receivables turnover ratio might also suggest that an organisation typically operates on a cash basis.

(j)  *Budget Variance*: This metric is a periodic measure applied by the public and private sectors at an organisational, department, or responsibility unit level to compute the difference between budgeted and actual figures for a particular accounting category. It can also be utilised as a project management KPI to reveal how projected budgets differ in comparison to actual budget totals, thus assessing whether the baseline values of expenses or revenue have been achieved. A favourable budget variance is achieved when actual revenue is greater than the budget and/or when the actual cost is less than the budget. A budget variance is frequently caused by bad assumptions, optimistic estimates, poor leadership decisions or inappropriate budgeting, such as using politics to derive an unusually easy budget target. This means that the baseline against which actual results are measured is not realistic. Budget variance can be classified under two general categories, namely controllable or uncontrollable variances. Budget variances are controllable when the underlying costs and revenues are directly under the influence of management, such as working at overtime rates. On the other hand, uncontrollable budget variances occur when the underlying costs and revenues are not under the influence of management, such as expenses resulting from change in law (i.e., statutory wage increases) or industrial disputes, or higher material costs (i.e., price of steel). There is no definite figure as to what an acceptable variance is, since it all depends on the industry and specific circumstances (i.e., COVID-19). Many organisations view an acceptable variance (for revenue, expenses, and cash flow) as being ± 5% to 10%. However, for a well-defined construction project, the variances tolerance could range from ± 3% to 5% percent. In a research and development project, acceptable variances may increase to around ± 10% to 15%.

(k)  *Line Items in Budget*: A line item is an item listed in a budget, such as, salaries, materials and supplies, utilities (water and electricity), fuel, vehicle maintenance, and many others. A line item can be an item of revenue or expenditure in a budget or other financial statement or report. Line items can be expressed as a general description or be in detail. For example, revenue may be considered as a general level line item; however, this line item may be expressed in sub-line items by specific products or services. The same may be said for expenses. Furthermore, the categories of line items may be expressed at an organisational, departmental, sectional, and responsibility unit levels. Hence, line items in a budget assist managers and project leaders to monitor expenditures and revenue in a very detailed way to provide a better overview (or a detailed one if deemed necessary) of where the money is being earned and spent. Additionally, a detailed budget makes it easier for an organisation to address the appropriate departments and projects when implementing austerity measures. When combined with a standard costing-based system, these line items will provide a sophisticated method for variance analysis and for revealing the reasons for such variances to permit management to take timely and corrective action.

(1) *Sales Growth*: This metric measures the ability of the sales/service team to increase revenue over a fixed period by showing the change in total sales generated over a certain period. Hence, the Sales Growth provides the percentage of the current sales period compared to the previous one, giving the growth or decrease in total sales. The Sales Growth can be displayed by the individual (or group of) products or services within a specific segment of the organisation. However, most consider Sales Growth as a strategic indicator that may be applied by senior management (executives and the board of directors) in its decision making and greatly impacts the preparation and implementation of the organisation strategy. Sales growth is calculated by firstly subtracting the net sales of the prior period from that of the current period, and then dividing the result by the net sales of the prior period, and multiplying the result by 100 to get the percent sales growth (i.e., Sales growth = [(Net Sales for current period − Net Sales for prior period) ÷ Net sales of the prior period] X 100). Generally, growth rates depend on the industry type and organisation size. However, certain research literature suggests that a sales growth of 5% to 10% is normally seen as being acceptable for very large organisations, while sales growth of over 10% is more applicable to smaller organisations. Other research literature suggests that as a general benchmark, organisations should have on average between 15% and 45% of year-over-year growth, with

organisations of less than $2 million annually tending to have higher growth rates. Because sales growth discloses the increase in sales over a specific period, it provides an investor with an indication of whether the demand for the organisation's products and/or services will be increasing in the future.

(m) *Days Sales Outstanding (DSO)*: This metric provides the average number of days required for customers to pay an organisation (or segment of an organisation) from the date of receiving the invoice until the date the full payment is made. The DSO is related to the supply chain since it reflects a working capital ratio that quantifies the number of days that an organisation takes, on average, to collect its accounts receivable. The DSO is calculated by dividing the average accounts receivable during a given period by the total value of credit sales during the same period and multiplying the result by the number of days in the period being measured (i.e., DSO = [Total accounts receivable during a certain period ÷ Total value of credit sales for that period] x Number of days in period being assessed). The period used to measure DSO can be monthly, quarterly, or annually. The DSO measures the effectiveness of the organisation's payment collections process and keeps track of its cash flow but needs to be supplemented by other indicators for evaluating the organisation's performance or liquidity. The lower the DSO ratio, the more the organisation can focus on its growth and procuring additional supplies. An organisation with a high DSO is an indication of poor invoice management and/or challenging market conditions where customers are finding it difficult to pay their bills on time.

(n) *Payment Error Rate*: This KPI shows the percentage of incoming or outgoing payments that were not completed due to a processing error. If an organisation's Payment Error Rate increases over time, it may indicate that a business process reengineering exercise is required to review the payment processing system. Often, the reason for payment failures is a lack of authorisation, missing data or reference, and poor documentation. Research shows that most organisations reveal an average payment error rate of more than 1%, with some reporting between 2% to 4%. To mitigate the payment error rate the organisation needs to have a proper approval system in place to ensure that all purchases go through an approval method; have a central repository for all documents related to payments that groups transactions to reflect the organisation's structure, such as departments, budgets, workflow, products, and services;

introduce a three-way matching process for checking that the purchase order, shipping order, and invoice all have the same amounts (and reference) on them; and conduct frequent audits to ensure that procedures are being conducted correctly and to identify common mistakes and any spurious spending that may be taking place.

The above are financial KPIs that may be used at various levels of the organisation structure, such as department, section, responsibility unit, product, and service. It is also suggested that three non-financial KPIs are also used as follows:

(a) *Sickness Absence Rate*: This KPI would measure the percentage hours of sick leave taken in a specific period. Firstly, work out the total number of days/hours lost to sickness absence and divide this by the number that should have been worked (multiply result by 100 to calculate a sickness absence percentage). Therefore, the Sickness Absence Rate = Sick Leave Hours taken during a specific period ÷ Total possible working hours during a specific period. For example, assume that that a responsibility unit within the organisation has 5 employees working on a 40 hour per week basis and that 4 hours of sick leave have been reported during the week for this responsibility unit. Therefore, the Sickness Absence Rate = 4 hours reported sick leave ÷ (10 employees X 40 hours) = (4 ÷ 400) x 100 = 1%. Generally, a 1.5% absence rate is an acceptable rate. Illness is impossible to prevent 100% and taking 3 to 4 days per year off because of a severe cold or another ailment is fine. However, the Sickness Absence Rate depends on the industry the organisation belongs to. Therefore, it would be appropriate to compare the Sick Leave Rate with the industry average.

(b) *Injury Hours*: This refers to incidents that result in a disability or an employee missing work due to an injury. To calculate the lost time injury rate, divide the total number of lost time injuries (in a specified period) by the total number of hours worked (in that period) and multiply by 100.

(c) *Employee Turnover Rate*: This metric measures the percentage of employees who leave an organisation during a certain specified time. Organisations usually include voluntary resignations, dismissals, non-certifications, and retirements in their turnover calculations. Organisations should aim for 10% for an employee turnover rate. However, often the employee turnover rate is in the range of 12% to 20%. Note that certain industries report higher employee turnover rates because of the nature of the job. The immediate consequences of a high employee turnover rate are loss of valuable knowledge and experience, loss of morale for those employees left working in the organisation, and loss of confidence in the team's competence and ability to perform. The employee turnover rate is calculated by dividing the number of employee terminations during a specific period by the number of employees at the beginning of that period. For example, if at the start of the year there are 150 employees, and during the year, 5 people ceased their employment, the turnover is $5 \div 150 =$ approximately 0.03, or 3%.

The above KPIs will provide a comprehensive understanding of the way the organisation is performing and may suggest to management certain actions that need to be taken to improve the performance of the organisation or segment of the organisation. Note that for simplicity, management may need to restrict the number of KPIs that are reported.

## Standard Cost Systems and Variance Analysis as KPI Measuring Tools

Standard costs are viewed as predetermined costs, since they are target costs that should be incurred under efficient operating conditions. In other words, they are target costs for each operation that can be built up to produce a product standard cost. Since they are target costs, these costs can be viewed as KPIs for a specific activity. On the other hand, a budget relates to the cost for the total activity, whereas a standard relates to a cost per unit of activity. Therefore, by establishing standard costs for each unit produced, it is possible to analyse in detail any differences between budgeted costs and actual costs. This process is referred to as variance analysis and enables cost to be controlled more effectively, and the performance of a specific cost centre to be determined accurately.

Standard costing is most suited for organisations whose activities consist of a series of common or repetitive operations and the input required to produce each unit of output can be specified. Standard costing systems are most suited to manufacturing but are also applicable to service industries, such as banks, hospitality, public services, amongst many others. However, it is emphasised that they are not suited to activities that are of a non-repetitive nature. Hence, standard costing systems can be applied to organisations that produce many different products providing production consists of a series of common operations. Generally, the operation of a standard costing system consists of several specific processes.

Firstly, the standard costs for the actual output in a particular period are traced to the managers of responsibility centres, who are responsible for various operations. It should be noted that the actual costs are also charged to the responsibility centres. Secondly, the standard and actual costs are compared, and any variances are reported. Thirdly, all variances would be investigated to determine why they have occurred, and once a variance is investigated, corrective action is taken. Finally, standards are continually monitored and adjusted to reflect the actual process. It should be noted that if an operational process is changed in any way, then the standard must be reviewed to ensure it reflects the changed operational process.

A standard costing system has several objectives, namely it provides the expected future costs that can be applied for decision-making; thus, it is a very useful way of predicting costs related to estimating product or service quotations. It provides a demanding target that employees are motivated to achieve. Research suggests that having demanding goals is likely to motivate higher levels of performance rather than having no targets at all. A standard costing system assists in establishing budgets and evaluating managerial performance at a responsibility centre level. Thus, budgetary preparation time is considerably reduced if standard costs are available because the standard cost of operations may be accumulated to provide total costs of any budgeted volume and product mix. A standard costing system also acts as a cost control tool by highlighting those activities that do not conform to the designated plan. Hence, managers are alerted to those situations that may be 'out of control' and in need of corrective action.

Finally, a standard costing system simplifies the task of tracing costs to products to measure profit and inventory valuation. Since most firms prepare monthly internal profit statements, inventories and cost of goods sold are recorded at standard cost and converted to actual cost by writing off all variances arising during the period as a period cost. These objectives contribute to helping management to monitor and achieve higher performance levels.

As stated previously, standard costs may be used for inventory valuation and profit measurement by firstly maintaining the product costs at standard cost and recording the inventories and cost-of-goods-sold at standard cost. Converting these standard costs to actual cost is achieved by writing off all variances arising during the period as a period cost. It should be noted that the variances from the standard cost are extracted by comparing the actual with standard costs at responsibility centre level, and not at the product level. Hence, actual costs are not assigned to individual products.

### Variance Analysis as KPI Tools

It should be noted that with variance analysis, the KPIs are established when defining the standard cost for the product or service. Hence, variance analysis takes into consideration the KPIs contained in the standard cost card and compares them with the actual outcome. The variance being the difference between the actual and the established standard (KPI). However, variance analysis goes one step further by determining the likely reason for the difference (i.e., variance). This enables management to take the appropriate corrective action that will impact future activities.

Figure 5.14 provides a breakdown of the profit variance into component cost and revenue variances that can be calculated for a standard variable costing system. Typically, the profit variance is the difference between budgeted and actual profit. Figure 5.14 illustrates that the profit variance consists of

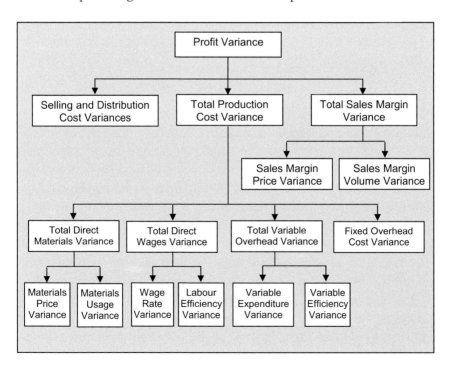

Figure 5.14  Variance Analysis for a Standard Variable Costing System by Category

three components, firstly the selling and distribution cost variances. These standards are only viable if the activities are repetitive and are calculated in a similar way to the production variances. However, if standards are not viable at this level, the costs are monitored and controlled by comparing the budgeted figures with the attained actual. The other two components are the total production cost variance and the total sales margin variance. Note that the total sales margin variance consists of two sub-components, namely, sales margin price variance and sales margin volume variance.

The total production cost variance is comprised of four sub-components, namely the total direct materials variance, the total direct wages variance, the total variable overhead variance, and the fixed overhead expenditure variance. Each of these sub-component variances consists of two further elements. For materials there is the material price and usage variances; for labour there is the wage rate and labour efficiency variances; and for the variable overhead variances there are the variable expenditure and variable efficiency variances. The fixed overhead expenditure variance has no sub-components under the marginal costing approach. However, it has several sub-components under absorption costing. The focus at this stage is the marginal costing approach, which assumes only variable costs as product costs.

### *Example: Standard Cost Approach Using Variance Analysis as KPI Tools*

To illustrate the standard cost approach using variance analysis as KPI Tools, it is best to take an example. Assume that a company manufactures a single product, which is known as Part-X and this product has a single operation. Furthermore, the company uses a marginal costing system for internal profit measurement purposes. The standard cost card for this operation is shown at Table 5.2. Note that normally a company would manufacture many products and each product would be made through several operations. Hence, the example being considered has a very simple structure. However, the principles are the same for a single product with a single operation as for a multi-product and multi-operation environment.

Further assume that the company plans to produce and sell 10,000 units of Part-X in the month of March. The annual budgeted fixed overheads are $1,920,000 and are assumed to be encountered evenly throughout the year

Table 5.2  Standard Cost Card for Part-X: Operation 1

| Standard Cost Card: Part-X Operation 1 (KPI Details) | $ |
|---|---|
| (a) Direct Materials: | |
| 2.5Kg of Material-A at $9.50 per Kg. | 23.75 |
| 1.25Kg of Material-B at $14.75 per Kg. | 18.44 |
| (b) Direct Labour (2.5 hours at $7.50per hour) | 18.75 |
| (c) Variable Overhead (2.5 hours at $1.80 per direct hour) | 4.50 |
| (d) Total Standard Variable Cost (a + b + c) | **65.44** |
| (e) Standard Contribution Margin (f − d) | **24.06** |
| (f) Standard Selling Price | **89.50** |

Table 5.3  Budgeted Costs Based on the Standard Cost Card for Part-X: Operation 1

| Budgeted Costs Based on Standard Cost for Part-X: Operation 1 | $ | $ | $ |
|---|---|---|---|
| (a) Sales (10,000 units at $89.50 per unit): | | | 895,000 |
| (b) Direct Materials: | | | |
| Material-A: 25,000 Kg at $9.50 per Kg. | 237,500 | | |
| Material-B: 12,000 Kg at $14.75 per Kg. | 184,375 | 421,875 | |
| (c) Direct Labour (25,000 hours at $7.50 per hour) | | 187,500 | |
| (d) Variable Overhead (25,000 hours at $1.80 per direct hour) | | 45,000 | 654,375 |
| **(e) Budgeted Contribution (a − d)** | | | **240,625** |
| **(f) Fixed Overheads ($1,920,000 ÷ 12 = $120,000)** | | | **160,000** |
| | | | 80,625 |

(i.e., $160,000 per month). The budgeted costs based on the information contained in the standard cost card are shown at Table 5.3. Moreover, the actual results for the month of March are shown at Table 5.4. Note that the manufacturing overheads are charged to production based on direct labour hours and that actual production and sales for the period were 9,750 units.

Table 5.4 Actual Costs and Profit for Part-X: Operation 1

| Actual Costs and Profit for Part-X: Operation 1 | $ | $ | $ |
|---|---|---|---|
| (a) Sales (9,750 units at $90 per unit): | | | 877,500 |
| (b)  Direct Materials: | | | |
| Material-A: 23,000 Kg at $9.75 per Kg. | 224,250 | | |
| Material-B: 11,500 Kg at $15 per Kg. | 172,500 | 396,750 | |
| (c) Direct Labour (23,000 hours at $7.65 per hour) | | 175,950 | |
| (d) Variable Overhead | | 54,000 | 626,700 |
| (e) Contribution (a − d) | | | 250,800 |
| (f) Fixed Overheads | | | 155,000 |
| (g) Profit (e − f) | | | 95,800 |

## Material Variances

The first step is to calculate the material variances. Note that the cost of materials used to manufacture the product is determined by two factors, namely the price paid for the materials and the quantity of materials used in production. However, actual cost may differ from the standard cost because the actual quantity of materials used may differ from the established standard quantity and/or the actual price paid may be different from the standard price. Therefore, there is need to calculate two variances, namely the material price variance and material usage variance:

(a) The Material Price Variance = (SP − AP) x QP where SP = Standard price; AP = Actual Price; QP = Quantity of material purchased.

For Material-A: Standard price Material-A is $9.50 per kg; actual price Material-A is $9.75 per kg; and amount of Material-A purchased is 23,000 kg. Therefore, Material-A price variance = (SP − AP) x QP.

Material-A price variance = ($9.50 − $9.75) x 23,000 kg = $5,750 A (adverse).

(b) For Material-B: Standard price Material-B is $14.75 per kg; actual price Material-B is $15 per kg; and amount of Material-B purchased is 11,500 kg. Therefore, Material-B price variance = (SP − AP) x QP.

Material-B price variance = ($14.75 − $15) x 11,500 kg = $2,875 A (adverse).

It is important that variances are reported as quickly as possible so that any inefficiencies are revealed, and corrective action taken by management.

However, a difficulty arises when material purchased in a period may be used in subsequent periods. For example, if 10,000 units of a material are purchased in Period-01 at a price of $1 per unit over standard and 2,000 units were used in each Period 01 to 05, the following two options may be used to calculate the price variance: (i) the full amount of 10,000 units is reported in Period-01 with the quantity being determined as the quantity purchased; and (ii) the price variance is computed with the quantity used. Hence, the unit price variance of $1 is multiplied by the quantity used (i.e., 2000 units), which would mean that a price variance of $2000 is reported for each Period 01 to 05. It is recommended that this approach is used so that the price variance is reported in the period in which it occurs and ensures that reporting total variance is not delayed until all the material is utilised, thus enabling corrective action to be taken earlier.

(c) The Material Usage Variance = $(SQ - AQ)$ x SP where SQ = Standard Quantity; AQ = Actual Quantity; and SP = Standard price of material.

For Material-A: Standard quantity Material-A is 24,375 kg usage (i.e., 2.5 kg x 9,750); actual quantity Material-A is 23,000 kg; and standard price Material-A is $9.50. Therefore, Material-A usage variance = $(SQ - AQ)$ x SP.

Material-A usage variance = $(24,375 - 23,000)$ x $9.50 = $13,062.50 F (favourable).

(d) For Material-B: Standard quantity Material-B is 12,187.5 kg usage (i.e., 1.25 kg x 9,750); actual quantity Material-B is 11,500 kg; and standard price Material-B is $14.75. Therefore, Material-B usage variance = $(SQ - AQ)$ x SP.

Material-A usage variance = $(12,187.5 - 11,500)$ x $14.75 = $10,140.63 F (favourable).

Material usage variance is under the full control of the responsibility centre manager. There are several reasons for adverse variance regarding material utilisation. These include procuring poor quality materials; irresponsible handling of materials by production employees; petty theft; modifying quality control specifications; and variations in production methods. Note that separate material usage variances must be computed for each material type used by each responsibility centre.

Another concern with material usage variance is identifying the responsibility centre that is accountable for the usage variation. Hence, the analysis of material variance into price and usage components is not entirely accurate because there may be a multiparty responsibility for the variance. For example, assume that for Material-A, 24,375 kg of a material are required (i.e., 2.5 kg x 9,750), at a standard price of $9.50 per kg and 23,000 kg are used, at a price of $9.75 per kg. The procurement staff may accept responsibility for the price variance of $0.25 for 24,375 kg but not for the 23,000 kg (extra 1375 kg). Hence, the usage variance of 1375 kg may be viewed as being the responsibility of the production foreman. This difficulty may be resolved by reporting a joint price/quantity variance of $343.75 (1375 kg @ $0.25) separately and not charge it to either responsibility centre. Therefore, the analysis of the original price variance would be as shown as Joint price/usage variance = $(SP - AP) \times (AQ - SQ)$, which would be ($9.50 - $9.75) x (23,000–24,375) = $343.75 F (favourable).

For Material-B the Joint price/usage variance = $(SP - AP) \times (AQ - SQ)$, which would be ($14.75- $15.00) x (11,500 − 12,187.5) = $171.88 F (favourable).

(e) Total Material Variance: The total material variance is the variance before it is analysed into the respective price and usage material variance and can be used to verify the overall calculations. Total material variance = SC − AC where: SC = standard material cost; and AC = Actual material cost.

Hence, for Material-A: SC = ($9.50 x 2.5 kg per unit) x 9750 units = $231,562.5; and AC = $224,250. Therefore, the Total Material-A variance = $231,562.5- $224,250 = **$7312.50 F**. This agrees with the price variance of $5750 A + usage variance of $13,062.50 F, which equals **$7312.50 F**.

Hence, for Material-B: SC = (€14.75 x 1.25 kg per unit) x 9750 units = $179,765.63; and AC = $172,500. Therefore, the Total Material-B variance = €179,765.63- €172,500 = **$7265.63 F**. This agrees with the price variance = $2875 A + usage variance of $10,140.63 F = **$7265.63 F**.

Note that if the price variance is calculated on the actual quantity purchased instead of actual quantity used, the price variance plus usage variance will agree with total variance only when the quantity purchased is equal to quantity used.

## Wage Rate and Labour Efficiency Variances

The next step is to calculate the wage rate and labour efficiency variances. The cost of labour is determined by two factors, namely the price paid for labour and the quantity of labour used in the production process. Like material variances, actual cost of labour may differ from the standard cost because the actual quantity of labour applied may differ from the established standard quantity due to likely inefficiencies in the production process; and/or the actual price paid may be different from the standard price due to likely wage increases. Therefore, two variances need to be calculated, namely the labour wage rate variance and the labour efficiency variance.

The wage rate variance can be calculated by the following equation: Wage Rate Variance = (SR − AR) x AH where SR is the standard wage rate per hour; AR is the actual wage rate; and AH is the actual number of hours worked. The wage rate variance is probably the least variance that is subject to control by management due to the statutory wage increases or wage increases due to industrial disputes. Continuing with the Part-X example for March, the variables for wage rate variance have the following values: SR is $7.50 per hour; AR is $7.65 per hour; and AH is 23,000 hours. Hence, the wage rate variance = ($7.50 − $7.65) x 23,000 hours = $3450 A.

The labour efficiency variance is equivalent to the quantity variance for direct labour. In other words, the quantity of labour that should be used for the actual output as expressed in terms of standard hours produced. Hence, the labour efficiency variance is equal to (SH − AH) x SR where SH is the standard labour hours for actual production; AH is the actual number of hours worked; and SR is the standard wage rate per hour. In this example, SH is 2.50 hours times 9750 units to give 24,375 standard hours; AH is equal to 23,000; and SR is $7.50 per hour. Therefore, the labour efficiency variance = (24,375 − 23,000) x $7.50 = $10,312.50 F. It should be noted that the labour efficiency variance is normally under the control of the production responsibility centre manager and is often caused by using inferior quality materials; having different grades of labour with varying experience levels; frequent breakdowns due to the failure of maintaining machinery in a proper condition; installing new equipment or tooling that require a learning process; and unreported alteration in the production process.

The total labour variance is the variance before it is divided into the wage rate and efficiency elements. Hence, total labour variance equals

SC − AC where SC is the standard labour cost and AC is the actual production labour cost. Hence, SC is \$7.5 x 2.5 hours X 9750 units giving \$182,812.50 and AC is \$175,950. Therefore, Total Labour Variance is equal to (\$182,812.50 − \$175,950) = **\$6862.50 F**. This agrees with the summation of the Wage Rate variance and Labour Efficiency variance (i.e., \$3450 A + \$10,312.50 F = **\$6862.50 F**).

### Variable Overhead Variances

The next group of variances to be calculated is the variable overhead variances. Generally, the variable overhead expenditure varies with direct labour and machine hours of input. The variable overheads are also determined by two factors, namely the price variance (i.e., actual overhead cost being different from budgeted cost) and the quantity variance result from actual direct labour or machine hours of input being different from the hours of input which have been used. Therefore, these two factors give rise to two sub-variances, the variable overhead expenditure variance and the variable overhead efficiency variance.

To calculate the variable overhead expenditure variance and therefore compare the actual overhead expenditure with the budgeted expenditure, it is necessary to flex the budget. A flexible budget varies with changes in the amount of actual revenue earned. Hence, in its basic form, the flexed budget will apply percentages of revenue for certain costs, rather than the usual fixed values, to provide a better method of comparing the budgeted and actual results. A flexible budget approach is required because the initial assumption given by the data was that the variable overheads will vary with direct labour hours of input. Hence, the budget is flexed on this basis.

The Variable Overhead Expenditure variance is calculated by BFVO − AVO where BFVO is the budgeted flexed variable overheads for the actual direct labour hours of input and AVO is the actual overhead costs incurred. AVO is \$54,000 resulting from 23,000 direct labour hours of input. Hence, at this level of activity, BFVO is 23,000 hours times \$1.80 to give \$48,400 (i.e., 23,000 hours are used and not 25,000 hours due to the flexed budget). Therefore, the Variable Overhead Expenditure variance is equal to \$41,400 minus \$54,000 to give \$12,600 A. Hence, if the budgeted and the actual overhead costs for 23,000 direct labour hours of input are compared, the efficiency content is eliminated from the variance. In other words, the difference can only be due to the actual variable overhead spending being different from the budgeted variable overhead spending.

Note that the variable overhead expenditure consists of a diverse number of individual cost items, such as, indirect labour (e.g., management supervision); indirect materials (e.g., grease and oil for machinery; cleaning fluids; and oil rags); electricity; and maintenance, amongst many others. The variable overhead expenditure variance occurs due to several reasons, namely, increase in the prices of individual overhead items; unproductive utilisation of the individual overhead items; and wasteful use of utilities, such as leaving lights on during lunch breaks. The variable overhead expenditure on its own is not very informative, but comparing the actual expenditure for each individual item of variable overhead expenditure against budget, one may reveal the cause of the variance and the corrective action that is required.

The other variance under this classification is the variable overhead efficiency variance. The variable overhead efficiency variance is calculated by the equation: (SH − AH) x SR where SH is the standard hours of output; AH is the actual hours of input for the period; and SR is the standard variable overhead rate. SH is 24,375 hours (i.e., 9750 units x 2.5 hours); AH is 23,000 hours to produce 9750 units; and SR is $1.80 per hour. Therefore, the Variable Overhead Efficiency variance is equal to (24,375 − 23,000) x $1.80 = $2475F. Like the labour efficiency variance, it is assumed that variable overheads will vary with the direct labour hours of input. Hence, the possible causes for the variable overhead efficiency variance are the same.

The total variable overhead variance is calculated like the material and labour variances. The total variable overhead variance is equal to SC minus AC where SC is the standard variable overheads charged to production; and AC is the actual variable overheads incurred. Therefore, SC is 9750 units x 2.50 Hrs x $1.80 per unit produced, which equals $43,875, and AC is equal to $54,000. Therefore, the Total Variable Overhead variance is $43,875 − $54,000, which is equal to $10,125 A.

## Other Variances

This section addresses other variances, such as fixed overhead expenditure variance and those variances related to sales, namely sales margin and sales volume. One needs to note that with a margin or variable costing system, fixed manufacturing overheads are not unitised and allocated to products but arc charged as an expense in the period in which they are incurred. Moreover, fixed costs are assumed to remain unchanged in the short-term in response to changes in the level of operational activity, but they may change in response to other factors. For instance, a price increase for indirect materials and labour may trigger an increase in fixed overheads costs.

The fixed overhead expenditure variance explains the difference between the budgeted fixed overhead costs and the actual fixed overheads incurred. Hence, Fixed Overhead Expenditure Variance is equal to BFO − AFO where BFO is the budgeted fixed overheads and AFO is the actual fixed overhead spending. In the example, BFO is $160,000 and AFO is $155,000. Therefore, the Fixed Overhead Expenditure variance is $160,000 minus $155,000 to give $5000 F. The fixed overhead expenditure variance on its own is not very informative. However, it becomes meaningful when one compares each item of fixed overhead expenditure against the budget. The differences may be due to a modification in the salaries paid to supervisors, such as an appointment (or promotion) of additional supervisors. Generally, fixed overhead expenditure tends to be uncontrollable in the short-term.

Sales variances are often applied to analyse performance of the sales function or revenue centres, with their most significant feature being that they are calculated in terms of profit or contribution margins rather than sales values. For example, consider the budgeted sales for a company as being $121,000 consisting of 11,000 units at $11 per unit, with the standard cost per unit as $7. Also assume that the actual sales are $130,000 (13,000 units x $10 per unit) with the actual cost per unit being $7. The calculation of the variance on the sales value would be based by comparing budgeted sales value of $121,000 with actual sales of $130,000, giving **$9,000F**. However, this ignores the impact of the sales effort on profit. Hence, the budget profit contribution is $44,000 (i.e., 11,000 units at $4 being the difference between $11 budgeted sales − $7 standard cost). But the actual impact of the sales effort in terms of profit margins is $39,000 (i.e., 13,000 units x $3 that is $10 actual sales minus $7 standard cost giving $39,000), giving a variance of **$5000A** ($39,000 actual profit margin - $44,000 budget profit contribution).

This simple example illustrates that the selling prices have been reduced but this has not led to an increase in the total sales, instead it led to a reduction in total profits. It must be understood that the aim of the selling function is to favourably influence total profits. Hence, it is more meaningful to measure sales performance in terms of profit or contribution margins rather than sales revenue.

Continuing with the Part-X example, it is now appropriate to calculate the remaining two variances, namely the sales margin price variance and the sales margin volume variance. The sales margin price variance is computed by the following: (ASP − SSP) x AV where ASP is the actual sales price; SSP is the standard selling price; and AV is the actual sales volume. The information provided shows that ASP is $90; SSP is $89.50 and AV= 9,750 (see data). Therefore, the sales margin price variance is equal to ($90 − $89.50) x 9,750, which is $4,875 F variance.

The sales margin volume variance is computed by the following: (AV − BV) x SM, where AV is the actual sales volume; BV is the budgeted volume; and SM is the standard contribution margin. The information provided shows that AV is 9750; BV is 10,000 units; and SM is $24.06. Therefore, the sales margin volume variance is equal to (9750 − 10,000) x $24.06 giving $6015A. The use of the formulae ensures that the volume variance is not affected by any changes in the actual selling price.

With a marginal costing system, the total sales margin variance seeks to identify the impact of the sales function on the difference between budget and actual profit contribution. Hence, in the Part-X example, the total sales margin variance is equal to (ASR − SCOS) − BC where ASR is actual sales revenue; SCOS is the standard variable cost of sales; and BC is the budgeted profit contribution. The data shows that ASR is $877,500 (see Table 5.4); SCOS is $638,040 (i.e., 9750 units x $65.44 standard variable cost from Table 5.2); and BC is $240,625 (see Table 5.3). Therefore, the total sales margin variance is equal to ($877,500 − $638,040) − $240,625, which gives $1,165A.

Note that the sales function is accountable for the sales volume and the unit price, but not for the unit cost to manufacture the item. Hence, it is the standard cost of sales and not the actual cost of sales that is deducted from the actual sales revenue. Using the standard cost of sales ensures that the variances related to production do not distort the computation of the sales variances. Therefore, it is important to note that the sales variances only result from changes in those variables that are controlled by the sales function (e.g., selling prices and sales quantity).

The use of variance analysis as a supporting tool for KPIs is important, but caution should be exercised when analysing total sales margin. It is contended that there is no point in classifying total sales margin variance into the price and volume elements because changes in selling prices are more than likely to affect sales volume. Furthermore, the sales variances may arise from external factors that may not be under the management's control, such as variations in selling prices, which may be the result of a response to variations in the competitors' selling prices and/or an economic recession that was not anticipated when preparing the budget. These factors may adversely impact both the price and volume of the product. Therefore, it is argued that for control and performance appraisal, it may be better to compare the actual market share with target market share for each product and monitor the trend in market share while comparing selling prices with competitors' prices.

Finally, the variance analysis is concluded by preparing a reconciliation statement of budgeted and actual profit to verify the calculations, and providing management with sufficient detail for them to investigate the variances further and take appropriate action. Table 5.5 illustrates the reconciliation statement, which shows the budgeted net profit adjusted for the various variances to provide the actual profit. It should be noted that the actual profit figure for the period reconciles with the profit figure at Table 5.4, which depicts the actual costs and profit for Part-X (operation-1). The reconciliation statement provides executive management with the reasons why actual profit is different from budgeted profit.

Also note that the example has only one product with single operation. Therefore, the KPIs established by the standard card (Table 5.2) and the budgeted costs (Table 5.3) are monitoring performance at a very low level (by product and operation) that represents a responsibility (cost) centre. In practice, entities have many products with multiple operations per product. Hence, the reconciliation statement may be compiled to show a summary of the variances for many responsibility centres with the option of drilling down (i.e., performance analytics) to a single responsibility centre. Hence, a reconciliation statement may provide a broad picture to top management that explains the major reasons for any differences between budgeted and actual profits and gives them the opportunity to explore deeper to precisely determine the cause for the over or underperformance. Once the reconciliation statement is concluded (at any desired level) the various variances may be transformed into a meaningful KPI dashboard to assist managers in their day-to-day performance decision-making process.

Figure 5.15 shows the KPIs performance dashboard for Product-X (Operation-1). The performance dashboard indicates that this responsibility centre has underperformed in relation to the standard process and rates

Table 5.5  Reconciliation of Budgeted and Actual Profit Using Variances for Part-X: Operation 1

| Reconciliation for Part-X: Operation 1 | $ | $ | $ |
|---|---|---|---|
| (a) Budgeted Net Profit: | | | 80,625 |
| (b) Sales Variances: | | | |
| Sales Margin Price | 4875.00F | | |
| Sales Margin Volume | 6015.63A | 1140.63A | |
| (c) Direct Cost Variances | | | |
| Material-A Price | 5,750.00A | | |
| Material-B Price | 2,875.00A | | |
| Material-A Usage | 13,062.50F | | |
| Material-B Usage | 10,140.63F | 14,578.13F | |
| Labour Rate | 3,450.00A | | |
| Labour Efficiency | 10,312.50F | 6,862.50F | |
| (d) Manufacturing Overhead Variances | | | |
| Fixed Overhead Cost | 5,000.00F | | |
| Variable Overhead Cost | 12600.00A | | |
| Variable Overhead Efficiency | 2,475.00F | 5,125.00A | 15,175 |
| (e) Actual Profit | | | 95,800 |

but has overperformed on efficiency in the use of material and labour (and related variable overhead costs). The sales volume is down but the organisation managed to keep the product price below standard. Overall, the performance dashboard shows an 18.82% improvement in actual profit when compared to the budgeted amount.

## Performance Analytics as a Performance Management Tool

Organisations have a wealth of data at their disposal and are very eager to exploit it to the maximum. Management has the capability to transform corporate data into an insight generating mechanism that drives business performance management and the decision-making process. There are various types of analytics, such as descriptive, diagnostic, predictive, and prescriptive

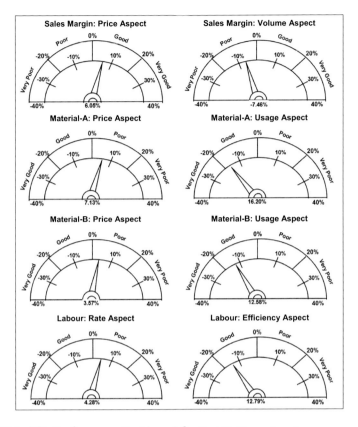

Figure 5.15a  KPIs Performance Dashboard for Part-X: Operation 1

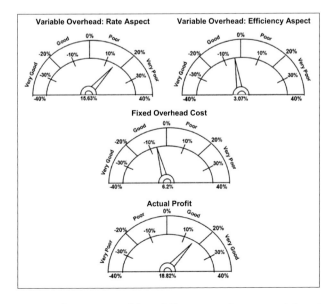

Figure 5.15b  KPIs Performance Dashboard for Part-X: Operation 1 (continued)

that are based on having a repository of data that reflect the past optimisation strategies of an organisation. Having a business performance analytics capability is essential for making correct and rapid decisions. However, not all organisations are successful in utilising their data to gain optimum benefits.

Business performance analytics is a cross-functional discipline aimed at improving an organisation's performance towards achieving its strategic and tactical objectives. It includes a wide range of activities, such as the analysis of past performance information; the identification of data-set relationships and patterns and associated key performance indicators; the definition of hypothesis about data interrelationships, cause-and-effects associations, and the generation of future performance scenarios; and formulating a plan of action that will enable the achievement of the desired outcomes.

Traditional financial analysis and business performance analytics have a similar purpose but are very different. Business performance analysis caters for much larger data volumes and has the capacity to gather, store, and process data using state-of-the-art processes and technologies. This gives business performance analytics the capacity to have greater processing power of modern technologies; delve deeper into the available data because it can handle a larger number of data points that were not previously available; is more accurate due to superior algorithms that are able to make the most of different data types (i.e., structured, and unstructured data); and is more reliable because of its facility to iteratively adapt the logic to perform multiple tests, and leverage the scale of digital solutions.

An analytics-driven approach to performance improvement is a contemporary methodology for increasing an organisation's performance level because it permits superior visibility of costs and provides management with a unique opportunity to link financial data with operational and at times unstructured data (text or images). For example, preventative maintenance scheduling under an analytics-driven approach may focus on equipment with the highest risk, which means spending the maintenance effort on equipment about to breakdown. This may be done because the equipment status can be detected through special sensors that reveal under which operational conditions it is functioning, and therefore the probability of an upcoming breakdown. This provides a more accurate resource allocation approach resulting in the reduction of overall cost, while concurrently mitigating the risk of interruption and downtimes.

Performance analytics can also be applied for improving customer service levels by proactively detecting potential supply chain issues and taking corrective action before customers are impacted. Other applications include: Decreasing inventory levels by having better sales forecasts and effective supply planning; reducing inventory write-offs by highlighting likely obsolete items in a timely manner; and optimising the logistics route network and making better decisions regarding what objects are shipped from where, thus decreasing transportation costs. There are five important prerequisites for using and maximising the full capability of business performance analytics, namely:

- *Align with business objectives.* Business performance analytics is a strategic tool and therefore its resultant outcomes must support the business objectives of the organisation. Without this essential linkage, the technique becomes just an accounting or data manipulation exercise and will not contribute to how the organisation's goals are to be achieved. Hence, when the organisation's objectives change, the analytics stratagem and tactics must be reviewed to ensure that they are aligned with the amended objectives.
- *Data integrity.* The adage 'garbage-in-garbage-out' principle applies. Data is the raw material of analytics, which means having the right data available, that it is of the correct quality and reliability, and ensuring that the data is relevant and meaningful to the business needs. This also means that everyone in the organisation sees the same version of the data (timeliness).
- *Consistent processes.* Having the right and timely data available may require a business process reengineering exercise to ensure that the data is generated and captured correctly and consistently. Hence, the analytical model applied should be viewed as part of a holistic business framework that encompasses all the input and output processes.
- *Stakeholder support.* Stakeholder support and end-to-end integration are of immense importance when making generalised inferences from the analysis of voluminous cross-functional data. It is important that data definitions, identified assumptions and hypotheses, interpretation of findings, and their impact on business goals are fully understood and agreed to by all concerned and are linked with the strategic objectives.
- *Data-driven decision-making culture.* The capacity to gain an accurate and deep understanding of what is taking place will depend on the analytics model. However, it is important for management to change its decision-making

abilities to a data-driven approach. This requires management to fully understand the assumptions underlying the analytics model, the logic applied to reach a conclusion, and the linkage between the results and business outcomes. It is only through this approach that buy-in from the management is attained. However, a data-driven decision-making environment is achieved gradually and not overnight. It requires commitment from the top, supported by investing in the skills and ability of employees, and encouraging an experimental mindset.

The above illustrates that the voluminous amount of data currently available has the capacity to profoundly change organisations and their respective business models. Data has always been important, but the modern concept of data availability and its implications presents an enormous challenge to organisations in terms of how data is handled, processed, stored, evaluated, and utilised. The current and anticipated flood of data and its subsequent utilisation requires innovative technologies that rapidly process, store, retrieve, and analyse this data content to unearth significant and constructive business insights that transform the organisation into a data-driven entity.

### Performance Management in a Data-Driven Organisation

Pugna, Dutescu, and Stanila (2018) argue that new information technologies are changing the way organisations are perceiving management and business models. They view cloud computing, Big Data, high-performance computing, and powerful analytics as being the pertinent drivers to performance improvement and strategic development scenarios. They further claim that Business Intelligence and Business Analytics are transforming the paradigms organisations are using to define their strategy and to analyse their performance, both for management and integrated financial reporting scope. The performance management systems of the past are no longer applicable. Most organisations are using performance management systems to integrate management methods, techniques, support tools, and Business Intelligence components to manage and measure their performance.

These innovative performance management systems have several significant features that include collecting and storing on a frequent basis various measures regarding the business activities of the organisation; gathering and storing benchmarks, threshold values, and business rules for comparing outcomes between current performance indicators and projected values; to support datamining methods through roll-ups and drill-downs of analysed indicators together with hierarchical aggregation criteria (structured Performance Measurements); and permit management to swiftly appraise which business processes are successful, and which require attention.

Sharda, Delen, and Turban (2015) presented a conceptual framework of performance management as illustrated at Figure 5.16. This framework maintains the notion that business performance information systems support decision-making at the strategic level by comparing a mixture of key performance indicators with an established number of objectives and industry benchmarks. Figure 5.16 illustrates that the BPM framework has a closed-loop cycle with emphasis on strategy. This framework supports the overall theme of this chapter.

Sharda, Delen, and Turban argue that BPM encompasses a closed loop set of processes that link strategy to execution in order to optimise business performance. They claim the loop implies that optimum performance is achieved by setting goals and objectives (i.e., strategise), establishing initiatives and plans to achieve those goals (i.e., plan), monitoring actual performance against the goals and objectives (i.e., monitor), and taking corrective action (i.e., act and adjust). Hence, the unbroken and recurring nature of the cycle infers that the conclusion of an iteration leads to a fresh and upgraded one (supporting the continuous process enhancement efforts).

The BPM framework has four key components, namely define the strategy, plan, monitor, and act and adjust. The fundamental component is

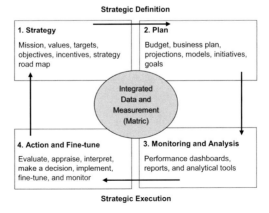

Figure 5.16  Conceptual Framework of Business Performance Management (BPM)

STRATEGIC MANAGEMENT AND BUSINESS PLANNING    227

the organisational (corporate) strategy. Basically, strategy is the road map that defines where the organisation wants to go (direction). Hence, it is a high-level long-term plan of action that identifies the goals which are to be achieved during the period. The strategy of an organisation is influenced by the political, economic, social, and technological environment (i.e., PEST Analysis) and how this environment is likely to impact the goals to be achieved. An essential element for defining the strategy is the MOST analysis, namely the mission (and vision), objectives, strategy (at different organisational levels), and operational tactics. These are all aimed at achieving the defined strategic objectives. The strategy is often defined by senior executive management and must go through the strategy approval process of the specific organisation (depending on its structure and whether it is a public or private entity).

The next stage of the BPM is defining the plan. Normally, the planning cycle matches the strategic planning cycle. Hence, if the strategy is for a duration of three financial years, the plan is normally for three years as well, but with a focus on the current financial year and reviewing the remaining planning years to keep the plan on track with the strategy. Hence, the plan should be viewed as a short-term segment of the strategy. The plan outlines how the strategy is to be achieved (i.e., defines how the entity is to get to where it wants to be) by defining in detail the operational and financial proposals. Hence, the plan describes the tactics and initiatives that will be followed to achieve the performance goals defined by the strategic plan and the expected financial results once the tactics and initiatives are implemented.

The operational plan reflects the organisation's strategic objectives and consists of detailed tactics and initiatives, the resources required, and the projected results for the defined period (normally a financial year). It is essential that all activities undertaken by the organisation support the agreed strategy. On the other hand, the financial planning and budgeting process use the operational plan as a key input to determine the costs for generating the estimated revenue or income. Furthermore, management would also determine the overhead costs and the cost of the required capital improvements. The planning process requires a collaborative approach from the various departments within the organisation. This means that the strategy is communicated to everyone within the organisation and that it is clearly understood.

It must be noted that a plan is theoretical; reality sets in when the plan is being implemented. Therefore, management must have a mechanism in place to ensure that the implementation of the plan (reality) converges with the defined plan (theory). Hence, the next stage in the BPM is the regular monitoring and analysis of the planning implementation process. This stage addresses the issue of how well the organisation is doing. In other words, how well is the organisation performing? This can only be answered by regular and continuous monitoring. The key issue here is, what is to be monitored and how is this monitoring going to take place? The first issue regarding what is to be monitored is addressed by selecting a number of key performance indicators (KPIs). The second issue regarding the monitoring methods is related to the tools that may be applied, such as variance analysis, balanced scorecard, and many other approaches. The final stage is related to making practical decisions when the monitoring stage is being conducted. Here the issue that is being addressed is what the organisation needs to do differently. In other words, what action and adjustments need to be carried out to respond to the results of the monitoring and analysis activities?

The key output from the Business Performance Information Systems are the reports, dashboards, and scorecards amongst others. The types of output required depend on characteristics of the management team. For instance, reports tend to provide an in-depth analysis of a specific metric that some management members may prefer. However, others may prefer dashboards that provide a pictorial view of selected KPIs. Still other managers may prefer scorecards that tend to be designed for many different verticals of a business, and track progress towards goals with the aim of identifying sensitive areas. There are no specific preferences for the numerous tools that are available. Dashboards have the advantage of cascading through the organisation's hierarchy by having customised metrics and goals that are directly linked to the strategy. They are simple and easy to use and are designed to be generally utilised by everyone in the organisation who has a monitoring role, and/or is responsible for the management and analysis of business processes.

Sharda, Delen, and Turban argue that as organisations move into the age of Big Data, analytics is changing the way organisations are applying the sophistication of information technologies to acquire insight (and in many cases foresight) from their data repositories to support successful decision-making. Innovative organisations are instituting a 'data-driven' culture so that they may take suitable action to ease the demands of persistent changing markets and their desire to take a more active role regarding social responsibility. Organisations have made an increasing effort of being more transparent in conducting their operations and to improve their engagement with their customers to comprehend their specific needs. This desire is consistently being included in the strategic vision of many organisations and the use of performance analytics is helping these organisations to achieve this vision.

According to Sharda, Delen, and Turban, management must integrate new variables that impact the conceptual layout of the reports and dashboards, supplementing the volume and the currency of data that must be processed. However, they argue that organisations are tempted to include too many variables in the strategic equation, when big data does not simply demand more variables, but more meaningful variables that add value to the analytical sphere. Big data analytics has moved away from the traditional methods of processing and analysing data; Artificial Intelligence technologies are being applied to explore and discover data patterns and to predict the future in the absence of an interpretation process. Thus, in this new evolving analytical environment, human judgement, intuition, and expertise in interpreting the analytical findings is repositioned.

Some researchers advocate that business analysts must not question the results that are provided but instead rely on them completely. The use of performance dashboards for visualising KPIs has facilitated the decision-making process for managers. However, for proper decisions to be made, the manager must not only consider these performance dashboards but must have a thorough knowledge of the organisation to be able to assimilate the knowledge gained from different sources (even intuition-based) for making the appropriate decisions. The concept of transforming data to information, and information to knowledge, and knowledge to wisdom still holds and must be strengthened in the Big Data environment. It should be noted that knowledge leads to 'insight' and wisdom leads to 'foresight.' It is important that human intuition is not removed from the decision-making equation even though knowledge and wisdom are needed to make sense of the explanations that analytics provides.

Ernst & Young (2015, p. 5) argue that analytics can enable an organisation to effectively grow, optimise, and protect value. They argue that decision-making is no longer reliant on merely 'gut feeling' and contend that big data provides a far-reaching view of market conditions, customer needs and preferences, and potential project risks. Hence, organisations can understand and embrace emerging opportunities and align products and services with changing customer needs, creating additional value for stakeholders in the process (Ernst & Young, 2015, p. 5). Furthermore, they view big data as helping organisations to protect value based on effective risk mitigation and compliance in-line with the ever-changing regulations, particularly the implications of the European Union (EU) General Data Privacy Regulation.

Moreover, Ernst & Young (Ibid.) contend that analytics can assist organisations to uncover and measure intangible sources of value more successfully by combining factual data from the financial statements with a variety of qualitative evidence. Hence, they argue that the outcome of analytics is a more thorough knowledge of what drives an organisation's valuation, whilst providing a well-defined approach for managing value and communicating it to its stakeholders.

Ernst & Young (Ibid., p. 7) commissioned a study regarding big data that sought the views of senior executives, of which 270 responded to questions on all aspects of their data strategy. The findings from this study revealed that about 68% of respondents were active stakeholders in big data projects, and all departmental functions and industry sectors are represented, with most respondents working in finance, marketing, and IT, as well as in cross-departmental management roles. Figure 5.17 shows the results of the Ernst & Young study related to the top ten drivers for organisations to implement big data analytics.

The findings suggest that understanding the customer better and improving the products and services were the top two drivers for organisations to implement big data analytics (73% and 72% respectively); these were followed way down in ranking by improving the management of existing data, creating new revenue streams, and necessity for their business model (47%, 41%, and 40% respectively). Improving the detection and prevention of fraud featured last at a low of 20%.

Figure 5.18 reveals further results of the Ernst & Young study related to various issues. A large majority of executives noted that data should be at the heart of all decision-making (81%), followed equally by poor data quality as a key concern and return-on-investment (ROI) as a key challenge

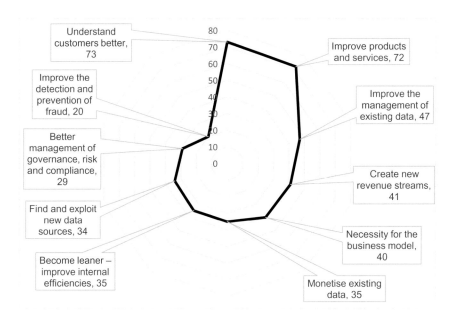

*Figure 5.17* Top Ten Drivers for Organisations to Implement Big Data Analytics

to projects (both 50%). This implies that a significant number of executives are not sure whether the ROI, which measures performance used to evaluate the efficiency or profitability of an investment, is sufficient for them to undertake a big data analytics project. Additionally, adapting the organisational culture to integrate big data and recognising the financial value of big data have been noted as key challenges (47% and 35% respectively).These findings suggest that there is a long way to go before Big Data Analytics is the accepted norm in organisations. Chris Mazzei, Global Chief Analytics Officer, EY summed up the general situation when he stated that: '*Analytics is changing how organisations make decisions and take actions. Data by itself has limited value but when managed as a strategic asset, data can change how organisations compete and win*' (Ernst & Young, 2015, p. 24).

## *Analytical Insights to Boost Business Performance*

The current availability of big data requires systems that enable analysts to effortlessly access and retrieve relevant information that is transformed to knowledge and ultimately transformed to wisdom (insights and foresights).

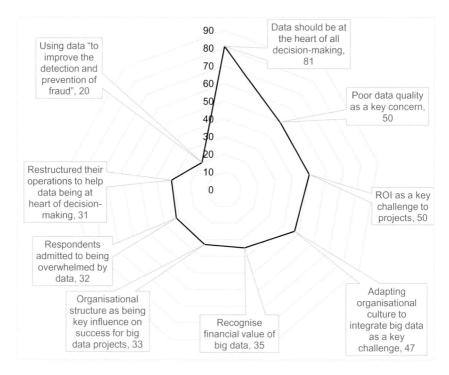

Figure 5.18  Further Findings of Ernst & Young (2015) Study Related to a Mixture of Issues

This will enable a new breed of management to comprehend, analyse, and interpret the available data and information to define realistic plans that are achievable and generate tangible business value. Management recognises that the utilisation and innovative analysis of data to mitigate risk and increase performance in an organisation is an important tangible asset. However, special skills and an investigative mindset are required to take advantage of this analytical environment.

BearingPoint (2019) argue that organisations that can leverage analytics and governance to manage the overwhelming volume and complexity of data will dominate the market, particularly those organisations that use data and analytics effectively. It must be stressed that using data and analytics effectively is not an IT function. The IT department has the function of facilitating the availability, storage, and retrieval of information. But it is management's responsibility and function to use the available information by accessing the relevant data, applying the applicable analytical tools, and interpreting the findings for decision-making purposes.

Król and Zdonek (2020) contend that the implementation analytics effectiveness is mainly determined by the evaluation of an organisation's position in the analytics continuum. They argue that an organisation's analytics maturity evaluation permits management to plan the respective project scope and the implementation rate. Basically, the initial aim is to take a snapshot or inventory of the existing state of play. According to Król and Zdonek, understanding an organisation's capability to make use of data analytics to increase innovation and the competitive advantage requires an assessment of the position it takes in the so-called analytics continuum. Figure 5.19 illustrates that the data analytics continuum consists of five categories that are defined by tools, techniques, and the approach to data analytics, namely, descriptive analytics, diagnostic analytics, predictive analytics, prescriptive analytics, and cognitive analytics.

As an organisation moves from descriptive analytics to the cognitive analytics, the beneficial value to the organisation increase from hindsight to foresight. Furthermore, as an organisation moves towards cognitive analytics, the maturity level in terms of the analytical environment increases but is more difficult to attain. In a practical sense, the different analytics categories co-exist and complement each other. Each stage on the maturity path progresses the organisation towards the solutions that allow soundly-based decisions to be taken faster (on-demand enterprise) (Król and Zdonek, 2020). Figure 5.19 also shows the different types and the purpose of the report tools.

According to Król and Zdonek, the growth in the use of analytics in organisations is not a linear process, because the implementation of organisational change differs in terms of the order and intensity, depending on both an organisation's specificity and the business context. For instance, descriptive analytics contributes to the knowledge and understanding of reality by examining what took place (hindsight) through the exploration of data patterns and utilising technology, such as Relational Database Management Systems (RDBMS), ODS (Operating Data Store) being the earliest data warehouse model, and On-Line Analytical Processing (OLAP).

Descriptive analytics is viewed as the initial primary source of information for management by revealing what happened and is widely applied in exploring different scenarios regarding customer profiling and operational

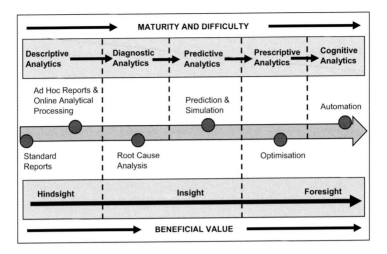

Figure 5.19  Illustration of the Data Analytics Continuum

efficiency. On the other hand, diagnostic analytics examines data by taking a step further to investigate why an event has happened. Root cause analysis is a common tool for doing this, where a certain delay in decision-making is evident, since the data needs to be gathered, structured, analysed, and interpreted. Thus, diagnostic analytics permits historical data to be analysed with the aim of revealing symmetries and quantitative relationships between variables. It should be noted that it is the manager who interprets the resultant information to decide its applicability.

Predictive analytics is a further progression and involves defining a model for undertaking simulations and forecasts. With predictive analytics, both current and historical data are analysed to discern what may happen in the future. Although its focus is on gaining an insight into what happened, it is inclined towards the attainment of foresight. This advancement takes place due to a further evolution of the available technology, such as NoSQL, which is a schema-free database, and NewSQL, which is a hybrid of a schema-fixed as well as a schema-free database. As the name implies, predictive analytics is all about forecasting future events and trends. Hence, it entails searching for relationships and data patterns in historical data (i.e., the past) and applying them to a specific model, such as simulation systems, for generating forecasts and making better decisions.

Prescriptive analytics is a higher level of sophistication and builds upon the predictive model by using simulation and machine learning (artificial intelligence) to propose actions to be taken to achieve wanted results. This utilises a Simulation-Driven Analysis and Decision-making tool by using a mature Data Lake approach. Data Lakes permit the storage of a conglomeration of relational data, such as operational databases and data from a line of business applications, and non-relational data, such as mobile apps, Internet-of-things (IoT) devices, and social media. Hence, they provide the ability to recognise and comprehend the data in the lake through crawling, cataloguing, and indexing of data.

Prescriptive analytics focuses on recommending the actions that should be taken in specific situations. An even higher level of innovative sophistication is cognitive analytics. Cognitive analytics makes extensive use of artificial intelligence (AI) and high-performance data analysis to systematise the decision-making process. This escalates the efficiency level of decisions taken through the application of intelligent machines, such as having algorithms that perform tasks a person could reasonably deem to require intelligence if a human were to do them. Cognitive systems can be used to monitor interactions between the customer and the organisation in real time to analyse the context and customer's behaviour patterns and select an appropriate action that is optimal at a given time. Most organisations are still at the descriptive and diagnostic analytics stage. Hence, there is still a long way to go. However, those who have progressed beyond the diagnostic analytics stage have reported extensive benefits to their organisations. Artificial intelligence is currently viewed as being the emerging technology and it will take some time before it will become the accepted norm.

## Performance Analytics in the Public Sector

Performance management in government is not a recent practice. However, the widespread applicability of performance analytics is a rather recent event. Most performance management frameworks have some kind of management system that ensures continuous improvement, establishes efficient and effective operations, and engages stakeholders, particularly the customer. Furthermore, these performance management systems process data and analyse information, thus they feature an analytics component. Hence, the difference between normal performance management in government and the concept of performance analytics is the extent, intensity, and sophistication of the information management structure and the analytical tools applied. Therefore, government entities need to have better expertise in managing information and analysing this information. Hence, the focus of government systems should not be merely operational or administrative enhancement, but should encompass a higher level of information management and analytics, using data warehousing and data-mining concepts.

A data warehouse is predominantly a data management system that is designed to enable and support business intelligence (BI) activities, particularly analytics. Data warehouses contain a vast volume of historical data and have several key functions, namely, to perform interrogations, clean and maintain the database, manipulate and transform the information content, and analyse the data. On the other hand, datamining is the process of discovering actionable information from large sets of data using mathematical analysis to derive data patterns and trends. These data patterns cannot be revealed by traditional data exploration methods because the relationships between them are too complex and voluminous. The data patterns and trends are usually gathered and defined as a datamining model that may be applied to specific scenarios, such as forecasting service levels; identifying vulnerable customers; recommending the services that should be escalated to a higher priority; and analysing and determining customers' social needs.

In government, analytics should be a fundamental key ingredient for all managerial functions (junior and senior management posts). Hence, it is not just a matter of having a list of KPIs and an attractive dashboard. Government entities need to go beyond just having lengthy meetings, reporting, and examining the metrics. They need to use analytical tools to determine the insights (and foresights) underlying the data, which can assist public servants to redesign services for much better outcomes. Therefore, performance analytics for government entities is to continuously examine how they can function better and inject the gained insights into both the strategic and operational decision-making processes. Figure 5.20 and the above explanation have illustrated that there is a difference between performance management and performance analytics. Figure 5.20 shows that a more sophisticated level of information management through a data warehouse and datamining is required. Datamining techniques will permit a higher quality analytical approach to be taken, resulting in descriptive, diagnostic, predictive, prescriptive, and cognitive analysis. These have already been described in Section 5.5.2.

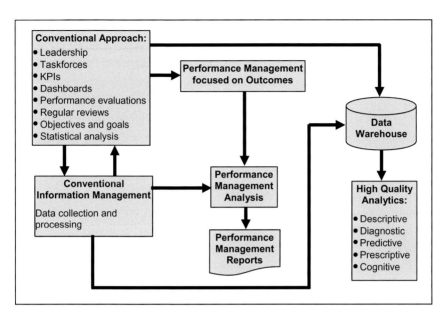

*Figure* 5.20  Performance Management and Performance Analytics Process

Both the conventional and innovative approach shown in Figure 5.20 require several key prerequisites. Firstly, an executive champion is required who has a clear vision and purpose to provide a cohesive strategic direction and robust objectives. This person needs to have a senior position with authority and influence, such as a Minister, Secretary, Governor, Permanent Secretary, Head of Department, or Mayor, amongst other possible positions depending on the governmental system applicable. Secondly, there has to be commitment and accountability for the analytics project, with clear-cut responsibilities (ownership), processes, and performance action plans.

The greatest challenge is to instil cultural change throughout the organisation that fosters a learning organisational mindset by introducing best practices and peer evaluations by assessing performance against external criteria such as benchmarking or other similar alternative methods. There needs to be a culture where managers question why certain events occur, possibly through Root Cause Analysis. Thirdly, management must engage the employees within the organisation through different communication approaches that ultimately lead to transparency and mutual trust by providing access to performance management reports and other information related to the decision-making process. Hence, executive management needs to establish a proper organisational environment for the performance analytics process to succeed.

Apart from this humanistic-management leadership aspect that is required, care must be taken to have a suitable analytical mechanism in place to ensure that the organisation has the necessary analytical tools and skills. Data availability, the cost of storing it, and the tools necessary to retrieve it are no longer a major concern. The major challenge for government organisations is to attract talented and qualified employees who are highly competent in the use of datamining and the associated anaytical skills. This may mean paying above average industry salaries to acquire these scarce competences, which are essential for transforming data and information to insight and ultimately to foresight. The competencies to turn data into insight and foresight include having technological ingenuity and agility by recruiting highly qualified employees for conducting descriptive, diagnostic, predictive, prescriptive, and cognitive analysis; fostering a problem solving mindset, such as applying Root Cause Analysis; having a creative and enquiring mentality by fostering employees to question why certain events occur and exhibiting an ability to ask 'why not?'; and having a successful communications mechanism that encourages teamwork and conveys an atmosphere of trust and organisational proficiency.

## Stat Program Implementation Initiative

In the United States of America (USA), a Stat program was developed about two decades ago, named CompStat, for use by the New York City Police Department. This programme was swiftly taken up by other police agencies across the world as well as by other agencies within New York City. It was also adapted by the City of Baltimore, which created CitiStat, the first application of this leadership strategy to an entire jurisdiction. According to Keegan (2015), governments at all levels employ PerformanceStat, which is a focused effort by government executives to exploit the power, purpose and motivation, responsibility and discretion, data and meetings, analysis and learning, feedback, and follow-up, with the aim of improving the government's performance.

PerformanceStat leadership strategy is not straightforward to implement but must be customised to fit an organisation's specific environment. Firstly, it requires government executives to make an unequivocal and specific commitment. According to Behn (2014), the PerformanceStat leadership strategy is all about taking responsibility to achieve specific public purposes, which means that for government executives, embracing this responsibility puts them out there with no place to hide. Keegan argues that PerformanceStat is not a system, and it is not a model or leadership strategy, nor is it solely a performance measurement tool either. He contends that PerformanceStat is a leadership strategy that is designed to fulfil specific public purposes by producing specific results.

In other words, it is aimed at achieving explicitly defined results based on a government executive having a specific purpose in mind that dovetails with their agency's mission (Keegan, 2015). Keegan explains that the PerformanceStat practice is based upon having a series of regular integrated meetings to discuss what's effective and identify specific problems, together with the causes of the problems, all the way developing strategies that might help solve a particular problem. He states that these meetings should follow up on previous targets, review commitments, and assess progress, as well as always trying to figure out what the next issue is that can be addressed and how to bring the PerformanceStat approach to bear as a leadership strategy.

Johns Hopkins University (2022) argues that when governments have the fundamentals, they know exactly what they want to achieve, how they will achieve it, and how they will know when it is achieved. They contend that when governments have strong teams and robust analysis feeding decision-makers, they can add evidence to the suite of ingredients that factor into sound decision-making. However, they stress that increasing the effectiveness of governments based on evidence requires sound management, which inherently requires routinely convening the managers. It is important to recognise that managers as decision-makers are not convened for the sake of just having a meeting, but to discuss a very clear objective, such as crime reduction, traffic control, or climate change amongst many others. At these meetings the entire team is assembled with the goal of having an open and collective dialogue about mutual objectives and impediments. At the end of these meetings, actions are assigned to individuals or responsibility centres that are regularly monitored and followed up.

Johns Hopkins University has developed a guide to help interested governments decide whether they are ready for Stat program implementation. Figure 5.21, which is an adaptation from Johns Hopkins University,

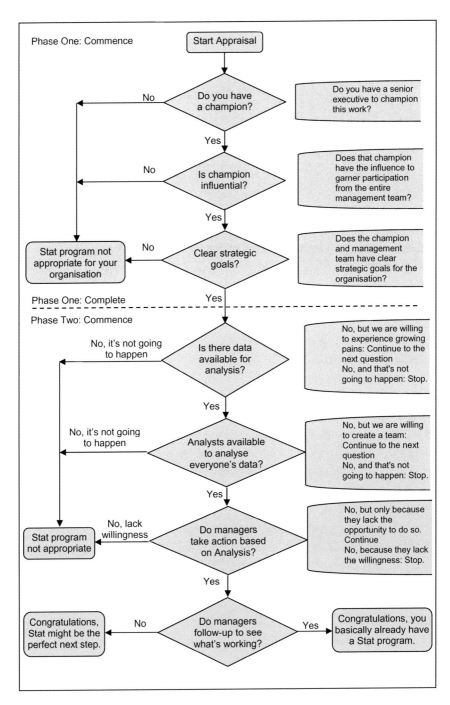

Figure 5.21 Flowchart of Stat Program Appraisal Process – Readiness for Implementation

presents a flowchart of the Stat program appraisal process that has been developed by them. Figure 5.21 illustrates that the appraisal process consists of two phases. The first phase is defined by the first three questions to establish whether the organisation is ready for the Stat program; that is, if the answer to any of these three questions is negative then the organisation is clearly not ready to undertake the Stat program. These three questions basically focus on the current leadership attributes in terms of commitment level, degree of influence within the organisation, and the intensity of having clear strategic goals. Without these characteristics as defined by these three questions, the organisation cannot possibly be ready to undertake the Stat program.

The second phase is undertaken if the answer to the three previous questions is 'yes.' This phase consists of four specific questions regarding two aspects, namely the data and management attributes. The answers to the questions for the second phase will determine whether the Stat program might be an appropriate next step for the organisation under examination. The first question in phase two is to determine whether there is data available for analysis. It the data is available or will become available with a sustained effort, the assessment may proceed to the next question. However, if the data is not likely to be made available then the organisation is not ready for a Stat program, since the data (and the analysis of it) is a critical ingredient to the success of Stat programs. Hence, the organisation must focus on its data inventory and management before considering a Stat program. The second question is related to the existing analytical skills and competencies available to the organisation to analyse all the data available to the organisation.

If these analytical skills and competencies are available or could become available, the assessment may proceed to the next question. However, if the analytical skills and competencies are not going to be available, then the organisation is not ready for a Stat program since data without analysis is useless, and analysis requires people. If the organisation is not keen to establish analytical support and is not prepared to empower a team of analysts to examine the data from across the organisation, then the level of commitment required is not appropriate for a Stat program. The third question in the second phase is to assess whether the managers and executive champion act on the findings of the data analysis. If the managers and executive champion act on the findings of the data analysis or their inaction is because they lack the opportunity to do so, the Stat program might be the perfect next step for the organisation because it creates that opportunity to make decisions based on the latest information. However, if the response to this question is 'no' because they lack the willingness to do so, then it may be indicative that the organisation's leadership is not ready for a Stat program.

There may be several reasons for this, such as not trusting the data, or they may be anxious about making the wrong decision. However, whatever the reason, an unwillingness to act based on data and evidence is a serious barrier since headway requires leaders to be risk takers. The final question is to assess whether the managers and executive champion routinely follow up to reflect on what is working or not. If the response is 'yes' then the organisation already has the basic elements for the Stat program to be in place. It may need some fine-tuning but basically the processes are working. On the other hand, if the response is 'no' then a Stat program might be the perfect next step for the organisation, since routine follow-up and creating opportunities to reflect on progress are essential requirements.

Government offers a wide spectrum of services ranging from public transportation, education, cleaning, safer streets, playgrounds, housing, potable water, sewage, electricity, economic development, emergency services, and public utilities, amongst many others. Moreover, citizens demand indefinite timely and high-quality service delivery. Additionally, finances and resources are not infinite. Hence, there is the need for judicious management practices to ensure that government achieves more with less. Also, over the years, citizens have developed sophisticated habits, with demands for diverse and new services being endless. Therefore, governments continuously need to establish priorities and delivery targets to ensure that service delivery is enhanced for all.

Performance management has become an essential tool for ensuring that managers are held accountable. Johns Hopkins University (2022) views PerformanceStat as a vital process of setting goals, identifying metrics, assessing performance, and evaluating employees' performance and program outcomes to informed decision-making. According to Johns Hopkins University, PerformanceStat is a continuous process where government executives work with their staff to deliver results to their citizens. They argue that currently, managers are focused on leveraging data, analysis, responsibility, discretion, and power to convene follow-ups to improve performance with the various Stat models and itemise reasons why governments should consider establishing a Stat program (see Table 5.6).

Table 5.6  30 Reasons Why Governments Should Consider Establishing a Stat Program

| |
|---|
| Enhances the effectiveness of governance and helps to accomplish objectives. |
| Provides opportunities to communicate constraints and negotiate solutions. |
| Promotes rapid deployment of resources and direct focus to areas ensuring big wins. |
| Promotes government accountability, transparency, and responsiveness. |
| Offers opportunities for capacity development for management and staff. |
| Helps residents to engage and learn of how taxes are managed to deliver service. |
| Ensures the setting of performance standards and benchmarks for managers. |
| Encourages tactical problem solving, process improvement, and proactive solutions to maximise residents' experience. |
| Increases communication between agencies, departments, and residents. |
| Provides an effective tool to increase management responsibility by setting performance targets and tracking progress against those targets. |
| Allows for the setting of clear expectations from managers, and senior staff. |
| Provides direction and pathways for managers to adapt to maximising their performance and helping them to monitor the progress of their staff as well. |
| Provides opportunities for the removal of barriers to improving productivity. |
| Helps managers to become more aware of targets and expectations. |
| Facilitates the process of identifying resources, training, and logistics necessary for managers to achieve objectives. |
| Allows for the measuring of progress, helping managers to understand how they are doing and what they should be doing to improve outcomes for citizens. |
| Improves productivity, maximises results and enhances efficient use of resources. |
| Promotes and facilitates communication between executives, managers, and staff. |
| Ensures staff understand the importance of their contribution to achieving objectives. |
| Provides opportunities for recognising and rewarding dedicated managers. |
| Enhances teamwork and increases staff productivity while improving collective accountability and responsibility. |
| Identifies concerns earlier and addresses them before they get out of control. |
| Promotes efficient use of time, money, and resources. |
| Allows for an opportunity to provide feedback to managers to better align their strength and competencies to improve work outcomes. |

(Continued)

*Table 5.6*  (Continued)

| |
|---|
| Helps to better communicate strategic goals and priorities to managers and promote understanding of what needs to be done at specified periods. |
| Enables open conversation between executives, managers, and staff about priorities and promote harmony in a manner that contributes to achieving objectives. |
| Enables executives to increase quality of service and improved value to residents. |
| Helps better manage scarce resources and drive down cost of operations. |
| Fosters timely intervention into practices so that managers stay on track to achieving set targets and results. |
| Provides opportunity for developing strategies and tactics for achieving outcomes. |

Performance management applying the PerformanceStat approach means that management is compelled to address three essential questions, namely: Who is responsible for what? Who will follow up to make sure it got done? When can we expect to see results? There are different 'Stat' programs. Some governments apply a 'Stat' program as a meeting and decision-making forum, where decision makers regularly meet to review analysis and together, they collaborate to address and resolve specific problems. However, these 'Stat' programs are not easy to apply and require a high level of discipline and needs to be harmonised with the organisation's current or desired culture. There are two basic models of PerformanceStat approaches, namely 'gotcha' and 'no surprises,' both having their own specific risks and benefits.

According to Johns Hopkins University (2022), 'Gotcha' is viewed as an unpleasant surprise, usually a disconcerting challenge, attempting to expose something, such as underperformance or poor management. Thus, it implies someone is after you and you must figure out how to avoid any negative implications. The objective of the gotcha-style stat is to urge a high-level of preparation and a deep understanding of operations for both the meeting leadership and participants. To prepare for the meeting, executives must acquaint themselves with the organisation's operations and data, including work records, reports, and input from others who are familiar with the manager's work.

Often, an analyst prepares notes and tester lines of questioning for the organisation's leadership team, which identify concerns and data of critical interest to be discussed at the meeting. At times, the information is collected without the manager knowing and the analyst's notes are not distributed to the relevant organisation. Hence, managers required to address the issues during the meeting must prepare their own notes without knowing the questions that will be put to them during the meeting. This approach is viewed as providing the motivation for managers to keep their house in order. According to Johns Hopkins University (2022), several benefits of the 'Gotcha' approach have been identified and include:

- Urges managers to effectively prepare for the meeting. Managers knowing that they will be publicly questioned about tomorrow regarding programs they are responsible for today necessitates sufficient and continuous preparation. Thus, they do not know the questions that will be put to them, but they are expected to shrewdly answer them. This requires them to foresee the questions, to think smart, and confer with subordinates. It also necessitates that they develop effective and convincing responses. Hence, managers become aware that there is no room for complacency and ample groundwork is crucial to circumvent possible embarrassment at the meeting.
- Inspires managers at various organisational levels to meticulously analyse all their data. Exhibiting a deficiency of knowledge about the data of their own organisation may depict managers as not fulfilling their duties well, which could be awkward. Managers need to examine and analyse their data, reveal trends and new patterns, and identify those sections where resources and focus may be necessary.
- Simplifies the process to reveal performing and non-performing agencies. Since the analysis and questions are not provided to managers beforehand, a PerformanceStat meeting will reveal the performance level of managers by the way they reply to the various questions about the analysis and data from their own entities. Thus, a PerformanceStat meeting will highlight which agencies are meeting expectations, achieving targets, and delivering the required outcomes. This process compels executives to painstakingly explain and engage managers at various levels regarding how they could improve their effort.
- Discloses organisational segments for improvement that may be challenging to discover. A PerformanceStat meeting will provide executives with comprehensive insight into the operations of the organisation by evaluating the progress being made towards achieving the agreed goals and concurrently detecting areas for improvement.

- Provokes improved supervision. At the PerformanceStat meeting, managers are expected to take full responsibility for the successes and failures of their organisation. This motivates managers to make sure that their subordinates meet the agreed expectations.
- Supports collective accountability. Organisations will only succeed if all employees perform their work according to their role. A manager's role is to link up consequences to collective results and assist subordinates to perform their role adequately. Employees must focus on their organisation's success and not on their personal goals. Ultimately, managers must assume responsibility for their organisation. Therefore, being aware of this assists them to recognise the importance of consulting with anyone (employees or others) whose collaboration is required to achieve the organisation's targets.
- Facilitates managers to keep track and update their data. Monitoring progress towards the achievement of agreed organisational targets requires continuous tracking of tasks and updating performance information. This allows management to assess whether the organisation's operations are achieving the anticipated outcomes, and which projects are effective, or what modifications are necessary to make them effective. Managers should be aware that accurate and timely information is the basis of data-driven decisions.
- Avoids omitting critical issues. A PerformanceStat meeting tends to go beyond discussing a predefined range of problems that concern the participating organisation. This is essential to systematically focus on performance challenges that may have been unobserved by confining discussions to prearranged concerns only.
- Encourages managers to frequently assess their approach for finding innovative answers to persistent difficulties. The leadership team will make a persistent effort to determine whether managers are making prudent use of the limited resources available to them or whether they are squandering resources on the same problems. Hence, managers being aware of this scrutiny would find innovative ways to detect and resolve problems that otherwise may have been repeated.
- Encourages managers to focus more on outcomes and less on the process. At a PerformanceStat meeting, the executive team would want to reveal whether managers are achieving the agreed outcomes. On the other hand, managers would want to implement the right metrics that focus on highlighting that the expected outcomes are being achieved.

Although the 'Gotcha' approach has significant benefits, Johns Hopkins University also highlights several risks:

- Needlessly springs surprises for managers that may lead to confrontation. Therefore, instead of being motivated, managers and their teams are challenged with data and analysis that has the potential to cast doubt on their work performance. Thus, they may tend to become defensive and dispute with executives rather than discuss the issues.
- Increases the managers' anxiety due to them not knowing what to expect, especially when quizzed publicly.
- May create a culture of fear and low morale by exposing performance deficits.
- Inhibits innovation and risk-taking because managers would not risk being seen as underperforming or exposed to public ridicule. Thus, they tend to confine themselves to specified and narrow goals within their control.
- Liable to reach inaccurate conclusions because when managers are confronted with data that they have no knowledge of and are queried about it, their standard response is likely to be 'I don't know.' This may give the wrong impression to those asking.
- Delayed feedback for performance improvement is likely to result, because managers are confronted with issues that they know little about.
- Focuses on performance issues that managers may often not be proud of and ignores important areas of progress, leaving them feel unfairly judged. This may be counter-productive to getting things done in a more timely and constructive manner.

According to Johns Hopkins University, the 'no surprises' approach takes an opposite style to the 'Gotcha' method. The 'no surprises' approach gives emphasis to full disclosure to managers on all matters and potential issues that would be addressed during the meeting. Therefore, before a meeting takes place, managers are presented with the potential questions and issues to be discussed. Hence, managers turn up at the meeting knowing exactly what data and issues they are going to present and discuss. Johns Hopkins University argues that this approach has distinct benefits.

For instance, it eliminates uncertainties and mitigates the manager's anxieties, thus providing a lot of comfort, which enhances the manager's ability to perform at optimum levels. It also gives managers the opportunity to adequately prepare for the performance meeting and thus the meetings are more productive. The 'no surprises' approach tends to encourage collaboration and cooperation between managers and senior executives, thus building a sense of trust, which is viewed as being essential for achieving the agreed goals. The method also permits managers to address potential performance shortfalls before the meeting commences, since it provides managers with the opportunity to obtain feedback on their progress towards established goals. The 'no surprises' approach eliminates the manager's fear of humiliation, and instead builds trust and confidence in the process by having continuous two-way communication about what is necessary to achieve the performance expectations.

Moreover, managers become aware of the resources and operational capacity needed to address problems because they can conduct the necessary research to identify resources needed to achieve the agreed objectives. Finally, the 'no surprises' approach encourages a culture of trust and openness, because having no surprises enables managers to function effectively by enhancing their ability to be innovative and being risk takers. Johns Hopkins University identifies several risks with the 'no surprises' approach. They view the method as being time consuming since a lot of time is usually consumed in writing and confirming responses to the issues that would be raised during the performance meeting. The method may also lead to duplication and waste of resources since the meetings may be viewed as merely reinforcing the answers to questions that have already been addressed. The 'no surprises' approach may also be susceptible to cover-up of critical details from the executive team, because issues that could reveal critical details with the potential for exposing weaknesses in performance may not be discussed or are carefully avoided by the skilful managers.

Furthermore, the range of issues that organisations are meant to respond to may be narrowed since executives may not be thoroughly abreast of key issues that are crucial to address performance deficits. Moreover, the 'no surprise' approach may give more emphasis to recent work and accomplishments because managers often get uncomfortable with having to answer repeated questions, hence they tend to focus on recent accomplishments. Finally, the method may not place enough importance on objective feedback to managers because the method is disposed to highlighting achievements that managers know are deserving of praise from executives. Thus, this does not encourage objective feedback necessary for managers to improve performance.

Johns Hopkins University argues that the goals driving effective PerformanceStat meetings are to provide operational updates, reveal deficiencies, highlight areas for improvement, and create accountability. Hence, they contend that the focus should be on what the organisation needs to do to achieve its goals of providing quality service to its citizens by identifying the relevant data, analysis, and performance deficits that departments need to address. They argue that it is all about exploring alternatives for eliminating or mitigating the deficiencies that exist, learning from what has worked, considering strategies for future improvement, and recognising managers and departments that are making progress. Johns Hopkins University accentuates that the meeting must be conducted to ensure that every manager is focused on creating meaningful and realistic results. They argue that there is no one size fits all approach to conducting a PerformanceStat meeting, but these meetings should be tailored to ensure that everyone is committed to achieving the organisation's performance targets. Johns Hopkins University contends that the benefit for these Stat meetings is that managers have an opportunity to be accountable for their data.

Finally, one needs to make a choice between the 'Gotcha' and 'no surprises' approaches after taking into consideration their respective advantages and disadvantages. Johns Hopkins University argues that the choice of the approach must depend primarily on solving specific problems, identifying the root causes of these problems, exploring alternative solutions, determining capacities and resources that exist to address the issues, and assigning responsibilities.

## *Performance Analytics in Managing Projects*

The objective of this section is to illustrate how performance analytics using datamining and knowledge management concepts may be applied in a project-oriented environment for both the private and public sectors. According to Bala (2008), datamining deals with the principle of extracting knowledge from a large volume of data and picking out relevant information that finds application in various business decision-making processes. On the other hand, a project-oriented environment deals extensively with data, information, and knowledge for a wide spectrum of decision-making scenarios. This direct linkage between datamining and a project-oriented environment will be illustrated by showing how datamining may be applied to resolve issues ranging from assessing whether a proposed project is aligned with the strategic direction of an organisation to the delivery of the project outputs and outcomes.

A project management environment provides many challenges. As a project moves through its life cycle the issues involved become numerous. Some of these issues include managing the project portfolio; having a mechanism in place to capture and share project lessons learnt; maintaining the critical project data flow processes; defining project scope; preparing project bids; planning and controlling projects; and assessing project risk. Hence, the road leading to success in a project-oriented environment is a long and difficult one. Many of the concerns related to the issues highlighted above may be mitigated through the application of analytics through sifting and analysing data related to projects previously undertaken.

Private and public sector organisations that are involved in delivering projects normally possess an enormous amount of data related to past and current projects. This voluminous historical projects data is often by itself of low value. However, its hidden potential needs to be exploited for various purposes within the project life cycle to ensure the achievement of the business objectives and more specifically corporate success. Executive management must seek ways to exploit data to add value to processes and create a new reality in terms of establishing innovative practices by capturing intelligence and knowledge across the organisation. Hence, the project-oriented environment, with its extensive data generating capability and capacity, has a direct potential link with performance analytics by applying datamining concepts for private and public sector organisations.

Cooke-Davies (2002) argues that the aim of an organisation should be to introduce practices and measures that allow the enterprise to resource fully a portfolio of projects that is rationally and dynamically matched to the organisation's business objectives and corporate strategy. These practices and measures cover a spectrum of tasks, such as transforming data to information and information to knowledge, thus optimising the information value chain of an organisation and therefore its ability to bring projects to a successful conclusion. Sutton (2010) identifies four distinct levels of project success, with each level having its own discipline, tools, and techniques.

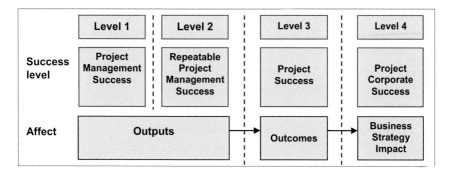

Figure 5.22  Project Success Road Map – Sutton's Project Success Framework

Thus, excellence at each level is viewed as being critical for absolute project success.

The project success framework put forward by Sutton, shown in Figure 5.22, takes a holistic corporate approach by linking project delivery to corporate strategy. It provides a road map which leads to an organisation being successful in a project-oriented environment. The objective is to apply analytics as one travels along the project success road map.

It is important to note that there is a definite tangible distinction and focus between the four success levels proposed by Sutton. Project management success refers to whether a specific project has produced the desired output (project deliverables) while project success refers to whether a specific project has produced the desired outcomes (project objectives). Hence, project output and outcomes are viewed as being separate. Repeatable project management success refers to the organisation's ability to consistently execute projects that have produced the desired output. Furthermore, project corporate success refers to whether the outcomes produced have the intended impact on the business strategy of the organisation. Sutton insists that project failure may occur at any one of the four levels. Therefore, managers are to understand where and how they are failing and then target the measures that produce the greatest likelihood of success. The application of performance analytics is viewed as providing an opportunity for management to produce the best likelihood of success at each of the four project success levels. Therefore, the objective is to identify how performance analytics may be applied at each project success level to facilitate corporate success.

Furthermore, an organisation's value chain becomes an important notion when examining the application of performance analytics to the project-oriented environment. One should note that when referring to an organisation's value chain we are referring to two separate concurrent but complementary value chains. One portrays the physical value chain and the other depicts the informational value chain. Hence, the physical value chain is the transformation of tangible resources, such as materials and labour, to a finished product or service; while the informational value chain consists of the data necessary to transform tangible resources to a finished product or service. Both value chains are necessary, each supporting the other, and ultimately, they shape the basis of the organisation's business survival.

Pyle (2003) refers to the knowledge value chain where data is viewed as a detailed record of selected events that is first identified and created, is summarised and structured into information for a specific purpose, and is then transformed into knowledge from information by a structured framework. Reference to the informational value chain in this text should be viewed as incorporating the notions presented by these researchers. Datamining or knowledge discovery refers to the process of finding interesting information in large repositories of data (Ayre, 2006). Therefore, the informational value chain is viewed as fundamental to the application of datamining in private and public sector entities. Furthermore, datamining is the process of analysing data from different perspectives and summarising it into useful information; information that can be used to increase revenue, cut costs, or both (Palace, 1996). Hence, the focus of analytics through datamining in the project-oriented environment context is the exploitation and application of the organisation's vast repository of projects data to the projects that are in the pipeline or are being implemented. The aim is to ensure the maximum return on project completion with the consequence that the undertaken projects will have the intended impact on the private and public sector organisations' business strategy.

Managers are not interested in what datamining (performance analytics) is; rather, they want to know what it will do for their organisation (Pyle, 2003). Performance analytics through datamining is used to search for valuable information from the mounds of data collected over time, which could be used in decision-making (Keating, 2008). This implies that it permits private and public sector users to analyse large databases to solve business decision concerns with the aim of increasing revenue and/ or decreasing costs. Furthermore, a project-oriented environment incorporates an organisation's informational value chain to provide timely and complex analysis of an integrated view of data to strengthen the organisation's competitive position. It is important to address two essential aspects. The first aspect is related to the contents of the data warehouse and the organisational processes that contribute to populating it. The second aspect is the application of performance analytics through datamining methods as a project moves along the four project success levels.

Let us discuss the first aspect related to the processes and the projects' data warehouse, which is considered the heart of the matter. Management has six types of resources at its disposal to carry out the projects under its responsibility. These are money, people, materials, equipment, energy, and data. Our focus is data and the processes needed to support the data flow. Datta (2008) refers to the basic elements of datamining, two of which are (a) extracting, transforming, and loading transaction data onto the data warehouse system; and (b) storing and managing the data in a multidimensional database system. However, for these elements to occur, management must have the proper processes in place. These processes permit the communication and dissemination of information and knowledge to the relevant people, thus achieving the three remaining datamining elements, namely, data access by relevant professionals; analytics being the analysis of data by suitable application software; and presenting results in a meaningful format, such as dashboards, to various organisational users. In an environment where projects are conducted by individuals in isolation, the processes will most likely be undemanding and involve only a few persons. However, in project-oriented organisational environments the processes that determine the information flow can be quite intricate.

Figure 5.23 provides a concise view of the complexity of the functions and processes that control project information flow in a private or public sector project-oriented environment. Each functional area may generate a combination of data, information, and knowledge that are required to be stored in a projects data warehouse for retrieval, analysis, and compilation of meaningful reports to resolve complex problems. Figure 5.23 shows the strong integration of the various functional areas that contribute to the physical and informational value chains. The informational value chain consists of data from external and internal sources that combine to provide

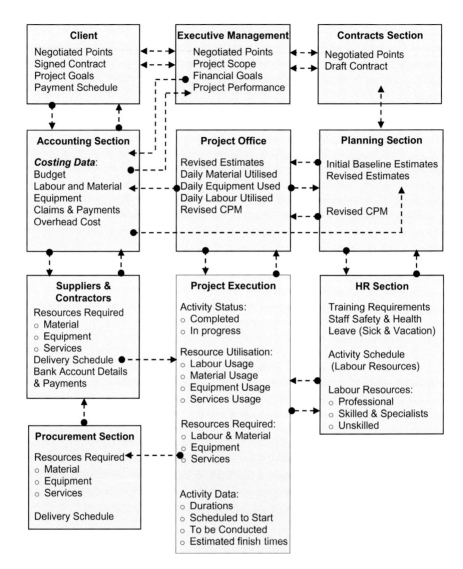

Figure 5.23  Processes Controlling Project Information Flow and Data Warehouse
Contents

a holistic and complete picture of the organisational project-oriented environment at any one point in time.

Furthermore, Figure 5.24 illustrates that ICT plays a crucial role in bringing together the processes and data to populate the projects data warehouse that may be mined to determine operational patterns and resolve specific

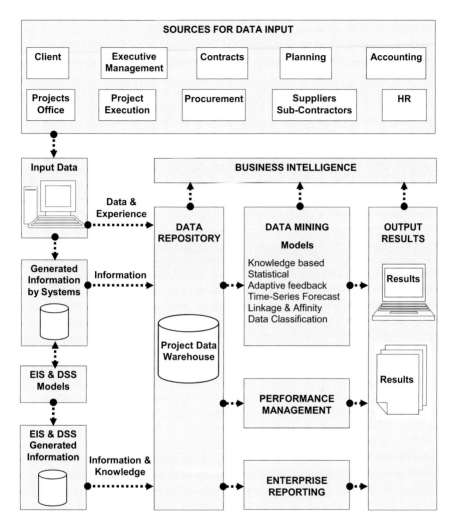

Figure 5.24  Project Data Warehouse and Datamining

concerns for private and public sector organisations. Figure 5.24 demonstrates several fundamental features. Firstly, input data may consist of raw data that act as the input transactions for Management Information Systems (MIS) that generate the transactional databases and/or may consist of documented project experiences, such as business strategies; contracts and projects scopes; various concerns and solutions; and various conflicts and conflict resolutions that are entered directly into the projects data warehouse without an MIS filtering.

Secondly, MIS provides information for the projects data warehouse and may also utilise its transactional databases as an input source for Decision Support Systems (DSS) and Executive Information Systems (EIS). Thirdly, DSS and EIS may after executing the relevant business models provide information and knowledge to the projects data warehouse. Finally, the projects data warehouse will consist of data, information, and knowledge that will be used by data mining methods for the resolution of a wide spectrum of project-related concerns. The long-term objectives are to reconcile the varying views of data; provide a consolidated view of enterprise data; create a central point for accessing and sharing analytical data; and develop an enterprise approach to business intelligence and reporting.

This concept is in line with the five-tier knowledge management hierarchy of Hicks et al. (2007), where the data warehouse is populated from various sources, including individuals' experience; databases; learning systems; DSS and EIS; knowledge pooling; best practices; expert systems and corporate strategy. It is important to note that the processes needed to support the data flow and the respective critical data sets that are generated by them are essential to the four project success levels. Furthermore, the concept is applicable to both the private and public sectors, irrespective of the industry or government department they represent. Sutton's project success Levels 1 and 2 refer to the project management function. Success Level 1 refers to the successful completion of an individual project. However, Success Level 2 refers to repeatable project management success; that is, the organisation's ability to consistently execute projects that have produced the desired deliverables.

The emphasis of Success Level 1 is related to the tasks that achieve project scope; project planning and control; and project risk management. Meanwhile, the focus of Success Level 2 is having a definite project management standard and ensuring its compliance throughout the organisation. Both success levels are related to project planning, control, and execution. The literature revealed several potential areas where performance analytic through datamining applications may be applied to project management success. These potential datamining application areas are discussed below.

## Project Proposal Preparation and Project Scope

Project proposal and project scope are interconnected. A project proposal is an initial definition of the project outputs and outcomes and precedes the project scope. Project scope defines in detail what needs to be done and what is excluded from the project. A project scope is only undertaken when a project proposal has been accepted by the client and is usually an annex of a formal legal contract between the client and the organisation executing the project. If a project proposal is issued as part of a competitive tender process, then timeliness, quality, and accuracy of the bid preparation become critical. However, at the project scope stage, quality and accuracy become the most important elements. It should be emphasised that the project proposal and project scope establish the overall project time and cost parameters, and normally also define the payment terms and payment schedule. Therefore, an organisation must overcome three major hurdles: To outclass its competitors by promptly providing a precise and accurate project bid; to be awarded the project; and to execute the project within the defined project scope and the established contractual parameters to achieve its estimated profit margin.

Nemati and Barko (2002) argue that we are living in an age where information is quickly becoming the differentiator between industry leading firms and second-rate organisations. The application of performance analytics using datamining at this level would focus on the analysis of the projects data warehouse to find similar project requirements configuration for projects that have already been undertaken by the organisation. This may be achieved through text mining and rules generation using classification and association of the projects data warehouse (previous project scopes and contracts). A software tool may be used to automatically summarise text data and extract valuable rules that may be further transformed into a semantic network which may provide a concise and accurate summary of the analysed text.

Nayak and Qiu (2004) have successfully applied this datamining technique to analyse software problem reports in pure text for the accurate prediction of time and cost in fixing software problems at a global telecommunication company. This datamining application goes beyond the concept of exploring patterns and relationships within the projects data warehouse to discover hidden knowledge; it would aim at enhancing the decision-making process by transforming data and information into actionable knowledge and gaining a strategic competitive advantage. The application of datamining tools for the project proposal preparation and project scope would allow the project management team to prepare project bids and project scopes quickly, accurately and at a lower cost before the competitors, and to be aware of specific concerns related to a particular project type. Moreover, this datamining application would mean that project bids may be submitted to a higher level of quality before competitors, thus conveying a positive image for the organisation to potential clients with a resultant increase in good will.

### Accurate Estimation of Time and Cost to Project Completion

Traditionally project management success and failure are seen as being dependent on the accurate estimation of the time and cost of the works to be completed and ensuring that works execution does not exceed these estimates. Thus, to deliver a project on time and within budget requires the application of best project management practices and tight control of the projects undertaken. An essential step within the project planning stage is the accurate preparation of activity utility data. The preparation of activity utility data is concerned with estimating the duration and cost that each activity within a project will take to be completed. Furthermore, an individual activity may be conducted by alternative methods using different types and combinations of resources. Hence, the duration and cost activity estimate will need to be established for each alternative method. These calculations become important during project execution particularly when a project slips behind schedule and certain critical activities need to be expedited. However, a large and complex project may consist of hundreds of activities, with many activities having different execution methods. Therefore, the preparation of activity utility data for a particular project becomes a mammoth task both in terms of work effort and cost; and is open to the risk of errors and inaccuracies.

Hence, at the project planning stage, datamining may be applied for the preparation of utility data for current project activities by analysing the projects data warehouse and using cluster analysis to identify similar activities that had been conducted in previous projects and extracting the related estimate data and alternative methods of executing the planned activities of the current project. This datamining application may be particularly beneficial to construction industry projects, where the resultant analysis may provide a combination of ways of executing activities utilising different equipment, crew sizes, and working hours. Admittedly, the resultant activity estimates and alternative methods would still need to be reviewed, but the overall effort and cost to conduct this essential planning task would be significantly decreased. Furthermore, datamining becomes extremely beneficial at the project implementation stage in situations where critical project activities are close to (or are) running behind schedule or when non-critical activities are approaching being critical. In this situation datamining may be utilised to analyse similar activities from the projects data warehouse of current and previous projects and suggest alternate methods to carry out the specific activity to recover lost time at an optimal cost. The overall objective in the application of datamining at this level is to ensure that the optimum economic project solution is being implemented with a change in project circumstances.

The application of datamining methods for the project planning and control stage embraces several different approaches. Iranmanesh and Mokhtari (2008) contend that traditional methods to deal with the complex task of controlling and modifying the baseline project schedule during project execution to measure and communicate the real physical progress of a project are not adequate, since these methods often fail to predict the total duration of a project to completion. These researchers have applied the decision tree, neural network, and association rule datamining tools to predict the total project duration in terms of time-estimate at completion. To calculate the time-estimate at completion, the Iranmanesh and Mokhtari model applies six input parameters, namely, actual cost of work performed; budget cost of work performed; budget cost of work scheduled; actual duration; earned duration; and planned duration.

The three datamining methods provided consistent results in that the neural network showed that the cost performance index (budget cost of work performed divided by actual cost of work performed) had the largest weighting among all indexes to predict project completion time; whilst the decision tree and the association rule methods predicted consistent Time Estimate at Completion results. The objective of the study was to enable the applied datamining tools to accurately forecast the project completion time during the project execution stage so that the project team may assess and monitor project risk by measuring project progress in time and monetary terms and take proactive preventative actions to mitigate any adverse conditions.

## *Occupational Health and Safety*

Many projects involving the output of physical items, such as in the engineering and construction environments, regularly encounter occupational health and safety issues. The consequences of accidents during project execution may turn out to be very harmful both in terms of human causalities and project cost escalation. For example, the West Gate Bridge in Melbourne, Australia collapsed during construction in 1978. Approximately 2000 tonnes of steel and concrete came crashing down, taking the lives of 35 workers with many others injured. The report from the Royal Commission (VPRS 2591/P0, unit 14) stated: 'Error begat error ... and the events which led to the disaster moved with the inevitability of a Greek Tragedy.' The project was finally completed after 10 years at a cost of A\$202 million. While project cost escalation issues may somehow be resolved in the long-term, human lives are irreplaceable.

A datamining method that may be applied to reduce such tragic incidents would be very cost-effective in terms of human causalities and project expenditure. NASA Engineering and Safety Center (NESC) was established to improve safety through engineering excellence within NASA programs and projects (Parsons, 2007). One of NESC's objectives is to find methods that enable it to become proactive in identifying areas that may be precursors to future problems. Parsons (2007) argues that problems are better prevented than solved. Hence, the goal is to find a method to uncover adverse patterns. Parsons contends that NASA's research findings indicate that clustering techniques in their environment are a key component. However, he cautions that there is a disparity between the generation of data and true interpretation (or understanding) of the meaning within the data.

The findings suggest that when data is dynamic, voluminous, noisy, and incomplete, then learning algorithms are the most ineffective and discovery algorithms such as clustering are optimal. Furthermore, when the datamining objective is exploration, clustering should be used as the optimal unsupervised learning technique (Parsons, 2007). Hence, in a project-oriented environment, performance analytics using datamining tools such as learning and discovery algorithms may be used to determine which project activities, skills, and/or resources may be more prone to occupational health and safety issues so that appropriate steps are taken to mitigate or prevent adverse occurrences.

Furthermore, decision trees and association rules may be used to detect anomalies in the way project activities are being carried out in relation to past projects and current regulatory standards (e.g. engineering, construction, and occupational health and safety standards). However, the data-mining methods applicable will depend on the organisational environment in terms of the data, information, and knowledge characteristics, such as quality, volume, integrity, and completeness.

## Preventative Maintenance of Plant and Equipment

Many project-oriented organisations, particularly those involving engineering and construction, increasingly rely on profits generated from the high utilisation of plant and equipment. The unscheduled disruption in the use of plant and equipment during project execution not only incurs direct costs of labour, replacement parts, and consumables, but also the consequential costs of delays to contract, possible loss of client goodwill and ultimately, loss of profit. The findings of a study conducted by Barber et al. (2000) regarding the cost of quality failures in two major road projects suggest that the cost of failures may be a significant percentage of total costs, and that conventional means of identifying them may not be reliable. Moreover, these types of costs will not be easy to eradicate without widespread changes in attitudes and norms of behaviour within the industry and improved managerial co-ordination of activities throughout the supply chain.

Srinivas and Harding (2008) propose a datamining integrated architecture model that provides a mechanism for continuous learning and may be applied to resolve concerns regarding process planning and scheduling, including extracting knowledge to establish rules for identifying maintenance interventions. Wang (2007) illustrates the use of datamining to solve a scheduled maintenance problem in a manufacturing shop which may also be applicable to a project environment. Wang's datamining application has two objectives: Classification – to determine what subsystems or components are most responsible for downtime, the 'root cause'; and prediction – to forecast when preventative maintenance would be most effective in reducing failures. Finally, the generated information may be used to establish maintenance policy guidelines, such as planned plant and equipment maintenance schedule. In this example classification and prediction were achieved by utilising decision trees.

Wang applied the decision tree approach to classify machine health, with equipment availability being the target dependent variable. The developed model determined the most sensible plant and equipment that are most responsible to the low equipment availability. Therefore, the aim was to detect the plant and equipment with a low availability index, thus focusing on specific apparatus (or group of apparatus) to make the maintenance effort more effective, thus saving time and cost. The generated nodes on the decision tree consisted of the different plant and equipment that are classified by the evaluation of the equipment availability value. Hence, those responsible for maintenance can examine specific plant and equipment responsible for the low availability in this part of the classification and take the necessary action. Furthermore, the model can provide accurate knowledge about the specific component that is the 'root cause' of failure within the indicated plant and equipment.

## Project Risk Management

According to Hubbard (2009, p. 46) risk management is the identification, assessment, and prioritisation of risks followed by coordinated and economical application of resources to minimise, monitor, and control the probability and/or impact of unfortunate events. There are many causes of negative risks in project execution, including delays in the delivery of adequate supplies; inadequate quality levels of procured items; high turnover of project team members; and a host of other potential adverse elements. These risk sources can be damaging to a project, such as having delays in project delivery dates and budget overruns. The consequences of these risk occurrences include financial loss; demoralisation of project team members; and harming the reputation of the project manager. Project risk management endeavours to foresee and deal with uncertainties that jeopardise the objectives, and the time and cost schedules of a project.

The basis for the project risk management process is information and knowledge. Earl (2001) argues that knowledge is a critical organisational resource and mentions examples from industry about how various organisations build and utilise their knowledge base. For example, he refers to BP Amoco's philosophy of productivity through knowledge reuse and accelerated learning, which is articulated by their expression: 'Every time we drill another well, we do the next one better.' Earl illustrates how a typical productivity-through-knowledge project at BP follows several stages, including: Documenting the current work process; gathering, summarising, and codifying knowledge and expertise on critical tasks; and conducting post-project reviews to assess initial goals, examine what happened, and assess the variance between outcome and intent.

Hence, both the positive and negative aspects of executed projects are documented for future utilisation. Furthermore, this process ensures that new learning and experience is added and validated by the project team and expert facilitators. This way a projects data warehouse is maintained with knowledge and expertise that has the potential, if suitably applied, to identify and quantify risk so that an appropriate risk response may be undertaken by the project manager.

Datta (2008) identifies risk analysis as a key datamining application area where hidden rules may not be obvious to the decision maker. Datamining is extremely useful in facilitating project risk management. For instance, risk identification basically addresses the question: What might go wrong? The aim of this process is to identify and specifically name the project risks and their characteristics. Datamining can be applied through the analysis of the projects data warehouse, seeking learning classification and association rules to determine the attributes of the potential identified risks. The analysis would closely examine the current project plan for areas of uncertainty when compared to projects that have already been implemented. Hence, the objective of the analysis would be to examine the project plans to search for issues that could cause the project to be behind schedule. The outcome of the analysis would be a full risk inventory that would categorise risk under several major headings consisting of two components; namely, the likely cause of the specific condition, for example, a sub-contractor not meeting the delivery schedule; and the general impact of the risk on the project, for example, milestones will not be achieved and/or the budget will be exceeded.

When the risk identification process is completed, the project manager will closely interpret the analysis containing the resultant risk inventory and decide on a risk-by-risk basis for which project risks are to be further investigated through risk quantification. The risk quantification process will result in a prioritised list of project risk elements that will need a response from the project manager to take advantage of the risk if it has a positive trait or to take action to mitigate any adverse circumstances should the risk have a negative attribute. Turner and Zizzamia (2008) apply a similar approach using a datamining predictive modelling for an insurance claims management scenario.

They maintain that predictive modelling provides a better understanding of a claim, allowing it to identify and prioritise an appropriate and immediate response. Their predictive model has the potential to analyse hundreds of risk attributes based on the available data to produce a numerical (and rational) score indicating exposure level and complexity. Turner and Zizzamia argue that by using the predictive model to explore and pinpoint exposure, risk managers can optimise resource deployment and minimise the process duration.

In a project management scenario, decision tree analysis provides a way of presenting a balanced view of the risks and pay-outs associated with each possible alternative strategy. This type of application has the objective of answering the following questions: What is the probability of meeting the project scope, considering all known and quantified risks? By how much will the project be delayed? What level of contingency does the organisation need to allocate in terms of time and cost to meet the desired level of certainty taking into consideration the predicted project delay? Where in the project are the most risks, taking into consideration the project network and all the identified and quantified risks?

Using decision tree analysis as a datamining tool is valuable because it visibly defines the decision to be resolved by showing all options and associated cost calculations; permits management to fully assess all the likely consequences of a decision; provides a feasible framework for calculating the outcome values and respective probabilities of achieving them; and help management to evaluate the available information to arrive at the best decisions by selecting the better alternative. Statistical methods can also be used to assess the impact of all identified and quantified risks. The outcome of the statistical analysis is a probability distribution of the project's cost and completion date based on project risks to predict schedule risk. Schedule risk is the probability that a project will go beyond its calculated time schedule and cost.

The datamining application may also provide the possible risk response based upon the project risk identification and quantification, thus itemising the options available and defining the appropriate actions to enhance the opportunities and minimise the threats. The aim of the project manager at this stage would be to closely examine the datamining results and select the best approach to address each risk that merits attention and propose actions for implementing the selected risk policy. Furthermore, the project risk datamining application should be viewed as being a continuous process that will regularly monitor and control risk during the entire project implementation life cycle.

The continuous monitoring and control of risks will identify any change in the risk status or if a particular risk has developed into an issue. The inventory of project risk is not static and constantly changes as the project is being implemented, thus new risks evolve, and other risks disappear. Hence, the datamining risk reviews allow the project manager to reassess and modify the risk ratings and prioritisation throughout the project life cycle until its successful completion.

## Repeatable Project Management Success

As stated previously, repeatable project management success is the organisation's ability to consistently execute projects that have produced the desired output. The emphasis here is on 'consistency' in implementing projects successfully. Consistency in a project management context is normally achieved by having and adhering to a uniform project management standard throughout the organisation. Therefore, the objective is to ensure that the stages and steps in the project implementation life cycle do not deviate from the project management standard by detecting anomalies in the way the project is being implemented. This is particularly applicable to projects that have a specific implementation framework, for instance, computer application software development and conducting research and development projects.

According to Eberle and Holder (2007), detecting anomalies in various data sets is an important endeavour in datamining, particularly for handling data that cannot be easily analysed. Anomaly detection in datamining is related to the discovery of events that generally do not conform to expected normal behaviour. Such events are often referred to as anomalies, outliers, exceptions, deviations, and other similar designations depending on the application domain. Although deviations may be infrequent events, their occurrence may have serious consequences and therefore their detection becomes extremely important. Most anomaly detection methods use a supervised approach that requires some sort of baseline of information from which comparisons or training can be performed (Eberle and Holder, 2007). There are generally two steps in anomaly detection schemes:

- Building a profile of the 'normal' behaviour. These profiles may be patterns or summary statistics of the overall population.
- Using a 'normal' profile to detect anomalies. Anomalies being observations whose characteristics differ significantly from the normal profile.

In a project management standard compliance application, anomaly detection can be based on supervised learning whose goal is to develop a group of decision rules that can be used to determine a known outcome. For instance, the project management standard would form the basis of the datamining learning model, defining classes, and providing positive and negative examples of objects belonging to the classes. Supervised learning algorithms can be utilised to construct decision trees or rule sets that work by repeatedly subdividing the data into groups based on identified predictor variables which are related to the selected group membership. The supervised learning algorithms, such as classification, create a series of decision rules that can be used to separate data into specific determined groups.

Typically, the major difficulty in detecting anomalies in a datamining context is to know what is 'normal.' For instance, Eberle and Holder (2007) assume that an anomaly is not random and that an anomaly should only be a minor deviation from the normal pattern. They argue that anyone who is attempting to hide devious activities would not want to be caught, and therefore, they would want their activities to look as real as possible. This does not appear to be a concern in a project management standard compliance application, since the normal' is established by the project management standard being used. Another concern is having noisy data that may hamper efforts to detect deviations. However, the type of data being generated in a project-oriented environment will be mostly filtered and therefore clean, hence noisy data should not present an obstacle for this type of application.

Furthermore, the project management standard may be codified or labelled through a standard work breakdown structure (WBS) framework that would be mirrored by the WBS milestones for the projects being implemented. Hence, the detection of any deviation from the project management standard by a specific project is a practical application that may be easily achieved by the above datamining method. This would ensure that projects are implemented to the desired quality at a cost-effective level; and that the organisation's ability to consistently execute projects that have produced the desired output is realised, thus achieving the primary objective of repeatable project management success.

## Project Success (Outcomes)

This is Sutton's (2010) project success Level 3. Project management is often viewed as the application of knowledge, competencies, methods, and tools to achieve the defined project tasks to satisfy stakeholder requirements and expectations from a project. This view takes into consideration two aspects; namely, project outputs – that is, the actual deliverables – and project outcomes – that is, the project purpose and objectives. The previous section addressed how datamining tools may aid in attaining the project outputs; this section will focus on how datamining may aid in achieving the project outcomes.

An essential factor to a project's level of success will depend on the perceptions of different stakeholders that have an interest in the project. Therefore, a critical consideration is whether the project achieves its purpose and objectives; that is, does the project do what it is supposed to do? The answer to this question is very subjective because it depends on the eyes of the beholder, namely the different stakeholders' perceptions. For example, in a building construction project, the outcomes are closely related to the users of the building. Is the building functional for the purpose it was built for? Does it accommodate different individuals' general needs? For instance, does the building design cater for individuals with special needs? Hence, project outcomes are more difficult to achieve because they take into consideration the operational aspects of the deliverables after projects have been implemented.

The difficulty with achieving project success as distinct from project management success is the variety of the stakeholders that need to be satisfied. These stakeholders may include consumer groups, environmentalists, local communities, public, mass media, shareholders, creditors, and many others depending on the nature of the project. Hence, each industry type may have different active stakeholders. However, it should be noted that individual entities normally conduct projects that are specific to their industry. Therefore, these individual entities can identify and know their influential and active stakeholders.

According to Rennolls and Shawabkeh (2008), knowledge of various forms is recognised as a crucial business asset, to be utilised for the development of new products and services, and hopefully leading to competitive advantage. They argue that knowledge management has been high on corporate agendas, with the main concerns (apart from IT infrastructure) being people and culture, and communication and collaboration. Hence, gaining knowledge of the stakeholders' needs, characteristics, and attitudes are achievable and are fundamental in influencing their perceptions. This may be translated into the application of datamining methods to establish a mechanism for building a knowledge warehouse and developing a learning organisation and utilising it for the purpose of facilitating the achievement of the project outcomes. This process may consist of capturing, storing, analysing, and sharing project lessons learnt about past project outcomes and profiling stakeholders' needs, attitudes, and characteristics.

The generation of a knowledge warehouse and the development of a learning organisation require continuous attention and effort. The major reasons for this are: (i) knowledge may be obtained from both the organisation's internal and external environments, therefore knowledge is infinite; and (ii) knowledge must be relevant to the organisation's needs; however deciding what is relevant may not be a straightforward matter. Hence, perfection is not entirely possible. Having said this however, even the imperfect achievement of a knowledge warehouse and the creation of a learning organisation will have a tremendous positive effect on the project success performance rating.

Currently, the maturation of datamining supporting processes that would consider human and organisational aspects is still living its childhood (Pechenizkiy et al., 2008). There are several activities that may help an organisation to build and retain knowledge and thus develop a learning organisation. For example, knowledge about project outcomes may be possible by collecting and storing remarks (and their source) appearing in the mass media, such as the press, internet, virtual media, and televised and broadcast media about projects that are relevant to the industry with which the organisation is involved. These projects may include project proposals or projects being undertaken within a similar cultural and operational environment, and not necessarily conducted by the organisation itself.

Academic literature suggests that a learning organisation knows how to retain knowledge, appreciates the value of sharing collective knowledge, and grows more knowledgeable with each activity it performs (Day and Rogers, 2006). The aim is to build a knowledge warehouse about the outcomes of projects, and the identification and profiling of influential stakeholders. The knowledge source in this case will be mainly external and could come from anywhere and at any time. The type of knowledge to be collected will vary but the content of critical reviews and their source are obviously most relevant. This will enable the organisation to gain knowledge about what society thinks about specific projects (likely outcomes) and identify the influential stakeholders. However, in generating a knowledge warehouse it is important to examine ethical considerations, particularly data protection legislation in relation to the creation of stakeholder profiles.

It is emphasised that reference about influential stakeholders should not be viewed as individuals but as generic designations. Another means of collecting knowledge is through the maintenance of an electronic journal, documenting specific unique experiences during project implementation. This knowledge will be mainly from internal sources; however, external information sources are also possible, particularly from contractors and sub-contractors that are involved in the project. This knowledge source will involve projects specifically undertaken by the organisation. Special focus should be given to factors related to satisfying project outcomes and specifically to remarks and other feedback from clients, potential end users of the project deliverables, and society in general.

Finally, the creation of a learning organisation is facilitated by conducting a post-project implementation review, specifically when the project outputs have shifted to the operation stage, where project outcomes are brought to fruition. The post-project implementation review evaluates the project at completion to assess what went right and wrong with the project so that experience gained from a project is not lost. The organisation should have the proper mechanisms for capturing lessons learnt through the documentation of the good and bad things in the management of the project and capture all comments and recommendations for improvements. Day and Rogers (2006) suggest that project reviews should occur after major events and milestones because data collected close to the event eliminates the bias of hindsight. Such a process facilitates a commitment to long-term relationships amongst the project teams and stakeholders, with the primary objective of having continuous improvement through learning from project experience.

This datamining mechanism ensures that knowledge gained by individuals is retained for the benefit of the organisation. A lack of such a mechanism will mean that knowledge is likely to be lost, especially if the individual ceases membership of the organisation. When employees leave an organisation, they carry with them invaluable tacit knowledge that is often the source of competitive advantage for the business (Nagadevara et al., 2008). Knowledge lost to the organisation is likely to be knowledge gained by a competitor. Therefore, datamining in a project management environment has the potential of allowing the storage, retrieving, and analysing of project experience and knowledge that is shared throughout the organisation for the achievement of the defined project outcomes and not hoarded by any individual.

The terminology of machine learning and datamining methods does not always allow a simple match between practical problems and methods; while some problems look similar from the user's point of view, but require different methods to be solved, some others look very different, yet they can be solved by applying the same methods and tools (Van Someren and Urbancic, 2006). Applying the appropriate datamining tools for problem solving in practice depends on experience and an innovative approach in the way a knowledge warehouse is utilised. The focus in the utilisation of the knowledge warehouse to achieve project success is to share project lessons learnt about the outcomes from previous projects and stakeholder profiling. The aim is to predict stakeholder reactions to a project, taking a proactive approach to mitigate any adverse stakeholder reactions to the project, thus influencing the eventual project outcomes.

According to Datta (2008), datamining can facilitate in identifying and exploring patterns of information from massive client focused databases and can help to select, explore, and model large amounts of data to discover previously unknown patterns, for the advantage of business. This application would be like a marketing environment related to launching a new product or service, where predicted reactions to the project by different stakeholders are viewed as the likely project outcomes, and the stakeholders are associated with different types of clients, with each stakeholder type having different requirements, attitudes, and attributes.

The objective of this datamining application would be to identify the various stakeholders that are likely to have an interest in a proposed project; to identify the likely attitude to a proposed project by the identified stakeholders; to ascertain the characteristics of each stakeholder type; to itemise decisions taken in prior projects and their respective impact on stakeholder attitudes and project outcomes; and to provide suggestions that are likely to have a positive impact in changing stakeholder attitudes and therefore are likely to influence project outcomes.

Stakeholder segmentation analysis would be an appropriate method in this situation. The stakeholder segmentation analysis would aim at identifying groups of stakeholders that have common attributes and that have an interest in a proposed project. The stakeholder attributes are likely to represent attitudes and resultant behaviours. This stakeholder segmentation analysis may be based on supervised learning algorithms that take the form of a hierarchical decision tree structure such that small segments form larger stakeholder segments, with each small segment representing a stakeholder type. Furthermore, using the knowledge about the attributes of each stakeholder type and the decisions taken in former projects and their respective impact on stakeholder attitudes and project outcomes, this datamining application may create a series of decision rules that may be used to generate ideas that are likely to positively change stakeholder attitudes to the proposed project for each stakeholder segment, with the aim of favourably impacting the outcomes of the proposed project.

## Project Corporate Success

Project corporate success is Sutton's (2010) project success level 4. The consequence of business endeavours that do not support the business strategy is the misuse and underutilisation of corporate resources. Hence, it is essential that projects are aligned with the organisation's strategic direction and that their completion results in a positive impact on the organisation's business objectives (Cleland and Ireland, 2006). Applying datamining methods in a project-oriented environment can facilitate corporate success. In a practical sense, this means using datamining techniques to sustain organisational initiatives by having proper project selection processes and best practice in project portfolio management.

According to Cleland and Ireland (2006), projects are essential to the survival and growth of organisations. They argue that failure in the management of projects in an organisation will impair the ability of the organisation to accomplish its mission in an effective and efficient manner. Datamining may be used to determine if a project proposal is aligned with the corporate business strategy before a decision is made about whether to pursue it. Like the other datamining examples, this application is based on having and utilising the relevant information stored in the projects data warehouse (refer to Figure 5.24).

A combination of decision tree learning and statistical methods may be used to construct a predictive model. The aim of this application is to conduct an analysis of the project proposal and the relevant information items held in the projects data warehouse to determine a strategic fit index for project proposals. The strategic fit index would be based on assessing the following:

(a) The extent to which a proposed project fits within the organisation's activity boundary.
(b) Human and financial resource implications of the proposed project to ensure that it does not expose the organisation to the risk of economic non-sustainability.
(c) Stakeholder values and expectations related to the proposed project to ensure that unrealistic project execution time frames that often lead to ineffective outcomes do not occur.
(d) Long-term influence of the proposed project on the organisation to ensure that undertaking a major project does not restrict the organisation from conducting other concurrent projects and hence adversely impact the organisation's potential for future growth.

This datamining application will evaluate the strategic fit of a proposed project and will also rank proposals in order of priority, since a high strategic fit index means a higher project ranking. Undertaking a major project can be viewed as a partnership between the project owner (client), the organisation executing the project, and suppliers. The failure of one partner could be detrimental to the project and is likely to result in a financial loss to some or all the partners. The extent of harm to the project will depend on the failing partner. For example, if the client fails, the project will likely be abandoned. However, if a supplier fails, the project will probably experience a delay with a resultant financial loss, but the project will likely survive.

Project portfolio management in this text will take the view of the organisation executing the project and consider a datamining application for determining the financial reliability of the client and contractors in the supply chain. Van Someren and Urbancic (2006) cite an example that uses datamining for predicting financial risk in the banking industry by evaluating credit worthiness to forecast the financial state of a person, company, or other entity by exploring the characteristics of their current financial state and economic conditions. This example is based on a Bayesian model using information about similar clients and contractors whose status is known to establish a comparable appraisal baseline. The input to the model is a mixture of numerical and nominal data that is normally available in financial statements. Furthermore, Hensher and Jones (2007), using published financial data, apply a mixed logit model (or random parameter logit) to predict corporate bankruptcy. They argue that the development of more powerful and accurate forecasting methodologies to predict corporate bankruptcy is of importance to a range of user groups, including shareholders, creditors, employees, suppliers, ratings agencies, auditors, and corporate managers.

A similar approach may be used to assess the financial reliability of the project partners, in this case, the client and contractors in the supply chain. However, it should be noted that the generated knowledge from the prediction model will need to be presented in a manner that is easily understood by the decision makers. There is no doubt that these datamining applications will enable the organisation to understand and assess the financial reliability of potential partners and enable private and public sector organisations to choose their partners carefully and thus avoid partial or project failure.

The applications described above are based on the ability to have a well synchronised team utilising the extensive knowledge that an enterprise possesses. To engage in innovative project management practices, such as supply chain management and the sharing of information and knowledge across the entire organisation, requires the acceptance of a collaborative spirit. Computer-supported cooperative work (CSCW) systems are computer-based tools that support collaborative activities that meet the requirements of normal collaborative efforts among people (Zhu, 2006). Future research should attempt to link datamining tools to CSCW. The future widespread use of datamining lies in the ability and capacity of an organisation to implement an enterprise knowledge framework that permits individuals to collaborate in the gathering, storing, analysing, and sharing of data, information, and knowledge across the organisational boundaries, be they private or public entities. An enterprise approach to knowledge management will increase an organisation's capacity to apply datamining tools for strengthening its competitive position and thus ensure corporate success.

This section has examined datamining and the project management environment. It has shown several applications where datamining and knowledge learning may be used at various stages in the project management life cycle, with the goal being to achieve corporate success in private and public sectors. Some of the major organisational issues that are applicable to both the private and public sectors include:

(a) Ensuring that performance analytics using datamining applications focus and support the strategic direction of the organisation to gain a competitive advantage and meet clients' satisfaction.
(b) Recognising that data, information, and knowledge are corporate assets that should be proactively managed like every other major organisational asset.
(c) Respecting ethical values by ensuring that individuals are not the end target of profiling exercises, since this may conflict with data protection legislation.
(d) Ensuring the support of executive management for sharing data, information, and knowledge across the organisational boundaries.
(e) Recognising that performance analytics using datamining applications do not follow the conventional data processing way of thinking but require an innovative and creative mindset.
(f) Recognising that information and particularly knowledge are dynamic and therefore must be constantly rejuvenated through continuous regeneration.
(g) Recognising that the contents of a data warehouse depend on well-defined data flow procedures and processes.
(h) Ensuring that appropriate security measures and procedures are in place to protect the data warehouse from unauthorised access and/or deliberate and non-deliberate destruction.
(i) Ensuring that an appropriate organisation structure is in place for knowledge management and its associated datamining functions.
(j) Selecting suitable analytical software tools that are compatible with the existing ICT infrastructure and the projects' data warehouse.

Finally, it is essential to have a senior management executive who will act as the organisation's performance analytics champion to guarantee the long-term sustainability of the warehousing and datamining investment. These measures will ensure that using performance analytics in a project-oriented environment will help an organisation to achieve corporate success at unprecedented levels.

## Performance Reporting as a Performance Management Tool

Performance reporting is an integrated system of planning and reporting that is specifically tailored for achieving outcomes. It involves a spectrum of tasks that entail detailed planning, such as the generation of the priorities and strategies outline report (applicable to private and public sector entities) and supplemental information for a legislative review programme (applicable to public sector entities), apart from the normal regular reporting on the plans, including the compilation of the annual report. Hence, performance reporting is a comprehensive systematic process that is intended to explain organisational goals and policies; communicate the organisation's priorities; monitor progress and generate continuous improvement; promote budgeting and resource allocation decisions; and present information to legislators (in case of public entities), the public, media, and other stakeholders about the function of the organisation.

Planning and reporting are fundamental functions of an organisation's ongoing operations and decision-making, with reporting on performance being an essential component of effective management and accountability. A critical aim of performance reporting is not only to show how an organisation is progressing, but it should encourage a 'continuous improvement' mentality. This is achieved through a continuous feedback loop, where reports on the organisation's activities and performance provide essential information to management to allow them to make the best possible decisions in preparation for the next planning cycle. Performance reporting should be viewed as an integral part of the planning process, with the plan leading the process and reporting being at the tail end of the process, within a continuous recurring loop. Hence, the plan will outline the organisation's priorities, objectives, and actions aligned with the current and anticipated circumstances and available resources. The plan is theoretical, but once the implementation phase commences it becomes reality, and the organisation will need to have a process for monitoring progress and adjusting the plan as deemed necessary. At the end of the financial year, the organisation will need to report on the priorities, objectives, actions, and performance of the organisation (i.e., reporting on the realisation of the plan).

It should be noted that the report will likely influence future planning and resource allocation. In fact, in a performance reporting model, planning and reporting are two ends of the same process, within a continuous cyclic feedback loop. It should be recognised that planning and performance reporting are conducted across organisations and are compiled in various structures for a diverse number of purposes. Moreover, best management practice and accountability has resulted in the generation of considerable quantities of performance information. This performance information has been exploited for strategic and operational decision-making and has facilitated a greater level of accountability within the organisation. The performance reports are prepared for a mixed audience. For the private sector, the performance reports are mainly for internal consumption. On the other hand, for the public sector, the performance reports would likely be made available to members of the Legislature (or Parliament) depending on the type of democratic system, the public, and media.

### *Performance Reporting Deployment*

O'Mahony and Lyon (2015) argue that performance reporting at its best should enable an organisation to link its operational activity and decision-making with the attainment of its strategy. Hence, they contend that this provides organisations with the essential information to make more confident and effective decisions, focuses the attention of management on activities that truly matter, and provides a consistent view of actual performance across the business. However, their research, which was conducted across 50 countries with over 1100 finance professionals, revealed that despite the ever-increasing volumes of data and disruptive technologies, current Performance Reporting processes are flawed, and many enterprises continue to proceed with 'information' that is ineffective in the support of rapid and informed decision-making. Hence, O'Mahony and Lyon argue that the findings suggest missed value delivery opportunities and slow responses to emerging threats.

Their findings indicate that there are three critical areas that needs to be focused on to enhance current Performance Reporting capability and provide the organisation with information that can drive value, namely: Building the right data and governance foundation; structuring the delivery model for success; and empowering finance professionals to collaborate with the business effectively.

### Building the Right Data and Governance Foundation

In their survey, O'Mahony and Lyon (2015) found that over 71% of respondents perceive that their organisation applies a common set of KPIs consistently. This supports their contention that in a knowledge-based economy, organisations make better decisions, create competitive advantage, and successfully deliver their strategy when they optimise and make appropriate use of data. Hence, they conclude that for Performance Reporting to be effective, a common data hierarchy must be successfully deployed across the organisation applying the appropriate KPIs of the organisation, which in practice is strengthened by data that supports the representation of a single version of the reality.

Applying a common set of KPIs consistently across the organisation is important since it permits management to compare and understand performance across the organisation on a coherent basis. Additionally, transparent metrics allow management to have a clear view of how the holistic strategy is impacting the organisation by the operational activity. Despite this, there are three issues that must be addressed, namely that the KPIs being used are aligned to the organisation's strategy; that the data supporting these KPIs is coherent and reliable; and that the organisation is managing its data at an adequate quality level. However, one must be aware that although organisations may have coherent and reliable KPIs, there is a risk that these KPIs may depict an ambiguous representation of performance if they are not determined properly. For instance, organisations should be careful not to apply measures that are too inwardly focused without considering their competitors.

On the other hand, those with too outward a focus risk ignoring the detail with the consequence that the measures are not aligned with the corporate strategy. Therefore, management must be aware that inferior data will generate inconsistent measures, even if they are labelled as the same KPI. Hence, the reason for ensuring that the basic data structures and data feeds are correct, because they are very critical in supporting decisions that management can have confidence in. Therefore, there must be a strong focus on gathering the data that really matters to the organisation; in other words, collecting the data that maintains an integrated set of defined KPIs. Furthermore, this assumes that data is of high quality and that a robust data governance structure is in place to guarantee the integrity of the data, since data is the fundamental basis for the Performance Reporting process.

## Structure the Delivery Model for Success

In their survey, O'Mahony and Lyon (2015) found that over 55% of the respondents perceive there is a duplication of reporting between finance and the organisation (business). O'Mahony and Lyon argue that the management needs performance information that is consistent, controlled, timely, relevant, complete, and delivered in a cost-efficient manner. They also contend that success is determined by how well the Finance function is structured, and how efficiently and effectively it delivers its Performance Reporting capability. Having a centralised finance function facilitates the issue related to comparability and consistency of the information being produced if this centralised structure has the objective of increasing the quality of the data basis and not as a cost saving measure. The research findings suggest that many organisations have outsourced transactional Finance activities, but very few have done the same for Performance Reporting. This is mainly due to concerns over data security, loss of potential intellectual property, and cultural change issues.

O'Mahony and Lyon argue that often there is a perception that the Finance function imposes the Performance Reporting process on the enterprise with little regard to integrating into the wider business. However, the findings suggest that senior management tends to set the overall strategy, with the Finance team having the function of establishing a transparent Performance Reporting process that is cascaded throughout the organisation to support decision-making at all levels. However, many respondents perceive Finance to be a great challenge. These respondents perceive that weak core data puts into question the relevance of metrics and the whole Performance Reporting process. Therefore, this loss of trust in the effectiveness of the process increases the risk that the Finance team will be perceived as mere data providers, fit only to perform basic analysis.

This is confirmed by the findings in that respondents suggested that Finance personnel are still not partnering with the rest of the organisation effectively to support consistent KPIs and an increasing use of technology, which are both viewed as the backbone of Performance Reporting. The O'Mahony and Lyon study reveals that over 56% of respondents believe the Finance team is perceived principally as gatekeepers of data or providers of basic financial analysis at best. Therefore, it is important that there is total commitment to the Performance Reporting process across the organisation by having the appropriate structures.

## Empower Finance Professionals to Collaborate with the Business Effectively

In their survey, O'Mahony and Lyon (2015) found that only 45% of respondents' reports are driven directly from the source systems and that over 67% of respondents either did not know or disagreed that cloud solutions have the required functionality to complete the performance reporting processes. This supports the O'Mahony and Lyon argument that building the right data foundations, putting in place robust governance structures, and adapting the delivery model might provide the backbone for delivering effective Performance Reporting, but Performance Reporting will only prosper if Finance personnel are properly equipped to deliver high-quality insight that supports decision-making empowered with the deployment of reporting technologies. A key success factor is the deployment of reporting technologies such as cloud computing. The key goal of Performance Reporting is timeliness and excellence of decision-making in the organisation to deliver a sustainable competitive advantage. This can only be achieved by having Finance professionals with the right level of competences and comportments, supported by the applicable technologies.

O'Mahony and Lyon contend that organisations must ensure that Finance personnel involved in Performance Reporting should devote a significant proportion of their time to collaborating with the business and should not be tied up in transactional activities, such as data extraction and manipulation or traditional month-end activities. The research study revealed that most respondents continued to extract data and manipulate offline, rather than use source systems, resulting in more inefficiency, higher risk of error, less timely provision of information to management, and poor confidence in the reporting process. A good reporting tool minimises manual intervention to derive the required information. However, the research study by O'Mahony and Lyon suggests that the provision of reports for 'on-the-move' viewing is still not occurring in most organisations and that mobile friendly reporting has not yet become a mainstay in Performance Reporting.

### *Performance Reporting Principles*

There are several principles that define the performance reporting framework. These key principles are depicted in Figure 5.25 and described below. Firstly, there must be a clear definition of the organisation's vision and mission, including an outline of its business strategy. This provides the raison d'être of the organisation and clearly communicates this to all stakeholders. The outline of the organisation's strategy must describe the purpose of the organisation, the organisational structure and key reporting relationships, the general customer profile, and service/product delivery method. If the organisation is a public sector entity, the strategy must clearly identify who the organisation serves, including the stakeholders who rely on the government-sponsored programmes, products, and services. It must also identify and explain those services that are delivered through another entity and how these services are provided (e.g., health and educational services). Additionally, it must define the communication approach that describes the governance structure of the organisation, including the relevant legislations.

The second principle is regarding the establishment of priorities in relation to the defined strategic direction. This ensures that operational activities are aligned with the strategic direction. Performance reporting must indicate how the holistic priorities of the organisation are being achieved. If the organisation is a public sector entity, management must ensure that department priorities are congruent with the general strategic direction of government. The third principle defines the objectives for each organisational priority and identifies the tasks required to achieve them. A priority is viewed as a results-oriented statement that describes each key focus area of the organisation. It expresses the desired outcomes, stating in practical terms what the organisation expects to achieve. On the other hand, a task or action refers to an identifiable initiative, strategy, or program that is intended to press forward the objective. It is essential that priorities, objectives, and tasks are linked in an ambiguous manner that illustrates how the

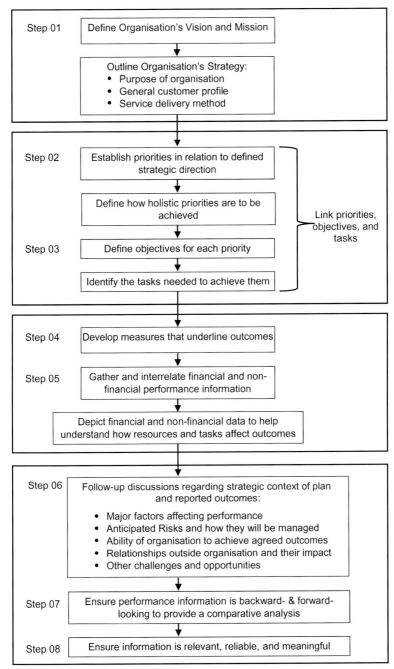

Adapted: Manitoba Treasury Board Secretariat. (2008). Performance Reporting Principles & Guidelines. https://www.gov.mb.ca/chc/grants/pdf/performance_reporting_guide.pdf

Figure 5.25  Principles Defining the Performance Reporting Framework

organisation will focus its efforts to ensure that the effort of the organisation remains focused on its priorities and intended outcomes.

The fourth principle is related to the development of measures that underline the outcomes on selected critical aspects of performance. Measures indicate the degree to which the identified tasks are being implemented towards the achievement of the organisation's objectives and desired outcomes. Measures should be unambiguous and to the point, exhibiting pertinent and meaningful information on important aspects of the organisation to relevant stakeholders. Therefore, a suite of measures should be a balance between inputs, outputs, and outcomes in a results-oriented organisational environment. The fifth principle is regarding the conjoining of financial and non-financial information. It is important that financial and non-financial performance information and the application of resources about the tasks being conducted by the organisation are gathered and interrelated. Financial and non-financial information needs to be depicted in a manner that helps the user understand how resources and tasks affect outcomes. This will facilitate the evaluation of the impact of resource allocation and improve decision-making regarding future tasks and resource requirements. It is important to establish whether planned, actual, and variance expenditure information has been provided. It is also essential to know which tasks are consuming most of the funding and whether the organisation provides information to support the key operational assumptions that drive the financial plan.

The sixth principle is related to having follow-up discussions that are to take place regarding the strategic context for the plan and the reported outcomes. It is important to have information about the strategic context of the organisation so that management may comprehend the difficulty and level of uncertainty that is associated with the development and implementation of initiatives, services, and the decision-making process of the organisation in that specific strategic environment. These discussions are to include the major factors affecting performance; the risks to be encountered and how these will be managed; the capability of the organisation to achieve the agreed outcomes; the relationships that occur outside of the organisation and how these relationships affect organisational tasks; and other challenges and opportunities that may be presented at any point in time.

The seventh principle is based upon the concept of having performance information that is backward- and forward-looking in time to provide a comparative analysis about prior years and predicted performance, with the predicted performance integrating future expectations. This will indicate whether organisational performance is stable, improving, or declining. The final principle is about ensuring that the information is relevant, reliable, and meaningful. Hence, the information should be expressed in simple and uncomplicated written language that is easily understood. The information sources should be clearly disclosed, and a balanced assessment of performance provided without the use of emotional writing. Ideally, performance information should be focused on a few critical aspects based upon measured data and presented in a clear and consistent fashion by comparing one period to the next with the variations explained. Therefore, organisational performance information must be comprehensible, accurate, and must depict a reliable evaluation existing at that point in time as a snapshot.

Table 5.7, which is adapted from Manitoba Treasury Board Secretariat (2008), provides a self-diagnostic assessment questionnaire to evaluate whether the organisation has the desired capacity to apply the Performance Reporting principles defined above. The basic notion to keep in mind when devising an assessment scheme is that *what cannot be measured cannot be managed and what cannot be managed cannot be changed.* Therefore, the assessment of whether the organisation has the desired capacity to apply the Performance Reporting principles requires the development of a balanced set of measures for each of the eight principles illustrated by Table 5.7. The self-diagnostic assessment questionnaire is divided into eight segments, with each segment representing one of the key principles described above. Each segment has several questions that must be answered by respondents to assess whether the organisation has the desired capacity to apply the Performance Reporting principles.

Each question is scored by a number from zero (0) to ten (10), with zero being the lowest score and ten the highest. For example, to the question: 'To what extent have the organisation's vision, mission, and mandate been clearly/explicitly stated?', a zero would mean that the organisation's vision, mission, and mandate have not at all been clearly/explicitly stated. An easy way of conducting this assessment is by administering the diagnostic questionnaire to employees in the organisation ranging from middle to executive management.

The diagnostic questionnaire has been designed to make it user-friendly for respondents to complete. It is best to administer the diagnostic questionnaire as part of an information seminar on performance management. This procedure would allow a facilitator the opportunity to explain the

*Table 5.7a* Self-diagnostic Assessment Questionnaire for Performance Reporting Framework

| Statement | | Score |
|---|---|---|
| **Defining the Organisation's Vision and Mission** | | |
| 1. | To what extent have the organisation's vision, mission, and mandate been clearly/explicitly stated? | |
| 2. | To what extent have the core values (if applicable) of the organisation been stated? | |
| 3. | To what extent has an overview of programs, products, or services been included? | |
| 4. | To what extent is it clear who the organisation serves – including clients or stakeholders who rely on programs, products, and services? | |
| 5. | To what extent has the governance structure of the organisation (including legislation, organisational structure, and key reporting relationships) been communicated clearly? | |
| 6. | If services are delivered through another organisation, to what extent has it been explained how those services are delivered? | |
| **Establishing organisational priorities in relation to the defined strategic direction** | | |
| 1. | To what extent are the organisation's priorities related to overall priorities provided by the organisation? | |
| 2. | In reporting on performance, to what extent has the organisation referenced how the overall priorities have been advanced? | |
| **Defining the objectives for each priority** | | |
| 1. | To what extent has the organisation clearly indicated what its priorities are? | |
| 2. | To what extent are the priorities, objectives, and actions well-defined and do they support the purpose (i.e., vision, mission, and mandate) of the organisation? | |
| 3. | To what extent is there a clear link between the overall organisation's priorities and department priorities, objectives, and actions? | |
| 4. | To what extent has the organisation outlined realistic, result-oriented objectives under those priorities? | |

| | | |
|---|---|---|
| 5. | To what extent has the organisation described specific and financially feasible actions that will be or have been undertaken to achieve the objectives? | |
| **Developing measures that underline outcomes** | | |
| 1. | To what extent are the measures aligned with the organisation's priorities? | |
| 2. | To what extent are measures aligned with what is important to the organisation at a high level as reflected in the organisation's overall priorities? | |
| 3. | To what extent is there a clear link between priorities, objectives, actions, and measures? | |
| **Gathering and interrelating financial and non-financial performance information** | | |
| 1. | To what extent has planned, actual, and variance expenditure information been provided? | |
| 2. | To what extent is it clear what key activities account for most of the funding? | |
| 3. | To what extent does the organisation explain the key operational assumptions that drive the financial plan? | |
| 4. | To what extent is financial and non-financial information presented in such a way as to help the reader understand how resources and activities affect results? | |

*Table 5.7b* Self-diagnostic Assessment Questionnaire for Performance Reporting Framework (continued)

| Statement | Score |
|---|---|
| **Following up discussions regarding strategic context of plan & reported outcomes** | |
| 1. To what extent has the organisation outlined the key factors that affect performance in a concise manner? | |
| 2. To what extent has the organisation identified key risks and how they are being managed or addressed? | |
| 3. To what extent has the organisation taken steps to develop capacity to meet expected challenges? | |

(Continued)

*Table 5.7b* (Continued)

| | Statement | Score |
|---|---|---|
| 4. | To what extent have external events or circumstances affected activities and results? | |
| 5. | To what extent has the organisation dealt with the external events or circumstances? | |
| 6. | To what extent has the organisation identified areas where there are cross-department or inter-organisational initiatives? | |
| 7. | To what extent does the organisation explain the impact these relationships have on performance? | |
| 8. | If services are delivered through another organisation, to what extent have the responsibilities for service delivery and performance been explained? | |
| **Ensuring performance information is backward- and forward-looking to provide a comparative analysis** | | |
| 1. | To what extent does the performance measure include baseline data and trend information? | |
| 2. | To what extent does the organisation discuss future expectations, goals, or previously stated targets? | |
| 3. | To what extent does the information enable the external reader to understand if performance is improving, declining, or remaining stable? | |
| 4. | To what extent has the organisation provided comparative information regarding the performance of other organisational segments where it is useful or applicable? | |
| 5. | To what extent have any inconsistencies in data or the presentation of data been explained? | |
| 6. | To what extent has the organisation discussed significant variances between actual and expected results? | |
| 7. | In the information presented, to what extent has the organisation considered lessons learned? | |

purpose of the diagnostic questionnaire and how it may be completed. Furthermore, it would give the respondents the opportunity to ask further questions should they not fully understand the meaning of any question. It is best to have the respondents complete the diagnostic questionnaire on a voluntary basis and, most importantly, anonymously. The information

*Table 5.7c*  Self-diagnostic Assessment Questionnaire for Performance Reporting
Framework (Continued)

| Statement | | Score |
|---|---|---|
| **Ensuring information is relevant, reliable, and meaningful** | | |
| 1. | To what extent does the information avoid jargon, acronyms, and overly technical descriptions? | |
| 2. | To what extent is the information presented succinctly? | |
| 3. | To what extent is information presented in a manner that helps the reader understand the content and appreciate its significance? | |
| 4. | To what extent are successes and shortcomings reported in a balanced way? | |
| 5. | To what extent were charts, graphs, or other visuals used in a way that enhanced the understanding of the document? | |
| 6. | To what extent was there an explanation why measures were chosen and what limitations might exist with the data/indicators? | |
| 7. | To what extent are performance measures relevant, and to what extent do they measure what they purport to measure? | |
| 8. | To what extent are measures consistent from year to year? | |
| 9. | To what extent is the performance information sourced? | |
| 10. | To what extent is the data accurate, recent, and of sufficient quality? | |

seminar programme would ensure that the length of the diagnostic questionnaire (43 questions) does not pose any difficulties to the participants and make their participation more interesting for them. Having the information seminar conducted in a comfortable conference room environment with all the necessary facilities would also ensure that the participants complete the questionnaire fully and accurately.

The respondents will be requested to answer each question of the diagnostic questionnaire by assessing each question with a score ranging from 0 to 10, as explained previously. The scores from each of the completed respondents' diagnostic questionnaires are entered in a database, as shown in Table 5.8. For example, a row in Table 5.8 represents an individual respondent's scores for the questions. The responses for each question for all respondents are added and divided by the number of respondents to

*Table 5.8* Database for Responses of Self-diagnostic Assessment Questionnaire

| Respondent | Principle 1 | | | | | | | Principle 2 | | | Principle 3 | | | | | | Principle 4 | | | | Principle 5 | | | | |
|---|---|---|---|---|---|---|---|---|---|---|---|---|---|---|---|---|---|---|---|---|---|---|---|---|---|
| | Q1 | Q2 | Q3 | Q4 | Q5 | Q6 | Ave. Score | Q1 | Q2 | Ave. Score | Q1 | Q2 | Q3 | Q4 | Q5 | Ave. Score | Q1 | Q2 | Q3 | Ave. Score | Q1 | Q2 | Q3 | Q4 | Ave. Score |
| 1 | | | | | | | | | | | | | | | | | | | | | | | | | |
| 2 | | | | | | | | | | | | | | | | | | | | | | | | | |
| 3 | | | | | | | | | | | | | | | | | | | | | | | | | |
| 4 | | | | | | | | | | | | | | | | | | | | | | | | | |
| 5 | | | | | | | | | | | | | | | | | | | | | | | | | |
| . | | | | | | | | | | | | | | | | | | | | | | | | | |
| . | | | | | | | | | | | | | | | | | | | | | | | | | |
| . | | | | | | | | | | | | | | | | | | | | | | | | | |
| . | | | | | | | | | | | | | | | | | | | | | | | | | |
| . | | | | | | | | | | | | | | | | | | | | | | | | | |
| . | | | | | | | | | | | | | | | | | | | | | | | | | |
| . | | | | | | | | | | | | | | | | | | | | | | | | | |
| . | | | | | | | | | | | | | | | | | | | | | | | | | |
| . | | | | | | | | | | | | | | | | | | | | | | | | | |
| . | | | | | | | | | | | | | | | | | | | | | | | | | |
| . | | | | | | | | | | | | | | | | | | | | | | | | | |
| . | | | | | | | | | | | | | | | | | | | | | | | | | |
| . | | | | | | | | | | | | | | | | | | | | | | | | | |
| . | | | | | | | | | | | | | | | | | | | | | | | | | |
| . | | | | | | | | | | | | | | | | | | | | | | | | | |
| . | | | | | | | | | | | | | | | | | | | | | | | | | |
| Ave. Score | | | | | | | | | | | | | | | | | | | | | | | | | |

| Principle 6 | | | | | | | | | Principle 7 | | | | | | | | Principle 8 | | | | | | | | | | |
|---|---|---|---|---|---|---|---|---|---|---|---|---|---|---|---|---|---|---|---|---|---|---|---|---|---|---|---|
| Q1 | Q2 | Q3 | Q4 | Q5 | Q6 | Q7 | Q8 | Ave. Score | Q1 | Q2 | Q3 | Q4 | Q5 | Q6 | Q7 | Ave. Score | Q1 | Q2 | Q3 | Q4 | Q5 | Q6 | Q7 | Q8 | Q9 | Q10 | Ave. Score |
| | | | | | | | | | | | | | | | | | | | | | | | | | | | |
| | | | | | | | | | | | | | | | | | | | | | | | | | | | |
| | | | | | | | | | | | | | | | | | | | | | | | | | | | |
| | | | | | | | | | | | | | | | | | | | | | | | | | | | |
| | | | | | | | | | | | | | | | | | | | | | | | | | | | |
| | | | | | | | | | | | | | | | | | | | | | | | | | | | |
| | | | | | | | | | | | | | | | | | | | | | | | | | | | |
| | | | | | | | | | | | | | | | | | | | | | | | | | | | |
| | | | | | | | | | | | | | | | | | | | | | | | | | | | |
| | | | | | | | | | | | | | | | | | | | | | | | | | | | |
| | | | | | | | | | | | | | | | | | | | | | | | | | | | |
| | | | | | | | | | | | | | | | | | | | | | | | | | | | |
| | | | | | | | | | | | | | | | | | | | | | | | | | | | |
| | | | | | | | | | | | | | | | | | | | | | | | | | | | |
| | | | | | | | | | | | | | | | | | | | | | | | | | | | |
| | | | | | | | | | | | | | | | | | | | | | | | | | | | |
| | | | | | | | | | | | | | | | | | | | | | | | | | | | |
| | | | | | | | | | | | | | | | | | | | | | | | | | | | |
| | | | | | | | | | | | | | | | | | | | | | | | | | | | |
| | | | | | | | | | | | | | | | | | | | | | | | | | | | |
| | | | | | | | | | | | | | | | | | | | | | | | | | | | |
| | | | | | | | | | | | | | | | | | | | | | | | | | | | |
| | | | | | | | | | | | | | | | | | | | | | | | | | | | |

obtain an average score for each question. An overall average score for a particular principle is calculated in a similar manner. It is suggested that an EXCEL spreadsheet is used for entering the responses and calculating the total and average scores.

### Interpreting the Diagnostic Questionnaire for the Performance Reporting Framework

The best way to explain how to interpret the diagnostic questionnaire is through an example. For simplicity, let us assume that after all the responses from the middle and senior management have been collected and entered, the average scores are as shown in Table 5.9.

The overall average scores for each principle shown in Table 5.9 are plotted as shown in Figure 5.26 to provide a graphical view of the overall appraisal of whether an organisation is adequately prepared for implementing a Performance Reporting Framework. This appraisal (see Figure 5.26) indicates that while the organisation is generally prepared to implement the Performance Reporting Framework, it needs to review and improve several principles and specific aspects, namely Principle 1: Enhancing the definition of the organisation's vision and mission; Principle 3: Enhancing the definition of the objectives for each priority; Principle 6: Improving the processes for following up discussions regarding strategic context of plan and reported outcomes; Principle 7: Improving the attributes of performance information so that it is backward- and forward-looking to provide a comparative analysis; and Principle 8: Refining the quality of information to ensure it is relevant, reliable, and meaningful.

Moreover, Figure 5.27 to Figure 5.31 analyse the data deeper in relation to those principles and aspects that need further review and improvements (i.e. review of each specific relevant question with a score of 6 or less). For example, Figure 5.27 reveals that Principle 1, Defining the Organisation's Vision and Mission, has three shortcomings (or weaknesses) that need improvement, namely that there is a need to provide an adequate overview of the programs, products, or services; that the governance structure of the organisation needs to be communicated better; and that an explanation as to how services are to be delivered when these services are being provided through another organisation. Once these weaknesses are corrected, this Principle would be confirmed. Similarly, Figures 5.28

STRATEGIC MANAGEMENT AND BUSINESS PLANNING    291

Table 5.9  Average Scores Computed in the Database of Responses of Diagnostic Assessment Questionnaire

| Principle 1 | Q1 | Q2 | Q3 | Q4 | Q5 | Q6 | Ave. Score |
|---|---|---|---|---|---|---|---|
| Ave. Score | 9 | 8 | 6 | 7 | 6 | 6 | 7 |

| Principle 2 | Q1 | Q2 | Ave. Score |
|---|---|---|---|
| | 9 | 7 | 8 |

| Principle 3 | Q1 | Q2 | Q3 | Q4 | Q5 | Ave. Score |
|---|---|---|---|---|---|---|
| | 8 | 6 | 7 | 8 | 6 | 7 |

| Principle 4 | Q1 | Q2 | Q3 | Ave. Score |
|---|---|---|---|---|
| | 9 | 8 | 7 | 8 |

| Principle 5 | Q1 | Q2 | Q3 | Q4 | Ave. Score |
|---|---|---|---|---|---|
| | 9 | 9 | 6 | 8 | 8 |

| Principle 6 | Q1 | Q2 | Q3 | Q4 | Q5 | Q6 | Q7 | Q8 | Ave. Score |
|---|---|---|---|---|---|---|---|---|---|
| Ave. Score | 6 | 7 | 8 | 8 | 8 | 6 | 6 | 7 | 7 |

| Principle 7 | Q1 | Q2 | Q3 | Q4 | Q5 | Q6 | Q7 | Ave. Score |
|---|---|---|---|---|---|---|---|---|
| | 7 | 6 | 8 | 7 | 8 | 8 | 5 | 7 |

| Principle 8 | Q1 | Q2 | Q3 | Q4 | Q5 | Q6 | Q7 | Q8 | Q9 | Q10 | Ave. Score |
|---|---|---|---|---|---|---|---|---|---|---|---|
| | 6 | 5 | 8 | 5 | 8 | 6 | 8 | 8 | 7 | 9 | 7 |

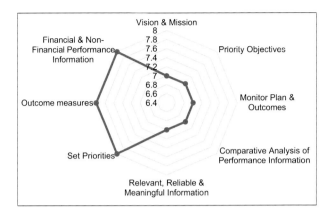

Figure 5.26 Organisation's Readiness for Implementing a Performance Reporting Framework

to Figure 5.31 provide the diagnosis for the other principles that revealed specific shortcomings.

The above has provided a simple but effective method of ascertaining an organisation's preparedness for implementing the Performance Reporting Framework. The suggested diagnostic model takes a holistic view in the way the proposed Performance Reporting Framework may improve the organisation's performance. Furthermore, an alternative method of administrating the diagnostic questionnaire is by holding a focus group meeting managed by a trained facilitator. The facilitator would discuss each individual question with the focus group members and record the group's response. Therefore, instead of having everyone completing the diagnostic questionnaire, the focus group would discuss each item (question) in detail and document a single group (consensus) response. If this method is used, the facilitator must be careful to ensure that each member of the focus group participates in the discussion and the final response decision (for every question) and that no one single person(s) dominates the discussion and resultant responses.

The careful application of the suggested diagnostic questionnaire will provide a simple but effective assessment method for determining how prepared the organisation is for implementing the Performance Reporting Framework. The diagnostic questionnaire will reveal the strengths and weakness within each specific principle so that appropriate action may be taken to maintain the strengths and transform the identified weaknesses into sustainable strengths.

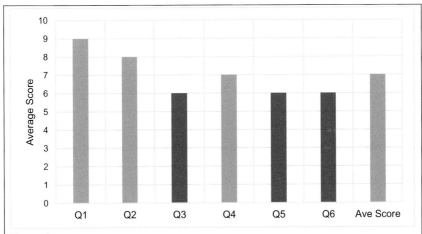

**Diagnosis:**

An overview of programs, products, or services has not been adequately included.

The governance structure of the organisation (including legislation, organisational structure, and key reporting relationships) has not been adequately communicated.

Services delivered through another organisation have not been adequately explained as to how these services will be delivered.

Figure 5.27  Diagnosis Principle 1: Defining the Organisation's Vision and Mission

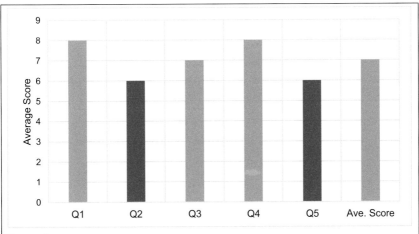

**Diagnosis:**

The priorities, objectives, and actions are not adequately defined, and they are not clearly supportive of the organisation's purpose.

The organisation has not adequately described specific and financially feasible actions that will be or have been undertaken to achieve the objectives.

Figure 5.28  Diagnosis Principle 3: Defining the Objectives for Each Priority

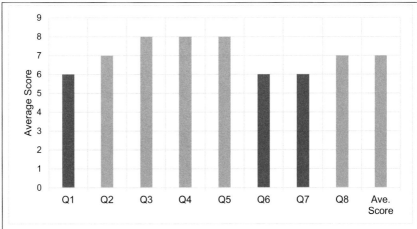

**Diagnosis:**

The organisation does not adequately outline the key factors that affect performance in a concise manner.

The organisation does not adequately identify areas where there are cross-department, or inter-organisational initiatives.

The organisation does not adequately explain the impact the relationships have on performance.

*Figure 5.29*  Diagnosis Principle 6: Discussing Strategic Context of Plan and Reported Outcomes

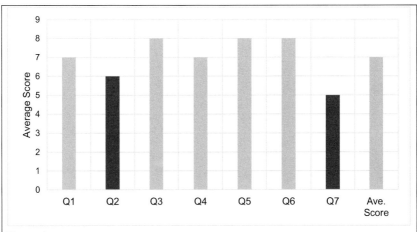

**Diagnosis:**

The organisation does not adequately discuss future expectations, goals, or previously stated targets.

The organisation does not adequately consider lessons learned regarding the information presented.

*Figure 5.30*  Diagnosis Principle 7: Ensuring Performance Information Provides a Comparative Analysis

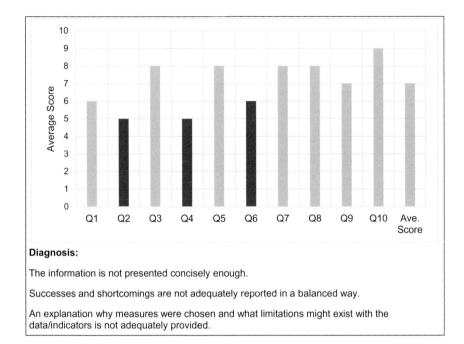

Figure 5.31 Diagnosis Principle 8: Ensuring Information is Relevant, Reliable, and Meaningful

# Conclusion

This chapter discussed in detail several performance management tools that are directly linked to the strategic direction of an organisation. These related performance management tools included strategic planning; business planning (including variance Analysis); performance analytics; and performance reporting. It is important to note that the performance management tools presented are applicable to both the private and public sectors. However, management must adapt them to their specific operational environment. The next chapters under Part II will discuss specific individual performance management tools, which may be considered as add-ons to the performance management tools covered in this chapter.

# References

Ayre, L.B. (2006). *Data Mining for Information Professionals*. Available at: https://www.researchgate.net/publication/228386369_Data_Mining_for_Information_Professionals (Accessed 22 November 2023).

Bala, P.K. (2008). 'A Technique for Mining Generalized Quantitative Associated Rules for Retail Inventory Management.' *International Journal of Business Strategy*, 8(2), pp. 114–127.

Barber, P., Graves, A., Hall, M., Sheath, D., and Tomkins, C. (2000). 'Quality Failure Costs in Civil Engineering Projects.' *International Journal of Quality & Reliability Management*, 17(4/5), pp. 479–492.

BearingPoint (2019). *Data & Analytics. Analytical Insights to Boost Your Business Performance*. Available at: https://www.bearingpoint.com/files/Data_and_Analytics_boost_your_business_performance.pdf (Accessed 21 November 2023).

Behn, R.D. (2014). *The PerformanceStat Potential: A Leadership Strategy for Producing Results*. Washington: Brookings Institution Press.

Cleland, D.I. and Ireland, L.R. (2006). *Project Management: Strategic Design And Implementation*. Fifth Edition. Clarksville, TN: McGraw-Hill.

Cooke-Davies, T. (2002). 'The "Real" Success Factors on Projects.' *International Journal of Project Management*, 20, pp. 185–190.

Datta, R.P. (2008). 'Data Mining Applications and Infrastructural Issues: An Indian Perspective.' *ICFAI Journal of Infrastructure*, VI(3), pp. 42–50.

Day, R and Rogers, E. (2006). 'Enhancing NASA's Performance as a Learning Organization.' *NASA Ask Magazine*, 22, pp. 36–39.

Drury, C. (2012). *Management and Cost Accounting*. Eighth Edition. Cengage India (1 January, 2012).

Dusenbury, P. (2000). Governing for Results and Accountability: Strategic Planning and Performance Measurement. *The Urban Institute Washington, USA*.

Dye, R., and Sibony, O. (2007). 'How to Improve Strategic Planning.' *The McKinsey Quarterly* (3), p. 41–49.

Earl, M. (2001). 'Knowledge Management Strategies: Toward a Taxonomy.' *Journal of Management Information*, 18(1), pp. 215–233.

Eberle, W. and Holder, L. (2007). Discovering Structural Anomalies in Graph-based Data. Published in: *Seventh IEEE International Conference on Data Mining Workshops (ICDMW 2007)*, Omaha, NE, USA.

Ernst & Young (2015). *Becoming an Analytics Driven Organization to Create Value: A Report in Collaboration with Nimbus Ninety*. Ernst & Young Global Limited, UK.

Hensher, D.A. and Jones, S. (2007). 'Forecasting Corporate Bankruptcy: Optimizing the Performance of the Mixed Logit Model.' *ABACUS*, 43(3), pp. 241–264.

Hubbard, D. (2009). *The Failure of Risk Management: Why It's Broken and How to Fix It*. Hoboken, NJ: John Wiley & Sons.

Hicks, R.C., Dattero, R., and Galup, S.D. (2006). 'The Five-tier Knowledge Management Hierarchy.' *Journal of Knowledge Management*, 10(1), pp. 19–31.

Hicks, R.C., Galup, S.D., and Dattero, R. (2007). 'The Transformations in the Five Tier Knowledge Management Transformation Matrix.' *Journal of Knowledge Management*, 8, p. 1.

Iranmanesh, S.H. and Mokhtari, Z. (2008, August). 'Application of Data Mining Tools to Predicate Completion Time of a Project.' *Proceedings of World Academy of Science, Engineering and Technology*, 32, pp. 234–239.

Johns Hopkins University (2022). *What Is Performance Analytics?* Centre for Government Excellence, Johns Hopkins University. Available at: https://centerforgov.gitbooks.io/performance-management-getting-started/content/introduction-to-performance-management.html (Accessed 21 November 2023).

Keating, B. (2008). 'Data Mining: What Is It and How Is It Used?' *The Journal of Business Forecasting*, 27(3), pp. 33–35.

Keegan, M.J. (2015). *Introduction Perspective on the PerformanceStat Potential: A Leadership Strategy for Producing Results.* Available at: https://www.businessofgovernment.org/sites/default/files/Perspectives_0.pdf (Accessed 23 November 2023).

Król, K. and Zdonek, D. (2020). 'Analytics Maturity Models: An Overview.' *Information 2020*, 11, p. 142.

Nagadevara, V., Srinivasan, V., and Valk, R. (2008). 'Establishing a Link between Employee Turnover and Withdrawal Behaviours: Application of Data Mining Techniques.' *Research and Practice in Human Resource Management*, 16(2), pp. 81–99.

Nayak, R. and Qiu, T. (2004). Data Mining Application in a Software Project Management Process. Published in: *Proceedings of Australian Data Mining Conference*, Cairns, Australia.

Nemati, H.R. and Barko, C.D. (2002). 'Enhancing Enterprise Decisions through Organizational Data Mining.' *Journal of Computer Information Systems*, Summer, pp. 21–28.

O'Mahony, J. and Lyon, J. (2015). *Performance Reporting: An Eye on the Facts.* KPMG LLP, UK. Available at: https://assets.kpmg/content/dam/kpmg/pdf/2015/11/performance-reporting-an-eye-on-the-facts.pdf (Accessed 21 November 2023).

Palace, B. (1996). *Data Mining: What is Data Mining?* Anderson Graduate School of Management at UCLA. Available at: http://www.anderson.ucla.edu/faculty/jason.frand/teacher/technologies/palace/datamining.htm (Accessed 21 November 2023).

Parsons, V.S. (2007). 'Searching for "Unknown Unknowns".' *Engineering Management Journal*, 19(1), pp. 43–46.

Pechenizkiya, M., Puuronenb, S., and Tsymbalc, A. (2008). 'Towards more Relevance-oriented Data Mining Research.' *Intelligent Data Analysis*, 12, pp. 237–249.

Pirtea, M., Nicolescu, C., and Botoc, C. (2009). 'The Role of Strategic Planning in Modern Organisations.' *Annales Universitatis Apulensis Series Oeconomica*, 11(2), pp. 953–957.

Pugna, I.B., Dutescu, A., and Stanila, G.O. (2018). Performance Management in the Data-driven Organisation. Published in: *Proceedings of the 12th International Conference on Business Excellence 2018*, Bucharest.

Pyle, D. (2003). 'Making the Case.' *IBM Database Magazine*, 8(4). Available at: https://www.researchgate.net/publication/293125552_Making_the_case (Accessed 22 November 2023).

Rennolls, K. and AL-Shawabkeh, A. (2008). 'Formal Structures for Data Mining, Knowledge Discovery and Communication in a Knowledge Management Environment.' *Intelligent Data Analysis*, 12, pp. 147–163.

Sharda, R., Delen, D., and Turban, E. (2015). *Business Intelligence and Analytics: Systems for Decision Support*. 10th Edition. New York: Pearson Education.

Srinivas and Harding, J.A. (2008). 'A Data Mining Integrated Architecture for Shop Floor Control.' *Proc. IMechE Part B: J. Engineering Manufacture*, 222(5), pp. 605–624.

Sutton, B. (2010). *Why Projects Fail – Mastering the Monster (Part 1): Examining the Underlying Reasons for Project Failure, and How to Use That Knowledge to Get Your Projects Back On Track*. ArchItect, Bearpark Publishing Ltd. Available at: https://www.developerfusion.com/article/84858/why-projects-fail-8211-mastering-the-monster-part-1/ (Accessed 22 November 2023).

Turner, K. and Zizzamia, F. (2008). 'Predicting Better Claims Management.' *Risk Management*, 55(7), pp. 52–55.

Van Someren, M. and Urbancic, T. (2006). 'Applications of Machine Learning: Matching Problems to Tasks and Methods.' *The Knowledge Engineering Review*, 20(4), pp. 363–402.

Wang, K. (2007). 'Applying Data Mining to Manufacturing: The Nature and Implications.' *Journal of Intellectual Manufacturing*, 18, pp. 487–495.

Wong, H.K. (2004). 'Knowledge Value Chain: Implementation of New Product Development System in a Winery.' *The Electronic Journal of Knowledge Management*, 2(1), pp. 77–90.

Zhu, H. (2006). 'Role Mechanisms in Collaborative Systems.' *International Journal of Production Research*, 44(1), pp. 181–193.

# 6

## CRITICAL SUCCESS FACTORS FOR ESTABLISHING AND APPLYING KPIS

'Numbers have an important story to tell. They rely on us to give them a clear and convincing voice.'

Stephen Few
Author and I.T. Innovator

The focus of the previous chapter was limited to several performance management tools that were directly linked to the strategic direction of an organisation. These related performance management tools included strategic planning, business planning (including Variance Analysis), performance analytics, and performance reporting. It was also demonstrated that these performance management tools were applicable to both the private and public sectors. This chapter will discuss the use of Critical Success Factors (CSFs) as a means of establishing and applying Key Performance Indicators (KPIs) as a performance management tool. CSFs and KPIs are both useful tools that may be applied to achieve organisational success at every level within the entity. They both contribute to the growth of the organisation by providing a control mechanism for mitigating costs and

DOI: 10.4324/9781032685465-8

maximising opportunities. Generally, CSFs are the critical elements or activities that are required to ensure the success of an organisation.

Rockart (1979, p. 85) defined CSFs as those critical areas whose high performance or success is essential since they determine the success of an organisation. CSFs are viewed as being the elements needed to ensure success. On the other hand, KPIs indicate the level of success and are viewed as the necessary tools to measure the performance of any organisation. KPIs help an organisation to obtain consistent and acceptable results that will eventually enable the organisation to grow and succeed in a competitive and turbulent environment.

Ascertaining the CSFs is seen as being important because it permits the organisation to focus its efforts on developing its capabilities to match the critical success factors. However, successful outcomes may only be realised when employees work together as a well synchronised team that constantly achieves the organisational strategic objectives and goals through the achievement of CSFs via the established KPIs. Keep in mind that a KPI is a computed measure to assess how well individual goals and/or the organisational targets are being achieved. Normally, managers do not rely on just one CSF or KPI, but tend to define several CSFs that are supported by KPIs to determine how well departments, work teams, or individual employees are faring at performing the tasks allocated to them.

## Introduction

It is important to recognise that CSFs and KPIs are not the same. They both complement each other. In combination they provide a very powerful performance management tool for the organisation. Both are essential for attaining organisation success. The identification of CSFs permits the organisation to focus its efforts on building its capabilities to meet the defined CSFs. On the other hand, the defined KPIs provide the measures to determine whether the organisation is achieving its defined CSFs.

CSFs can be defined as those specific areas or aspects that are essential to the success of an organisation. Hence, the concept is based on the premise that for an organisation to achieve the desired performance, it must dedicate special attention and involvement to those areas that have an impact and are the determining elements for the organisation's present and future success. Thus, CSFs are highly significant for the realisation of the established strategic goals and aspirations of the organisation. On the other hand, KPIs are viewed as a collection of events or actions that play an important role in the success of organisations of today and tomorrow (Parmenter, 2007, p. 3). Moreover, a KPI is a definite method to quantify and qualify the tactical goals of an organisation reflecting its priorities. Hence, a KPI is specifically used to measure performance, with the CSFs being an aid for management to reveal aspects that are to be improved so that the success of the organisation is ensured.

Figure 6.1 illustrates that there are two concurrent processes, both starting with the definition of the organisation's strategy and ending with the outcome of the strategy. Each process branch has a distinct focus, one related to strategy implementation (action execution) and the other focusing on the performance (CSFs and KPIs). Furthermore, the focus of performance monitoring is through the KPIs. For example, from a CSF and KPI perspective, an organisation's CSFs may target specific aspects, such as the reliability of its applied information technology and the associated information systems, system utilisation, and several human resource aspects.

However, the KPIs related to these specific aspects may include: (a) for information technology reliability: Uptime of 99.9% for file server and WAN, less than three seconds response time, and no reported or observed security violations; (b) for information system reliability: Uptime of 99.9% for application systems, less than five seconds response time per transaction,

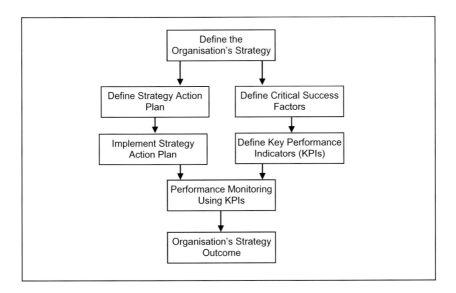

*Figure 6.1* Relationship between Strategic Planning, CSFs, and KPIs

Table 6.1 Different Notions the CSFs and KPIs Represent

| | Critical Success Factors | KPIs |
|---|---|---|
| Issue to be addressed | What should be done to be successful? | Level of success |
| Core role | Identify prerequisites for success | Specify what is being done |
| Category of measurement | Qualitative (characteristics or features) | Measurable |
| Reliance | Standalone | Contingent on benchmarks |
| Business visions | Utilise visions | Generate visions |

and no reported or observed security violations; (c) for system utilisation: System penetration growth rate per month of 1.5%; and (d) for human resource aspects: Less than 10% staff turnover rate, an average of less than two days' sick leave per worker, an average of less than 50 client complaints per month, and an average decrease in operational cost per year of 7.5%.

Table 6.1, which has been adapted from BSC Designer, shows the different notions that the concepts of CSFs and KPIs represent. CSFs and KPIs are different and have a different purpose. They complement each other; hence both are needed and rely on each other. It is essential that management recognises and knows the differences and details of these two different concepts. The differences between CSFs and KPIs are as follows:

- CSFs are the basis for organisational success and what is needed (action) for the success to happen. However, KPIs are the consequences of the action taken. Hence, they indicate what is being done (KPI) and not what should be done (CSF). A CSF tells management what should be done to be successful and a KPI tells management whether they are succeeding.
- CSFs are general in nature and focus on specific aspects. However, KPIs are established in harmony with the identified priorities of a particular organisation.
- A CSF is normally qualitative and describes an aspect such as 'customer loyalty' that can only be discussed or analysed but not measured. On the other hand, KPIs are usually quantitative, representing numerical values.

- CSFs indicate what needs to be accomplished to succeed as an independent aspect. However, KPIs are dependent on other data for comparison purposes. The KPI can be considered as a benchmark that needs to be compared with what has been achieved (performance).
- CSFs consist of several KPIs and can be utilised by management to improve performance. Hence, the information conveyed by the KPIs is applied by the CSF to upgrade itself.
- CSFs do not usually change, but at times they may be changed when an organisation sets up a new goal. However, CSFs transform in a cyclic manner contingent on the needs of customers or the environment. On the other hand, KPIs are constantly changing since they are measured again and again on a timely basis.

After an organisation establishes its vision and strategies, it then identifies the CSFs that determine what should be done to achieve the goal. This enables the organisation to measure the success rate (or performance) by monitoring progress, which informs the organisation its position in relation to the agreed goal. KPIs do not improve performance themselves but they reveal if the organisation must improve or if the goal is achieved. CSFs are a strategic tool and guide the organisation on how to achieve the strategic goals. CSFs are an approach that is used externally by the customers to judge how well the organisation is progressing. However, a KPI is used internally by the organisation, hence CSFs are common, general, and sometimes universal. Therefore, designing CSFs is more crucial to the performance of the organisation, hence managers should devote more time to them.

## Types of Critical Success Factors

Rockart (1979) identified five main types of CSFs that organisations are required to consider, namely: The industry, competitive strategy and industry position, environmental factors, temporal factors, and managerial position (if considered from an individual's point of view). The industry factors reflect the specific attributes of the industry that need to be accomplished to sustain the organisation's competitive position within the market. For example, a high technology start-up organisation may perhaps ascertain 'innovation' as a CSF. Furthermore, different industries are likely to have unique, industry-specific CSFs. Hence, the unique attributes of a specific industry will likely result in defining its own specific CSFs. On the other hand, different industries will have diverse CSFs.

For example, research studies have shown that while industry sectors of retail, manufacturing, education and health, and financial services had common CSF themes, such as market orientation, learning orientation, entrepreneurial management style, and organisational flexibility, their specific CSFs were found to be different. These findings suggest that each organisation has its specific unique goals. Although organisations operating within the same industry are likely to have several common CSFs, it is also probable that even though there may be some type of industry standard, not all firms in one industry will have identical CSFs.

Environmental factors are the outcome of macro-environmental effects on the organisation, such as the economic performance of country, industry regulation, political development, and demographic changes. A PEST analysis will indicate the environmental factors that have an impact on the organisation and help management to understand the magnitude of their influence, and possibly identify several CSFs for the organisation. The PEST analysis will examine the business climate, the economy, the competitors, and technological developments. Environmental factors depict the external environment and are not under the control of the organisation. However, these environmental factors cannot be ignored, and management must take them into account when developing CSFs.

An example of environmental factors affecting an organisation could be the liberalisation of financial institutions and the regulatory requirements regarding mergers. Strategic factors are the outcome of the organisation's competitive strategy. Hence, the organisation's circumstances and its position in the marketplace or its adopted strategy to increase its market share bring about several CSFs. For instance, the approach an organisation prefers to position and market itself, such as whether it is a high-volume, low-cost producer or a low-volume, high-cost one will influence the identification of the CSFs. Therefore, differing strategies and positions in the marketplace generate distinctive CSFs. Hence, not all organisations in a particular industry will have the same CSFs. The values of an organisation and its target market, amongst other aspects, will influence the CSFs that are suitable for the specific organisation at a given point in time. Hence, an organisation will define its CSFs to reflect its specific circumstances.

The temporal factors result from the organisation's internal driven changes and development. Temporal factors are normally encountered in relation to short-term circumstances, such as an operational crisis. Hence, these CSFs may be important, but are usually short-lived. For example, a rapidly expanding business might have a CSF that sought to increase its international sales with urgency. Furthermore, temporal factors are of a temporary nature or one-off CSFs that result from a specific event that necessitate their inclusion. In these crisis circumstances, specific obstacles, disputes, and inspirations will essentially determine these CSFs.

For example, an organisation that is aggressively undertaking to develop a new innovative product would have a need for an R & D team to undertake this development. Thus, it would have the CSF of 'establishing a dynamic R & D team to develop a specific product' and it may have this CSF for different product development programmes. The final type of CSF is related to the managerial role or position. These types of CSFs are important if they consider an individual manager's point of view. Hence, an individual managerial role may generate several CSFs if the performance is related to the specific manager's area of responsibility, and which may be deemed critical to the success of an organisation. For example, an individual manager's qualities become important in situations where the organisation has established CSFs related to product quality, inventory control, and cash control. Similarly, in organisations with departments focused on customer relationships, an individual's manger's qualities become essential, especially if a CSF is defined in relation to customer relationship management. Remember that things that are measured get done more often than things that are not measured. Hence, each CSF should be measurable and associated with a target goal (KPI).

It is important that CSFs are written in a clear and meaningful manner. Hence, to write good CSFs, it is essential that you have an exceptional understanding of the organisation and its associated industry. The analysis of the external environment related to the industry sector for defining CSFs is typically available from the public domain through the internet, such as industry associations, trade associations, prospectuses of competitors, news media, and equity/analyst reports. These will provide management with sufficient information for conducting a PEST analysis, thus building adequate knowledge regarding the economic environment, the industry, and competitors. Conducting a SWOT analysis will also enable management to analyse both the internal (SW: Strengths and weaknesses of the organisation) and external (OT: Opportunities and threats) environments.

The accumulated information regarding the internal and external environments provides the basis from which management can generate discussions to identify and define the CSFs. It has already been shown that there are five types of CSFs that reflect the environment the organisation and associated industry are operating in. These provide the fundamental basis for generating good CSFs. It has also been illustrated that those organisations that belong to the same industry sector may have common CSFs, but most CSFs are unique to the organisation, since they are highly dependent on the vision of those leading the organisation. Hence, it is important to customise the CSFs to your specific organisation and individuals based upon the strategic and operational uniqueness of the organisation. It is also critical to accumulate knowledge about the competitors in the industry, such as their general market position, their resources, capacity and capabilities, and their strategy. Such knowledge can have an impact on the organisation's own strategy and resultant CSFs.

CSFs should be defined in a way that results in observable differences. Keep in mind the principle that elements which get measured are more likely to be achieved in comparison to factors that are not measured. Hence, it is important to identify CSFs that are observable or possibly measurable in certain aspects so that they are defined in terms that would facilitate their measurement. Firstly, define the CSFs that have the greatest impact on the organisation's performance, since CSFs are viewed as the most critical factors for organisations or individuals. However, since CSFs are typically qualitative, care should be taken in identifying them to ensure that all likely CSF alternatives are included in subsequent discussions. An effective and pragmatic CSF begins with an action verb, which should clearly and briefly express what is essential and where the focus of attention should be placed, such as 'monitor consumer needs and future trends.' Examples of action verbs include such words as monitor, deploy, increase, manage, and perform, amongst many others.

The term 'Critical Success Factor' is often viewed as being synonymous with the term 'Key Performance Indicator.' However, they are completely different and dependent on each other. Therefore, make sure you do not confuse the terms (i.e., a CSF is not a KPI). CSFs originate from the organisation's mission and objectives and are critical components for a strategy to be successful. Therefore, they specify what needs to be done to be successful and tend to be widespread across organisations. On the other hand, KPIs are measures that quantify objectives and enable the measurement and extent of strategic performance achievement.

Once an organisation's CSFs are identified and defined, management can utilise them to develop more specific and precise KPIs. These are the explicit measures that managers and organisations apply to assess performance, and as has already been shown, they often differ from organisation to organisation. Hence, KPIs tend to be unique for each individual organisation. KPIs provide the data that enables an organisation to determine whether the CSFs have been sustained, and if the goals have been attained. KPIs can also be applied at different organisational levels. For instance, they can be applied to explain strategic organisation-wide goals, or to drill down into an organisational division, unit, team, and individual objectives. Therefore, KPIs are normally much more detailed and are quantitative in format than CSFs. For example, the CSF 'Increase sales in the national market' could generate the KPI 'Increase sales revenue in the national market by 10 percent year-on-year.'

## Implementing Critical Success Factor Model

As explained previously, CSFs are operational issues or aspects that need to be always conducted correctly, continuously, and repeatedly by the staff in the organisation. It is important that CSFs are aligned with the strategic direction of the organisation and are recognised as the basis of all important performance measures, such as the KPIs. Typically, an organisation has five to eight CSFs, and from these CSFs several KPIs are established. This section will describe the CSFs methodology framework, and links the strategy, CSFs, and KPIs to ensure that the strategic objectives are achieved.

The concept regarding the CSFs approach was introduced by Ronald Daniel, Senior Partner of McKinsey & Company in a Harvard Business Review article of 1961, titled 'Management Information Crisis.' Daniel (1961) examined the issue of inadequate management information for identifying objectives, defining strategies, decision-making, and measuring outcomes against established targets. He argued that organisational planning information must focus on 'success factors' that were described as 'three to six factors that determine success… key jobs [that] must be done exceedingly well for a company to be successful.' Rockart (1979) from MIT Sloan School of Management refined Daniel's (1961) concept to aid senior managers in defining their information needs to better manage their organisations. He argued that the success factor concept had a boarder application base other than gathering information needs for management decision-making. Hence, the CSFs approach has been successfully applied for strategic planning.

The CSFs methodology framework is based on the concept that a CSF is a high-level objective feature that is vital for an organisation or project to achieve its mission. Thus, CSFs are those few events that must happen as expected to ensure success for a manager or an organisation. Therefore, CSFs signify those managerial or enterprise areas, which must receive special and continual attention to bring about high performance and include those concerns that are most important to an organisation's current operating activities and to its future success. The CSFs methodology is a sophisticated tool that is easy to apply. However, for the methodology to be effective, CSFs must have high-level objectives; be essential to the organisation's success; be holistically beneficial to the organisation or a division; and be directly linked to the organisation's business strategy. Furthermore, CSFs should be expressed as action aphorisms that define the method, desired outcome, and the action to be taken (e.g., increasing current operational efficiency by 30%).

The CSF methodology is put into operation as a team effort. Hence, it is necessary to establish a team of individuals who will be working together on identifying and defining the CSFs. It is important that this team has a mixture of individuals, ranging from typical shop floor workers to senior management. Moreover, the team discussion may be led by a facilitator who would have the necessary experience to stimulate discussions and generate feedback from the team members. Caralli et al. (2004) contend that the goal of the CSF method is to tap the knowledge and intuition of the organisation's managers.

They argue that many experienced managers act with a 'sixth sense' that makes them successful; thus, the CSF method attempts to make this 'sixth sense' explicit so the organisation can use it as an aid in setting strategic direction and in directing resources to those activities that can make it successful (Caralli et al., 2004). Hence, CSFs are derived from the organisation rather than created, because every organisation already has a set of CSFs but may not know them, particularly the industry CSFs that the organisation inherits (Ibid.).

Caralli et al. argue that the CSF method is a way to harvest these factors from a review and analysis of the goals and objectives of key management personnel in the organisation. Moreover, CSFs are revealed by talking and listening to key management employees to discover what is important in their specific domain and discussing the barriers they encounter in achieving their goals and objectives. Figure 6.2 illustrates the Critical Success Factors Methodology Framework that consists of five critical processes, each one being related to the other:

1.  Objectives: Where do we want our organisation to go? This is the overall target of what the organisation is trying to achieve.
2.  Strategy: How are we going to get there? These are measures that will be taken by the organisation to achieve the overall target.
3.  Identify the CSFs: What must be done absolutely right? These are the tasks that support the attainment of the measures being taken by the organisation to achieve the overall target.

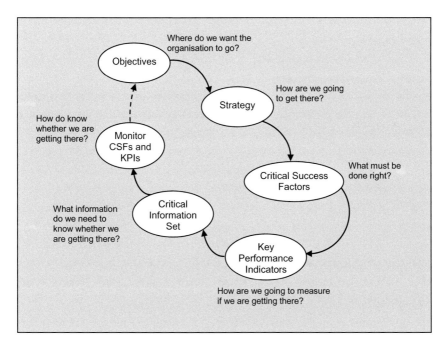

Figure 6.2  Critical Success Factors Methodology Framework

4.  Define the key performance indicators (KPIs): How do we measure if we are getting there? These are the measures that are established to evaluate whether the tasks are being achieved.
5.  Determine the critical information set: What information should be collected to track progress of each individual CSF? Thus, the information collected should be sufficient to verify whether the KPIs are being achieved.

## Strategic Objectives

Strategic objectives are the holistic or big-picture goals for the organisation. In other words, they are goals that can affect the overall success of an organisation or project aim, rather than focusing on minor details. Strategic objectives describe what the organisation will do to endeavour to fulfil its mission. Strategic objectives are typically some kind of performance goals, for example, launching a new service. Organisations are inclined to pursue several key strategic objectives, namely operational excellence, new products and services, business models, and customer and supplier intimacy. To generate successful strategic objectives, it is important for management to define the current position of the organisation in consultation with its key stakeholders.

Next, management must define the desired future position of the organisation. This will provide a basis for generating strategic objectives. It is important to actively involve the key stakeholders. Keep in mind that strategic objectives are purpose (intention) statements that will aid management to generate an overall vision and an agreed set of goals and measurable steps for the organisation as a means of achieving the desired outcome. A strategic objective has the greatest effect when it is quantifiable either by statistical or observable data.

## Strategy

The organisational strategy is a roadmap that defines how management will achieve the desired objectives. Generally, a strategy is a plan of action that is intended to achieve a long-term or overall aim. There is limited consensus about the exact meaning of strategy. However, Michael Porter views strategy as an instrument that defines and communicates an organisation's unique position in the industry, and defines how organisational resources, skills, and competencies should be merged to generate a competitive advantage. There are different levels of strategy. The focus here is on two specific strategies, namely corporate and divisional (business unit).

The corporate strategy refers to the overall strategy of an organisation, which will likely consist of several business divisions or units, operating in various markets. The corporate strategy outlines how the holistic organisation supports and develops the value of the business units within it. The corporate strategy addresses the issue of how the organisation will be structured so that all its units, through synergy, generate more value together than they would individually. At a corporate level, the strategy is focused on how the various business units should fit together, and to utilise the available resources to generate the utmost possible value. This is achieved by defining forceful values that all in the organisation can support, developing robust internal competences, leveraging technologies and resources between departments and teams, creating durable relationships in teams and between teams, forming and sustaining a compelling corporate brand, and acquiring capital from investors.

At a divisional (or business unit) level, the strategy focuses on competing successfully in the individual markets and examines the issue of how each division is to increase its market share. It is essential that the divisional strategies are linked to the objectives defined in the corporate strategy. Competitive analysis needs to consider the core competencies of each division and how these may be utilised to address the customers' needs. A SWOT analysis will reveal the strengths and weaknesses of the divisions and will also reveal the opportunities and threats. It is important that employees are involved in defining the divisional strategy and that the final version is communicated to all so that employees within each unit are able to link the strategy and the work that they are performing. This will likely foster a highly productive and motivated workforce, especially when at a later stage the CSFs and KPIs are identified and defined to support the divisional strategy.

### *Identify CSFs*

As stated previously, the CSFs are the aspects that must be executed correctly. Therefore, it is important that the CSFs are identified and clearly defined. Firstly, research and examine closely the organisation's mission, values, and broad strategy. Determine the main challenges and key priorities that the organisation needs to currently focus on. If necessary, conduct a PEST analysis to understand the external market forces that are currently impacting the organisation. It is also suggested that a SWOT analysis is carried out to establish whether the organisation has the competencies to address the market challenges. Moreover, evaluate the organisation's strengths and weaknesses. This exercise will help management to shed light on what enhancements need to be made and where.

Secondly, explore and review the defined strategic objectives and identify possible candidate CSFs by listing the organisation's key strategic goals. These are typically related to the organisation's mission and values. Determine a possible approach for achieving each individual objective. This may indicate several activities that need to occur for the organisation to achieve each strategic objective. The outcome of this exercise is a list of candidate CSFs. For example, if a strategic objective is to 'increase the current operational efficiency,' it is likely that several CSFs are required to achieve this, such as investing more in information technology and systems, improving the legal and governance framework, and investing more in a staff development programme.

The next step is to evaluate, refine, and prioritise the identified CSFs. Examine each CSF and select those that accurately reflect and are essential to the organisation's success. As each CSF is examined, assess whether there is some association between them or if they are interdependent. This will help in establishing the priority of the CSFs to enable the organisation to truly focus on the aspects that contribute to its success. It is suggested that the number of CSFs is limited to six or fewer to ensure that each CSF provides a clear focus on the agreed priorities.

The fourth step is related to communicating the CSFs to the relevant stakeholders. It is essential to identify those individuals and/or units that can contribute to the achievement of the CSFs. Each CSF should have an owner who is accountable for its achievement. This may require an exercise to review various operational activities, including modifying individual roles and responsibilities. The final step is related to the monitoring of the CSFs. Hence, the CSFs together with the associated KPIs need to be monitored so that progress may be ascertained. However, at this stage one only needs to consider the approach that will be taken to monitor and measure each CSF. This can be challenging because CSFs are usually broad statements and often are likely to require feedback from various sources (i.e., business units, divisions, and other stakeholders) throughout the organisation. In any case, CSFs are often monitored by referring to related KPIs. KPIs are addressed in the next section.

## Define KPIs

KPIs are a quantifiable measure of performance over time for a specific objective that are closely related to CSFs. KPIs provide the goals for the work teams to aim for, milestones to gauge progress, and insights that help people across the organisation to make better decisions. An effective method to monitor and measure organisational progress is establishing several KPIs as an offshoot of each identified CSF. For example, if one of the CSFs is to increase revenue, management may generate a KPI to provide more detail, such as 'Increase revenue by 25% by 2025.' KPIs are important since they act as a scorecard for organisational health; measure progress by the tracking of metrics; help to identify when to make adjustment to the CSFs; and recognise and analyse performance trends.

## Determine the Critical Information Set

It is also essential to have a monitoring system to keep track of progress in relation to the identified CSFs and associated KPIs. This requires two elements; namely, to determine the critical information set to be collected from the various information systems and making someone accountable for monitoring progress. A KPI is a target measure, which needs to be compared with actual outcomes. Hence, a system needs to be in place that collects actual information to be compared with the established KPI target. This task needs to be assigned to a specific individual within the organisation who will be responsible for gathering data and regularly monitoring the organisation's progress in relation to the specific CSFs and KPIs.

### *Example One: Applying the Critical Success Factor Methodology Framework*

Let us assume that the senior management at the Inland Revenue Department (IRD) would like to increase the Department's current operational efficiency. Using Critical Success Factors Methodology as shown at Figure 6.2, the following procedure would be adopted:

1. Step One: Where does the IRD management want the organisation to go?
   *Establish an overall general objective*: IRD management would like to increase their current operational efficiency by 30%.
2. Step Two: How does the IRD management propose to achieve the objective defined in Step One?
   *Define the implementation strategy*: IRD management is adopting a strategy where it would be encouraging at least 65% of all individual tax payers to electronically lodge all IRD-related activities, such as submitting tax returns, making enquiries, lodging complaints and objections, making payments, and receiving payment receipts, and receive acknowledgements and other notices electronically by 2025.
3. Step Three: What must IRD management do correctly to support the attainment of organisational objective?
   Define a set of CSFs that must be achieved by IRD:
   - *Information Technology*: Ensure that a reliable and robust wide area network (WAN) is in place that provides 24 Hours/7 days a week service; has a fast operating system response time, and has high security with electronic signatures.
   - *Information System*: Ensure that a reliable and robust application system is in place that operates on a wide area network configuration and has a fast application system response time, and has high access and authorised user security.
   - *Legal Framework*: Ensure that appropriate laws are in place to support the electronic transactions policy.
   - *Organisational Structure*: Ensure that an appropriate organisation structure with highly trained, committed, and motivated staff is in place.
   - *Clients*: Ensure that an external communications strategy is in place to make certain that application users (clients) are highly informed and trained in the use of the system.

4. Step Four: How would IRD management measure if it is progressing towards achieving the CSFs?

Define key performance indicators (KPIs) that must be achieved by IRD:

- *Information Technology*: Ensure that File Server and WAN has an uptime of 99.9%; less than five seconds response time; and no reported or observed security violations.
- *Information System*: Ensure that the application system has an uptime of 99.9%; less than five seconds response time; and no reported or observed security violations.
- *Legal Framework*: Ensure that appropriate laws are in place to support the electronic transactions policy with no legal challenges in court regarding transaction authentication and verification policies.
- *Organisational*: Ensure that the appropriate human resource policies are in place that result in less than 10% staff turnover rate; an average of less than two days sick leave per worker; an average of less than 50 client complaints per month; and an average decrease in operational cost per year of 7.5%.
- *Clients*: Ensure a system penetration growth rate per month of 1.5%.

5. Step Five: What information is to be collected by IRD management to track the progress of CSFs and therefore whether the KPIs are being achieved?

This basically involves defining the critical information set that is required to be collected by IRD management through the various established ICT mechanisms, such as:

- *Information Technology*: Network management system that gathers statistical information regarding the performance of the ICT WAN network. Information required is actual average File Server and WAN up-time per day; average transaction response time in seconds per day; and number of reported or observed security violations per day.
- *Information System*: MIS Performance System that gathers statistical information regarding the performance of the application system. The information required is the actual average information system uptime per day; average transaction response time in seconds per day; and number of reported or observed security violations per day.

- *Legal Framework*: IRD legal support office is to provide daily statistics regarding the number of court legal challenges related to transaction authentication and verification policies.
- *Organisational*: The critical data set required under 'Organisational' is extensive and is dependent on a number of application systems being in place, such as: (i) Human Resource Management Information System (HRMIS) to provide monthly statistics regarding the staff turnover rate per month; average length of sick leave per worker per month; average number of client complaints per month; (ii) Financial Management Information System (FMIS) to collect information regarding the average decrease in operational cost per year for IRD; and (iii) Customer Management Information System (CMIS) to provide statistics on the number of client complaints received by IRM per month.
- *Clients*: Departmental Market System that gathers statistical information regarding the penetration growth rate per month.

Defining the critical information set as a basis for comparing them with the KPIs is a relatively simple matter. However, implementing the various mechanisms and application systems to collect the defined critical information set is a very complex matter that requires a great deal of effort with the appropriate ICT investment funding. Moreover, there is no other way of monitoring whether the KPIs are being achieved without having these support systems in place.

In implementing the CSF methodology, it is suggested that an individual is appointed with the overall responsibility of putting into practice the whole process and that a focus group discussion takes place to consider each of the steps outlined above. The focus group should be given the authority to consult with various individuals in the organisation who may have specialist knowledge of the particular step. Table 6.2 provides an indication of the support the focus group may need as it proceeds through the various CSF methodology steps. Furthermore, Table 6.3 illustrates the steps in the CSF methodology and the outcome of the organisational support required for the IRD example. The IRD example illustrates that the CSF methodology provides a systematic framework for establishing objectives and the associated mechanism to ensure that the progress of these objectives is monitored and measured, until their eventual accomplishment.

*Table* 6.2  Steps in CSF Methodology and Organisational Support Required

| Steps in CSF Methodology | Support Required |
| --- | --- |
| 1. Step One: Objective | • Individual is appointed with the overall responsibility of putting into practise the whole process.<br>• Focus Group to hold brainstorming sessions to establish objectives.<br>• Establish objectives in measurable terms.<br>• Engage a facilitator to control and document brainstorming sessions (Define Overall Objectives). |
| 2. Step Two: Strategy | • Focus Group to invite members of staff who have specialist knowledge of each particular objective.<br>• Hold separate brainstorming sessions for each identified objective.<br>• Establish strategic goals in measurable terms.<br>• Engage a facilitator to control and document brainstorming sessions (Define Strategic Goals). |
| 3. Step Three: Identify CSFs | • Focus Group to invite members of staff who have specialist knowledge of each particular strategic goal.<br>• Hold separate brainstorming sessions for each identified strategic goal.<br>• Identify CSFs for each strategic goal.<br>• Engage a facilitator to control and document brainstorming sessions (Define CSFs per Strategic Goal). |
| 4. Step Four: Define KPIs | • Focus Group to invite members of staff who have specialist knowledge of each particular CSF.<br>• Hold separate brainstorming sessions for each identified CSF.<br>• Establish KPIs for each CSF in measurable terms.<br>• Engage a facilitator to control and document brainstorming sessions (Establish KPIs per CSF). |
| 5. Step Five: Establish critical information set | • Focus Group to invite members of staff that have specialist knowledge of each particular CSF and current processes and Information Systems.<br>• Hold separate brainstorming sessions for each identified CSF and matching KPIs.<br>• Identify information source to correspond with each CSF and matching KPIs in measurable terms.<br>• Engage a facilitator to control and document brainstorming sessions (Establish Critical Information Set). |

*Table 6.3a* IRD Example: Steps in CSF Methodology and Support Required

| Steps in CSF Methodology | Outcome of Support Required |
| --- | --- |
| 1. Step One: Objective | Define Overall Objectives:<br>• Increase current operational efficiency by 30%. |
| 2. Step Two: Strategy | Define Strategic Goals:<br>• 65% of all individual tax payers to electronically lodge all IRD-related activities by 2025. |
| 3. Step Three: Identify CSFs | Define CSFs per Strategic Goal:<br>• Information Technology:<br>   ◦ Reliable and robust wide area network (WAN).<br>   ◦ WAN availability 24 Hours, 7 days a week.<br>   ◦ Fast operating system response time.<br>   ◦ High level of security with electronic signatures.<br>• Information System:<br>   ◦ Reliable and robust application system.<br>   ◦ Application system to run on WAN configuration.<br>   ◦ Fast application system response time.<br>   ◦ High level of security (authorised users only).<br>• Legal Framework:<br>   ◦ Laws to support electronic transactions.<br>• Organisational Structure:<br>   ◦ Highly trained, committed, and motivated staff.<br>• Clients:<br>   ◦ Formulate external communications strategy.<br>   ◦ Informed and trained clients to use system. |

Table 6.3b  IRD Example: Steps in CSF Methodology and Support Required

| Steps in CSF Methodology | Outcome of Support Required |
|---|---|
| 4. Step Four: Define KPIs | Define KPIs per CSF:<br>• Information Technology:<br>  ○ WAN uptime 99.9%.<br>  ○ Less than five seconds response time.<br>  ○ No reported or observed security violations.<br>• Information System:<br>  ○ Application system uptime 99.9%.<br>  ○ Less than five seconds response time.<br>  ○ No reported or observed security violations.<br>• Legal Framework:<br>  ○ No court cases.<br>• Organisational Structure:<br>  ○ Less than 10% staff turnover rate.<br>  ○ Less than two days sick leave per worker.<br>  ○ Less than 50 client complaints per month.<br>  ○ Decrease in operational cost per year of 7.5%.<br>• Clients:<br>  ○ System usage growth rate of 1.5% per month. |
| 5. Step Five: Establish critical information set | Define Critical Information Set (data source):<br>• IT: Network Management System:<br>  ○ WAN uptime; response time; security violations.<br>• IS: MIS Performance System.<br>  ○ Uptime; response time; security violations.<br>• Legal Support Office:<br>  ○ No court cases.<br>• Organisational Structure Information Source:<br>  ○ HR Management Information System.<br>  ○ Financial Management Information System.<br>  ○ Customer Management Information System.<br>• Clients: Departmental Marketing System:<br>  ○ Penetration growth rate per month. |

### *Example Two: Applying the Critical Success Factor Methodology Framework*

Let us assume that a restaurant owner would like to increase business profit by 7.5% by the end of the financial year, as a result of increasing the patronage for lunch and dinner trade by 15% without reducing the gross margins. Using Critical Success Factors Methodology as shown in Figure 6.2, the following procedure would be adopted:

1. Step One: Where does the restaurant owner want the organisation to go?
   *Establish an overall general objective:* The restaurant owner wants to increase business profit by 7.5% by the end of the financial year.
2. Step Two: How does the restaurant owner propose to achieve the objective defined in Step One?
   *Define the implementation strategy:* The restaurant owner is adopting a strategy to increase the patronage for lunch and dinner trade by 15% without reducing the gross margins through better exposure, better service, and better-quality meals.
3. Step Three: What must the restaurant owner do correctly to support the attainment of organisational objectives?
   Define a set of CSFs that must be achieved by the restaurant owner:

   - *Market Share:* Increase market share through more exposure in the surrounding district.
   - *Customer Satisfaction:* Increase customer satisfaction though the provision of a better service.
   - *Meal Quality:* Increase the quality of the meals being provided to customers.
   - *Organisational Structure:* Ensure that an appropriate organisation structure with committed and motivated staff is in place.

4. Step Four: How would management measure if they are progressing towards achieving the CSFs?
   Define key performance indicators (KPIs) that must be achieved by IRD:

   - *Market Share:* Ensure that the percentage increase of customers within a 3.5 km radius is 15%.
   - *Customer Satisfaction:* Ensure that the customer satisfaction rating is 95%.

- *Meal Quality*: Ensure that the meal rejection rate due to poor quality is below 1.5%.
- *Organisational Structure*: Ensure that there is less than 10% staff turnover rate per annum; an average of less than two days sick leave per worker per month; an average of less than five client complaints per month.

5. Step Five: What information is to be collected by management to track the progress of CSFs and therefore whether the KPIs are being achieved? This basically involves defining the critical information set that is required to be collected by the restaurant owner through various mechanisms, such as:

- *Market Share and Customer Satisfaction*: Administer a simple customer satisfaction survey to each customer that notes the customer business/home location; the extent customers are satisfied with the service provided in terms of cleanness, waiter courtesy, and service waiting times through a rating range of 0 to 10 (10 being maximum satisfaction); whether the customer has any complaint; and suggestions to improve service.
- *Meal Quality*: Head waiter is to note any occurrence of meal rejection and the reason for such rejection; the waiter taking the initial order and the chef preparing the meal; and the type of sitting, whether lunch or dinner.
- *Organisational Structure*: The critical data set required under 'Organisational' is mainly through the HR Management Information System (HRMIS) to provide monthly statistics regarding the staff turnover rate per month; average length of sick leave per worker per month; average number of client complaints per month. The Financial Management Information System (FMIS) would be used to assess whether the target profit increase of 7.5% is being achieved.

It is essential that in implementing the CSF methodology, an individual is appointed with the overall responsibility of putting into practice the whole process. In this case it could be the restaurant owner. Hence, the restaurant owner (or other responsible senior person) must process the collected data to evaluate whether the CSFs and KPIs are being achieved, and implement any action deemed necessary to bring all the targets on track. It is also important that employees are involved in the CSF methodology process so that everyone is focused on achieving the desired outcome. Once again, this example illustrates that the CSF methodology provides a systematic framework for establishing objectives and the associated mechanism to ensure that the progress of these objectives is monitored and measured, until their eventual accomplishment.

### *Example Three: Applying the Critical Success Factor Methodology Framework*

Let us assume that a Whitegoods manufacturer would like to increase net operating profit by 8% for the Deluxe Refrigerator model product line over the strategic planning period of three years. Using Critical Success Factors Methodology as shown in Figure 6.3, the following procedure would be adopted:

1. Step One: Where does the Whitegoods manufacturer want the organisation to go?
   *Establish an overall general objective*: The Whitegoods manufacturer wants to increase net operating profit by 8% for the Deluxe Refrigerator model over the strategic planning period of three years.
2. Step Two: How does the Whitegoods manufacturer propose to achieve the objective defined in Step One?
   *Define the implementation strategy*: The Whitegoods manufacturer is adopting a strategy to increase the product quality, increase processing efficiency by boosting output and lowering production costs, and expanding the market share.
3. Step Three: What must the Whitegoods manufacturer do correctly to support the attainment of organisational objectives?
   Define a set of CSFs that must be achieved by the Whitegoods manufacturer:

   * *Market Share*: Increase market share.
   * *Product Quality*: Lower the number of warranty claims.
   * *Production*: Increase production output and lower production cost.

4. Step Four: How would management measure if they are progressing towards achieving the CSFs?
Define key performance indicators (KPIs) that must be achieved by IRD:

- *Market Share*: Increase market share by 20% through an increase in advertising budget of 25% and offering minimum discounts of 10%.
- *Product Quality*: Number of warranties claims per 100 units not to exceed three units.
- *Production*: Achieve 95% production capacity rating and maintain an average variable costs of less than $475 per unit.

5. Step Five: What information is to be collected by management to track the progress of CSFs and therefore whether the KPIs are being achieved? This basically involves defining the critical information set that is required to be collected by the Whitegoods manufacturer through the production and financial management information systems:

- *Market Share*: The information related to the advertising budget expenditure and minimum discounts quantities and values are collected through the financial management information system. The overall market share information is gathered through Industry Association sources and specific market research.
- *Product Quality*: The information regarding the number of warranties claims per 100 units is collected through the financial management information system, more specifically the Sales Client subsidiary information system module.
- *Production*: The information regarding utilised production capacity rating is collected from the production control information system and variable costs per unit is collected through the financial management information system.

Implementing the CSF methodology requires the appointment of an individual with the overall responsibility of putting into practice the whole process, specifically monitoring the various information systems to gather the relevant information for comparison with the KPIs. Hence, a responsible senior management person must be responsible for processing the collected data to evaluate whether the CSFs and KPIs are being achieved, and

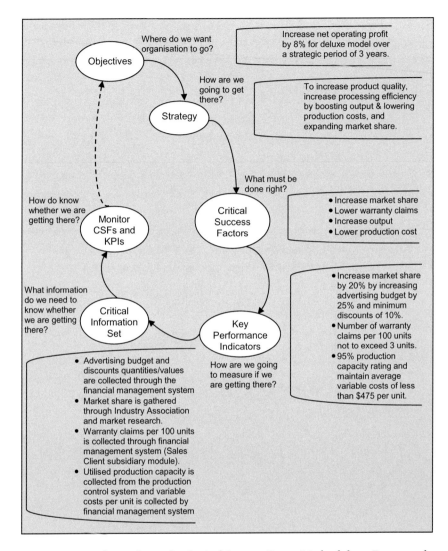

*Figure 6.3* Example Applying the Critical Success Factor Methodology Framework

implementing any action deemed necessary to ensure all the targets are on track. It is also important that employees are involved in the CSF methodology process so that everyone is focused on achieving the desired outcome. Once again, this example illustrates that the CSF methodology provides a systematic framework for establishing objectives and the associated mechanisms to ensure that the progress of these objectives is monitored and measured, until their eventual accomplishment.

# Conclusion

This chapter discussed the application of CSFs as a means of establishing and employing KPIs as a performance management tool. It was shown that CSFs and KPIs are both useful tools for achieving organisational success at every level within the entity and contribute to its growth. They provide a control mechanism for mitigating costs and maximising opportunities. CSFs are viewed as being the components required to ensure success, whilst KPIs indicate the level of success and are viewed as the necessary tools to measure the performance of any organisation. Normally, managers define several CSFs that are supported by KPIs to determine how well departments, work teams or individual employees are performing the tasks allocated to them. The identification of CSFs permits the organisation to focus its efforts on building its capabilities to meet the defined CSFs. On the other hand, the defined KPIs provide the measures to determine whether the organisation is achieving its defined CSFs.

CSFs are a strategic tool and guide the organisation towards achieving the strategic goals. The CSFs approach is used externally by the customers to judge how well the organisation is progressing, while a KPI is used internally by the organisation to measure the success of implementing the CSFs. This chapter also described the CSF methodology framework (refer to Figure 6.2), which is based on the concept that a CSF is a high-level objective feature that is vital for an organisation or project to achieve its mission. The CSFs methodology is a sophisticated tool that is easy to apply. However, for the methodology to be effective, CSFs must have high-level objectives; be essential to the organisation's success; be holistically beneficial to the organisation or a division; and be directly linked to the organisation's business strategy. Furthermore, CSFs should be expressed as action aphorisms that define the method, desired outcome, and the action to be taken.

The model presented in Figure 6.2 indicates that there is a close relationship between the CSFs and the KPIs, which reveal how the organisation is going to measure if the individual CSFs are being achieved. Furthermore, it is important for the organisation to have the appropriate mechanisms in place to collect information to ensure that actual performance (KPIs) is being achieved by comparing the collected measures with the defined KPIs. Hence, the CSFs and KPIs need to be closely monitored by an individual who is responsible for this specific function. The chapter also presents three examples regarding the implementation of the CSFs methodology framework. The first example is related to a public sector organisation and the final two examples are related to the private sector; thus demonstrating that the methodology is applicable to both the public and private sectors.

# References

Caralli, R.A., Stevens, J.F., Willke, B.J., and Wilson, W.R. (2004). *The Critical Success Factor Method: Establishing a Foundation for Enterprise Security Management. Technical Report.* CMU/SEI-2004-TR-010 ESC-TR-2004–010, Carnegie Mellon University.

Daniel, D.R. (1961). 'Management Information Crisis.' *Harvard Business Review*, 39(5), pp. 111–121.

Parmenter, D. (2007). *Key Performance Indicators (KPI): Developing, Implementing and Using Winning KPIs.* Hoboken, NJ: Wiley, John & Sons, Inc.

Rockart, J.F. (1979). 'Chief Executives Define Their Own Data Needs.' *Harvard Business Review*, 57(2), pp. 81–93.

# 7

# BALANCED SCORECARD AND BENCHMARKING

## BASIS FOR APPLYING KPIS

'Performance management metrics aren't just historical, but they are also forward-looking projections so that managers can know who has a positive trajectory.'

Professor Dr John Sullivan
Corporate Speaker, and Advisor

This chapter examines the Balanced Scorecard and Benchmarking methods as a performance management approach through the application of KPIs. According to Poister (2003), the usefulness of any given performance measure rests on how this measure will be applied. Therefore, for performance measures to have significance and provide valuable information, they must be compared with a robust base. Thus, the undertaken comparisons may be used to assess progress in attaining the agreed objectives or goals, review trends in performance over a given duration, or consider the performance of one entity contrasted to another.

It is worth mentioning at this stage that such comparisons are applicable both for the public and private sector. For example, the Government

DOI: 10.4324/9781032685465-9

Performance and Results Act (GPRA) that was enacted in 1993 throughout the United States Federal Government established the requirement for performance measures to assess how well departments and agencies are achieving their stated goals and objectives. This Act was designed to improve program management, with agencies being required to develop a five-year strategic plan outlining their mission, long-term goals for the agency's major functions, performance measures, and reporting results. Moreover, the strategic plan was to be updated every three years. Besides the strategic plan, agencies must also submit an annual performance report to the Office of Management and Budget with the established fiscal year performance goals, objectives on how to achieve these goals, and an explanation of how performance is measured and verified. Thus, the focus of the GPRA performance measures is on output and outcome measures at the program level.

The private sector has embraced the concept of performance measures as an integral aspect of performance management for decades and well before the public sector. It is generally recognised that performance measures employed as a management tool must be extended to incorporate both input and process measures. One method exploited is the application of the scorecard that consists of multiple measures. This may take the form of a Balanced Scorecard or Benchmarking.

The Balanced Scorecard evaluates an organisation and its programs from four different viewpoints, namely the customer, employee, process, and finance. According to Kaplan and Norton (1996, p. 148), the scorecard generates a holistic model of the strategy that permits all employees to understand how they contribute to organisational success. Kaplan and Norton highlight that the approach focuses on change efforts, and stress that if the right objectives and measures are identified, successful implementation will probably come about. On the other hand, Benchmarking is also seen as a core component of continuous improvement programs. Watson (1992) argues that Benchmarking is a key component of quality assurance and process improvement. The role of Benchmarking in improving processes is synonymous to the Six Sigma process improvement methodology. This aspect will be explored in more detail later in this chapter.

## Introduction

The use of the Balanced Scorecard and Benchmarking as a tool provides organisations with an approach that supports their performance management process. It must be recognised that the Balanced Scorecard (BSC) is a strategic planning and management methodology that is used by organisations to communicate their objectives and goals; to align the day-to-day work with strategy; to prioritise the undertaken projects, products, and services; and to measure and track progress concerning strategic targets. The term 'Balanced Scorecard' refers to the notion of examining strategic measures in addition to traditional financial measures to obtain a more 'balanced' view of performance.

The concept of Balanced Scorecard has grown from the simple application of management viewpoints to a holistic system for managing the strategic direction of an organisation. As such, the Balanced Scorecard methodology consists of a systematic framework that provides organisations with a process of bringing together a lot of pieces of information from the various components of strategic planning and management. This results in having a visible link between the projects and programs that employees are engaged on; the measurements being applied to monitor success (KPIs); the strategic objectives and goals the organisation is aiming to accomplish; and the mission, vision, and strategy of the organisation.

The BSC concept was first proposed in an article entitled 'The Balanced Scorecard: Measures that Drive Performance' that appeared in the January-February 1992 edition of Harvard University Business Review contributed by David Norton and Robert Kaplan. These authors utilised previous metric performance measures and adapted them to include non-financial information and provided business executives with a complete framework that transforms the organisation's strategic objectives into a coherent set of performance measures. The success in the use of the BSC concept has resulted in its wide acceptance and is now applied in commercial entities, government, and not-for-profit organisations around the world.

Conventionally organisations applied short-term financial performance as a measure of success, but the BSC introduced additional non-financial strategic measures to the assortment of performance measures to enhance management's focus on long-term success. Thus, the BSC method provided a clear direction as to what organisations should measure to 'balance' the financial performance perspective. The methodology has developed over the past three decades and is currently viewed as a fully integrated strategic management system.

The BSC system proposes that an organisation is examined from four key standpoints to aid in the development of organisational objectives, measures (KPIs), goals, and initiatives relative to these standpoints. First standpoint is financial (or stewardship), which examines an organisation's financial performance and the use of financial resources. The next standpoint is the customer and other stakeholders, which assesses organisational performance from the customer or key stakeholders' point of view that the organisation is designed to serve. The third standpoint is related to the internal process, which considers the quality and efficiency of an organisation's performance related to the product, services, or other key business processes. The final standpoint is regarding organisational capacity (or learning and development) that considers human capital, infrastructure, technology, culture, and other capacities that are key to breakthrough performance. The examination of these four standpoints provides a holistic view of the organisation's strategic standing and, more importantly, act as an assessment system to determine whether the organisation is achieving its strategic objectives. In subsequent sections a more detailed examination of the BSC concept will be provided, including applicable practical examples.

The other important tool that will be examined in this chapter is Benchmarking. Like BSC, Benchmarking is a performance assessment tool. It is a systematic method of measuring key organisational metrics and practices and comparing them within the various organisational areas or against a competitor, industry peers, or other entities to understand how and where the organisation needs to change to improve its performance. It is a methodology that is aimed at achieving continuous improvement by identifying internal opportunities that lead to better performance. Benchmarking is an essential component of a total quality management process, and includes several key elements, namely focusing on processes rather than outcomes; facilitating information sharing; and implies a willingness to change and a desire to implement best practices. It must be noted that benchmarks and KPIs are different but may complement each other.

Benchmarking establishes points of reference for comparing the organisation's performance with the performance of other organisations, preferably with those that apply best practices. Furthermore, there are different levels of Benchmarking. Hence, benchmarks can compare processes, services, products, or operations, and these comparisons can be applied in contrast to other parts of the same organisation, external organisation (such as competitors or similar organisations), or industry best practises.

Benchmarking can also be used to evaluate customer satisfaction, costs, and quality of service or product. On the other hand, KPIs are mainly used as monitoring tools and facilitate decision-making by scrutinising the organisation's performance in relation to its strategic goals. KPIs highlight the events that may not be on the proper path and therefore require corrective action. Thus, KPIs act as a warning system to ensure that appropriate action is taken. Therefore, KPIs are used to compare progress against a specific goal, while benchmarks are used to compare what is happening in the organisation as compared with other organisations. Hence, KPIs are used to establish targets, while Benchmarking is used to compare the extent of achievement of these targets when compared to others; thus complementing each other. Note that both benchmarks and KPIs are applied for identifying opportunities to enhance performance.

Benchmarks typically consist of two broad categories, namely internal and external. Internal Benchmarking compares performance, processes, and practises against other divisions or departments within the same entity. Internal Benchmarking can also be used to compare work teams, business units, or individuals. For example, benchmarks could be used to compare processes and services in one health clinic with another health clinic within the same group of health clinics. On the other hand, external Benchmarking compares organisational performance with other entities, such as competitors or best practice entities in other jurisdictions. External Benchmarking can also be used to compare performance, processes, and practises across different industries. Irrespective of whether Benchmarking is internal or external, they can be applied for several purposes. For instance, it may be adapted for Benchmarking a process in an operational area. In this case, one would compare the processes for delivering a specific product or service with another functional area (internal or external) to determine an approach for optimising and improving the existent processes. However, the comparable functional area selected for Benchmarking must be a topmost performer, otherwise there is no point in using Benchmarking. The aim is to improve your organisation's processes by making them more efficient and responsive.

Another purpose for using Benchmarking is to benchmark performance in terms of outcomes. This is a broad application base and can cover every operational aspect of an organisation, ranging from customer care to growth in profitability. Furthermore, the outcomes may be compared with both internal and external functional areas, such as marketing and human resources, amongst many others. Finally, Benchmarking may be used for strategic purposes. This basically compares strategies and their implementation approaches to ensure that the organisation intensifies and supports its strategic planning approach and establishes realistic strategic priorities. Thus, this approach enables management to reveal any breaches in performance and highlight opportunities to improve the organisation's overall performance. Having said this, Benchmarking must be used in conjunction with KPIs so that one may monitor performance to ensure that the agreed goals are achieved.

## Balanced Scorecard

According to Kaplan and Norton (1993), managers recognise the impact that measures have on performance, but they rarely think of measurement as an essential part of their strategy. They argue that executives may introduce new strategies and innovative operating processes intended to achieve breakthrough performance, then continue to use the same short-term financial indicators they have used for decades, measures like return-on-investment, sales growth, and operating income. However, they contend that these managers fail not only to introduce new measures to monitor new goals and processes, but also to question whether their old measures are relevant to the new initiatives.

Kaplan and Norton maintain that effective measurement, however, must be an integral part of the management process. These ideas were central to Kaplan and Norton's development of the Balanced Scorecard. Kaplan and Norton argue that BSC provides executives with a comprehensive framework that translates a company's strategic objectives into a coherent set of performance measures. They view the Balanced Scorecard as a management system that can motivate breakthrough improvements in such critical areas as product, process, customer, and market development. Generally, the Balanced Scorecard (BSC) is an organisational framework utilised for monitoring and managing an organisation's strategy.

The word 'Balanced' is used because the basis of the BSC framework is the balance between leading and lagging indicators that are viewed as the drivers and outcomes of an organisation's goals. Note that leading indicators convey what is necessary for achieving the goals that lead to achieving results; whereas lagging indicators are outputs that measure the results. Hence, when these key indicators are applied in the Balanced Scorecard framework, they reveal whether the organisational goals are being achieved and whether management is on the right path to achieving the future goals. When applied correctly, the BSC framework gives management the ability to define the organisation's strategy, measure the progress being made in implementing the strategy, and monitor the activities being taken to improve the organisation's strategic outcomes. Hence, the BSC framework is predominantly forward-looking, taking a proactive perspective rather than a reactive one.

The BSC provides management with four distinctive viewpoints, with each viewpoint having its own unique measures that may be selected by management. It is important to note that BSC supplements traditional financial indicators with other performance measures related to customers, internal processes, and innovation and improvement activities. These other performance measures differ from the traditional financial measures. Firstly, the traditional financial measures are generated from a bottom-up approach and originate from processes when necessary. On the other hand, the BSC measures are part of a continuous process that are based on the organisation's strategic objectives and competitive pressures. Hence, the BSC measures help management to focus on the strategic vision. Moreover, the traditional financial measures are historical; they describe what happened in the last period without suggesting ways that managers can improve performance in the future, such as the next period. Thus, BSC operates as the foundation of the organisation's present and future success.

Additionally, the information generated from the four views provides a balance between the internal measures and external measures. Hence, this balanced set of measures discloses the adjustments that management have currently made among the performance measures and urges them to achieve their future goals without making compromises among key success factors. The BSC approach can facilitate an organisation's endeavours to integrate the implementation of internal improvement programs, such as business process reengineering, total quality management, and employee empowerment by explaining and communicating priorities to management, employees, investors, and where feasible, to customers. Many organisations that have adopted the BSC approach no longer view the annual budget as the primary management planning device, but rather view BSC as the benchmark against which all new projects and undertakings are evaluated.

Kaplan and Norton argue that BSC is not a template that can be applied to organisations in general or industry-wide, since different market situations, product strategies, and competitive environments require different scorecards. They contend that organisational units formulate the scorecards to fit their mission, strategy, technology, and culture. Kaplan and Norton maintain that a critical test of a scorecard's success is its transparency, in that with 15 to 20 scorecard measures, an observer should be able to see through to the business unit's competitive strategy.

## Roadmap for Applying the Balanced Scorecard Methodology

According to Rohm (2008), co-founder and president of the Balanced Scorecard Institute (BSI), the Balanced Scorecards, when developed as strategic planning and management systems, can help align an organisation to support a shared vision of success by prompting employees to work on what is important and focusing on outcomes. He argues that a scorecard is a synchronised system, consisting of people, strategy, processes, and technology. Furthermore, he maintains that the Balanced Scorecard system is based on a disciplined framework that supports a systematic step-by-step approach. A scrutiny of the Balanced Scorecard functions reveal that it encompasses a wide application spectrum. It ranges from a measurement-based Balanced Scorecard that supports a specific performance measurement framework for classifying current measures into identifiable categories and depicting the measures graphically.

These are often illustrated as a dashboard like those shown in Chapter 5. These are typically input, output, and process measures of an operational nature rather than being strategic, and are mainly utilised to monitor production, operations, and service delivery. The other end of the spectrum consists of applications related to a holistic organisational strategic plan, including its management, execution, and associated communications strategy. These strategic applications align the employee work activities with the organisational vision and strategy, communicate the strategic goals to external stakeholders and across the organisation, and provide a robust basis for supporting strategic objectives with the necessary resources. Maximum benefits accrue from balance scorecard systems when they are applied as an organisational strategic planning and management tool that focuses on outcomes. Moreover, the development of a Balanced Scorecard system is based upon several fundamental principles.

## First Principle

The first principle is based upon developing the appropriate organisational environment. This basically consists of recognising the fact that a Balanced Scorecard system is transformational. Transformational change means that management will completely reshape the business strategy and processes, often resulting in a shift in work culture; whereas incremental change attempts to solve problems with small, systematic steps that provoke change over time to mitigate risk. The introduction of a Balanced Scorecard system cannot be incremental; it must be transformational because it will change entirely the way the organisation will be managed.

For transformational change to occur, three things must happen. firstly there must be an engaging leadership style that facilitates, strengthens, connects, and inspires employees to increase their work engagement. Secondly, there is a need for interactive communication throughout the organisation that inspires an exchange of ideas where participants are active and can influence one another. The third prerequisite is a robust change management process that incorporates overcoming resistance, engaging employees, implementing the change, and effectively communicating the change. Often, a Balanced Scorecard system fails because the appropriate organisational environment has not been created. Regrettably, creating the appropriate organisational environment is not straightforward and is not easily achieved because it is about changing the attitudes of many individuals.

## Second Principle

The second principle is related to having a results-oriented perspective as depicted in Figure 7.1. It starts with defining the desired results (outcomes) of the process and considers five specific aspects. To ensure that the outcomes are attained, it is vital to define the performance measures, targets, and thresholds. The performance measures must be linked to the strategic objectives and permit management to measure what matters and monitor progress towards the desired strategic outcomes. The targets and thresholds

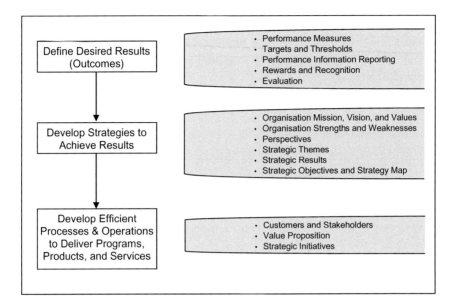

*Figure 7.1* Balanced Scorecard Results-oriented Perspective

specify the basis for the visual interpretation of performance data, and to transform the data into business intelligence. The desired results must also be reported by having a performance information reporting mechanism.

This mechanism consists of computerised data collection and reporting processes that are utilised to depict performance information and to keep the decision-makers throughout the organisation better informed. Linked to performance are the rewards and recognition practices. These practices and the related incentives prompt the strategy to become an actionable instrument with a practical value by ensuring buy-in from employees and make the change process more acceptable to them. This contributes towards building a high-performance organisation. The final aspect related to defining the desired results is the evaluation process. Since the outcomes of the organisation are more strategy-focused, they need to be evaluated so that adjustments may be made to the strategy, the gathered measures, and the strategic initiatives to promote a learning environment throughout the organisation.

Once the desired results are defined, management must develop the strategies to achieve them. Developing the strategies requires various activities, namely defining the organisation's mission, vision, and values; identifying the strengths and weaknesses of the organisation; describing the organisational perspectives, strategic themes, and strategic results; and defining the strategic objectives and related strategic map. The organisation's mission, vision, and values often reflect the leadership style and personalities of those responsible for the running of the organisation. The mission statement conveys the purpose of the organisation, with the vision statement providing an insight into what the organisation desires to achieve or become in the future, while the values statement reflects the organisation's core principles and ethics. These three organisational features must be closely bonded and are extremely important for aligning all employees in the organisation towards the defined strategy.

Without a shared vision the Balanced Scorecard development process will likely fail. It is also vital to identify the strengths and weaknesses of the organisation. These define the internal environment and reveal the competencies or lack of competencies that the organisation possesses, which will influence the strategy definition process and the approach that will be undertaken to achieving future results. An important feature of the Balanced Scorecard is to view the strategy from different perspectives. Hence, the identification of the perspectives, strategic themes, and strategic results are important to facilitate management's view of the strategy through different performance lenses. Collectively, they provide the motivation that transforms the organisation strategy into operational actionable drivers for all employees. The strategic objectives are fundamental to the strategy, and when considered collectively they provide the basis for the cause-effect relationships to produce the strategy map, which reveal the processes of how an organisation generates value for its customers and stakeholders.

The final activity related to the Balanced Scorecard is the results-oriented perspective illustrated by Figure 7.1. This activity develops efficient processes and operations for the delivery of programs, products, and services. The processes and operations must cater for needs of the customers and other key stakeholders. An effective functional strategy must encompass a view from the customer and stakeholder viewpoint that includes an inherent understanding of customer requirements regarding the products and services and their specific characteristics, the preferred relationships, and the desired image that the organisation wants to depict. The desired image is the impact of the policies, personnel, and operations of the organisation that is imparted to its employees and the public. Furthermore, this activity must also reveal the strategic initiatives, which are to transform the strategy into operational terms by specifying a base for prioritising the budget and identifying the most important projects for the organisation to undertake.

## Third Principle

The third principle is regarding the focus of the Balanced Scorecard in relation to the four perspectives that are to be addressed by the system. These four perspectives consist of financial; customer; internal processes; and learning and growth. A common oversight when using the Balanced Scorecard is to treat the method too simplistically as if the four views can be addressed in quasi-isolation. The four perspectives are often seen as having a simple link to provide a Balanced Scorecard of the organisation performance, with each perspective having its own list of strategic objectives, undertakings, and KPIs that employees independently execute.

This approach views the end goal as being an endeavour to balance each perspective, resulting in improved performance. However, this approach is erroneous because the Balanced Scorecard is not a succession of equally weighted perspectives. On the contrary, the Balanced Scorecard is a process that has its starting point at the bottom, and one would work up through each perspective with the objective to delivering the topmost perspective, being 'Financial Gain' in the case of the private sector. Therefore, the four perspectives should be viewed as a pyramid starting from the bottom and moving up. Figure 7.2 illustrates that each perspective unfastens management's capability to deliver effectively against the layer above it. Therefore, the Balanced Scorecard should be visualised from a strategy mapping point of view.

## Fourth Principle

The fourth principle is regarding the Balanced Scorecard cascading model. Cascading a Balanced Scorecard is to transform the corporate-wide scorecard (referred to as Tier 1) down to first business units, support units or departments (Tier 2), and then teams or individuals (Tier 3). The outcome should be a focus across all levels of the organisation that is consistent. Cascading facilitates the alignment of the balance scorecard system throughout the organisation through the strategy, utilising the strategy map, performance measures and targets, and initiatives. Scorecards are applied to

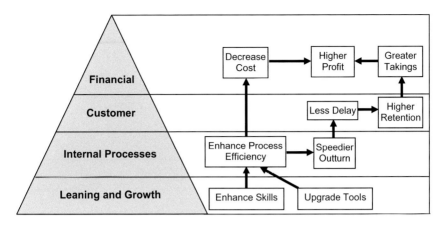

*Figure 7.2*  Balanced Scorecard Perspectives Pyramid

enhance transparency and accountability. This is achieved by the relationship between the 'objective and performance measure ownership,' with
the required employee behaviours to be incentivised by recognition and
rewards.

The central issue to be addressed at this stage is related to organisational
alignment. However, the actual success of using the Balanced Scorecard as
an alignment tool depends very much on the strategic focus of the scorecard. Simple performance measurement dashboards are not inclined to be
very helpful. The extent of the success of the Balanced Scorecard implementation is whether the organisation successfully cascades the scorecard. Figure 7.3 illustrates that the cascading model focuses the complete
organisation on strategy and generates a visible horizon between the tasks
employees perform and the desired higher-level outcomes.

As the process is cascaded down through the various hierarchical organisational levels, the objectives become more operational and tactical, supported by the respective operational and tactical performance measures.
Transparency and accountability monitor the objectives and measures since
ownership responsibility is clearly defined at each level. There must also
be a comprehensive communications strategy within the organisation to
ensure that the focus on outcomes and the strategies required to generate
the results are unambiguously communicated throughout the organisation.

There are several common obstacles that organisations need to address
with cascading. These include inadequate planning for implementing the

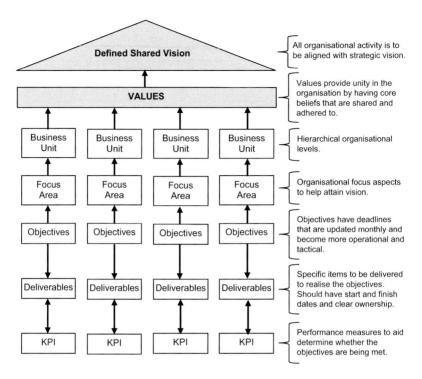

Figure 7.3  Balanced Scorecard Cascading Process

cascading configuration; a lack of sufficient understanding by employees about the process; delegation and administration concerns that disrupt the link between the various tiers; inconsistent success rate in implementing the approach across the organisation; and the consolidated organisation level Balanced Scorecard is not sufficiently understood or is difficult to communicate to employees.

## Fifth Principle

Rohm (2008) argues that doing the right things and doing things right is a balancing act and requires the development of good business strategies (doing the right things) and efficient processes and operations to deliver the programs, products, and services (doing things right) that make up the organisation's core business. The previous four principles have already demonstrated this. However, the fifth principle takes a step further. Kaplan and Norton (1993) in Figure 7.4 illustrate that each individual perspective is

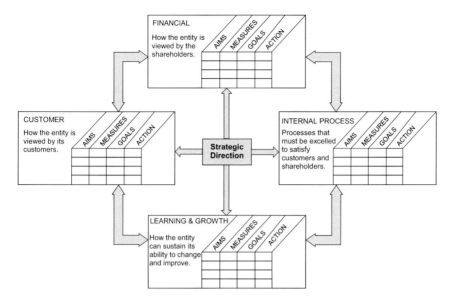

*Figure 7.4*  Balanced Scorecard Activity Framework

linked to the vision and strategy of the organisation and with each other as a two-way process. This implies that the whole process is an iterative one. This suggests that management is using an iterative development approach to create, test, and revise the balance score card system until they're satisfied with the result and therefore can apply it to manage organisational strategic performance. Additionally, each individual perspective has its own defined objectives, measures, targets, and initiatives, all of which are targeted at achieving the organisational vision and strategy.

One should note that the Balanced Scorecard system includes a strategy map, to illustrate how value is created for the customers; strategic objectives to identify and define what needs to be achieved to produce value; what performance measures are to be applied to evaluate progress against targets; and what strategic initiatives are to be undertaken to render the strategy actionable and operational. It is also important to recognise that the implementation of Balanced Scorecard systems is applicable for the private and public sectors, and for non-profit organisations. Admittedly, there are differences between the sectors in the way they operate and their ultimate raison d'être, but the disciplined and systematic process can be adapted to all types and sizes of organisations. The five fundamental principles described above illustrate that creating a Balanced Scorecard system is like solving a jigsaw puzzle: The outcome to be achieved is known before-hand, but care must be taken to fit the various pieces together in an effective manner to form a complete picture that reflects the vision and strategy of the organisation.

### Example: Applying the Balanced Scorecard Methodology – Private Sector

Pinnacle, a wholly owned subsidiary of a national construction company, is a national leader in high-quality residential construction. Mark Smith, who was recently engaged as CEO, has extensive knowledge of the residential construction industry and is aware that the industry's competitive base has been changing considerably, given the innovative developments in building techniques and materials. Just a few years ago the residential construction industry was relatively stable, but the discovery of new materials, innovative building techniques, and new regulatory requirements has seen intense competition within the industry, with many smaller companies being forced out.

In addition, the focus of the competition has changed. Residential construction companies have been inclined to foster long-term strategic partnerships with their suppliers and sub-contractors that warrant higher quality rather than opting for suppliers and sub-contractors based on low-price rivalry. Mark gathered his senior management team and together they developed a more appealing vision: 'To be the builder most trusted by value minded clients and high performing employees.' Together the senior management team also defined a strategy to implement this vision. The strategic objectives are as shown in Figure 7.5.

Pinnacle's senior management team then went through the process of translating this vision and strategy into the Balanced Scorecard's four sets of performance perspectives (see Figure 7.6):

- **Financial Measures:** The financial perspective included three categories of measures that are of importance to the shareholder. These are liquidity (Cash Flow); capital structure (Gearing); and profitability (Return-on-capital-employed, Project Profitability, Production Cost Effectiveness, and Performance Consistency). These reflect the preferences for short-term and medium-term outcomes, while Production Cost-Effectiveness and Performance Consistency signify management's

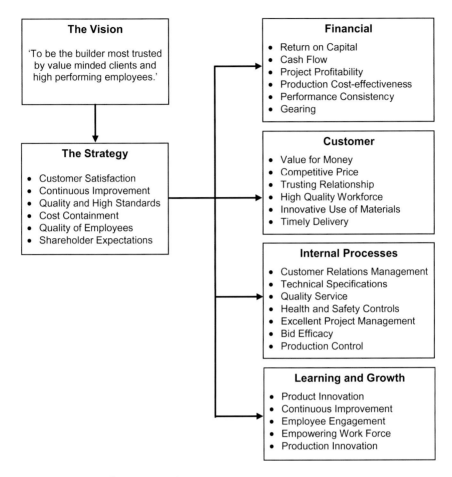

**The Vision**

'To be the builder most trusted by value minded clients and high performing employees.'

**The Strategy**

- Customer Satisfaction
- Continuous Improvement
- Quality and High Standards
- Cost Containment
- Quality of Employees
- Shareholder Expectations

**Financial**

- Return on Capital
- Cash Flow
- Project Profitability
- Production Cost-effectiveness
- Performance Consistency
- Gearing

**Customer**

- Value for Money
- Competitive Price
- Trusting Relationship
- High Quality Workforce
- Innovative Use of Materials
- Timely Delivery

**Internal Processes**

- Customer Relations Management
- Technical Specifications
- Quality Service
- Health and Safety Controls
- Excellent Project Management
- Bid Efficacy
- Production Control

**Learning and Growth**

- Product Innovation
- Continuous Improvement
- Employee Engagement
- Empowering Work Force
- Production Innovation

*Figure 7.5*  Pinnacle's Strategic Objectives

desire to achieve repeatable project management success and mitigate uncertainty caused by unforeseen variations in performance. Moreover, Project Profitability shifts the focus on the multi-project environment of the organisation to ensure adequate planning and control, specifically related to the application of resources, thus helping to lessen uncertainty of performance.

- **Customer Satisfaction**: Pinnacle want to distinguish between its two types of customers: Tier I customers are those who trust the company through repeat business (loyalty), and Tier II customers are those who prefer suppliers based on value through competitive pricing and quality. A price indicator based upon market research was maintained to

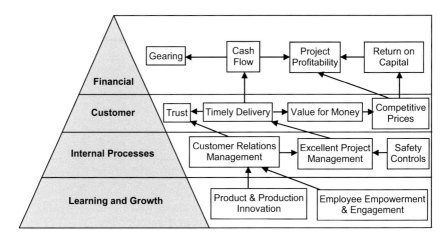

Figure 7.6  Pinnacle's Balanced Scorecard Perspectives Pyramid

safeguard that Pinnacle could still hold on to Tier II customers' business when required by competitive circumstances. The company's strategy focused on value-based business to remain competitive and build trust (customer loyalty). A market research company was engaged to conduct a biannual survey to determine Pinnacle's standing in terms of quality, use of innovative materials, and timely delivery. The survey also aimed to rank customers' perceptions of Pinnacle's services compared to those of its competitors, including value for money. Additionally, customers were asked to rate the company in terms of satisfaction and performance ratings. Pinnacle's management team viewed these ratings as essential since they considered them to be a direct link with their customers and their respective needs. The market research, combined with the important customer accounts, provided Pinnacle with tangible evidence that enhancements in customer satisfaction were being transformed into visible benefits.

- **Internal Processes**: To develop measures of internal processes, Pinnacle's management identified the project life cycle of a typical residence construction project focusing on the information flows throughout the organisation. Measures were devised for each of the key business-process phases of a typical project cycle:

  a) Project Scope: number of hours discussing with customer for new work.
  b) Quotation Bid: Quotation bid success rate.

c)  Project Organisation: project performance effectiveness index, rescheduled work, safety control.
d)  Project Closure: length of project closeout phase.

The internal business measures focused on aspects that integrated key business processes within a typical project life cycle that aimed for timely delivery within the establish budget that mitigated variances. The development of a robust 'cost-time-quality' index of project performance effectiveness was a key core competency for Pinnacle. Pinnacle's management believed that apart from safety, customer relations was a key competitive factor.

Furthermore, internal findings showed that the re-work costs and costs due to accidents could be many times the direct production costs. The scorecard included a production and safety indices, derived from a detailed production and safety measurement methodology that could identify and classify all risk occurrences with the possibility for impairment to employees, assets, or process. The management team also desired a metric that would convey to Pinnacle's employees the importance of developing relationships with customers and satisfying their needs. It was decided to base this measure on quality time spent with customers. This was viewed as a prerequisite for affecting outcomes. This input measure was seen as a way of educating employees about the value of satisfying customer needs.

- **Learning and Growth**: The learning and growth objectives have the intention of urging improvement in the financial, customer, and internal process performance perspectives. At Pinnacle, such enhancements derived from product and production innovation that would generate continuous improvement of processes and thus develop new possibilities of gaining revenue and market expansion. These were measured by percentage of revenue from new products and a continuous improvement index that signified the rate of improvement of several key operational measures, such as safety and rescheduled work. Moreover, product/production innovation and operational improvements were pushed by a supportive environment of empowered and motivated employees. A quarterly employee attitude survey and a metric to measure the number of employee suggestions was used to determine whether such an environment climate was being generated. Additionally, revenue per employee and employee turnover measured the effects of employee commitment and training programs.

Figure 7.7, applying the Kaplan and Norton model, illustrates the Balanced Scorecard system adopted by Pinnacle's management. Generally, the Balanced Scorecard system helped Pinnacle's management to give emphasis to a process view of operations, motivate its employees, and incorporate

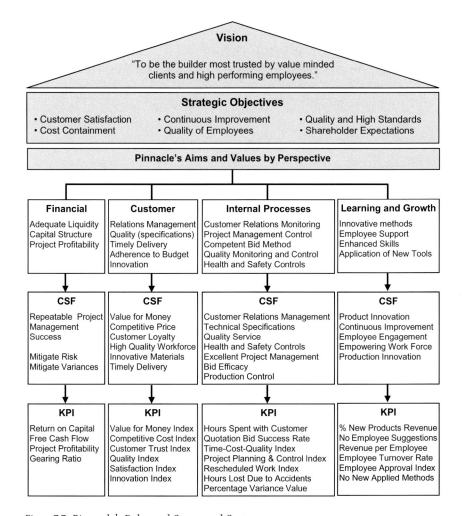

Figure 7.7  Pinnacle's Balanced Scorecard System

a customer feedback loop into its operations. It also created consensus on the need to generate partnerships with key customers, the importance of repeat orders based upon trust and loyalty, and the need for improved process management at every phase of project implementation in a multi-project organisational environment. Smith views the Balanced Scorecard as an irreplaceable tool to support his company to achieve its mission: 'To be the builder most trusted by value minded clients and high performing employees.'

## Applying the Balanced Scorecard Methodology in the Public Sector

Various researchers have promoted the use of the Balanced Scorecard (BSC) as having the potential to support performance management in the public sector. According to Northcott and Taulapapa (2012, p. 167), the BSC is understood to present a multi-dimensional view of performance across different objectives and stakeholders, as is required for many public sector organisations. Additionally, they hold the view that because BSC focuses on key performance indicators (KPIs), it directs management's attention to important drivers of organisational outcomes and informs performance management by linking these KPIs in causal relationships with desired outcomes.

As one may recall, Figure 7.2 highlights the fact that the BSC concept places the financial objectives as the endpoint of the BSC's performance management objectives. This seems to be inconsistent with the aims of most public sector organisations. However, while Kaplan and Norton (p. 98) confirm that the concept was initially envisaged for profit-making organisations, they argue that the BSC can be easily adapted for use in public sector organisations simply by modifying the scorecard to have customers or constituents at the top of the hierarchy, instead of financial. Hence, it is argued that through this minor restructuring, the BSC can be applied to both the public and private sector contexts as a measurement instrument to guide performance.

BSC is viewed by many researchers as supporting a multi-dimensional concept that secures non-financial aspects of performance and defines a few selected KPIs that give an unambiguous focus for achieving organisational strategy irrespective of the operating environment complexity. Research has

shown that the success factors for implementing BSC include top management commitment; employee buy-in; an emphasis on performance excellence; adequate training; a simple BSC design; clear organisational strategy
and goals; links to incentive schemes; and adequate resourcing. According to Northcott and Taulapapa (p. 169), other research suggests that the
main reasons for not implementing BSC include inadequate information
systems, inadequate sponsorship of the BSC by senior managers, and a lack
of time, while unsuccessful implementations are attributed to poor linkage
to employee rewards, uncertainty about the choice of suitable KPIs, and
organisational resistance to change.

It is noted that all the above factors are associated with the first principle
discussed previously regarding the development of an appropriate organisational environment. Many management tools, including BSC, require an
appropriate organisational environment as a mandatory starting point. Furthermore, many of the above suggested reasons for BSC success or failure
apply equally in both the private and public sectors. Northcott and Taulapapa (p. 170) contend that the literature has acknowledged some weak
research areas regarding BSC implementation in public sector contexts, and
that few studies have assessed how BSC has been adapted to the public sector
in practice. Specifically, the re-orientation of BSC away from financial goals
obscures the perception of causality between KPIs within its four dimensions, thus diminishing its usefulness as a performance management tool.

Northcott and Taulapapa conducted a study of the applicability of BSC
in the New Zealand Local Government scenario. The results of their study,
which are shown in Table 7.1, illustrate that they surveyed 73 local government bodies with 48 providing usable responses, giving a response
rate of 65.8%. Their research found that only 16.67% of the respondents

Table 7.1  BSC Usage by Local Government Bodies

|  |  | Current Users | | Previous Users | | Non-Users | |
|---|---|---|---|---|---|---|---|
|  | Usable Responses | n | % | n | % | n | % |
| City Councils | 11 | 3 | 27.3 | 1 | 9.1 | 7 | 63.6 |
| District Councils | 37 | 5 | 13.5 | 0 | 0.0 | 32 | 86.5 |
| Total | 48 | 8 | 16.7 | 1 | 2.1 | 39 | 81.3 |

apply BSC. Table 7.1 shows the full extent to which BSC is used within the studied context. Their findings also suggest that larger organisations, which have a higher degree of strategic orientation and more resourcing, are more inclined to adopt BSC. The reason for this may be due to the circumstance of public entities, where a competitive market is fictional, and many longer-term operating requirements are imposed by legislation or policy rather than directed by management.

The findings of Northcott and Taulapapa's study suggest that the current BSC users perceived the BSC to be highly useful to their organisations for several reasons, including that the BSC provides focus and clear lines of accountability and the ability to measure the achievement of agreed outcomes (District Council); gives management a concise set of information to gauge performance and direct improvements; enables more comprehensive reporting to stakeholders and informs staff as to how successful the organisation has been (City Council); and helps clarify key measures that suggest whether the strategy is working (City Council). Additionally, the findings revealed performance measurement to be the main perceived benefit of using BSC, followed by strategic management and reporting.

The Northcott and Taulapapa study also found that the two key factors that contributed to the successful implementation of BSC were the modification of the BSC to align with the respective organisational needs; and undertaking the applicable learning, both prior to implementing the BSC and while using it. The modification aspect of BSC is in line with the Kaplan and Norton recommendation of placing the customer perspective at the ultimate target level and if necessary, expanding it to account for the multiplicity of services, users, and stakeholders in public sector contexts. However, they contend that there has been little empirical research into how such modifications to the BSC framework are affected in the public sector. Northcott and Taulapapa found that the respondents using the BSC observed that the modifications made to their BSC systems reflected the general nature of local government services and aims.

The findings suggest that these organisations developed their BSC system to support the mandatory Local Government documentation related to Long Term Community Council Plans and annual plans under the Local Government Act of 2002, which required local government to identify outcomes and then monitor achievement of outcomes for reporting. Northcott and Taulapapa noted that BSC appeared to be an effective method to achieve this. A Local Government Organisation modified the title of the perspective, while another added a fifth dimension of 'leadership and governance' as an additional perspective. This seems to suggest that the BSC methodology can be adapted to help to secure a successful and sustained implementation of BSC and can become a learning experience platform rather than necessarily offering an immediate, complete performance management solution.

Another Local Government Organisation applied an incremental-learning approach based on the experiences of others. This suggests that researching previous BSC implementations and benchmarking against best practice, attending seminars and training sessions, and seeking assistance from experts may be a worthwhile approach for other councils who are considering the application of BSC. Northcott and Taulapapa found that the main barriers to implementing BSC in local government include the following:

- Applicability of alternative systems that did not incorporate BSC.
- Size of the organisation did not warrant a BSC system.
- Lack of adequate resources to support information gathering and processing for a BSC system.
- Scarcity of time since managers were mostly occupied with more immediate operating concerns.
- Inadequate top management support for promoting BSC and providing the resources to sustain its use.

Most of the identified obstacles are related to the first principle regarding having an appropriate organisational environment that often requires a significant culture change. Moreover, Northcott and Taulapapa also identified two serious concerns, namely that related to complications in adapting the BSC structure to a public sector context, and problems with identifying and incorporating meaningful causal relationships between KPIs within the various BSC dimensions.

The necessity to modify the BSC structure and terminology to conform to public sector organisations has already been mentioned. However, the findings revealed that a main difficulty in implementing BSC is adapting to a new managerial philosophy that required a move from the traditional inputs focus to a focus on outcomes approach, which is the basis for BSC.

The study also revealed that the development of strategy maps at an organisational and business group level was a worthwhile exercise for considering 'how' the delivery of products and services are undertaken. But a shortcoming with BSC was related to providing a link or a means for comprehensive business planning.

Additionally, the study revealed that some managers found it difficult to construct a BSC with dimensions and measures that were appropriate to the aims and activities of their specific organisations. They found the range of the perspectives limiting. Generally, Northcott and Taulapapa found that local government managers struggled to adapt to the BSC's outcomes-based philosophy; define their 'customer'; identify appropriate BSC dimensions; and select a workable number of useful KPIs, which are all necessary in translating the BSC to suit their organisations' needs. Northcott and Taulapapa argue that the challenge of adapting the BSC framework needs special consideration in public sector organisations. Hence, adapting BSC to local government requires some creative thinking and the support of experts who are familiar with local government applications.

The second serious challenge revealed by the Northcott and Taulapapa study is how to identify and incorporate causal relationships within a public sector BSC (mapping causality). Kaplan and Norton contend that the cause-and-effect links amongst the performance measures are critical to the performance management objective of BSC since it allows managers to focus on the leading indicators that facilitate prediction, learning, and innovation. Although this contention is recognised by local government managers, they find that identifying these causal relationships and building them into the BSC is a significant practical challenge. However, the study revealed that this challenge can be overcome and is not unique to the public sector.

This study has highlighted several implications regarding the application of BSC in the public sector. The Northcott and Taulapapa study and others have revealed that BSC is not widely used in the public sector. However, those making use of it found it a useful performance measurement and management tool, and that BSC can be a valuable external reporting tool for public sector organisations that operate in the absence of competitive markets. Northcott and Taulapapa argue that for public sector managers to take advantage of the full potential of the BSC, more attention must be given to the issues that support or hinder its implementation in practice.

They contend that several issues impacting BSC adoption have been observed in previous BSC research of both public and private sector. They noted that the main implementation success factors included:

- A participative pre-implementation decision process to ensure support for BSC.
- Learning from others' experience regarding BSC implementations and benchmarking best practice.
- Robust and compelling management support.
- Sufficient resources to support the BSC initiatives.
- Modifying the standard BSC model to harmonise with the organisation's context and strategy.
- Continuous in-use learning and training.
- Undertaking a post-implementation review.

The Northcott and Taulapapa study has highlighted several implementation important challenges for the public sector that are described below. Firstly, given that BSC is based upon an organisation's strategy, a lack of a perceived strategic orientation within public sector organisations may act as a barrier to BSC adoption. Hence, it is important for public sector organisations to define their strategy and communicate it clearly, so that mangers see their roles and activities as linked to key strategic outcomes and are therefore better placed to exploit the potential benefits of the BSC as a performance management tool.

Secondly, it is essential that modifications of the BSC are made to fit an organisation's context. Some managers mentioned difficulties with deciding on suitable dimensions to include in the BSC, defining the customer, and identifying a manageable number of appropriate KPIs given the range and complexity of organisational activities. Therefore, it is suggested that public organisations commence with a BSC template that has been adapted for the similar attributes to their own organisation, rather than using the standard Kaplan and Norton model as a departure point. Thus, the public sector managers may learn from the experiences of other similar organisations and use this as a benchmark.

Thirdly, BSC causality may be poorly understood and under-developed in the public sector. While causal links between the dimensions are viewed as critical to the BSC's performance management role, performance measures are seen as imitative from assumed cause-and-effect relationships, noting that these assumptions may eventually turn out to be incorrect. Thus, to correct any improper assumptions, it is suggested that organisations try to confirm (where possible) assumed causal relationships when performance data becomes available over time. This continued use of the BSC is essential to collect the longitudinal performance data required for such testing, so a period of commitment to BSC development is required.

The Northcott and Taulapapa study has shown that the potential for the BSC to support the performance management aims of public sector organi sations is well recognised in the literature and has also been recognised by the managers who participated in their research. However, it must also be recognised that BSC has a low penetration rate amongst public sector organisations for various reasons that have been explained previously. It is important to note that although several challenges have been identi fied, none of them are insurmountable, given that sufficient support from experts is solicited.

## Example: Applying Balanced Scorecard (BSC) Methodology in the Public Sector

The public sector requires managers to use modern methods for increasing efficiency in functioning of public organisations due to more stringent pro cedures of spending and controlling public funds; the competition between public organisations for obtaining limited public funds; and the increasing demand of citizens for better and responsive services. An increasing trend of public management towards improving the effectiveness and efficiency of functioning of the public sector is through innovative solutions bor rowed from the private sector. The previous section examined the possible application of the Balanced Scorecard in the local government environment and highlighted the challenges encountered by the public sector for intro ducing such methods.

This section will illustrate the use of the Balanced Scorecard at a local government level using a hypothetical example. It has already been dem onstrated that a public organisation that has a defined strategy of operation with associated key themes is able to commence the BSC process. It has also been previously noted that a suitable organisational environment must be created for the BSC process to be implemented successfully, such as top management support amongst several other factors. According to Rohm (2008), the implementation of BSC consists of several basic steps, namely: strategic analysis; identification of customers and associated value proposal; defining the organisation's vision and mission statements; identifying the strategic themes; defining suitable perspectives and strategic objectives; generating a strategic map, including the targets and relevant measures for achievement; developing strategic initiatives for specific areas of organisational activity; cascading the Balanced Scorecards at lower organisational levels; appraising the results of the undertaken activities; and undertaking corrective action as necessary.

## Public Sector Example

The example presented in this section is for a hypothetical local government scenario for the municipality of Silverton. As stated previously, the first step is to develop the appropriate organisational environment. Silverton's executive management must recognise that a BSC system is transformational and therefore will completely reshape the organisation's strategy and processes, resulting in a shift in work culture. This will require having an engaging leadership style; having interactive communication throughout the organisation that inspires an exchange of ideas; and having a robust change management process that incorporates overcoming resistance, engaging employees, implementing the change, and effectively communicating the change.

The next step is for the organisation to develop its strategy by defining the strategic themes of possible action, followed by defining the mission and vision statements in relation to its customers, which will give rise to the identification of the strategic issues. The strategic issues are the key themes based on which the organisation will develop its strategy. The strategy will be developed by analysing the internal and external environments, using two major tools, namely SWOT (strengths, weaknesses, opportunities, and threats) and PEST (political, economic, social, and technology) analysis. The resulting strategy represents the chosen options that the public organisation wants to realise to fulfil its vision and mission statements.

The strategic issues may be viewed as the vision and mission of the organisation transformed into operational terms. These postulate the answer to the following question: 'How does the organisation want to pursue its mission statement?' In Silverton's case its vision and mission statement conveyed the aspiration of the city to ensure high-quality public services, through which the city would be the best place to live, work, and relax through leisure time. The city council resolved that Silverton city should allocate its limited financial resources to those initiatives that are likely to provide the greatest impact on the realisation of their vision. The city council selected several themes out of the possible numerous proposed themes that included: Public safety; transportation; economic development; upgrading older areas of the city; and the restructuring of local government.

A taskforce was established to implement the five goals effectively. The taskforce was to transform the selected strategic themes into strategic goals. Since the organisation was a local government entity, it was decided to give more emphasis to the Citizen. Therefore, the taskforce agreed to place the customer perspective at the top of the scorecard. The city council of Silverton felt that this customer focus represented a logical relationship between the mission statement and its role as a local government unit and the construction of the BSC. However, it was also recognised, being a public organisation, that Finance is the only means to achieve the needs of its citizens. Figure 7.8, using the Kaplan and Norton approach, illustrates the general structure of the BSC for Silverton city as a public entity.

In the case of a public organisation, the BSC signifies the measure of success in public entities that have a customer's perspective as the main theme and not the financial perspective as displayed for the private sector. As shown in Table 7.2, Arveson (2003) found that the focus of the BSC for the private and public sectors is somewhat different.

It should be noted that public organisations perspectives in BSC may differ significantly, depending on the function and responsibility the organisation plays regarding its customer base. Furthermore, Northcott and Taulapapa revealed that the number of perspectives may be bigger than the traditional four of the basic BSC set. However, the common view of developing a BSC is to have a chain of cause-and-effect linkages between perspectives aimed at an effective strategy implementation. Therefore, after identifying and defining the strategic themes and perspectives, it becomes essential to generate strategy maps. These describe in detail how the strategy is to be implemented, by the creation of targets for each of the selected perspectives. Thus, a strategy map, as suggested by Kaplan and Norton in

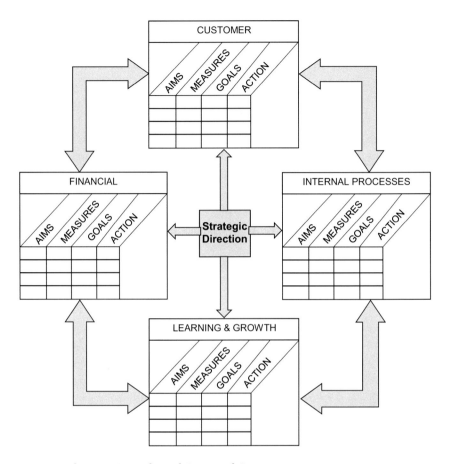

*Figure 7.8*  Silverton City Balanced Scorecard Structure

*Table 7.2*  Difference in the Focus of the BSC for the Private and Public Sectors

| Feature | Private Sector | Public Sector |
|---|---|---|
| General Strategic Goals | Competitiveness; Uniqueness | Mission Success; Best Practices |
| Financial Goals | Profit; Growth; Market Share | Productivity; Efficiency; Value |
| Stakeholders | Stakeholders; Buyers; Managers | Taxpayers; Recipients; Legislators |
| Desired Outcome | Customer Satisfaction | Customer Satisfaction |

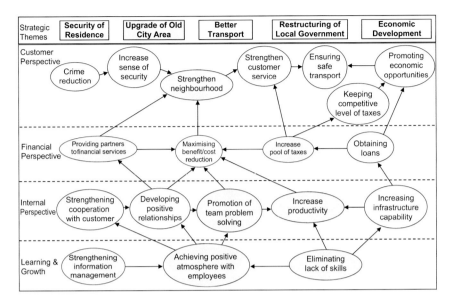

*Figure 7.9* Strategy Map for the City of Silverton

Figure 7.9, shows the cause-and-effect linkages between the objectives in the perspectives of the organisation, in this case Silverton City.

The objectives for the City of Silverton that were included in the customers' perspective consisted of the main services that the city had decided to provide to its residents. The realisation of the financial objectives allowed the city to achieve the objectives identified in the customers' perspective. The financial objectives incorporated the provision by the city of paid services at reasonable prices, providing financial assistance of external partners. Additionally, the objectives of the internal processes' perspective and the learning and growth perspective sustained the objectives that were included in the financial perspective and in the customers' perspective.

The taskforce developing the BSC generated descriptions of each objective contained in the BSC (Kaplan and Norton, 2001). They also included a financial perspective objective aimed at reducing costs. This illustrates the manner the organisation views itself, its services, and its responsibility to its residents within the scope of managing its limited resources. This dimension is seen as emulating the operations of a public organisation to that of a private entity. Hence, a public service needs to be given at the finest quality and with a judicious use of public resources.

A BSC caters for all facets of the attainment of the objectives, categorised into perspectives that does not exclude any of them. The cause-and-effect linkages covered by the strategy map permit all to comprehend what the strategy of a public organisation is all about and depicts the way that one may help in its implementation. The strategy map makes it easier for management to present the organisation's strategy in a clear and unambiguous manner. It also provides all those assessing local government actions with visible measures for evaluating its activities in terms of implementing various programmes and the extent and approach of implementing the objectives that were defined by the organisation itself. It must be recognised that a strategy map does not absolutely cover all the services provided by a public organisation, such as a municipality.

The BSC for Silverton only covers the themes related to those services that the City Council wish to improve with the intention of turning Silverton into the ideal place to live, work, and relax in. Therefore, the BSC should be viewed as providing a general summary of what (and how) the Silverton City Council wants to achieve. A complete BSC considers the synergistic linkage of the objectives with the specific perspectives across the strategic themes. For example, the elements in Figure 7.9 that are shaded in grey reflect the theme related to 'upgrading of old city area' in the BSC.

The next step in the strategic planning process when applying the BSC approach is to establish measures to ensure that the objectives are achieved. The strategy map depicted the objectives and their mutual linkages. However, this poses an important issue that must be addressed, namely, exactly how will the organisation determine whether the objective has been achieved. Once the strategic objectives and the respective measures for their implementation have been determined, management may define the operational objectives that deal with a shorter period. These address the strategic initiatives, which are viewed as tangible activities intended to achieve the agreed objectives. These take various forms, contingent on whether they refer to the activities that encompass the whole organisation, or elements of the BSC for individual departments.

The transformation from the strategic objectives to the strategic initiatives for Silverton applying the Naukowa et al. (2014) model is shown in Figure 7.10. Figure 7.10 illustrates the 'Customer' orientation approach for the BSC. It also shows how one may combine the strategy for the different perspectives with the measures, operational objectives, and initiatives

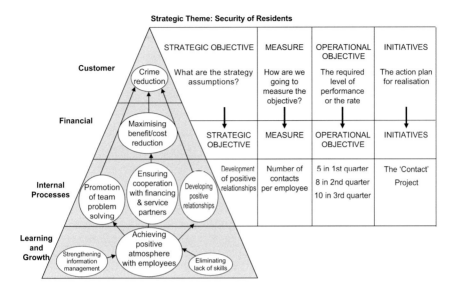

Strategic Theme: Security of Residents

*Figure 7.10* Transformation from Strategic Objectives to the Strategic Initiatives for Silverton

for each of the strategic objectives for a specific strategic theme (example Security of Residence).

The cascading process of assigning the scorecards to the various organisational levels commences when the strategy maps and the key linkages leading to the achievement of the objectives contained in it and joint initiatives for the entire organisation have been identified, as illustrated by Figure 7.10. The key issue that needs to be addressed at this stage is how a specific department contributes to the implementation of the strategy. This establishes the foundation for assigning the specific objectives to every individual department contingent to meeting the strategic assumptions.

This encourages management to review the organisational structure because it replaces the vertical division of the functional areas of management with initiatives for strategy implementation. Thus, the organisation's strengths that stimulate growth, development, or change within the organisation transform and the synergistic relationships between its parts occur. The development of BSC for individual departments and individuals commences after the structure of the organisation to address the new challenges is modified according to the new circumstances. The modification to the organisation structure is not complex, because the operation improvement areas are delimited by the internal processes and learning and growth levels. Therefore, after establishing the strategic objectives under its responsibility and using the strategic maps, each individual organisational area will describe how it will achieve the strategic goals, ascertain the operational objectives and associated measures, and define the strategic initiatives.

The choice of measures depends on the perspective and the operational targets that are established once these have been determined. It should be noted that the operational targets reflect a shorter time horizon and depict the development of the organisation with a view to reaching the objective planned in the strategy. These objectives are achieved by undertaking several initiatives, which are viewed as the assignments that have the goal of implementing the operational objectives in the short-term and the strategic goals in the long-term. Each initiative has an associated plan that describes the budget, sponsor, deadlines, and resources. Moreover, each initiative is focused on the implementation of the operational objectives that consist of the tasks required to achieve the strategic objectives. Note that the implementation of the strategic objectives contributes to the achievement of the strategic themes, which are the outcome of the transformation of the vision statement into operational terms as illustrated in Figure 7.10.

BSC are developed for business units, teams, and individuals, which provide the basis for strategy cascading to lower operating levels. Hence, the BSC for the various levels of the organisation are an expansion of the main holistic organisational BSC. Figure 7.11, applying the Naukowa, et al. (2014) approach, illustrates a system of creating BSCs by generating 'cascades' that move down to the lower organisational levels. The BSCs at each level are coherent and implement a single strategy that provides value to the customer, and are an effective way of communicating between business units or departments. To maintain a BSC system, the organisation requires an information management system that gathers, processes, and displays various variables that are relevant to the BSC system.

It should be noted that strategy-oriented organisations have an integrated process of budget and operations management that, together, support strategic management. The reporting system is a key feature and is based upon a strategic BSC that monitors the progress being made in the implementation of the strategy and taking corrective action when needed.

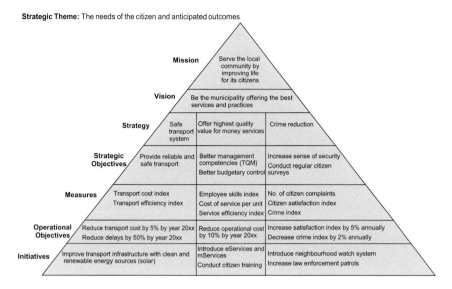

*Figure 7.11*  Transformation of Strategy into Operational Terms

This strategy-oriented approach incorporates three solutions that are essential for the management system (Kaplan and Norton, 2001, p. 147):

- Linking the strategy with the budget by having robust objectives of the BSC to combine the strategy rhetoric with the budget objectivity (see Figure 7.12 using the Arveson [2003] method).
- Strategic feedback systems that incorporate a new basis for reporting and a new kind of board meetings. Hence, managers are no longer held accountable for managing functional siloes, but take responsibility for strategic management activities (see Figure 7.13 applying the Arveson model).
- Testing, learning, adapting. The BSC defines in explicit terms the strategy hypotheses. Hence, managerial teams can test these hypotheses more analytically using feedback from the BSC. Additionally, the strategy evolves in real time when new ideas and suggestions flow from the organisation.

Anderson and McAdam (2004) provide some additional common non-financial measures that may be used by management to assess performance on certain specific aspects as shown by Table 7.3. Management must choose the best measures that make most sense for the agreed strategy.

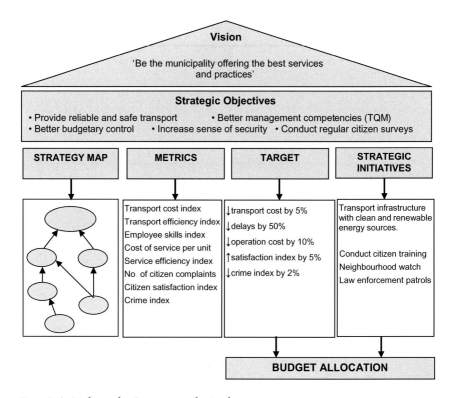

Figure 7.12  Linking the Strategy to the Budget

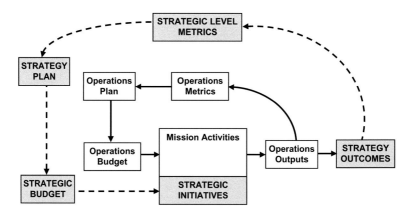

Figure 7.13  Operational and Strategic Feedback Systems

The BSC has four perspectives; however, Table 7.3 only considers the non-financial views. According to Naukowa et al. (2014) and Northcott and Taulapapa (2012), the BSC has been successfully applied in local government units in the United States of America and New Zealand. The BSC is

Table 7.3  Difference in the Focus of the BSC for the Private and Public Sectors

| Customer Perspective | Internal Processes Perspective | Learning & Growth Perspective |
|---|---|---|
| **Conversion Rate**: The percentage of interactions that result in a sale. Conversion Rate = (Interactions with Completed Transactions) / (Total Sales Interactions) | **Customer Support Tickets**: Number of new tickets, number of resolved tickets, and resolution time. | **Salary Competitiveness Ratio (SCR)**: The competitiveness of compensation options. SCR = (Average Company Salary) / (Average Salary Offered from Competitors or Industry) |
| **Retention Rate**: Portion of persons who remain customers for an entire reporting period. Customer Retention Rate = (Customers Lost in a Given Period) / (Number of Customers at Start of a Period) | **Product Defect Percentage**: Percentage of defective products in a specified timeframe. Product Defect Percentage = (Number of Defective Units in a Given Period) / (Total Number of Units Produced in a Given Period) | **Employee Productivity Rate**: Workforce efficiency measured over time. Employee Productivity Rate = (Total Company Revenue) / (Total Number of Employees) |
| **Contact Volume by Channel**: Number of support requests by phone and email in a given period. | **On-Time Rate**: Percentage of time products were delivered as scheduled. On-Time Rate = (Number of On-Time Units in a Given Period) / (Total Number of Units Shipped in a Given Period) | **Turnover Rate for Highest Performers**: The success of retention efforts for top performers and plans for talent replacement. High Performer Turnover Rate = (Number of High Performers Who Departed in Past Year) / (Total High Performers Identified) |

(Continued)

Table 7.3   (Continued)

| Customer Perspective | Internal Processes Perspective | Learning & Growth Perspective |
|---|---|---|
| **Customer Satisfaction Index**: The entity's success at meeting the customers' needs. This is normally found through a regular customer survey. | **Efficiency Measure**: This varies by industry. Manufacturing industry may measure efficiency by analysing how many units are produced every hour and the plant's uptime percentage. | **Average Time to Hire**: The efficiency of the hiring process measured by time to recruit, interview, and hire. |
| **Net Promoter Score**: The likelihood that customers will recommend a brand to others. A score from 1–10 that qualifies promoters (usually 9–10) and detractors (under 6).<br><br>Net Promoter Score = (Number of Promoters) – (Number of Detractors) | **Overdue Project Percentage**: Number of projects that are behind schedule.<br><br>Overdue Project Percentage = (Number of Overdue Projects in a Given Period) / (Total Number of Projects in a Given Period) | **Internal Promotion Rate**: Successful retention and growth of top performers.<br><br>Internal Promotion Rate = (The Number of Promoted Individuals) / (Total Number of Employees) |

viewed as facilitating the realisation of the strategic vision of the organisation. It is also argued that the BSC assists managers to focus on those things that have the greatest impact on the municipality. There is no doubt that the BSC has helped in implementing the agreed strategy, but it is seen as a concept for action as an action-focused strategy.

## Benchmarking

Like every management tool, the usefulness of any specified performance measure depends on how it is used and how well it will be applied. It has long been accepted that for performance measures to have significance and provide practical information, it is necessary for management to make comparisons. These comparisons may assess the progress being made in achieving given agreed targets, evaluate performance trends over time, or contrast the performance of two or more organisations. These type of performance measures have been exploited by the private sector for many decades. However, this practice is becoming more common in the public sector as well.

For example, in the United States of America, the Government Performance and Results Act of 1993 (GPRA) made it mandatory for management in the public sector to establish performance measures to assess how well departments and agencies are achieving their declared goals and objectives. However, the focus of GPRA performance measures is on output and outcome measures at the program level rather than processes. Therefore, there is a need for performance measures to be widened in scope to include input and process measures. As illustrated in previous sections of this chapter, one method is to use an assortment of measures, such as the Balanced Scorecard, which assess an organisation and its programs from different perspectives. According to Kaplan and Norton (1996, p. 148), if the right objectives and measures are identified, successful implementation will likely occur.

Another approach that may be used for measuring and improving performance at a process level is Benchmarking. Benchmarking is viewed as a key element of continuous improvement programs and has a similar role to the Six Sigma methodology that will be described in detail in the next chapter. The focus of this section is Benchmarking as a performance measurement and management tool. Sarkis (2001) argues that from a manager's viewpoint, Benchmarking has been defined as a continuous, systematic process for evaluating the products, services, and work processes of organisations that are recognised as representing best practices, for the purpose of organisational improvement.

Benchmarking has also been described as a structured process. However, there seems little consensus regarding the definition of Benchmarking because the literature suggests that there are different categories of Benchmarking that have a different meaning and use. Anderson and McAdam (2004), after reviewing the literature related to Benchmarking and the different typologies of Benchmarking, agree on the classification as shown in Table 7.4, which shows five different types of Benchmarking that may be applied for four different management purposes.

Table 7.4 suggests that Lead Benchmarking is highly relevant for the five different types of Benchmarking. According to Anderson and McAdam (2004), a working definition of lead Benchmarking is Benchmarking that focuses on analysing forward-looking, predictive, and future performance comparisons. However, a closer examination of the various definitions will be discussed after some basic Benchmarking concepts are provided. Benchmarking can be a powerful tool if one is pursuing continuous improvements in the organisational processes. However, it is a waste of time and resources if the organisation is only Benchmarking against itself.

Generally, Benchmarking is a process of measuring the performance of an organisation's products, services, operations, processes against other organisations that are recognised as the best in their sector or the wider

*Table 7.4* Relevance of Use for Different Categories of Benchmarking and Different Management Purposes

|  | Internal Benchmarking | Competitor Benchmarking | Functional Benchmarking | Generic Benchmarking | Performance Benchmarking |
|---|---|---|---|---|---|
| Performance Benchmarking | Medium | High | Medium | Low | Medium |
| Process Benchmarking | Medium | Low | High | High | Medium |
| Strategic Benchmarking | Low | High | Low | Low | Medium |
| Lead Benchmarking | High | High | High | High | High |

marketplace. There are various metrics that are used for Benchmarking, with the more frequent being cost per unit, time to produce, product/service quality, effectiveness, time to market, customer satisfaction, loyalty, and brand recognition. Applying Benchmarking as a comparison with leading organisations will provide specific insights to assist management's understanding of how their organisation's brand, product, or other elements compare with others, irrespective of whether they belong to the same or a different industry or have a different customer base. Hence, Benchmarking is the process for acquiring a measure or set of measures, known as a benchmark or benchmarks. Therefore, Benchmarking specifies the process of how the measure was obtained, and benchmarks are the measures themselves (i.e., the 'what').

Benchmarking will facilitate management's endeavours to have more efficient processes and improve quality, which in turn is likely to result in lower costs and higher revenue. The key element to the success of Benchmarking is to identify the best-in-class organisations and observe why their processes work so well. This may not be straightforward and will require substantial effort, but it will give your organisation the opportunity for continuous improvement regarding new innovative processes; upgrading basic product or service features to surpass the competitor's product or service; enhancing communication through social media innovations; and incentivising employees, amongst many others.

Generally, if used effectively, Benchmarking may be exploited to improve processes and operations; enhance efficiency, lower operating costs, and improve quality; determine the effectiveness of past performance; understand how key competitors operate; and strengthen customer satisfaction and loyalty. It should be noted that Benchmarking is a continuing process that requires constant monitoring for identifying industry standards that at minimum should be met, with the aim of surpassing them. The aim is to identify what the competitors are doing right so that the organisation may emulate their success, and to recognise what the organisation is doing wrong so that corrective action may be taken. Benchmarking supports the business goals by continuously improving processes.

## *Benchmarking Classification*

Briefly, Benchmarking is a process used to measure the quality and performance of an organisation's products, services, processes, and other selected features. On their own these measurements do not have much value. However, their value increases dramatically when compared against some type of standard (i.e., a benchmark). Hence, a way of knowing your organisation's standing on several characteristics is to compare against other data, such as the time it takes another organisation to provide a similar service. For example, if another organisation can provide the same type of service in less than 20 minutes, then this time can be used as a benchmark for measuring your own organisation's methods, processes, and practices.

Hence, the objective of Benchmarking is that by using the data gathered in the Benchmarking process, management will be able to identify those areas where improvements can be made. For example, by establishing how and where other organisations are realising higher performance levels than your own organisation; by comparing the competitor's procedures, processes, and strategies with your own organisation; and by exploiting the collected, processed, and analysed information, to undertake a detail comparison exercise for implementing a change management strategy to continually improve your organisation's operations.

Benchmarking is not a one-off exercise; it is a continuous activity to help an organisation's management to improve its processes and procedures; assess the effectiveness of its past performance; and to provide it with better knowledge and understanding of how the competition operates to assist management to identify best practices for increasing performance. Table 7.4 indicates that there are many different types of Benchmarking that fall into several primary categories. Table 7.4 also provides an indication, according to Anderson and McAdam (2004), of their effectiveness as benchmarks for the various types and purposes of Benchmarking. A brief description of each benchmark's type and purpose is provided below.

### Internal Benchmarking

Generally, Benchmarking can be internal or external. Internal Benchmarking compares performance, processes, and practises against other units within the same organisation. The organisational units can be different teams, business units, groups, or even individuals. For example, benchmarks may be used to compare the average project delay time of one division with that of another division within the same organisation, or to compare processes in one service centre with other service centres within the same organisation. Internal Benchmarking is very useful where no external benchmarks are available.

Internal benchmarks can be used as a preliminary start for a quantitative process analysis, where trends can be identified, and the impact of performance-improving processes can be evaluated. External Benchmarking is covered when discussing competitor Benchmarking. On the other hand, external Benchmarking compares performance of one organisation against other external organisations. Very often these external organisations are peers or competitors. However, this is not always the case. For example, Benchmarking can be used to compare performance, processes, and practises across different industries. External benchmarks provide the added benefit of comparing against competitors to gain a better understanding of what constitutes 'good' performance.

## Competitive Benchmarking

Competitive Benchmarking examines closely an organisation's competitors, not only to improve its internal operations but also to understand the competitors better. Therefore, this type of Benchmarking conducts a comparison of products, the organisation's position within its industry, and what the organisation may need to do better to increase its productivity. For example, an organisation may compare the customers' satisfaction with a competitor's product with its own. If the competitor is receiving better customer reviews, the organisation will need to analyse what the difference is and think of ways to improve the quality of its own product.

Competitive Benchmarking is different from competitor analysis. Competitor analysis focuses specifically on a brand and endeavours to secure a competitive edge by entering niche areas, such as new markets and new product or service features. In contrast, competitive Benchmarking requires an organisation to collect insights to illustrate how the competitor's processes work, compared to its own, with the aim of identifying industry performance standards. In other words, an organisation would compare its products, services, processes, and methods with those of its key competitors to identify its position in the industry and determine how to increase productivity and marketing success. For example, an organisation would collect data regarding the customer sentiment towards the competitor's brand and its own in terms of being positive, negative, or neutral.

The analysis of this data would reveal whether the competitor's rating is better and allows management to decide how to improve.

## Functional Benchmarking

Functional Benchmarking is a procedure for comparing similar practices within the same organisation or different organisations or industries. For example, a health institution may want to improve its debt collection procedures. This may be achieved by comparing its debt collection process with that of a corporate business that specialises in debt collection. Hence, comparing the same function but in different organisations and industries.

## Generic Benchmarking

The objective of generic Benchmarking is to identify excellent work processes that do not need to be in the same industry or job function. Hence, generic Benchmarking is the process of analysing two organisations in different industries and comparing their general operational and administrative functions. The comparison may be made on any type of function or feature that is common across industries, such as website functionality, recruiting practices, and accounting administrative processes.

## Performance Benchmarking

Performance Benchmarking involves the collection of information regarding how well the organisation is achieving in terms of outcomes and comparing these outcomes with other organisations internally or externally. Outcomes cover a range of elements from revenue growth to customer satisfaction. Performance Benchmarking requires the collaboration of the entire organisation. Its key aim is to motivate change in the organisation by collecting insights, which if managed correctly will bring about improvements. The term performance Benchmarking may also refer to functional performance Benchmarking. For example, Benchmarking the performance of the Human Resource section, using measures such as the employee net promoter score or staff engagement surveys or the Marketing section, by evaluating the net promoter score or brand awareness.

## Process Benchmarking

Process Benchmarking results from a detailed analysis of the organisation's key processes and comparing their performance against internal and external benchmarks. The objective is to discover a method that will optimise and improve the organisation's processes. Hence, by understanding better how top performers complete a process, the organisation can find ways to make its own processes more efficient, quicker, and more effective.

## Strategic Benchmarking

Strategic Benchmarking compares an organisation's strategies, business approaches, and business models with key competitor organisations to strengthen the organisation's own strategic planning and determine its strategic priorities. The objective is for the organisation to understand what strategies support successful companies (or teams or business units) and then compare these strategies with its own to find a means for the organisation to be more successful. For strategic Benchmarking to be applied successfully, the comparison must be conducted against best practice organisations. Furthermore, the comparison should not be limited to other organisations within the same industry. Management should be on the lookout for products, services, or brands that have proved successful in a specific process.

This Benchmarking approach should be applied when the organisation needs to view beyond its own industry to identify first-class performance and best practices to discover innovative ways of adapting its methods to its own procedures and processes. Strategic Benchmarking aims to improve the holistic performance of the organisation by considering long-term strategies compared to others, and will help the organisation to review and improve its core competencies and new product/service development. Ghete (2014) cited an example where Southwest Airlines, realising a need to improve its performance, consulted NASCAR to examine how pit crews were able to service race cars so swiftly. They discovered that the process depended on the ability of each pit crew member to achieve a specific task within precise time intervals (12 to 16 seconds) of all the four streamlined processes for gate maintenance, plane cleaning, and passenger boarding.

## *Lead Benchmarking*

Lead Benchmarking focuses on analysing forward-looking, predictive, and future performance comparisons. Anderson and McAdam (2004) argue that lead measures are proactive and preventive in nature and help to antic-ipate and impact future desired results. They contend that lead measures are needed to drive performance throughout the organisation and provide information on incremental steps towards larger goals. Hence, an entity must be organised to respond to change in a timely manner, with the cost of responding to change being smaller if the change period is longer. Lead Benchmarking helps to forecast change in a timely manner, thus gaining a longer change period when compared to a more costly quick response, after a competitor's reaction to change is detected. This is achieved by the continuous monitoring of the organisation, thus permitting a longer change period.

Anderson and McAdam contend that opportunities for creating value are shifting from managing tangible assets to managing knowledge-based strategies that develop an organisation's intangible assets, such as customer relationships, innovative products and services, high quality and responsive operating processes, information technology and databases, and employee capabilities, skills, and motivations. They maintain that these intangible assets are important elements within lead Benchmarking. Anderson and McAdam also argue that lead measures could be branded as performance measurement gaps, in that there is a failure to apply the proper meas-ure, so that something that may be important for the organisation stays neglected, but needs to be further identified, assessed, and developed by the organisation.

## **The Benchmarking Process**

Benchmarking is viewed as systematic process for measuring an organi-sation's performance when compared with recognised leaders with the objective of determining best practices that lead to superior performance when adapted and applied. This implies that Benchmarking must be imple-mented as a structured and systematic process. Hence, Benchmarking will not succeed when implemented in an improvised manner. Figure 7.14 pro-vides a systematic method to successfully implement Benchmarking based on the Benchmarking pioneering work of Camp (1989) at Xerox.

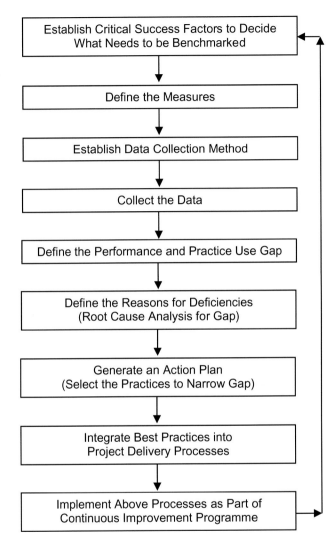

*Figure 7.14* Systematic Model for Implementing Benchmarking Successfully

Often Benchmarking is based on best-practice organisations as the comparison baseline. Hence, the method is based on comparing an organisation with the best-in-class. Additionally, Benchmarking is not a one-off exercise but forms part of a continuous management improvement programme that includes a feedback loop, as illustrated by Figure 7.14. As stated in the previous section, Benchmarking can be internal or external. Internal Benchmarking means that organisations benchmark against their own projects, processes, and other factors.

On the other hand, with external Benchmarking, organisations seek projects, processes, and other factors from external organisations for comparative analysis. Internal Benchmarking is viewed as beneficial when no external benchmarks are readily available, and is often exploited to commence quantitative analysis by identifying trends over time and evaluating the impact of processes that are meant to improve performance. External Benchmarking is generally considered better, because it provides the added advantage of comparing against competitors, thus giving an organisation's managers a better understanding of what constitutes 'good' practice.

Figure 7.14 illustrates that the first step of Benchmarking is for management to understand what is important to the organisation, by defining the organisation's critical success factors (CSFs) and therefore deciding what is to be benchmarked. These CSFs provide the basis for measuring performance. Hence, the next step is related to defining the measures that will be used in the comparison exercise. Once the measures have been identified, management will need to devise a process for collecting the required data and commence collecting the data, storing it in an appropriate format for later retrieval when needed. A Benchmarking approach requires the support from a computer system designed to collect, retrieve, and process the collected data. The collected data will consist of two key components, namely the measures collected from internal sources related to one's organisation and the comparative data collected from the sources related to the best-in-class organisation, which can be an internal or external entity depending on whether internal or external Benchmarking is being used.

The gap between actual performance (own organisation) and preferred achievement (comparative organisation) is generally examined to identify the opportunities for improvement. The Root Cause Analysis is undertaken to evaluate the cause of the actual performance, which may be unsatisfactory or satisfactory. This analysis will commence a search for best practices if the performance is unsatisfactory and will be used to help address the identified performance problems. Three more activities are required to complete the Benchmarking process cycle. These consist of preparing an action plan to select the practices that are aimed at narrowing the performance gap; integrating the identified best practices into a project or process delivery approach; and implementing the holistic processes as part of a continuous improvement programme. However, for these latter activities to be successful, Benchmarking requires buy-in from the senior and middle management at the various levels of the organisation. Hence, senior management commitment is a critical factor, particularly when a culture change is necessary. Furthermore, senior management's commitment must be supported by middle management and the employees.

The success of a Benchmarking system depends on the accuracy and timeliness of the benchmarked data. The benchmark data is collected through several ways, including a survey instrument administrated by the organisation itself or through a market research firm, the contents of which are then analysed by an expert team. The analyst team is interviewed to explain and resolve issues. It is essential that this step is conducted carefully because its objective is to validate the collected data and its analysis. It may be worthwhile for the organisation to engage an independent reviewer to carry out this function to ensure that the data and its analysis are complete and accurate, to maintain consistency across the organisation.

Many organisations mistakenly think that Benchmarking is a straightforward process and easy to implement. Unfortunately, this is not the case, and the successful implementation of Benchmarking needs to overcome several obstacles. A major concern of private sector management is related to disclosing and sharing information, which they view as giving them a competitive advantage. Others are concerned that sharing information may reveal their organisational weaknesses. These concerns may be mitigated by applying an identity-blind process, which is designed to ensure the data are posted without ascription or acknowledgement. A major barrier is that some organisations may be complacent and falsely view their organisation as being the best, so they do not see a reason why they should benchmark. There are also organisations that are unaware of the benefits of Benchmarking and view Benchmarking systems as ineffective for focusing on their specific requirements. Lack of resources to undertake a continuous Benchmarking programme is also a key obstacle, particularly if the organisation does not have the computer systems that may easily be modified to support Benchmarking. Hence, it is important that a suitable champion from the senior management ranks is found and appointed to promote the use of Benchmarking and other performance measurement and management tools.

## *Benchmarking Challenges*

There are some important prerequisites for the successful implementation of Benchmarking, some of which have been mentioned previously. Firstly, it is important to have senior management buy-in and support. It is important to identify suitable Benchmarking campions from senior management who have the vision and energy to generate the enthusiasm needed to push the Benchmarking methodology throughout the organisation. It must be recognised that the Benchmarking process within the various departments is similar, hence the learning curve should not be a prolonged one in any specific department. Benchmarking depends on complete and accurate data; hence a high code of ethics is essential to ensure that the data is not tampered with. For Benchmarking to be sustainable in terms of resources requirements, it should be implemented as an integral part of an organisation-wide information management system, with performance measures being used in a structured Benchmarking process. This will facilitate the data collection and analysis process, and minimise manual intervention, thus Benchmarking becomes cost-effective, adding value to the data being collected and processed.

Benchmarking must overcome several challenges if its full potential is to materialise. Benchmarking is versatile, so it is important that the organisation implements the Benchmarking process that suits its environment. Moreover, organisations must avoid the temptation of applying Benchmarking up to the KPI comparison step without moving on to the discovery steps to reveal and adopt best practices. The aim of Benchmarking is to have a continuous improvement process by adopting best practices that are constantly changing over time. Organisation must focus on the objective of Benchmarking. Benchmarking is not just about attaining targets but is also about improving performance. Therefore, the focus of the organisation is on performance improvement.

Organisations must be careful to select the proper benchmarks. Available benchmarks are not always the best to use. Hence, it may be worthwhile for the organisation to hire professionals to attain the proper benchmark data that is valid and reliable. The above highlight that Benchmarking needs to be viewed in its proper perspective. Remember that Benchmarking is a systematic process for measuring an organisation's performance when compared with recognised leaders, with the objective of determining best practices that lead to superior performance when adapted and applied. This definition stresses the need for Benchmarking and provides a clear sense of why it is undertaken.

# Conclusion

This chapter examined the Balanced Scorecard and Benchmarking methods as the basis for applying KPIs as a performance management approach. It has been illustrated that the usefulness of any given performance measure depends on how this measure is computed and applied. Hence, for performance measures to have meaning and provide helpful information, they must be compared against a robust base. Comparisons might be used to assess progress in attaining the agreed objectives or goals, review trends in performance over a given duration, or consider the performance of one entity contrasted to another.

This chapter has also demonstrated that comparisons are applicable both for the public and private sectors. It is argued that performance measures employed as a management tool must be extended to incorporate both input and process measures. One method exploited is the application of the scorecard that consists of multiple measures. This may take the form of a Balanced Scorecard or Benchmarking. The Balanced Scorecard evaluates an organisation and its programs from four different viewpoints, namely the finance, customer, employee, and process. The Balanced Scorecard generates a complete organisational holistic model of the strategy. This specifically permits all employees to understand how they contribute to organisational success and focuses on change efforts. Hence, if the right objectives and measures are identified, successful implementation will likely result. Benchmarking, on the other hand, is also viewed as a core component of continuous improvement programs and is considered an important performance assessment tool.

The application of the Balanced Scorecard and Benchmarking provide organisations with an approach that supports their performance management process. This chapter has shown that the Balanced Scorecard is a strategic planning and management methodology used by organisations to communicate their objectives and goals; align the day-to-day work with strategy; prioritise the undertaken projects, products, and services; and measure and track progress concerning strategic targets. The concept of the Balanced Scorecard has developed into a holistic system for managing the strategic direction of an organisation and consists of a systematic framework that provides organisations with a process of bringing together diverse items of information from the different components of strategic planning and management. This provides a visible link between the projects and programs being worked upon; the measurements being applied to monitor success (KPIs); the strategic objectives and goals the organisation is aiming to accomplish; and the mission, vision, and strategy of the organisation.

In contrast, Benchmarking is a systematic method of measuring key organisational metrics and practices and comparing them against various organisational areas or against a competitor, industry peers, or other entities to understand how and where the organisation needs to change to improve its performance. Benchmarking aims to achieve continuous improvement by identifying internal opportunities that lead to better performance. Benchmarking provides points of reference for contrasting an organisation's performance against the performance of other organisations, preferably those that apply best practices.

Benchmarking can be applied at various organisational levels, such as processes, services, products, or operations, and these comparisons can be applied in contrast to other parts of the organisation, external organisation (such as competitors or similar organisations), or industry best practises. This chapter has also illustrated that Benchmarking typically consist of two broad categories, namely internal and external. Internal Benchmarking compares performance, processes, and practises against other divisions or departments within the same entity. On the other hand, external Benchmarking compares organisational performance with other entities, such as competitors or best practice entities in other jurisdictions. External Benchmarking can also be used to compare performance, processes, and practises across different industries.

It must be recognised that both the Balanced Scorecard and Benchmarking have their own challenges to overcome. They both need a suitable organisational environment with a culture that embraces a continuous improvement programme. They both need the support of senior management to promote their proper use as an effective performance management tool. The next chapter will examine another significant performance management tool, namely Six Sigma. It will examine how the Six Sigma methodology can be applied to complement the Balanced Scorecard for managing and improving organisational performance.

## References

Anderson, K. and McAdam, R. (2004). 'A Critique of Benchmarking and Performance Measurement: Lead or Lag?' *Benchmarking: An International Journal*, 11(5), pp. 465–483.

Arveson, P. (2003). *An Introduction to the Balanced Scorecard for City & County Governments*. Cary, NC: Balanced Scorecard Institute.

Camp, R.C. (1989). *Benchmarking the Search for Industry Best Practices That Lead to Superior Performance*. White Plains, NY: Quality Resources.

Ghețe, A. (2014). Southwest Airlines: From Benchmarking to Benchmarked. *Performance Magazine – The KPI Institute*. Available at: https://www.performancemagazine.org/southwest-airlines-from-benchmarking-to-benchmarked/ (Accessed 22 November 2023).

Kaplan, R.S. and Norton, D.P. (1993). 'Putting the Balanced Scorecard to Work.' *Harvard Business Review*, September–October 1993 issue.

Kaplan, R.S. and Norton, D.P. (1996). *The Balanced Scorecard*. Boston, MA: Harvard Business School Press.

Kaplan, R.S. and Norton, D.P. (2001). 'Transforming the Balanced Scorecard from Performance Measurement to Strategic Management: Part 1.' *Accounting Horizons*, 15(1), pp. 87–104.

Northcott, D. and Taulapapa, T.M. (2012). 'Using the Balanced Scorecard to Manage Performance in Public Sector Organisations: Issues and Challenges.' *International Journal of Public Sector Management*, 25(3), pp. 166–191.

Poister, T.H. (2003). *Measuring Performance in Public and Non-profit Organizations*. San Francisco, CA: Jossey-Bass.

Rohm, Howard. (2008). *Using the Balanced Scorecard to Align Your Organisation*. Cary, NC: Balanced Scorecard Institute.

Sarkis, J. (2001). 'Benchmarking for Agility.' *Benchmarking: An International Journal*, 8(2), pp. 88–107.

Watson, G.H. (1992). *The Benchmarking Workbook: Adapting Best Practices for Performance Improvement*. Portland, OR: Productivity Press.

# 8

## SIX SIGMA

### BASIS FOR CONTINUOUS PROCESS IMPROVEMENT

'Measurement is the first step that leads to control and eventually to improvement. If you can't measure something, you can't understand it. If you can't understand it, you can't control it. If you can't control it, you can't improve it.'

Dr H. James Harrington
Author & Management Mentor

This chapter continues and elaborates on the theme of performance management using well test tools, which may be applied in conjunction with KPIs as performance measures. Often the fact that an entity has implemented some form of performance measurement becomes itself an impulse for the employees to perform better. Additionally, by evaluating the outcome of this performance measurement activity, an organisation is likely to improve its efficiency. This chapter will discuss Six Sigma as a performance management tool and will attempt to reveal how it may be used to improve the effectiveness of an organisation, both in the private and public sectors.

Six Sigma is viewed as a quality control mechanism that is applied to various business verticals. Vertical markets, or 'verticals,' are viewed as business

DOI: 10.4324/9781032685465-10

niches where the product or service provider focuses on a specific audience and their set of needs. An organisation may be described as 'vertical' if it is structured in a highly hierarchical manner. This type of organisation places more emphasis on clearly established authority. Hence, while subordinates may be treated with benevolence and esteem, their acquiescence to their superiors is critical. The definition of vertical is highly applicable to public sector organisations, which normally operate in a highly hierarchical manner and their departments are inclined to focus on specific audiences and issues. Furthermore, the vertical markets are progressively being serviced through eCommerce in the private Sector or eGovernment in the public sector (or mobile apps), because they can reach a wider range of audiences and minimise overhead costs by leveraging technology.

Apart from the public sector example, other generic examples of business verticals include the aerospace industry, agriculture, chemical manufacturing, defence industry, energy production and distribution, healthcare, real estate, and transportation. As one may appreciate, Six Sigma was originally conceived for the manufacturing industry due to the rigid and disciplined production methodology, but it has since evolved to be used in all other types of industries as well. Six Sigma focuses primarily on streamlining processes, to ensure that the desired output of those processes is achieved consistently every time. This chapter will examine the various features of Six Sigma and how these features may be applied in a practical manner.

## Introduction

The information age and digital transformation have become the common catchwords in the management of organisations. New technologies and a diverse arsenal of tools are being regularly introduced to help management in its expedition towards transformation, irrespective of whether they are running small or large organisations. Their primary objective is to achieve growth. However, the transformation process will not succeed unless it is supported by methodologies that foster quality and business transformation. Six Sigma is such a tool that was initially developed by Motorola in 1986 (and later trademarked in 1993) to keep in tune with emerging markets and processes related to quality management. Since its initial conception, Six Sigma has been refined and matured into an accepted robust theory of principles and methods, aimed at business transformation through a clearly defined systematic process.

Six Sigma is specifically a quality management methodology that is applied for helping organisations to improve their current processes, products, or services by revealing and eradicating defects. The primary objective is to streamline quality control in manufacturing or business processes to make sure that there is almost no variance throughout. Its key aim is having constant processes.

Six Sigma is named after the Greek letter sigma ($\sigma$), which is a statistical symbol for standard deviation. One of the basic principles in statistics is the Normal Distribution (the Bell-shaped graph). In fact, many statistical methods are based upon the assumption that the data adheres to the Normal Distribution. It is common practice to accept the probability of 99.73% of all outcomes that fall within three standard deviations of the mean (above or below). This is known as Three Sigma, which for most applications is acceptable. However, there are several circumstances where 99.73% accuracy (certainty) is not acceptable, such as in manufacturing and computing, particularly where safety is an issue. The Six Sigma approach ensures that 99.99966% of the processes or components function as intended. In other words, six standard deviations from the mean. This lowers parts per million (PPM) defects to 3.4, which is a more acceptable number and one that is difficult to outdo.

The objective of the Six Sigma approach is like business process reengineering, which focuses on streamlining processes and ensuring that only value-added activities are conducted. This means that the desired output of these processes is achieved each time in a highly consistent manner by making each process as constant as possible, and thereby reducing the number of defects. The term 'defects' has a special meaning in the Six Sigma method. In the production of physical components or objects, reducing defects becomes obvious due the physical tangibility of the outcome. However, reducing defects in service industries is not a straightforward matter. Six Sigma has redefined the word 'defect' to include any output (not necessarily tangible) that did not achieve what the customer desired. Therefore, when referring to defects, it is not necessarily the case that reference is being made to objects like components.

Under the Six Sigma definition, defects include a defective procedure outcome. The literature shows that there are two fundamental approaches when using Six Sigma: One related to existing processes (DMAIC) and the other for creating new processes (DMADV). Measurement is a key aspect of each Six Sigma approach and is an integral part of the system adopted.

Measurement in the Six Sigma method includes the documentation of the quantifiable facets of the process for supplementary analysis. Moreover, this measurement activity must assess and incorporate all the elements that may bias or prejudice the process outcome, with each element being regarded as a variable in an equation. This procedure ensures that the performance measurement is far more meaningful at a later Six Sigma procedural stage.

The literature suggests that most organisations adopting Six Sigma encounter problems at the performance measurement stage. These problems are more pronounced when applying Six Sigma in a service industry. Often a major obstacle that organisations encounter is identifying a suitable variable that may be used for performance measurement, which is critical for the application of the Six Sigma model. The reason for this is that in the absence of a suitable performance measurement, the issue of how much a process has improved becomes evasive.

There are several broad categories of metrics that may be used for performance measurement, including the improvement in quality; process variability; finances; acceleration of process time; and assessment of productivity. The improvement in quality category fits in seamlessly in the Six Sigma environment, because the original aim of Six Sigma is quality enhancement, and this category is merely the calculation of the number of defects. Since the defects are defined during the initial application stages, the numbers can be easily compared without too much effort. The process variability category does not present a difficulty either, because a key element of the Six Sigma methodology is ensuring constant processes with no or very little deviation, thus attaining the minimum number of defects.

It is an accepted fact that financial quantifiers are fundamental and widely used as a performance measurement metric. Therefore, the finance category is clearly attainable, and an organisation may simply evaluate the cost elements of a process when compared with the process that was in place beforehand. The adage that 'time is money' holds for the Six Sigma environment because time is viewed as a valuable resource. In other words, streamlining processes and conducting only value-added activities have the potential of reducing time significantly in the operations of an organisation, irrespective of whether the organisation is production- or service-oriented. Moreover, time is also a simple quantifiable metric.

The performance metric related to the assessment of productivity category basically evaluates whether an improved process makes use of the available resources more effectively and produces more for less raw material. The above illustrates that the underlying principles of Six Sigma do not present any major difficulties in their implementation. In the sections to follow, the chapter will probe deeper into the topic of Six Sigma.

## Establishing Goal Values for Six Sigma

Some years ago, the common trend was towards customer orientation instead of production orientation. This basically meant that the customer did not have to wait too long in a queue to be served. Waiting in a queue often feels like eternity, particularly if you are accompanied by younger children. This is the type of experience that people dislike and is often encountered at establishments, such as drive-in fast-food businesses. You wait, the queue grows longer. Some endure the wait; others decide to go elsewhere. The outcome is lost sales and the perception of bad quality for the service provider, even though the food served may be of above standard quality. On the other, if the food is served too swiftly, there would be doubt about its freshness. This example illustrates those processes should match the service goals, which in this case was a fast service. In other words, organisations need to establish their service goals according to the service level they wish to provide to maintain the desired quality for the customer.

Goal values are the KPIs that define the service boundaries required to attain the quality required by customers. Additionally, goal values should be decided by the customer. In other words, goal values should reflect the customers' expectations. This is the reason why goal values are highly dependent on what is being measured and the method adopted to measure the service. For example, the response time a user expects from a system may be set at three seconds from the time one hits the enter key on the keyboard. Once the three-second mark passes, the user will start getting anxious and will likely give up entirely after the seven-second mark. Hence, the user has an in-built tolerance, after which the user will simply give up. In our example, the tolerance is likely to be between three to five seconds.

In the fast-food example, a customer may expect an eight-minute service time and will likely be tolerant with a 10-minute service time, but once the 10-minute time limit is exceeded, the customer will get anxious and start to grumble. Hence, the goal value must be established within the expected customer time frame, including the tolerance limit. Obviously, the goal values will depend on the process type and the customers' expectation.

Zomes (2021) refers to target vales, rather than goal values. However, a closer examination of the Zomes concept reveals that both are referring to the same issue. According to Zomes, there are three types of target values; namely, Smaller is Better; Larger is Better; and Nominal is Best. Smaller is Better refers to waiting time, such as waiting in a queue. Hence, when examining Small is Better the process will always have an upper measurement limit, which is close to zero, and the distribution will be depicted as right or positive skewed (refer to Figure 8.1).

For example, late flight departure times from an airport would have a target value of zero. However, airports must allow for some variation and therefore will often schedule connecting flights not to depart in less than 30–60 minutes from the first landing. According to Zomes, the target value for Larger is Better is skewed to the left, creating a negative distribution and in which the target value will always have a lower specification limit (refer to Figure 8.2). Therefore, if a process falls below the target value, customers are likely to feel that they received less than what they expected.

According to Zomes, the final type of target value is Nominal is Best, which often is applied in the manufacturing industry where a process has pre-defined parameters that the organisation must adhere to (refer to Figure 8.3). For example, a producer may make a product where the target content is 40 items with a tolerance of $\pm$ 5 items. Therefore, a customer receiving a packet with 38 items would feel deceved, whereas if the content was 45 items, the producer would be making a loss on that packet. In the Nominal is Best case, both the lower and upper limits are shown, and

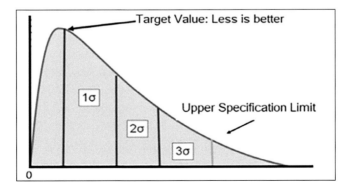

Figure 8.1 Smaller is Better: Depicting the Target Value and Upper Specification Limit

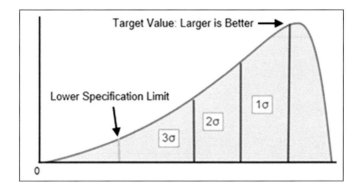

Figure 8.2  Larger is Better: Depicting the Target Value and Lower Specification Limit

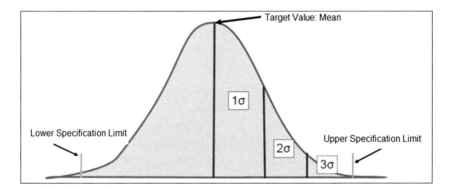

Figure 8.3  Nominal is Best: Depicting the Upper and Lower Specification Limits and Target Values

the distribution would depict a Normal (bell-shaped) distribution with no skewness.

An important issue is when to use the Goal (or Target) Values. As stated previously, the target value is established by the recipient of the service or product (i.e., the customer) and is determined when applying Six Sigma instruments, such as Critical to Quality (CTQ) Trees, Kano Diagrams, or customer surveys. These tools are all focused on determining customer target values. The CTQ Trees can help you to design customer-centric, quality products and services by identifying the needs of the customer and translate that information into measurable product and process requirements. A CTQ tree allows organisations to understand the characteristics of a product or service that most drives quality for customers. Figure 8.4

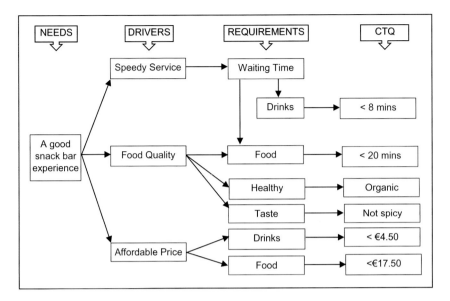

Figure 8.4 Example Critical to Quality (CTQ) Tree

illustrates an example of a CTQ tree, showing the customer needs, service drivers, service requirements, and resultant Critical to Quality measures. Likewise, Figure 8.5, which is an adaptation of the Kano Diagram, is an analysis tool to explore and measure customer needs and identify the fundamental requirements of customers, including performance and anticipation (stimulation) requirements.

When applied for existing processes, the Six Sigma comprises of five phases, namely Define, Measure, Analyse, Improve, and Control (DMAIC). The concept of Target Values is addressed during the Define and Measure phases. Hence, after a profound and exhaustive reflection during the Define phase, the Six Sigma practitioner will be in a good position to reveal the Target Values the customer expects. Once the Target Values are defined by the customer, the Measure phase can commence. This phase has the objective of establishing the Upper and Lower Specification Limits around the mean value of the process; the mean value being the Target Value.

The above may be illustrated through an example. Mark Smith is CEO of Pinnacle, which is a wholly-owned subsidiary of a national construction company that is a national leader in high-quality residential construction. Mark, as CEO, administers the operations of several procuring agents and

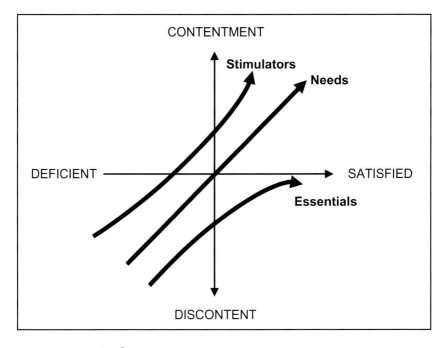

Figure 8.5  Example of a Kano Diagram

desires to improve the existing processes and thus enhance the procurement team's performance by applying the Six Sigma methodology. The Six Sigma approach consists of five phases, starting with the 'Define' phase. In conducting the Define phase, Mark held several meetings and discussions with the construction supervisors to comprehend how the team's operations can be better supported. Several tools were used, including the CTQ tree and questionnaires.

The outcome of these tools showed that the workers often moaned about receiving finishing materials a few days late. Mark applied the gained information to target the lead time for the construction team to receive the required finishing goods. The information received by Mark enabled him to measure the duration of time it took the procurement people to respond to the requests for purchasing the material needed. Mark cautiously measured the duration of time the procuring agents took to respond to the purchase suggestions. He found that it took on average eight days to generate the purchase orders, which was three days more than the target maximum of five days. Mark plotted the data and found that his procuring agents were over the established tolerance. Mark analysed the collected data to demonstrate its statistical significance by testing the null hypothesis that the procuring agents were not performing to their optimum level. Mark discussed the results with the procuring agents and held several brainstorming sessions with them to find a solution whereby the five-day tolerance limit will be adhered to.

After implementing several ideas and monitoring the performance of the procuring agents for an eight-week duration, he found that the procuring agents' performance was on target. To ensure that the performance level of the procuring agents was maintained, Mark implemented control charts to track the procurement function and confirmed that the procurement of finishing materials was within the established tolerance.

This section has provided a general description of the Six Sigma approach, focusing on establishing goal or Target Values. In the sections to follow, the Six Sigma approach will be examined in more detail.

## The Key Principles of Six Sigma

Six Sigma is a quality management methodology that is used for improving organisational operations by mitigating the possibility of error. It consists of a set of management tools and techniques to assist organisations to improve current processes, products, or services by revealing and removing defects. This is achieved by streamlining the quality control process in manufacturing or business processes with the aim of having little or no variance throughout the process. Furthermore, it is a data-driven approach that applies a statistical approach for removing defects or erroneous processes. The statistical basis of Six Sigma is the Normal Distribution (Bell curve), where one Sigma represents one standard deviation from the mean. Hence, if the process has six Sigma(s), three above (+) and three below (-) the mean, the error or defect rate is considered as 'extremely low.'

The above implies that the objective of Six Sigma is to transform the organisation's operational environment to achieve optimal customer satisfaction by delivering near-perfect goods and services. Six Sigma aims to remove the inconsistencies in the achievement of quality by getting rid of the defects that are causing these variations. These aims are achieved by addressing two key issues, namely identifying the concern and solving the concern. In identifying the concern, two further issues are addressed.

These are: Where does a process or function deviate from 'what should be' to 'what is,' and is it important enough to require corrections? Moreover, solving the concern also requires two further actions; these are: Modifying the status of the process or function from 'what is' to 'what should be' and making sure the modification is executed for the achievement of the desired goals.

The previous section has already explained the concept related to Target Values, namely 'smaller is better,' 'larger is better,' or 'nominal is best.' It was explained that:

- 'Smaller is Better' generates an 'upper specification limit,' such as having a target of zero for defects or rejected parts.
- 'Larger is Better' contains a 'lower specification limit,' such as test results, where the target is 100%.
- 'Nominal is Best' takes the middle ground. For instance, a customer care operator must spend sufficient time with a customer to resolve a problem, but not so long that there is a loss in productivity.

The whole process is intended to integrate data and statistics to assist in objectively identifying errors and defects that have an impact on quality. Six Sigma has matured to an extent that it is applicable to a variety of organisational settings that permits them to define objectives around specific industry needs. The Six Sigma concept is based upon five fundamental principles:

- *Customer Orientation*: This reflects the importance that should be given to the customer in every business. Conventionally it means the assurance to provide good products or services. However, with the evolving technology it means a lot more than just products or services. The key objective is bringing maximum benefit to the customer. However, for this to happen, an organisation must understand and know its customers, their needs, and what drives customer loyalty and the demand for services or products. Hence, there is a need to establish a standard of quality that is defined by what the customer or market demands.
- *Measure Value Stream and Reveal Your Problem*: This requires that the organisation maps the steps in each process to ascertain the areas of waste. It is important that the data is collected to uncover the specific area of

concern, which needs to be addressed and transformed. Conduct a root cause analysis, to precisely identify the problem and the approach to resolve it.

- *Remove Non-Value-Added Activities*: Remove activities in the process that do not add value to the customer. The value stream should identify the problem area. However, if it does not, use appropriate tools to reveal anomalies and problem areas, streamlining functions with the aim of achieving quality control and efficiency.
- *Continue Activity or Process*: Adopt a standard process where team members collaborate and contribute their varied expertise for resolving the identified problem. It is important to involve all relevant stakeholders and to provide specialised training to team members in the use of Six Sigma.
- *Adopt a Flexible and Responsive Ecosystem*: The aim of Six Sigma is transformation and change, which is achieved by removing the faulty and inefficient processes through the introduction of better work practices and improved employee approach. A robust culture of flexibility and responsiveness to changes in procedures is required to ensure a streamlined project implementation where processes are designed for rapid and seamless adoption.

The above permit an organisation to implement continuous improvements that allow it to adjust its methods and processes to gain a competitive edge.

## The Six Sigma Methodology

The Six Sigma methodologies consist of two distinct approaches, with each having its own set of procedures that, when implemented, achieve organisational transformation. The first methodology is DMAIC, which is a data-driven approach to enhance existing products or services to achieve better customer satisfaction. DMAIC is an acronym for the five phases of the methodology, namely: D – Define, M – Measure, A – Analyse, I – Improve, C – Control. This approach is applied in the manufacturing of a product or delivery of a service. The second methodology is DMADV, which is used to design or re-design a new set of processes for manufacturing a product or delivering a service. This methodology is part of the Design for Six Sigma (DFSS). DMADV is also an acronym for the five phases of the methodology, namely: D – Define, M – Measure, A – Analyse, D – Design, V – Validate. This methodology is applied when the existing processes fail to meet customers' requirements, even after optimisation, or when it is necessary to develop new methods.

The Six Sigma process of organisational transformation is a relatively straightforward methodology, but it requires a high level of discipline. Additionally, while Six Sigma has two derivatives to reveal deviations and solve problems, the DMAIC approach is the standard methodology used by Six Sigma practitioners. As stated previously, Six Sigma uses a data-driven management process that is applied for optimising and improving business processes. The DMAIC approach has a very strong customer focus and dynamic utilisation of data and statistics. The focus of this section will be on the application of the DMAIC method that consists of the following phases and as illustrated by Figure 8.6:

(a) *Define*: As illustrated by Figure 8.6, the Define phase is the start of the Six Sigma process and is focused on a customer-centric approach that consists of three key steps. The first step is to identify and define in detail the organisational concern from the perspective of the customer. Once this is completed, establish the goals, in terms of what is to be achieved and what resources are required to achieve these goals. The final step in the Define phase is to map the process and to obtain confirmation from the stakeholders to ensure its accuracy.

(b) *Measure*: The focus of the second phase is on the measurement system (metrics) and the tools to be exploited in the measurement process in terms of how the process may be improved and how these improvements may be quantified. This phase also consists of three steps, starting with measuring the identified concern in numerical terms or other supporting data. This step is followed by defining the performance benchmark and establishing the tolerance limits. The final step in the Measure phase is to evaluate the measurement system to be applied by appraising whether the system can assist in achieving the desired outcome.

(c) *Analyse*: The third phase analyses the process to reveal the variables that impact it. There are three steps to the Analyse phase. Firstly, it is important to determine whether the process is efficient and effective, assessing how the process may help achieve what is needed. The second step

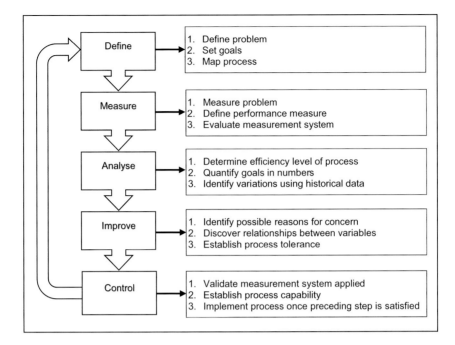

*Figure 8.6* DMAIC Phases and Their Respective Steps

is related to quantifying the agreed goals in numerical terms. The Final step focuses on identifying the variations using historical data.

(d) *Improve:* This phase examines how the change in the process impacts the outcome by identifying how one can improve the process implementation. This phase consists of three steps. Firstly, identify possible reasons for the concern by identifying the relationship between the variables. Secondly, establish the process tolerance. The tolerance must be defined precisely within the acceptable parameters (i.e., the quality of any given service). Finally, define the operating conditions that may influence the outcome.

(e) *Control:* Control is the final phase. In the Control phase it is important that the performance objective identified in the previous phase is implemented successfully and that the designed improvements are practical and sustainable. This phase also consists of three steps, starting with the validation of the measurement system to be applied, followed by the establishment of the process capability by ensuring that the goals are met. Finally, once the goals are satisfied the process is implemented.

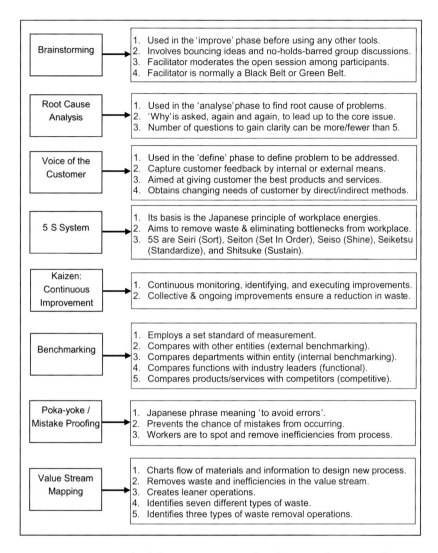

*Figure 8.7* Six Sigma Methodology: Key Statistical and Data Evaluation Tools

Figure 8.7 illustrates that the Six Sigma methodology utilises an assortment of statistical and data evaluation methods in combination with the Six Sigma methodology, some of which have been addressed separately in previous chapters. All the itemised tools have a common theme, namely, to identify those concerns that are causing inefficiencies and eliminating them. Therefore, on an organisational basis, management would have a continuous improvement process in place.

The Six Sigma methodology is not a straightforward process and requires an escalating training programme that conforms to specified training requirements, education criteria, job standards, and eligibility, starting at the White Belt level and progressing to the Master Black Belt status. The White Belt is the basic level, where a newcomer may join a team that focuses on problem-solving projects. The team participant at the White Belt level must understand the basic Six Sigma concepts. The next level of proficiency is the Yellow Belt. The participant at this level contributes as a project team member and specifically reviews process improvements, thus gaining a good understanding of the various methodologies and DMAIC.

After attaining the Yellow Belt, a participant can work towards the Green Belt level. To gain the Green Belt, an individual must work a minimum of three years of full-time employment; understand the tools and methodologies utilised for problem-solving; have hands-on experience working in projects that require some level of business transformation; lead Green Belt teams or projects; and provide support for Black Belt projects regarding data collection and analysis. The next level is the Black Belt. A Black Belt practitioner must have a minimum of three years of full-time employment; have gained work experience in a core knowledge area; have proof of contributing to a minimum of two Six Sigma projects; demonstrate expertise at applying multivariate metrics to various organisational change scenarios; have proof of leading varied teams in problem-solving projects; and have participated in training and coaching project teams.

The top level of Six Sigma competency is the Master Black Belt level. To gain a Master Black Belt, the participant must be in possession of Black Belt certification; have a minimum of five years of full-time employment, or proof of completing a minimum of ten Six Sigma projects; hold a proven work portfolio, with individual specific requirements, such as having coached and trained Green Belts and Black Belts; developed key metrics and strategies; and worked as an organisation's Six Sigma technologist and internal business transformation advisor. For example, a DMADV project is executed by Six Sigma Green Belts and Six Sigma Black Belts and under the supervision of Six Sigma Master Black Belts.

The Six Sigma belt system of competencies is essential to sustain an exceptional level of implementation success of the Six Sigma quality excellence. However, a key component of successful Six Sigma implementation is the buy-in and support from the organisation executives. It has also been observed that the Six Sigma methodology does not work very well when the organisation experiences pockets of resistance to the implementation process. Training of employees at all levels of the organisation is an essential factor. It is important that the organisation has a Six Sigma certification process that allows enough employees to be certified at the various Belt levels. White Belts and Yellow Belts usually gain an introduction to process improvement theories and Six Sigma terminology, while the Green Belts normally support the Black Belts on projects, assisting with data collection and analysis.

The Black Belts act as the project leaders, while Master Black Belts examine various approaches to apply Six Sigma across an organisation. Thus, Six Sigma transforms the organisation's employees into quality improvement experts and provides them with a toolbox that is loaded with principles and instruments to resolve quality problems by mitigating defects. Hence, a lower defect rate facilitates organisations to produce more and better goods or services at a lower cost, resulting in overall profitability growth.

## Six Sigma Case Studies

There are numerous documented case studies related to the Six Sigma methodology. This section will describe several case studies that apply the Six Sigma approach for streamlining the activities of the applicable organisation.

### *Six Sigma Methodology: Reducing Inventory Levels*

Inventory in organisations can result in tying up a substantial amount of working capital. Hence, having an optimum level of inventory is likely to release much needed working capital to be used elsewhere. This case study is related to reducing inventory levels in the mining industry, without increasing the risk of lowering the production service levels. This case study examines a medium size company that trades in the mining industry by selling drilling fluids and compounds to land mining exploration companies. The supply chain channel for this company is shown in Figure 8.8.

Figure 8.8 indicates that the items sold to the customer are on consignment, with the inventory being owned by the supplier until it is used and consumed by the customer. Mining operations are usually located in

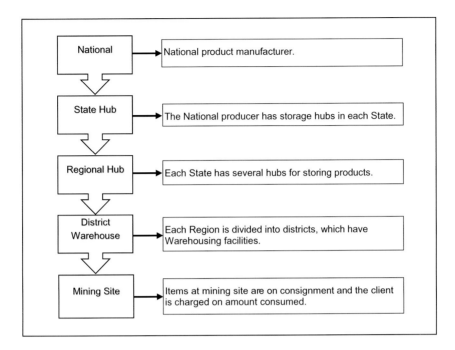

*Figure 8.8* Case Study: Supply Chain Channel

remote areas, and therefore if the mining site runs out of drilling fluids and other compounds, it may cost the drilling company thousands of dollars per hour. Hence, to avoid running out of stock, the drilling fluids company stocked higher levels of compounds than what was actually required, to ensure supply. One should note that these products were high-value and bulky items that required large warehouses to host them. The inventory records indicated that on average, the product stock movement is about 12 months before being consumed by the mining operations.

A brainstorming session was conducted that involved all the stakeholders in the supply chain as well as the employees at the mining site. The aim was to have continuous monitoring, identifying, and executing improvements with the final goal being to implement collective and ongoing improvements to ensure a reduction in waste. Value stream mapping was conducted for the complete procurement process taking into consideration everyone's input. This mapping process had the objective of charting the flow of materials and information to design new process; removing waste and inefficiencies in the value stream; creating leaner operations;

identifying the different types of waste; and identifying the types of waste removal operations. The value stream mapping indicated all the process steps, lead times, and issues, amongst other things that can take place from the time the need for a product arises until the time the product is actually consumed by the mining operation.

A comprehensive statistical analysis of inventory levels contrasted with the variable lead time demand was conducted. Each storage point was analysed separately, which revealed that they were all holding slightly more stock than was required for a 99% service level. However, when the whole supply chain was analysed holistically, it was found that the total stock which was being held was multiple the quantities of what it needed to be for the same service level. The analysis showed that there was too much buffer stock being held at too many points (locations), leading to enormous overstocking.

The mapping data provided information for new procurement plans to be generated for each item. This revealed that the majority of the items were under the periodic order and order-up-to inventory models, contingent on the specific attributes of the product and its particular supply chain. This exercise promoted smaller and more frequent orders, keeping in view the economic order quantities. Furthermore, a proactive inventory optimisation model was implemented for project managers to provide an early warning system regarding when to purchase product, with the aim of keeping a 99% service level. The future value stream mapping process was monitored to confirm the initial results achieved. It was found that within a four-month period the company's inventory status improved by over 190%. Continuous monitoring is indicating a continuous slower upwards trend, resulting in millions of dollars in cash savings and working capital reduction.

### Six Sigma Methodology: Reducing Call Centre Responses

The public and private sectors both apply call centres as a major source of customer care. This case study examines how a call centre was able to significantly reduce the average handling time of inbound calls. The call centre in this Six Sigma case study handles thousands of calls per day related to government services. This call centre is a private company but was awarded a tender by the government to handle customer care enquires regarding various government services.

Over the past three years, this call centre has grown at a huge rate as more government services are integrated within this customer care system.

Hence, the only way to keep up with the increase in service requirements has been to engage more call agents and increase the number of workstations. However, this required further investment and extensive training that cost a substantial amount of funding. To remain competitive and retain its contract with government, the call centre had to find a way to increase its capacity without additional cost and capital.

A project team was established to examine ways of reducing one of the main metrics at the call centre, namely the average handling time (AHT). However, it was noted that the AHT was not the only output. The project team had to ensure that mitigating the AHT did not have a negative effect on any other company output, such as customer satisfaction. Since the AHT metric was measured automatically by the system from the start to end of every call, the project team members were very confident of the measurement system and could move straight to the analyse phase. An analysis of variance (ANOVA) was conducted to test significance of many possible input variables. The project team found that the 'call type' was the essential input that had the most impact on the amount of time a call took.

The project team generated value stream maps for the top four call types with the longest total call times. This mapping process had the objective of charting the flow of the call information to design new process; removing waste and inefficiencies in the value stream; creating leaner operations; identifying the different types of waste; and identifying the types of waste removal operations. The project team found that many of the process steps had substantial waste, where they did not add any value to that particular call type. Hence, a streamlining process was conducted where non-value-added steps were taken out of the process and the future state map was generated. The project team verified that taking out the non-value-added steps did not have an adverse impact on any other metrics. Once this was confirmed, the project team implemented the future value stream map. The result of the Six Sigma approach was a reduction in the average handling time by 20%, resulting in an increase in capacity of the call centre by 20%, which resulted in millions of dollars being saved each year.

## Conclusion

This chapter elaborated on the theme of performance management using the Six Sigma methodology and has demonstrated how one may improve the effectiveness of an organisation both in the private and public sectors.

Six Sigma is a quality control mechanism that is applied to various business verticals that are structured in a highly hierarchical manner where more emphasis is placed on clearly established authority. The advantage of Six Sigma is that it focuses primarily on streamlining processes, to ensure that the desired output of those processes is achieved consistently every time. It is very similar to business process reengineering, which not only focuses on streamlining processes but ensures that only value-added activities are conducted. This means that the desired output of these processes is achieved each time in a highly consistent manner by making each process as constant as possible, and thereby reducing the number of defects. However, in Six Sigma, the term defects has a specific meaning; in manufacturing defects are related to components, but defects in service industries include any output (not necessarily tangible) that did not achieve what the customer desired. Thus, under the Six Sigma definition, defects include a defective procedure outcome.

This chapter has shown that there are two fundamental approaches when using Six Sigma, one related to existing processes (DMAIC) and the other for creating new processes (DMADV). Measurement is a key aspect of each Six Sigma approach and is an integral part of the system adopted. In the Six Sigma environment, measurement includes the documentation of the quantifiable facets of the process for supplementary analysis. Hence, the measurement activity must assess and incorporate all the elements that may bias or prejudice the process outcome, with each element being regarded as a variable in an equation. This ensures that the performance measurement is far more meaningful at a later Six Sigma procedural stage. The performance measurement stage appears to be problematic for many organisations using the Six Sigma approach, particularly in the service industry.

A major obstacle regarding this issue is the identification of a suitable variable that may be used for performance measurement, which is critical for the application of the Six Sigma model. The reason for this is that in the absence of a suitable performance measurement, the issue of how much a process has improved becomes evasive. However, there are several broad categories of metrics that may be used for performance measurement, including the improvement in quality; process variability; finances; acceleration of process time; and assessment of productivity.

The improvement in quality category fits in seamlessly in the Six Sigma environment, because the original aim of Six Sigma is quality enhancement, and this category is merely the calculation of the number of defects. Since the defects are defined during the initial application stages, the numbers can be easily compared without too much effort. The process variability category does not present a difficulty either because a key element of the Six Sigma methodology is ensuring constant processes with no or very little deviation, thus attaining the minimum number of defects. It is an accepted fact that financial quantifiers are fundamental and widely used as a performance measurement metric. Therefore, the finance category is clearly attainable, and an organisation may simply evaluate the cost elements of a process when compared with the process that was in place beforehand.

The adage that 'time is money' holds for the Six Sigma environment because time is viewed as a valuable resource. In other words, streamlining processes and conducting only value-added activities have the potential of reducing time significantly in the operations of an organisation, irrespective of whether the organisation is production- or service-oriented. Moreover, time is also a simple quantifiable metric. The performance metric related to the assessment of productivity category basically evaluates whether an improved process makes use of the available resources more effectively and produces more for less raw material. The above illustrates that the underlying principles of Six Sigma do not present any major difficulties in their implementation, but the Six Sigma approach requires a level of discipline in the way organisational activities are conducted.

## References

Heavey, C. and Murphy, E. (2012). 'Integrating the Balanced Scorecard with Six Sigma.' *The TQM Journal*, 24(2), pp. 108–122.

Kano, N., Seraku, N., Takahashi, F., Tsuji, S. (1984). 'Attractive Quality and Must-be Quality.' *Journal of the Japanese Society for Quality Control*, 14(2), pp. 147–156.

Six Sigma Daily. (2020). *What is Six Sigma?* Available at: https://www.sixsigmadaily.com/what-is-six-sigma/ (Accessed 22 November 2023).

White, K.S. (2018). What is Six Sigma? *Streamlining for Quality. CIO.com.* Available at: https://www.cio.com/article/227977/six-sigma-quality-management-methodology.html (Accessed 22 November 2023).

Zomes, T. (2021). Target Values. *6σSTUDY GUIDE.COM. Target Values – What You Need to Know to Pass a Six Sigma Certification.* Available at: http://sixsigmastudyguide.com (Accessed 22 November 2023).

# 9

## BUSINESS EXCELLENCE MODELS, ENTERPRISE RISK MANAGEMENT, AND PROGRAMME MANAGEMENT AS A BASIS FOR PERFORMANCE IMPROVEMENT

'Performance management starts from the top by tailoring strategies which can be translated into meaningful targets, and trickles down to managers for setting goals & making this process effective by helping them understand the big picture and owning up careers of their team members.'

Colin Mendes
Head HR, Voltas Beko

This is the final chapter regarding the theme of performance measurement and management using well-tested tools that may be applied in conjunction with KPIs as performance measures. It should be stated once more that there is no magic wand for improving an organisation's performance. No one singular tool will lead an organisation to excel. It will take several such tools in combination with commitment and determination to achieve the desired level of performance improvement. The performance-inducing tools that are available to management are numerous and the circumstances in which such tools may be applied are also plentiful. Therefore, it is important to match the performance tool being applied with the circumstances

DOI: 10.4324/9781032685465-11

being encountered by the organisation. Furthermore, certain performance improvement tools are applicable to specific organisational functional areas. For instance, the tools used to improve and measure performance in a Human Resources department are different from those used in a Finance department, in a Production department, or in a Marketing department.

This chapter will discuss three important tools, namely, the use of the Business Excellence Models, Enterprise Risk Management, and Programme Management as the basis for performance improvement. The original Business Excellence Model was developed by the European Foundation for Quality Management (EFQM). According to EFQM, the model's objective is to support the management of Western European organisations in accelerating the process of making quality a decisive influence for achieving global competitive advantage.

The Business Excellence Model is based upon a self-assessment approach that allows management to compare the organisation with the Model. The foundation of the Model is reasonable logical thinking, where results are achieved through acting on enablers. The results are measured through financial measures, customer satisfaction, people satisfaction, and the impact on society, whereas the enablers are leadership, policy and strategy, people management, and resources and process management. The Business Excellence Model is based upon the view that by improving the 'how' this would improve the results in terms of the 'what.'

The Enterprise Risk Management (ERM) framework complements the Business Excellence Model. The ERM framework permits management to optimise its strategy and performance by increasing awareness of the opportunities to build organisational value. This framework is based on the principle that organisations which embrace change can manage the unpredictable unknowns with enhanced awareness of the overall business risks. The ERM framework is able to integrate with the organisation's strategy and performance system and add value to the organisation and the overall risk program objectives. One needs to appreciate that metrics improve the understanding of the organisation and stimulates productive discussions between senior leadership and relevant stakeholders, thus generating better overall outcomes.

Another important tool to improve organisational performance is programme management. Programme management is the holistic management of several interrelated projects that make up a portfolio of these connected projects (i.e., the programme). Often programme management includes the integration of organisational change within the business areas affected by a specific project, to ensure the successful implementation of the project and its consequential change. Programme management also encompasses a systematic project management approach for planning and implementing the various activities.

It is important that any undertaking is aligned with the organisation's strategy, otherwise management would be misusing resources. Programme management provides the necessary layer of governance above the specific projects and ensures that the portfolio of projects is executed effectively. This chapter will examine the above three tools in detail to illustrate how their specific features may be applied in a practical manner to enhance the performance of the organisation.

## Introduction

The fundamental basis for performance improvement is the improvement of a business process, function, or procedure with the objective of improving overall outcomes at an organisational level. In other words, performance improvement focuses on business processes to ensure that only processes that add value are being conducted. Performance improvement is an integral component of performance management, where management explores various means to improve the process itself. Moreover, performance improvement can take place at any level within an organisation and in any division or department.

One must also be mindful that performance improvement is different from a performance improvement plan. The latter signifies a plan to assist a specific employee to improve their job performance. Hence, there is a need to address the performance improvement plan as a distinct function that identifies the underlying issues, sets clear objectives, involves relevant employees, establishes a focused training programme with adequate organisational support, and has a mechanism for regularly reviewing progress.

Performance improvement is not difficult to achieve if it is tackled in a rational and disciplined manner. Firstly, a plan must be created that specifically shows the current state and the expected state of the function being addressed. Secondly, there is a need to establish the key performance indicators (KPIs) that are measurable, relevant, and achievable for that function.

Thirdly, seek and implement solutions that will advance the process closer to a specific end-goal. Finally, implement an improvement strategy with the aim of achieving the envisaged benefits, such as improved productivity, increased efficiency, and decreased process costs.

These steps help to make the organisation much leaner, more efficient, more cost-conscious, and achieve a realisable growth in profit. Hence, performance improvement is viewed as a method for analysing performance concerns and establishing systems to ensure better performance. Research shows that performance improvement is most effectively applied in organisational environments where employees are organised in teams within the same organisation, or where employees are performing analogous jobs.

There are several approaches for improving the performance of organisations, teams and individuals, such as industrial engineering, quality assurance, training, and human resources development. These all focus on performance gaps in their own specific way. However, performance improvement is different from these approaches, since it applies a systematic procedure to reveal the root causes of a performance concern and then implements a solution that targets a specific performance shortfall. Quality control is the most common type of performance improvement that can be implemented because of a formal process or through a real-time system that continuously seeks ways of increasing efficiency and output. In the sections that follow, we shall discuss in detail three important performance improvement tools, namely, the Business Excellence Models, Enterprise Risk Management, and Programme Management.

## Development of Business Excellence Models

Business Excellence Models are a recent development dating back to the mid-80s. They came about with the upsurge of the quality movement in the Western World, as a reaction to Japan's innovations in quality and its vigorous competitive efforts. Business Excellence Models have evolved from the Total Quality Management (TQM) models, and in fact have replaced them. Quality is viewed as a national target leading to national competitiveness. This is why excellence models are seen as a key mechanism in many developed countries for improving performance in organisations and as a way of enhancing national competitiveness as a reaction to globalisation.

The evolution of quality management emerged from the concept of the value chain, more specifically value-added activities. A value added activity is any action taken that increases the benefit of a good or service to a customer. Hence, a business entity can greatly decrease its cost and increase its profitability by identifying those activities that increase value and which do not and stripping away the non-value-added activities. For example, inspection activities do not add value. Thus, the evolution of quality management commenced with the introduction of the principles of Inspection, Quality Control, and Quality Management, which later expanded further by a greater impetus in terms of the Total Quality Management (TQM) movement.

The TQM movement was a result of the work conducted by contemporary quality gurus such as Deming, Juran, Crosby, and other quality experts, such as Japan's Toyota Production Model (TPS). Edwards Deming, Joseph Juran, and Philip B. Crosby designed and promoted statistical quality control and structured approaches to the improvement of quality by introducing zero-defects programs. They demonstrated that there was more than one approach to improving quality. However, the greatest influence for the shift from TQM to Business Excellence was the national emphasis for promoting greater competitiveness as a general national policy to take advantage of the opportunities that globalisation has to offer in terms of cross-border trade in goods and services, technology, and flows of investment, people, and information.

### *Business Excellence Model*

The Business Excellence Model has become critical for many organisations because the British and European Governments are committed to encouraging organisations within their respective jurisdictions to apply it for improving organisational performance. The Model has its origins in the private sector but is also applicable for public and voluntary sector organisations. Therefore, irrespective of the industry sector and the size, structure, or maturity of organisations, it is essential to institute a suitable management system to ensure a successful venture. This is precisely the aim of the Excellence Model. The term 'excellence' is used because the Excellence Model focuses on what an organisation does, or could do, to provide an excellent service or product to its customers, service users, or stakeholders.

It is a practical tool to assist organisations to be successful by assessing and measuring where organisations are on its path to Excellence; aiding these organisations to understand the gaps; and then inspiring them to find appropriate solutions. The Business Excellence Model was formulated by the British Quality Foundation (BQF), with the support of the European Foundation for Quality Management (EFQM). These institutions are committed to researching and upgrading the Model with the contributions of tested good practices from thousands of organisations, both within and outside of Europe, to make sure that the Model remains dynamic and in line with modern management thinking.

The Business Excellence Model is non-prescriptive and therefore it can be used with a degree of flexibility, since it does not involve following a set of precise rules or standards but provides a broad and coherent set of assumptions about what is required for a good organisation and its management. Moreover, each organisation can adapt it to fit its own needs for managing and developing improvement, under the control of the internal organisational users, rather than an external assessor.

Figure 9.1, applying the EFQM Model, illustrates that the model is an all-embracing framework based on various criteria. The first group of these criteria refer to the enablers and remaining criteria refer to results (or outcomes). The enablers address what an organisation does (its activities) and consist of individuals, strategy and planning, and alliances and resources. The results criteria address what an organisation achieves. The rationale is that the results or outcomes are caused by the enablers. The objective of the model is to 'support the management of Western European organisations in accelerating the process of making quality a decisive influence for achieving global competitive advantage' (EFQM, 2021). The Model recognises that there are many ways of achieving sustainable excellence in all the facets of performance and is based on the proposition that excellent results regarding performance, clients, individuals, and the general public (society) are realised through leadership by driving the strategy and business plan; that is delivered through individuals, alliances and resources, and organisational processes. The arrows in Figure 9.1 highlight the dynamic characteristics of the model, which imply an innovative and learning organisation as facilitating the improvement of the enablers, in turn leading to improved outcomes.

Figure 9.1 represents a high-level explanation of the model. However, each criterion is supported by several sub-criteria. These sub-criteria present

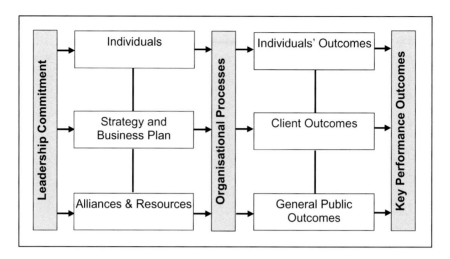

*Figure 9.1* Example of the EFQM: Business Excellence Model

several questions that need to be considered when making an assessment. Moreover, each sub-criterion provides a list of possible areas to address. These areas are not mandatory nor are they exhaustive. However, they are intended to further illustrate the meaning of the specific sub-criterion. The enablers consist of leadership; strategy and business planning; individuals; alliances and resources; and organisational processes. The outcomes are categorised under four headings, namely: Client outcomes; individual outcomes; general public outcomes (Society); and Key Performance Results. The EFQM framework recognises that there are many approaches to achieving sustainable excellence. Additionally, within this non-prescriptive framework there are several fundamental concepts that support the EFQM Model. These fundamental concepts are itemised in Table 9.1. Note that the order in which the concepts are presented has no significance and the list presented is not exhaustive, since the concepts will change as organisations develop and improve on their course towards excellence. Furthermore, at the centre of the self-assessment method is the rationale of the process, known as RADAR, that has the following components: Results, Approach, Deployment, Assessment, and Review.

The fundamental idea behind the Model is that management conducts a Self-Assessment of the organisation by comparing the organisation to the Model. Thus, the Model is the benchmark that management uses to compare their organisation with. Hence, the Model presents a conceivable

*Table 9.1* EFQM Framework: Fundamental Concepts

| *Results Orientation* | *Management by Processes and Facts* | *Partnership Development* |
|---|---|---|
| Excellence is achieving results that delight all organisations' stakeholders. | Excellence is managing the organisation through a set of interdependent and interrelated systems, processes, and facts. | Excellence is developing and maintaining value-adding partnerships. |
| Customer Focus | People Development and Involvement. | Corporate Social Responsibility. |
| Excellence is creating sustainable customer value. | Excellence is maximising the contribution of employees through their development and involvement. | Excellence is exceeding the minimum regulatory framework in which the organisation operates and to strive to understand and respond to the expectations of their stakeholders in society. |
| Leadership and Constancy of Purpose | Continuous Learning, Innovation, and Improvement. | |
| Excellence is visionary and inspirational leadership, coupled with constancy of purpose. | Excellence is challenging the status quo and effecting change by using learning to create innovation and improvement opportunities. | |

logic, where Results (i.e., financial, customer satisfaction, people satisfaction, and impact on society) are achieved through the Enablers (i.e., leadership, policy and strategy, people management, resources, and process management). Exponents of the model argue that by improving the 'how,' this will improve the results (i.e., the 'what'). The central issue that needs to be addressed is how well does a Self-Assessment outcome describe the relationships between results and enablers? In other words, are managers able to act with assurance that their actions will lead to improvement? The outcome from the model is not instantaneous.

Management needs to carry out regular reviews and take stock of what the organisation is getting out of the effort that the model requires. It may take several cycles and constant refinements before the desired results from the model are achieved. Priority should be given to defining the processes and focusing on ensuring that only value-added activities are processed. Hence, conducting a business process engineering (BPR) exercise with the objective of streamlining the process cycle is essential. Therefore, it is advisable to start with BPR exercise (i.e., knowing the 'what and why' of the current performance) and once the new processes are in place and working, conduct the comparison of these processes with the model. The logic of RADAR states that an organisation should firstly determine the Results it is aiming for. However, this requires management to implement an integrated set of sound Approaches to deliver the required results. Furthermore, it is important that management Deploy the approaches systematically, and Assess and Review the effectiveness of the approaches.

### Emergence of Other Business Excellence Models

Generally, Business Excellence or Performance Excellence refer to 'excellence' in three specific aspects, namely, strategies; business practices; and stakeholder-related performance results that have been validated by assessments and use proven business excellence models, which achieve sustainable world-class performance. Therefore, Business Excellence models provide guidance to organisations for achieving sustainable world-class business results and are based on sound business principles that have been proven in practice.

The core concepts, which are the business principles, are very similar for most Business Excellence models and are designed to steer the organisation to help it improve its performance. Worldwide there are some eighty recognised Business Excellence frameworks. Most Business Excellence models have been developed by national bodies to improve national economic performance and as a basis for award programmes. These award programmes have the following objectives:

- Communication, publication, and sharing of best practices.
- Fostering of continuous management, organisational quality, and process improvement.

- Promotion of an awareness of quality management.
- Promotion, support, strengthening, and enhancement of competitiveness.
- Recognition of performance excellence, best practices, and benchmarks.
- Understanding the requirements for performance excellence.

The award programmes and the methodology applied for business excellence models generate several benefits for the organisation. These benefits include the following: (i) Providing a basis for developing organisational performance; (ii) Proposing a robust structure for developing and improving different performance functional areas; (iii) Assisting management to attain organisational goals; (iv) Revealing interdependencies and relationships between various organisational components as a holistic approach to analysis that focuses on the way a system's constituent parts interrelate and how systems work over time and within the context of larger systems; and (v) Providing a performance benchmarking schedule that regularly reviews and assesses the business against the key aspects of the model.

Often organisations use the self-assessment Business Excellence Model to ascertain their strengths and reveal opportunities to improve. Once the self-assessment is completed, management would define and implement the improvement action plans. The Business Excellence Model is also utilised for implementing an organisation's 'improvement culture' by: (i) generally focusing on encouraging the use of best practice in various functional areas where the effect will be of most benefit to performance; and (ii) by adopting the model's core principles as a way of doing business and entrenching these principles as part of the organisation's culture. Table 9.2 provides details of the internationally popular models that are used in various countries. As stated previously, all the models tend to be based on the same core principles. However, they may differ in the way that they are implemented.

### Varying Approach to Implementing Business Excellence Models

Seddon (2022), who is renowned for his critical view of ISO 9000, does not overtly criticise the Business Excellence Models. However, he contends that the Business Excellence Models have two basic concerns, namely Content and Method. Seddon argues that he does not fault Business Excellence

*Table 9.2*  International Business Excellence Models

| Country | Partnership Development |
|---|---|
| USA | Baldrige Criteria for Performance Excellence (BCPE) |
| European Union | European Foundation of Quality Management's EFQM Excellence Model |
| Japan | Deming Prize and The Japan Quality Award |
| India | Indian Industry Confederation award, Bank Award for Business Excellence |
| South America | Iberoamerican Excellence Model for Management (IEM) |
| Singapore | Singapore Quality Award Criteria (SQAC) |
| Australia | Australian Business Excellence Framework (ABEF) Baldrige Criteria for Performance Excellence (BCPE [NZ]) Singapore Quality Award Criteria (SQAC) |
| New Zealand | New Zealand Business Excellence Foundation (NZBEF) New Zealand Organisation for Quality (NZOQ) Centre for Organisational Excellence Research (COER, Massey University) Business Performance Improvement Resource (BPIR.com) |

Models in the same way as ISO 9000 because, unlike ISO 9000, the Business Excellence Models have no theory and are very flexible in the way they may be implemented. However, he argues that it is important to get it right first time by having the correct implementation process in place.

Consequently, Seddon developed the Vanguard Method in the late 1980s, which is viewed as a combination of systems thinking and intervention theory. The uniqueness of the method is its key objective to transform organisations by changing management thinking, to assist executive management to design more effective services with extraordinary consequences for performance leading to swift, tangible, and sustainable results. The most important feature of the Vanguard Method is the eradication of 'failure demand.'

The Vanguard Method has been applied worldwide in eleven countries, generating significant results in a broad range of service organisations, from telecommunications, utilities, and financial services to health and care, council services, emergency services, and public housing providers.

The success of the method has been achieved in both the private and public sectors. In the private sector, the Vanguard Method directs users to redesigned customer-shaped services to provide a better approach for attracting, acquiring, growing, and retaining customers. This has transformed customer satisfaction ratings and staff morale with a resulting growth in profits.

On the other hand, when used in public sector and non-profit organisations (which are 'people-centric systems'), the Vanguard Method provides an opportunity to significantly reduce costs and to improve people's lives by helping public leaders to design public services that work. Seddon contends that not only does the Vanguard Method eradicate the strangling effect of high failure demand, but that fewer people experience problems. Hence, the general outcomes of providing services that work is that demand falls. The Vanguard Method applies certain principles from the Toyota Production System and the work of Deming, which have been transposed to be used within service industries. The Vanguard Method has recently worked with the Central Otago District Council in New Zealand, and in the UK it has been applied to several social housing groups. The latter assignment was reviewed by the UK Office of the Deputy Prime Minister Review (Systematic Approach to Service Improvement – 2005), which concluded: 'The pilots indicated that systems thinking has the potential to deliver wholesale efficiencies in service delivery...'

As mentioned previously, Seddon contends that the Business Excellence Models have two basic concerns, namely Method and Content. Seddon argues that the self-assessment approach, by comparing the current operational status of the organisation with the Model, is an unreliable method for initiating change, since it does not lead to a good understanding of what is going on in an organisation. Hence, he contends that this leads managers to decisions and actions that have little or no basis in knowledge, with the consequence that often plausible but fruitless actions for improvement are conducted. He maintains that the Vanguard Guide to Business Excellence encourages managers to start the process of Self-Assessment in a different place, by first having a thorough understanding of the 'what and why' of current performance, to comprehend their current organisation as a system (including its weaknesses). In other words, the organisation must be prepared for the change in every aspect of its operations, including the behavioural features, such as motivation and organisational commitment, amongst others. Seddon contends that taking a systems view of the organisation provides a wholly different picture, with the starting point being to look outside-in. This prompted the development of the Vanguard approach to self-assessment.

Figure 9.2, which applies Seddon's approach, provides an outline of the Vanguard method to self-assessment by conducting an organisational review and understanding the organisation as an operational system. Figure 9.2 illustrates that the Vanguard method has two parallel action branches: One that is associated with change, and the other associated with the Model to establish a culture of continuous improvement. A systems perspective of the organisation will guide managers to redesign the work effort. Hence, the first step is to establish what work had to be carried out to resolve each concern. A Root Cause Analysis may be required to investigate every aspect that is causing a problem. This approach allows managers to understand the work of the organisation as a system, something that could not have been achieved from the usual method of Self-Assessment. Hence, managers can act on the system, producing improvements in work efficiency and simultaneously addressing other behavioural concerns.

The second concern identified by Seddon was content. Seddon views quality as a better way to conduct work. He argues that quality educates

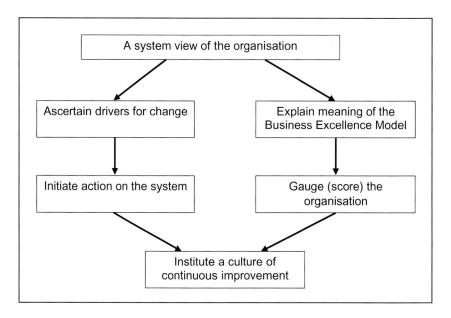

Figure 9.2  Vanguard Method to Self-Assessment: Performance Improvement

*Table 9.3* Comparison between Traditional Thinking and Systems Thinking

| Traditional Thinking | Features | Quality Thinking |
|---|---|---|
| Top-down chain of command | **Standpoint** | Value co-creation with customers |
| Functional specialism & processes | **Outline of work method** | Exigency, significance, and flow |
| Contractual | **Customer Mindset** | What matters? |
| Separated from work | **Come to a decision** | Incorporated with work |
| Output, targets, activity, standards: Related to budget | **Quantify** | Ability, change: Related to goal |
| Contractual | **Supplier Mindset** | Collaborative |
| Control budgets, manage people | **Management values** | Learn through action on system |

managers to work in a different and better way, as illustrated by Table 9.3. Table 9.3 provides a comparison between traditional thinking and systems thinking. Seddon argues that rather than thinking top-down, managers should think outside-in, with the work design being less concerned with functional issues and more concerned with the nature of demand and flow. Thus, Seddon maintains that to work this way requires different and better measures regarding capability and variation, which are distinct and different from the traditional mass-production thinking, which is diametrically opposed to and cannot co-exist with these measures.

The concern with the Business Excellence Model is that it is interspersed with 'mass production' (traditional) ideas and thinking. Hence, he recommends that when implementing the Business Excellence Model, there should be an explicit distinction between traditional thinking and systems thinking. Seddon argues that the Business Excellence Model urges the use of targets and standards; however, it is more important to know what is predictably to be achieved rather than to set arbitrary targets and standards. He contends that managers must understand the pitfalls of arbitrary targets and standards and need to develop more useful measures (of capability and variation). It is also important that management should not be viewed as a 'review' function but should be composed of hands-on leaders, since this is likely to achieve better outcomes in terms of staff morale and performance improvement. Furthermore, people management and work design should be seen as two distinct functions to mitigate dissent in the workplace.

Moreover, Seddon suggests that organisations which are not involved in manufacturing can achieve swift change by merely changing the work methods in accordance with quality thinking. He argues that managers need practical contrasts between what they do today and what they might do instead if they are to change the way they think and work. The Vanguard Guide compares the traditional interpretations of the Business Excellence Model with a quality thinking approach to the interpretations of the Business Excellence Model. Hence, the concern is not the Business Excellence Model itself but the approach and attitude in the way Business Excellence Model is interpreted and implemented. Hence, Seddon argues that managers can thus make their own choices for interpretation and can test the value of their assumptions in terms of impact on performance, which is the fundamental reason why any manager ought to be interested in quality. He contends that if managers do not get value from their experience with the Business Excellence Model, it will pass into history as just another fad. It is also important to understand that the Business Excellence Model may be used in conjunction with other tools that were discussed in previous chapters, such as Root Cause Analysis, Six Sigma, and Lean Six Sigma.

## Other Business Excellence Models Framework

The models and tools are not mutually exclusive, and they complement each other. In fact, many organisations make use of one or more of the models. However, it is critical to appreciate what each model is best used for and how the models support the organisation to improve. Figure 9.3 illustrates the Baldrige Excellence Framework (2021) for Performance Excellence, which is very similar in many aspects to the EFQM Business Excellence Model Framework. Figure 9.3 illustrates the key functional elements of the criteria for performance excellence and exhibits the significantly imperative alignment between the categories.

The factors from 1 to 6 are viewed as the enablers (predictor variables) and factor 7 the business results (response variables). It is noted that empirical studies have validated the relationships between the 'enablers'

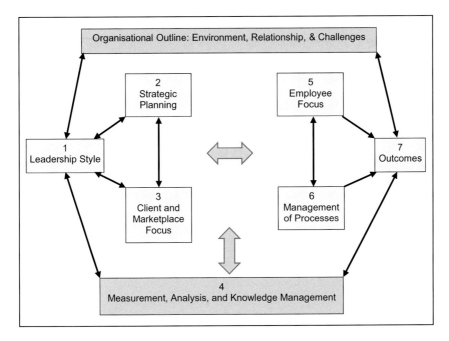

*Figure 9.3*  Example of the Baldrige Criteria for Performance Excellence

and 'business results' in the Business Excellence models. It is essential that one understands the alignments between the business functions to enable a holistic approach to business improvement. The Baldrige Business Excellence model consists of eleven interrelated Core Values and Concepts as follows:

- Visionary leadership.
- Customer-driven excellence.
- Organisational and personal learning.
- Valuing workforce members and partners.
- Agility.
- Focus on the future.
- Managing for innovation.
- Management by fact.
- Social responsibility.
- Focus on results and creating value.
- Systems perspective.

These values and concepts are embedded in systematic processes (criteria) generating the performance results (factor 7) and ideally should be viewed as entrenched beliefs and behaviours that are found in high-performing organisations. Additionally, they are considered as the basis for the integration of key requirements within a results-oriented framework that creates a foundation for action and feedback, which is an objective of the Business Excellence models. It should also be noted that each criterion in the model has several sub-elements that define that criterion. For example, in the model in Figure 9.3, the Leadership criteria would solicit the following questions:

- How do an organisation's senior leaders guide and sustain that organisation?
- How do senior leaders communicate with the work force and encourage high performance?
- What are the governance structures and how does the organisation address its ethical, legal, and community responsibility?

Moreover, the significance is not only the fact that there is a procedure in place, but the focus must be on the achieved results and the level of deployment of the procedures across the organisation. What is more, the principles, core concepts, and criteria (concepts and constructs) are very similar across most Business Excellence models. However, the major difference is the method in which the criteria (constructs) are measured. For instance, an examination of Figure 9.1 (EFQM model) and Figure 9.3 (Baldrige model) reveals close similarities.

### Other Considerations Regarding Business Excellence Models

Undertaking a Business Excellence model process is a critical and major decision for the organisation. Therefore, it is important that the management team and the respective organisation are prepared for such an undertaking. The following are the key issues when contemplating the implementation of business excellence in an organisation: What is the available support structure or system in the organisation? What are the core principles and processes regarding quality improvement? What tools would be useful to help in the deployment process?

Organisations must also decide which of the following aims they desire: (a) good management encompassing quality improvement principles and processes; (b) an agreed organisational quality improvement model, such as EFQM or Baldrige or another suitable model (see Table 9.2); (c) independent accreditation for the model; and (d) public recognition of achievement through Awards. The organisation must also decide whether there are standards and accreditation that the organisation requires to do business and determine how these relate to what the organisation desires.

Business Excellence models have already been applied in more than 80 countries. These models have the primary objective of fostering and guiding organisations to improve in all aspects of their operations, by assisting them to identify their strengths and the areas that require improvement. The models are flexible, which allows them to be applied in any type of organisation, irrespective of sector (private or public), industry, size, and nature of operation. The models also foster and assist organisations to embrace self-assessment on a continuous basis, thus making sure that improvement and benefits are measured. It is observed that while some organisations implement Business Excellence models to improve and seek accreditation through awards, the majority of the organisations just desire to improve performance and competitiveness. Readers should recall that excellence models are seen as a key mechanism in many developed countries for improving performance in organisations and as a way of enhancing national competitiveness as a reaction to globalisation.

## Enterprise Risk Management

Gordon et al. (2009) argues that managing risk is a fundamental concern in today's dynamic global environment. This view complements and supports the importance of business excellence models for improving performance in organisations and as a way of enhancing national competitiveness as a reaction to globalisation. Hence, enterprise risk management supports business excellence models' concepts to ensure enterprise success. Stanton (2012) views risk management as a process by which an organisation identifies and analyses threats, examines alternatives, and accepts or mitigates the identified threats. It is important to recognise that organisations need to understand the risks they encounter, and this understanding capability is a fundamental prerequisite and reflects management's ability to successfully attain the identified business objectives.

Furthermore, every choice management makes on behalf of the organisation carries with it the possibility of risk. Therefore, it is important to ensure that a risk management strategy is in place and that it is congruent with and supports the organisation's performance objectives. Risk mitigation should be aimed at helping management to achieve its objectives and should not be viewed as consuming management's effort away from these objectives. In other words, risk mitigation is a necessary management activity that should be present in every aspect of management's undertakings. Hence, it is critical for management to define an enterprise risk management strategy that will facilitate its efforts to mitigate risk, adapt to change, accelerate growth, and enhance performance throughout all the functional levels of the organisation.

The purpose of enterprise risk management frameworks is to permit management to enhance its strategy and performance by escalating the level of understanding of the dynamic and ever-changing opportunities to generate value. Management's ability to establish an organisation that is adaptable to change reflects management's capacity to manage the unpredictable unknowns with enhanced visibility to the holistic business risks. Hence, it is important for management to prepare an enterprise risk management framework that integrates with strategy and performance to add value to the holistic risk plan.

### Enterprise Risk Management Theory and Concepts

Culp (2008) contends that Enterprise Risk Management is perceived as a key factor of successful organisations that enables them to view all the risks that may be encountered by them through a corporate plan. Enterprise Risk Management addresses the limitations of silo-based traditional risk management. In other words, it treats risk management on a holistic basis. Additionally, risk management is viewed as a value adding mechanism that has the objective of creating additional benefits to the organisation by providing management with an overview of all the risky activities, preparing recovery plans, and regular monitoring of the day-to-day operations. Risk management is viewed as being an important development in the overall management process.

Nocco and Stulz (2006) contend that risk management has fully comprehended a new variety of multiple risks and risk measures over the last ten years. While Liu (2012) argues that risk management has developed as the most important factor of how to deal with risks, and understanding their characteristics has currently become a priority for organisations. On the other hand, Aabo et al. (2005) claim that it has become evident that risk is considered a primary threat to organisations, but if handled properly, could result in an opportunity. However, Kalita (2004) maintains that enterprise-wide risk management seems to be the trend in organisations, rather than managing risk individually. It is noted that enterprise risk management has the potential to create higher shareholder value by instituting an organisational risk portfolio, maintaining some risks while mitigating the others.

Organisations have recognised the importance of Enterprise Risk Management, and many have established a team, headed by a Chief Risk Officer, to ensure that risk structures and links are instituted throughout all the organisational levels. However, it is vital for the organisation to have a mechanism to measure several variables to calculate the efficiency level of the risk management process. Gordon et al. (2009) conducted a study to assess the impact of enterprise risk management on organisational performance by generating a class of models that could uncover the real effect. The findings of this study demonstrated that organisations with a higher performance level were fully committed to implementing enterprise risk management and its associated policies.

Moreover, these organisations also made a serious effort to increase their level of risk managements efficiently and adopted the process as a best practice model. Additionally, Gates et al. (2012) found that there was a significant and positive relationship between organisational performance and enterprise risk management. Lukianchuk (2015) argues that Enterprise Risk Management may be too sophisticated for small organisations, since they may lack the experience needed in this area. However, other researchers, such as Weidner (2010), contend that it is possible for SMEs to implement useful risk management techniques that go well beyond simple SWOT analysis, since Enterprise Risk Management can protect organisational investments and increase the organisation's value.

Lukianchuk argues that for small- and medium-sized organisations to flourish, grow, and become large corporations, they need to focus on three key elements: (i) safeguarding of resources; (ii) having operational objectives, especially when dealing with large players on the market; and (iii) identifying strategic objectives to enhancing organisational value and achieving new goals. However, the above illustrates that Enterprise Risk

Management is beneficial for the long-term survival of the organisation and will provide the organisation with the opportunity to grow and prosper.

## Difference between Risk Management and Enterprise Risk Management

It is noted that traditional risk management occurs within an isolated location or organisation silos, such as a department or business unit, and focuses mainly on exposure risks. Hence, this approach to risk management concentrates on a specific segment of the organisation and diminishes management's capacity to evaluate a collaborative effort on a specific risk function on the holistic risk level of the organisation. Gensuite (2020) contends that enterprise risk management functions augment the traditional risk management method by allowing management to focus on three key aspects:

- *Strategic applications*: Enterprise risk management facilitates the achievement of value-based objectives and supports continuous review because it is enterprise-wide and not just limited to individual departments.
- *Risks are taken into account*: Enterprise Risk Management permits organisations to devote time and energy into key components to attain their goals since the process considers all types of risks.
- *Performance metrics*: Enterprise Risk Management focuses on results-based performance measurement by signifying whether a risk management technique became active during the attainment of a business goal. Enterprise Risk Management assists in mitigating the undesirable effects of missed opportunities and lessening residual uncertainty throughout the organisation.

The above explains how enterprise risk management takes a holistic approach and supplements the traditional risk management method to provide a complete system for managing risk.

## Advantages of an Enterprise Risk Management Framework

Strategic thinking is the biggest challenge facing most organisations and enables management to use critical thinking to solve complex problems and plan for the future. These skills are essential for the attainment of business objectives, surmounting complications, and addressing obstacles. Hence, the process of defining and attuning a strategy that is compatible with the current business environment is a common challenge for organisations worldwide. Therefore, simplifying this strategic process and streamlining it necessitates the most advantageous framework for enhancing performance through strategy. COSO (2017) maintains that Enterprise Risk Management facilitates and contributes to this simplified strategic process by:

- Enhancing enterprise strength and robustness by consolidating an organisation's capacity to predict and respond to change.
- Increasing the scope of opportunities available to an organisation by considering all options, both positive and negative, and evaluating the forthcoming plan of action.
- Identifying and managing risk on a holistic organisational basis by considering the likely impact of risk on each functional aspect of an organisation, irrespective of the circumstances that it occurs in.
- Increasing the positive outcomes and taking advantage of and mitigating negative disclosures due to increased reliability of risk identification and risk control measures.
- Lowering performance fluctuations by predicting risks that may impact performance and implementing plans to mitigate disruptions and enhance access to opportunities.
- Optimising the utilisation of resources, evaluating the holistic organisational requirements, better resource application, and optimum allocation of resources to functional areas.

Enterprise Risk Management is an effective tool for taking advantage of strategic opportunities by giving management the ability to evaluate their responses to the difficulties they may encounter proactively and meticulously. and to exploit the many opportunities that are presented to them.

### *Integrating Strategy and Performance into Enterprise Risk Management*

COSO (2017) argue that strategy selection is about making choices and accepting trade-offs, with Enterprise Risk Management being the best approach for untangling the art and science of making well-informed choices. Although risk is viewed as a significant factor in defining an organ-isation's strategy, often risk is assessed mainly on its potential to impact an existing strategy. However, COSO contend that organisations must address several questions that are fundamental to conducting a strategy, such as: Has management modelled customer demand accurately? Will the organi-sation's supply chain deliver on time and on budget? Will new competi-tors emerge? Is the organisation's technology infrastructure up to the task? COSO further argue that risk to the chosen strategy is only one aspect to consider. They maintain that there are two other facets to Enterprise Risk Management that may have much greater impact on an organisation's value, such as the possibility of the strategy not aligning, and the implica-tions from the strategy chosen.

Like every other major undertaking, the success of defining and imple-menting an Enterprise Risk Management framework depends on aligning it with the organisation's mission and vision, strategy, and performance. Therefore, an Enterprise Risk Management framework must be synchro-nised with the organisation's strategy. The chosen strategy must support the organisation's mission and vision. A misaligned strategy increases the pos-sibility that the organisation may not realise its mission and vision, or may compromise its values, even if a strategy is successfully carried out (COSO, 2017). Therefore, the Enterprise Risk Management framework must address the possibility of it not being congruent with the organisation's strategy (i.e., not aligning with the organisation's mission and vision) and must also examine the consequences of such a strategy, and the management of risk to define the strategic objectives.

Accordingly, each alternative strategy has its own risk profile, i.e. the implications arising from the strategy. Executive management must deter-mine if the chosen strategy functions in accordance with the organisation's risk preference, and in what manner will it assist the organisation to deter-mine its objectives and optimise the allocation of its resources. The aim is to ensure that the organisational strategy and the Enterprise Risk Management framework converge until they are fully aligned through anterativee process.

Enterprise Risk Management is as much about understanding the impli-cations from the strategy and the possibility of the strategy not aligning as it is about managing risks to set objectives (COSO, 2017). Ultimately, the Enterprise Risk Management framework aims to assist the management team of an organisation in identifying, assessing, and managing the risks of the chosen strategy. COSO argue that the Enterprise Risk Management framework adheres and identifies with the principles that can be classified into five interrelated components, all of which must be considered during development to ensure alignment with strategy and performance:

a)  *Governance and Culture*: This assists in the application of board risk oversight, to establish operating structures, demonstrate commitment to core values, and define the desired culture.
b)  *Strategy and objective setting*: This helps to analyse the business context, define risk capacity, evaluate alternate strategies, and formulate business objectives.
c)  *Performance*: This identifies and prioritises risks, assesses their severity, and implements risk responses and control measures.
d)  *Review and revision*: These aid management to evaluate substantial change, review risk and performance, and pursue improvement in the overall Enterprise Risk Management frameworks.
e)  *Information, communication, and reporting*: These help to leverage information and technology, communicate risk data, and report on risk, culture, and performance.

Gensuite (2020) argue that adhering to the principles within these five components during the development of the organisation's Enterprise Risk Management framework provides management with the understanding required to manage and mitigate the risks associated with the defined strategy and business objectives. COSO maintain that Enterprise Risk Management has assisted organisations to identify, assess, and manage risks to the strategy. However, they argue that the most significant causes of value destruction are embedded in the possibility of the strategy not supporting the entity's mission and vision, and the implications from the strategy (COSO, 2017). Enterprise Risk Management improves the strategy selection process by facilitating a structured decision-making methodology that analyses the ever-present risk and ensures that the resources are utilised to support the mission and vision of the organisation.

### Implementation of the Enterprise Risk Management Framework

Like every other key reform, implementing an Enterprise Risk Management framework is a major challenge for an organisation. The implementation of an Enterprise Risk Management framework requires careful planning and total commitment from all employees involved in the process; but most of all it requires strong leadership. The advantages of Enterprise Risk Management that have been outlined previously make the effort worthwhile. Gensuite (2020) suggests the following prerequisite activities:

- Define the value the organisation will attain from the Enterprise Risk Management framework.
- Research and comprehend the various guidelines/standards and frameworks that are available.
- Take stock of the risk management action the organisation is currently undertaking.
- Seek support, keep the process simple, and start small to ensure consistency and accurate reporting.

Furthermore, Gensuite recommends that throughout the process of researching and selecting the framework that suits the organisation, management must dedicate sufficient time and energy towards:

- Identifying a common risk vocabulary.
- Defining risk appetite statements together with organisational objectives.
- Revealing the benefits/value of Enterprise Risk Management (e.g., cultural issues increasing risk).
- Determining ownership for each risk type and taking follow-up actions.
- Defining risks and quantifying probable damage.
- Ranking risks and ascertaining priorities throughout the organisation.
- Formulating risk management plans to ensure proper control.
- Determining the information that needs to be shared through risk reporting, and how it is to be done.

It should be noted that risk appetite is the extent of risk an organisation is willing to take in pursuit of the objectives that it deems to have value. In other words, risk appetite is the organisation's risk capacity, or the maximum amount of residual risk it will accept after controls and other measures have been put in place. According to Gensuite, an appropriate Enterprise Risk Management solution assists management to identify and mitigate risks; put in place individualised control measures; assess the effectiveness of these measures; and evaluate and rate their effectiveness on performance. Additionally, they argue that implementing a suitable Enterprise Risk Management software facilitates the establishment of a successful Enterprise Risk Management framework that will aid the organisation to adjust and adapt to the future, irrespective of the nature it takes.

### *Outlook for Enterprise Risk Management Framework*

According to COSO (2017), organisations will continue to face a future full of volatility, complexity, and ambiguity, which supports the premise that Enterprise Risk Management will be an important part of how an organisation manages and prospers through these times. They argue that regardless of the type and size of the organisation, strategies need to fully support the organisation's mission. COSO suggest that all organisations must display a tendency towards having an effective response to change, including swift decision-making, the ability to respond in a cohesive manner, and the adaptive capacity to revolve and reposition while maintaining high levels of trust among stakeholders. COSO identify four key trends that will influence Enterprise Risk Management as follows:

a) *Management of Voluminous Data*: Enterprise Risk Management needs to adapt to an environment where the propagation of data is constantly growing and the speed at which this new data can be analysed is increasing. There are two data sources, namely from inside and outside the organisation, and this data will be structured in new ways. Advanced analytics and data visualisation tools will constantly evolve and will assist management to understand the risk and its impact, irrespective of whether the impact is positive and/or negative.

b) *Leveraging artificial intelligence and automation*: It is important for management to review Enterprise Risk Management practices and consider the impact of these future technologies and leverage their capabilities. New technologies can shed light on previously unrecognisable relationships, trends, and patterns by providing a rich source of information critical to managing risk.

c) *Managing the cost of risk management*: The cost of risk management, compliance processes, and control activities in comparison to the value gained, is a common management concern. Enterprise Risk Management practices involve many activities related to risk, compliance, control, and governance. It is essential that these activities are carried out efficiently and coordinated to provide maximum benefit to the organisation, thus justifying the cost. It is through such a process that Enterprise Risk Management re-evaluates its importance to the organisation, especially in view of the change it brings about.

d)  *Building stronger organizations*: The integration of Enterprise Risk Management with strategy and performance provides an opportunity for the organisation to strengthen its robustness. Enterprise risk management permits management to understand the risks that will have the greatest impact on the organisation and assist them to implement capabilities that allow them to act early and take advantage of the new opportunities that are presented by the circumstances.

According to COSO (2017), Enterprise Risk Management will need to change and adapt to the future to consistently provide the benefits outlined in the Framework. They contend that with the right focus, the benefits derived from Enterprise Risk Management will far outweigh the investments and provide organisations with confidence in their ability to handle the future.

## Programme Management

The final topic to be discussed in this chapter is programme management. Performance management often focuses on processes rather than project-oriented undertakings. Process-type work is normally undertaken by service or manufacturing industries. Therefore, it is important to open a discussion regarding non-process types of work, such as those found at construction organisations and organisations that are project-orientated irrespective of the work they undertake. Firstly, it is essential to clarify what is meant by a 'programme.' Successful programmes facilitate transformational (or innovative) change within an organisation. The purpose of a programme is to coordinate, direct, and oversee the implementation of a group of interrelated projects to deliver outcomes and their resultant benefits that are aligned to the organisation's strategic objectives. For instance, implementing an Enterprise Risk Management framework consists of several interrelated projects that may be classified as a programme. Note that like Enterprise Risk Management, the strategic link is extremely important.

A programme may consist of projects that cut across organisational boundaries and therefore involve different areas of the organisation. For example, initiating a new product or service may depend on several inter-related projects that are being executed by various organisational divisions, such as sales, marketing, distribution, and IT departments. These organi-sational functional divisions would be focused on delivering the outcome required by the programme (i.e., a set of related projects). It should be noted that a programme can be standalone or form part of a portfolio. Moreover, whilst an individual project is usually focused on delivering a specific out-put on its own, a programme may deliver ongoing outcomes and organisa-tional benefits over a typical period of between one and two years.

Now that the difference between a project and a programme has been established, it is opportune to address the meaning of programme management. In simple terms, programme management is the holistic management of the interrelated projects that constitute a programme. Programme management entails bringing together the organisational change functions within the impacted functional areas to ensure that the changes are correctly implemented. A common characteristic that is shared by project management and programme management alike is the importance of meticulous planning. However, the work carried out by pro-gramme management is very closely affiliated to the organisation's ongo-ing strategy, whereas project management focuses on specific deliverables.

### Key Attributes of Programme Management

A key distinguishing attribute of programme management is its capac-ity to provide a level of governance above the specific projects that con-stitute the programme to make sure that they are executed successfully. Rather than focusing on shortening the individual project implementation duration, programme management focuses on the optimum utilisation of resources and the holistic programme duration. Like project manage-ment, the objectives and anticipated benefits of a programme are defined in the programme's proposal document (i.e., Business case), with the vision statement defining the overall required outcome once the programme is completed.

The programme's proposal document also identifies the anticipated achievements once the programme and its respective individual projects are finalised. Other key aspects of programme management include: (i) Governance, which defines the programme tasks and responsibilities, including the procedures and measures to evaluate performance; (ii) Management, which consists of planning the holistic programme, including the individual projects to make sure that stakeholders are involved, and regular reviews are conducted; (iii) Financial management for managing programme costs, including the processes to track and control them; and (iv) Infrastructure support to ensure the right work environment is in place to support the holistic programme planning process, based on the specific projects, resources, timescales, and controls.

### Programme Management Operational Aspects

It is common practice for a Programme Office to be established to support the programme of works, with the responsibility for coordinating programme activities and monitoring performance in terms of the achievement of benefits as defined in the implementation plan. The Programme Office also acts as a central information repository by collecting information to enable benefits reviews to be conducted and for generating performance reports required by the programme manager. It also manages the programme change control process and maintains the appropriate audit trails emanating from the respective change. The Programme Office ensures that the required resources are made available as and when necessary, particularly for defining the programme plans, and facilitating the impact assessments of change on the defined plans and maintaining configuration control of the plans. The Programme Office has a key governance role with a focus on creating a centre of excellence and facilitating the proper implementation of the programme's principles, governance themes and transformational flow.

Like project management, a senior manager in the organisation needs to promote the programme and act as the programme sponsor. The programme sponsor signifies a strong commitment to the programme at a senior management level within the organisation and must ensure that the programme achieves the objectives and benefits that are defined in the proposal document (or business case). Furthermore, the programme sponsor must provide support to the programme manager, specifically allowing the programme manager to escalate problems through the sponsor that cannot be resolved at programme manager level. Hence, the programme manager is responsible for day-to-day administration of the programme and has the specific function of coordinating all the individual projects within the programme. As implied previously, any difficulty being encountered by the programme manager that is beyond the programme manager's control is escalated to the programme sponsor.

Like every other management position, a programme manager requires resilient leadership, communication, and interpersonal skills. These skills are a necessity because the programme manager will be leading the programme team that may consist of several individual project teams that constitute the holistic programme. Therefore, expertise of programme and project management frameworks are a must in combination with knowledge related to financial management (budgeting); procurement procedures; and resource allocation and levelling techniques. Additionally, programme managers need to be aware of risk management procedures so that they may be able to guide their project teams, specifically to predict concerns and to suggest a response to these concerns. The above skills are required because programme managers need to plan the holistic programme, including the individual projects, and assign sufficient resources to all of them. Resource allocation and resource levelling are serious challenges for programme managers, since the optimum use of resources becomes a specific focus.

### Programme Management System of Measurement

The above illustrates that program management covers a spectrum of tasks, and although tracking these tasks and adhering to the planned completion dates are important, the optimisation in the use of resources to achieve more, faster, better, and higher profitability are by far more important aspects. There is an urgent need to develop program management metrics to enhance the program management team's performance. Strategic program management metrics are an important element that is needed during and after project execution. Metrics assist program managers to ensure that the holistic programme and its individual projects: (i) are on track and on budget; (ii) help resolve challenges before they become hindrances; and

(iii) use trends and patterns to adjust processes or resources for improving future performance. Program management metrics have a scientific basis that helps management to make projects more predictable, sustainable, and productive. Mavenlink (2019) recommends eight practical steps to assist management in defining programme management metrics, as shown in Figure 9.4 and described below:

- *Step 1: Identify Programme Management Goals.* It is essential to commence by understanding what is strategically important to the organisation regarding programme fulfilment, since this will guide management to select the required metrics and how these may be analysed.
- *Step 2: Ascertain the Programme Management Metrics.* Selecting the relevant metrics is critical. There is a need to match the programme management metrics with the programme goals. Hence, management must decide the project management metrics to be generated for measuring performance related to these goals. Only high-impact essential measures should be selected since this simplifies the tracking and analysis process.
- *Step 3: Choose Metrics to Track Ongoing Programme Performance.* Programme management metrics are defined at two levels: (i) metrics that track progress as the programme is being implemented to ensure it is on track regarding costs, timeline, and resource management; and (ii) metrics that provide information at the end of the project. One should also reflect on scope change, deadline/budget changes, and changes in resources, amongst others.
- *Step 4: Choose How Each Metric Will be Measured.* Management needs to decide on a standard of measurement for each programme management metric. For instance, measuring completed tasks as a number of total tasks or as a percentage of total project/programme that is complete; and deciding whether to round up hours to the nearest 15 minutes or measured to two decimal points, and whether the cost variance is measured by a monetary currency or by percentage. Management must also decide how to measure programme satisfaction.
- *Step 5: Design Methods for Collecting Programme Management Metrics.* It is important that the methods used to track and measure the organisation's programme management process are relatively simple to collect and compare. They need to be reliable, unambiguous, and equitable to all

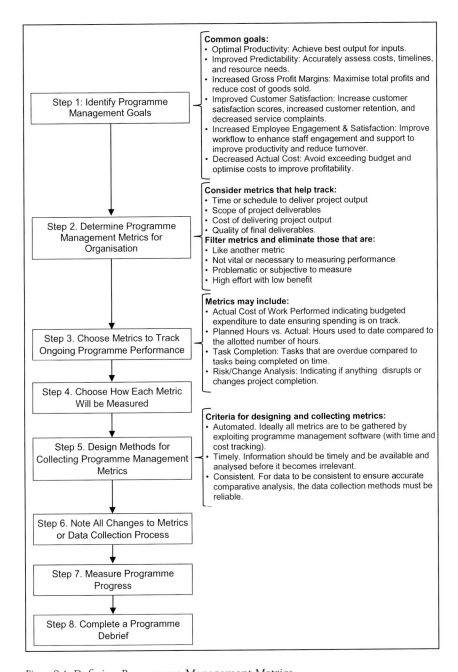

Figure 9.4  Defining Programme Management Metrics

users and should be supported by evidence-based data and measured in a replicable way.

- *Step 6: Note All Changes to Metrics or Data Collection Process.* Programme management metrics are utilised to compare performance over time. Hence, any metrics that are modified must be clearly noted in the reports to aid management trace discrepancies in comparative analysis.
- *Step 7: Measure Programme Progress.* The frequency for measuring programme progress is contingent on the holistic duration of the programme and the quantity/value of the resources involved. Longer and complex programmes must have mid-programme metric reporting to track actual progress compared to budget and scope. This will help management to resolve bottlenecks, mismanagement of resources, or other areas where adjustments may be made to improve project outcomes.
- *Step 8: Always Complete a Programme Debrief.* Organisations must not only track programme management metrics at mid-programme milestones, but a detailed programme review should be conducted to determine what went right and wrong with the programme, and whether certain tasks could have been carried out differently and better to improve long-term performance.

Management must address several issues when implementing a programme. According to Mavenlink (2019), these issues may include: (a) Risk Analysis to ascertain whether there were any unforeseen risks or challenges encountered that stopped or delayed progress on the programme and its respective projects; (b) Budget Analysis to determine whether the programme and its respective projects were achieved on budget (or above or below budget); (c) Resource Analysis to evaluate which resources performed as planned, and those that under or overperformed; (d) Programme Analysis to establish whether the final programme and its respective projects were conducted according to the specifications; and (e) Trend Analysis to ascertain whether there were any trends between this programme (and its projects) and others that might highlight a need to make adjustments to resources, budgeting, or scoping, amongst others.

When implementing programmes, be careful to select the optimum number of metrics (KPIs), otherwise the performance review process will become difficult to manage. Therefore, only measure the metrics that are absolutely required to optimise systems, measure changes in performance, and measure important milestones that inform business decisions. Ensure that performance targets are calculated on normal conditions that are as realistic as possible (i.e., not tight or generous). Managers should exploit the metrics provided to ensure that matters are moving according to the agreed plan. Any highlighted variances (positive or negative) should be carefully investigated to determine the cause, since they may provide an opportunity for doing things better. Information is the critical component in doing things better, faster, and more sustainably; therefore, the best organisations are those that do what they do well, do it consistently, and are always seeking to find ways to improve (Mavenlink, 2019).

## Conclusion

This is the final chapter regarding the use of performance management tools using three distinct but related methods, namely Business Excellence Models, Enterprise Risk Management, and Programme Management. This chapter has illustrated that these tools can be exploited as a basis for performance improvement. There are various business excellence models. However, the original model was developed by the European Foundation for Quality Management (EFQM). All the models have a common objective, namely, to support the management of organisations in accelerating the process of making quality a decisive influence for achieving global competitive advantage.

Most business excellence models are based upon a self-assessment approach that allow management to compare their organisation with the Model. The foundation of the models is reasonable rational thinking, where results are achieved through several enablers, with the results being measured by financial measures, customer satisfaction, people satisfaction, and the impact on society. The enablers are leadership, policy and strategy, people management, and resources and process management. Business excellence models are based upon the view that by improving the 'how' this will improve the results in terms of the 'what.'

The Enterprise Risk Management (ERM) framework supplements business excellence models. The ERM framework permits management to optimise its strategy and performance by increasing awareness of the opportunities to build organisational value. This framework is based on the principle that organisations which embrace change can manage the unpredictable unknowns with enhanced awareness of the overall business risks. The ERM framework is able to integrate with the organisation's strategy and performance system and add value to the organisation and the overall risk program objectives. One needs to appreciate that metrics improve the understanding of the organisation and stimulate productive discussions between senior leadership and relevant stakeholders, thus generating better overall outcomes.

The other important tool to improve organisational performance that was discussed in this chapter is programme management. Programme management is the holistic management of several interrelated projects that make up a portfolio of these connected projects (i.e., the programme). Often programme management includes the integration of organisational change within the business areas affected by a specific project, to ensure the successful implementation of the project and its consequential change. Programme management also encompasses a systematic project management approach for planning and implementing the various activities. It is important that any undertaking is aligned with the organisation's strategy, otherwise management will be misusing resources. Programme management provides the necessary layer of governance above the specific projects and ensures that the portfolio of projects is executed effectively.

It should be noted that these three tools can be implemented in combination or separately. Furthermore, the numerous tools discussed in Part II of this book can be used separately or in conjunction with others, depending on the circumstances of the organisation, the various processes that are in operation, and the challenges being encountered by management from time to time.

# References

Aabo, T., Fraser, J.R.S., and Simkins, B.J. (2005). 'The Rise and Evolution of the Chief Risk Officer: Enterprise Risk Management at Hydro One.' *Journal of Applied Corporate Finance*, 17(3), pp. 62–75.

Baldridge Excellence Framework (2021). *Baldrige Performance Excellence Program, Gaithersburg, Maryland*. Available at: https://www.nist.gov/baldrige/publications/baldrige-excellence-framework/businessnonprofit (Accessed 22 November 2023).

COSO (2017). *Enterprise Risk Management Integrating with Strategy and Performance.* Available at: https://aaahq.org/portals/0/documents/coso/coso_erm_2017_main_v1_20230815.pdf (Accessed 22 November 2023).

Culp, C.L. (2002). 'The Revolution in Corporate Risk Management: A Decade of Innovations in Process and Products.' *Journal of Applied Corporate Finance*, 14(4), pp. 8–26.

EFQM (2021). *The EFQM Model. London.* EFQM Revised 2nd edition. Available at: https://www.scribd.com/document/526358941/EFQM-Model-Revised-2nd-Edition-Free-English (Accessed 22 November 2023).

Gates, S., Nicolas, J., and Walker, P.L. (2012). 'Enterprise Risk Management: A Process for Enhanced Management and Improved Performance.' *Management Accounting Quarterly*, 13(3), pp. 28–38.

Gensuite. (2020). *Enterprise Risk Management – Integrating Strategy.* Available at: https://www.gensuite.com/enterprise-risk-management-performance-strategy/ (Accessed 22 November 2023).

Gordon, L.A., Loeb, M.P., and Tseng, C. (2009). 'Enterprise Risk Management and Firm Performance: A Contingency Perspective.' *Public Policy*, 28, pp. 301–327.

Kalita, M. (2004). 'Enterprise-Wide Risk Management: Myth or Reality?' *Business Credit*, 106(3), pp. 22–23.

Liu, J. (2012). 'The Enterprise Risk Management and the Risk Oriented Internal Audit.' *iBusiness*, 4, pp. 287–292.

Lukianchuk, G. (2015). 'The Impact of Enterprise Risk Management on Firm Performance of Small and Medium Enterprises.' *European Scientific Journal*, 11(13).

Mavenlink. (2019). *8 Steps for Practical Program Management Metrics.* Available at: https://www.mavenlink.com/blog/article/8-steps-for-practical-program-management-metrics (Accessed 22 November 2023).

Nocco, B.W. and Stulz, R.M. (2006). 'Enterprise Risk Management: Theory and Practice.' *Journal of Applied Corporate Finance*, 18(4), pp. 8–20.

Seddon, J. (2022). *Vanguard Set Up the Beyond Command-and-Control Network.* Available at: https://beyondcommandandcontrol.com/john-seddon-and-the-vanguard-method/ (Accessed 22 November 2023).

Stanton, T.H. (2012). *Why Some Firms Thrive While Others Fail.* Oxford: Oxford University Press.

Weidner, S. (2010). *Risk Management for Small and Medium Sized Incoming Tour Operators: Shown at the example of Skylimit Travel S.A., Isla Margarita, Venezuela.* GRIN Verlag OHG.

# PART III

## PRACTICAL APPLICATION OF PERFORMANCE MANAGEMENT TOOLS AND FUTURE TRENDS

Part I of this book, which consisted of four chapters, laid the foundation regarding performance management and measurement principles. These chapters explained that key performance indicators (KPIs) may be defined at different levels of the organisation, such as corporate, divisional, departmental, activity, and individual levels. It was also shown that KPIs may also be defined on a product or service level or for specific customers. This illustrated that KPI methodologies are extremely flexible and have a resourceful characteristic that may be adapted for the private and public sectors. KPIs are about accountability of those who are responsible for a specific duty, role, or segment of the organisation. Hence, the success of the KPI process is contingent on the management team and employees being highly committed towards having a KPI methodology as the performance management appraisal system.

Furthermore, a performance management system must be aligned with the strategic objectives of the organisation and how the specific function of all employees contributes towards the achievement of these strategic

DOI: 10.4324/9781032685465-12

objectives. This is the primary reason why the contribution of the employees to the achievement of the organisation's strategic objectives, and the respective defined KPIs, have become the fundamental basis for measuring performance either at an individual level or at various organisational functional levels. It must be recognised that KPIs provide a common thread between the various performance management systems and their associated tools. Performance management systems are still evolving with the objective of significantly increasing organisational effectiveness and employee productivity. Part I concluded with the formulation of a performance management framework that is robust and flexible, and yet easy to apply and applicable to both the private and public sectors, and that can be implemented progressively throughout the organisation.

Part II examined in detail various performance management tools that are viewed as being critical for the successful implementation of the proposed performance management framework described in Part I. An important principle of the proposed performance management framework is to separate the various functions within the organisation and implement a performance management system for each function (and in many cases sub-functions) with their own limited number of objectives and resultant KPIs. Part II illustrated that each organisational function or sub-function may utilise different tools and methods for establishing and monitoring performance through KPIs. For example, some organisational functional areas may use balanced scorecards, others may utilise a standard costing system and associated variance analysis, yet still other functions may use benchmarking, and so on.

This basic principle of segmenting an organisation into functional units (and even sub-units) for the purpose of performance management will permit the same performance management framework to be used by both the Private and Public Sectors. Hence, Part II described the application of various performance management and measurement tools and focused on Stage Three of the proposed performance management framework, specifically the action plan for KPIs, monitoring the action plan, and the post-implementation review of the action plan.

Part III is the final segment of this book and will consist of three chapters. The first two chapters will focus as much as practically possible on the application of the performance management tools described in Part II. The methodology used in Part III is based upon selecting two authentic organisations, one from the private sector and the other from the public sector. Hence, a chapter will be dedicated to each industry segment, namely from one each from the private and public sectors.

The actual names of the organisations will be changed to conceal their identities. The information regarding these organisations will be mainly extracted from their latest annual report, through the internet. Using this information, the chapters will analyse these annual reports and attempt to apply as much as practically possible from the information available the performance management tools described in Part II. The purpose of these two chapters is to explain the application of the performance management tools and illustrate their use. The final chapter of Part III will focus on the future development trend of performance management systems, so that readers become aware of the changing nature in relation to how organisational performance will be evaluated in the future and the role Artificial Intelligence is likely to play.

# 10

## APPLICATION OF THE PERFORMANCE MANAGEMENT TOOLS

### PRIVATE SECTOR

'To win in the marketplace you must first win in the workplace.'

Douglas R. Conant
Business Leader and Author

The focus of this chapter is to apply the various performance measurement and management tools in a private sector environment, namely a manufacturing company that is listed with the United States of America Securities and Exchange Commission. The identification of the selected organisation has been changed to provide anonymity. The information regarding the chosen organisation has been chiefly obtained from one of its annual reports. Furthermore, certain original data items have been modified and new fictional information has been introduced to permit the use of various techniques for illustration purposes. Therefore, the final analytical results from this case study should not be construed to be a real assessment of the chosen organisation.

DOI: 10.4324/9781032685465-13

## Description of the Organisation

The selected organisation, which will be referred to as GeoMed Limited, is a global provider of customised engineered solutions located in North America, Europe, Asia, and the Middle East. The company designs, engineers, and manufactures mechatronic products and components for Original Equipment Manufacturers (OEMs). Examples of mechatronic systems include robots, digitally controlled combustion engines, machine tools with self-adaptive devices, contact-free magnetic bearings, and automated guided vehicles, amongst others. Typically, these require the integration of a high amount of system knowledge and software that is necessary for their design. The company's products are utilised by end markets within the transportation industry, construction equipment, infrastructure, cloud computing, consumer appliances, and medical devices.

### *Operating Segments of Organisation*

The operating segments of the organisation include medical, automotive, interface, and industrial. The Medical segment consists of the medical device business that specialises in surface support technology aimed at pressure injury prevention. This technology is utilised by patients who are immobilised or are at risk for pressure injuries, including those undergoing long-duration surgical procedures. The Automotive segment provides electronic and electro-mechanical devices and associated components that are used by automobile OEMs. These products have different uses and include integrated centre consoles, various switches, LED-based lighting, power transmission lead-frames, and sensors that feature magneto-elastic sensing and other technologies to monitor the status or operation of a system or a specific component.

The Interface segment produces an assortment of copper-based transceivers and related accessories for cloud computing hardware apparatus and telecommunications broadband equipment, user interface systems for the appliance, commercial food provision, point-of-sale equipment providers, and fluid-level sensors for the marine, recreational vehicle, and sump pump markets. The Industrial segment produces external lighting systems, braided flexible cables, current-conducting laminated busbars and devices, and custom power-product assemblies. It also specialises in industrial safety radio remote controls, high-current low-voltage flexible power cabling systems, and powder-coated busbars that are used in various industrial sectors and applications, including aerospace, cloud computing, commercial vehicles, industrial, military, power conversion, and transportation.

The organisation's sales initiatives are managed by inhouse sales executives who are supported by expert application engineers and technical personnel, who work directly with customers to design products for their specific systems. The application engineers also assist management to identify emerging markets and new specialised products. Since the organisation produces specialised components that are often customised products, most sales are made through the organisation's sales department. However, the organisation also utilises independent manufacturers' sales agents through a global sales distribution network.

## *Other Organisational Characteristics*

The organisation specialises in the manufacture of unique products and components; therefore, the organisation is highly dependent on patents, licenses, trademarks, trade secrets, and non-disclosure agreements to safeguard its intellectual property and proprietary products. Patents have been attained in Europe, United States of America, and Asia, and many more patents are pending processing and approval in various continents. The organisation has a diverse number of patents to ensure that it is not dependent on a single product and to ensure that the expiration of a particular patent does not have an adverse material effect on the organisation and its ability to compete.

Being a specialised component manufacturer, the organisation is affected by the seasonal fluctuations of the sales and production schedules of its customers. Hence, the organisation's diversification strategy is aimed at mitigating any occurring seasonal fluctuations. The organisation is highly dependent on a single vehicle manufacturing customer, which may place the organisation at risk, should this customer experience a sales downturn. It is also important for the organisation's engineering division to work closely with the customer's design team to ensure that the right products are developed for the specific future vehicle models. This will ensure that the organisation's order book is continually full. Moreover, the organisation has in place long-term supply agreements to ensure that its manufacturing facilities operate at an optimum level. However, the long-term agreements may not always result in firm orders and the OEM customers are not obliged to procure a minimum number of components from the organisation.

This flexibility is essential for its customers to mitigate any adverse effects of an economic downturn in the national and global economies. However, firm orders are secured when there are authorised customer purchase orders that are normally based on the customer production release schedules. A major objective of the organisation is to satisfy these orders as rapidly as possible according to the just-in-time policy of the customer. Hence, a backlog of orders at any given time is not a meaningful indicator of future earnings. The markets the organisation operates in are highly competitive and are characterised by the continuous and swift technological changes and developments. The competition is normally based upon the price, service, and product performance. The organisation competes with a significant number of manufacturers that have much larger resources. However, the organisation has a significant research and development programme to counter this considerable competition. This research and development programme is undertaken with the participation of several highly qualified employees who are mainly involved in enhancing existing products and developing new products and processes.

The organisation must comply with various government regulations from a diverse number of countries from which the organisation operates. Currently, compliance to these regulations has not had a material impact upon the organisation's outcome of operations, competitive position, and capital expenditures. Moreover, the organisation does not expect any material capital expenditures for environmental control facilities in the short-term. However, this situation regarding compliance with existing or future governmental regulations cannot be guaranteed in the medium- to long-term.

The organisation has over 7000 fulltime employees globally, most of whom are in Europe and Asia. However, not all employees are covered by a collective bargaining agreement. The corporate culture is dedicated to conducting business with honesty, collaboration, and performance excellence. Hence, the management team and employees are required to demonstrate the principles of equity, uprightness, and integrity in the activities undertaken by the organisation. In addition, the employees must abide by the organisation's code of conduct that deals with various themes, such as harassment, discrimination, anti-corruption, privacy, protecting confidential information, and proper use of the organisation's assets. The organisation has in place an annual training programme that focuses on preventing, identifying, reporting, and ceasing any type of unlawful discrimination or unethical actions.

The organisation tries to induce and retain capable and experienced people to manage and support its operations. Hence, the organisation's recruitment strategy is centred on attracting the best talent, acknowledging, and rewarding their performance while constantly developing, engaging, and retaining them. The organisation has a global talent review and succession planning process in place to ensure that it has the appropriate human resources to satisfy its current and future business strategies. The organisation has a diversity and inclusion policy to allow it to develop and empower its workforce. This policy makes use of the unique backgrounds, experiences, ideas, and talents of the employees. Hence, employees are valued and esteemed for their individual contributions to innovate, expand, and sustain the organisation's business and improve its performance.

The health and safety of the employees is very important to the organisation and is a key contributing factor to its business success. The organisation creates an environment that mitigates workplace incidents, risks, and hazards by regularly training employees on safety-related topics and continuous monitoring of the effectiveness of the health and safety policy. The organisation offers a competitive compensation and benefits package to its employees commensurate with their location, grade, qualifications, and experience. This helps to attract, retain, and motivate employees. Apart from a generous salary and wages package, the organisation provides other benefits such as life, disability, and health (medical, dental, and vision) insurance; a retirement savings and investing plan; paid study sabbatical; tuition reimbursement; military leave; and holiday pay.

## *Organisational Risk Factors*

Key risk factors that are classified by specific themes have been identified by the organisation, which are shown in Table 10.1 and Table 10.2.

*Table 10.1* Key Operational and Industry Risk Factors Identified by GeoMed Limited

| Risk Description |
| --- |
| Inability of the organisation's supply chain, or customers' supply chain, to deliver key components, such as semiconductors, could materially adversely affect business, financial condition and results of operations and cause significant cost increases. |
| COVID-19 pandemic has adversely affected, and may continue to adversely affect business, financial condition, and results of operations. The extent of these effects on business depends on future events that continue to be highly uncertain and beyond the organisation's control. |
| Susceptible to trends and factors affecting industry the organisation operates in. |
| Inflation may adversely impact business, financial condition, and results of operations. |
| Loss or insolvency of major customers, or a significant decline in the volume of products purchased by these customers, would adversely affect future results. |
| Inability to attract/retain key employees and a highly skilled workforce may have an adverse effect on business, financial condition, and results of operations. |
| Global nature of operations exposes organisation to political, economic, and social risks that may adversely affect business, financial condition, and results of operations. |
| Organisation is dependent on the availability and price of raw materials. |
| Organisation or customers' inability to effectively manage timing, quality, and cost of new program launches could adversely affect financial performance. |
| Businesses and markets in which organisation operates are very competitive. If entity is unable to compete effectively, sales and profitability could decline. |
| Future price reductions and increased quality standards may reduce profitability and have a material adverse effect on business, financial condition, and results of operations. |
| Organisation's ability to market its products is subject to a lengthy sales cycle that requires significant investment prior to reporting sales revenues, and there is no assurance that components will be implemented in any product. |
| Inability to capitalise on prior or future acquisitions or any decision to strategically divest one or more current businesses may adversely affect business, financial condition, and results of operations. |
| Customers may cancel their orders, change production quantities or locations or delay production. |
| A catastrophic event or significant business interruption at any of the facilities could adversely affect business, financial condition, and results of operations. |

*Table 10.2*  Other Key Risk Factors Identified by GeoMed Limited

| *Risk Description* |
| --- |
| **Technology and Intellectual Property Risk Factors** |
| Organisation's operations could be negatively impacted by IT service interruptions, data corruption or misuse, cyber-based attacks, or network security breaches. |
| Organisation may be unable to keep pace with rapid technological changes that could adversely affect business, financial condition, and results of operations. |
| Inability to protect intellectual property or infringement, or alleged infringement, on another person's intellectual property; the organisation's competitive position and results of operations may be adversely impacted. |
| **Legal, Regulatory, and Compliance Risks** |
| Organisation is subject to government regulations, including environmental, health, and safety laws and regulations, that expose organisation to potential financial liability. |
| Organisation operates business on a global basis and changes to trade policy, including tariffs and customs regulations, could have a material and adverse effect on our business. |
| Climate change issues and regulations may adversely impact business and results of operations. |
| Products the organisation manufactures may contain design or manufacturing defects that could result in reduced demand for products or services and liability claims against the organisation. |
| **Financial Risks** |
| Organisation has significant goodwill and other intangible assets, and future impairment of these assets could have a material adverse impact on financial condition and results of operations. |
| Organisation has incurred indebtedness, and its level of indebtedness and restrictions under our indebtedness could adversely affect operations and liquidity. |
| A significant fluctuation between the US dollar and other currencies could adversely impact business, results of operations, and financial condition. |
| Performance-based awards under a long-term incentive plan may require significant adjustments to compensation expense that could have a material adverse impact on results of operations. |
| Restructuring activities may lead to additional costs and material adverse effects. |
| Changes in the effective tax rate may adversely impact the organisation's results of operations. |
| Organisation's judgements regarding the accounting for tax positions and the resolution of tax disputes may impact the results of operations and financial condition. |

## Financial Condition and Results of Operations

The organisation's financial condition and results of operations are based upon the consolidated financial statements that were prepared in accordance with US GAAP. It is noted that the organisation procures its components from external sources globally. Hence, the organisation's financial condition and results of operations may materially be adversely impacted due to the inability of the organisation's supply chain and that of its customers to provide key components, such as semiconductors. This inability to attain key components may cause the organisation to incur significant cost increases because it will be difficult for it to meet production schedules and it would need to expedite deliveries at significant additional expenses and other related costs.

Thus, any significant interruptions to such supply chains could materially negatively affect the organisation's business, financial condition, and results of operations. There is an ongoing significant global shortage of semiconductors due to the complexity of the semiconductor supply chain, with capacity constraints occurring throughout due to the substantial competition within the automotive and commercial vehicle supply chains and with other industries. This competitive environment for semiconductors is likely to negatively affect the organisation's business, financial condition, and results of operations. Table 10.3 to Table 10.8 provide the consolidated

Table 10.3  Comparison of the GeoMed Limited Results of Operations for Fiscal Years 2022 and 2021

|  |  Fiscal Year |  |
| --- | --- | --- |
| Details ($ in millions) | 2022 | 2021 |
| Net sales | 1163.60 | 1088.00 |
| Less: Cost of products sold | 898.70 | 813.90 |
| Gross profit | 264.90 | 274.10 |
| Less: |  |  |
| Selling and administrative expenses | 134.10 | 126.90 |
| Amortisation of intangibles | 19.10 | 19.30 |
| Interest expense, net | 3.50 | 5.20 |
| Other income, net | −10.30 | −12.20 |
| Income tax expense | 16.30 | 12.60 |
| Net income | 102.20 | 122.30 |

Table 10.4  Comparison of the GeoMed Limited Cashflows for Fiscal Years 2022 and 2021

| | Fiscal Year | |
|---|---|---|
| **Details ($ in millions)** | **2022** | **2021** |
| **Operating activities:** | | |
| Net income | 102.20 | 122.30 |
| Non-cash items | 66.40 | 50.70 |
| Changes in operating assets and liabilities | −69.80 | 6.80 |
| *Net cash provided by operating activities* | **98.80** | **179.80** |
| Net cash used in investing activities | −37.40 | −24.80 |
| Net cash used in financing activities | −114.60 | −142.90 |
| Effect of foreign currency exchange rate changes on cash & cash equivalents | −8.00 | 3.80 |
| *(Decrease) increase in cash and cash equivalents* | **−61.20** | **15.90** |
| Cash and cash equivalents at beginning of the period | 233.20 | 217.30 |
| *Cash and cash equivalents at end of the period* | **172.00** | **233.20** |

Table 10.5  GeoMed Limited Current (2022) Contractual Obligations

| | Payments Due by Period | | | | |
|---|---|---|---|---|---|
| ($ in millions) | Total | 1 year | 1–3 years | 3–5 years | 5 years |
| Finance leases | 0.80 | 0.40 | 0.30 | 0.10 | 0.00 |
| Operating leases | 24.00 | 6.50 | 7.30 | 3.20 | 7.00 |
| Debt (1) | 211.40 | 13.00 | 197.10 | 0.40 | 0.90 |
| Estimated interest on debt (2) | 5.60 | 3.70 | 1.70 | 0.10 | 0.10 |
| Deferred compensation | 8.00 | 1.60 | 1.90 | 1.80 | 2.70 |
| **Total:** | **249.80** | **25.20** | **208.30** | **5.60** | **10.70** |

Table 10.6  GeoMed Limited Consolidated Balance Sheet Statement

| Details ($ in millions) | 2022 | 2021 |
|---|---|---|
| **ASSETS** | | |
| **Current assets:** | **629.00** | **674.00** |
| Cash and cash equivalents | 172.00 | 233.20 |

*Table 10.6*  (Continued)

| Details ($ in millions) | 2022 | 2021 |
|---|---|---|
| Accounts receivable, net | 273.30 | 282.50 |
| Inventories | 158.50 | 124.20 |
| Income taxes receivable | 8.30 | 11.50 |
| Prepaid expenses and other current assets | 16.90 | 22.60 |
| **Long-term assets:** | **760.10** | **793.00** |
| Property, plant, and equipment, net | 197.00 | 204.00 |
| Goodwill | 233.00 | 235.60 |
| Other intangible assets, net | 207.70 | 229.40 |
| Operating lease right-of-use assets, net | 20.00 | 22.30 |
| Deferred tax assets | 36.80 | 41.20 |
| Pre-production costs | 27.20 | 25.00 |
| Other long-term assets | 38.40 | 35.50 |
| **Total assets** | **1389.10** | **1467.00** |
| **LIABILITIES AND SHAREHOLDERS' EQUITY** | | |
| **Current liabilities:** | **188.60** | **222.70** |
| Accounts payable | 108.50 | 122.90 |
| Accrued employee liabilities | 30.00 | 33.50 |
| Other accrued liabilities | 24.50 | 25.00 |
| Short-term operating lease liabilities | 6.00 | 6.10 |
| Short-term debt | 13.00 | 14.90 |
| Income tax payable | 6.60 | 20.30 |
| **Long-term liabilities:** | **286.70** | **326.30** |
| Long-term debt | 197.50 | 225.20 |
| Long-term operating lease liabilities | 14.80 | 17.50 |
| Long-term income taxes payable | 22.10 | 24.80 |
| Other long-term liabilities | 14.00 | 20.50 |
| Deferred tax liabilities | 38.30 | 38.30 |
| **Total liabilities** | **475.30** | **549.00** |

(Continued)

Table 10.6  (Continued)

| Details ($ in millions) | 2022 | 2021 |
|---|---|---|
| **Shareholders' equity:** Common stock, $0.50 par value, 100,000,000 shares authorized, 38,276,968 shares & 39,644,913 shares issued as of 30 April 30 2022 & 1 May 1 2021, respectively. | 19.20 | 19.80 |
| Additional paid-in capital | 169.00 | 157.60 |
| Accumulated other comprehensive (loss) income | −26.80 | 6.10 |
| Treasury stock, 1,346,624 shares as of 30 April 2022 and 1 May 2021 | −11.50 | −11.50 |
| Retained earnings | 763.90 | 746.00 |
| **Total shareholders' equity** | **913.80** | **918.00** |
| **Total liabilities and shareholders' equity** | **1389.10** | **1467.00** |

Table 10.7  GeoMed Limited Consolidated Income Statement

| | Fiscal Year | | |
|---|---|---|---|
| **Details ($ in millions)** | **2022** | **2021** | **2020** |
| | (52 Weeks) | (52 Weeks) | (53 Weeks) |
| Net sales | 1163.60 | 1088.00 | 1023.90 |
| Cost of products sold | 898.70 | 813.90 | 741.00 |
| **Gross profit** | **264.90** | **274.10** | **282.90** |
| Selling and administrative expenses | 134.10 | 126.90 | 116.80 |
| Amortisation of intangibles | 19.10 | 19.30 | 19.00 |
| **Income from operations** | **111.70** | **127.90** | **147.10** |
| Interest expense, net | 3.50 | 5.20 | 10.10 |
| Other income, net | −10.30 | −12.20 | −11.70 |
| **Income before income taxes** | **118.50** | **134.90** | **148.70** |
| Income tax expense | 16.30 | 12.60 | 25.30 |
| **Net income** | **102.20** | **122.30** | **123.40** |
| | | | |
| **Basic and diluted income per share:** | | | |
| Basic | 2.74 | 3.22 | 3.28 |
| Diluted | 2.70 | 3.19 | 3.26 |
| Cash dividends per share | 0.56 | 0.44 | 0.44 |

Table 10.8  GeoMed Limited Consolidated Cashflow Statement

| Details ($ in millions) | 2022 | 2021 | 2020 |
|---|---|---|---|
| **Operating activities:** | 52 Weeks | 52 Weeks | 3 Weeks |
| Net income | 102.20 | 122.30 | 123.40 |
| *Adjustments to reconcile net income to net cash:* | | | |
| Depreciation and amortisation | 52.60 | 51.50 | 48.30 |
| Stock-based compensation expense | 11.80 | 6.80 | 0.30 |
| Change in cash surrender value of life insurance | 0.10 | -2.00 | 0.00 |
| Amortisation of debt issuance costs | 0.70 | 0.70 | 0.70 |
| (Gain) loss on sale of business/investment/property | −0.30 | 1.30 | -0.40 |
| Impairment of long-lived assets | 3.10 | 0.00 | 0.00 |
| Change in deferred income taxes | −2.10 | −9.60 | 8.00 |
| Other | 0.50 | 2.00 | −0.20 |
| **Changes in operating assets and liabilities:** | | | |
| Accounts receivable | −2.00 | −81.90 | 27.40 |
| Inventories | −39.30 | 11.30 | −15.80 |
| Prepaid expenses and other assets | 1.50 | 17.90 | −3.60 |
| Accounts payable | −8.70 | 44.00 | −15.50 |
| Other liabilities | −21.30 | 15.50 | −32.00 |
| **Net cash provided by operating activities** | **98.80** | **179.80** | **140.60** |
| **Investing activities:** | | | |
| Purchases of property, plant, and equipment | −38.00 | −24.90 | −45.10 |
| Sale of business/investment/property | 0.60 | 0.10 | 0.60 |
| **Net cash used in investing activities** | **−37.40** | **−24.80** | **−44.50** |
| **Financing activities:** | | | |
| Taxes paid related to net share settlement of equity awards | −0.30 | −3.90 | −0.40 |
| Repayments of finance leases | −0.70 | −0.50 | −0.70 |
| Proceeds from exercise of stock options | 0.50 | 0.80 | 0.00 |
| Purchases of common stock | −64.50 | −6.70 | 0.00 |
| Cash dividends | −20.40 | −17.40 | −16.30 |

(Continued)

*Table 10.8* (Continued)

| | | | |
|---|---|---|---|
| Proceeds from borrowings | 0.00 | 1.50 | 157.50 |
| Repayments of borrowings | −29.20 | −116.70 | −98.40 |
| **Net cash (used in) provided by financing activities** | **−114.60** | **−142.90** | **41.70** |
| Effect of foreign currency exchange rate changes on cash and cash equivalents | −8.00 | 3.80 | -3.70 |
| **(Decrease) increase in cash and cash equivalents** | **−61.20** | **15.90** | **134.10** |
| Cash and cash equivalents at beginning of the year | 233.20 | 217.30 | 83.20 |
| **Cash and cash equivalents at end of the year** | **172.00** | **233.20** | **217.30** |
| | | | |
| **Supplemental information. *Cash paid during period for:*** | | | |
| Interest | 3.60 | 5.30 | 9.90 |
| Income taxes, net of refunds | 32.30 | 16.00 | 21.10 |

financial data related to the organisation, which were extracted from Form 10-K, United States Securities and Exchange Commission (real company name not identified).

## Application of the Performance Management Tools: Private Sector

This section will apply several performance management tools using GeoMed Limited data described above, including strategic planning and business planning (including Variance Analysis).

### Strategic Planning as a Performance Management Tool

As discussed in Chapter 5, it is important to avoid several mistakes that are normally made by organisations. When applying KPI models the following criteria must be adhered to:

- Defined KPIs must be aligned with the strategic objectives.
- Should not limit the selected KPIs to those that are easily measured (e.g., also use non-financial KPIs, such as customer satisfaction).

- KPIs should not give excessive significance to past events (e.g., also use KPIs that are based on trends, such as customer orientation).
- KPIs should not be used as a mechanism for controlling employees.
- Distinguish strategic KPIs from operational KPIs.

It is critical for KPIs to be integrated in the strategic management framework adopted by the organisation to ensure that there is a rigorous process in place for selecting the appropriate KPIs. Note that too many KPIs will make the performance management system unmanageable; on the other hand, too few KPIs will make it meaningless. Therefore, there must be a fine balance regarding how many KPIs are selected and a balanced combination of forward-looking (future) and backward-looking (past) KPIs. Figure 10.1,

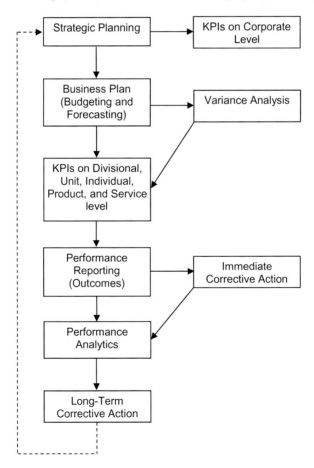

Figure 10.1 Integrated Strategic and Business Planning Performance Management Model: GeoMed Limited

which was described in Chapter 5, provides a model for integrating the strategic and business planning processes with their respective performance management systems, utilising various tools that range from KPIs at various levels to performance analytics and performance reporting. The aim for this chapter is to apply this model to GeoMed Limited.

## Financial and Non-Financial Strategic KPIs for GeoMed Limited

This section will examine GeoMed's financial statements and other related data to determine the organisation's KPIs. Figure 10.2 provides a summary of the different categories of financial ratios, whilst Table 10.9 shows

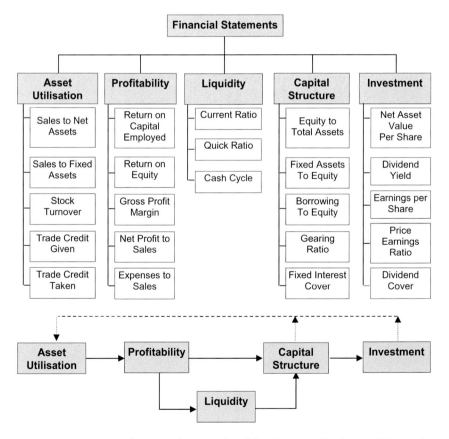

*Figure* 10.2  Summary of Financial Ratios (KPIs) by Category for GeoMed Limited

Table 10.9a Financial Ratios (KPIs) by Application Category for GeoMed Limited

| Financial Ratio | Formulae | Ratio | Interpretation and/or Remarks |
|---|---|---|---|
| **Liquidity:** | | | |
| Current Ratio | Current Assets ÷ Current Liabilities | 3.3 | A current ratio of between 1.5:1 and 2:1 is generally considered practical although this depends on the nature of the business. Current assets should always be greater than current liabilities. |
| Liquid Ratio (Quick ratio or Acid Test) | (Current Assets − Stock) ÷ Current Liabilities | 2.5 | A liquid ratio of 1:1 is normally considered satisfactory but may be allowed to fall to 0.9:1 if the debtors pay promptly and there is a regular inflow of cash from them. |
| **Profitability:** | | | |
| Return on Capital Employed (ROCE) | $\dfrac{\text{Profit Before Interest and Tax}}{\text{Capital Employed}} \times 100$ | 2022: 9.3% 2021: 10.3% | This ratio indicates management efficiency because it contrasts the earnings with the funds utilised to generate that profit. As a minimum management will aim to maintain the ROCE level. Capital Employed = Total Assets − Current Liabilities. |
| Return on Equity (ROE) | Profit Before Tax (after preference dividends) ÷ (Ordinary Share Capital + Reserves) | 14.8% | The ratio measures profitability by revealing how much profit a company generates with the money shareholders have invested. Net income is for the full fiscal year (before dividends paid to common stock holders but after dividends to preferred stock.) Shareholder's equity does not include preferred shares. |
| Gross Profit Margin | Gross Profit ÷ Sales | 23% | The ratio shows the margin that is being earned on sales. It measures a company's manufacturing and distribution efficiency during the production process. Note that gross margin tends to remain stable over time. |
| Net Profit to Sales | Profit Before Interest and Tax ÷ Sales | 10% | The ratio indicates the overall performance of the company. |
| Expenses to Sales: Operating Expenses Selling/Distribution Cost Administrative Expenses Finance Charges | Total Operating Expenses ÷ Sales Selling & Administrative Expenses ÷ Sales Finance Charges ÷ Sales | 77% 12% 0.3% | Only three ratios are shown and focus on the performance of the company in terms of the proportion of each particular expense to sales. Other ratios may include any other expense item. These ratios provide a view of the company's cost structure. |

Table 10.9b  Financial Ratios (KPIs) by Application Category for GeoMed Limited (continued)

| Financial Ratio | Formulae | Ratio | Interpretation and/or Remarks |
|---|---|---|---|
| **Asset Utilisation:** | | | |
| Sales to Net Assets | Sales ÷ Net Assets<br>Where: Net assets = Total Assets − Total Liabilities. | 1.3 | Unless the firm is over trading, a high ratio is a healthy indication. A low ratio may indicate unused capacity, especially if accompanied with a high ratio of fixed overheads to sales. |
| Sales to Fixed Assets | Sales ÷ Net Fixed Assets<br>Where: Net Fixed Assets = Purchase price − Depreciation + Leasehold Improvements − Total Liabilities. | 4.1 | Measures the utilisation of fixed assets. A low ratio may suggest ineffective use of fixed assets. However, this may also be due to recent fixed capital investment. One may consider using the book value of the fixed assets for net fixed assets. |
| Stock Turnover (days) | (Average Stock ÷ Cost of Sales) X 365 days | 64 | Shows the number of days stock held before it is sold. Average Stock = (Opening Stock + Closing Stock) ÷ 2 |
| Trade Credit Given (days) | (Average Debtors ÷ Sales) X 365 days | 86 | Measures the collection period in days of debtors. Average Debtors = (Opening Debtors + Closing Debtors) ÷ 2 |
| Trade Credit Taken (days) | (Average Creditors ÷ Purchase) X 365 days | 44 | Measures the payment period in days of creditors. Average Creditors = (Opening Creditors + Closing Creditors) ÷ 2 |
| Cash Cycle Duration (days) | Stock Turnover + Credit Period Given − Credit Period Taken | 106 | Measures the period of time between the purchase of stocks and receipt of cash from debtors for goods sold. |

**Capital Structure:**

| | | | |
|---|---|---|---|
| Equity to Total assets | (Capital + Reserves) ÷ Total Assets | 66% | Shows the percentage of total assets financed by the shareholders. |
| Fixed Assets to Equity | Net Fixed Assets ÷ (Capital + Reserves) | 31% | Shows the percentage of fixed assets financed by the shareholders. |
| Borrowing to Equity | (Long Term Liabilities + Current Liabilities) ÷ (Capital + Reserves) | 0.52 | Shows the proportion of external financing versus internal financing. |
| Gearing Ratio | Long Term Liabilities ÷ (Capital + Reserves) | 31% | Measures financial leverage, demonstrating the degree to which a firm's activities are funded by owner's funds versus creditor's funds. |
| Fixed Interest Cover | Fixed Interest Expense ÷ Net Profit Before Interest | 3% | Indicates how easily a firm can pay interest on outstanding debt. |

Table 10.9c  Financial Ratios (KPIs) by Application Category for GeoMed Limited (continued)

| Financial Ratio | Formulae | Ratio | Interpretation and/or Remarks |
|---|---|---|---|
| **Investment:** | | | |
| Net Asset Value per Share | Net Assets ÷ No. of Ordinary Shares<br>Where: Net assets = Total Assets − Total Liabilities | 3.65 | Represents the value of a share and may be viewed as the price at which shares are bought and sold. |
| Dividend Yield | Dividend per Share ÷ Market Price per Share (approximate) | 3% | Measures the real rate of return on an investment since it is based on the market price and not the nominal value. |
| Earnings per Share | Net Profit After Tax ÷ No. of Ordinary Shares | 2.7 | Indicates level of profitability, but it is limited when compared to dividend yield since number of shares remain constant. |
| Price Earnings Ratio | Market Price per Share ÷ Earnings per Share | 4.95 | The lower the price earnings ratio, the quicker the capital outlay is recovered. |
| Dividend Cover | Net Dividend ÷ Net Profit After Tax | 4% | It shows the amount available for distribution and demonstrates the plough back and dividend distribution policies of the company. |

the various financial ratios that may be applied for strategic performance management. As stated above, management must be selective in the KPIs that are chosen for performance measurement otherwise the performance management system at a strategic level becomes unmanageable. It is therefore suggested that a brainstorming session is conducted by senior executive management with the objective of selecting around five KPIs for each division to assess strategic performance.

As explained previously, KPIs are meant to measure organisational performance and help management to identify certain aspects that require improvement in the organisation's operations. As Table 10.9 illustrates, there are many financial ratios that may be applied as KPIs, which may be used to ensure that the defined strategy is implemented as planned. Figure 10.2 shows that there are various categories of KPIs that may be applied, including asset utilisation, profitability, liquidity, capital structure, and investment. However, recall that our current focus is the strategic level (i.e., the big picture). Therefore, it is necessary to choose those key indicators that address the big-picture strategic planning for the future direction of the organisation. Figure 10.3 provides a typical dashboard for GeoMed Limited regarding various financial rations. Figure 10.3 may be enhanced by using a colour scheme to show the safe, warning, and danger zones, thus making it more meaningful for management. The presented dashboard illustrates the adage that a picture is worth a thousand words.

The selected KPIs in Figure 10.3 focus on four key strategic aspects of GeoMed Limited, namely profitability (return on capital and return on equity); liquidity (current ratio); capital structure (debt to equity); and asset utilisation (cash cycle duration, inventory turnover, and trade credit given). These KPIs provide a very good picture of the financial performance status of GeoMed Limited. The KPIs related to profitability demonstrate that GeoMed Limited needs to improve its operating profit. Depending on the nature of the industry, a return on capital employed of 15% or more is likely to mean that the company is generating a return well above its weighted average cost of capital. Therefore, the company's return on capital employed of 9.3% needs to be improved. This is also confirmed by the return on equity KPI, which measures the ability of management to generate income from the equity available to it. A return of between 15% to 20% is considered satisfactory, which means that the return of 14.8% is marginally acceptable.

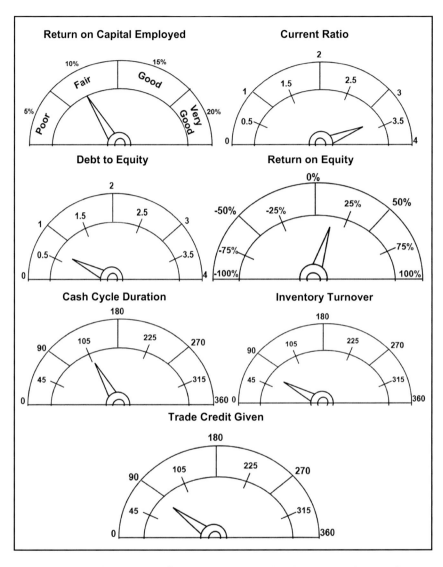

*Figure 10.3* Typical Dashboard for Financial KPIs Related to GeoMed Limited

The KPI regarding liquidity that is measured by the current ratio, which weighs all the company's current assets and liabilities suggests that GeoMed Limited has ample liquidity with a current ratio of 3.3. It is noted that a satisfactory current ratio is typically considered to be anywhere between 1.5 and 3. The capital structure KPI, which is measured by the debt-to-equity ratio, stands at 0.52. This suggests that GeoMed Limited is a low-risk investment for creditors and/or interested investors. This KPI reveals that for every $0.52 of debt, the company has $1.00 of assets.

As stated previously, the company's asset utilisation aspect is measured by three related KPIs, namely the cash cycle, inventory turnover, and trade credit given (accounts receivable). The cash cycle duration is normally measured in days. GeoMed's cash cycle stands at about 106 days, equivalent to 3.5 months, which is considered too long when compared to the normal benchmark of 30 to 45 days. A company with a shorter cash cycle has more working capital and less cash occupied in inventory and receivable accounts, which means it is less dependent on borrowed money. However, given the company's good liquidity position, this means the lengthy cash cycle is under control.

This is confirmed by the inventory turnover KPI, which stands at 64 days (about 2 months). Inventory turnover refers to the amount of time that occurs from the day an item is purchased by a company until it is sold. For most industries the inventory turnover cycle is 1–2 months. This provides a good balance between having enough inventory on hand and not having to reorder too frequently. The final KPI for the asset utilisation aspect is measured by the trade credit given (accounts receivable). The trade credit given measure refers to the money GeoMed's customers owe for goods or services they have received but not yet paid for. It is noted that a shorter average collection period (60 days or less) is generally preferable and indicates that the company has higher liquidity. Therefore, although the company's liquidity position is very good, it should try to reduce the trade credit given duration from 86 days to less than 60 days.

Moreover, the illustrated dashboards at Figure 10.3 may be enhanced by including a dial that shows the industry average (or the perceived best competitor in the industry). This enhancement would integrate the benchmarking concept with the desired KPIs for GeoMed Limited as an added technique for the representation of Strategic KPIs. If the information is available, the enhancement may also be applied to the non-financial KPIs. These non-financial KPIs are also important and need to be evaluated since they are useful in strategic planning and may be more department-specific. However, in this case study of GeoMed Limited the information related to these KPIs is not available. Therefore, fictitious data is being used for illustration purposes. Figure 10.4 shows various non-financial KPIs related to the customer and operations that may be depicted to management. The presented dashboard provides a simple but clear indication of the relationship between the organisation and the customer and operations.

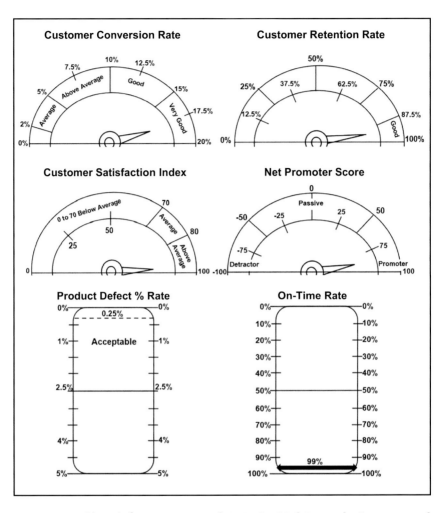

Figure 10.4 Dashboard for Non-Financial KPIs GeoMed Limited: Customer and Operations Category

The customer category non-financial KPIs consist of the customer conversion rate, customer retention rate, customer satisfaction index, and net promoter score, whilst the operations category consists of the product defect rate and the on-time delivery rate. The Conversion Rate KPI depends on the industry. However, generally a conversion rate of between 2% and 5% is considered average; 6% to 9% is considered above average; and anything over 10% is good. GeoMed's conversion rate at 18% is considered as being very good. The customer retention rate is the percentage of existing customers who remain customers after a given period. Generally, the better the customer retention rate, the more loyal the customers are. Generally, an employee retention rate of 90% or higher is deemed good, therefore at 98%, GeoMed's customer retention rate is very good and reflects the company's robust quality standards. The company's standing with the customer is also reflected by the customer satisfaction index, which is calculated at 99%.

This indicates an above average satisfaction rate. The final KPI for the customer category is the Net Promoter Score (NPS), which measures customer experience and predicts business growth. It provides an indication of the likelihood that customers will recommend a brand or service to others. With a score of 90, GeoMed's customers are classified as Promoters, who are loyal enthusiasts and will likely keep buying (or use the service) and refer others, thus fuelling growth. Figure 10.4 also shows the two selected KPIs for the operations category, namely the product defect rate calculated at 0.25% and the on-time delivery rate calculated at 99%. A product defect percentage rate of 1% is considered as good. Hence, GeoMed's KPI rate of 0.25% is considered to be excellent. The on-time delivery rate measures the percentage of time products were delivered promptly as scheduled and is shown as 99%. This again illustrates the excellent performance of GeoMed Limited for this aspect. Figure 10.5 is a continuation of the non-financial KPIs but in this case, they are related to the human resources category aspect of the company.

The KPIs for human resources have the objective to provide general performance information regarding learning and employee development growth. The salary competitiveness ratio (SCR) measures the extent that the current salary being offered by the organisation is competitive when compared with the salary being offered by competitors or the industry average. This KPI for GeoMed has been determined at 12.5%. Typically, the organisation should aim to offer employees a competitive salary of between 5% to 10% above the industry averages. Hence, GeoMed Limited is considered as a good employer in terms of salary. The employee productivity rate KPI measures workforce efficiency over time and provides the organisation a clear view of whether the company's employees are doing their job effectively. Generally, the average worker productivity rating is 60% or less each day. Therefore, GeoMed's productivity rating of 85% is very high. This score may also reflect the fact that the salaries paid are far above the industry average and that the company's production incentive scheme is giving the desired results.

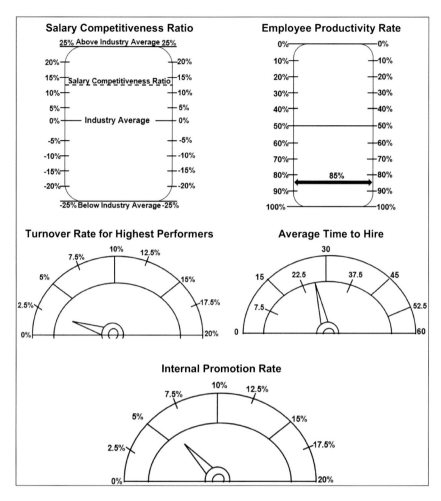

Figure 10.5  Dashboard for Non-Financial KPIs GeoMed Limited: Human Resources
Category

Another informative KPI is the turnover rate for highest performers. This
KPI measures the success of the retention efforts to hold on to top performers and the plans for talent replacement. This KPI is normally computed
annually or at any given time when the HR team fails to retain its valuable
human assets. It is desirable that the turnover rate for the highest performers is 0%. However, at times a 3% rate is acceptable. Therefore, a 2% rating
for GeoMed's turnover rate for highest performers is marginally acceptable
and management needs to investigate further to determine the cause and
lower the turnover rate further. The average time to hire KPI measures

the efficiency of the overall recruiting process of an organisation in relation to the time to recruit, interview, and hire. The measurement value of
the average time to hire KPI depends on the industry type. For instance,
research shows that the manufacturing industry value of the average time
to hire is 30.7 days. Therefore, GeoMed's average time to hire being 25
days is below the industry average. One should note that fast hiring might
mean that the organisation is not screening candidates thoroughly enough
and risks making bad hires.

On the other hand, slow hiring could result in competitors securing the
best candidates. Hence, the objective is to speed up administrative tasks
and streamline communication to candidates. The final KPI for the human
resources category is the internal promotion rate. This measures the opened
positions in an organisation that are filled internally by selecting the best
talent to fill vacant positions. This process aids organisations to assess the
internal talent's capability to satisfy different roles. Generally, research
suggests that organisations promote 8.9% of employees internally, while
new recruits are typically at 30.2%. At the supervisory levels, organisations
promoted more internally than they hired externally (17.2% of managers
are promoted, while 15.6% are new hires). Therefore, GeoMed's internal
promotion rate of 5.5% is rather low and should be improved as this might
boost overall employee motivation.

As one may appreciate, there are many more KPIs that may be calculated and provided to management. However, it is important that the performance management rating process is manageable. Therefore, there is a
need to be selective and that only the important strategic KPIs should be
displayed, otherwise the system will become unwieldy. There are literally
hundreds of KPIs to choose from, so focus on the ones that make the most
substance for your organisation's strategy.

## KPIs for Budgeting and Forecasting at Departmental Level for GeoMed Limited

KPIs for budgeting and business planning are very useful for monitoring
and regulating the organisation's financial health and operational efficiency.
These KPIs can provide organisations, irrespective of their size, with the
ability to gain quick insights into their internal operations. For illustration purposes, five additional KPIs have been selected that may be applied
to individual departments or responsibility units in relation to budgeting

Table 10.10  Additional KPIs for GeoMed Limited Related to Budgeting and Forecasting

| Financial Ratio | Formulae | Ratio | Interpretation and/or Remarks |
|---|---|---|---|
| Operating Cash Flow (direct method) | OCF = Total Revenue – Operating Expenses<br><br>OCF ratio = OCF ÷ Current Liabilities | 1.5 | OCF shows the total earnings generated by a specific responsibility unit from its daily business operations. OCF ratio should be close to 1:1, since a much smaller ratio suggests that the responsibility unit is obtaining most of its cash flow from sources other than its core operating capabilities. |
| Net Profit Margin | (Net Profit ÷ Revenue) x 100 | 8.8% | This KPI shows how much net profit is generated as a percentage of revenue and reveals the efficiency of the organisation at generating profit compared to its revenue. A net profit margin greater than 10% is viewed as excellent but it depends on the industry. |
| Gross Profit Margin | (Gross Profit ÷ Sales) x 100 | 23% | The ratio shows the margin that is being earned on sales. It measures a company's manufacturing and distribution efficiency during the production process. Note that gross margin tends to remain stable over time. |
| Current Accounts Receivable Turnover | Net credit sales ÷ average accounts receivable<br><br>Net credit sales = sales on credit – sales returns – sales allowances | 4.2 | In general, a higher accounts receivable turnover ratio is favourable, and companies should strive for at least a ratio of 1.0 to ensure it collects the full amount of the average accounts receivable at least one time during a period. |
| Sales Growth | (Current sales – Sales previous period) ÷ Sales previous period) | 6.9% | The metric measures the ability of the sales/service team to increase revenue over a fixed period by showing the change in total sales generated over a certain period. A sales growth of 5% to 10% is normally seen as being acceptable for very large organisations, while sales growth of over 10% is more applicable to smaller organisations. |

and forecasting to determine whether they are achieving the prerequisite targets for maintaining profitable operations. Unfortunately, the data available is related to the holistic organisation and is not on a departmental basis. However, the techniques being illustrated below may be applied at a responsibility unit or department level depending on the level of detail and quality of the available data. Table 10.10 shows how these additional KPIs may be calculated. It should be noted that the resulting calculations are based upon the data from GeoMed's financial statements that are illustrated in Table 10.3 to Table 10.8. The accuracy of the computations is dependent on the level of data available and some modifications have been made for illustrative purposes.

The additional KPIs are related to operating cash flow (OCF) using the direct method; net profit margin; gross profit margin; current accounts receivable turnover; and sales growth. The dashboard for these KPIs is shown at Figure 10.6. The objective of the OCF is to provide the total amount of earnings generated by a department or specific responsibility unit from its daily business operations. OCF is calculated by two methods, namely the direct or indirect approach. In the example provided the direct approach is being used. The OCF ratio is calculated by dividing OCF by the current liabilities.

This KPI implies whether a segment (department or responsibility unit) of an organisation can sustain a healthy cash flow position required to take advantage of growth opportunities or needs external financing to deal with the outstanding expenses. In other words, OCF ratio assesses the department's (or responsibility unit's) ability to generate sufficient cash inflow through its business activities. Preferably, the OCF ratio should be close to 1:1, since a much smaller ratio suggests that the department or responsibility unit is obtaining a great deal of its cash flow from sources other than its core operating capabilities. GeoMed's OCF ratio stands at 1.5, which suggests that the company as a whole is generating cash flow from its core operating capabilities. As stated previously, if the data was available, this KPI should be calculated on a responsibility unit (or department) basis to illustrate if there are any weak operational segments within the organisation. It is also suggested that OFC is contrasted to total capital employed to evaluate whether the department or responsibility unit is generating sufficient capital to maintain positive accounts.

The net profit margin measures how much net income or profit is generated as a percentage of revenue and reveals the efficiency of the

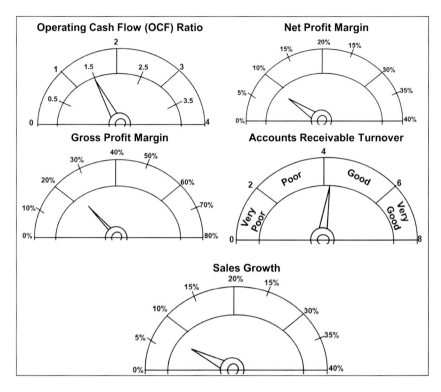

Figure 10.6  Dashboard for Additional KPIs Related to Budgeting and Forecasting for GeoMed Limited

responsibility unit (or department) at generating profit compared to its revenue. However, once again the level of data detail has prevented the calculation from being computed on an organisational segmentation basis. This KPI highlights how much of each currency unit earned (e.g., dollar) by a specific organisational segment translates into profits; thus reflecting the organisation's profitability and suggesting the rate at which the organisation may grow in the long-term. Generally, a net profit margin greater than 10% is viewed as excellent; however, it depends on the industry and the structure of the organisation being examined. Therefore, GeoMed's net profit margin of 8.8% is regarded as being very good.

The gross profit margin KPI measures the profitability of an organisation (or organisation segment) by revealing the amount of revenue remaining in an accounting period after the organisation pays for the cost of goods sold. The ratio indicates the percentage of each currency unit (e.g., dollar) of revenue that the organisation retains as gross profit. This metric is a better indicator of an organisation's financial health because it shows whether an organisation has the capacity of paying its operating expenses while having funds left for growth. Hence, the higher the percentage, the more the organisation retains on each currency unit of sales to service its other costs and obligations.

Typically, organisations have a somewhat stable gross profit margin statistic unless the organisation has made several radical changes that affect production costs or pricing policies. GeoMed's gross profit margin stands at 23%, which means that for every dollar of revenue generated, $0.23 is retained while $0.77 is attributed to the cost of goods sold. It is also noted that GeoMed's gross profit margin has been constantly decreasing since 2020. Its gross profit margin was recorded at 28%, 25%, and 23% for 2020, 2021, and 2022 respectively. This decrease is likely to be due to the COVID-19 pandemic. However, one should note that a gross profit margin ratio of 50% to 70% would be considered healthy for many types of businesses, such as retailers, restaurants, manufacturers, and other producers of goods. Therefore, GeoMed needs to determine whether the concern is a general occurrence or whether certain organisational segments are the cause of the concern.

The accounts receivable turnover KPI reveals the organisation's effectiveness in collecting debts and extending credits. Accounts receivable turnover ratio suggests how many times the accounts receivables have been collected during an accounting period. GeoMed has an accounts receivable turnover of 4.2, which is considered as being good. Companies should strive for at least a ratio of 1.0 to ensure that they collect the full amount of the average accounts receivable at least one time during a period. Thus, the higher the turnover, the faster the business is collecting its receivables and the less likely that the organisation is striving to collect debts and payments, and the more likely it is to have liquidity for investing in growth and innovation.

The last metric shown is sales growth. This metric measures the ability of the sales/service team to increase revenue over a fixed period by showing the change in total sales generated over a certain period. The sales growth metric provides the percentage of the current sales period compared to the previous one, giving the growth or decrease in total sales. Like the other KPIs, if the data is available, the sales growth metric can be displayed by the individual (or group of) products or services within a specific segment of the organisation. Certain research literature suggests that a sales growth of 5% to 10% is normally seen as being acceptable for very large organisations, while sales growth of over 10% is more applicable to smaller organisations. Therefore, GeoMed's sales growth of 6.9% is within the normal acceptable range. Because sales growth discloses the increase in sales over a specific period, it provides an investor with an indication of whether the demand for the organisation's products and/or services will be increasing in the future.

## Standard Cost Systems and Variance Analysis at Component Level for GeoMed Ltd

Chapter 5 provided an overview of standard cost systems and the associated variance analysis calculations. GeoMed's data does not provide information at a component level. Therefore, the information to illustrate the standard cost and variance analysis approach will need to be based upon assumptions. However, the application of the standard cost and variance analysis approach is still valid and applicable to a variety of organisations. The standard cost approach is based upon the concept of having target costs for each operation that can be built up to produce a product standard cost. These targeted costs are established after a detail study of the production (or service) process.

In manufacturing industries, industrial engineers conduct a scientific study of the operation to establish the standard cost of the operation. Hence, production budgets are based upon the established standard cost of the operations to produce a component or product or service. Therefore, by establishing standard costs for each unit produced, it is possible to analyse in detail any differences between budgeted costs and actual costs. This process is referred to as variance analysis and enables cost to be controlled more effectively, and the performance of a specific cost centre to be determined accurately. Standard costing is suited for organisations whose activities consist of a series of common or repetitive operations and the input required to produce each unit of output can be specified. Standard costing systems are most suitable to manufacturing but are also applicable to service industries, such as banks, hospitality, and public services, amongst many others as long as their processes are repetitive operations and the input required to produce (or service) each unit of output can be specified.

This section will consider a single component that is manufactured by GeoMed Limited. The information related to this component is shown below. It should be noted that GeoMed Limited may have hundreds of components that are part of their standard cost system. In such an environment a comprehensive computerised system would be implemented. Furthermore, the computerised system would produce exception reports related to those operations that are above or below the established standard. It should be noted that a standard cost system reports on operations related to responsibility unit. Therefore, this specifically addresses the performance of an individual or team and the responsibility unit manager.

## Selected Component Information

Variance Analysis takes into consideration the standard cost card (KPIs) and compares them with the budgeted and actual outcome to determine the likely reason for the difference (i.e., variance). This enables management to take the appropriate corrective action that will impact future activities. Figure 5.14 (from Chapter 5) provides a breakdown of the variances into component cost and revenue variances that can be calculated for a standard variable costing system. The emphasis for this section is the various levels of the total production cost variance. GeoMed Limited produces several automobile switches. Table 10.11 shows the company's standard cost card for one of the components GeoMed Limited manufactures in a single operation. Overhead is applied to the products based on direct labour hours with the level of activity being 4100 hours. In March, GeoMed Limited produced 3050 components. The fixed overhead expense budget was $24,600. The actual costs in March are shown at Table 10.12. The variance analysis calculations using the standard and actual cost data for March is found at Table 10.13.

Table 10.11  GeoMed Limited Standard Cost Card for a Component Manufactured in a Single Operation

| Standard Cost Card for Component-X: Operation 1. | $ |
|---|---|
| (a) Direct Materials 6 items per component at $0.50 per item. | 3.00 |
| (b) Direct Labour (1.3 hours per component at $8.00 per hour) | 10.40 |
| (c) Variable Overhead (1.3 hours per component at $4.00 per hour) | 5.20 |
| (d) Fixed manufacturing overhead (1.3 hours per component at $6.00 per hour) | 7.80 |

Table 10.12  GeoMed Limited Actual Cost for March for a Component Manufactured in a Single Operation

| Actual Cost for Component-X: Operation 1. | $ |
|---|---|
| (a) Direct Materials 25,000 items at $0.48 per item. | 12,000.00 |
| (b) Direct Labour (4,000 hours) | 36,000.00 |
| (c) Variable manufacturing overhead | 17,000.00 |
| (d) Fixed manufacturing overhead | 25,000.00 |

Table 10.13  GeoMed Limited Variance Analysis Calculations for March for the Manufactured Component

| Variance Details | Formulae | Outcome |
|---|---|---|
| Price Material Variance: | (Actual Qty X Standard Price) − (Actual Qty X Actual Price) | $500 Favourable |
| Quantity Material Variance: | (Standard Qty X Standard Price) − (Actual Qty X Standard Price) | $3350 Adverse |
| Labour Rate Variance: | (Actual Hrs X Standard Rate) − (Actual Hrs X Actual Rate) | $4000 Adverse |
| Labour Efficiency Variance: | (Standard Hrs X Standard Rate) − (Actual Hrs X Standard Rate) | $280 Adverse |
| Fixed Budgeted Overhead Variance: | (Denominator level of activity X Standard Rate) − (Actual Fixed Overhead Cost) | $400 Adverse |
| Fixed Volume Overhead Variance: | (Standard Hrs X Standard Rate) −- (Denominator level of activity X Standard Rate) | $810 Adverse |
| Variable Expenditure Variance: | (Denominator level of activity X Standard Rate) − (Actual Fixed Overhead Cost) | $600 Adverse |
| Variable Efficiency Variance: | (Standard Hrs X Standard Rate) − (Denominator level of activity X Standard Rate) | $540 Adverse |

## Interpretation of Variance Analysis Findings

Management would need to examine the outcome of the variance analysis results (as shown in Table 10.13) to determine the cause of both the favourable and adverse variances. In a practical environment only those above or below an established tolerance (say ±5%) would be examined, otherwise the system would become unmanageable. Note that in the above case study there are four categories of variances, namely material, labour, variable overheads, and fixed overheads. Looking specifically at the material variances, these consist of the material usage and material price variances. The material usage variance is under the full control of the responsibility centre manager.

Furthermore, there are several reasons for an adverse (or favourable) variance regarding material utilisation. Considering the material usage variance from an adverse viewpoint, possible reasons include procuring poor quality materials; irresponsible handling of materials by production employees; petty theft; modifying quality control specifications; and variations in production methods. Note that separate material usage variances must be computed for each material type used by each responsibility centre. An adverse material price variance may result from demand-supply considerations (e.g., a shortage of supply or high demand) or carelessness of the procurement department.

Like the material variance, a labour variance may be due to the applicable rate (price) and efficiency. It should be noted that the labour efficiency variance is normally under the control of the production responsibility centre manager and an adverse variance is often caused by using inferior quality materials; having different grades of labour with varying experience levels; frequent breakdowns due to the failure to maintain machinery in a good condition; installing new equipment or tooling that requires a learning process; and unreported alteration in the production process. An adverse labour rate variance is often caused by having a relaxed overtime policy. Another cause could be due to wage adjustments that have not been reflected in the labour standard.

The next group of variances is related to the variable overheads. Generally, the variable overhead expenditure varies with direct labour and machine hours of input. The variable overheads are also determined by two factors, namely the price variance (i.e., actual overhead cost being different from budgeted cost) and the quantity variance resulting from actual direct labour or machine hours of input being different from the hours of input that have been used. Therefore, these two factors give rise to two sub-variances, the variable overhead expenditure variance and the variable overhead efficiency variance. Note that the variable overhead expenditure consists of a diverse number of individual cost items, such as indirect labour (e.g., management supervision); indirect materials (e.g., grease and oil for machinery; cleaning fluids; and oil rags); electricity; and maintenance, amongst many others.

An adverse variable overhead expenditure and efficiency variance may occur due to several reasons, namely, increase in the prices of individual overhead items; unproductive utilisation of the individual overhead items; and wasteful use of utilities, such as leaving lights on during lunch breaks. The variable overhead expenditure on its own is not very informative, but comparing the actual expenditure for each individual item of variable overhead expenditure against budget may reveal the cause of the variance and the corrective action that is required.

With a variable costing system, fixed manufacturing overheads are not unitised and allocated to products; rather they are charged as an expense in the period in which they are incurred. Moreover, fixed costs are assumed to remain unchanged in the short-term in response to changes in the level of operational activity, but they may change in response to other factors. For instance, a price increase for indirect materials and labour may trigger an increase in fixed overheads costs. The fixed overhead expenditure variance explains the difference between the budgeted fixed overhead costs and the actual fixed overheads incurred. The fixed overhead expenditure variance on its own is not very informative. However, it becomes meaningful when one compares each item of fixed overhead expenditure against the budget. The differences may be due to a modification in the salaries paid to supervisors, such as an appointment (or promotion) of additional supervisors. Generally, fixed overhead expenditure tends to be uncontrollable in the short-term.

Considering GeoMed's variance analysis results at Table 10.13, it is noted that the quantity (usage) material variance and the labour rate variance are somewhat high and need further investigation. As stated previously, the material usage variance is under the full control of the responsibility centre manager. Unless the quality control specifications and/or product methods have been modified, a possible cause of the adverse material usage variance is the irresponsible handling of materials by production employees and/or petty theft. However, the favourable material price variance may indicate that cheaper (lower quality) material was procured, leading to poor labour handling and higher wastage. This is somewhat confirmed by the rather high adverse labour rate variance (coupled with an adverse labour efficiency variance), which is likely to be due to the use of inferior quality materials, particularly if different grades of labour with varying experience levels are being utilised for the process. A detailed investigation into the production process would reveal the true cause for the variances.

### General Lessons Learnt from the GeoMed Ltd Case Study

The GeoMed Ltd case study has demonstrated that performance management tools using KPIs may be applied at three general organisational levels. Figure 10.7 explains this three-level concept. At an organisational holistic level, it is possible to monitor the organisational strategic plan by using financial and non-financial strategic KPIs. These are illustrated by the dashboards at Figure 10.3 to Figure 10.5. The selected KPIs in Figure 10.3 focus on four key strategic aspects, namely profitability; liquidity; capital structure; and asset utilisation. These KPIs provide a very good holistic picture of the financial performance status of GeoMed Ltd. The KPIs at the business planning divisional level are very useful for monitoring and regulating the

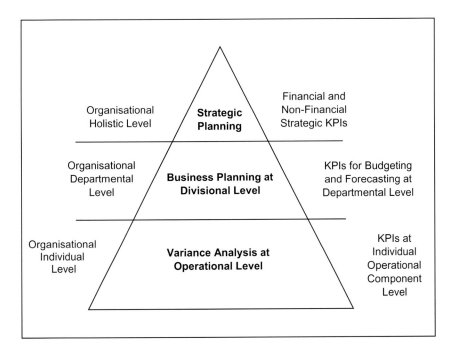

Figure 10.7 Application of Performance Management Tools Using KPIs at Three Organisational Levels

organisation's financial health and operational efficiency on a divisional (departmental) and/or sub-departmental level.

These KPIs can provide organisations, irrespective of their size, with the ability to gain quick insights into their internal departmental operations. Figure 10.6 shows the dashboard for the KPIs related to budgeting and forecasting for GeoMed Limited. For illustration purposes, five additional KPIs have been selected that may be applied to individual departments or responsibility units in relation to budgeting and forecasting to determine whether they are achieving the prerequisite targets for maintaining profitable operations.

The third level is more detailed and is applicable to components and individual operations that comprise each component. In a practical sense, this level may be applied to individual operators or teams of operators, under a responsibility cost centre, namely the unit manager or foreman. This may be achieved by applying a standard costing system and implementing a variance analysis operations management control process. The standard costing system would establish the KPIs for each operation that comprises a component and can be extended to a product level by the accumulation of the costs (and their respective KPIs) that comprise all the components within the product. It should be noted that an organisation may have hundreds of components (and numerous operations that make up a component) that may form part of their standard cost system.

In such an environment, a comprehensive computerised system would be required. Moreover, the computerised system would produce exception reports related to those operations that are above or below the established standard. It should be noted that a standard cost system reports on operations related to responsibility unit. Therefore, this specifically addresses the performance of an individual or team and the responsibility unit manager.

## *Other Applicable Performance Management Tools for GeoMed Ltd*

As stated at the beginning of this chapter, the GeoMed Ltd case study is based on available and created information. Therefore, only a limited number of performance management tools using KPIs could be demonstrated. The previous chapters have covered numerous other performance management tools using KPIs that could not, for practical reasons, be demonstrated in this particular chapter. These additional performance management tools using KPIs include: The Critical Success Factors methodology; Balanced Scorecard and Benchmarking; Six Sigma methodologies; Business Excellence Models; Enterprise Risk Management; and Programme Management. However, each of these additional performance management tools have been individually addressed in sufficient detail in the various chapters.

## Conclusion

The objective of this chapter was to illustrate the use of the various performance management tools that were described in previous chapters and apply them in a private sector environment. A case study approach was utilised to demonstrate the utility of the performance management tools selected.

## References

Camilleri, E. and Camilleri, R. (2017). *Accounting for Financial Instruments: A Guide to Valuation and Risk Management*. Oxford and New York: Routledge.

# 11

---

# APPLICATION OF
# THE PERFORMANCE
# MANAGEMENT TOOLS

## PUBLIC SECTOR

'Designing a winning strategy is the art of asking questions. Experimenting and then constantly renewing the thinking process by questioning the answers. No matter how good today's strategy is you must always keep reinventing it.'

Constantinos Markides
Academic and Author

This chapter will focus as much as practically possible on the application of the performance management tools in a public sector environment. The public sector is a critical and essential part of the economy, which is comprised of both public services and public enterprises. The distinction between public services and public enterprises is important due to the strategic and operational differences. Most public enterprises operate on a similar basis as private enterprises. Hence, public enterprises, or state-owned enterprises, are self-financing commercial enterprises that are under public ownership, which provide various private goods and services for sale and usually operate on a commercial basis.

DOI: 10.4324/9781032685465-14

They are managed by a Board of Directors, headed by an executive or non-executive chairperson. Therefore, the performance management tools applicable are similar to the private sector enterprises. On the other hand, public services are provided by government departments, within a Ministry, such as infrastructure, public education, health care and those working for the government itself, such as elected officials. Public sector departments are normally headed by a permanent secretary, with each department being administered and managed by a Director General and several directors according to an annual government budget allocation.

This chapter will focus on the government of an EU member state and specifically on public service provision, such as health and education. The actual name of the country will not be revealed and the information regarding the selected organisation will be extracted from published financial estimates (i.e. budget) and other relevant reports. Various data will at times be modified to accommodate the use of various techniques. Furthermore, additional fictional information may be included to substitute missing data and other information to permit several analytical approaches to be conducted for illustrative purposes. Accordingly, a complete case study will be defined from the accumulation of all this information with the objective of explaining the application of the performance management tools and demonstrating their use. The final analytical results from this exercise should not be construed to be a real assessment of the selected organisation.

## Description of Selected Governmental Organisation

The selected governmental organisation is an EU member state within the Euro zone with a unicameralism type of legislature that consists of a democratically elected House of Representatives. By constitutional law, all government ministers, including the Prime Minister, must be members of the House of Representatives. The House of Representatives is presided over by the Speaker of the House and the President is appointed for a five-year term by a resolution of the House. The president is the constitutional head of state and is responsible for the appointment of the judiciary. Executive authority is nominally vested in the President, but is in practice exercised by the Prime Minister.

The Public Administration consists of the public service and the public sector, which engages approximately 22% of the total number of gainfully occupied persons in the country. The public service acts as the backbone of the country's economy through the generation and implementation of government policy. The public service under examination consists of employees who serve in departments, directorates, schools, and health centres, among others, whereas the public sector consists of agencies, authorities, and entities where the government is the main shareholder. Hence, the focus of this chapter is the public service.

The public service consists of public officers who endeavour to provide a service of excellence to the general public and is guided by the core values of integrity, respect, loyalty, trust, quality, accountability, impartiality, and non-discrimination. The leadership of this governmental organisation necessitates the setting out of a strategy with the appropriate vision and mission as a roadmap to guide the way towards the achievement of the various initiatives and projects. The focus of the strategy has aimed at increasing the number of services provided online and accessible 24/7 from anywhere, and the continual improvement in service delivery to achieve a service of excellence.

## Applicable Strategic Performance Management KPIs for the Public Service

This section will focus on several strategic performance management KPIs for government, specifically the public service. A government KPI is a quantifiable measure that the public service applies to evaluate its general performance. It should be noted that government KPIs have the same objective as those KPIs used by the private sector. Typically, government KPIs demonstrate the organisation's overall performance and its accountability to its stakeholders. They serve two important purposes; namely they report important information to citizens and provide information that directly describes the government's activities.

Democratic governments are mainly accountable for the social welfare and growth of society. The citizens and the business community cannot assess their government's performance unless they have access to regular reporting on measurable key performance metrics. In other words, there is an essential need for society to generally understand and evaluate significant strategic KPIs so that an assessment may be made as to whether governments are fulfilling their commitment to responsible spending and transparency, and for the citizen to verify whether the required services are being effectively delivered.

Governmental KPIs have two significant characteristics; namely that they govern what is essential and critical to the success of the target organisation and specify the projected level of performance that needs to be achieved. However, it is important that government has a mechanism in place to ensure that the information available is of the highest quality and that an appropriate business intelligence engine is secured. Moreover, it is important that suitable metrics are identified that are predictive (leading) and corrective (lagging) with the aim of forecasting and reporting performance. These suitable metrics are to focus and underline the application of the available resources to indicate their level of efficiency and to exhibit how these resources have achieved the desired results to demonstrate their effectiveness. Furthermore, it is necessary that the selected metrics are cross-sectional by ensuring that the KPIs cover each individual division and department within the organisation.

It should be noted that some KPIs have a higher influence on the success of the organisation. Therefore, it may be necessary to assign weight to the selected KPIs. Furthermore, it is essential that the metrics reflect the organisation's mission. It should be recognised that missions and strategies change. Therefore, organisations need to regularly review whether their KPIs are valid and ensure that circumstances have not changed and that they are still aligned with the operational strategies. This approach will enable management to determine whether the measures within various teams are contributing towards strengthening accountability in every department and are permitting all employees to share in the organisation's success. This action-feedback approach allows the government management team to review and substantiate if the selected KPIs are balanced, weighed, and current. Obviously, the frequency of action-feedback reviewing cycle is normally dependent upon the available resources and the budget cycle.

It is also important that all KPIs have a target and a stretch value assigned to them. It is wrong to assume that all KPIs should be stretch targets, meaning that they are only achievable through radical change or innovation. Hence, if government achieves its KPI targets, it is successful. However, if it achieves its stretch values, it is performing exceptionally well. This requires a very high degree of buy-in, knowledge, support, and belief. Therefore, governments should apply broadly accepted and evidence-based benchmarks for their target and stretch values.

It is also critical to define a baseline for each KPI as soon as it is identified and defined. This KPI baseline is used for comparison purposes and will facilitate the analysis of the metrics. Hence, in order to comprehend and recognise the current performance status of an organisation, it is essential for management as decision-makers to assess the KPIs and their trend through time. Management needs to explore the analysis in depth since KPIs will reveal bits and pieces of where the organisation has been and where it will be proceeding. Therefore, management needs to take appropriate action on the revelations that KPIs provide. Management must have faith and trust the KPIs when it comes to decision-making and view them as an opportunity to improve and maximise performance. Exploiting and tracking an organisation's KPIs will give management the opportunity to improve matters and achieve a high-performing organisation.

The public service covers an enormous scope of activities. Hence, there is a vast repository of government KPIs that may be chosen. Therefore, the following sections will focus on a selected number of governmental KPIs that are classified into five categories: Finance, operations, services, citizens, and human resources, to give a cross-sectional view of the organisation under study. These five categories of KPIs will be examined at three levels, namely national, ministerial, and departmental. Further levels may be possible depending on the information available. However, for the purpose of demonstrating the application of KPIs to determine the entity's performance, the three mentioned levels will be used. Moreover, the KPIs at a national level will be compared with several countries. Note that this comparison is only possible at a national level since the portfolio of the various ministries within a country tends to differ from country to country.

## Cross-Sectional Categories of KPIs for Public Service: National Level

Table 11.1 provides an itemised list of cross-sectional categories of KPIs for the public service. As stated previously, five categories of KPIs will be discussed that include: Finance, operations, services, citizens, and human resources. Furthermore, Table 11.2 shows the various KPI values for each category related to the target country and three other countries for comparison purposes.

*Table 11.1* Cross-Sectional Categories of KPIs for the Public Service

| KPI Details | Formulae |
|---|---|
| Financial Category | Budgeting ratio = Operating Cost ÷ Revenue<br>Revenue per capita = Revenue ÷ Population<br>Operating cost per capita = Operating cost ÷ Population<br>Near-term solvency = Short term debt ÷ Revenue<br>Debt per capita = Total Gov Debt ÷ Population<br>Personnel and administration cost ratio = Personnel and administration ÷ Operating Cost<br>Bond rating |
| Operational Category | Audit findings resolved (%)<br>Ombudsman findings resolved (%) |
| Service Category | Government effectiveness<br>Provision of public services (%)<br>User-centricity of government digital services (index)<br>Digital public services for citizens (0–100)<br>Digital public services for business (0–100)<br>E-Government users interacting with public authorities (%) |
| Citizen Category | National voter turnout (%)<br>Public satisfaction (%)<br>Transparency of government (0-100)<br>Tendency to trust national government (%)<br>Tendency to trust the public administration (%) |
| HR Category | Employee retention rate = number of employees who have left the workforce ÷ total number of staff (%)<br>Women in senior administrator positions (%)<br>Share of government employees under 39 years (%)<br>Share of government employees over 55 years (%) |

*Table* 11.2  Values for Cross-Sectional Categories of KPIs Related to Target Country and Other Countries

| KPI | Formulae | Countries | | | |
|---|---|---|---|---|---|
| | | Target | 1 | 2 | 3 |
| Financial Category | Budgeting ratio (%) | 110.7 | 101.6 | 149.4 | 80.90 |
| | Revenue per capita | 9692 | 5167 | 3719 | 953 |
| | Operating cost per capita | 10726 | 5252 | 5482 | 771 |
| | Near-term solvency (%) | 12.0 | 12.8 | 14.3 | 17.8 |
| | Debt per capita | 15431 | 28201 | 43215 | 46687 |
| | Personnel & administration cost ratio (%) | 25.0 | 22.0 | 29.7 | 30.7 |
| | Bond rate (%) 10-year average | 2.85 | 2.15 | 2.67 | 4.18 |
| Operation Category | Audit findings resolved (%) | 80 | 82 | 75 | 55 |
| | Ombudsman findings resolved (%) | 93 | 85 | 70 | 45 |
| Service Category | Government effectiveness (%) | 77.88 | 87.98 | 86.06 | 64.90 |
| | Provision of public services (%) | 69.0 | 66.0 | 42.0 | 30.0 |
| | User-centricity of government digital services (index) | 100 | 88.0 | 90.4 | 90.8 |
| | Digital public services for citizens (0–100) | 99.6 | 41.0 | 35.8 | 48.3 |
| | Digital public services for business (0–100) | 95.0 | 80.0 | 88.6 | 84.6 |
| | % eGovernment users interacting with public authorities | 63.0 | 66.0 | 64.1 | 58.6 |
| Citizen Category | National voter turnout (%) | 85.5 | 55.5 | 72.0 | 63.8 |
| | Public satisfaction (%) | 79.0 | 35.0 | 31.5 | 57.0 |
| | Transparency of government (0–100) | 97.1 | 66.6 | 69.5 | 75.3 |
| | Tendency to trust national government (%) | 46.0 | 50.0 | 24.0 | 25.0 |
| | Tendency to trust the public administration (%) | 56.0 | 64.0 | 67.0 | 42.0 |
| HR Category | Employee retention rate (%) | 97.8 | 90.0 | 91.0 | 96.0 |
| | Women in senior administrator positions (%) | 44.6 | 30.0 | 36.8 | 28.0 |
| | Share of government employees under 39 years (%) | 56.1 | 40.5 | 48.2 | 38.9 |
| | Share of government employees over 55 years (%) | 15.6 | 35.0 | 33.8 | 45.2 |

Note: Some country figures are fictitious and are used for illustrative purposes.

## *Finance Category*

The finance category consists of seven individual KPIs, namely the budgeting ratio; revenue per capita; operating cost per capita; near-term solvency; debt per capita; personnel and administration cost ratio; and bond rating. The *budgeting ratio* is basically a ratio of the public sector operating cost as a proportion of its revenue. This metric consists of two components, namely government revenue and government operating cost. Government revenue is mainly generated through the application of taxes and awarded grants. For example, the allocation of funds or subvention to the local councils by the central government. Another example is the grants provided by the European Union to a number of its member countries.

In many countries, central governments have the sole authority to apply taxes. This is known as tax autonomy. A local or regional government that is able to define its own tax bases, tax rates, and other characteristics of a tax has a high degree of tax autonomy or taxing power. Hence, governments that have tax autonomy are authorised to initiate or abolish a tax or establish tax rates. Where countries share taxes between central and sub-central governments, the sub-central governments do not have tax autonomy, but they may be able to negotiate a tax sharing system with the central government. The other component of the budgeting ratio is government operating cost. Public service operating cost is basically the amount expended on administration, personnel, and logistics. Governments need to monitor their budgeting ratio to ensure the highest level of transparency and accountability to its citizens.

Table 11.2 illustrates that the target country has a budgeting ratio (expressed as a percentage of revenue) of 110.7. When compared with the other three countries, the budgeting ratio appears high with two of the benchmark countries. It should be noted that a rising budgeting ratio indicates a potential expenditure mismanagement concern and must be addressed with urgency. On the other hand, a decreasing budgeting ratio may indicate better control on expenditure. However, an acute decreasing budgeting ratio may suggest that the government is not spending enough to improve the quality of life of its citizens. It should be noted that the budgeting ratio is the most important financial key performance measure for government organisations, since it monitors the amount of income and expenditure of the organisation. In the example from Table 11.2, the target country is spending more than what it is collecting as revenue. However, this situation is likely to be a short-term manoeuvre as a result of the COVID-19 pandemic.

The next KPI is *revenue per capita*, which is calculated by dividing government revenue by the country's population size. A rising revenue per capita is a desirable feature since it indicates that a government is in position to expand its range of services. Table 11.2 suggests that the target country has a much higher revenue per capita when compared with the benchmark countries, indicating that the target country is in a better position to expand its services to its citizens. It should be noted that a declining revenue per capita is worrying and should be identified immediately since it hampers the government's capacity to deliver on its electoral promises. Closely related to the revenue per capita KPI is the *operating cost per capita*. This KPI is calculated by dividing the operating cost by the population size. Table 11.2 shows that the target country has a much higher operating cost per capita than the three benchmark countries. This confirms that the government is expanding its services and delivering on its electoral undertakings. Care needs to be taken to ensure that the operating cost per capita is close to the revenue per capita. However, this situation is likely to be a result of the COVID-19 pandemic and is likely to be resolved in the short-term.

Another important KPI is the *near-term solvency* rate. This public service KPI indicates the government's capacity to settle its short-term obligations. Table 11.2 shows that the target country has a near-term solvency rating of 12%, which is somewhat lower than the benchmark countries. The figures suggest that the target country is in a good position to meet its short-term obligations. However, it must monitor this KPI closely to reassess its priorities and avoid ending up in a situation where it is grappling with its debt. Therefore, the public service organisation must regularly conduct a risk analysis, and a debt management strategy must be defined and implemented. The *debt per capita* takes into account the total government debt divided by its population. This measure provides government with a good understanding of the size of the government debt relative to the number of citizens. Table 11.2 shows that the target country has a debt per capita which is much lower than the benchmark countries. Thus confirming the previous indicators that the government's debt is under control.

The next KPI is *personnel and administration cost ratio*, expressed as a percentage (%). This government KPI provides the proportion of the personnel and administration cost to the operating cost of the public service. The cost of labour is a significant segment of the government operating cost. Hence, any fluctuation in this cost element tends to influence the performance of the public service. Table 11.2 shows that the target country has a personnel and administration cost ratio of 25%, which is comparable to the benchmark countries. One should note that this ratio may indicate the administrative efficiency of government employees. However, if the employee cost and operating cost do not increase or decrease proportionally, the government's capacity to deliver its services or maintain its budget will weaken.

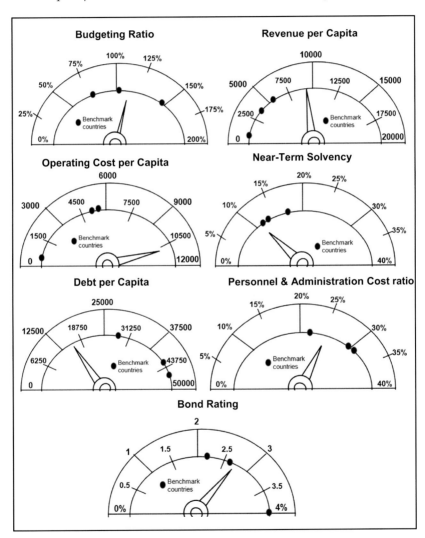

Figure 11.1  Typical Dashboard for the Finance Category KPIs Showing Target and Benchmark Countries

The final KPI to be considered within this category is the bond rating, which measures financial stability and denotes the credit quality of the government. Table 11.2 indicates that the bond rating for the target country is 2.85%, which is on a par with two of the benchmark countries and is much lower than the third benchmark country. This suggests that the interest rates are low and thus the government's ability to pay the bond's principal and interest is high.

Figure 11.1 provides a typical dashboard for the KPIs discussed under the finance category. The dashboard also shows the benchmark countries for comparative purposes. The performance of the target country appears to be very good when compared to the benchmark countries, particularly in relation to revenue per capital, operating cost per capita, and debt per capita. The debt per capita for the target country is much lower than the benchmark countries. Hence, on a national level the public service entities in relation to financial management are performing at a more than adequate rate.

### Operations Category

The operations category KPIs are based upon two elements, namely the percentage of national audit authority findings resolved and the percentage of national ombudsman findings resolved. Both of these public service KPIs are important, since all public entities are scrutinised by an independent review of their operation in the case of the audit KPI and citizens are able to lodge a complaint through the ombudsman if they feel aggrieved. The purpose of these reviews either through an audit or investigation is not only to examine the government on its inadequacies but also to bring awareness to opportunities for improvement. Table 11.2 indicates that 82% of the recommendations made by the National Audit Office are implemented outright. The other 20% are either challenged or under further consideration. This KPI compares favourably with the benchmark countries. Table 11.2 also demonstrates that 93% of the ombudsman's findings are accepted and implemented by government, and this figure is much better than that of the benchmark countries.

Figure 11.2 shows a simple dashboard for this category and depicts the target country performance for this category in comparison with the benchmark countries. Figure 11.2 suggests that the target country is performing at a much higher level than the benchmark countries.

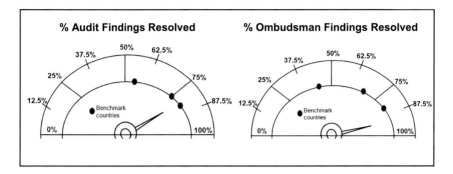

*Figure* 11.2   Typical Dashboard for the Operations Category KPIs Showing Target and Benchmark Countries

## Public Services Category

Public services category KPIs are extremely important because the fundamental purpose of public entities is to serve their citizens and business community to ensure their prosperity. These services embrace many aspects of day-to-day living, such as the environment, health, education, transportation, and housing amongst many others. The public service category being illustrated consists of six primary KPIs, namely government effectiveness; provision of public services; user-centricity of government digital services; digital public services for citizens; digital public services for business; and eGovernment users interacting with public authorities. There are many other KPIs that may be selected depending on the government's current circumstances, national characteristics, and culture.

The government effectiveness KPI captures perceptions of the quality of public services, the quality of the public service and the degree of its independence from political pressures, the quality of policy formulation and implementation, and the credibility of the government's commitment to such policies. The target country government effectiveness KPI is 77.88%. When compared with the three benchmark countries (87.98%, 86.06%, and 64.90% respectively), the data indicates that the target country needs to improve its effectiveness. The government effectiveness index is computed by the World Bank and consists of many variables. Hence, a more detailed examination of the World Bank government effectiveness variables would reveal the relevant weaknesses of a particular country, in this case the target country.

The provision of public services KPI refers to the presence of basic government functions that serve the people. It includes the provision of essential services, such as health, education, water and sanitation, transport infrastructure, electricity and power, and internet and connectivity. This KPI also considers the level and maintenance of general infrastructure to the extent that its absence would negatively affect the country's actual or potential development. The target country provision of public services KPI is recorded as 69%, compared with the benchmark countries with a rating of 66%, 42%, and 30% respectively. Whilst this data suggests that further improvement is required, it also illustrates that the target country's performance is relatively better than the benchmark countries.

The KPIs related to digital services are also considered to be important metrics. These consist of four KPIs, namely, user-centricity of government digital services; digital public services for citizens; digital public services for business; and eGovernment users interacting with public authorities. One should note that the eGovernment infrastructure KPIs are becoming increasingly important for governments to provide reliable online services to their citizens and the business community.

It is recognised that online platforms offer a convenient and easy approach to communicate critical information and undertake transactions. These KPIs need to be closely monitored and continuously improved, and include various aspects, such as capacity that takes into consideration the bandwidth for providing uninterrupted online services; accessibility that takes into account the government's ability to perform its important services online; interconnectivity and interoperability that assesses the ease of connection between multiple branches of the government; and security, which evaluates the level and quality of protection that the government has in place to secure data. The data at Table 11.2 indicates that the target country has high scores in all of these KPIs, with the exception of eGovernment users interacting with public authorities. Generally, the target country has a better performance than the benchmark countries.

Figure 11.3 shows the dashboard for the public services category, depicting the target country's performance for this category in comparison with the benchmark countries. Figure 11.3 indicates that generally, the target country is performing at a better and higher level than the benchmark countries.

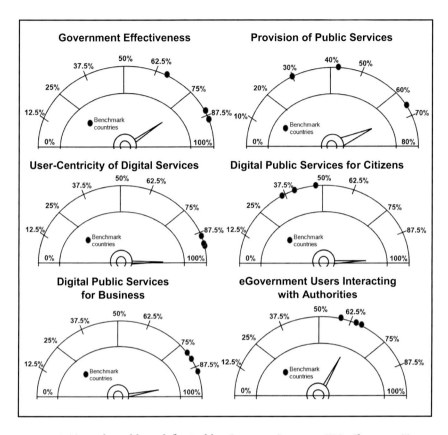

*Figure 11.3* Typical Dashboard for Public Services Category KPIs Showing Target and Benchmark Countries

## Citizens Category

The citizens category KPIs for the public service indicates the relationship between the citizens and government. One needs to recognise that citizens need to be viewed as shareholders, similar to the shareholders of private entities. Hence, the citizens must be treated with due respect and be included in the government's decision-making process. They must be given the opportunity to express their views, particularly their concerns. This category consists of five KPIs, namely, national voter turnout; public satisfaction; transparency of government; tendency to trust national government; and tendency to trust the public administration. The voter turnout KPI is very closely related to public participation, since it measures the involvement of the citizens in choosing the government, particularly the direction that the government will be taking through its election manifesto.

A high voter turnout points to a more engaged public, and if the government administration is re-elected, it shows that the government is performing its functions well. The target country has a national voter turnout of 85.5%, which is much higher than the three benchmark countries, as shown in Table 11.2. Moreover, the public satisfaction and transparency of government KPIs for the target country (79% and 97.1% respectively) suggest that it is performing better than the benchmark countries. The tendency to

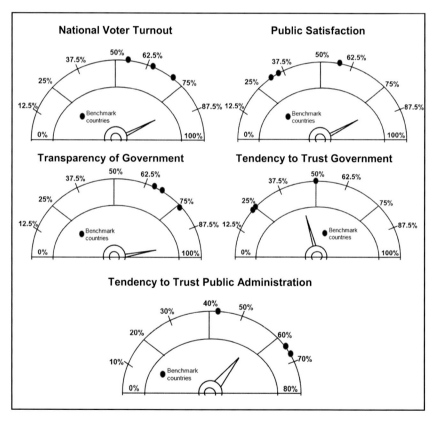

Figure 11.4  Typical Dashboard for the Citizens Category KPIs Showing Target and Benchmark Countries

trust national government and the public administration KPIs illustrate that the target country is performing well but needs to improve its rating when compared with some of the benchmark countries. Figure 11.4 shows the dashboard for the citizens category KPIs, showing the target country performance for this category in comparison with the benchmark countries. Figure 11.4 indicates that generally, the target country is performing very well in comparison with the benchmark countries.

## *Human Resources Category*

The human resources KPIs for the government is the final category of KPIs to be considered. Similar to the private sector, the public service is highly dependent on the quality and level of commitment of its employees. This category of consists of four KPIs, namely, the employee retention rate; the level of women in senior administrator positions; the share of government employees under the age of 39 years; and the share of government employees over the age of 55 years. The data in Table 11.2 shows that the employee retention rate for the target country is higher when compared with the benchmark countries. This government KPI measures the government's ability to retain its employees. A high retention rate indicates a committed workforce, which is indicative of a healthy and thriving workplace. A low retention rate points to concerns regarding employee satisfaction and motivation, indicating a need for revamping the management team.

Furthermore, the target country data shows that the percentage of women holding senior positions in the public service is relatively high and is higher than the benchmark countries. It is also noted that the target country has a relatively younger public service than the benchmark countries. The share of government employees who are older than 55 years is much lower than the benchmark countries.

Figure 11.5 shows the dashboard for the human resources category KPIs, illustrating that the target country performance for this category in comparison with the benchmark countries is much better. Figure 11.5 indicates that generally, the target country is performing very well for this category of KPIs but needs to improve the proportion of women holding senior positions to bring it at par with the male gender.

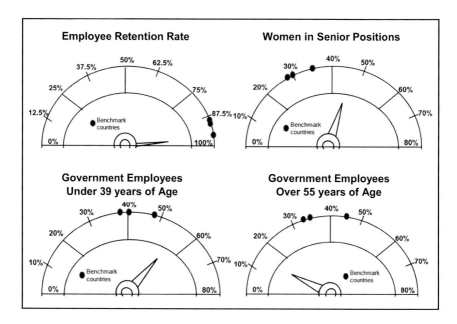

*Figure 11.5*  Typical Dashboard for Human Resources Category KPIs Showing Target and Benchmark Countries

## Cross-Sectional Categories of KPIs for Public Service: Ministerial Level

The previous section addressed KPIs on a central or national government level. Therefore, the selected KPIs were mostly of a strategic nature and at the highest organisational level. This section will address KPIs at a level below the national government and will focus on ministries within the national government hierarchy, such as health services. As one will appreciate, due to the limited space, it is not possible to address every government ministry. However, the example provided will illustrate how KPIs may be applied to enhance the performance management system of government entities.

Governments worldwide have adopted budgetary and reporting mechanisms designed to make government operations as transparent as possible and demonstrate in a realistic manner how public funds are being utilised to accomplish their policy objectives. Government budgetary management trends have seen a conceptual shift towards a results-orientated approach that are designed to provide government decision-makers and other stakeholders, such as parliaments and citizens, with an unambiguous depiction of what governments accomplish for the public funds that are consumed in their operational undertakings. Therefore, performance measurement and the utilisation of KPIs are a fundamental basis of these results-oriented models, since they provide continuous and regular feedback; thus enhancing public service delivery and keeping stakeholders informed by fostering accountability and illustrating in explicit terms the results the government is achieving through its ministries. KPIs are measures that are essential for monitoring progress in achieving an organisation's strategic goals and should be widely used at different levels within an organisation.

The government ministries are under intense pressure to deliver a variety of complex services. This environment has enabled the use of KPIs to be aggressively exploited to improve performance. This is driven by various factors, such as raising claims for government accountability; intensifying legislative scrutiny of government operations; a continuous trend towards results-oriented fiscal allocations; and having austerity economic policies for reducing government spending and focusing on delivering public services as efficiently and effectively as possible. As implied in previous chapters, well selected and designed KPIs have the objective of helping the decision-makers within each ministry to establish current baseline information for comparison with performance being achieved; establish performance standards and goals to stimulate constant improvement; measure and report progress over time; compare performance across the various departments and functions; benchmark performance in comparison with best practice peer organisations; and permit a wide range of stakeholders to impartially evaluate ministerial performance.

Stakeholders in a ministerial environment may include parliament, national audit office, business and civil society, those receiving the particular service, the budget office at the ministry of finance, and the media. KPIs should aim to gather and report information that help to emphasise the relationship between resources, activities, and outcomes. Thus, KPIs allow the various ministries to demonstrate how the application of allocated resources impact outcomes and help to predict the resources that would be needed to sustain service standards and maintain current and future workloads. This provides decision-makers with resilient information for sustaining investments in expanding their services, improving processes, and implementing technology upgrades. However, KPIs must be supported by political constraints as a key driver of policy and budgetary decisions.

Designing and applying KPIs requires a systematic process for gathering, managing, analysing, dispersing, and reporting performance information. Chapter 6 regarding the use of the Critical Success Factors model provides a description of this systemic process. It is essential that when KPIs and the respective goals have been defined, it is also critical to identify the data to be collected; ascertain the data sources; define the data collection methodology; and establish the policies, competences, and infrastructure required to process and manage the data and be able to retrieve the processed information.

An essential element, once a systematic process has been established, is to perform rigorous analysis of the gathered data and the interpretation of the resulting performance information. There is no point in having good indicators and goals without a rigorous analysis and respective interpretation procedure in place that addresses multiple audiences, such as the professionals in a particular field of interest, policymakers, program managers, budget analysts, citizens, and politicians.

The following section addresses some of the critical KPIs that may be applied in the health care sector. The primary aim of a health care KPI is to provide a precise performance measurement that is used to monitor, analyse, and optimise all relevant health care processes to enhance patient satisfaction. Health care professionals must focus on managing their data and generated information to provide the best health care possible, manage costs effectively, and ensure sustainable hospital performance. Hence, having a suitable health care dashboard will enable health care managers to improve their processes and deliver significant value for hospitals and patients.

Table 11.3 provides a critical set of health care KPIs that health care managers and professionals need to help them carry out their functions effectively. Furthermore, Table 11.4 presents various critical KPI values for the health services being offered, including the benchmark values for comparison purposes. Both tables provide the basic information for defining and designing the health services dashboards regarding the hospital offering the health services and the patient as the recipient of the health care services. Note that the data presented by Table 11.4 are arbitrary figures, some are based on research but are not applicable to any specific organisation. The reason for this is that such data is normally used for internal management utilisation and, unlike budgetary financial information, is not made available on the public domain. However, the presented figures are useful for illustration purposes and are used to design the relevant dashboards.

Figure 11.6 and Figure 11.7 illustrate the resultant dashboards. The trend data for the dashboards is characteristically arbitrary in nature and is

Table 11.3a  Critical Set of Healthcare KPIs

| KPI | Details |
|---|---|
| Average Hospital Stay | Measures the average time spent by a patient in a specific medical facility. It is important to break down this KPI by diverse categories of stay, procedures, and operations to have a more accurate result. |
| Bed Occupancy Rate by Month | Shows percentage number of beds occupied during a specific period. A high occupancy rate may indicate a pandemic. Aim is to balance the use of hospital resources and the general pressure on the medical facility. |
| Medical Equipment Usage | Monitor the application and use of medical equipment to assess the asset management procedures. It is important to optimise the usage of medical equipment and allocate it to areas where it is required most. |
| Patient Medications Cost Per Stay | Enhance the medications cost management system to track their cost. |
| Patient Treatment Cost | Measures treatment costs for patients using a specific medical facility. The objective is to highlight and address irregular or inflated expenses. The patient treatment costs trends are to be analysed by various treatment categories, including by patient age-groups. |
| Patient Bed Set-up Rate | This measures the cost of preparing a patient bed when a previous patient is discharged that includes cleaning, assessing apparatus/equipment, and reviewing/adjusting medical materials applicable to a specific patient. The objective is to ensure a cost-effective, swift, and high-quality process that mitigates the risk of infections. |
| Outpatient Rate | This is related to follow-up treatment of patients who have been discharged from hospital as an inpatient, such as consultations, check-ups, and blood tests, among other forms of treatment. |
| Hospital Readmission Rate | This is the percentage of admitted patients who return to the hospital within seven days of discharge. The percentage of admitted patients who return to the hospital within seven days of discharge will remain constant or decline as changes are made to improve patient flow through the system. This KPI indicates the quality of care being administered by a facility. |

*Table 11.3b* Critical Set of Healthcare KPIs (continued)

| KPI | Details |
|---|---|
| Patient Wait Time | This measures the time from when a person registers at the hospital to when they are seen by a doctor to attain treatment. This is particularly relevant for the emergency department to assess how quickly the hospital can deliver urgent services to patients. |
| Patient Satisfaction Rate | This measures the patients' overall perception of the service being given in terms of excellent, good, neutral, bad, very bad. Patients may be asked to rate the care being given, the meals, and how long it took hospital staff to explain their medical status. |
| Treatment Error Rate | This measures the number of mistakes that are made by medical staff in treating a patient. Mistakes may include wrong diagnoses, providing the wrong treatment, and prescribing the wrong medication or dosage. |
| Patient Mortality Rate | This monitors the number of patients who died while being treated at a medical facility. This indicates the capability of medical staff to stabilise a patient in critical condition or follow the operations or interventions processes. |
| Clinical Staff-to-Patient Ratio | This measures the effectiveness of the clinical staff management processes to determine whether the hospital is under- or over-staffed. |
| Cancelled/missed appointments rate | This measures the number of outpatients who do not attend their scheduled appointment. |
| Patient Safety Rate | This measures the ability of the health facility to deliver quality care to patients by keeping them safe from contracting a new infection, post-operation complications, or some type of sepsis. |
| Emergency Department Wait Time | Similar to Patient Wait Time. Monitor this KPI by time of day to assess rush period. |

*Table* 11.4a  Values for the Critical Set of Healthcare KPIs and their Benchmark Target

| KPI | Details | Target Hospital | Benchmark |
|---|---|---|---|
| Average Hospital Stay | This KPI will vary depending on the type of stay and treatment. Hence, itemise this KPI by different categories of stay and treatment, procedures, and operations. This KPI can be measured by different departments. | 4.0 days | 4.5 days |
| Bed Occupancy Rate by Month | This shows the bed occupancy rate by month. The aim is to control the occupancy rate due to the risk of acute facility pressure and higher rates of infection. 85% is generally considered to be the point beyond which safety and efficiency are at risk. | 60% | 65% |
| Medical Equipment Usage | The equipment usage rate is critical for applying better asset management practises. However, this depends on the equipment type and application. | 65% | 70% |
| Patient Medications Cost Per Stay | Relevant medications are necessary, else patient care will deteriorate and hospitals will experience budget pressures that will eventually result in a shortage of staff. | $825 | $950 |
| Patient Treatment Cost | The objective is to detect deviant or overstated expenses and address them. The analysis conducted may be by category, such as department, operation, or age group. | $15,500 | $17,500 |
| Patient Bed Set-up Rate | This is the rate of preparing a room for another patient to enter when discharging a previous occupant. The aim is to have a rapid and high-quality process that mitigates risk of infections. | 50 minutes | 45 minutes |
| Outpatient Rate | Outpatient treatments may include check-ups, blood tests, new prescriptions, or consultations. | 45% | 35% |
| Hospital Readmission Rate | The readmission rate correlates with an increased risk of various adverse health outcomes, including increased patient stress and higher mortality rates. However, a reduced readmission rate is associated with greater patient satisfaction and improved outcomes. | 12% | 16% |

Note: Figures quoted above do not represent the true cost status but are simply used for illustration purposes.

*Table 11.4b*  Values for the Critical Set of Healthcare KPIs and their Benchmark Target (continued)

| KPI | Details | Target Hospital | Benchmark |
|---|---|---|---|
| Patient Wait Time | This measures the time it takes for a person to see a doctor and get treatment after registering at the hospital. Low customer satisfaction results if the figure is too high. | 45 minutes | 50 minutes |
| Patient Satisfaction Rate | Patients are asked to rate how they felt while being taken care of in terms of care and meals. | 65% | 75% |
| Treatment Error Rate | A high treatment error rate may cause an increase in costs from needless readmissions. Review the errors being made in each facility so that preventive measures may be implanted to mitigate errors. | 9% | 12% |
| Patient Mortality Rate | The patient mortality rate monitors the number of people who died while being treated at a health facility. It is essential to analyse data by age group. | 2% | 2.5% |
| Clinical Staff-to-Patient Ratio | This indicates whether the hospital is under- or over-staffed. It is essential to analyse data by type of care. For instance, at the ITU it should be 1:1. It is best to compare with the previous month to examine why there is a drop or increase. | 1:6 | 1:5 |
| Cancelled/ missed appointments rate | It is important to examine the reason for the cancelled or missed appointments. | 12% | 15% |
| Patient Safety Rate | This depends on the type of treatment the patient is receiving. Hence, it is important to break down this KPI by distinct categories of service provided. | 3% | 5% |
| Emergency Department Wait Time | Same as Patient Wait Time | 60 minutes | 90 minutes |

Note: Figures quoted above do not represent the true cost status but are simply used for illustration purposes.

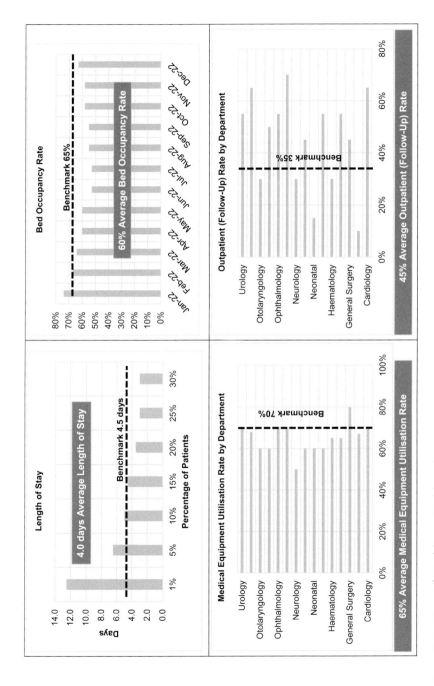

Figure 11.6a  Hospital Healthcare Dashboard

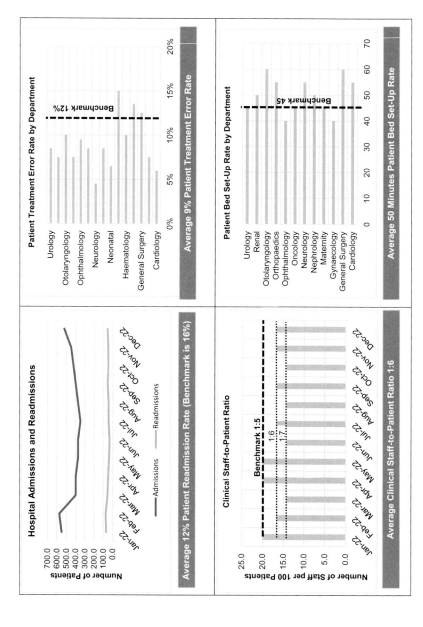

Figure 11.6b  Hospital Healthcare Dashboard (continued)

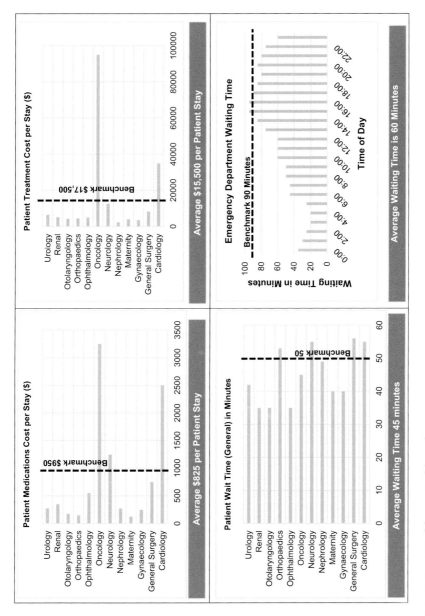

Figure 11.7a  Patient Healthcare Dashboard

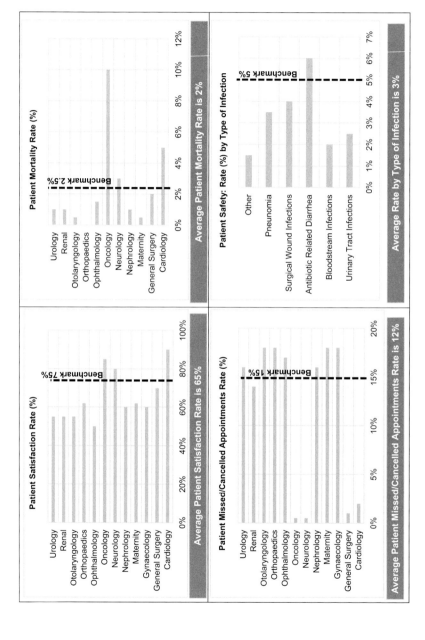

Figure 11.7b  Patient Healthcare Dashboard (continued)

mainly used to depict the specific dashboard design. Figure 11.6 is related to the general performance of the hospital and in some cases to specific departments, whilst Figure 11.7 is related to the performance related to the recipient of the healthcare service, namely the patient.

The Hospital Healthcare Dashboard (Figure 11.6) consists of eight charts (KPIs) that generally depict the performance of the target organisation. Each chart measures a particular hospital activity that show the activity trend data, the average for the element being measured, and the benchmark data for comparison purposes. The activities depicted in Figure 11.6 include the Length of Stay, Bed Occupancy Rate, Medical Equipment Utilisation Rate by Department, Outpatient (follow-up) Rate by Department, Hospital Admissions and Readmissions, Patient Treatment Error Rate by Department, Patient Bed Set-Up Rate by Department, and Clinical Staff to Patient Ratio.

The Hospital Healthcare Dashboard suggests that generally the target organisation is performing at an adequate level, but some elements of the activities need improvement. For example, the medical equipment utilisation rate for most Departments needs to increase. Furthermore, the outpatient follow-up rate for several departments needs to decrease to at least the established benchmark level of 35%. Moreover, the patient treatment error rate for the Maternity, Gynaecology, and General Surgery departments requires some improvement to bring them to the benchmark level of 12%. Additionally, the clinical staff to patient ratio needs regular monitoring to ensure appropriate action is taken to recruit the necessary clinical staff in a timely manner.

The Patient Healthcare Dashboard (Figure 11.7) also consists of eight charts that typically show the performance of the target organisation related specifically to the patient. Each chart measures a specific patient-related activity that illustrates the activity trend data, the average for the element being measured, and the benchmark data for comparison purposes. The patient-related activities depicted in Figure 11.7 include the Patient Medications Cost Per Stay, Patient Treatment Cost Per Stay, Patient Wait Time (excluding Emergency Department), Emergency Department Patient Waiting Time, Patient Satisfaction Rate by Department, Patient Mortality Rate by Department, Patient Missed/Cancelled Appointments Rate by Department, and Patient Safety Rate by Type of Infection.

Generally, the Patient Healthcare Dashboard suggests that patient care at the target organisation is performing at a very good level, but some service elements require improvement. For example, the patient waiting time for the orthopaedics, neurology, general surgery, and cardiology require a further decrease in waiting time to bring them into line with the benchmark of a maximum of 50 minutes. The patient satisfaction rating is very good, but some improvement is required for oncology, neurology, and cardiology. These departments are highly sensitive and further effort is required to address this specific weakness. The patient mortality rate chart suggests that extensive improvement is required for the oncology, neurology, and cardiology departments. However, these healthcare aspects are highly dependent on research developments that may be external to the target organisation.

The chart related to patient missed/cancelled appointments also suggests that although the average of 12% is below the 15% benchmark, several departments require significant improvement. It may be worthwhile for management to conduct a survey amongst patients to establish why they missed or cancelled their appointments. Patient safety is within the 5% benchmark except for the antibiotic-related diarrhoea. This aspect may require further study to establish the steps that may be taken to mitigate this safety risk element.

As stated previously, this section addressed the KPIs at a level below the national government and has focused on a particular ministry within the national government hierarchy, namely the health services. The next section will examine the KPIs at a lower level to a specific department.

## Cross-Sectional Categories of KPIs for Public Service: Departmental Level

The objective of this chapter is to discuss the application of KPIs as a performance management tool for the public sector. Like the private sector, the application of KPIs can be used at different organisational levels, such as the holistic organisation, division, department, unit within a department, team within a unit, and individual person. In a public sector environment this translates to: Central Government; Ministry; Department; Section; team; and individual person. In the long-term, an effective performance management system should be implemented at all these levels if it is practical to do so. Thus, it is best to adopt a five-year performance management implementation strategy that implements a level at a time. The speed of implementing an all-embracing performance management system depends on the resources, in terms of the financial funding and human power that management has at its disposal.

The previous two sections addressed KPIs on national government and ministerial levels. This section will discuss the implementation of KPIs at a Departmental level by focusing on a particular department, namely Higher Education. As was stated previously, governments have a wide spectrum of functions and services they offer. Therefore, it is not possible to address every organisational level in this book, particularly all the government departments. Nevertheless, the department selected (Higher Education Department) will illustrate how KPIs may be applied to enhance the performance management system of government entities at a departmental level.

For the purposes of this chapter, the KPIs for the Higher Education Department will include eight categories that are specific to education management. Although there are hundreds of KPIs that may be applied for education, one needs to be selective to ensure that the performance management system is meaningful and manageable. Figure 11.8 illustrates the eight categories that are applicable to managing an education institution. It also includes the critical KPIs that are required for the performance management system that are associated with each category. Moreover, Table 11.5 shows the descriptions of each individual KPI, including the performance level attained by the target education institution (i.e. department) and the defined benchmark level to be achieved for each KPI. The data contained at Table 11.5 provides the basic information necessary for defining and designing the required dashboard for each of the eight categories of KPIs.

The Education Institution Dashboard (Figure 11.9) consists of eight categories of charts with each representing several critical KPIs that generally depict the performance of the target institution. The eight categories of charts and their associated KPIs are as follows: Scholastic; Financial Resources; Students and Staff; Study Programmes; Academic Staff; Amenities and Services provided; Technology; and Accommodation. Hence, each

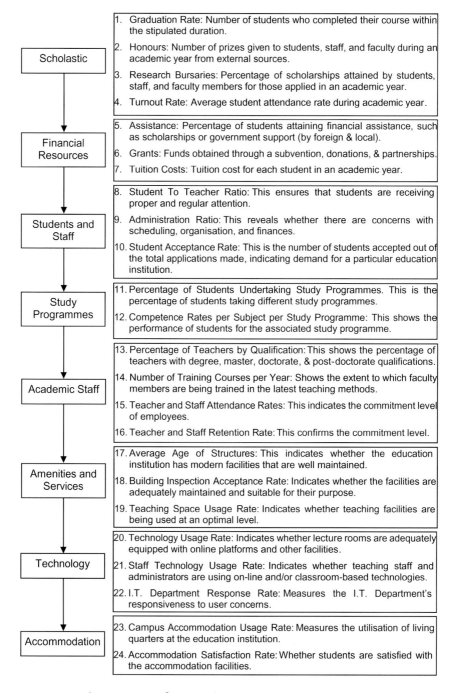

Figure 11.8  Eight Categories of KPIs Applicable to Managing an Education Institution

Table 11.5  Critical Set of KPIs for Managing an Education Institution

| KPI | Details | Target Institution | Benchmark |
|---|---|---|---|
| Graduation Rate | Students finishing course within stipulated duration | 90% | 95% |
| Honours Received | Prizes given to students, staff, and faculty during an academic year from external sources | 8 | 14 |
| Research Bursaries | Percentage of scholarships attained by students, staff, and faculty members in an academic year. | 7.7% | 12% |
| Turnout Rate | Average student attendance rate in academic year | 84% | 95% |
| Assistance | Students receiving financial assistance | 33% | 45% |
| Grants | Funding from subvention, donations, & partnerships | 20% | 35% |
| Tuition Costs | Tuition cost for each student in an academic year | $12,900 | $11,000 |
| Teacher to Student | Average number of students assigned per lecturer | 1:25 | 1:20 |
| Administration | Percentage number of administration staff | 25% | 20% |
| Students Accepted | Number of students accepted rate | 72% | 80% |
| % Students taking Study Programmes | Percentage of students taking different study programmes | n/a | n/a |
| Competence Rates | Performance of students for study programme | 68% | 75% |
| Teacher Qualifications | Percentage of teachers with degree, master, doctorate, and-post doctorate qualifications | n/a | n/a |
| Training Courses | Extent to which faculty members are being trained | 6 | 8 |
| Attendance Rates | Attendance rate of teachers and staff | 81% | 95% |

(Continued)

Table 11.5  (Continued)

| KPI | Details | Target Institution | Benchmark |
|---|---|---|---|
| Staff Retention | Teacher and Staff Retention Rate | 90% | 98% |
| Age of Structures | Indicates if modern facilities are available | 21.5 years | 20 years |
| Building Inspection | Indicates maintenance level of buildings | 89% | 98% |
| Space Usage Rate | Utilisation of teaching space | 88% | 90% |
| Technology Usage | Technology capacity utilisation level | 85% | 95% |
| Staff Usage of Technology | Usage of technology by employees | 88% | 95% |
| I.T. Department Response Rate | I.T. Department responsiveness to user concerns | 28 minutes | 15 minutes |
| Accommodation Usage Rate | Utilisation of Campus Accommodation Facilities | 68% | 85% |
| Satisfaction Rate | Satisfaction with the accommodation facilities | 91% | 95% |

Note: Figures quoted above do not represent the true status but are simply used for illustration purposes.

category of chart measures a particular education activity aspect that shows the specific trend data for each activity, the average for the element being measured, and the benchmark data for comparison purposes. The dashboards for each category of KPIs are found in Figure 11.9.

The Scholastic category KPIs suggests that generally the target institution is performing well, but various aspects require improvement. For example, the graduation rate of each faculty is generally rather high, but only two faculties are within the benchmark of the institution, which is established at 95%. Hence, the institution is aiming for a very high standard, with the Economics and Accountancy faculty needing a significant improvement. Several other faculties require a slight improvement to reach the benchmark target.

Furthermore, the number of prizes attained by students and the percentage number of research bursaries received require a significant

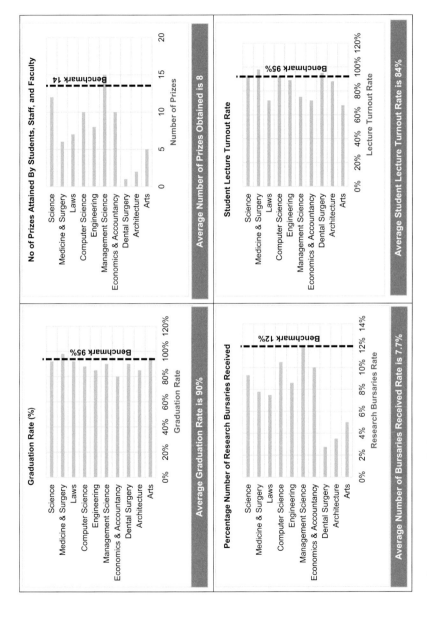

Figure 11.9a  Education Institution: Scholastic Category

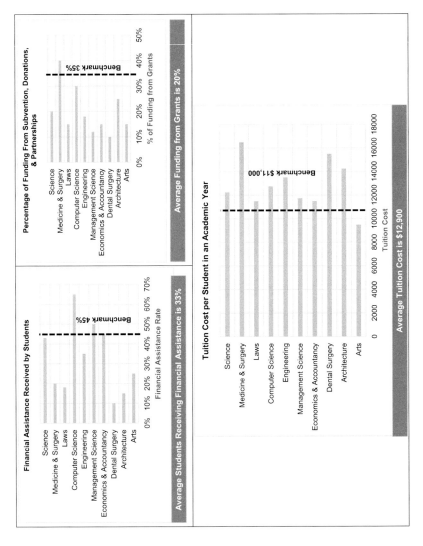

Figure 11.9b Education Institution: Financial Resources Category (Continued)

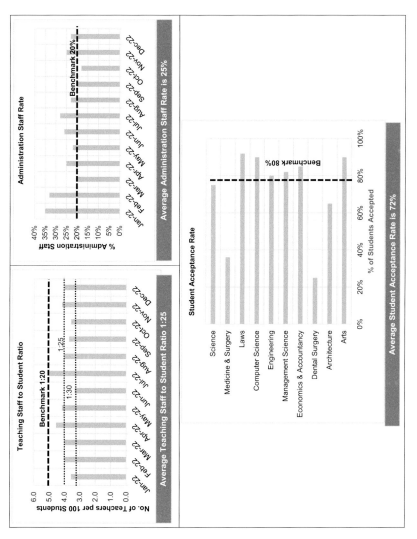

Figure 11.9c  Education Institution: Students and Staff Category (Continued)

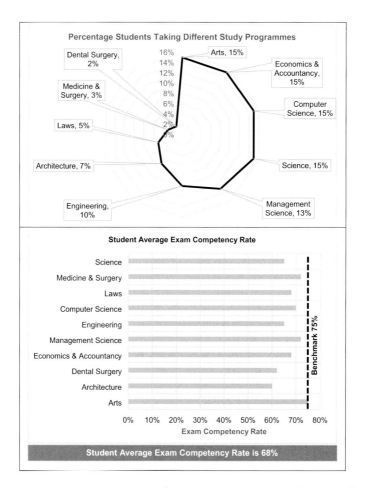

*Figure 11.9d* Education Institution: Study Programmes Category (Continued)

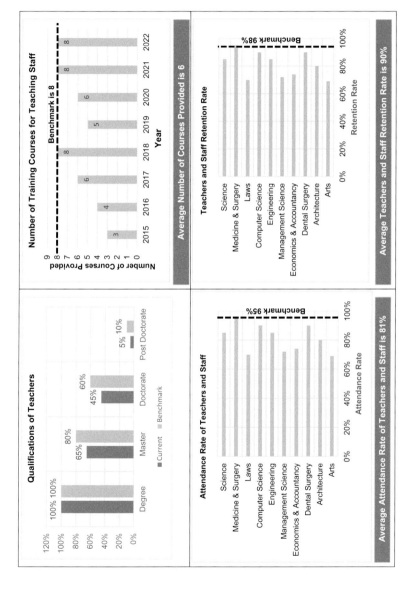

Figure 11.9e  Education Institution: Academic Staff Category (Continued)

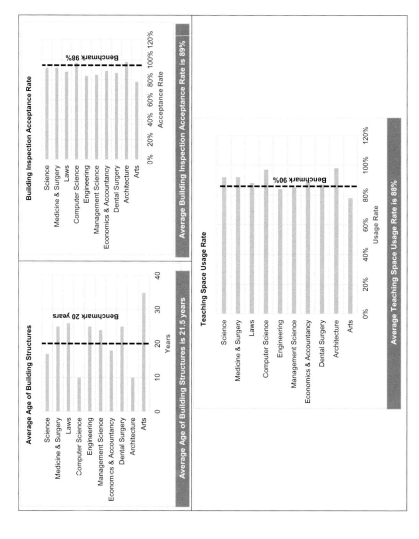

Figure 11.9f  Education Institution: Amenities and Services Provided Category (Continued)

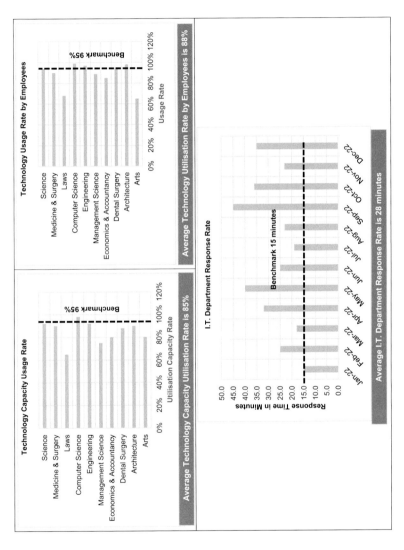

Figure 11.9g  Education Institution: Technology Category (Continued)

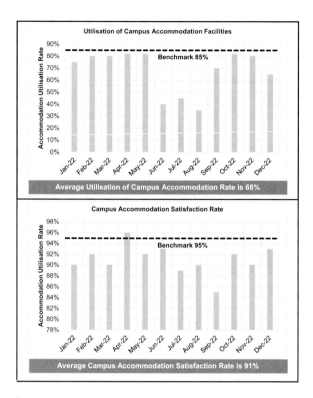

*Figure* 11.9h  Education Institution: Accommodation Category (Continued)

improvement. The Management Science faculty is outperforming the other faculties in these aspects. The students lecture turnout rate is at an acceptable level but requires a significant improvement from several faculties, specifically the Art, Economics and Accountancy, Management Science, and Law faculties. Management needs to investigate the reasons for this situation and adopt a strategy to improve the current position.

The Financial Resources Category indicates that most of the students do not receive financial assistance. This confirms the figures related to the prizes and research bursaries received. Additionally, more effort needs to be made by the Institution to secure supplementary donations and encourage partnerships with the industrial sector. Moreover, a sustained effort needs to be made to lower the tuition cost per student, particularly if the Institution is not able to increase funding from sources, such as subvention, donations, and partnerships.

The Students and Staff Category dashboard suggests that there is a consistent need for recruiting qualified lecturing staff, since the benchmark of having one lecturer to twenty students has been achieved only for one month in the depicted academic year. The dashboard indicates that currently the education institution is achieving one member of teaching staff to twenty-five students, which is far below the established benchmark. Furthermore, the administration staff rate is on average 25%, which is significantly above the benchmark of 20%. It is noted that the target benchmark has been achieved for only three months of the year being depicted. Achieving the benchmark of 20% would result in cost savings for the Education Institution being examined. The student acceptance rate is at an average of 72%, which is significantly lower than the established benchmark of 80%. The dashboard indicates that several faculties, namely Science, Medicine and Surgery, Dental Surgery, and Architecture, are required to take the appropriate action to attract a higher calibre of student applicants to achieve the 80% benchmark.

The examination of the Study Programmes category suggests that there is an imbalance in the percentage of students taking the different study programmes being offered by the education institution under scrutiny. More effort needs to be taken by several faculties, namely Dental Surgery, Medicine and Surgery, Law, Architecture, and Engineering to attract more students to their faculties. This also confirms the previous remark that these faculties are required to take the appropriate action to attract a higher calibre of student applicants. Furthermore, this particular dashboard indicates that more effort is required to increase the student exam competency rate. The average student exam competency rate is 68%, which needs to increase to the established benchmark of 75%. This KPI may be related to a previous comment regarding the need to increase the teaching staff to student ratio, from the current 1 teacher to 25 students to 1 teacher to 20 students.

Reviewing the Academic Staff dashboard highlights several concerns. Firstly, the Education Institution under review needs to attract higher qualified teaching staff at three levels, namely Master Degree, Doctorate Degree, and Post-Doctorate Degree. These qualification levels are significantly below the established benchmark. Having highly qualified teaching staff will increase the reputation of the education institution and attract a higher calibre of student applicants. The dashboard suggests that the education institution under review has a concern regarding teaching staff's organisational commitment. This is reflected by the average attendance rate of teaching staff of 81%, compared with a benchmark of 95%, and the average teacher and staff retention rate of 90% compared with a benchmark of 98%. Teaching staff organisational commitment may be increased by attracting more highly qualified staff, lowering the teacher to student ratio to 1 teacher per 20 students, and implementing a comprehensive teacher development training programme.

The Amenities and Services Provided Category dashboard indicates that the education institution under review must make more effort in securing funds for investing in the building structures to ensure that modern premises and amenities are provided. This would be an important factor for attracting more high calibre students and teaching staff. The average building inspection acceptance rate is 89% compared with a benchmark of 98%, thus confirming the suggestion that more investment is required to upkeep the building structures and amenities being provided.

The Technology Category dashboard indicates that the overall technology capacity usage rate of 85% is below the 95% benchmark. Moreover, the average I.T. Department response rate to a reported concern is 28 minutes compared with a benchmark of 15 minutes. This lengthy response rate may be indicative of the disappointing technology capacity usage rate being significantly below the benchmark. Generally, the education institution is required to improve its I.T. services by investing in more advanced technology and I.T. support staff. These findings also confirm the findings of the Amenities and Services Provided Category.

The final dashboard presented is related to the Accommodation Category. The average utilisation of the campus accommodation facilities is 68% compared with a benchmark of 85%. It is difficult to achieve the benchmark due to the scholastic calendar. However, the accommodation utilisation also depends on the allocation system being applied by the education institution. In other words, whether the accommodation facility is managed as a boarding house or as an aparthotel. The former use type would make it more difficult to achieve the benchmark, whereas the latter use type may allow more flexibility for utilising the accommodation facilities. The average campus accommodation satisfaction rate is 91% compared with a benchmark of 95%. Although the current satisfaction rate of 91% is slightly below the benchmark, it may be concluded that the accommodation facilities are at a high standard. This indicates that the accommodation standard is not a concern but that a solution needs to be found for increasing the utilisation rate of the accommodation facilities.

Generally, the education institution under examination is performing adequately but requires improvement in several aspects. This education institution needs to reduce its recurrent administration cost and increase its capital expenditure by investing more in its building programme, I.T. services, and support staff, and improving its amenities. Moreover, it needs to upgrade the general qualifications standard to its teaching staff and recruit additional teaching staff to attract a higher calibre of students, thus resulting in attaining a higher percentage of research bursaries and student scholarships.

Furthermore, this would attract and secure more supplementary donations and encourage research partnerships with the industrial sector. Emphasis should be given to attracting highly qualified teaching staff since this will increase the reputation of the education institution and attract a higher calibre of student applicants. The above will also contribute towards improving staff motivation and organisational commitment.

## Conclusion

The purpose of this chapter was to apply some of the main features that were explained in previous chapters, specifically those appropriate to the public sector environment. It is an accepted fact that the public sector is a critical and essential part of the economy, which comprises of both public services and public enterprises. This chapter has focused on public services, since most public enterprises operate on a similar basis to private enterprises and use the performance management tools applicable to the private sector enterprises. On the other hand, public services are provided by government departments within a Ministry, such as infrastructure, public education, health care, and those working for the government itself, such as elected officials. Public sector departments are normally headed by a permanent secretary, with each department being administered and managed by a Director General and several directors according to an annual government budget allocation.

Hence this chapter has focused on specific segments of government related to public service provision, specifically health and education. It should be noted that the actual identity of the entities being described are not revealed and the information regarding the selected organisation was extracted from published financial estimates (i.e. budget) and other relevant reports. However, when the required data was not available, fictional information was utilised to permit several analytical approaches to be conducted for illustrative purposes. Therefore, the analytical results contained in this chapter should not be construed to be a real assessment of the selected organisation.

## References

insightsoftware. (2021). *10+ Government KPIs for 2021 Reporting.* Available at: https://insightsoftware.com/blog/10-government-kpis-for-2021-reporting/ (Accessed 22 November 2023).

Jackson, T. (2022). *Key Performance Indicators for Schools & Education Management.* Available at: https://www.clearpointstrategy.com/key-performance-indicators-in-education/ (Accessed 22 November 22, 2023).

Rozner, S. (2013). *Developing and Using Key Performance Indicators: A Toolkit for Health Sector Managers.* Bethesda, MD: Health Finance & Governance Project, Abt Associates Inc.

# 12

## PERFORMANCE MEASUREMENT AND MANAGEMENT

### FUTURE TRENDS

'Research indicates that workers have three prime needs: Interesting work, recognition for doing a good job, and being let in on things that are going on in the organisation.'

Zig Ziglar
Author and motivational speaker

This chapter is the end of our journey regarding the exploration of the various performance measurement and management concepts and tools. Thus, this chapter will focus on consolidating the knowledge gathered regarding performance measurement and management and will examine the likely future trends regarding this critical and important topic. According to Cappelli and Tavis (2016), the focus of performance measurement and management is shifting from accountability to learning. They contend that traditional performance appraisals have been abandoned by more than a third of US companies and are viewed by these companies and their employees as a nuisance.

DOI: 10.4324/9781032685465-15

Cappelli and Tavis view the annual review requirement as the prime limitation of the traditional performance appraisals. They argue that the emphasis on holding employees accountable for what they did last year, at the expense of improving performance now and in the future, is a regressive feature of traditional performance appraisals. Hence, the reason why numerous organisations are changing to a more frequent, development-focused conversations between managers and employees.

As we have seen in previous chapters, performance management is a set of tools that management apply to make sure that the identified and defined strategic goals and targets for their organisation are achieved. Therefore, performance management typically commences at the strategic management stage, cascading down to employees that are viewed as the actual performers. Performance management practices are based on the concept of having a set of evaluation procedures that are applied to the organisation's employees. The evaluation procedures encompass various tasks, such as planning, monitoring, developing, assessing, and rewarding the organisation's employees.

Effective employee performance management depends on the organisation's ability to achieve an optimum motivational level of its employees through a higher intensity of involvement and providing them with an appropriate reward. This requires the establishment of measurable and practical KPIs and having a monitoring system that continuously assesses their performance. Performance should not be viewed as a static component but must be seen as a dynamic factor that may be further improved through well designed development programmes that focus on improving the employee's knowledge, skills, and competencies by taking advantage of the benefits that state-of-the-art systems are able to provide. Hence, established KPIs must be periodically reviewed to ensure that employees are assessed and appraised against an appropriate performance scale (KPIs) and rewarded according to the appraisal reports.

The new trends in performance management are basically dependent on the continuous evolution of systems that reflect a new generation of performance measurement and management software that has computerised most of the HR function, which was previously carried out manually through laborious paperwork. The evolution of systems is continuous (never ending) and new advancements in such areas as artificial intelligence are a constant development, particularly in the human resources (HR) segment. Hence, the HR function is increasingly being integrated as part of an enterprise management system that seamlessly joins together the HR, accounting, financial, and production functional segments.

This enterprise management system is envisaged to integrate the traditional management functions with the support of a sophisticated learning system through the use of artificial intelligence. An enterprise management system is applicable to both the private and public sectors. Such a system would help to retain employees and reduce the costs of acquiring new workers when needed.

## Introduction

Performance measurement and management, like every other management tool, is greatly influenced by technology trends. People management consists of various aspects that need to be closely monitored and regularly reviewed to permit the organisation to execute its processes effectively. It must also be recognised that tasks related to people management are applicable to all types and sizes of organisations. No matter how many employees an organisation has, there is a need to have a proper monitoring system in place to regulate the organisation's employees, since processes tend to rotate around the employees themselves or the work they perform.

The difference between small and large organisations in relation to their employee management is the level of automation of the respective systems. Larger organisations tend to have more complex and sophisticated systems to manage their daily voluminous transactions, whereas very small (micro) organisations may have a manual-based system. But whatever the size, an appropriate system (computerised or manual) is required.

Managing the performance of employees is a primary function of managers, since appraising the performance of the employees is an effective way for managers to identify an organisation's weaknesses and success factors. However, adequate evaluation tools are essential because such tools provide the means for managers to obtain a clear picture of the work being performed and to take suitable decisions. It is important to stress that without these effective evaluation tools in place, the information generated may be misleading. Hence, the reason why technology is playing such an important role in managing performance is because modern technology can provide timely, accurate, and complete information that knowledgeable managers are able to harness and use to help them make the correct decisions.

Performance measurement and management is viewed as a strategic function since the performance of employees is directly interconnected to the strategic objectives of the organisation. This strategic link has been emphasised in previous chapters, where is has been illustrated that the starting point of a performance management system is the identification and definition of the organisation's strategic objectives that are linked to the functions performed by the respective employees. All activities carried out in an organisation must support the strategic objectives of that organisation. In other words, waste in the application of resources results when there are activities being conducted that do not support the strategic objectives of the organisation.

An effective employee performance management system mitigates HR resource wastage by identifying those areas (through KPI dashboards) that do not contribute towards the achievement of the organisation's strategic objectives. Studies have shown that organisations with an inadequate growth rate tend to have unresponsive and ineffective performance management systems. These organisations are inept at identifying what changes are required and what measures need to be taken, thus these organisations are stuck in their current position.

Technology is an essential element and game changer in the performance evaluation cycle. A typical performance evaluation cycle is shown in Figure 12.1, which consists of four critical activities that are continuously in operation. The first activity is regarding the task of data gathering. Data gathering is not a simple activity and integration with other systems becomes essential in order to avoid duplication of effort in entering data and ensuring its timeliness, completion, and accuracy. Every effort should be made to mitigate the need for manual data entry. However, if this cannot be avoided, it is essential to make sure that the data entry is secure, timely, validated, and verified. Hence, the reason for the desire to have the highest level of system integration. The next critical activity is defining the objectives through clearly, timely, and measurable goals.

The goals should support the organisation's strategic objectives and must be attainable. These goals must also be supported by the data gathering task and are able to be compared with what is being collected, to determine whether the specific goals are being attained. These goals should provide a critical link between employees with the aim of collectively achieving the defined goals. Hence, each employee is to have a clearly defined role and responsibility that can be measured, and any weakness detected.

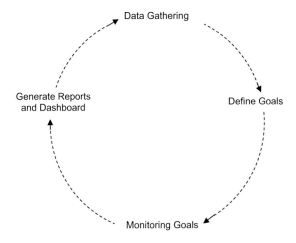

*Figure 12.1* Typical Performance Evaluation Cycle

The next activity is regarding the continuous monitoring of the defined goals. This is basically a comparison of the targets (goals) with what is being achieved. Continuous monitoring means having regular short performance evaluation intervals. The performance evaluation intervals depend on the nature of the organisation and the organisational activities being conducted. Hence, it could be daily (or shorter), weekly, or longer. This is possible with the proper technological systems in place and these systems will help the organisation to grow faster. Hence, by comparing what is being achieved by an employee with the defined goals assigned to each employee, the manager or supervisor may monitor the progress of the work being conducted under the prevalent operational circumstances.

This means that managers and supervisors can identify weaknesses and can take timely corrective decisions on the activities that they find are performing inadequately, irrespective of whether work is being conducted on site or remotely. The final activity is the generation of reports, particularly the relevant dashboards. An efficient and flexible report generator will not only minimise the manual effort but will also allow the individual managers to design (customise) the reports according to their individual requirements. The reports may take the form of visual displays or hard copy. The flexibility of the available software will help managers to avoid hard copy reports and allow them to produce exception reports that avoid voluminous output that contribute to making the system unmanageable.

Performance management has been revolutionised by modern technology in various ways. There is no doubt that the productivity of employees is affected by using the latest systems, because performance appraisal is in real-time mode with progress monitoring being unrestricted by a given schedule and the outcomes displayed are based purely on a factual data-driven mechanism, without subjectivity. However, goals must be clearly established, and tasks allocated in a timely fashion without any ambiguity. Modern systems help to enhance transparency and encourage employee engagement.

Research has shown that employees' trust increases when they perceive that they are being treated equitably, particularly when they are able to observe their specific appraisal factors. Thus, a culture of transparency and fairness is fostered throughout the organisation, where employees do not feel that they are being manipulated. This type of environment will help to develop work motivation amongst employees and will encourage them to do their best in performing their specific tasks. Furthermore, employee engagement is likely to grow as the employees' efforts are increasingly recognised and appreciated by everyone. However, it is essential that complete and accurate output is generated by the performance management system and weaknesses are identified and corrective action taken. It is important for management to know what has worked well and what has not, so that various processes may be modified to reflect the desired outcomes and the risk of erroneous decisions is mitigated.

The system must also be employee-goal driven, with the employee-goals aligned with the strategic objectives of the organisation. Note that the starting point to establishing a performance management system is to examine the needs of the organisation and the needs of the employee and aligning these two sets of needs. Therefore, it is essential that goals and objectives are defined in specific and measurable terms since the ultimate performance evaluation must be based on the assigned goals and related tasks. Keep in mind that organisational objective achievement is measured by metrics, such as KPIs, which determine whether the agreed goals have been achieved. Ideally, these goals should be defined as the 'Objectives and Key Results' (OKRs) for the organisation, which are viewed as milestones to be reported on, preferably at short time intervals (i.e., monthly, quarterly, or bi-annually). However, it should be recognised that not all the work effort in an organisation directly contributes to the strategic objectives of the organisation.

The work effort can be classified into two categories. There is work effort that is directly linked to strategic objectives (OKRs), such as the core activities (primary activities), and there is work effort that contributes to supporting the organisation, such as business-as-usual processes and jobs-to-be-done that maintain and improve specific areas of responsibility (secondary activities). Thus, in some cases, employees may have a mixture of the two categories of work effort. Therefore, it is important that every employee knows where they fit in the scheme of things and know how their work effort contributes to the organisation's success. For this to happen, employees must know in clear terms their specific role and associated goals, and how their work effort contributes to the organisation's business plan. This provides the employees' raison d'etre, their purpose in the organisation, which in turn is found to be rewarding and positively affects their job satisfaction, resulting in productivity gains. Having a clear role and explicit goals ensures that the employee's work effort is relevant and is fully directed to achieving the organisational plans and strategic objectives.

Current technology allows employees to access systems at any time from anywhere. Today's mobile phone can be considered a computational tool. Not only due to its networking capabilities, but because of its processing power through the execution of various Apps and its internet connectivity capacity. Technology has empowered employees and the employees' dependency on the managers has been reduced. Thus, they can review and track their own performances. This technological enhancement allows organisations to embrace a remote working environment that permits teams to work effectively.

The COVID-19 pandemic provided the opportunity and right conditions for the development and enhancement of an effective remote working model allowing organisations to operate in an uninterrupted manner. Hence, while teams worked remotely, the system permitted managers to constantly monitor the work being performed by employees. This effective remote working model has enhanced the use of communication tools and improved the processes related to document sharing and task management, which facilitated the performance review process.

## *Remodelling Performance Management*

Buckingham and Goodall (2015) examined the performance management process at Deloitte, where they found that the system used at Deloitte to evaluate the work of employees and then training them, promoting them, and paying them accordingly was increasingly out of step with their objectives. According to Buckingham and Goodall's study, many entities are discovering the same situation. Deloitte's management sought a quicker and more innovative system, which was real-time and tailored for their type of industry, and focused more on the individual. They sought a system that stimulated future performance rather than appraising the past. They wanted to move away from the concept of having cascading objectives that were established at the highest level of the organisation, where supporting goals are created for every team and individual within the organisation. They did not want a system with an annual review or 360-degree feedback tools. They wanted a system that was timely and responsive, supporting a one-size-fits-one concept with continuous learning. A one-size-fits-one approach avoids the frequently isolated and specific design solutions that are focused to meet the needs of those 'on the margins.' However, their concept needed to be supported by a novel way of gathering reliable performance data.

According to Buckingham and Goodall, the design for Deloitte's new performance management system was based upon three essential factors, namely, an easy and straightforward method of counting hours, reviewing research about the various methods regarding ratings, and a meticulous operations review of its own organisation. Their investigation revealed that Deloitte was consuming about two million hours a year on performance management, and that 'idiosyncratic rater effects' (i.e. ratings given by different supervisors for the same performance that do not align) often led to ratings that divulged more about team leaders (supervisors) than about the individuals they were rating.

The empirical study about Deloitte's high-performing teams revealed that three items correlated best with high performance for a team: 'My co-workers are committed to doing quality work,' 'The mission of our company inspires me,' and 'I have the chance to use my strengths every day.' The study showed that the third item was the most powerful across the organisation. This empirical study provided the evidence required to design a radical new performance management system. A crucial issue encountered by Deloitte in designing the performance management system was deciding what features were to be included or excluded from the new system, given the fact that they run a talent-dependent business.

When examining how two million hours a year on performance management was consumed, it was revealed that most of the hours were spent on three tasks, namely filling forms, holding meetings, and ratings. However, it became evident that a significant amount of activity within these three tasks was taken up by leaders' discussions behind closed doors about the outcomes of the processes. Hence, management questioned the utility of this activity and whether it made more sense to focus on open dialogue with the employees about their performance and careers rather than on discussing ratings behind closed doors. In other words, they needed to focus on the future rather than the past.

The analysis of the process also revealed inconsistencies in the assessment of the employees' skills, since those rating the skills of employees have different characteristics that lead to varying ratings. In other words, it is unlikely that two persons rating the same individual will come up with the same outcome. Some 'raters' are tough, whilst others are more lenient or have a different experience base that affects the assessment. The 'halo' effect also often comes into play, where one trait of a person is used to make an overall judgement of that person, which may support biased appraisals. Research shows that over 60% of the performance ratings variance may be due to the distinctiveness of perception experienced by the person conducting the rating exercise, with only about 21% of the variance being due to performance. This research illustrated that ratings reveal more about the person rating the employee rather than the person being rated. Although the best person to rate an employee's performance was the immediate team leader; the challenge was to find a method that mitigates the distinctive effects of the person rating the employee.

It was also important to not only focus on the performance of employees but to examine the characteristics of the organisation as a whole to determine what elements contribute in creating high-performing teams. The examination of Deloitte's work teams suggested that the teams were strengths-oriented, with team members sensing the continual need for them to give their best effort. Extensive longitudinal empirical research by Gallup regarding high-performing teams revealed that individuals comprising high-performance teams strongly cherished the opportunity to do what they do best every day at work. Moreover, these individuals were significantly more likely to attain high customer satisfaction scores, and more likely to experience high employee retention rates and be industrious.

Buckingham and Goodall conducted a similar study to Gallup, but on a smaller scale, specifically at Deloitte's. They administered a six-item survey to a representative sample of 1954 employees who embodied all parts of the organisation. Three items of the survey correlated best with the concept of high-performance teams, namely, commitment to doing quality work; being inspired by the organisation's mission; and being given the opportunity to use one's strengths every day. However, of these three items, the most powerful across the organisation was being given the opportunity to use one's strengths every day. Hence, the new design needed to focus on assisting employees as team members to use their strengths by having better clearness of purpose and expectations and to have a simple and swift method of gathering reliable and differentiated performance data. With this in mind, they went about designing a new system.

Buckingham and Goodall, in radically designing Deloitte's performance management approach, commenced by defining the ultimate purpose of performance management in the context of Deloitte's organisation. They defined several key system objectives, namely:

(a)  To allow them to acknowledge performance, particularly through variable compensation.

(b)  To mitigate the 'idiosyncratic rater' effect by referring only to the immediate team leader and asking him/her to respond to four future-focused statements about each team member at the end of every project or once every quarter for long-term projects. Thus, the questions are asking team leaders what they would do with each team member rather than what they think of that individual. The four questions are as follows:

  •   Given what I know of this person's performance, and if it were my money, I would award this person the highest possible compensation increase, and bonus. This was intended to measure overall performance and unique value to the organisation on a five-point Likert scale from 'strongly agree' to 'strongly disagree.'

  •   Given what I know of this person's performance, I would always want him or her on my team. This measures the ability to work well with others on the same five-point scale.

  •   This person is at risk for low performance. This identifies problems that might harm the customer or the team on a yes-or-no basis.

  •   This person is ready for promotion today. This measures potential on a yes-or-no basis.

(c) To streamline the process of evaluation, project rating, consensus meeting, and final rating. The data points are cumulated over a year, weighting each according to the duration of a given project. Thus, providing a simple, effective, and consistent method of rating. This rating method provides a basis for the team leaders to define succession planning, development pathways, or performance-pattern analysis. Hence, the collective data is viewed as the initial point for compensation, not the ending point with the definitive outcome being made by the team leader who knows each individual or by a panel of leaders.

(d) To implement a tool that enabled team leaders to strengthen performance. Buckingham and Goodall found that the best team leaders conduct regular check-ins with each team member by engaging in brief conversations that allow leaders to set expectations for the upcoming week, review priorities, comment on recent work, and provide course correction, coaching, or important new information. Thus, in designing the performance management system it was essential for every team leader to check in with each team member once a week as an integral part of their work. Thus, if team leaders desire employees to engage and talk about how to do their best work in the near future, they need to talk often, hence the weekly requirement. Thus, the new system would provide a place for people to explore and share what is best about themselves.

Figure 12.2 depicts the fundamental principles of the proposed performance management system. It shows the three objectives that form the basis of performance management, which are supported by the three interlock processes to support them. Hence, the Buckingham and Goodall proposed system swung from a batched focus on the past events to a continual and persistent focus on the future by frequent evaluations and regular weekly check-ins. Buckingham and Goodall tested the system as a pilot project on a selected segment of the organisation and extended the system across Deloitte, noting the evolutionary change that took place.

However, Buckingham and Goodall noted that the issue of transparency is a concern in relation to assigning a number when rating individuals. In addressing this concern, they solicit an answer to the question: What do we see when we try to quantify a person? They argue that in certain circumstances, such as sports and medicine, quantification is possible, but

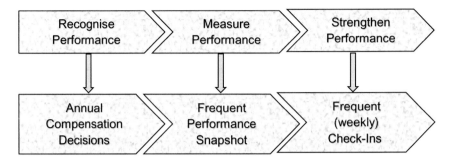

Figure 12.2 Objectives and Interlocking Procedures of Performance Management System

in a work environment quantifying performance in a single number is difficult to explain (and possibly justify). Two-way feedback between the team leader and employee may help to mitigate this genuine concern, but it is not the full solution. Buckingham and Goodall contend that the debate about performance management has been characterised as a debate about ratings, that is whether or not they are fair, and whether or not they achieve their stated objectives. However, they argue that the issue may not so much be that ratings fail to convey what the organisation knows about each person, but that as presented, that knowledge is sadly one-dimensional.

The Buckingham and Goodall Deloitte case study focuses on the individual and how a particular individual is rated. However, it should also be noted that Deloitte as an organisation is mainly performing a jobbing function (or more precisely a mixture of projects ranging from small to large). The primary driver in the Buckingham and Goodall performance management model is to create an environment that encourages employees to do their best in carrying out their specific role. However, the underlying performance targets are the defined estimates and identified project milestones for each of the projects being undertaken.

Therefore, these defined estimates and identified project milestones act as the de facto KPIs for an individual or team of individuals, depending on the amount of planning detail that is conducted when preparing the quotation for a specific job (or project). Hence, rating an individual to a single figure may be possible and justified if the rating also takes into consideration the key performance indicators (in Deloitte's case, the defined estimates and identified project milestones), with the underlying objective and assumption that employees are doing their best in carrying out their specific role.

## Performance Management Transformation

According to Cappelli and Tavis (2016), traditional performance assessments have been discarded by more than a third of US companies. They contend that from Silicon Valley to New York, and in offices across the world, firms are replacing annual reviews with frequent, informal check-ins between managers and employees. They argue that traditional performance assessments are detested by both executive management and their employees. The major shortcoming with this traditional approach is its emphasis on the past (i.e., holding employees accountable for what they did last year) and neglecting the future (i.e., discarding the opportunity to improve current and future performance).

Cappelli and Tavis argue that there is an urgent need to transform performance management systems into frequent, development-focused exchanges between managers and employees, with the objective of looking after employees by keeping them happy and preparing them for advancement; having frequent check-ins with employees to ensure that the organisation is responsive to the constant change in its business environment; and fostering teamwork by giving precedence to improvement rather than accountability. A performance management system must at minimum meet several objectives, including the achievement of the organisation's strategic goals through the alignment of individual and organisational goals; rewarding employees on merit; pinpointing good and poor performers; and treating employees equitably.

According to Cappelli and Tavis, the evolution of performance management over the last century has been greatly influenced by the changing historical and economic environment. They argue that when human capital was abundant, the emphasis was on deciding which employees to retain and which to reward. Under this scenario the traditional assessment approach that focused on individual accountability appeared to function adequately. However, as economic recovery took hold and gigantic technological advances were made that resulted in a scarcity of skilled labour, organisations were faced with the urgent need to develop their workforce and have a performance management system that reflected this need.

Also according to Cappelli and Tavis, the first significant divergence from traditional reviews occurred at Adobe in 2011. They claim that Adobe broke down its projects into 'sprints' that were immediately followed by debriefing sessions, and this was developed into a regular assessment and feedback method, forming the basis for their performance management, with frequent check-ins replacing annual appraisals. Cappelli and Tavis reveal that the Adobe approach was taken up by others, such as Juniper Systems, Dell, and Microsoft. It is proposed that modern performance management systems are driven by business needs, rather than being imposed by the HR Department. Cappelli and Tavis argue that there are three clear business constraints that are influencing companies to discard performance appraisals:

(a) Firstly, the need to develop talent in the organisation to keep up with the rapid pace of technological developments in areas such as knowledge work and big data analysis. Hence, this approach needs valuable feedback from supervisors, which is ameliorated by frequent, informal check-ins rather than by annual reviews. Thus, having a system with a feedback mechanism that is provided immediately after an assignment assists supervisors to enhance their coaching of subordinates and permits subordinates to decipher, understand, and utilise the advice given by the supervisor more effectively.

(b) Secondly, the need for organisational responsiveness. Organisations must continually change in response to technological developments, since innovation is a source of competitive advantage. It must be recognised that businesses no longer have clear annual cycles, since many projects tend to be of a short-term nature and are inclined to change during their implementation. Hence, employees' goals and tasks are unlikely to be accurately defined a year in advance.

(c) Thirdly, the need to promote teamwork and abandon forced ranking and appraisals that focus on individual accountability. In retail companies, leading-edge customer service requires frontline and back-office employees to work as a well synchronised team to keep shelves stocked and manage customer flow. Hence, the system needs to enhance performance at a team level and facilitate the tracking of collaboration between the relevant sections.

The three reasons for discarding annual appraisals support the concept of closely following the natural cycle of work rather than having a fixed annual cycle. Thus, two-way communication between supervisors and employees takes place when projects finish and/or milestones are reached, and/or when challenges are encountered, thus permitting employees to resolve current concerns that may affect performance while concurrently enhancing their skills for the future. However, essentially organisations are revamping their performance management system as a proactive measure because their businesses require the change.

According to Cappelli and Tavis, the greatest resistance to discarding traditional appraisal systems does not come from the supervisors or employees, but from the HR Department, simply because the procedures that HR has built over the years revolve around these traditional appraisal systems. Furthermore, Cappelli and Tavis argue that replacing the performance management system with a contemporary approach presents several challenges, as described below:

(a) Achieving congruency of individual and organisational goals. In the traditional model, business objectives and strategies were defined in a top-down manner. Thus, the business objectives and strategies would cascade down the organisation with the business units and respective employees establishing their targets to reflect and support this top-down direction. It is argued that this top-down approach succeeds when business goals are easily defined and are held constant over a financial year. However, when employee targets are linked to specific projects or milestones, it may not be possible to hold the targets constant for a financial year since circumstances are constantly changing. Hence, as projects are being implemented and circumstances change, aligning individual priorities with organisational goals becomes difficult, particularly when organisational objectives are linked to specific projects or milestones that are not interrelated to a specific financial year.

(b) Rewarding performance. Organisations may have their own particular pay-for-performance model and are unsure how the new practices will affect their reward model. Often organisations rely on the managers' qualitative assessment rather than numerical ratings. However, in a project-oriented environment, where specific project plans identify tasks, including their cost and time estimates, it may be possible to utilise these estimates as KPIs and thus have accurate numerical ratings as a performance base.

(c) Identifying poor performers. HR departments consistently complain that line managers do not use the appraisal process to document poor

performers and often wait until the end of the year before highlighting a concern. As stated previously in a project-oriented environment
it is possible to establish KPIs based upon defined tasks and milestones.
Hence, poor performers are easily identified, monitored, and coun-
selled regularly, thus mitigating the possibility of discharges. Cappelli
and Tavis argue that 'performance improvement plans' for employees
remain universally problematic, because many issues that cause poor
performance cannot be solved by management intervention.

(d) Mitigating the risk of legal troubles. A common concern within HR
departments is that discrimination charges will increase if they cease
basing pay increases and promotions on numerical ratings that appear to
be objective. It is argued that appraisals have not prevented discrimina-
tory practices. Hence, no matter what system is applied, there is always
a significant amount of discretion that is subject to bias, which is inherent to the process. Cappelli and Tavis claim that considerable evidence
shows supervisors discriminate against some employees by giving them
undeservedly low ratings. They contend that formal ratings may do more
to reveal bias than to curb it and if a company has clear appraisal scores
and merit-pay indexes, it is easy to see if women and minorities with
the same scores as white men are getting fewer or lower pay increases.
Hence, linking KPIs with an employee appraisal system may mitigate
discrimination because all employees are evaluated on the same basis.

(e) Managing the feedback pipeline. It is essential that performance management systems permit continuous feedback to facilitate the employee
check-ins approach. The technology is currently available to permit
the employee check-ins approach to happen. Cappelli and Tavis (2016)
claim that General Electric have developed an app (PD@GE) that permits managers to call up notes and materials from prior conversations
and summarise that information, and allows employees to ask for
direction when they need it. However, they argue that not all employers face the same business pressures to change their performance processes, and some industrial segments still focus on accountability and
financial rewards for individual performers. However, it is argued that
accountability should be a collective concept and that supervisors need
to improve their subordinates' coaching and developing skills.

(f) Ideology at the top matters. Cappelli and Tavis explain that at Intel,
employees got feedback but no formal appraisal scores and supervisors

had no difficulty with their performance-based pay system without these ratings. However, they revealed that Intel company executives returned to the ratings approach, because they viewed ratings as creating healthy competition and clear outcomes.

Cappelli and Tavis contend that the above challenges need to be addressed as performance management systems evolve over time. They argue that it will be interesting to see how well these 'third way' approaches work; however, the degree to which these new concepts will work depends on the support of senior leadership, reinforced by organisational culture. They stress that holding on to the old systems may not be a good option for most organisations.

## Contemporary Performance Management and Measurement Trends

Key Performance Indicators (KPIs) are about gathering knowledge and exploring the best way to achieve organisation goals (Idrees, 2016). In the previous introductory chapters addressing performance measurement concepts, four levels or types of performance measures were identified, namely:

- Key result indicators (KRIs) that inform managers how they achieved the quantitative results of business actions to help them track progress and attain the organisational goals.
- Result indicators (RIs) that inform managers what they have completed.
- Performance indicators (PIs) that inform managers what they must carry out.
- KPIs that inform managers what they must carry out to substantially increase performance.

Idrees (2016) uses the onion analogy to explain how these four levels of 'performance measures' function. She describes the outside skin as the overall condition in terms of a KRI with the other layers providing more detailed information. Hence, the layers are viewed as representing the various performance and result indicators, with the core denoting the key performance indicator. Thus, she argues that KPIs act as a set of measures that focus on organisational performance aspects that are critical for the success of the organisation. Hence, she contends that KPIs are seldom new to the organisation but may not have come to the attention of management. However, KPIs are but one component of the performance phenomena, which goes beyond just KPIs, extending into the realm of Performance Measurement and Management (PMM).

According to Taticchi et al. (2012), organisations that try to use PMM systems report experiencing implementation problems, including goal incongruence. They argue that research in PMM has become increasingly important because of its significant impact on competitive strategy and operations of organisations in the current global business environment. They contend that there is a need for a holistic approach to PMM, which requires an intensive and deep comprehension of the key activities in the organisation and their related drivers. Taticchi et al. (2012) cite the Balanced Scorecard (BSC) approach as having received considerable attention and having been applied successfully in numerous industries. Their research revealed that performance management frameworks in the first decade of the twenty-first century had several common attributes, such as linking strategy to operations and recommending a balanced set of financial and non-financial measures.

These models also encountered some common challenges, such as struggling to create quantitative relations incorporating performance indicators and addressing performance measurement as a rational process. Taticchi et al. argue that the models that emerged since the year 2000 embody further improvement in understanding of the process, such as the dynamic performance measurement system (DPMS), which aims to ensure that the gains achieved through improvement programmes are maintained. They contend that the DPMS attempted to merge all the strengths of the previously developed frameworks, by integrating the use of Information and Communication Technology (ICT) infrastructure and a quantitative model to manage cause-effect relations of performance metrics. Applying the Taticchi and Balachandran (2008) methodology, Taticchi et al. identified five essential milestones of an 'ideal' PMM system as follows:

(a) **Assessment**: PMM systems are to have an assessment stage to evaluate the capability of the current system in order to define a base for planning improvement. This clarifies at the conceptual stage what the actual PM architecture can offer and what efforts and actions need to be taken in order to improve it.

(b) **Design**: PMM systems must reflect the organisation's business activities. Hence, the need to design specific architecture and relevant measures. Typical elements of these frameworks are: The relationship of strategies to operations, the consideration of differing stakeholder perspectives, the use of financial and non-financial indicators, and the integration of external and internal parameters. The PMM system must have several processes, namely a performance measurement framework and strategy maps, measures and targets, alignment and integration, and the information infrastructure.

(c) **Implementation**: This step involves having clearly articulated guidelines for successful implementation. For an effective implementation of a PMM system several processes are required, namely top manager agreement and commitment; the 3 E's: empower, enable, and encourage; and an effective two-way communication process.

(d) **Communication/Alignment**: PMM systems must provide clear unambiguous guidelines to effectively communicate performances inside the organisation, with the aim of achieving organisation alignment. The communication aspect includes the application of a single indicator to enable mutual understanding, and the use of dashboards for managers or the use of icons and smiles with employees. Communication is an essential driver to achieve organisational alignment to strategy, combined with an incentive compensation system to promote organisational alignment and performance growth.

(e) **Review**: PMM systems must have a review stage for assessing both the architecture and measures as a consequence of environmental or strategic changes. This provides a means of avoiding any misalignment of the PMM system with the organisation's business activity and as a way of confirming whether the PMM system is contributing to an overall improvement in performance.

Taticchi et al. found poor consistency between the various PMM systems investigated. Their research revealed that none of the models/frameworks reviewed presented concurrently all the milestones that a PMM system should encompass. Hence, they suggest several attributes that a PMM system should possess and provide guidelines for future design. They strongly advocate that to create a total performance measurement and management system, integration with other systems is a prerequisite. Indeed, Taticchi and Balachandran (2008) had emphasised that for a complete PMM system, a multi-level model is required that incorporates a framework integrating five specific systems, namely a performance system; cost system; capability evaluation system; benchmarking system; and planning system.

Furthermore, an extensive comprehension of the business is indispensable for implementing the framework. Hence, if you do not understand the basis of the problem, there is no way of resolving it. Therefore, it is imperative that a detailed operational review of the organisation is undertaken that analyses the organisation's business activities and their respective drivers. Organisations that have implemented an Activity Based Costing approach will find this to be a great advantage. Taticchi et al. contend that the proposed framework defines 'what' information should be analysed, 'how' it should be processed, and 'how' it could be integrated to generate value information for managerial actions.

Figure 12.3 illustrates the Taticchi and Balachandran PMM method, which uses a multi-level model. Taking a bottom-up approach, the model commences with the value chain processes. These processes provide the input to the three upper systems of analysis, comprising of the capability evaluation system, cost system, and the performance system. These three systems are closely integrated, passing information to each other. Note that the value chain processes must be examined by focusing on the activities and related drivers to present an across-the-board understanding of the organisation's business operations.

Taticchi et al. argue that unfortunately many organisations, particularly small and medium enterprises, do not have their processes and activities well defined. Hence, they contend that an effort should be made in order to identify the organisation's value chain, and associated processes, activities, and related drivers. The identification of the processes will permit their evaluation by the performance system to report the results achieved. The performance system should focus on the measurement of the organisation's processes, specifically the identified KPIs. Taticchi et al. advocate that a good performance measurement system should not only be limited to a list of KPIs, but should identify relations between them and their level of impact over the organisation's business activities.

To comprehend the information generated by the performance system, the results have to be examined in comparison with the 'physical

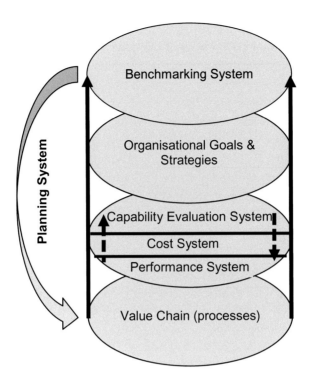

*Figure* 12.3  Integration of Systems in a Multi-Level Systems Environment

capabilities' of the organisation that limit the performance of a specific process. The resources responsible for limiting output should be identified. These 'physical capabilities' constraints are referred to as Limiting or Scarce factors. Within the short-term period it is unlikely that these 'physical capabilities' constraints can be removed and additional resources acquired. Therefore, the aim is to focus on those products or services that yield the largest contribution per limiting factor. The 'physical capabilities' limitations may be due to several aspects, namely technological, materials available, and human resources, as well as others.

The Cost System is a critical source of information for supporting managers in their decision-making processes, since it provides the information regarding process and activity costs. These costs are vital for determining the interchange when comparing the findings of the Performance and Capability Systems, and thus deciding which products or services yield the largest contribution per limiting factor. Hence, the outcome of this comparison analysis provides a clear understanding of the process performance, which is necessary for knowing the action required to optimise the performance and the identification of likely physical limitations that may be eliminated on a contribution (cost and revenue) basis. The output from the performance system and the comparative analysis are to be evaluated in combination with the organisation's strategies and goals, to make certain that there is alignment of the overall structure.

Moreover, the performances achieved should be benchmarked with top-performing-organisations to establish additional targets that consistently take into consideration the organisation's capabilities. The planning aspect is also important to ensure the achievement of the latest identified goals. Planning should be viewed as a holistic activity related to business planning, taking into account financial and non-financial budgeting factors. Taticchi et al. argue that the integration of the proposed five systems is an essential guideline for future PMM system design. They contend that by optimising and integrating the characteristics of each of the systems, researchers could develop comprehensive systems of performance measurement and management.

Let us take an example to illustrate how the proposed framework would work in a practical situation. This example is related to the production of components. In the short-term, sales demand may be in excess of current productive capacity. Productive capacity may include skilled labour, materials, equipment, and floor space. Firstly, the resources responsible for limiting output should be identified. These are referred to as Limiting or Scarce factors. Note that within the short-term period it is unlikely that production constraints can be removed and additional resources acquired. Hence, the aim is to focus on those products or services that yield the largest contribution per limiting factor.

Let us assume that a department supplies components to firms in the automobile industry. The cost system report is shown at Table 12.1 and the capability evaluation system report is depicted at Table 12.2. The information shown in Table 12.1 and Table 12.2 is related to anticipated demand and productive capacity for the next quarter regarding the three components that are manufactured. However, the performance system report at Table 12.3 shows that the machine hours capacity for its special purpose machines is 33% below the normal requirement due to a breakdown of one of the special purpose machines.

Table 12.1 Cost System Report for Producing Required Components

| Cost Details | Part X | Part Y | Part Z |
|---|---|---|---|
| Contribution per unit of output | $12 | $10 | $6 |
| Estimated sales demand in units | 2,000 | 2,000 | 2,000 |

Table 12.2 Capability Evaluation System Report for Producing Required
 Components

| Capacity Utilisation Details | Part X | Part Y | Part Z |
|---|---|---|---|
| Machine hours per unit of output | 6 | 2 | 1 |
| Required machine hours per quarter | 12,000 | 4,000 | 2,000 |

Table 12.3 Performance System Report for Producing Required Components

| Special Purpose M/Cs | Actual | Budget | Gap | Status | Outlook | Strategic Impact | Capabilities Related |
|---|---|---|---|---|---|---|---|
| Machine hours available | 12,000 | 18,000 | -33% | | | High | Machine Capacity |

Therefore, the limiting factor in this case is machine hours, which is limited to 12,000 machine hours for the period. Based on budgeted (planned) values of the special purpose machines indicators, the performance system indicates a warning related to the insufficient special purpose machines hours to meet the sales demand. Thus, the production manager needs to advise management on the mix of products that should be produced during the period to maximise the total contribution.

To provide the required advice, the production manager needs to focus on integrating the available information generated by the three systems, namely the cost, capability evaluation, and performance systems. The example illustrates that the special purpose machine breakdown is a concern and is highlighted as being the limiting factor. Hence, maximising the total contribution should not be based upon the contribution per unit of output (see Table 12.1), but on the contribution per limiting factor, in this case contribution per special purpose machine hours. Therefore, the organisation's ability to increase its output, net cash inflows, and profits is limited by the special purpose machine capacity.

To determine the optimum production plan, first calculate the contribution per limiting factor for each component. Hence, the contribution per machine hour = Contribution per unit output ÷ Machine hours per unit of output. For Part X: Contribution per machine hour = 12 ÷ 6 hours = $2 per hour; for Part Y: Contribution per machine hour = 10 ÷ 2 hours = $5 per hour; and for Part Z: Contribution per machine hour = 6 ÷ 1 hour = $6 per hour. These calculations and respective production priority rankings are shown at Table 12.4. Note that Table 12.4 indicates that to maximise the total contribution for the organisation, the production plan should rank the production of the components in order of profitability based on: Part Z at €6 per hour; Part Y at €5 per hour; Part X at €2 per hour. Therefore, the production manager is now in a position to allocate the 12,000 scarce special purpose machine hours in accordance with the calculated ranking as shown in Table 12.5.

Table 12.4  Contribution per Special Purpose Machine Hours for Producing Required Components

| Contribution Details | Part X | Part Y | Part Z |
| --- | --- | --- | --- |
| Contribution per unit of output | $12 | $10 | $6 |
| Machine hours per unit of output | 6 | 2 | 1 |
| Contribution per machine hour | $2 | $5 | $6 |
| Production priority | 3 | 2 | 1 |

Table 12.5  Production Plan for Producing Required Components to Maximise Total Contribution

| Production Details | Machine Hours Used | Contribution |
| --- | --- | --- |
| 2 000 units of Z at €6 per unit contribution | 2,000 | $12,000 |
| 2 000 units of Y at €10 per unit contribution | 4,000 | $20,000 |
| 1 000 units of X at €12 per unit contribution | 6,000 | $12,000 |
| Total: | 12,000 | $44,000 |

As the example illustrated, the limited special purpose machine hours were the cause of the concern. The production manager should make some further recommendations to top management to mitigate the highlighted concern. These recommendations may include:

(a) Working overtime or introduce an extra work shift. However, this would increase the production cost.
(b) Having a buffer stock of each component to ensure that orders are met. However, this would negatively impact working capital.
(c) Enter into a back-up agreement with the machine supplier or a collaborative arrangement with a producer who may not be a direct competitor.
(d) Increase capacity but have under-utilised equipment on stand-by.

The production manager needs to consider the consequences from the proposed production plan, particularly, if the lower production-ranked components are for longstanding loyal customers. It may be better for the organisation to encounter higher production costs and lower contribution margins rather than losing loyal customers. This example shows that information from integrated systems is essential for making the correct decisions. Furthermore, qualitative factors are an important consideration and should be brought to the attention of the eventual decision-maker to ensure that all customers are satisfied with the service provided.

Taticchi et al. identify several challenges for the future design of performance measurement and management systems. They argue that the first challenge to improve the effectiveness of performance measurement and management models is related to creating the right organisational environment. Admittedly, this challenge is a common factor in the introduction of any type of major change within an organisation. It normally boils down to equipping the organisation and its employees with the appropriate Information Management Technology methods required to gather, process, retrieve, and analyse data that depicts their business. Hence, Enterprise Resource Planning (ERP) and Business Intelligence (BI) software supported by an effective database engine can significantly contribute to supporting the performance measurement and management initiatives.

Taticchi et al. contend that the second challenge is the need for performance measurement and management models to incorporate logical interrelationships of cause and effect between actions and results. They argue that management should sanction their organisation to recognise relationships between processes and the fundamental basis of their business so that they can really contribute to accomplishing the 'knowing-doing' gap. The 'knowing-doing' gap signifies the concern of managers in successfully understanding the information coming from the measurement of processes into operational tasks. In other words, the gap between knowledge and action (i.e., the gap between what is known and what is actually applied). Hence, the concern is not in acquiring a suitable set of KPIs for monitoring the organisation's processes, but in understanding the cause-effect relationships of what value each indicator is based on.

Figure 12.4 illustrates that management information systems must be capable of handling voluminous transactions on an enterprise-wide basis by adopting a concept supporting the integration of systems and backed by a data warehouse that permits data integration and data sharing across

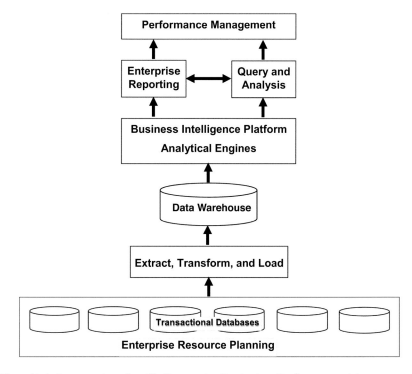

Figure 12.4  Overcoming the Challenges in Designing Performance Measurement and Management Models

the organisation. The data warehouse philosophy needs to have the ability to record all transactions down to sub-process level and extract data from different sources, with the capability to store and transform the data for analytical purposes.

It is essential that a Business Intelligence Platform is implemented with the necessary analytical tools and having a flexible and powerful report generator that is operable at a user level to permit enterprise reporting and query analysis to answer ad hoc queries. This concept will support a performance measurement and management model to track, monitor, and analyse key financial goals and objectives. A prime objective is knowing what drives the organisation's business to be able to reduce costs, add value, create new reality, and minimise risk.

The overall aim is to create a data warehouse from the data generated by the enterprise-wide systems and their respective transaction databases. Once this data warehouse transformation mechanism is in place, the data warehouse may be utilised to create a comprehensive business intelligence repository. This business intelligence repository is itself used in making effective management decisions. Hence, the data warehouse provides the data, information, and intelligence (knowledge), but to use this vast amount of data, information, and intelligence repository a datamining tool is require to extract the knowledge that is required for a specific decision. However, the majority of current performance measurement and management models take a narrow viewpoint and restrict their focus to the performance system.

This approach does not fully utilise the valuable generated information for realising optimal likely effectiveness. The above illustrates that performance measurement and management systems need a high level of integration between systems, to allow management to better understand and analyse the intricacy and distinctiveness of their business activities. This would provide robust operational support to management in making their decisions. Additionally, the integration of systems through an enterprise model allows management to fully understand the available data and information, which is a conceivable way forward in shifting from performance measurement to performance management.

Murtala (2017) conducted research studies at various companies to examine new trends in the performance measurement system over the traditional system, how corporate organisations respond to the emerging trends, how the changes impact their businesses performance in the challenging contemporary business environment, and identify the new approaches adopted to manage the changes. Murtala confirms the findings of Taticchi et al. A summary of Murtala's research findings is shown in Table 12.6. Murtala argues these findings indicate that:

- Traditional performance measurement systems such as profitability, cash flow, and return on capital employed were falling short of meeting the needs of managers in a turbulent business environment.
- The trend is towards developing systems of performance measurement that reflect the growing complexity of the business environment, and monitor their strategic response to this complexity.
- The need for good performance management is an ongoing issue where poor performance needs to be addressed.
- Providing honest and timely feedback to trigger behavioural change is key.
- The current emphasis is individual check-ins, team touch points, and individual development plan (IDP).
- A performance management system that focuses on behaviour in addition to results becomes a business-risk management tool or a business-risk mitigation tool.

Murtala contends that corporate organisations are progressively realising that much of their strategic value rests in their people, systems, processes, and ability to innovate. Hence, integrating the appraisal of behaviour in performance management becomes a valuable instrument for building and sustaining a culture valued by consumers, potential investors, shareholders, regulators, and other external interest groups. Murtala argues that negative behaviours which may impact performance include insubordination, having turbulent relationships, being individualistic, working in a silo, passing the buck, and nonchalant attitude, amongst others, while positive behaviours include diligence, being industrious, teamwork, having a robust reputation for being collaborative, and being emotionally intelligent, amongst others. He argues that performance is a direct consequence of behaviour and therefore it is essential to measure the behaviours that result in performance, because it may have positive or negative consequences for the business. He notes that results measure past performance, while behaviour points to future performance.

*Table* 12.6  Summary of Murtala's (2017) Research Findings Regarding Big
            Companies

| Organisation | Findings |
|---|---|
| Lafargeholcim Group: Swiss Building Materials Manufacturer | Initial finding was that traditional performance management practice was ineffective at boosting performance. They replaced their system by focusing on the following areas: To identify what to do and how to do it. Having regular Individual Check-ins and Team Touch Point between employee and line manager, and between team and line manager. |
| Cargill, Inc.: US food producer and distributor | Transformed its traditional performance management by removing performance ratings and annual review forms and focusing on managers having frequent on-the-job chats and giving regular, constructive feedback. |
| Adobe Systems: US multinational computer software firm | Abandoned annual performance appraisals and replaced them with regular 'check-ins' supported by frequent feedback, both positive and constructive. There are no ratings and different parts of the organisation are able to determine frequency of check-in conversations according to their work cycles. |
| Accenture Group: Irish global professional services company | Disbanded ranking and once-a-year evaluation process, replacing them with frequent feedback and chats at the heart of their new process, and focusing on performance development, rather than performance rating. |
| Deloitte: UK audit, consulting, financial advisory, risk management, tax, and related services company | Scraped once-a-year performance reviews, 360-degree feedback, and objective cascading, replacing them with check-ins between team leaders and each team member once a week to discuss near-term work and priorities, comment on recent work, and provide coaching. Check-ins are initiated by the team members rather than the team leaders. |
| General Electric Group: US multinational company | GE replaced the annual appraisal system with frequent feedback and regular conversations called 'touch points' to review progress against agreed goals. |

According to Ossovski et al. (2016), organisations' strategies tend to be designed to promote their deployment in measures that will lead to actions for the achievement of targets. They argue that Measurement System Strategic Performance (MSSP) stimulates the development of a more comprehensive strategic agenda within the organisation, consisting not only in the formulation of the strategy but also in defining how this strategy will be deployed and implemented, bringing 'action,' 'monitoring' and 'evaluation' of the results as part of the processes. Hence, they conclude that the implementation of an MSSP creates a significant alignment between the long-term strategy of the organisation and other aspects and stages infused in a performance measurement system, namely the deployment in targets, measurements, assessments, actions, reviews, and learning, including the active commitment of the top management. The active commitment of the top management is particularly important because it acts as a motivating factor for the entire chain such as managers, experts, operational staff, customers, and suppliers, becoming a crucial element to achieve success while implementing a performance measurement system in an organisation.

Ossovski et al. view the alignment of strategic analysis and performance measurement as an essential ingredient to organisational success because it steers managers to focus on the future, promotes a more precise communication flow, and optimises a holistic coordination process. Ossovski et al. (2016) maintain that a performance measurement system progresses through five key phases, namely: Design, implementation, use of performance measures, review, and learning. Moreover, not all phases are executed in a sequential manner but may overlap with other phases, with several phases being implemented before others. Figure 12.5 illustrates the five phases of the performance measurement system as defined by Bourne et al. (2000), Farris et al. (2011), and Ossovski et al.

The design stage commences with an operations review of the organisation to identify the requirements of the customers and stakeholders, thus confirming the alignment with the organisation's strategy. This enables management to define a new set of objectives for the organisation. Bourne et al. suggest that the design stage can be further sub-divided into the identification of key design objectives and measures design. Substantial literature recommends the approach applied by Neely et al. (1997). These recommendations maintain that performance measures must be derived from the strategy; provide updated feedback; be quantifiable; reflect the organisational activities; be specific, relevant, simple, and objective; have

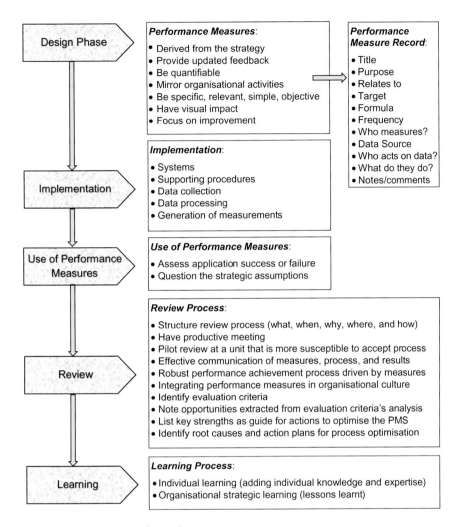

**Design Phase**

**Performance Measures:**
- Derived from the strategy
- Provide updated feedback
- Be quantifiable
- Mirror organisational activities
- Be specific, relevant, simple, objective
- Have visual impact
- Focus on improvement

**Performance Measure Record:**
- Title
- Purpose
- Relates to
- Target
- Formula
- Frequency
- Who measures?
- Data Source
- Who acts on data?
- What do they do?
- Notes/comments

**Implementation**

**Implementation:**
- Systems
- Supporting procedures
- Data collection
- Data processing
- Generation of measurements

**Use of Performance Measures**

**Use of Performance Measures:**
- Assess application success or failure
- Question the strategic assumptions

**Review**

**Review Process:**
- Structure review process (what, when, why, where, and how)
- Have productive meeting
- Pilot review at a unit that is more susceptible to accept process
- Effective communication of measures, process, and results
- Robust performance achievement process driven by measures
- Integrating performance measures in organisational culture
- Identify evaluation criteria
- Note opportunities extracted from evaluation criteria's analysis
- List key strengths as guide for actions to optimise the PMS
- Identify root causes and action plans for process optimisation

**Learning**

**Learning Process:**
- Individual learning (adding individual knowledge and expertise)
- Organisational strategic learning (lessons learnt)

Figure 12.5  Five Phases of a Performance Measurement System

visual impact; and focus on improvement. These recommendations are supported by a Performance Measure Record Sheet that strives to define what a good performance measure should embrace.

The implementation phase comprises of the systems and supporting procedures to collect and process the data that generate the measurements to support the defined strategy. According to Ossovski et al., the application of the performance measures consists of two tasks, namely to assess the success or failure of the implementation and to question the strategic assumptions. Hence, one must assess the extent to which the performance management system suits the organisational operation by providing the scores that permit senior management, managers, and employees to determine whether the defined goals were realised. The review phase is triggered if the goals were not realised.

Questioning the strategic assumptions will help management to realise that by examining the results and the extracted measures of the implemented performance management system, they can take appropriate action, including changing direction to improve the organisational performance. The review process is undertaken to improve management's understanding of the performance measurement system to enhance its expertise on the applicability of the measures. The review phase consists of two aspects, namely, preparing for the review process and having an approach to analyse the shortcomings of the performance measurement system to determine what needs to be modified or optimised for improvement. The review process facilitates the organisational learning process and is an important component for changing organisational culture.

There are two aspects to learning, namely individual learning and organisational strategic learning. According to Ossovski et al., individual learning occurs when employees absorb new knowledge through experience in their daily lives and from other sources, thus increasing the intelligence and ability of the individual. On the other hand, strategic learning is achieved by reviewing the lessons learnt from success and failure. In other words, management must determine what went right, including the reasons for the success and similarly what went wrong and why. The performance management system is an excellent vehicle for the strategic learning process, intensifying the knowledge about current measures and the enhancement of the identified opportunities, which lead to change and innovation, and better understanding of the performance management system as a whole.

Ossovski et al. propose a performance measurement system conceptual model from the strategic management viewpoint. Their proposed conceptual model consolidates the phases depicted by Figure 12.5, which can be used by different types of organisations as a guide when developing or reviewing a performance measurement system process. The performance measurement system conceptual model proposed by Ossovski et al. is illustrated by Figure 12.6, which itemises key actions as a checklist to avoid critical points in the process from being overlooked or neglected. Ossovski et al. contend that the proposed model can be utilised to support a

| Stages | Key Actions | Specific Actions |
|---|---|---|
| ➢ Long-Term Strategy: Top Management | ○ Align strategy with support from management for PMS support | ✓ List inhibiting factors for PMS to assess resistance by management |
| ➢ Long Term Strategy – Senior Managers | ○ Execute Business Strategy, Corporate / Process / Employees Goals, to support PMS | ✓ List inhibiting factors for PMS to assess resistance by operations |
| ➢ Traditional and Non-Traditional Measures | ○ Analyse organisation's method and objectives to set measures | ✓ Choose between traditional and non-traditional measures |
| ➢ Performance Measures | ○ Ensure compliance with attributes of defined measures | ✓ Highlight specific attributes to suit business scenario and strategies |
| ➢ Design | ○ Use recommendations for the performance measures design<br>○ Use record sheet for the performance measures<br>○ Analyse existing PM models and apply best option | ✓ Confirm creation of goals that are simple & are essential measures<br>✓ Register established measures ensuring their clarity |
| ➢ Implementation | ○ Employ design definitions, system model selected, & data allocation | ✓ Follow up design planning<br>✓ See if adjustments are needed |
| ➢ Use | ○ Classify results<br>○ Use analysis & process upgrading for low performances | ✓ Confirm data accuracy, results analysis, & hold regular meetings<br>✓ Team motivation focusing on improvements, not pointing fingers |
| ➢ Review – Preparation | ○ Assess preparation for process review abiding by proposed guidelines | ✓ Set what, when, why, where, how<br>✓ Have constructive meetings<br>✓ Identify business unit for review |
| ➢ Review – Systematic | ○ Utilise systematic process review | ✓ Use assessment criteria<br>✓ Identify strengths & opportunities for improvement<br>✓ Choose key opportunities<br>✓ Find root cause and use action plans for improvement |
| ✓ Learning | ✓ Ascertain opportunities for enhancement & innovation based on PMS review | ✓ Deploy improvement projects and progress of measures<br>✓ Use PMS and adjust as expertise increases and variation raises |

Figure 12.6  Proposed Performance Measurement System Conceptual Model

performance measurement system process review for those organisations that have already developed their own systems and are willing to add modifications and/or enhancements.

## Artificial Intelligence: The Future in Performance Management

According to Tabassum and Ghosh (2018), the quality of employee performance measurement and management has invariably improved due to the integration of advanced technologies like machine learning and artificial intelligence (AI), which enables the adoption of predictive analytics in emphasising employee performance. They argue that redesigning performance management is considered high priority. They contend that the company's capacity to improve performance management has improved by 10% when compared to 2015. Tabassum and Ghosh argue that the impacts of new performance practices are high, with 90% of companies having redesigned their performance management process. Of these companies, 96% have recorded benefits due to streamlined processes that make their performance management simpler to manage, and 83% have noted an upward trend in the quality of conversations between employees and their managers.

Tabassum and Ghosh argue that 91% of companies have adopted continuous performance management that provide better data for decision-making purposes, by eliminating the bias and discrimination in promotion and career advancement. Tabassum and Ghosh argue that increasing the performance feedback frequency and gratification will lead to increased usage of individual employee performance metrics. They propose that the organisation must recruit managers with strong coaching and communication skills and develop digital dexterity across the workforce; review compensation practices to make new performance management alternatives more effective; re-evaluate practices and policies around data sharing with individuals and teams; and balance the risk of oversharing and undersharing while supporting the need for greater transparency.

It is observed that organisations have become increasingly employee-focused and less process-driven, with the emphasis shifting from quantity to quality of conversations and feedback. The employee-focused approach is doing away with annual appraisals and is focusing on more regular 'check-ins' and frequent real-time feedback. The new performance management systems aim to provide both employees and managers with a framework for having high-quality discussions and effective feedback. Additionally, the performance management systems must promote a future-focused approach with developmental dialogue supported by real-time qualitative feedback.

New performance management software tools are being rapidly adopted to make performance measurement as effortless as possible, and to permit agile objectives and shorter-term priorities to be agreed and monitored. The new generation of performance management tools allows employees to receive and request feedback in real-time, send automated email reminders to ensure employees and their managers check-in with each other regularly, provide online agendas for effective one-to-one conversations, and give HR and senior management visibility of whether regular performance discussions are taking place, thus moving away from the annual goal-setting cycle approach.

AI and other new related technologies will have a huge impact on performance management of organisations. Arnauts (2019) argues that the look of enterprise performance management is changing as new technologies, specifically in the scope of AI and advanced data analytics to mine previously untapped organisational data and take future-oriented decisions, meet growing demands for better, more agile, and more change-oriented enterprise-wide performance management approaches. The approach that organisations can take to move from strategy to strategic actions, while concurrently forecasting, monitoring, and managing performance, will require more than what enterprise performance management formerly permitted.

Arnauts claims that AI will have a huge impact on performance management because it will allow organisations to correlate information and create insights that weren't possible before, so that they can take the best possible decisions. He argues that the causes for the different approaches in enterprise performance management include the variation in the extent of digital business transformation; the increasing demand for holistic, real-time, and future-oriented customer and business insights to guide better decisions; and the constant demands generated by the ever more dynamic markets. Whilst the concepts of enterprise performance management are not new, there is on one hand the evolution in the reality and needs of enterprise performance management, and on the other hand the technologies that enable operational excellence and holistic change in a highly data-driven and insights power-driven way. However, it must be recognised that gaining the strategic, financial, analytical, and business intelligence to make better business decisions is only one part of the equation.

AI in enterprise performance management is all about forward-thinking organisations that look to the future. AI in performance management is transformational. Hence, it is not just a matter of learning from the past and present but, more importantly, to understand and plan for the future using the proper KPIs (Arnauts, 2019). According to Arnauts, allowing AI to get into the core of an organisation's enterprise performance management cycle enables management to harness all available data in the organisation's ecosystem in order to take the best possible decisions in previously unforeseen ways.

Furthermore, Gartner (2023) defines enterprise performance management as an umbrella term that describes the methodologies, metrics, processes, and systems used to monitor and manage the business performance of an enterprise. Hence, they view enterprise performance management as consisting of applications that enable them to translate strategically focused information to operational plans and send aggregated results. Additionally, these applications are also integrated into many elements of the planning and control cycle. Therefore, enterprise performance management must be supported by a suite of analytical applications that provide the functionality to support these processes, methodologies, and metrics.

It must be noted that enterprise performance management is not synonymous to performance management in the sense of HR and employees, but takes a more holistic view. However, one may note that performance management in the sense of HR and employees is a particular aspect that utilises the application of AI and may be an integral part of enterprise performance management. Enterprise performance management encompasses business intelligence and exploits the functionalities associated with monitoring, forecasting, and managing the identified key performance indicators of the organisation.

AI extends beyond the sphere of historical information in enterprise performance management. It has the ability to detect patterns; perform statistical forecasting; and analyse considerable volumes of data, including automated decision-making. Thus, decisions can move away from the prime sphere of historical information and not only enable management to gain the insights that earlier went unnoticed, but also enable them to look into the future (Arnauts, 2019). Arnauts claims that enterprise performance management assists the organisation to achieve its strategic objectives at a time when change, change management, and the redefinition of KPIs (including their tracking) to optimise performance are broadly required by the organisation's ecosystem. Moreover, he argues that strategies need to be translated into decisions and actions, while monitoring, forecasting, and managing these enterprise performance parameters, including correcting decisions and to some extent automating them.

The application of AI is also being applied at a lower hierarchical level in performance reviews. Once again, this applicability of AI is fundamentally dependent mainly on the data collection process. More specifically, a performance management system is based upon a set of processes that include tracking and monitoring performance of an individual or set of individuals as a team or department or as an organisation. However, it should be noted that different organisations follow different processes, with the goals always being aligned with the organisational strategic objectives.

The traditional performance management system process typically has four common steps, including objective setting; self-evaluation; manager evaluation; and discussion and sign off. However, this traditional approach has serious limitations since the entire process is based upon on a predominate manual method that tends to be a lengthy process spread over a year, with its inherent errors in the process flow. With the traditional method, managers and the individuals concerned tend to recall the recent achievements, and the rating of the individuals is merely based on this recall. Furthermore, many employees, including the respective supervisors, do not take this annual activity seriously but see it as a necessary nuisance, with irrelevant and biased feedbacks. Hence, the entire process fails to consider the potential of the individual employee.

It must be recognised that the key objective of an employment performance review is to know the individuals and their performance at a personal level in terms of what they have achieved, what they are capable of achieving, and how they contribute to the organisation. These influence the individual's behaviours that eventually lead to success or failures not just in respect to their goals and objectives, but also regarding their coherence with the team and their alignment with the organisational goals. However, this demands the collection of considerable amounts of data, which is only the starting point of the performance review. Effective performance management and engagement with employees is contingent on seeing matters from their point of view, and foreseeing what they would require from the review process. But it is also important to note that individuals from different age groups are likely to have different priorities and aspirations.

Therefore, management requires a tool that analyses the data and provides meaningful conclusions to enable them to refine the performance of employees and facilitate their ability to make correct decisions, generating a positive performance culture, and establishing objectives for the future that are based on the existing performance. AI, supported by its accompanying software, is considered an appropriate tool for effective performance reviews. A data-driven appraisal or review system facilitates transparency, avoids any sort of misunderstanding or doubts, and assists in avoiding bias, such as the 'halo effect' and 'stereotypes.' AI is not the be-all-end-all to performance management, but it provides several advantages that management can benefit from, which include:

(a) Elimination of human errors: An AI performance-management-based system is entirely data driven. It has no bias but gathers data from various sources, eradicating the room for error in the data. Thus, AI facilitates the managers' function to provide objective feedback and draw insights that can be of value to the employees and the organisation.

(b) Forecasts are based on a more all-inclusive data: An AI-driven system searches and evaluates across an enormous quantity of data to generate projections based on the progress of the employees' performance since the beginning of their career in the organisation and the current performance review. Hence, the AI system identifies the employees' potential and defines the most fitting goals that can further assist the manager to identify promotions and determine incentives in an equitable manner.

(c) Continuous reviews and real-time assessment: AI provides managers with the facility to continuously acquire data from numerous sources, including written formatted and unformatted communication with employees amongst others. Hence, the AI system can provide real-time insights into the individuals' performance to assist managers in making rapid decisions and delivering feedback immediately. Thus, the AI system removes the need for a physical periodic performance review with employees, where they have to recall information and authenticate this information with the appropriate sources.

(d) Effective management: An AI system assists managers to double-check their adjudication and confirm whether their feedback is accurate. This helps managers to improve their effectiveness by viewing and comprehending a broader range of information about the employees being reviewed. The AI system may provide dashboards with the details of employees' performances, potentials, and trends.

(e) Improved employee engagement: An AI system contributes to the continuous performance review approach by conducting regular intelligence surveys to collect feedback in real-time. This provides the AI system with the facility to share individualised perceptions to the employees based on the conducted surveys and/or self-assessments.

(f) Keeping to established timelines: Objectives or milestones are normally associated with an achievement timeline. An AI-driven performance management system facilitates in monitoring these objectives by sharing real-time feedback about the amount of activity that has been achieved and yet to be achieved. An AI-based system may recommend rewards for overachievers. However, if performance is not on track or is losing on time, then the system can notify the individual about this and suggest ways for increasing the outcome.

(g) Enhanced employee development: The AI system is able to assist managers to identify skill gaps and provide individualised training recommendations by analysing the employees' career progression data from previous performance reviews, interests, and skill sets. Hence, performance management is improved by identifying employee competencies and noting where employees can improve.

Unfortunately, an AI performance management system also has several disadvantages. Being new, an AI system is expensive to acquire and operate. Furthermore, an AI system tends to lack a human element, thus the managers' role is diminished from being the one responsible for performance reviews to being a moderator or facilitator. Hence, when employees have complaints about their assessment, the loss of the human component in the review process creates disengagement between the employee and the organisation. In addition, the AI system can learn and function based on its software programme. Hence, whether the AI system is as resourceful as human intelligence is still unknown and the absence of human intelligence may have a negative long-term impact on the employees. Moreover, an AI system may not cater for all the diverse situations and may at times require human intelligence intervention to make decisions.

One needs to note that an AI system lacks emotional intelligence to deal with situations where organisations need to show empathy for what the employees are encountering and therefore will need to modify the performance reviews accordingly. However, as AI systems progress and are further developed through self-learning systems, the above identified disadvantages are likely to be mitigated. The most serious disadvantage of an

AI system is related to ethical standards. AI systems are designed to collect and decipher large amounts of data, principally personal data. Therefore, these types of systems can become extremely intrusive, particularly if an AI system is intended to track the work behaviours of employees using connected devices, such as the amount of time a person is away from their work desk. Performance reviews linked to such data can reflect negatively on employees and can result in the erosion of employees' trust in the organisation and its management team. Therefore, it is essential that such AI systems supplement human intelligence that assists managers to carry out their jobs and make decisions better, rather than performing their roles and becoming intrusive during the data collecting process.

AI has an important role to play in performance management. It can monitor the activity of employees constantly and can provide insights for both employees and supervisors with consistent feedback, progress status reviews, and suggestions for improvement. AI has the capability to coordinate feedbacks and reviews of the various stakeholders on a frequent and regular time interval that facilitates human reviews at the concluding performance review meeting. AI examines data from various sources and is unlikely to generate a biased evaluation. AI and data analytics are linked through two key technologies, namely machine learning and predictive modelling. Machine learning analyses data sets to find patterns that reveal how the data will perform under certain scenarios. With the accumulation of more data, the machine learning algorithm analyses that data and continues to adapt and learn.

On the other hand, predictive modelling is driven by the machine learning algorithm to help generate real-time forecasts utilising the data gathered by the machine learning algorithm. Hence, the greater the information that the machine learning algorithm accumulates, the accuracy of the predictive models and data analysis increases. Thus, the system is constantly evolving and improving as it gains more knowledge. Therefore, when an AI is driving the data analytics, the system can learn more from the data, make key decisions based on this data, and forecast what will probably occur in the future. Hence, AI can be applied as part of the performance management system.

Typically, the manager conducts employee performance reviews, defines employee roles, determines fair compensation, makes promotion decisions, and defines the business goals. A vast majority of these functions have already been incorporated through the performance management software. However, AI supports the performance management system to attain additional functionality as previously mentioned. Using AI to analyse performance management data is a relatively new phenomenon that will provide many benefits and overcome the many challenges that are encountered by the HR Department. AI and machine learning can streamline the processes associated with performance management and allows management to utilise a data-driven system to engage and manage its employees as an approach to secure and maintain transparency and mitigate bias.

## Conclusion

This chapter is the end of our journey in exploring the various performance measurement and management concepts and tools. This chapter focused on consolidating the knowledge gathered regarding performance measurement and management and examined the likely future trends regarding this critical and important topic. Previous chapters examined performance measurement and management, and applied and illustrated various tools that management may apply to make sure that the defined organisational strategic goals and targets are achieved. Performance management typically commences at the strategic management stage, cascading down to employees who are viewed as the actual performers.

This chapter illustrated that performance management practices are based on the concept of having a set of evaluation procedures, which encompass various tasks, such as planning, monitoring, developing, assessing, and rewarding the organisation's employees. Thus, effective employee performance management is highly dependent on the organisation's ability to achieve an optimum motivational level of its employees through a higher intensity of involvement and providing them with an appropriate reward.

This requires the establishment of measurable and practical KPIs and having a monitoring system that continuously assesses their performance. It is important to recognise that performance should not be seen as a static component but must be viewed as a dynamic tool that can be further enhanced through well designed development programmes that focus on improving the employee's knowledge, skills, and competencies by taking advantage of the benefits that state-of-the-art systems are able to provide. Therefore, the defined KPIs must be periodically reviewed to ensure that employees are assessed and appraised against an appropriate performance scale (KPIs) and rewarded according to the appraisal reports.

It is also important to recognise that new trends in performance management are fundamentally based on the continuous evolution of systems that reflect a new generation of performance measurement and management software associated with the HR function that was mainly conducted manually through laborious paperwork. The evolution of systems is continuous and new developments in such areas as artificial intelligence are a constant development, particularly in the human resource (HR) segment. Artificial Intelligence is an emerging technology that will play an important part in the future development of the HR Department. However, for this to happen, the HR function must be integrated as part of an enterprise management system that seamlessly joins together the HR, accounting, financial, and production functional segments to provide a true enterprise performance system. This enterprise performance management approach is envisaged to integrate the traditional management functions with the support of a sophisticated machine learning system through the use of artificial intelligence. Finally, such an approach is not just applicable to the private sector but is very relevant to the public sector as well. Such a system would help to retain employees and reduce the costs of acquiring new workers when needed.

## References

Arnauts, S. (2019). *Corporate Performance Management – The Impact and Role of AI and New Technologies.* Available at: https://www.i-scoop.eu/corporate-performance-management-ai-new-technologies/#:~:text=The%20face%20of%20corporate%20performance, and%20more%20change%2-Doriented%20enterprise%2D (Accessed 22 November 2023).

Bourne, M.C.S., Mills, J.F., Wilcox, M., Neely, A.D., and Platts, K.W. (2000). 'Designing, Implementing and Updating Performance Measurement Systems.' *International Journal of Operations & Production Management*, 20(7), pp. 754–771.

Buckingham, M. and Goodall, A. (2015). 'Employee Performance Management: Reinventing Performance Management.' *Harvard Business Review*, April 2015.

Cappelli, P. and Tavis, A. (2016). 'Employee Performance Management: The Performance Management Revolution.' *Harvard Business Review*, October 2016.

Farris, J.A., van Aken, E.M., Letens, G., Chearksul, P., and Coleman, G. (2011). 'Improving the Performance Review Process: A Structured Approach and Case Application.' *International Journal of Operations & Production Management*, 31(4), pp. 376–404.

Gartner. (2023). *Gartner Glossary.* Available at: https://www.gartner.com/en/information-technology/glossary/cpm-corporate-performance-management (Accessed 22 November 2023).

Idrees, A. (2016). 'A Survey on Exploring Key Performance Indicators.' *Future Computing and Informatics Journal*, 1(1).

Murtala, Z. (2017). 'New Performance Measurement Trends: Evidence from Selected Multinational Corporations.' *Journal of World Economic Research*, 6(4), pp. 54–58.

Ossovski, N.C., de Lima, E.P., and da Costa, S.G. (2016). *Performance Measurement System – A Conceptual Model.* Available at: https://www.semanticscholar.org/paper/Performance-measurement-system-%E2%80%93-a-conceptual-model-Ossovski/2a2b64f82fede4fb1c5ff7e344 80f157f8032a39 (Accessed 22 November 2023).

Tabassum, F. and Ghosh, N. (2018). 'Future of Performance Management in Artificial Intelligence ERA.' *International Journal of Arts, Science and Humanities*, 6(1).

Taticchi, P., Balachandran, K., and Tonelli, F. (2012). 'Performance Measurement and Management Systems: State of the Art, Guidelines for Design and Challenges.' *Measuring Business Excellence*, May 2012.

Taticchi, P. and Balachandran, K.R. (2008). 'Forward Performance Measurement and Management Integrated Frameworks.' *International Journal of Accounting and Information Management*, 16(2), pp. 140–154.

Taticchi, P., Tonelli, F., and Cagnazzo, L. (2009). 'A Decomposition and Hierarchical Approach for Business Performance Measurement and Management.' *Measuring Business Excellence*, 13(4), pp. 47–57.

# INDEX